Life Histories of

North American
Shore Birds

Life Histories of

North American

Shore Birds

BY

ARTHUR CLEVELAND BENT

QL
696
.L7
B36
v. 1

IN TWO PARTS

PART I

DOVER PUBLICATIONS, INC.

LIBRARY
LINCOLN MEMORIAL UNIVERSITY
Harrogate Tennessee 37752
73411

Published in Canada by General Publishing Company, Ltd., 30 Lesmill Road, Don Mills, Toronto, Ontario.

Published in the United Kingdom by Constable and Company, Ltd., 10 Orange Street, London WC 2.

This Dover edition, first published in 1962, is an unabridged and unaltered republication of the work originally published by the United States Government Printing Office. Part I was originally published in 1927 as Smithsonian Institution United States National Museum *Bulletin 142;* Part II was originally published in 1929 as Smithsonian Institution United States National Museum *Bulletin 146.*

International Standard Book Number: 0-486-20933-4
Library of Congress Catalog Card Number: 62-51562

Manufactured in the United States of America
Dover Publications, Inc.
180 Varick Street
New York, N. Y. 10014

ADVERTISEMENT

The scientific publications of the National Museum include two series, known, respectively, as *Proceedings* and *Bulletin*.

The *Proceedings*, begun in 1878, is intended primarily as a medium for the publication of original papers, based on the collections of the National Museum, that set forth newly acquired facts in biology, anthropology, and geology, with descriptions of new forms and revisions of limited groups. Copies of each paper, in pamphlet form, are distributed as published to libraries and scientific organizations and to specialists and others interested in the different subjects. The dates at which these separate papers are published are recorded in the table of contents of each of the volumes.

The *Bulletin*, the first of which was issued in 1875, consists of a series of separate publications comprising monographs of large zoological groups and other general systematic treatises (occasionally in several volumes), faunal works, reports of expeditions, catalogues of type-specimens, special collections, and other material of similar nature. The majority of the volumes are octavo in size, but a quarto size has been adopted in a few instances in which large plates were regarded as indispensable. In the *Bulletin* series appear volumes under the heading *Contributions from the United States National Herbarium*, in octavo form, published by the National Museum since 1902, which contain papers relating to the botanical collections of the Museum.

The present work forms No. 142 of the *Bulletin* series.

ALEXANDER WETMORE,
Assistant Secretary, Smithsonian Institution.

WASHINGTON, D. C., *November 15, 1927*.

TABLE OF CONTENTS

INTRODUCTION

This is the seventh in a series of bulletins of the United States National Museum on the life histories of North American birds. Previous numbers have been issued as follows:

107. Life Histories of North American Diving Birds, August 1, 1919.
113. Life Histories of North American Gulls and Terns, August 27, 1921.
121. Life Histories of North American Petrels, Pelicans and their Allies, October 19, 1922.
126. Life Histories of North American Wild Fowl, May 25, 1923.
130. Life Histories of North American Wild Fowl, June 27, 1925.
135. Life Histories of North American Marsh Birds, "1926." (=March 11, 1927).

The same general plan has been followed, as explained in previous bulletins, and the same sources of information have been utilized.

The classification and nomenclature adopted by the American Ornithologists' Union, in its latest check list and its supplements, have been followed, mainly, with such few changes as, in the author's opinion, will be, or should be, made to bring the work up to date, and in line with recent advances in the science.

The main ranges are as accurately outlined as limited space will permit; the normal migrations are given in sufficient detail to indicate the usual movements of the species; no attempt has been made to give all records, for economy in space, and no pretense at complete perfection is claimed. Many published records, often repeated, have been investigated and discarded; many apparently doubtful records have been verified; some published records, impossible to either verify or disprove, have been accepted if the evidence seemed to warrant it.

The egg dates are the condensed results of a mass of records taken from the data in a large number of the best egg collections in the country, as well as from contributed field notes and from a few published sources. They indicate the dates on which eggs have been actually found in various parts of the country, showing the earliest and latest dates and the limits between which half the dates fall, the height of the season.

The plumages are described only in enough detail to enable the reader to trace the sequence of molts and plumages from birth to maturity and to recognize the birds in the different stages and at the different seasons. No attempt has been made to fully describe adult plumages; this has been already well done in the many manuals. The names of colors, when in quotation marks, are taken from Ridgway's Color Standards and Nomenclature (1912) and the terms used to describe the shapes of eggs are taken from his Nomenclature of Colors (1886 edition). The heavy-faced type in the measurements of eggs indicates the four extremes of measurements.

Many of those who contributed material for former volumes have rendered a similar service in this case. In addition to those whose contributions have been acknowledged previously, our thanks are due to the following new contributors: Photographs, notes, or data have been contributed by W. B. Alexander, Clark Blickensderfer, C. E. Chapman, Karl Christofferson, C. W. Colthrup, Walter Colvin, W. M. Congreve, Joseph Dixon, J. G. Gordon, S. A. Grimes, W. C. Herman, Frank Howland, W. I. Lyon, T. R. Miley, D. J. Nicholson, R. H. Rauch, Russell Richardson, jr., W. A. Smith, J. D. Soper, E. S. Thomas, M. B. Trautman, C. F. Walker, F. M. Weston, H. F. Witherby, A. H. Wood, jr., and C. J. Young.

Receipt of material from over 250 contributors has been acknowledged in previous volumes.

Through the courtesy of the Biological Survey, the services of Frederick C. Lincoln were secured to compile the distribution paragraphs. With the matchless reference files of the Biological Survey at his disposal and with some advice and help from Dr. Harry C. Oberholser, his many hours of careful and thorough work have produced results far more satisfactory than could have been attained by the author, who claims no credit and assumes no responsibility for this part of the work. The few minor changes made in the system do not materially alter the general plan.

Dr. Charles W. Townsend has written the life histories of two species and the Rev. Francis C. R. Jourdain, a well-known British authority, has contributed the life histories and the distributions of six Old World species, which are known to us only as rare stragglers. Mr. J. H. Riley has furnished descriptions and measurements of some rare eggs in the National Museum. We are indebted to Mr. H. F. Witherby for the loan of the valuable photographs of the knot, taken by Admiral Peary, which the author publishes at his own risk, without permission.

As most of the shore birds are known to us mainly, or entirely, as migrants it has seemed desirable to describe their migrations quite fully. As it is a well-known fact that many, if not all, immature and nonbreeding shore birds remain far south of their breeding ranges all summer it has not seemed necessary to mention this in each case. Nor did it seem necessary to say that only one brood is raised in a season, as this is a nearly universal rule with all water birds.

The manuscript for this volume was completed in March, 1927. Contributions received since then will be acknowledged later. Only information of great importance could be added. When this volume appears contributions of photographs or notes relating to the gallinaceous birds should be sent to

THE AUTHOR.

Life Histories of

North American

Shore Birds

LIFE HISTORIES OF NORTH AMERICAN SHORE BIRDS

ORDER LIMICOLAE (PART 1)

By Arthur Cleveland Bent

Of Taunton, Massachusetts

Family PHALAROPODIDAE, Phalaropes

PHALAROPUS FULICARIUS (Linnaeus)

RED PHALAROPE

HABITS

The female red phalarope in her full nuptial plumage is, to my mind, the handsomest, certainly the most richly colored, of the three known species of phalaropes. The species is cosmopolitan, with a circumpolar breeding range; it is apparently homogeneous throughout its wide range except for a local race, breeding in Spitsbergen, which has been separated and named *Phalaropus fulicarius jourdaini* Iredale; this race is said to have paler edgings on the back, scapulars, and tertials. The species is commonly known abroad as the grey phalarope, an appropriate name for the bird in its winter plumage, in which it is most often seen.

It is less often seen in the United States than the other two species; its summer home is so far north that it is beyond the reach of most of us; and at other seasons it is much more pelagic than the other species, migrating and apparently spending the winter far out on the open sea, often a hundred miles or more from land. It seldom comes ashore on the mainland except when driven in by thick weather or a severe storm. Hence it is an apparently rare bird to most of us. But in its arctic summer home it is exceedingly abundant. Alfred M. Bailey (1925) says that "this was the most abundant of the shore birds at Wales, as at Wainwright, Alaska. As a person walks over the tundra there is a continual string of those handsome birds rising from the grass." Again he writes:

At Whalen, near East Cape, Siberia, we saw thousands of these beautiful little fellows on July 11. The day was very disagreeable, with a strong

1

wind off the ice and a drizzling rain. From the ship we could see waves of birds rising some distance off in such dense flocks that individuals could not be distinguished; the mass looked like a long, thin cloud swirling before the wind; one end of the line rose high in the air, while the other end swerved nearer to the water. They swung about with the erratic movements and wave-like flight so characteristic of black skimmers, now high in the air, again low over the water. As we worked along the shore, thousands that were feeding close along the beach rose and flew across the sand spit in front of us. There was a continual stream of them drifting by, like so much sand before a strong wind. They were, at this time, beginning to molt their breeding plumage.

Spring.—The migrations of the red phalarope are mainly at sea, usually far out from land. During the month of May enormous flocks may be seen on the ocean off the coasts of New England, but it is only during stress of weather that they are driven inshore. I can well remember a big storm, on May 21, 1892, which brought a large flight of these birds into Cape Cod Bay; Nat Gould killed a large number that day on Monomoy Island and I shot one at Plymouth Beach; others were taken at Provincetown. In pleasant weather these birds are well at home on the heaving bosom of the ocean, flying about in flocks, twisting, turning, and wheeling like flocks of sandpipers, or resting or feeding on the drifting rafts of seaweeds. On the Pacific coast these birds are even more abundant, if one goes far enough offshore to see them during April and May. They often congregate in considerable numbers about the Farallon Islands. W. Leon Dawson (1923) has drawn a graphic picture of them there, as follows:

Here in late spring thousands of these birds ride at anchor in the lee of the main island, along with other thousands of the other northern species, *Lobipes lobatus.* Of these some few scores are driven ashore by hunger and seek their sustenance in brackish pools, or else battle with the breakers in the little " bight " of the rocky lee shore. The date is May 23, and the company under survey numbers a few brilliant red birds in high plumage among the scores in unchanged gray, together with others exhibiting every inter-mediate gradation. When to this variety is added a similar diversity among the northerns, which mingle indiscriminately with them, you have a motley company—no two birds alike. Ho! but these are agile surfmen! Never, save in the case of the wandering tattler and the American dipper, have I seen such absolute disregard of danger and such instant adjustment to watery circumstance. Here are 30 of these phalaropes " fine mixed," threading a nar-row passage in the reefs where danger threatens in the minutest fraction of a second. Crash! comes a comber. Our little world is obliterated in foam. Sea anemones and rock oysters sputter and choke, and there is a fine fury of readjustment. But the phalaropes rise automatically, clear the crest of the crasher, and are down again, preening their feathers or snatching dainties with the utmost unconcern. Now a bird is left stranded on a reef, or now he is whisked and whirled a dozen feet away. All right, if he likes it; but if not, he is back again, automatically, at the old rendezvous. Life goes on right merrily in spite of these shocking interruptions. Food getting is the main business, and this is pursued with extraordinary ardor. The bird's tiny feet kick the water violently, and there is the tiniest compensatory bob for every stroke, so that their little bodies seem all a tremble. There seems to be no difference of opinion between the two species, but there is time for a good deal of amatory play between the sexes of the reds. It is always the bright-colored female who makes the advances, for the wanton phalaropes have revised nature's order, and the modest male either seeks escape by flight, or else defends himself with determined dabs. Here is the authentic lady for whom Shakespeare's "pilgrim" sighed.

Of their arrival on their breeding grounds in northern Alaska, E. W. Nelson (1887) writes:

It is much more gregarious than its relative, and for a week or two after its first arrival 50 or more flock together. These flocks were very numerous the 1st of June, 1879, at the Yukon mouth, where I had an excellent opportunity to observe them. In the morning the birds which were paired could be found scattered here and there, by twos, over the slightly flooded grassy flats. At times these pairs would rise and fly a short distance, the female, easily known by her bright colors and larger size, in advance, and uttering now and then a low and musical "clink, clink," sounding very much like the noise made by lightly tapping together two small bars of steel. When disturbed these notes were repeated oftener and became harder and louder. A little later in the day, as their hunger became satisfied, they began to unite into parties until 15 or 20 birds would rise and pursue an erratic course over the flat. As they passed swiftly along stray individuals and pairs might be seen to spring up and join the flock. Other flocks would rise and the smaller coalesce with the larger until from two hundred to three or even four hundred birds were gathered in a single flock. As the size of the flock increased its movements became more and more irregular. At one moment they would glide straight along the ground, then change to a wayward flight, back and forth, twisting about with such rapidity that it was difficult to follow them with the eye. Suddenly their course would change, and the compact flock, as if animated by a single impulse, would rise high over head, and, after a series of graceful and swift evolutions, come sweeping down with a loud, rushing sound to resume their playful course near the ground. During all their motions the entire flock moves in such unison that the alternate flashing of the underside of their wings and the dark color of the back, like the play of light and shade, makes a beautiful spectacle. When wearied of their sport the flock disbands and the birds again resume their feeding.

Courtship.—The well-known reversal of sexual characters in the phalaropes makes their courtship particularly interesting, as the large, handsome females press their ardent suits against the timid and dull-colored little males. A. L. V. Manniche (1910) has given us the best account of it, as follows:

June 19, 1907, early in the morning, I had the pleasure of watching for hours the actions of a loving couple of phalaropes on the beach of a pool surrounded by large sedge tufts, covered with long, withered grass. This act I found very funny, peculiar, and charming. When the male had been eagerly searching for food for some 20 minutes, often standing on his head in the water, like a duck, to fish or pick up something from the bottom, he would lie down on a tuft, stretching out his one leg and his one wing as if he would fully enjoy the rest after his exertions. The female for some moments was lying quietly and mutely in the middle of the pool; suddenly she began with increasing rapidity to whirl around on the surface of the water, always in the same little circle, the diameter of which was some 10 centimeters. As the male seemed to pay no attention to her alluring movements, she flew rapidly up to him—producing as she left the water a peculiar whirling sound with her wings and uttering short angry cries—pushed him with her bill, and then she returned to the water and took up her swimming dance. Now the male came out to her, and the two birds whirled around for some moments equally eager and with increasing rapidity. Uttering a short call, the female again flew to a tuft surrounded by water and waited some seconds in vain for the male; again she flew to the water to induce him with eager pushes and thumps to accompany her. They again whirled violently around, whereafter she, uttering a strong, alluring sound, flew back to the tuft, this time accompanied by the male—and the pairing immediately took place. In the matrimony of the grey phalarope the female only decides. She exceeds the male in size and brilliancy of plumage and has the decisive power in all family affairs. If she wants to shift her place of residence she flies up swift as an arrow with a commanding cry—which may be expressed as "*pittss*"—and if the male does not follow her at once she will immediately return and give him a severe punishment, which never fails to have the desired effect. It is a well-known fact that she completely ignores her eggs and young ones.

Nesting.—The same author describes the nesting habits of this species, in northeast Greenland, as follows:

It is peculiar, that the male has well-marked breeding spots before the breeding begins and certainly before the female has laid her first egg; but this fact has been proved by several solid examinations. June 26, 1907, I observed on the beach of the Bjergandeso in the Stormkap district, that the nest building was executed by the male. He was busy in building the nest on a low bank covered with short grass, while she paid no attention to his labor, but swam around the beach searching food. The male shaped a nest hollow by turning round his body against the ground on the place selected, having first by aid of the feet scraped away and trampled down the longest and most troublesome straws. He diligently used feet and bill at the same time to arrange the shorter fine straws, which are carefully bent into the nest hollow and form the lining of this. The nest was much smaller than that of *Tringa alpina* and contained one egg the next day. Along the beaches of a smaller lake not far from the ship's harbor I saw, June 30, three solitary swimming males, at least one of which showed signs of having a nest. I soon found this close to the place of residence of the male in question. The nest contained four fresh eggs and was built in exactly the same way as the before-mentioned nest. The male proved so far from being shy, that he could be driven to his nest and merely be caught by hand; having laid himself upon the nest he was still more fearless.

A breeding phalarope will lie motionless with his head pressed deep down against his back. He is almost fully covered by straws, which surround the nest, as he with the bill bends these over himself, besides he is so similar to the surroundings that no human eye is able to distinguish him from these, if the spot is not known beforehand.

July 9, 1907, I again found a phalarope's nest by the Bjergandeso; it contained four fresh eggs and was built a little differently from the two before-mentioned nests. These were found close to a lake on low banks covered with short grass, but this one was built on a tuft covered with long, withered grass, situated some 10 meters from the real lake, but surrounded by shallow water, that came from a little river running out from the lake and irrigating all the tufts, one of which contained the nest. This bird also kept very close on the nest, and did not leave it before I parted the long grass with my foot. When frightened up from the nest the bird for a short while lay screaming and flapping on the water not far from me; thereupon he flew away, silently and rapidly, to land on the opposite side of the lake. Having been absent for some five minutes he returned just as rapidly, flew a good way to the other side of the nest, sat down, and kept quiet for a couple of minutes, whereafter he again flew up and took the earth some 20 meters from the nest, which he then rapidly approached walking and swimming hidden by aquatic plants and tufts. All this was done in order to mislead me, who was lying some 15 meters from the nest without any shelter and therefore seen by the bird all the while.

C. W. G. Eifrig (1905) found the red phalarope breeding very commonly around Cape Fullerton and Southampton Island, Hudson Bay. "They nest around fresh water ponds, laying their eggs, without nesting material, in depressions in the sand or moss, often in lichens." John Murdoch (1885), on the other hand, says, at Point Barrow, Alaska, that—

The nest is always in the grass, never in the black or mossy portions of the tundra, and usually in a pretty wet situation, though a nest was occasionally found high and dry, in a place where the nest of the pectoral sandpiper would be looked for. A favorite nesting site was a narrow grassy isthmus between two of the shallow ponds. The nest is a very slight affair of dried grass and always well concealed.

In the Kotzebue Sound region Joseph Grinnell (1900) found three nests, of which he says:

The nests were all on higher ground and at a distance of 100 yards or more from the lagoons where the birds usually congregated for feeding and social purposes. The three nests agreed in situation, being rather deep depressions sunk into the tops of mossy hummocks. There was a thin lining of dry grasses, and in one case the drooping blades from an adjoining clumb of grass partially concealed the nest from view from above.

Miss Maud D. Haviland (1915) relates her experience with the nesting habits of this species, at the mouth of the Yenesei River, Siberia, as follows:

I found the first nest on Golchika Island early in July. My attention was called to it by the male bird, which flew round uneasily. Even when the nesting ground is invaded, this phalarope is very quiet and not very demonstrative. He flits round the intruder with a peculiar silent flight, rather like a big red moth, while he utters his chirruping alarm note—"zhit zhit." This call is shriller than that of *Phalaropus lobatus*, and quite recognizable where the two species breed side by side. I sat down on a log of driftwood, and in about half an hour was able to flush the bird from four fresh eggs. This nest, however, was not placed very well for photography, for about 50 yards away was a turf hut, which a Russian family had just taken possession of for the summer, and I dared not leave the hiding tent or apparatus near the spot. On the following day I was more fortunate, and found a nest which was also on the island but about half a verst away. It was in rather a dryer situation than the last, but like all the nests of this species that I saw, the eggs lay on quite a substantial platform of dead grass. In other cases the sites were so wet that the bird must have been sitting actually in water—and the photographer would have had to do likewise! In the photograph, the grass has been parted in order to show the eggs, but before this was done they were screened as carefully as the eggs of a redshank or reeve.

I pitched the tent at once, and went in to hide. The male phalarope stood on a tussock about 20 yards away and watched attentively, I should not thus have tackled the nest of any other wader, but I relied upon the confidence and simplicity of the phalarope, and I did not rely upon them in vain. In about 20 minutes I caught sight of the bird creeping round the tent, and a few minutes later he settled down upon the eggs. In this, my first glimpse of a grey phalarope at close quarters, two points struck me forcibly. One was the apparent extraordinary length of the bird. The single pair of legs in the middle seemed quite insufficient to support so long a body, and with his quaint perky gait, it seemed as if the bird swayed to and fro upon cee springs as he walked. The other was the peculiar harmony of the color of the mantle with the grass around, bleached or blackened by snow and thaw. The long, bladelike form of the secondary feathers, and the buff longitudinal shoulder bands seemed to emphasize the scheme until the bird was almost indistinguishable from his surroundings.

Herbert W. Brandt in his manuscript notes says:

The nest of the red phalarope is built either on dry ground or over shallow grass-grown water and is well concealed. Leading away from it usually are one or more runways which are either tunneled or open. The nest is fragile and very loosely made. The interior is moulded into a cup shape and the structure is made of grasses and often lined with moss stems, small leaves of the dwarf birch, cranberry, and other small, crisp leaves found there. Frequently, however, a simple depression in the moss or grass suffices to serve for the nursery. The range of measurements of 18 nests is: Height 3 to 5 inches; inside diameter 2½ to 3½ inches; depth of cavity, 2½ to 3 inches; but the nest is sometimes built up higher and is more substantial if placed directly over water. In fact, this little coot-footed bird sometimes builds a miniature cootlike nest. The male alone was noted building the nest, and he usually incubates, but on two occasions the female was observed on the eggs. The incubating bird is not a close sitter and departs from the nest long before the intruder arrives. In that jaeger-haunted land when the male phalarope returns to the nest he weaves so stealthily through the grass that it is almost impossible to follow his devious course so that two or three rapid charges are necessary by the watcher toward the supposed location of the nest before the incubating bird can finally be forced to rise directly from its eggs.

Eggs.—The red phalarope ordinarily lays four eggs, though three sometimes constitute a full set, and as many as six have been found in a nest, probably laid by two birds. They vary in shape from ovate pyriform to subpyriform and have a slight gloss. The prevailing ground colors range from " pale olive buff " to " dark olive buff "; in the darker sets they vary from " ecru olive " to " Isabella color "; in a few sets there is a greenish tinge approaching " light brownish olive ". The markings are bold, sharply defined and irregular in shape; they are most numerous and often confluent at the larger end; but some eggs are finely speckled over the entire surface. The prevailing colors of the markings are dark browns, from "warm sepia" or "Vandyke brown" to "bone brown" or "clove brown." Some eggs are marked with lighter or brighter browns, "hazel," "russet," or even "tawny." The drab under markings are hardly noticeable. The measurements of 148 eggs in the United States National Museum average 31.5 by 22 millimeters; the eggs showing the four extremes measure 35 by 22, 32 by 23 and 27.5 by 20.5 millimeters.

Young.—Authorities differ as to the period of incubation, which does not seem to have been definitely determined by anyone. Mr. Conover writes to me that "a nest located June 10, with three eggs, hatched on June 29." Incubation is performed almost wholly by the male, but Mr. Brandt (mss.) says: "The female, however, is, of course, the dominant member of the household, but she occasionally shares the cares of incubation, as I proved by collecting one from the nest; while later in the year I was successful in photographing a mother with a single chick. Perhaps it was a favorite child which she was taking for a walk while the father was mothering the rest of the family." Most observers agree that the male assumes full care of the young also; but Miss Haviland (1915) says: "It seems as if both male and female unite to care for the young, and when the breeding ground is approached they fly around and call anxiously." Probably the gaily dressed female is a poor mother at best and prefers to join the large flocks of her sex on the tundra pools.

Plumages.—The downy young red phalarope is the handsomest of its group, darker and more richly colored, as well as larger than the young northern phalarope. The upper parts show various shades of deep, warm brownish buff, darkest, "Sudan brown," on the crown, paling to "raw sienna," on the sides of the head, occiput, neck, thighs, and rump, and to "yellow ocher" on the rest of the upper parts; these colors shade off into "antimony yellow" or "warm buff" on the throat and breast and to buffy white on the belly; the down of the upper parts is tipped with black, except on the yellow ocher parts, and is basally dusky. It is boldly marked above with clear, velvety black; there is a large black patch back of the central crown patch of brown and a diminishing black stripe on each side of it; a narrow black stripe runs from the bill, over the eye, to the auriculars; another runs across the hind neck; a broad, but more or less broken and irregular, black stripe extends down the center of the back and a similar stripe down each side of it; there is also a large well-defined black patch on each side of the rump, above the thigh.

In fresh juvenal plumage, in August, the feathers of the crown, mantle, and scapulars are black, broadly edged with "ochraceous tawny"; the tertials, median wing coverts, upper tail coverts, and tail feathers are narrowly edged with paler shades of buff; the lesser wing coverts are narrowly edged with white; the forehead, lores, neck all around, upper breast, and flanks are suffused with grayish brown, varying from "fawn color" or "wood brown," on the throat, neck, and breast, to "vinaceous buff" on the head and flanks; the rest of the under parts are pure white. The sexes are alike in juvenal and winter plumages.

The tawny edgings of the upper plumage soon fade and wear away before the postjuvenal molt begins during August. I have seen birds in full juvenal plumage as late as September 15; the molt is usually not completed until late in October, but I have seen it well advanced by the middle of August. This molt includes nearly all of the contour plumage, but not the wings and tail, so that first-winter birds can be distinguished from adults by the juvenal wing coverts and tail.

The first prenuptial molt occurs mainly in April and May; it is sometimes completed by the last week in May, but more often not until early June; I have seen the full first-winter plumage retained until May 21. This molt involves the entire contour plumage, some wing coverts, and the tail; so that young birds in first nuptial plumage closely resemble adults and can be distinguished only by the presence of some old juvenal wing coverts. The sexes are quite unlike in this plumage and are probably ready to breed. Certain females, in which the black crown and white cheek patches are obscured with buff and rufous tints, but are otherwise in full plumage, are perhaps young birds.

At the following molt, the first postnuptial, the adult winter plumage is acquired, characterized by the bluish-gray mantle and the white under parts. This molt is complete; it begins in July and is sometimes completed in August, but more often it is prolonged into September or later. Adults have a partial molt in the spring, from March to May, involving the contour feathers, the tail, some of the tertials, and some of the wing coverts; the remiges are not molted, and some of the old scapulars are retained. The adult postnuptial molt, from July to December, is complete.

Food.—During the month or so that they are on their northern breeding grounds the red phalaropes are shore birds, feeding in the tundra pools or along the shores, but during the rest of the year they are essentially sea birds, feeding on or about the floating masses of kelp or seaweeds, or following the whales or schools of large fish; hence they are aptly called "sea geese," "whale birds," or "bowhead birds." They occasionally come in to brackish pools near the shore or rarely are seen on the sandy beaches or mud flats feeding with other shore birds. Outlying rocky islands are often favorite feeding places. Ludwig Kumlien (1879) writes:

Whalemen always watch these birds while they are wheeling around high in the air in graceful and rapid circles, for they know that as soon as they sight a whale blowing they start for him, and from their elevated position they can, of course, discern one at a much greater distance than the men in the boat. I doubt if it be altogether the marine animals brought to the surface by the whale that they are after, for if the whale remains above the surface any length of time they always settle on his back and hunt parasites. One specimen was brought me by an Eskimo that he had killed on the back of an *Orca gladiator;* the esophagus was fairly crammed with *Laernodipodian crus-taceans,* still alive, although the bird had been killed some hours; they looked to me like *Caprella phasma* and *Cyamus ceti.* According to the Eskimo who killed it, the birds were picking something from the whale's back. I have often seen them dart down among a school of *Delphinapterous leucas* and follow them as far as I could see. On one occasion a pair suddenly alighted astern of my boat and were not 3 feet from me at times; they followed directly in the wake of the boat, and seemed so intent on picking up food that they paid no attention whatever to us. They had probably mistaken the boat for a whale.

In northeastern Greenland, Manniche (1910) saw them hunt flying insects on land; he also says:

Some 20 analyses of stomachs proved that the phalaropes in the breeding season chiefly feed on small insects, principally gnats and larvae of these. The esophagus and stomachs of several birds killed were filled with larvae of gnats, which in vast multitudes live in the fresh-water ponds. In a few stomachs I also found fine indeterminable remnants of plants (Algae?).

W. Leon Dawson (1923) describes their feeding habits at the Farallones, as follows:

Three red phalaropes, all female I take it, although none of them in highest plumage, and one northern, also a female, just under "high," are pasturing at my feet in a brackish pool some 20 feet long, 10 feet wide, and 2 feet deep. The waters of the pool teem with a minute reddish crustacean (?) shaped like an ant, less than a thirty-second of an inch in length and incredibly nimble. The insects progress by leaps, and are visible only at the moment of arrival. Yet these birds gobble them up one at a time with unerring accuracy and with a rapidity which is nothing short of marvelous. The reds work habitually at the rate of five dabs per second, i. e., 300 a minute, while the northern, with a longer beak and a much daintier motion, works only half as fast.

The following observation was made on a California beach by Roland C. Ross (1922):

Kelp flies seemed to satisfy its sporting instincts and hunger, and the bird stalked them slowly and pointedly one by one. With bill and neck outstretched and lowered in line with a fly on the sand, a slow advance was made until with a pounce the hunt closed. If the fly escaped, the phalarope sometimes ran after it, bill out. Another pose interested me. On finding a kelp mass decaying and drawing flies, the phalarope approached closely and so low that his breast touched the ground, but the rear of the bird was high up. At times he would remain with breast down and pick at the flies much as a dusting fowl picks up a stray grain. Mr. L. E. Wyman reported similar "breast to ground" actions of two phalaropes he saw feeding by a kelp mass on the beach.

Alexander Wetmore (1925), in his report on the food of the red phalarope, analyzed the contents of 36 stomachs, mainly from the Pribilof Islands, with some from New York and Maine; they were collected from May to November, but mainly in August. Crustaceans made up 33.5 per cent of the food; beetles amounted to 27.3 per cent; flies formed 22.7 per cent; and 6.8 per cent consisted of tiny fishes, mostly sculpins. The food of this species therefore shows it to be harmless or neutral.

Behavior.—Phalaropes are active, lively birds in all their movements and they seem to be constantly on the move. They are all rapid fliers and this species is decidedly the swiftest on the wing of all three. As the restless flocks move about over the water, their aerial evolutions are well worth watching. Lucien M. Turner, in his Labrador notes, writes that he has seen them "ascend to a great height in increasing circles, darting in and out among each other and making a peculiar twitter as they ascend. When some suitable locality is discerned these birds descend almost perpendicularly and drop on the water as softly as a feather." They are so much like sandpipers in appearance and in manner of flight that one is always surprised to see them alight on the water.

Perhaps even more surprising than their peculiar marital relations are their aquatic habits. Their semipalmated and lobed toes are well adapted for swimming and the thick, compact plumage of their under parts protects them and buoys them up on the water. They float as lightly as corks, or as freshly fallen autumn leaves on a woodland pool, swimming swiftly and whirling rapidly, undisturbed by rushing currents or by foaming breakers. William Brewster (1925) has well described the behavior of a red phalarope on an inland stream at Umbagog Lake, Me.; he writes:

I strolled across a suspension footbridge that spans Bear River here, a shallow stream rippling over a rocky bed scarce 50 feet in width, beneath overhanging yellow birches and other deciduous trees. Returning a few minutes later I had reached the middle of the bridge when a grayish bird started directly under it and flew off down stream for a few rods, skimming close to the water and uttering a sharp *whit, whit*, which reminded me of the call of a spotted sandpiper concerned for the safety of its young. Almost at the first glance I recognized the bird as a red phalarope whose presence in such a place surprised me greatly, of course. Alighting, again, in the middle of the river it floated buoyantly and stemmed the swift current with apparent ease, although avoiding such exertion, whenever possible, by taking advantage of backward-flowing eddies. Presently it began working around the bases of some large boulders where it seemed to be obtaining abundant food by pecking rapidly and incessantly at their rough flanks, wetted by lapping waves. It also fed on the surface of the swirling eddies, paddling about very rapidly and in devious courses. It was most interesting to see a bird whose characteristic haunts, at least in autumn and winter, are boundless stretches of wind-swept ocean, thus disporting itself in a brawling mountain stream overarched by trees. Even a water ousel could not have appeared more perfectly at home there. Like most phalaropes this one was tame and confiding, but whenever I approached within 20 or 25 feet, it would rise and fly on a few yards, giving the *whit* call.

On land their movements are exceedingly rapid and graceful, though somewhat erratic; they run about excitedly with all the restless activity of sandpipers, nodding their heads with a pretty, dovelike motion. At such times they are remarkably tame, unsuspicious, and gentle birds; as they do not habitually come in contact with human beings, they are unafraid.

Voice.—The vocal performances of the red phalarope are not elaborate. As quoted above, Doctor Nelson (1887) describes its note as "a low and musical *clink*, *clink*, sounding very much like the noise made by lightly tapping together two small bars of steel." Mr. Brewster (1925) refers to the note as "an emphatic *zip*, *zip*, closely resembling that of Bonaparte's sandpiper . . . but louder and mellower." Again he says: "Once they rose and flew about the pond precisely like small sandpipers, one of them uttering a peep-like *tweet* just as it left the water." Charles W. Townsend (1920) saw one which "emitted a whistle which was clear and pleasant at times, and again sharp and grating; at times the note could be expressed as a *creak*."

Field marks.—In its nuptial plumage the red phalarope can be easily recognized by its brilliant colors; the male is smaller, his colors are duller, and his breast is mixed with white. In its winter plumage, in which we usually see it, it is likely to be confused with the northern phalarope or the sanderling. It is larger than the former, more stockily built and has a shorter, thicker bill, which is yellowish at the base. From the sanderling it can be distinguished by the gray markings on the head and neck, which are mainly white in winter sanderlings, by the darker gray of the back and by the yellow at the base of the bill. Phalaropes are usually tame enough to allow close study of these details. John T. Nichols suggests to me the following additional field characters:

This phalarope holds its gray plumage well into the spring and adults quickly resume same when they go to sea in late summer. Around the first of August flocks offshore are in gray and white "winter" plumage, but a few birds have a peculiar pink tone appreciable on the underparts at fair range, apt to be strongest posteriorly, and which is diagnostic. It is caused by scattered old red feathers overlaid by the delicate tips of new white ones. The white wing stripe is somewhat broader in this than in the northern phalarope and in gray plumage the upper parts are of so pale a tone that the wing pattern appears faint, something as it does in the piping plover. What seems to be a late summer plumage of birds of the year, on the other hand, is less white than the corresponding one of the northern. As the bird sits on the water the sides of its neck, breast, and sides appear brownish (not red or pink), the only touch of whitish it shows is on the flanks. At close range a curved phalarope mark behind the eye is just indicated, corresponding to the bold contrasting mark in the northern.

Enemies.—Phalaropes are not considered game birds, as they are too small and too seldom seen in large numbers to warrant pursuing them; so man should not be counted among their enemies. On their Arctic breeding grounds they evidently have plenty of avian enemies, such as jaegers, gulls, and various gyrfalcons. Mr. Manniche (1910) writes:

The two phalaropes observed were evidently very much afraid of larger waders as for instance knots. Several times I saw them rush together in terror and lie motionless on the water with their heads pressed down to their backs until the supposed danger—a passing knot—was past; then they continued their meal or love-making. The only enemy of the full-grown birds is the gyrfalcon (*Falco gyrfalco*), which will surprise and capture them when lying on the water. This I succeeded in observing one day in summer 1907; just as I was observing a male phalarope, which swam along the beach of a little clear pond hardly two paces from my feet, I suddenly heard a strong whistling in the air and saw an old falcon, that from a dizzy height shot like an arrow towards the surface of the water, caught the phalarope and again rapidly rose in the air carrying the bird in its talons. I saw the bird of prey descend and settle on the summit of a rock near the bay in order to eat its prey. The method, with which the falcon carried out its exploit, proved that several phalaropes before had the same fate. The gyrfalcon can certainly not catch a phalarope in flight.

Nature, however, sometimes takes her toll, as the following observation on the coast of California reported by L. W. Welch (1922) will illustrate:

There was an unusual migration of red phalaropes (*Phalaropus fulicarius*) this past fall. I saw about three hundred within an hour on the ponds of the Long Beach Salt Works. This was October 30. There was a great mortality among them this year. Dead birds were brought to the schools picked up by children in the streets or elsewhere. On the ponds mentioned above, dead birds were washed up in windrows. I could count 19 from one position and 21 from another. I counted 75 within half an hour. The birds had no shot holes in them, and showed no external evidences of having flown against wires, but all the birds examined were emaciated in the extreme.

Mr. Brandt in his manuscript notes writes:

I was told that the natives look upon the flesh of the red phalarope as the greatest delicacy, and it is considered the choicest food that can be placed before an honored guest. The little native boys have, as their most prized mark, this red-brown target. Inasmuch as this bird inhabits the small ponds just outside the villages, the young hunters have always easily stalked game available. The children begin to hunt the red phalarope as soon as they are large enough to pull a bow string. The chase is so alluring that the older boys in my employ could not resist the temptation whenever presented, to grab a bow and arrow from the youngsters, and stalk this little bird. The chase is not one sided, however, as the phalarope is as quick as a flash, and like cupid's arrows, many shots fail to reach their mark.

Fall.—The red phalaropes are the last of the waders to leave their Arctic breeding grounds, lingering until the lakes and shores are closed with ice, often well into October. These loiterers are all young birds; the adults leave early and are sometimes seen off the coasts of the United States in July. F. S. Hersey and I collected one at Chatham, Mass., on July 4, 1921; this may have been a loiterer from the spring flight, but probably it was an early fall migrant.

The fall migration is usually well out at sea, often hundreds of miles from land. Kumlien (1879) writes:

These birds were met with at great distances from land. The first seen on our outward passage was on August 4, 1877, in latitude 41° N., longitude 68° W.; here large flocks were met with. As we proceeded northward, their numbers increased till we reached Grinnell Bay. Off the Amitook Islands, on the Labrador coast, 200 miles from the nearest land, I saw very large flocks during a strong gale.

William Palmer (1890) met with it in great abundance between Cape Sable and Cape Cod on August 30.

Off the coast of California the flight begins in July or early August and continues through the fall; a few birds linger through the winter from Monterey southward. Throughout the great interior of North America migration records are scattering, hardly more than casuals. It is interesting, however, to note that Audubon (1840) saw his first birds of this species on the Ohio River near Louisville, Kentucky, where he killed 17 at one shot. I have an adult male in my collection which was shot on the Taunton River, near my home, on August 12, 1913.

Winter.—Our knowledge of the winter home of our American birds of this species is rather meager. They have been traced as far south as the Falkland Islands in the Atlantic Ocean and Juan Fernandez in the Pacific. Probably they are scattered over the warmer portions of both oceans, wherever they can find an abundant food supply.

A number of phalaropes, almost certainly of this species, were observed by Mr. Nichols in the Atlantic, off Cape Lookout, March 22, 1926. "They may winter here or, what is equally likely, arrive in spring to find the same feed which attracts the mackerel to the capes of the Carolinas in March or April."

Aretas A. Saunders writes to me of a similar observation made by him off the coast of South Carolina on March 5, 1908:

That day red phalaropes were abundant on the water, though we were out of sight of land. The sea was calm with a glossy surface, but a slight swell and flocks of from 10 to 50 birds rose from in front of the boat, at intervals all morning. They flew in compact flocks, low over the water, and alighted again when some distance away.

DISTRIBUTION

Range.—Arctic regions of both Old and New Worlds; south in winter to South Africa, India, China, and southern South America.

Breeding range.—In the Old World the red phalarope breeds on the Arctic coast from Iceland east to Nova Zembla, the Taimur Peninsula, and the islands and coast of Siberia to Bering Sea. The race, *jourdaini*, breeds in Spitsbergen, Iceland, and eastern Greenland.

In the Western Hemisphere the breeding range extends north to Alaska (probably St. Lawrence Island, Cape Prince of Wales, Cape Lowenstern, Point Barrow, and the Colville delta); Mackenzie (Rendezvous Lake and Franklin Bay); northern Franklin (Bay of Mercy, Winter Harbor, and Cape Liverpool); Grinnell Island (Fort Conger); and Greenland (Disco Bay, Godhavn, and probably Christianshaab). East to Greenland (Stormkap and probably Christianshaab); eastern Franklin (Exeter Sound, probably Nugumeute and Grinnell Bay); and Ungava (Port Burwell). South to Ungava (Port Burwell and probably Prince of Wales Sound); southern Franklin (Southampton Island and Cape Fullerton); and Alaska (Fort Egbert and Hooper Bay). West to Alaska (Hooper Bay, St. Michael, and probably St. Lawrence Island).

Winter range.—In the Eastern Hemisphere the winter range of the red phalarope seems to be principally at sea off the southern coast of Arabia and the west coast of Africa.

At this season in the Western Hemisphere it has been taken or observed north to Lower California (La Paz and Cape San Lucas); off the coast of Southern California (Point Pinos, Santa Cruz Islands, Anacapa Island, and San Diego); Alabama (Pickett Springs); Florida (Canaveral Light); and South Carolina (Mount Pleasant); and south to southern South America (Falkland Islands. Patagonia, and Chile).

Spring migration.—Early dates of arrival in North America are: North Carolina, Cape Lookout, May 29; Delaware, seen off the coast. May 9; New Jersey, Cape May, May 3, and Ocean City, May 6; New York, Shelter Island, March 25, and Montauk Point, April 30; Connecticut, Bridgeport, May 30; Massachusetts, Gloucester, April 2; Maine, York Beach, May 8; Nova Scotia, Halifax, June 10; Quebec, Prince of Wales Sound, May 31; Washington, Destruction Island lighthouse, May 8; and Alaska, Cape Constantine, May 15, Kodiak Island, May 16, near Kotlik, May 28, Prince Frederick Sound, May 29, and Point Barrow, June 3.

Fall migration.—Late dates of departure in the fall are: Alaska, Chatham Straits, September 9, Becharof Lake, October 6, Point Barrow, October 10, St. Michael, October 14, and Kodiak Island, November 4; Washington, Ilwaco, November 9, and Shoalwater Bay, November 24; California, Berkeley, October 27, Point Reyes, November 22, and Santa Barbara, November 30; Labrador, West Ste. Modiste, September 13; Prince Edward Island, North River, November 20; Nova Scotia, off the coast, September 16; Maine, Westbrook, September 26, Old Orchard, October 5, and Portland, October 16; Massachusetts, North Truro, October 15, near Nantucket, October 25, and Boston, December 30; Connecticut, Portland, October 21, and East Haven, November 24; New York, Oneida Lake, October 4, Branchport, October 12, Orient Point, October 15, Cayuga Lake, October 18, and Montauk Point, November 27; Maryland, White's Ferry, October 4; District of Columbia, Anacostia River, October 17; and Virginia, Blacksburg, September 21.

Casual records.—The red phalarope is rare or irregular anywhere in the interior but it has nevertheless been detected over wide areas on several occasions. Among these records are: Vermont, Woodstock, November 10, 1916; Pennsylvania, Bucks County, December 15, 1918; Ohio, Painesville, November 9, 1923; Ontario, Ottawa, October 21, 1886, and Hamilton, November 17, 1882; Michigan, Monroe, October 24, 1888, and October 25, 1890; Indiana, Jasper County, April 10, 1885, and Terre Haute, October 23, 1889; Wisconsin, Lake Koshkonong, September 3, 1891, Delavan, October 11, 1902, and near Cedar Grove, October 8, 1921; Kentucky, near Louisville, latter part of October, 1808; South Dakota, one taken near Rapid City (date unknown); Kansas, near Lawrence, November 5, 1905; Wyoming, Laramie Plains, fall of 1897; Colorado, Loveland, July 25, 1895; and Texas, Wise County, September 26, 1893. It also has been taken once in New Zealand, at Waimate, South Island, in June, 1883.

Egg dates.—Alaska: 152 records, May 25 to July 13; 76 records, June 14 to 30. Arctic Canada: 14 records, June 21 to July 14; 7 records, June 24 to July 6. Spitsbergen: 22 records, June 24 to July 18; 11 records, June 28 to July 11. Iceland: 17 records, June 1 to 25; 9 records, June 14 to 22.

LOBIPES LOBATUS (Linnaeus)

NORTHERN PHALAROPE

HABITS

This is the smallest, the most abundant, and the most widely distributed of the phalaropes; consequently it is the best known. Its breeding range is circumpolar, but extends much farther south than that of the red phalarope; it might be called sub-Arctic rather than Arctic. There seems to be only one homogeneous species around the world. It resembles the red phalarope in its habits, but is more often seen on inland waters than is that species.

Spring.—Countless thousands of these dainty little birds migrate northward off both coasts of North America in May, but very few ever come ashore except in bad weather. While cruising off the coast, 10 or more miles from land, one is likely to see them flying about in flocks, after the manner of small sandpipers, flitting about and alighting on drifting masses of seaweed or other flotsam, or swimming lightly on the smooth surface of the sea, darting hither and thither in a most erratic way, each seemingly intent on gathering its tiny bits of food. They are gentle, graceful, and charming little birds and well worth watching.

There is also a heavy northward migration through the interior during May. In Saskatchewan I saw a large flock at Quill Lake on May 28, 1917; and in the Crane Lake region we recorded it as an abundant migrant; it was seen migrating, on May 29, 1905, in large flocks with sanderlings; one was seen at Hay Lake on June 15; and two were taken on June 14, 1906, at Big Stick Lake, which were in breeding condition. C. G. Harrold writes to me that it is a common and rather late migrant in Manitoba. William Rowan's notes contain several references to the enormous flocks which pass Beaverhill Lake, Alberta, in May, mostly during the last two weeks.

Dr. E. W. Nelson (1887) has given us the following attractive account of the arrival of these birds in northern Alaska:

As summer approaches on the Arctic shores and coast of Bering Sea the numberless pools, until now hidden under a snowy covering, become bordered or covered with water; the mud about their edges begins to soften, and through the water the melting ice in the bottom looks pale green. The ducks and geese fill the air with their loud resounding cries, and the rapid wing strokes of arriving and departing flocks add a heavy bass to the chorus which greets the opening of another glad season in the wilds of the cheerless north. Amid this loud-tongued multitude suddenly appears the graceful, fairylike form of the northern phalarope. Perhaps, as the hunter sits by the border of a secluded pool still half covered with snow and ice, a pair of slight wings flit before him, and there, riding on the water, scarcely making a ripple, floats this charming and elegant bird. It glides hither and thither on the water, apparently drifted by its fancy, and skims about the pool like an autumn leaf wafted before the playful zephyrs on some embosomed lakelet in the forest. The delicate tints and slender fragile form, combining grace of color and outline with a peculiarly dainty elegance of motion, render this the most lovely and attractive among its handsome congeners.

The first arrivals reach St. Michaels in full plumage from May 14 to 15, and their number is steadily augmented, until, the last few days of May and 1st of June, they are on hand in full force and ready to set about the season's cares. Every pool now has from one to several pairs of these birds gliding in restless zigzag motion around its border, the slender necks at times darting quickly right or left as the bright black eyes catch sight of some minute particle of food. They may be watched with pleasure for hours, and present a picture of exquisite gentleness which renders them an unfailing source of interest. The female of this bird, as is the case with the two allied species, is much more richly colored than the male and possesses all the "rights" demanded by the most radical reformers.

Courtship.—The same gifted writer goes on to say:

As the season comes on when the flames of love mount high, the dull-colored male moves about the pool, apparently heedless of the surrounding fair ones. Such stoical indifference usually appears too much for the feelings of some of the fair ones to bear. A female coyly glides close to him and bows her head in pretty submissiveness, but he turns away, pecks at a bit of food and moves off; she follows and he quickens his speed, but in vain; he is her choice, and she proudly arches her neck and in mazy circles passes and repasses close before the harassed bachelor. He turns his breast first to one side, then to the other, as though to escape, but there is his gentle wooer ever pressing her suit before him. Frequently he takes flight to another part of the pool, all to no purpose. If with affected indifference he tries to feed, she swims along side by side, almost touching him, and at intervals rises on wing above him and, poised a foot or two over his back, makes a half dozen quick, sharp wing strokes, producing a series of sharp, whistling noises in rapid succession. In the course of time it is said that water will wear the hardest rock, and it is certain that time and importunity have their full effect upon the male of this phalarope, and soon all are comfortably married, while mater familias no longer needs to use her seductive ways and charming blandishments to draw his notice.

Mrs. Audrey Gordon (1921) made some interesting observations on the courtship of the red-necked phalarope, as this species is called abroad; she writes of her experiences in the Hebrides:

Three pairs were apparently in process of courting and their behavior was most interesting. Both cocks and hens were swimming in the water near the shore or in pools among the rushes. Suddenly a hen would raise herself in the water and flutter her wings at a great pace with her head held down and neck outstretched, all the while uttering a curious harsh call. She would then pursue the cock rapidly through the water for a few yards as though trying to attract his attention. At times the cock rose from the water and flew round about the pool where the hen was, with a low erratic flight and very slow wing beats, calling as he flew. This display only lasted a minute, when he would again alight on the water. Once after this flight the hen followed him closely and he turned and seemed to be about to mate her, but she would not let him. I saw no more on this occasion, but on June 18 I watched two hens and one cock in a pool. One of the hens kept close to the cock and whenever the other hen came nearer she would chase her away. Both the cock and the hen were seen to stand up in the water and flutter their wings as described above. The cock seemed to pay little attention to the hens and was busy pursuing, and picking up off the water, large black flies. Then, without any warning or unusual excitement on the part of either cock or hen, the nearest one to the cock suddenly put her head low down in the water with neck outstretched and made a curious single note. The cock at once swam to her and mating took place, the hen being submerged in the water except for her beautiful red neck. The cock fluttered his wings all the time; he then went ashore into the grasses. The second hen still kept in the neighborhood, though I imagine she must have realized she had lost her chance of a mate.

P. H. Bahr (1907) throws some light on the peculiar sexual relations of this species; he says:

On the 5th of June we watched the phenomena of polygamy, and of attempted polyandry in this species. At one end of the loch the former condition held sway, two energetic and quarrelsome females having attached themselves to one miserable-looking male, and it was ludicrous to behold the awe in which he held them. Once in particular he nearly swam between my legs in his efforts to avoid their attentions. Till our departure on the 27th, these three birds were constantly to be seen together. At the other end of the loch two males were seen continuously circling round the head of a female. I frequently observed the male performing evolutions, which I have previously described as the "marriage flight." Zigzagging from side to side with amazing rapidity he would hover with dangling legs over the head of the female, who, circling placidly in the water, appeared to take no notice of his attentions. Then settling beside her he would peck and chase her as if endeavoring to make her take to flight. Failing in this he would dash off once more across the marsh uttering a warbling sort of song much like that of the ringed plover. Then he would settle in a reedy spot, such as would be chosen for the nesting site, and would call vigorously, looking always in the direction of the female, as if expecting her to follow. I observed several pairs, behaving in this manner, and such was their fervor that the males continued this performance even in the midst of one of the worst storms we experienced. Often the female would resent these attentions, and a pitched battle would ensue.

Herbert W. Brandt (mss.) writes:

It is very interesting to watch a struggle between two female northern phalaropes over a solitary male. They fight by the hour, not after the manner of the males, which rush at each other and boldly lock in a mortal combat, but rather these females fight by flipping their wings and pecking at each other instead of laying hold with determination. This can be likened only to a feminine hair-pulling episode. One day I watched such a combat for an hour, and there were numerous occasions on which I thought that one of the birds would succumb; but the contest seemed to be very equal, and when a bird recovered from a hard onslaught it would return at once and take up the wing sparring. They would flutter here and there over the ground, first one then the other attacking, closely followed all the time by the shy but neutral male, the prize of the conflict. Natives informed me that they had never known of one's being killed by the other, but that the birds would fight all day long.

Nesting.—My personal experience with the nesting habits of the northern phalarope has been limited to what few nests we found in the Aleutian Islands in 1911. These birds were very scarce or entirely absent in the eastern half of the chain. We saw a few on Atka Island where several nests, with fresh eggs or incomplete sets, were found on June 18. On Kiska Island they were really abundant and we found them breeding about the small grassy ponds and wet meadows; fresh eggs were found on June 21. Their favorite resorts all through the western part of the chain were the wetter portions of the flat alluvial plains, near the mouths of the streams and about the marshy ponds. They were very tame everywhere and, about the ponds where they were breeding, they were very solicitous and noisy. Their simple nests were merely deep, little hollows, lined with a few bits of grass, in the little mounds or tussocks in the wet meadows around the borders of the ponds or near the small streams.

F. S. Hersey collected several sets of eggs for me near St. Michael, Alaska, in 1914 and 1915; most of the nests were in rather wet situations on the tundra, in or near marshy places, rather poorly concealed and scantily lined with grasses; others were well hidden in the clumps of scanty grass, or deeply sunken into the tundra mosses and lined with bits of leaves or well lined with grasses. Other observers have described the nesting habits of this species substantially as indicated above, except that Henry H. Slater (1898), who has "encountered 45 nests with eggs in them in one day, and considerably more than a hundred altogether", describes the nest as "a deep comfortable cup, concealed in a tuft of grass, or under a trailing branch of some dwarf Arctic shrub."

Eggs.—The northern phalarope lays four eggs almost invariably, rarely three eggs constitute a second set; as many as five and even seven eggs have been found in a nest, the largest number being the product of two females. The eggs vary in shape from subpyriform to ovate pyriform, are slightly glossy and are very fragile. The prevalent ground colors range from " pale olive buff " to " dark olive buff " or " ecru olive;" " olive buff " seems to be the commonest shade. In richly colored sets the colors range from " Isabella color," or " Dresden brown " to " buckthorn brown;" and in light buffy sets from " cream buff " to " cream color." The size, type, and arrangement of markings vary greatly in endless patterns. Some eggs, perhaps only one in a set, are evenly covered with small spots or dots, but more often these are mixed with larger, irregular spots or blotches. Some eggs are boldly marked with large irregular blotches. The colors of the markings range from " sepia," or " warm sepia," and " bister " to deep blackish brown, depending on the depth of the pigment. The underlying spots, in various drab shades, are small, inconspicuous and not numerous. In my series of over 50 sets there are two abnormal eggs; one is plain bluish white and unmarked; and another is similar except for one large blotch of " sepia " covering the large end. The measurements of 119 eggs, in the United States National Museum, average 29 by 20 millimeters; the eggs showing the four extremes measure 33 by 21, 28 by 22.5, 27 by 19, and 31 by 18.5 millimeters.

Young.—The period of incubation does not seem to be definitely known, but probably it is not far from 21 days. A set of four eggs found by H. B. Conover on June 10 hatched on the evening of June 30. Incubation is performed largely, but perhaps not wholly, by the male. H. H. Slater (1898) writes:

Jerdon asserts that the females (of all the phalaropes presumably) leave the care of the nests to the males and lead a club life in separate flocks. In the present species I have not found the sex to be so much "emancipated." I have never shot the red-necked phalarope off the nest, often as I have had a chance to do so, nor have I seen bare hatching spots on the breasts of either sex. I have no doubt that the males are the most attentive parents, but in the case of isolated nests the second bird makes its appearance before you have been there long, and I have repeatedly seen both with the young. In fact, I should have said that of all the birds I know the present species is the most connubial, and the mutual devotion of a pair is a most charming thing to see— in fact, quite touching. When not actively employed they treat themselves, and one another, to all manner of pretty and playful endearments.

Hugh S. Gladstone (1907) says:

Incubation is performed mostly, if not entirely, by the male. I flushed females off nests on two occasions, but in one case the full complement of eggs was not yet laid, and in the other I think they were only newly laid. The ground color of the eggs varied from stone to olive, and in one nest all four eggs were remarkably rotund. They take some 18 days to hatch, and only one brood is hatched in the season, though if the first sitting is destroyed the bird will lay again. The nestlings, although they can not fly for some days, are wonderfully precocious and can swim immediately. Their beautiful golden downy plumage becomes paler and paler, even after the first 24 hours.

When the nest contains eggs the female bird shows the greatest anxiety. She can be seen swimming about in the pools; or, rising without any splash, flying up and down quite close to one, uttering a low cry of "*plip, plip*," varied by a hoarse "*chiss-ick*." This cry warns the male, which never flies off the nest, but always creeps through the grass and rushes, to some pool, near one of which the nest is invariably placed. Here he will soon be joined by the female, and they will swim about trying to hide their anxiety by preening their feathers or pretending to feed.

Some observers have said that the young do not take to the water until they are fully fledged, but Mr. Hersey's notes say that: "They run lightly over the beaten down masses of grass around the tundra ponds and when they know they are discovered take to the water and swim as well as their parents."

Doctor Nelson (1887) writes:

Fresh eggs are rarely found after June 20th, and by the middle to 20th of July the young are fledged and on the wing. By the 12th to 15th of July a few of the ashy feathers of the autumnal plumage appear, and soon after old and young begin to gather in parties of from five to a hundred or more, and seek the edges of large ponds and flats or the muddy parts of the coast and borders of tide creeks. During August and September they are found on the bays, and the last are seen about the last of September or first of October.

Plumages.—The general color pattern of the downy young northern phalarope is similar to that of the red phalarope, but it differs in some details and the colors are lighter and more yellowish above. The colors vary from "ochraceous tawny," on the crown and rump, to "antimony yellow," on the rest of the upper parts, and to "Naples yellow" on the throat. The underparts are more extensively grayish white than in the preceeding species and there is considerable whitish between the black stripes on the back. There is more black in the crown, which is nearly surrounded by it, and the black terminates in a point on the nape. A very narrow black line runs from the bill to the eye; and there is a black auricular patch. The central black stripe on the back is broad, but the side stripes are narrow, and there are extensive black patches on thighs and wings.

I have seen no specimens showing the progress of development of the juvenal plumage. In the full juvenal plumage in August, the crown, occiput, and a space around the eye are black, the former faintly mottled with buff; the remainder of the head, throat, and under parts are white, more or less suffused with "light cinnamon drab" and gray on the sides of the neck, breast, and flanks; the feathers of the back and scapulars are brownish black, broadly edged with bright "ochraceous tawny," which gradually fades; some of the tertials are narrowly edged with the same color; the median and inner greater wing coverts and the central tail feathers are narrowly edged with pale buff or white.

A partial molt of the body plumage in September and October produces the first winter plumage, which is like that of the winter adult, except that the juvenal wings are retained. The sexes are alike in the juvenal and all winter plumages. A partial prenuptial molt, from February to June, involving the body plumage, some of the wing coverts and scapulars and the tail, produces the first nuptial plumage, in which the sexes differ, and which is nearly, if not quite, indistinguishable from that of the adult.

Adults have a complete molt from July to October and an incomplete molt from February to June, similar to that of the young bird, producing the distinct and well-known winter and nuptial plumages.

Food.—The northern phalarope obtains most of its food in the water, on the ocean or in bays or in brackish pools or in fresh-water ponds. Its characteristic and best-known method of feeding, on which many observers have commented, is to swim rapidly about in a small circle or to spin around in one spot, by alternate strokes of its lobed feet; this quick whirling action is supposed to stir up the minute forms of animal life on which it feeds and bring them within reach of its needlelike bill, which it jabs into the water two or three times during each revolution; the spinning motion is often very rapid and sometimes quite prolonged, a curious performance to watch. We saw this many times in the Aleutian Islands where small flocks were constantly seen spinning around about the old piers or feeding in the surf off the beaches where they floated buoyantly over the little waves or fluttered over the crests of the small breakers.

William Brewster (1925) describes an interesting feeding performance, at Umbagog Lake, Maine, as follows:

Alighting again, about 100 yards off, it began fluttering about in circles, now narrowly clearing the water for a yard or two, next hitting against or skittering over the surface, acting indeed, for all the world like some enfeebled butterfly or clumsy moth, alternately attracted and repelled by a forest pool lying in deep shadow. This singular performance was occasionally varied by more pronounced upward flights, extending to a height of several feet, and apparently undertaken in pursuit of flying insects, passing overhead.

Both the northern and the red phalaropes feed in large numbers at sea, often being associated together; their favorite feeding places are in the tide rips, on or around floating masses of seaweed, in the vicinity of whales or near schools of fish. George H. Mackay (1894) writes:

On May 25, 1894, about 10,000 (as carefully estimated) were observed resting on the water around the "pigs" (rocks lying off Swampscott), occupying an area of about a mile radius. They were feeding on the red whale bait (brit) some of which was taken from them. I am informed that these birds follow the mackerel, which also feed on this brit, by their pursuit of which it is driven to the surface, and is then obtainable by the birds. I am also told that in the Bay of Fundy the phalaropes so frighten the mackerel when they come to the surface in pursuit of the brit, that the fish sink themselves. To prevent this, the fishermen carry at times quantities of liver cut up, which they throw out to attract these birds and keep them away from the fish in order that they may be better able to capture the latter.

Dr. Alexander Wetmore (1925), in his report on the food of the northern phalarope, gives the results of the examination of 155 stomachs, collected in Alaska and in the United States, from May to October, inclusive; flies and the larvae of mosquitoes were the largest element, 32.8 per cent; the true bugs (*Hemiptera*) came next, 31.8 per cent, including water boatmen and back swimmers; beetles represented 16.5 and crustaceans 9.3 per cent; the remainder contained dragonfly nymphs, spiders, marine worms, small mollusks, a few small fishes and a few seeds. Various other insects and their larvae, many of which are injurious, are included in the food of this bird.

Behavior.—In flight these phalaropes remind one of the smaller sandpipers; their flight is swift and often erratic; when flying in flocks they twist and turn and wheel back and forth like a flock of peeps, flashing white or dark gray, as breasts or backs are turned toward the observer. Mr. Brewster (1883) has seen them pitch "down from a considerable height with closed wings, much as snipe will do under similar circumstances." Again he (1925) speaks of seeing one "rise abruptly to a height of 15 or 20 feet, and poise there for a moment, beating its wings and shaking its tail in a violent and peculiar manner."

It is while swimming on smooth water that the northern phalarope seems most at home, most graceful, charming, and confiding; it is usually very tame and easily approached, but sometimes, especially when in large flocks, it seems to be afraid of a boat and keeps beyond gun range. It swims lightly as a cork, its thick coat of breast feathers giving it great buoyancy, its head is held high and carried with a graceful nodding motion. When a flock alights on the water, the individuals soon scatter and swim about rapidly and independently in zigzag lines or circles, jabbing their bills into the water in a nervous and excited manner. I have never seen them dive and doubt if they can do so, as they seem to have great difficulty in getting under water, even to bathe. They frequently alight on floating masses of seaweed, where they run about and feed with all the nervous activity of small sandpipers on a mud flat. Roland C. Ross (1924) made some interesting observations in southern California; he writes:

The northern phalarope is quite fearless in this region, but seldom does one find the birds so confiding as in the following instance: Mr. Ray Francisco, the warden for the gun club on this marsh, was working in water a foot or two deep, pulling out sedges, dock, and arrowweed. The northern phalaropes took an interest in this roiled up water and drew close to dab at the surface and "whirligig" about in their unique way. As the man kept at work they drew nearer until actually about his feet. They stayed with him until he stopped work in that section. They were observed sleeping on land and water, bill along the back under a wing. Their ablutions were absurd attempts to get a swanlike breast and neck under water, when such airy grace and buoyancy forbade any subaquatic ventures. To get the proper ducking the phalarope stretches up and drives his pretty head and breast down in the water, which effort promptly forces his tail end up; whereupon like a cork he rebounds, to ride high and dry above the water with hardly a sign of moisture on the close-fitting plumage. At once he jerks up and ducks again, and again, all to little avail, seemingly. This up-jerk and ducking motion can be observed at a good distance, and the birds may be identified by it."

A curious little incident, observed in the Hebrides by Misses Best and Haviland (1914), is thus described:

On the south side of the loch, just where we had seen the pair of birds on our previous visit, we found a male and female in the long herbage at the water side. Perhaps we ought to reverse the usual order and say female and male, for the traditional dominance of the masculine sex is entirely unknown in this species. Certainly this cock bird was a most henpecked little fowl. Possibly he had been captured immediately on his arrival from the sea. At any rate, he was apparently tired out, and whenever the hen stopped, as she frequently did, to preen herself or feed, he sat down where he was, and tucking his bill under his feathers, went to sleep. Before he had dozed for more than a minute, however, the female would peck him awake, and, calling querulously, force him to follow her while she led the way through the marsh. Now and then she flew at him and chased him about, as if losing patience. This little scene was repeated three or four times, and the birds were so confiding that we were able to photograph them in the act.

Aretas A. Saunders writes to me:

I watched flocks of these birds on a small pond near the Priest Butte Lakes, in Seton County, Mont. They flew to the pond in a compact flock, scattered over the pond to feed, and evidently gathered insects from the surface of the water. When frightened by the approach of a marsh hawk the birds all rose, quickly formed the compact flock and flew away, returning later when the hawk had gone.

Voice.—The vocal performances of this little phalarope are not elaborate or striking. As it rises from the water it utters a plaintive and rather faint twittering note of one, two or three syllables, which has been variously noted as *tchip*, or *tchep*, or *pe-et*, or *pleep*, or *wit, wit*, or *quet, quet*. Charles W. Townsend (1920) says that it has a variety of notes. At times it twitters like a barn swallow, at times it emits a single harsh note like that of the eave swallow. Again a gentle *ee-ep* is emitted, or a sharp *quip*. According to Witherby's Handbook (1920), "Gladstone describes alarm note as a hoarse *chiss-ick*, and Aplin speaks of a short *quit*, a rapid *ket-ket, ket-ket*, and *chirra-chirra-chirra* at nesting places."

Field marks.—The northern is the smallest of the three phalaropes. It is the one most likely to be seen on inland ponds, except where the Wilson phalarope is common; but the latter is much larger and lighter colored, especially in fall and winter. The best field marks are small size, small head, slender neck and needlelike bill. The upper parts are blackish or dark gray (not pearly gray, as in the others) and in flight a white stripe shows conspicuously near the posterior border of the wing.

Fall.—Northern pharalopes are very abundant during August and September off the coasts of New England, but they seldom come near shore, except in severe storms. The main migration route is so far off shore, south of Cape Cod, that these birds are seldom seen in the Atlantic coast south of New England.

There is a heavy fall migration throughout the interior, which begins quite early. We found them abundant on both migrations in Saskatchewan and Alberta. After I left, Dr. L. B. Bishop saw a flock of 100 at Many Island Lake, Alberta, on July 13, 1905, the beginning of the fall migration; they were still more abundant at Big Stick Lake, Saskatchewan, on the 19th; nearly all of the birds taken on these two dates were adult females; many males were probably still tending broods of young. A. G. Lawrence writes to me that these birds are fairly common transients in southern Manitoba, from August 15 to the end of September.

H. L. Stoddard (1923) has published the following note:

Occasionally in August and September of past years large flocks of small shore birds have been seen a long way offshore in the sand-dune region of southern Lake Michigan circling and wheeling, flashing alternately snow-white breasts and darker backs. Long-range examination with binoculars showed rather prominent whitish wing bars, but the identity of the birds was never satisfactorily determined until the afternoon of August 28, 1921, when the writer was camping at the mouth of the above-mentioned Bar Creek, in Sheboygan County, Wis. About 2 o'clock in the afternoon a light fog drifted in, and soon after large numbers of small shore birds, similar in actions and appearance to those mentioned, were sighted executing extraordinary maneuvers close to the surface of the water about 500 yards out. They circled and recircled, turned and twisted, some of the flocks finally alighting in some smooth streaks in the water inshore of a long line of net stakes that extended about a mile out. Fully 500 of the birds, now recognized as phalaropes, were in sight. One specimen, a female in fall plumage, was finally secured by tying the shotgun onto driftwood pieces and swimming out among them. They were in no way disturbed at my presence until a shot was fired, and I fully satisfied myself that the bulk of the flock were of the same species as the one secured, northern phalaropes.

J. A. Munro tells me that these birds are irregular fall migrants at Okanagan Landing, British Columbia, from July 28 to September 18. Along the California coast the fall migration is heavy and prolonged from the latter part of July until late October or early November, the bulk of the flight passing during August and September. Grinnell, Bryant, and Storer (1918) say:

Heavy winds on the ocean sometimes prove disastrous to the migrating hosts of northern phalaropes. Chapman records finding many bodies of this species in the tide pools of the Farallon Islands. A heavy northwest wind had been blowing along the coast for the previous two weeks, and many of the birds had resorted to inland pools of water. The emaciated condition of the birds at the Farallones was probably due to their inability to procure food while on the open ocean in migration. Forbush records numbers of these birds as being killed on the Atlantic coast by dashing against lighthouses at night. In the Cape Region of Lower California, Brewster found that "most of the birds examined had lost one or more toes, and two or three an entire foot, and part of the tarsus also, while others showed gaping wounds on the breast. These mutilations were probably caused by the bites of fishes." Emerson records finding several of these birds killed by flying against the telephone wires strung across the salt ponds on the marshes west of Hayward, and says that very many of this and other species of birds are killed in this manner.

Winter.—Practically nothing is known about the winter home of this species in the Western Hemisphere. It is evidently south of the borders of the United States and probably south of the Equator on the open ocean. The few straggling winter records for California and South America give but a scant clue to the winter resorts of the vast numbers that pass us on migrations.

DISTRIBUTION

Range.—Distributed over both Old and New Worlds.

Breeding range.—Arctic regions of both hemispheres. In Europe and Asia the breeding range of the northern phalarope extends from Iceland, Spitsbergen, and Scandinavia, across northern Russia and Siberia to Bering Sea. South to Sakhalin Island, southern Russia (Orenburg), and the Outer Hebrides, Shetland, and Orkney Islands.

In North America the breeding range extends north to Alaska (Near Islands, St. Paul Island, Nelson Island, Pastolik, St. Michael, probably Golofin Bay, the Kowak Valley, Cape Blossom, Point Hope, Point Barrow, and the Gens de Large Mountains); Mackenzie (Franklin Bay); Keewatin (Cape Eskimo); probably Baffin Island (Cumberland Sound); and Greenland (North Star Bay, Upernavik and Jacob's Bight). East to Greenland (Disko Island); Labrador (Nain and Hopedale); and western Quebec (Fort George and Rupert House). South to western Quebec (Rupert House); northern Manitoba (York Factory and Fort Churchill); Mackenzie (Artillery Lake and Fort Rae); and Alaska (Nushagak and Kiska Island). West to Alaska (Kiska and Near Islands).

Winter range.—The winter range of the European and Asiatic birds appears to extend south to southern Japan, the north coast of New Guinea, Ceram, the coast of Beluchistan, the east coast of Arabia, and probably points in the northern part of the Indian Ocean.

The winter range of North American breeding birds of this species is more or less imperfectly known, and they are believed to winter largely at sea. It has been reported as wintering in southern California; it has been taken or observed in Costa Rica (Desamparados) and Peru (Tumbez); there is a specimen in the museum at Buenos Aires, Argentina, that was taken in Patagonia.

Spring migration.—Early dates of arrival in North America are: Florida, 175 miles west of Tampa, March 14; Bermuda Islands, March 18; South Carolina, near Chester, May 17; North Carolina, Cape Lookout, April 3; Maryland, Cumberland, May 23; New Jersey, 80 miles off Barnegat, May 6, and Cape May County, May 22; New York, Long Cave, April 2, Montauk Point, April 30, and Branchport, May 16; Connecticut, Quinnipiac Marshes, May 21; Massachusetts, near Boston, May 5, Marthas Vineyard, May 6, and Provincetown, May 21; Maine, near Milo, May 3; Quebec, Godbout, May 27; Nova Scotia, Halifax, May 12; Ohio, Youngstown, May 26; Nebraska, Lincoln, May 10; Manitoba, Shoal Lake, May 19; Saskatchewan, Indian Head, May 15, Osler, May 13, and Dinsmore, May 30; Colorado, Loveland, May 1, Denver, May 17, and Middle Park, May 26; Montana, Big Sandy, May 18, and Terry, May 21; Alberta, Beaverhill Lake, May 7; California, Monterey, April 9, Santa Barbara, April 24, Fresno, May 5, Los Banos, May 19, and Santa Cruz, May 22; Oregon, Klamath Falls, April 17, Malheur Lake, April 26, and Newport, April 30; Washington, Destruction Island Lighthouse, April 27, Shoalwater Bay, May 9, and Olympia, May 13; British Columbia, Okanagan Landing, May 18, and Mabel Lake, May 25; Yukon, Forty-mile, May 3; Alaska, Fort Kenia, May 3, Bethel, May 19, Kowak River, May 22, Igushik, May 23, St. Michael, May 14, Fort Yukon, June 1, and Point Barrow, June 11; and Greenland, North Star Bay, June 14.

Fall migration.—Late dates of departure are: Alaska, Pribilof Islands, August 31, Port Clarence, September 6, and Okutan, September 17; British Columbia, Okanagan Landing, October 15; Washington, Clallam Bay, October 28; Oregon, Oswego, September 25; California, Fresno, October 6, Watsonville, October 20, and Monterey, October 24; Montana, Priest Butte Lakes, September 4, Columbia Falls, September 13, and Corvallis, September 20; Idaho, Salmon River Mountains, September 5; Wyoming, Fort Washakie, September 13, and Yellowstone Park, September 18; Colorado, near Denver, October 13; Manitoba, Whitewater Lake, September 9, and Shoal Lake, September 21; North Dakota, Stump Lake, September 2; Nebraska, Lincoln, October 26; Minnesota, St. Vincent, August 31; Wisconsin, near Cedar Grove, September 23; Ontario, Ottawa, October 12; Ohio, Youngstown, October 9; Newfoundland, October 11; Ungava, mouth of the Koksoak River, September 19; Maine, near Pittsfield, September 3; New Hampshire, Lonesome Lake, September 22, Lancaster, October 8, and Dublin Pond, October 13; Massachusetts, Nantucket, September 20, near Springfield, September 23, Swampscott, September 26, Harvard, October 5, and Ware, October 13; Connecticut, Hartford, September 27; New York, Branchport, September 15, Athol Spring, September 24, Oneida Lake, September 21, Ithaca, September 27, Flushing, September 29, and Montauk Point, October 22; New Jersey, Stone Harbor, September 4, near Tuckerton, September 13, and 5-fathom Beach Light, October 12; Pennsylvania, Pittston, September 2, Beaver, September 26, Carlisle, October 1, and Erie, October 10; District of Columbia, Washington, August 31; West Virginia, near Parkersburg, September 26; North Carolina, Bladen County, September 23; and South Carolina, Frogmore, September 25, and Sea Islands, October 25.

Casual records.—The northern phalarope is apparently less common in the Mississippi Valley and the Southwest. Some records in these regions are: Michigan, Lenawee County, September 14, 1899, near Forestville, October 4, 1911, and October 28, 1911; Indiana, Fort Wayne, June 7, 1889; Illinois, Calumet Lake, September 27, 1903; Iowa, Burlington, August 10, 1894, and Omaha, May 6, 1896; Missouri, near St. Louis, October 9, 1878; Kansas, May 25, 1883; New Mexico, Las Vegas, August 31, 1903; and Arizona, Walker Lake, August 19, 1889.

Egg dates.—Alaska: 83 records, May 20 to July 23; 42 records, June 12 to 25. Arctic Canada: 58 records, June 16 to July 10; 29 records, June 23 to July 1. Iceland: 43 records, May 25 to July 12; 22 records, June 8 to 26. British Isles: 18 records, May 16 to July 12; 9 records, June 7 to 24.

STEGANOPUS TRICOLOR Vieillot

WILSON PHALAROPE

HABITS

I shall never forget my first impressions of a prairie slough with its teeming bird life, an oasis of moisture in a sea of dry, grassy plain, where all the various water birds of the region were thickly congregated. Perhaps 10 or a dozen species of ducks could be seen in the open water, gulls and terns were drifting about overhead, grebes and countless coots were scurrying in and out among the reeds, and noisy killdeers added their plaintive cries to the ceaseless din from swarms of blackbirds in the marsh. In marked contrast to the clownish coots and the noisy killdeers and blackbirds, the almost silent, gentle, dainty, little phalaropes stand out in memory as charming features in the picture, so characteristic of western bird life. The virgin prairies are nearly gone, but there are still left a few oases of moisture in our encroaching civilization, where these graceful birds may continue to delight the eye with their gentle manners.

Unlike the other two world-wide species, the Wilson phalarope is a strictly American bird, making its summer home in the interior of North America and wintering in southern South America. It differs from the other two also in being less pelagic and more terrestrial; it is seldom, if ever, seen on the oceans, being a bird of the inland marshes; and it prefers to spend more time walking about on land, or wading in shallow water, than swimming on the water. Hence its bill, neck and legs are longer, and its feet less lobed. It is a more normal shore bird.

Spring.—The spring migration seems to be directly northward from the west coasts of South America, through Central America, to the Mississippi Valley on one hand and to California on the other. Although it usually arrives in Manitoba during the first week in May, sometimes as early as April 27, I have found it common in Texas as late as May 17. Wilson phalarope are often associated with northern phalaropes on migrations, sometimes in considerable flocks, frequenting the temporary ponds made by heavy spring rains on the grassy meadows, rather than the larger ponds and lakes. The first arrivals are usually females, followed later by mixed flocks of both sexes, which soon scatter and separate into small parties of two or three pairs.

Courtship.—The pursuit courtship is thus described by Rev. P. B. Peabody (1903):

For some three weeks after their arrival, these birds gladden landscape and water scape, in care-free abandon. They are ever on the move, afoot or awing; and during these three weeks of junketing, the unique courtship is carried on. There is no more laughable sight, to one endowed with a modicum of the sense of humor, than that of a couple, or even three, of the brightly colored females, ardently chasing a single somber-plumaged male, who turns and darts, here and there, in arrowy flights apparently much bored by the whole performance. Meanwhile, the sometimes dangling feet and the ever tremulous wings of the amorous females bespeak an ardor that would be ridiculous, under the circumstances, were it not so desperately in earnest.

Dr. E. W. Nelson (1877), on the other hand, writes:

At these times the nearest aproach to pursuit is in a habit they have of suddenly darting off for a short distance at right angles to their general course, but this appears to be in mere sport, for nearly the same relative positions are kept by the birds, and this erratic course is rarely pursued beyond a few rods. In fact, throughout the pairing season I have always found the phalaropes very undemonstrative toward each other, the choice of mates being conducted in a quiet, unobtrusive way, quite unlike the usual manner among birds. The only demonstrations I have observed during the pairing time consist of a kind of solemn bowing of the head and body; but sometimes, with the head lowered and thrust forward, they will run back and forth in front of the object of their regard, or again a pair may often be seen to salute each other by alternately bowing or lowering their heads; but their courtship is characterized by a lack of rivalry and vehemence usually exhibited by birds. A male is often accompanied by two females at first, but as soon as his choice is made the rejected bird joins her fortunes with some more impressible swain.

During my various seasons spent on the western plains I have frequently seen these phalaropes flying about in trios, consisting of one male and two females, the male always in the lead, as if pursued. Females apparently outnumber the males; and, as nest building and incubation are entirely performed by the male, many of the females must remain unattached and unable to breed. I have actually seen the male building the nest and have never been able to flush a female from a set of eggs or a brood of young.

W. Leon Dawson (1923) writes:

We have already acknowledged that Mrs. Wilson wears the breeches and that she is more inclined to club life than she is to household cares. The case is, however, much more serious than we had at first suspected. I owe the original intimation of the true state of affairs to Mr. A. O. Treganza, the veteran oologist of Salt Lake City; and subsequent investigation of my own has abundantly confirmed his claims. Mrs. Wilson is a bigamist. Not occasionally, and of course not invariably, but very usually she maintains two establishments. Now that attention is called to it, we see that our notebooks are full of references to female phalaropes seen in company with two males. The association can not be accidental, for we are in the very midst of the breeding season. The males, frightened by our presence in the swamp, and not daring to remain longer upon their eggs, have sought the comforting presence of the head of their house. The three take counsel together, and it is only when the redoubtable lady announces that the way is clear that the dutiful cuckolds trail off to their nests. On the 6th and 7th of June, 1922, our M. C. O. party of three members gave close attention to a swamp in Long Valley, southern Mono County, at an altitude of 7,000 feet. We took 11 sets, of four eggs each, of the Wilson phalaropes, and we noted a distinct tendency of the nests to group themselves in pairs. In only one instance, however, were we able to trace clearly a connection between two occupied nests. These two, containing heavily incubated eggs, were situated only 42 feet apart, and the two males who were flushed from them by a surprise coup of ours joined themselves immediately to the only female who had shown any solicitude concerning this section of the swamp.

Nesting.—The Wilson phalarope is regarded by some egg collectors as an exasperating bird, because they have some difficulty in finding its nest. The nest is surprisingly well concealed, often in what seems to be scanty vegetation; and the eggs are good examples of protective coloration. I remember once crossing a moist meadow, covered with short grass which had been mowed the previous season; a male phalarope flushed from almost under foot, I threw down my hat to mark the spot and started hunting for the nest. I hunted in vain, until I gave it up and picked up my hat; there was the nest, with four eggs in it, under the hat and in plain sight.

In southwestern Saskatchewan in 1905 and 1906, we found some half dozen or more nests of this species, between June 8 and July 13. The nests were on the wet or moist meadows about the lakes and sloughs or on marshy islands; some of the nests were in practically plain sight in short grass; others were more or less well concealed in longer grass, which was sometimes arched over them; they were always difficult to find unless the incubating male was flushed. The nests were merely hollows in the damp ground, three or four inches in diameter, either scantily or well lined with dry grass.

Doctor Nelson (1877) gives a very good description of the behavior of these birds on their nesting grounds, as follows:

Incubation is attended to by the male alone. The female, however, keeps near, and is quick to give the alarm upon the approach of danger. The females are frequently found at this time in small parties of six or eight; and should their breeding ground be approached, exhibit great anxiety, coming from every part of the marsh to meet the intruder, and, hovering over his head, utter a weak nasal note, which can be heard to only a short distance.

The movements of the birds usually render it an easy matter to decide whether or not they have nests in the immediate vicinity. After the first alarm, those having nests at a distance disperse, while the others take their course in the form of an ellipse, sometimes several hundred yards in length, with the object of their suspicion in the center; and, with long strokes of their wings, much like the flight of a killdeer, they move back and forth. As their nests are approached the length of their flight is gradually lessened, until at last they are joined by the males, when the whole party hover low over the intruder's head, uttering their peculiar note of alarm. At this time they have an ingenious mode of misleading the novice, by flying off to a short distance and hovering anxiously over a particular spot in the marsh, as though there were concealed the objects of their solicitation. Should they be followed, however, and a search be there made, the maneuver is repeated in another place still farther from the real location of the nest. But should this ruse prove unavailing, they return and seem to become fairly desperate, flying about one's head almost within reach, manifesting great distress.

Aretas A. Saunders writes to me that, in Teton County, Mont., they nest in small colonies in grassy marshes, where alkaline soil prevents the grass, mainly species of *Carex* and *Juncus*, from growing tall.

Eggs.—The Wilson phalarope almost invariably lays four eggs, rarely only three. The shapes vary from ovate pyriform to ovate and there is a slight gloss. The ground colors vary from "cartridge buff" to "cream buff," rarely "chamois." The ground color is generally well concealed by numerous markings, more or less evenly distributed. Some eggs are uniformly covered with small spots and dots, but more often these are mixed with a few larger, irregular blotches. An occasional handsome set is boldly and very heavily blotched, sometimes almost concealing the ground color. The markings are usually in very dark, brownish black or blackish brown. In some handsome sets these dark markings are mixed with "bay" and "auburn" markings. The measurements of 57 eggs average 33 by 23.4 millimeters; the eggs showing the four extremes measure **36.2** by 23.7, 33 by **25.1**, **30** by 22.5 and 30.5 by **22** millimeters.

Young.—The period of incubation does not seem to be known. I can find no evidence that the female ever takes any part in it, but that she does not lose interest in her family is plainly shown by her demonstrations of anxiety when the nest is approached; probably she feels responsible for the faithful performance of his duties by her demure spouse. The male broods over the newly hatched young, protecting them from rain, or excessive heat or cold. But they are soon able to run about in a lively manner and care for themselves. Doctor Nelson (1877) writes that "the young have a fine, wiry peep, inaudible beyond a few feet." I believe that the young remain in the grassy meadows, where they can hide in safety, and do not take to the water until they are fully fledged.

Plumages.—In its natal down the young Wilson phalarope is entirely unlike the other phalaropes and quite different from any other young wader. The slender bill and long slender legs and feet are characteristic. It is prettily and distinctively colored also. The prevailing color of the upper parts and of a band across the chest is "ochraceous buff," deepening on the crown, wings, and mantle almost to "ochraceous orange," and paling to buffy or grayish white on the belly and to pure white on the chin and throat. There is a narrow, median, black line on the crown extending nearly or quite to the bill; this is continued in a broad, more or less broken, black stripe down the center of the back to a large black patch on the rump; a black spot on each side of the crown, one on the occiput and several more on wings, thighs, and sides of the back, sometimes run together to form stripes.

In fresh juvenal plumage, in July, the feathers of the crown, back, scapulars, tertials, and all wing coverts are dusky or nearly black, broadly edged with "light pinkish cinnamon" or "cinnamon buff," broadest and brightest on the scapulars; the under parts are white, but the throat, sides of the breast and flanks are washed with "pinkish buff," and the last two are mottled with dusky; the central tail feathers are broadly edged with "pinkish buff," bordered inwardly with a broad dusky band, surrounding a white area, with a dusky central streak invading it; the other tail feathers are similarly marked, but less completely patterned.

This plumage is worn for only a short time, as the body plumage and tail are molted during the last half of July and in August. By September young birds are in first winter plumage, which is like that of the adult, except that the entire juvenal wing is retained with the buff edgings faded out to white. The sexes are alike in juvenal and all winter plumages. A partial prenuptial molt in the spring, involving the body plumage and most, if not all, of the wing coverts and scapulars, makes the young bird practically adult.

Adults have a partial prenuptial molt in April and May, involving the tail, the wing coverts and all the body plumage, which produces the well-known brilliant plumage of the female and the duller plumage of the male. The complete postnuptial molt in summer produces the gray winter plumage in both sexes, in which the crown, back, and scapulars are "light drab" or "drab-gray," with narrow white edgings, and the upper tail coverts, as well as the under parts, are white. The sexes can be recognized in adult winter plumage by size only.

Food.—The other two species of phalaropes feed mainly on the water, but the Wilson phalarope is more of a shore bird and obtains most of its food while walking about on muddy shores or wading in shallow water. It does, however, adopt the whirling tactics of the others occasionally, concerning which Mr. Dawson (1923) says:

Instead of swinging from side to side with a rhythmical motion, as do the reds and northerns, the Wilson whirls all the way around. Moreover, he keeps on whirling, and though he pauses for the fraction of a second to inspect his chances, he goes on and on again like an industrious, mad clock. One bird which I had under the binoculars turned completely around 247 times in one spot, without stopping save for instantaneous dabs at prey. These dabs were directed forward or backward, i. e., with or against the direction of the body motion. A single gyration normally contains two such minute pauses, accompanied by a hitching motion of the head; and these are evidently the periods of maximum attention, since they are followed by, or rather flow into, the prey stroke, if game is sighted. "Game" is not always abundant nor certain, and I have seen a bird whirl a dozen times without a single stroke.

The method of feeding on mud flats or in shallow water is well described by Roland C. Ross (1924), as follows:

When feeding along the shallows with least, western, and red-backed sandpipers, they differed from them not only in size and color, but in their habit of steady, energetic walking and the constant "side sweeping" with the bill. Occasionally they picked objects from the surface with their needle bills, but this was not very actively pursued. In deeper water they fed among the northern phalaropes, knots, and dowitchers, wading along until they swam in places. However, they were able to wade where the northern swam. At such depths they feed with the head clear under and the energy of the feeding operation was indicated by the motion of the tail. They commonly walked steadily back and forth through the deeper sections of the ponds, and in such deep places they moved as headless bodies, evidently feeding as usual in the surface mud. From the vigorous side moves of the tail it would seem they were feeding in their usual manner as well; that is, "side sweeping." When the birds were standing to feed in the deeper places the tail was again much in evidence, and indicated the manner of feeding. This would seem to be a probing motion performed with some rapid vibration which was communicated to the tail as a series of quivers. It is rather a droll sight, and arresting as well, to see a certain area marked out by headless gray bodies buried in the water up to the bend of the wing, the vibrating tail indicating the vigorous operations being carried on down below. It seemed their best feeding was in the deeper waters.

The feeding habits of this and the other phalaropes are almost wholly beneficial. They live very largely on the larvae of mosquitoes. They also eat crane-fly larvae, which are often very destructive in grass lands and wheat fields. Predaceous diving beetles, which are a nuisance in fish hatcheries, are eaten by them. Dr. Alexander Wetmore's (1925) analysis of the contents of 106 stomachs showed that the food of the Wilson phalarope is mainly insects, of which various flies made up 43.1 per cent, aquatic bugs 24.4 per cent and beetles 20.1 per cent. The remainder of the food included brine shrimps, amphipods, eggs of water fleas, and seeds of various aquatic plants.

Behavior.—Much of the interesting behavior of the Wilson phala-ropes has been described under different headings above. In all its movements it is light, airy and graceful. Its flight is much like that of the lesser yellow legs, with which it is often associated; but, when suddenly alarmed, it sometimes flies hurriedly away in a zig-zag fashion. On its breeding grounds it often hovers, almost motion-less in the air, as the upland plover sometimes does. It swims lightly and buoyantly, but apparently does not dive. It walks about on land actively and daintly, where it is said to resemble the solitary sandpiper. It mingles freely on its feeding grounds with various other species of shore birds. Toward the close of the nesting season the females become very gregarious; as early as June 18, in southern Alberta, we saw them in large flocks, mixed with lesser yellow legs, flying about the marshy lakes.

Voice.—The only note I have recorded is a soft, nasal grunt or subdued quack. Dr. Walter P. Taylor (1912) describes a peculiar nuptial (?) call note " as *oit*, *oit*, *oit*, somewhat resembling the croak of a toad during the breeding season. At the instant of utterance of the note the bird which is calling raises its head somewhat, pauses momentarily in its flight, and its throat bulges slightly." Mr. Saun-ders calls it a low note sounding like *croo*, *croo*, *croo*.

E. S. Cameron (1907) writes:

The Wilson's phalaropes, both when feeding and when disturbed and circling on the wing, constantly uttered a low croaking, which at close quarters might be compared to the much louder note of the sandhill cranes, or, at a distance, to the faintly heard barking of a dog. On the other hand, I have heard them give a shrill and totally different call of indecision or satisfaction on their first arrival when hovering over a pool.

Field marks.—The Wilson is larger than the other phalaropes and has a longer bill, neck, and legs. It can be distinguished from other shore birds by its needlelike bill and small head and by the absence of white in its wings. Its spring plumage is, of course, well marked and very beautiful. John T. Nichols gives me the following field characters:

Very rare, but apparently regular on the south shore of Long Island in southward migration; those that I have known of have all been in pale gray and white plumage occurring singly about the marshes in flocks of the lesser yellow legs. Little smaller than that species, they are to be picked out in a flock of same at once by their much paler color. In alighting such a bird may swim on puddles of water between the stubble where the others are wading. At short range the long, straight, very slender bill and indications of a curved "phalarope" mark on the neck, backward and downward from the eye, are to be looked for. Large size and long, very slender bill should prevent confusion of this with other phalaropes in the field in any plumage.

Fall.—As soon as the young are able to care for themselves the males join the flocks of females and they all depart on their fall migration in August. Some individuals wander eastward to the Atlantic coast, but the main flight is southward along both coasts of Mexico to their winter home in Argentina, Chile, and Patagonia.

DISTRIBUTION

Range.—North and South America.

Breeding range.—The breeding range of Wilson's phalarope extends north to Washington (Bumping Lake); Alberta (Alix, Buffalo Lake, and Edmonton); Saskatchewan (Osler, Quill Lake, and Indian Head); Manitoba (Moose Mountain, Brandon, and Shoal Lake); North Dakota (Pembina); Minnesota (probably Leech Lake); Michigan (St. Clair Flats); and southern Ontario (Dunnville). East to southern Ontario (Dunnville); northern Indiana (Lake County); northern Illinois (West Northfield, Fox River, and Calumet Marshes); and formerly Missouri (Pierce). South to Indiana (Whiting); Missouri (formerly Pierce); rarely southern Kansas (Meade County); Colorado (Sterling, Barr, and San Luis Valley); southwestern Wyoming (Fort Bridger); northern Utah (Salt Lake City); Nevada (Washoe Lake); and California (Tahoe Lake and Los Banos). West to California (Los Banos, Lassen County, and Tule Lake); Oregon (Klamath Lake); and Washington (Conconully and Bumping Lake). It also has been reported in summer from southern California (Furnace Creek and Tulare Lake) and from central Mexico (Lerma).

Winter range.—The winter range of the Wilson phalarope is very imperfectly known. The few records available come chiefly from South America, but it also has been reported as wintering in Mexico (Mayorazgo, Ixtapalapa, and the City of Mexico); rarely southern Texas (Corpus Christi); and in southern California (Riverside). South American specimens have been taken or observed at this season in the Falkland Islands; Patagonia (Chupat); Argentina (Mendoza, Buenos Aires, Tucuman, Barracas al Sud, and Missiones); Chile (Valdivia); Bolivia (Alto Paraguay); Peru (Ingapirca); and Brazil (Caicara).

Spring migration.—Early dates of spring arrival are: Missouri, St. Louis, April 22, Corning, April 23, Independence, May 1, and Marionville, May 2; Illinois, Quincy, April 20, Chicago, April 21, Liter, April 27, Fernwood, May 1, and South Englewood, May 3; Indiana, Waterloo, April 27, and Kouts, April 30; Michigan, Ann Arbor, April 1, Detroit, May 1, and Iron Mountain, May 2; Ontario, Toronto, May 25; Iowa, Emmetsburg, April 24, Gilbert Station, April 27, Marshalltown, May 2, Sioux City, May 5, and Keokuk, May 6; Wisconsin, Delavan, April 26, North Freedom, April 29, and Whitewater, May 6; Minnesota, Heron Lake, May 8, Wilder,

May 8, Hallock, May 9, and Waseca, May 12; northern Texas, Gainesville, May 6, and Huntsville, May 7; Kansas, Emporia, April 23, Paola, April 28, Onaga, April 29, and Wichita, April 30; Nebraska, Dunbar, April 5, Badger, April 18, Callaway, April 19, Lincoln, April 22, and Valentine, May 1; South Dakota, Harrison, April 29, Vermilion, April 29, Forestburg, May 1, Pitrodie, May 3, and Huron, May 4; North Dakota, Menoken, May 1, Bismarck, May 3, Charlson, May 4, Antler, May 10, Cando, May 17, and Westhope, May 18; Manitoba, Oak Lake, April 27, Shoal Lake, May 7, Reaburn, May 16, and Winnipeg, May 22; Saskatchewan, Indian Head, May 12, Dinsmore, May 13, and Osler, May 19; New Mexico, Albuquerque, April 20, and Aragon, April 21; Arizona, Tucson, April 12; Colorado, Denver, April 25, Durango, April 25, Loveland, April 27, Boulder, May 3, and Salida, May 4; Wyoming, Lake Como, May 6, near Cokeville, May 7, Yellowstone Park, May 11, and Cheyenne, May 19; Idaho, Meridian, May 14; Montana, Billings, April 30, Great Falls, May 9, Fort Keogh, May 10, Big Sandy, May 14, and Terry, May 21; Alberta, Beaverhill Lake, May 7, Alliance, May 18, Veteran, May 22, and Stony Plain, May 23; California, Santa Barbara, April 26, Unlucky Lake, April 28, and Stockton, May 2; Nevada, Steptoe Valley, May 12, Washoe Lake, May 19, and Quinn River, May 20; and Oregon, Klamath Lake, April 30, Narrows, May 1, and Lawen, May 20.

Fall migration.—Late dates of fall departure are: Oregon, Malheur Lake, September 5; California, Santa Barbara, September 8, and near San Francisco, September 9; Montana, Milk River, July 21, and Great Falls, August 15; Utah, Great Salt Lake, September 16; Wyoming, Seven-mile Lake, September 14, and Yellowstone Park, September 27; Colorado, Denver, September 12; Arizona, Fort Verde, September 7; Saskatchewan, Ravine Bank, August 25; North Dakota, Grafton, September 11, and Westhope, September 24; South Dakota, Forestburg, August 13, Harrison, September 12, and Sioux Falls, October 14; Nebraska, Badger, August 30, and Gresham, September 1; Kansas, Emporia, August 31; Texas, Tivoli, September 14, and Corsicana, September 12; Minnesota, Lanesboro, September 13; Michigan, Kalamazoo County, September 8; and Ontario, near Toronto, September 23.

Casual records.—Although essentially a western species the Wilson phalarope has many times been detected in eastern localities. Among these are: Alabama, Bayou la Batre, September 5, 1911; South Carolina, Sullivans Island, September 7, 1910; North Carolina, near Church Island, August 25, 1910, and Currituck Light House, September 14, 1911; New Jersey, Ocean City, May 19, 1898, and Cape May, May 4, 1909; New York, Mastic, September 21,

1918, and August 23, 1920, Shinnecock, August 20, 1883, and August
15, 1885, Far Rockaway, October 10, 1874, East River, October 15,
1879, Onondaga Lake, September 2, 1886, Oneida Lake, October
6, 1883, Ithaca, fall of 1892, Atlanticville, August 15, 1885, and June
1, 1887, and Bronx Park, September 21, 1924; Connecticut, Bridgeport (Linsley); Rhode Island, Newport, August 2, 1880, August
20, 1883 and September 13, 1886, Sakonnet, August 24, 1899, and
Quonochontaug, August 28, 1909; Massachusetts, Chatham, October
19, 1888, Nantucket, August 31, 1889, Nahant, May, 1874, Salisbury
and Boston (Townsend); New Hampshire, Rye Beach, August 15,
1872; Maine, Sabattus Pond, September or October, 1906, and Scar-
borough, June 9, 1881; and Quebec, Montreal, August, 1869. It also
has been taken in British Columbia, Chilliwack, September 9, 1888,
and Osoyoos Lake, May 15, 1922 and May 18, 1922. It has been
detected a few times in Lower California, La Paz (date ?), and
San Jose del Cabo, one in spring and another in August, 1887.

Egg dates.—Saskatchewan and Alberta: 51 records, May 16 to
June 24; 26 records, June 5 to 11. Dakotas: 23 records, May 25 to
June 22; 12 records, June 3 to 12. Colorado and Utah: 20 records,
May 15 to July 10; 10 records, May 25 to June 8. California: 50
records, May 21 to June 22; 25 records, June 2 to 7.

Family RECURVIROSTRIDAE, Avocets and Stilts

RECURVIROSTRA AMERICANA Gmelin

AMERICAN AVOCET

HABITS

Wherever this large, showy bird is found it is always much in
evidence. Its large size and conspicuous colors could hardly be
overlooked, even if it were shy and retiring; but its bold, aggressive
manners force it upon our attention as soon as we approach its
haunts. Localities and conditions best suited to its needs are still
to be found in many places on the great plains and in the interior
valleys of the far west. Its favorite resorts seem to be the shallow,
muddy borders of alkaline lakes, wide open spaces of extensive
marshes, where scanty vegetation gives but little concealment, or
broad wet meadows splashed with shallow pools. If the muddy pools
are covered with reeking scum, attracting myriads of flies, so much
the better for feeding purposes. Dry, sun-baked mud flats or low,
gravelly or sandy islands, with scanty vegetation, furnish the desired nesting conditions. In such open spaces they can be seen from
afar and, long before we reach their haunts, the avocets are flying
out to meet us, advertising the fact that we are approaching their
home, making the air ring with their loud yelping notes of protest,
circling about us and darting down at us in threatening plunges.

Courtship.—Prof. Julian S. Huxley (1925), who has made a study of the European species, says:

The avocet has no courtship. There are no songs or aerial displays; no posturing by the male; no mutual ceremonies; no special courtship notes. There is some hostility and fighting; a peculiar action by the female which is a symbol of readiness to pair, followed by an excited action on the part of the male; and a special post-paring action by both birds; but of courtship in any accepted sense none whatever.

However that may be, our bird does indulge in actions and posturings which look very much like courtship. On May 29, 1905, we spent some time in watching the avocets in a colony on an alkali flat covered with a sparse growth of short, curly grass, near Hay Lake in southwestern Saskatchewan. We could not find any nests there at that time and concluded that the birds had not laid. They were apparently still conducting their courtships, wading about gracefully in the shallow water, frequently bowing or crouching down close to the water; sometimes they danced about with wings widespread, tipping from side to side like a balancing tight-rope walker; occasionally one, perhaps a female in an attitude of invitation, would lie prostrate on the ground or water for a minute or more, with the head and neck extended and wings outstretched. Frequently they fooled us by squatting down on the ground, as if sitting on a nest; if we went to investigate, they would run away and repeat the act elsewhere; perhaps this act carried the suggestion of mating as a part of the courtship ceremony.

Nesting.—We found no large breeding colonies in Saskatchewan but several small ones. The Hay Lake colony referred to above was perhaps the largest, containing 15 or 20 pairs. The nests, found here on June 15, were merely slight hollows in the sun-baked mud on the broad alkali flats bordering the shallow lake; they were scattered widely among the little tufts of short grass which scantily covered the flat; the hollows measured from 3 to 4 inches in diameter and were lined with a few dry grasses. Some of the nests were well formed and somewhat elevated. Although in plain sight, the eggs were not easy to find, as they matched their surroundings perfectly.

On June 14, 1906, we found an interesting little colony of avocets on an island in Big Stick Lake, Saskatchewan, which was also occupied by big colonies of California and ring-billed gulls, common terns, a few spotted sandpipers, and a few pairs of ducks. The avocets, terns, and sandpipers were all at one end of the island, a low grassy point; the ring-billed gulls and ducks were in the central, highest part; and the California gull colony was at the other end. The avocets' nests, ten or a dozen of them, were placed in the short grass near the edge of the beach or on the drift weed lying in windrows on the beach; one nest was partially under a fallen shrub or bushy weed. The nests were made of grasses, weed stems, straws and small sticks, with sometimes a few feathers, loosely arranged around small hollows, from 5 to 7 inches in diameter. Two of the nests held five eggs, the others three or four.

Robert B. Rockwell (1912) found an interesting colony of avocets on an island in Barr Lake, Colo., of which he says:

The nests were all located in very similar locations, among a young growth of cockle burrs not over six inches in height and which had probably grown at least half of that since the eggs were laid. The cockle burrs formed a belt about 10 yards wide clear around the island just below the dense blue-stem and other rank grass with which the island was covered and on ground that was under water during the high water of the spring although inundated for a short time only. Two of the nests were very crude affairs, being a mere shallow hollow in the sand with a very few dead weed stalks of short lengths arranged around the eggs. The other was constructed in the same manner, but was quite well lined with weed stems, so that the eggs did not touch the ground. There was no evident attempt at concealment, the nests all being placed in small open spaces from six inches to a foot in diameter, and with nothing to protect them; but the color of the eggs was sufficient protection to make them quite inconspicuous.

Dr. Alexander Wetmore (1925) writes:

The sites chosen often are subject to inundation by sudden floods, when the birds scurry about, seemingly in confusion, but in reality working actively to build up the nest in order to support the eggs above the level of the encroaching water. In some cases it may be necessary to erect a structure 12 or 15 inches in height. Weeds, small sticks, bones, or dried bodies of ducks or other birds, feathers, or any other materials available are utilized as building materials.

Eggs.—The American avocet lays three or four eggs, usually four and occasionally five. Numerous nests have been found containing seven or eight eggs, but these are probably products of two females. Edwin Beaupré writes to me that, in a colony of five pairs found by him on an island in a small lake in southern Alberta, the five pairs were occupying three nests; one contained eight eggs, another seven and the third four. The eggs vary in shape from ovate (rarely) to ovate pyriform and they are usually much elongated. The shell is smooth, but not glossy. The ground color varies from "Isabella color" to "deep olive buff." This is more or less evenly covered with irregular spots and blotches, in various sizes, of brownish black, blackish brown, or black, rarely "warm sepia" or "bister"; there are occasionally a few blackish scrawls, and numerous underlying spots of various shades of drab. The measurements of 55 eggs average 49.8 by 34 millimeters; the eggs showing the four extremes measure 56.3 by 34.6, 51.5 by 36.6, 43.2 by 33.4 and 47 by 31 millimeters.

Young.—The period of incubation of the American bird has apparently not been determined, but that of the European bird is said to be 28 days. I have no data as to how the sexes incubate. Young avocets are very precocial and leave the nest soon after hatching. They are expert at hiding, even on the open flats and beaches; and they take to the water at an early age, where they can swim and dive like young ducks. I have seen a brood of four young, that could not have been hatched more than a few hours, swimming out in a lake, as if very much at ease. They soon learn to tip up in shallow water and probe on the bottom, like their parents, for their insect food.

Plumages.—The downy young avocet is well colored for concealment on an open beach or alkaline flat. The colors of the upper parts are " cinnamon buff," " cream buff," and buffy grays, lightest on the crown and darkest on the rump; there is a distinct but narrow loral stripe of black; the crown is indistinctly spotted with dusky. Two parallel stripes of brownish black distinctly mark the scapulars and two more the sides of the rump; the wings, back, rump, and thighs are less distinctly spotted or peppered with gray and dusky. The under parts are buffy white, nearly pure white on the throat and belly.

In fresh juvenal plumage the crown is " light drab " with " pinkish buff " tips; the sides and back of the neck are deep, rich " cinnamon," deeper and richer than in the adult, shading off, on the upper back, throat, and upper breast, to a suffusion of " pinkish buff "; the chin and belly are white; the color pattern of the upper parts is similar to that of the adult, except that the dark feathers of the back, scapulars, and tertials are tipped with " pinkish buff"; and the greater and median wing coverts are narrowly so tipped.

This plumage is worn through the summer and fall without much change except by extensive fading and some wear. The cinnamon has nearly disappeared in September birds and all the buff edgings have faded or worn away. A body molt takes place in late winter or early spring which produces a first nuptial plumage much like the adult. Young birds can, however, be recognized by the worn primaries and by some of the juvenal scapulars and wing coverts. The first postnuptial molt, the following summer, is complete and produces the adult winter plumage.

Adults have a complete postnuptial molt, beginning in August, and a partial prenuptial molt, beginning in January, which involves the body plumage and some of the scapulars and wing coverts. The " cinnamon " colors of the head and neck are characteristic of the nuptial plumage and are replaced by pale gray in winter adults.

Food.—The feeding habits of the avocet are rather peculiar, as might be expected of a bird with such a peculiar bill. The bill is not so sharply upturned in life, as it is in some stuffed specimens and in some drawings. Dr. Frank M. Chapman (1891) has explained it very well, as follows:

The use of the avocet's recurved bill is clearly explained by the manner in which the bird procures its food. In feeding they wade into the water and drop the bill below the surface until the convexity of the maxilla probably touches the bottom. In this position they move forward at a half run and with every step the bill is swung from side to side sweeping through an arc of about 50° in search of shells and other small aquatic animals. The mandibles are slightly opened, and at times the birds pause to swallow their prey. It is evident that birds with a straight or a downward curved bill could not adopt this method of feeding.

Audubon (1840) describes it, as follows:

They search for food precisely in the manner of the roseate spoonbill, moving their heads to and fro sideways, while their bill is passing through the soft mud; and in many instances, when the water was deeper, they would immerse their whole head and a portion of the neck, as the spoonbill and red-breasted snipe are wont to do. When, on the contrary, they pursued aquatic insects, such as swim on the surface, they ran after them, and on getting up to them, suddenly seized them by thrusting the lower mandible beneath them, while the other was raised a good way above the surface, much in the manner of the black shear water, which, however, performs this act on wing. They were also expert at catching flying insects, after which they ran with partially expanded wings.

Doctor Wetmore (1925) found that, in 67 stomachs examined, animal food amounted to 65.1 per cent and vegetable food 34.9 per cent. Among the animal food were found phyllopods, dragonfly nymphs, back swimmers, water boatmen, various beetles and flies and their larvae. The vegetable matter consisted largely of seeds of marsh or aquatic plants. He says further:

Flocks of the birds search for food scattered about in shallow water, and do not hesitate to swim when necessary in crossing the deeper channels. Frequently a dozen or more feed in company, walking slowly along, shoulder to shoulder, as though in drill formation, at each forward step thrusting the head under water and sweeping the recurved bill along the bottom with a scythelike swing that must arouse consternation among water boatmen and other aquatic denizens of the bays and ponds. At times the writer has observed as many as 300 of these handsome birds feeding thus in a single company, a scene at once spirited and striking. As the birds feed much of the time by immersing the head, anything that may touch the bill is gathered indiscriminately, as in feeding they depend upon the sense of touch. From their manner of feeding, avocets are often scavengers, taking living or recently dead prey without much choice. The large tapeworms found almost without fail in the duodenum of the avocet are transmitted from one bird to another in this manner. The cast-off terminal segments of the worms (bearing the eggs) are picked up and swallowed by other avocets, a proceeding which the writer has personally observed. Avocets also pick up matter floating in the water, on or near the surface, or take insects and seeds from mud bars. The insects may be those living in such localities or may be individuals that have been washed up in drift.

Other observers have reported avocets as feeding on grasshoppers, predaceous diving beetles, crickets, centipedes, weevils, small snails, sea slugs, small crustaceans, and even small fishes.

Behavior.—Avocets are at all times tame and unsuspicious, very solicitous and aggressive on their breeding grounds, quiet and indifferent at other times, showing only mild curiosity. Their demonstrations of anxiety on their nesting grounds, particularly if they have young, are amusing and ludicrous. Utterly regardless of their own safety, they meet the intruder more than half way and stay with him till he leaves. W. Leon Dawson (1909) has described it very graphically, as follows:

The mother bird had flushed at a hundred yards, but seeing our position she flew toward us and dropped into the water some 50 feet away. Here she lifted a black wing in simulation of maimed stiffness, and flopped and floundered away with the aid of the other one. Seeing that the ruse failed, she ventured nearer and repeated the experiment, lifting now one wing and now both in token of utter helplessness. After a while the male joined her, and we had the painful spectacle of a crippled family, whose members were uttering most doleful cries of distress, necessitated apparently by their numerous aches and breaks. Once, for experiment's sake, we followed, and the waders flopped along in manifest delight coaxing us up on shore and making off through the sagebrush with broken legs and useless wings. But we came back, finding it better to let the birds make the advances. The birds were driven to the very limit of frenzy, dancing, wing trailing, swaying, going through last convulsions and beginning over again without regard to logical sequence, all in an agony of effort to divert attention from those precious eggs. As time elapsed, however, the color of the play changed. Finding that the appeal of cupidity was of no avail, the birds appeared to fall back upon the appeal to pity. Decoying was useless, that was plain; so they stood with upraised wings, quivering and moaning, in tenderest supplication. It was too much even for conscious rectitude and we withdrew abashed.

The flight of the avocet is strong, direct and rather swift, much like that of the greater yellow legs, with neck and legs fully extended, fore and aft. It can alight on or rise from the surface of the water with ease. On alighting its long, black and white wings are raised above its back, and slowly folded, as it settles itself with a nodding motion of the head, stands still and looks about it for a moment or two. No bird is better equipped for the amphibious existence that it leads; its long legs and webbed feet enable it to wade through soft muddy shallows of varying depths; and if it suddenly steps beyond its depth it swims as naturally as a duck until it strikes bottom again; the thick plumage of its under parts protects it and marks it as an habitual swimmer. It often feeds while swimming by tipping up like a surface-feeding duck and reaching down into the water with its long neck and bill. It can even dive when necessary.

Dr. Walter P. Taylor (1912) says that avocets "share with most other birds a dislike of owls. Three were seen pursuing a *Speotyto* over a wild hay meadow."

Dr. T. Gilbert Pearson (1916) noted an interesting flight maneuver:

Only a few weeks ago I was impressed anew with the beauty of these birds. While passing down the valley of Crane Creek, in southeastern Oregon, a flock of about 50 avocets arose and indulged in a series of evolutions which even the most casual observer would have paused to watch. In a fairly compact company they flew away for a short distance, then turned, and, after coming back almost to the starting point, dived toward the earth, arose again perhaps 50 yards in the air, then swung around and came back. These maneuvers were repeated at least three times. Their white and black plumage, flashing against the gray sagebrush of the desert mountain side, and sharply relieved as they skimmed over the alkaline creek, made a picture long to be remembered.

Charles E. H. Aiken (1914)

witnessed a curious performance of avocets in Utah. In September, 1893, he visited the mouth of Bear River where hundreds of acres of mud flats and shallow water offer an attractive resort for various water fowl. In a submerged grove where patches of mud appeared above the water hundreds of avocets were congregated. One little mud island that differed from others in that it was quite round seemed to have a fascination for the birds, and they were packed together upon it in a mass which covered the island to the water's edge. As the island was about 12 feet in circumference the number of birds probably approximated 150. This mass of birds continued to revolve about from left to right, and being so crowded the movement was rather slow and their steps short and measured, so that the impression was that they were all marking time in the marching. Birds on the rim of the circle avoided walking off in the water and crowded inward against the mass. Every moment or two birds would leave the milling body and fly to a neighboring mud island, and as many from near-by would fly to take their places and join the dance. Aiken advanced quietly to within 20 yards and viewed them for half an hour, but they continued undisturbed by his presence and he left them so. It appeared to be a diversion of the birds.

John G. Tyler contributes the following:

The avocet is evidently possessed of a very keen sense of hearing. On May 21, 1921, I discovered three or four pairs in an overflowed pasture not far from Fresno. Driving my car up to within about 100 feet of them I allowed my engine to die and sat perfectly motionless. In about 15 minutes the birds had become thoroughly accustomed to my presence and one bird finally took up a position on a small levee, tucked its bill under the feathers of its back, closed its eyes, and after raising the right leg and drawing it up close to the body, stood absolutely motionless and apparently asleep for several minutes. It was very much awake, however, for when I whistled softly through my teeth, making a rather squeaking noise, it immediately straightened up, opened its eyes, and gazed about in apparent astonishment. As I remained motionless the bird soon settled down and in the course of the next few moments I repeated the same experiment always with the same results. So long as one remains seated in the automobile and makes no noticeable movement it is possible to make close observation of these and several other species of shore birds, but the slightest movement or an attempt to get out of the car sends them away in the wildest confusion.

Voice.—The avocet's vocabulary is not so elaborate as it is impressive. The commonest note, heard on the breeding grounds as a note of alarm or protest, is a loud, shrill whistle or yelping scream, which I have recorded in my notes as *wheat, wheat, wheat.* Others have recorded it as *plee-eek, plee-eek,* or *click, click, click.* It is always sharp and vehement, implying anger. I have also heard a softer note, uttered in a conversational tone, like *whick, whick, whick,* or *whuck, whuck, whuck.*

Aretas A. Saunders contributes the following notes:

About the nest colony the adults flew closely about my head, calling a short staccato call that sounded like *pink, pink, pink.* One bird pretended wounded in a different manner from what I have seen it done by other species. The bird sat on the water, dropped its head and neck down to the surface, half spread its wings, also dropping them on the water, and, lying almost still, called *oo-oo, oo-oo, oo-oo,* over and over, as though suffering great pain. The voice was low and not very loud, and not at all like the *pink, pink* of the other birds.

Field marks.—The avocet, in its striking color pattern of black and white, could not be mistaken for anything else. A white tail, a black V on a white back, black wings with white secondaries and blue legs are all distinctive marks; the buff head and neck are nuptial adornments; in fall and winter these parts are grayish white. From the stilt it can be distinguished by its much stockier build, the absence of black on head and neck and by blue instead of pink legs.

Game.—Although it is a large, plump bird and would help to fill a game bag, there is no excuse for treating it as a game bird. It is so tame and so foolishly inquisitive that it would offer poor sport and would soon be exterminated. Furthermore its flesh is said to be worthless for the table. But above all, it is such a showy, handsome and interesting bird, that it ought to be preserved for future generations to enjoy. The destruction of its breeding grounds will exterminate it soon enough, as it has already been extirpated from its former range in the Eastern States.

DISTRIBUTION

Range.—North America to northern Central America.

Breeding range.—The breeding range of the avocet extends north to Washington (Moses Lake and probably Walla Walla); northern Idaho (Pend Oreille); Alberta (Red Deer, Buffalo Lake, and Flagstaff); Saskatchewan (Osler, Quill Lake, and Touchwood Hills); North Dakota (Kenmare and Cando); Minnesota (Brown's Valley,

Traverse County) ; and Wisconsin (Green Bay). East to Wisconsin (Green Bay) ; western Iowa (Sioux City) ; central Kansas (Larned and Dodge) ; and rarely to southern Texas (Corpus Christi and Isabel). South rarely to southern Texas (Isabel and Brownsville) ; New Mexico (Chloride) ; northern Utah (Salt Lake City) ; Nevada (Ruby Valley and probably Cloverdale) ; and southern California (Little Owens Lake, Kerrville, and Santa Ana). West to California (Santa Ana, Santa Cruz Island, Buena Vista Lake, Tulare Lake, Los Banos, Stockton, Amedee, Tule Lake, and Brownell) ; Oregon (Adel, Plush, Sumner Lake, and Christmas Lake) ; and Washington (Moses Lake). It has been recorded in summer north to British Columbia (Okanagan Landing) ; Manitoba (Brandon) ; and New York (Ithaca) ; while there also is an old breeding record for Egg Harbor, New Jersey.

Winter range.—North to Carolina (Novato and Stockton) ; and Texas (Houston). East to Texas (Houston, Corpus Christi, and Brownsville) ; Tamaulipas (Matamoros) ; and Guatemala (Chiapam). South to Guatemala (Chiapam) ; and Sinaloa (Escuinapa). West to Sinaloa (Escuinapa and Mazatlan) ; Lower California (San Jose del Cabo and La Paz) ; and California (San Diego, Morro Bay, San Francisco, and Novato.)

Spring migration.—Early dates of arrival are: Nebraska, Whitman, April 13, Long Pine, April 27, Alda, May 2, and Lincoln, May 5; South Dakota, Pitrodie, April 28, Huron, May 6, and Aberdeen, May 15; North Dakota, Marstonmoor, April 28; Manitoba, Margaret, May 5; Saskatchewan, Fort Carlston, May 4, and Dinsmore, May 9; Arizona, Ehrenburg, February 12, and Tucson, April 21; New Mexico, Albuquerque, April 14; Colorado, Loveland, April 9; and Denver, April 25; Utah, Salt Lake City, April 27; Wyoming, Huttons Lake, April 21, Lake Como, April 22, and Cheyenne, April 24; Idaho, Deer Flat, February 15, and Rupert, April 26; Montana, Great Falls, April 18, Fort Custer, April 26, Terry, May 1, Billings, May 3, and Big Sandy, May 18; Alberta, Beaverhill Lake, April 28, and Flagstaff, May 14; Nevada, Ash Meadows, March 15; Oregon, Klamath Falls, March 26, Narrows, April 11, Malheur Lake, April 17, and Lawen, April 19. Avocets have been noted at Lake Palomas, Chihuahua, on April 7, and at Gardner's Laguna, Lower California, on April 22.

Fall migration.—Late dates of departure are: Oregon, Forest Grove, September 28, Malheur Lake, October 26, and Klamath Lake, November 6; Alberta, Veteran, September 8; Montana, Fort Custer, September 9, and Great Falls, October 2; Idaho, Rupert, October 21; Wyoming, Fort Bridger, October 10; Utah, Provo, November 26; Colorado, Denver, October 3, and Mosca, October 20; New Mexico, Glenrio, October 11, Las Palomas, October 12, and Mesilla Park, November 9; Manitoba, Margaret, September 15; South Dakota, Harrison, October 28; Wisconsin, Waupaca County, October 21; Nebraska, Gresham, September 10, Long Pine, October 9, and Lincoln, October 27; and Kansas, Emporia, August 25. The arrival of avocets in the fall has been noted in the Valley of Mexico in August and September.

Casual records.—The avocet has on a number of occasions been reported or taken at points far outside of its normal range. Some of these records are: Cuba, once in the market at Havana and at Cardenas in August; Jamaica, reported in winter; Barbados, one in the fall of 1880 and again on October 1, 1888; Florida, one killed at Palm Beach Inlet in 1916; Georgia, St. Marys, October 8, 1903; North Carolina, six noted at Fort Macon on September 12, 1870; Virginia, two taken at Wallops Island in September, 1925; New Jersey, Barnegat, May 30, 1880; New York, Ponquoque, one in 1844, Carnarsie Bay, one in 1847, Long Beach, May 20, 1877, near Tuckerton, last of August, 1886, Renwick, September 16, 1909, and Ithaca, September 16, 1909; Connecticut, near Saybrook, 1871; Massachusetts, three at Ipswich Neck, September 13, 1896, Lake Cochituate, October 19, 1880, Natick, October 29, 1880, and Salisbury, May 23, 1887; Vermont, St. Albans, fall of 1875; Maine, Cape Elizabeth, November 5, 1878, and Calais, spring of 1862; New Brunswick, Quaco, in 1880; Louisiana, New Orleans, November 12, 1889, and November 7, 1819, Derniere Island, April 16, 1837, and Johnsons Bayou, November 26, 1882; Arkansas, a specimen was taken some time previous to 1847; Missouri, St. Louis, October 28, 1878, and Stotesbury, April 8, 1894; Illinois, St. Clair County, October 28, 1878, and two at Chicago, May 5, 1889; Indiana, one was taken at Calumet Lake; Ohio, St. Marys Reservoir, November 10, 1882, Oberlin, November 4, 1907, and March 16 to 21, 1907, Sandusky, May 24, 1914, and near Columbus, November 10, 1882; Michigan, St. Clair Flats, in 1874; Ontario, Toronto, last of May, 1881 and September 19, 1901; Mackenzie, Birch Lake, July 15, 1910, and Fort Rae; British Columbia, Okanagan, April 28, 1908, and mouth of the Fraser River, October 20, 1915. Avocets also have been reported from Greenland, but the records lack confirmation.

Egg dates.—Saskatchewan: 27 records, May 18 to June 16; 14 records, May 29 to June 14. Utah: 52 records, April 10 to June 15; 26 records, May 6 to 16. California: 35 records, April 22 to June 25; 18 records, May 5 to 29.

HIMANTOPUS MEXICANUS (Müller)

BLACK-NECKED STILT

HABITS

Although I first met the black-necked stilt in the Florida Keys in 1903, it was not until I visited the irrigated regions of the San Joaquin Valley in California in 1914, that I saw this curious bird living in abundance and flourishing in most congenial surroundings. It was a pleasant change from the cool, damp air of the coast region to the clear, dry warmth of this highly cultivated valley. The naturally arid plains between the distant mountain ranges had been transformed by irrigation into fertile fields of alfalfa and wheat, vast areas had been flooded with water from the melting snows of the Sierras, forming grazing lands for herds of cattle and endless marshes, wet meadows, ponds and creeks, for various species of water birds. As W. Leon Dawson (1923) puts it:

The magic touch of water following its expected channels quickens an otherwise barren plain into a paradise of avian activities. Ducks of six or seven species frequent the deeper channels; coots and gallinules and pied-billed grebes crowd the sedgy margins of the ponds; herons, bitterns, ibises, and egrets, seven species of *Herodiones*, all told, occupy the reedy depths of the larger ponds or deploy over the grassy levels. Rails creak and titter, red wings clink, yellow-headed blackbirds gurgle, wrangle, and screech; while the marsh wrens, familiar spirits of the maze, sputter and chuckle over their quaint basketry. The tricolored blackbirds, also in great silent companies recruited from a hundred acres, charge into their nesting covert with a din of uncanny preoccupation. Over the open ponds black terns hover, and Forster terns flit with languid ease. The killdeer is not forgotten, nor the burrowing owl, whose home is in the higher knolls; but over all and above all and through all comes the clamor of the black-necked stilt and the American avocet.

Of all these birds, the stilts were the most conspicuous in the wet meadows about Los Banos, where they were always noisy and aggressive. I have never seen them so abundant elsewhere, though I have seen them in similar situations in Florida and Texas, on extensive wet meadows where shallow water fills the hollows between myriads of little muddy islets and tufts of grass. Here they can wade about and feed in the water or build their nests on the hummocks above high-water mark, and here their young can hide successfully among the grassy tufts.

Nesting.—My first glimpse of a black-necked stilt was a complete surprise, and my first nest was in an unexpected situation. On May 8, 1903, we landed on Lake Key, in the Florida Keys, a low flat, open island with sandy shores and a lake in the middle of it. We walked across the beach, through a narrow strip of low red mangrove bushes and came to a little muddy pond, very shallow and dotted with little mangrove seedlings. Here we were delighted to see about half a dozen black-necked stilts, long slender birds, very striking in appearance and actions, the jet black wings contrasting finely with the pure white under parts and the long pink legs trailing behind. They seemed so much concerned, so unwilling to leave, and kept up such an incessant racket, that we felt sure that they were nesting there. A short search soon revealed two of their nests, both very conspicuously placed. The first nest, containing four quite heavily incubated eggs, was very prettily located under a little red mangrove root, just as it entered the ground; a hollow had been scraped in the sand and profusely lined with small bits of shell and pieces of dry sticks. The second nest was in plain sight on the open beach of finely broken shell in a small colony of least terns' nests, the three dark-colored eggs showing up very conspicuously on the white sand. The nest cavity measured six inches outside and four inches inside and was lined with pieces of shell, sticks, and fish bones, an odd and uncomfortable bed for the young. Besides the least terns, Wilson plovers were nesting close by, rather an unusual association for the marsh-loving stilts.

Gilbert R. Rossignol writes to me of a colony of some 23 nests that he found in a somewhat similar location on an island in Lake Kissimmee, Florida, on April 14, 1908. "The nests were all built high upon the gravelly beach and were lined with bits of fresh-water snails." This colony was wiped out later by a rise of water in the lake.

Herbert W. Brandt has sent me some notes on this species as he found it breeding in Kleberg County, Texas, on May 28, 1919. He found seven nests in a colony of about ten pairs on "a watery, marshy meadow covering about a square mile, the water being 6 to 12 inches deep." He describes one of the nests as "composed of sticks made up into a floating platform, about four inches high and well made The lining was small sticks and the top basin shallow and nicely made. The water, exceedingly high from recent rains, was up to the eggs, so that the nest was wet." I saw a similar colony near Brownsville, Tex.

Near Los Banos, California, stilts were nesting all over the flooded meadows, on little hummocks, on the muddy islands, and along the margins of ponds. On the drier shores and banks the nests were very simple structures, hollows in the ground, lined with small twigs, weed stems, and grasses; but in the wet places, where they were liable to be flooded, they were quite elaborately elevated to considerable heights. Mr. Dawson (1923) writes:

It is when the water rises that the birds rise to the occasion, and get busy with nest building. Sedges, sticks, water plants with clinging soil, anything movable, is seized and forced under the threatened eggs. Indeed, so apprehensive is the bird of the growing necessity, that as often as she leaves the nest she will seize loose material and fling it over her shoulder for future use. The eggs themselves, protectively colored in bister and black, are mauled about and soiled in the mud; but the day is saved. I have seen a stilt, painfully conscious no doubt, squatted on a truncated cone of vegetation 8 inches in height and as broad across the top, a veritable Noah's ark of safety.

John G. Tyler (1913) says:

Nesting colonies of these waders in the Fresno district are never very large, consisting of from 6 to 20 pairs, as a rule, the most extensive one of which I have any knowledge containing an average of about 30 pairs each season. Possibly the numerous small ponds will not support a great many birds, and as suitable pastures abound in certain sections it is not a difficult matter for all the birds to be accommodated without any crowding. As these nesting colonies of stilts are invariably in pastures with cattle tramping everywhere over the fields, it seems almost a miracle that any of the eggs escape being destroyed; and yet I have not one iota of positive proof of such a disaster ever overtaking a stilt's nest, while in many instances I have known the eggs to hatch safely almost under the feet of stock. It is known that few animals will purposely step on any living object of a size large enough to be noticed, and the writer is convinced that a stilt simply remains on her nest and by her vociferousness and possibly even with a few vigorous thrusts of her long bill causes a grazing cow to direct her course away from the nest. A lack of judgment causes many nests to be abandoned each year, and a colony of stilts that are not able to distinguish between a permanent pond and one that has been caused by irrigation is liable to find that by the time sets of eggs are complete the water has disappeared and a new nesting site must be chosen. Fortunately the larger colonies always seem to be located near the permanent ponds, but there are numerous scattering pairs that are deceived each summer.

I have often been surprised at the great diversity of nesting sites, even in the same colony, it being not an unusual occurrence to find nests entirely surrounded by water—little islands of mud and sticks often built up out of water several inches deep. Not less common are the platforms of dried grass placed just at the water's edge, or the slight excavations that, killdeerlike, are placed on the bare ground a hundred yards or more from the nearest water. In one colony the majority of the nests were built on a levee that extended through the pond and were so near the waters edge that, although most of the nests were quite elaborate platforms of dry grass and twigs, the lower parts of the eggs were wet. Undoubtedly a high wind would have caused the wavelets to break over the levee. At this same place there were several nests far out on the open dry ground without even a spear of grass for concealment or protection, and with hardly a vestige of nesting material under the eggs. At one pond where two pairs had taken up summer quarters there was one nest on the bare black ground where the white breast of the sitting female was the most conspicuous object imaginable and could be seen at a glance from a distance of three or four hundred feet. In direct contrast was the other nest; for it was artfully hidden among rather rank salt grass some distance from the pond, and when the sitting bird flattened herself upon it, as is the custom of this species when endeavoring to escape observation, she might have readily been overlooked from any near-by point.

The actions of different pairs of stilts when their nesting colonies are invaded are also variable. Sometimes a flock of noisy screeching birds will press close about the intruder, some hanging in the air on rapidly beating wings, others bouncing along the ground by leaps and bounds, raising and lowering their wings continually; while others go through every conceivable motion both on the ground and in the air. It seems that the larger the colony the more demonstrative the birds are; for in several instances where only one or two pairs were breeding the female would sneak from the nest in a guilty manner and quietly join her mate on the opposite side of the pond, where they would remain almost motionless or feed nervously along the margin of the pond.

Eggs.—Four eggs are usually laid by the black-necked stilt, sometimes five, rarely seven, and occasionally only three. The shape is ovate, often somewhat pointed, and there is little, if any, gloss. The ground color is dull "honey yellow," with an olivaceous tinge, or "cream buff." The eggs are irregularly spotted or covered with small blotches of brownish black or black. Sometimes there are a few blackish scrawls and usually a few underlying small spots of drab. They are often stained with mud. The measurements of 75 eggs, in the United States National Museum, average 44 by 30.5 millimeters; the eggs showing the four extremes measure 48 by 30, 47 by 32, 40.5 by 30, and 46 by 28 millimeters.

Young.—Incubation is shared by both sexes, but we have no accurate information as to its duration. Mr. Dawson (1923) says:

The infant can make shift to shuffle away from the nest and into cover within the hour, if need be, but he can not negotiate his stilts until several hours have elapsed after hatching; and he feels decidedly pale and tottery, like a young colt, until the day after.

Dr. Frank M. Chapman (1908) writes:

On May 23, their eggs were hatching, and in June the snipelike young were widely distributed over the marsh. They invariably attempted to escape observation by squatting with neck outstretched, but the parents, whether one approached their eggs or young, expressed their solicitude by a surprising extravagance of motion, all apparently designed to draw attention to themselves. I was at times surrounded by hopping, fluttering stilts, all calling loudly, waving their wings, bounding into the air to hang there with dangling legs and beating pinions, and executing other feats which would have done credit to acrobatic marionettes.

Dr. Alexander Wetmore (1925) says:

The young grow rapidly, and the increase in the length of their legs is amazing. Until the bones are well formed the young, when not feeding, prefer to rest with the full length of the tarsus extended on the ground, but even then appear as tall as other shore birds of similar body size. Stilts show considerable attachment for their young, and, unless dispersed by some untoward accident, frequently remain in family groups long after the young are able to care for themselves. As the latter become strong on the wing the family parties range over the country in search of suitable feeding grounds. As the nights grow cold in the North the birds band together in larger flocks and finally on some moonlit night in September, young and old may be heard calling as they pass overhead on their southward migration.

Plumages.—Robert Ridgway (1919) describes the downy young stilt as follows:

Upper parts light buffy grayish mottled with dusky, the back and rump with several large blotches of black; head, neck, and under parts buffy whitish or brownish white, the crown, occiput, and hindneck grayish, the crown with a mesial streak of black, the occiput with several irregular spots of the same.

The juvenal plumage appears first on the scapulars, back and breast; and the tail is the last to appear. The young bird is fully feathered, except the tail, by the time it is two-thirds grown. In fresh juvenal plumage the color pattern is much like that of the adult female; the crown, hind neck, back and wings are brownish black, all the feathers being edged or tipped with "cinnamon"; the edgings are narrowest on the head, upper back and wing coverts, and broadest on the scapulars and tertials; the face, sides of the head and all under parts are white; the central tail feathers are dusky and the others are white, washed with dusky near the tip, and all tipped with pinkish buff. This plumage is worn all through the fall and winter, with no change except by wear and fading; before winter the edgings have largely disappeared.

A partial prenuptial molt of the body plumage occurs in early spring, when young birds become indistinguishable from adults, except for some retained juvenal wing coverts. Adults probably have a partial prenuptial molt in early spring and a complete post-nuptial molt in late summer, but there are no well marked seasonal differences in plumage.

Food.—Doctor Wetmore (1925) writes:

Stilts feed by picking up insects on muddy shores or in shallow water, and though not averse to frequenting alkaline areas, on the whole prefer fresher water than do avocets. For detailed analysis, 80 stomachs of the black-necked stilt were available, distributed from March to August, and collected in California, Utah, Florida, and Porto Rico. Vegetable food in these amounted to only 1.1 per cent, whereas the animal matter formed 98.9 per cent. The birds are adept in seizing rapidly moving prey and in general are very methodical in their manner of obtaining food. Gravel is picked up to some extent to aid digestion, and part of the seeds taken may have been swallowed for the same purpose.

The animal food consisted mainly of insects, aquatic bugs and beetles making up the largest items; dragonfly nymphs, caddisflies, mayfly nymphs, flies, billbugs, mosquito larvae, and grasshoppers were included. Crawfishes, snails, and a few tiny fishes were eaten. The vegetable food consisted mainly of a few seeds of aquatic and marsh plants.

Behavior.—The flight of the stilt is steady and direct, but not particularly swift; the bill is held straight out in front and the legs are extended backwards, giving the bird a long, slim appearance. Over their eggs or young, stilts sometimes hover on steadily beating wings with dangling legs. In their excitement they sometimes climb up into the air and make startling dives.

But stilts are essentially waders; for wading they are highly specialized, and here they show to best advantage. At times they seem a bit wabbly on their absurdly long and slender legs, notably when trembling with excitement over the invasion of their breeding grounds. But really they are expert in the use of these well-adapted limbs, and one can not help admiring the skillful and graceful way in which they wade about in water breast deep, as well as on dry land, in search of their insect prey. The legs are much bent at each step, the foot is carefully raised and gently but firmly planted again at each long stride. The legs are so long that when the bird is feeding on land it is necessary to bend the legs backward to enable the bill to reach the ground.

Stilts can swim and even dive if necessary, but they are very awkward at both, as might be expected with such long legs and the absence of webbed feet; they never indulge in either action except in cases of dire necessity. They are usually gentle and unsuspicious birds, much more easily approached than most large waders. On their breeding grounds they are especially fearless and demonstrative. Some of their amusing antics are well described by Mr. Dawson (1923) as follows:

While all are shouting lustily, the birds whose nests are more immediately threatened are doing decoy stunts of several fascinating sorts. The favorite line of effort is the broken-leg act, in which the bird collapses suddenly, as though one of its little pipestem legs had snapped in two. The act is performed with such sincerity, even when the bird is standing in only an inch or so of water, that it never ceases to be amusing. Moreover, the trick is repeated diligently every few feet, so that it begins to look as though the bird had taken some fakir vow to prostrate itself every third or fourth step. The avocet, now that one thinks of it, does the same thing; but it does it awkwardly or, as it were, cautiously, and so unconvincingly. It has manifestly copied from its more agile neighbor. The second line of effort, most faithfully pursued, is wing fluttering. In this, again, the stilt is rather the mistress. It has perfected a trick of putting up one wing at a time and letting the wind towsle it about, as though it were really broken. Of course it also flutters both wings, and goes through other nondescript flopping and fluttering performances, such as are common to the family of shore birds.

Voice.—My first impression of the note as heard on the breeding grounds was recorded as a loud, guttural *whuck, whuck, whuck;* at other times it has seemed harsh and shrill. Audubon (1840) referred to their ordinary notes as "a whistling cry, different from the *cleek, cleek, cleek,* which they emit when they have nests or young." C. J. Maynard (1896), speaking of the breeding season, says: "The note at this time was quite different from that given earlier in the season, as they now uttered short syllables sounding like *put, put, put,* repeated rapidly, that of the males being harsh, while the females gave it shriller and more continuous."

Fall.—Stuart T. Danforth (1925), who made some studies of a breeding colony of stilts in Porto Rico, thus describes their departure in the fall:

By the latter part of June the adults had begun to flock again, and by the middle of September all the stilts at the lagoon (155 by actual count) had formed one compact flock. This count was made on September 17.. By September 20 only about 50 were left; on September 23 there were 20; on September 27 and September 30, 16; on October 7, 5. After that none were seen.

DISTRIBUTION

Range.—The United States, and Central and South America.

Breeding range.—North to Oregon (Klamath Lake, Burns and Malheur Lake); Utah (Brigham and Salt Lake City); Colorado (San Luis Lake and Fort Garland); Louisiana (Black Bayou, Calcasieu, Abbeville, and .Vermilion Bay); and Florida (Titusville). East to Florida (Titusville, Cape Canaveral, Kissimmee, Eden, and Lake Hicpoche); the Bahama Islands (Andros, Inagua and Green Cay); Cuba (Manzanillo); Porto Rico (Guanica lagoon); Venezuela (lagoon of Savonet and Curacao); Peru (Upper Ucayali River); and probably Ecuador (Guayaquil). South to probably Ecuador (Guayaquil); and probably the Galapagos Islands (Chatham and Albemarle Islands). West probably, to the Galapagos Islands (Albemarle Island); probably Nicaragua (Momotombo); probably Oaxaca (Tehuantepec); Tamaulipas (Tampico and Matamoras); probably lower California (San Quintin Bay); California (Santa Ana, Los Angeles, Castac Lake, Buena Vista Lake, Alila, Tulare Lake, Fresno, Los Banos, Stockton, Sutter County, and Tule Lake); and Oregon (Klamath Lake). There also is a breeding record for Saskatchewan (Fort Qu'Appelle, June 13, 1894).

Winter range.—The black-necked stilt is no doubt resident throughout most or all of its breeding range in Central and South America. At this season it has been detected north to lower California (San Jose del Cabo, Santiago, and Cape San Lucas); Sinaloa (Mazatlan and Escuinapa); Tamaulipas (Matamoras); Texas (Brownsville and Refugio County); rarely Louisiana (Grand Chenier); Florida (Fort Myers); and Porto Rico.

Spring migration.—Early dates of arrival are: California, Ojai, March 27, Daggett, April 10, Escondido, April 13, Stockton, April 13, Santa Barbara, April 14, and Fort Crook, April 19, Oregon, Narrows, April 8, and Malheur Lake, April 17; Arizona, Palo Verde, April 4; New Mexico, State College, May 17, and Lake Buford,

May 30; Colorado, Denver, May 5; Idaho, Rupert, April 28; and Montana, Billings, May 19. Migrants also have been observed to arrive at points on the Gulf coast as Texas, Port Lavaca, March 18; Louisiana, Sandfly Pass, March 16, and Vermilion Bay, April 27; and Florida, Merritts Island, March 10, and Titusville, March 11.

Fall migration.—Late dates of fall departure are: Oregon, Narrows, October 26; California, Fresno, September 15, Tulare Lake, October 7, Buttonwillow, November 13, and Riverdale, November 19; Utah, Ogden, October 8; Colorado, Windsor, November 5; and New Mexico, Jornada, September 25.

Casual records.—The black-necked stilt has been reported from many of the eastern States but some of these are indefinite or otherwise unsatisfactory. Among those that are considered valid are Mississippi, Vicksburg, July 13, 1913; Alabama, Leighton, August 26, 1892; South Carolina, Sullivans Island, May, 1881 (possibly breeding); New Jersey, Stone Harbor, April 24, 1894, and Cape May, July 21, 1843; New York, Great South Bay, two taken, one in 1843; New Hampshire, Rye Beach, reported as taken several years previous to 1902; Maine, Rockland, one taken early in May, 1889; New Brunswick, Maces Bay, one in September, 1880; Iowa, Hawarden, one in 1890, Webster County, several in the summer of 1898; Wisconsin, Racine, April, 1847; North Dakota, Hankinson, July 29, 1921; Kansas, Wichita, one killed in 1906; and Nebraska, a few occurrences around Omaha in 1893, 1894, and 1895. One also was taken on San Nicholas Island of the Santa Barbara group, California, on May 25, 1897.

Egg dates.—California: 140 records, April 26 to August 4, 70 records, May 21 to June 8. Utah: 12 records, May 10 to June 24, 6 records, May 14 to 23. Texas: 23 records, April 17 to June 11; 12 records, April 26 to May 28. Florida: 90 records, April 14 to June 25; 45 records, April 14 to May 6.

Family SCOLOPACIDAE, Snipes and Sandpipers

SCOLOPAX RUSTICOLA Linnaeus

EUROPEAN WOODCOCK

HABITS

This fine large member of the snipe family is widely distributed in Europe and Asia and has occurred as a straggler in North America half a dozen times or more at various points from Newfoundland to Virginia.

Seton Gordon (1915) gives a very good idea of its distribution and migrations, as follows:

The principal summer home of the woodcock is the northern portion of the Old World, for it is found extending from eastern Siberia to the western extremity of Europe. The woodcock nesting in Kamschatka migrate to Japan with the advent of the cold weather, those frequenting Mongolia to China, while those which have nested in western Siberia and on the plateau of Tibet move down to Burmah, India, Afghanistan, and Persia. Our own winter visitors are those birds which have bred in Scandinavia, Finland, and perhaps Russia. Those which press on south past our islands arrive in Palestine, in North Africa, and in Egypt. Throughout Russia the woodcock is found nesting, extending though in diminished numbers, as far south as the Caucasus and the Crimea. It also breeds in central France and in northern Italy. Some of its most distant nesting grounds are in Kashmir and Japan, while it has been found breeding in the Himalayas at the height of 10,000 feet. In the Faroe Islands it has occurred as a passing visitor and has also been recorded from Spitsbergen.

Courtship.—The same writer refers to a nuptial performance akin to the evening song flight of our woodcock, of which he says:

Immediately after sunset the entire male woodcock population leave their secluded haunts, and fly backwards and forwards over the same line of country, uttering a peculiar cry unheard except during the season of nesting. The notes may be termed the song of the males, and are uttered by the birds previous to their departure for their feeding grounds in the evening. The song commences with grunting cries, ending up with a sharp and penetrating note repeated maybe several times in quick succession, *pisick, pisick*. At times two cock birds during their aerial maneuvers cross one another's path, and then ensues a stern chase over the tree tops, the birds uttering repeatedly their chirping cries. The "roding" of the woodcock never takes place before the sun has set during the earlier part of spring, but at a more advanced period, in May, the birds commence their evening flights rather earlier. The flighting is continued till deep twilight has settled over the glen, but ceases before night. In the morning I, personally, have never heard this "roding," but it is said to be recommenced before daybreak, and to cease previous to full daylight. The woodcock when roding does not fly repeatedly over the same part of the wood; there is an interval between each of its appearances.

It is said to pass over the same country three times in the course of the evening. On the first visit it flies high and usually fast; on the second its progress is lower and more leisurely; while on the third and last the bird moves just above the trees.

Nesting.—In the southern portions of Great Britain the woodcock is a very early breeder, many birds nesting in March and some in February. Late nestings in July indicate the probability that two broods are sometimes raised, though this is unusual among waders. Mr. Gordon (1915) describes the nesting habits as follows:

The nesting ground is usually a wood, deciduous trees, being, I think preferred, owing to the soft layer of fallen leaves covering the ground. Close-grown plantations are rarely chosen as nesting sites, and small belts of birch and oak are favorite nesting grounds, provided that there is plenty of space between the trees. It is my experience that the birds dislike dense cover in which to nest; a few broken-down braken offer a suitable position, or the bird may scrape out a hollow amongst the deep layers of fallen beech and oak leaves which cover the ground beneath these trees. The eggs usually number four, but at times only three are found. Their ground color is normally buff colored, and they are liberally spotted and blotched by dark reddish-brown markings. Nothing more primitive than the nest of the woodcock can be found in the bird world. It is merely a slight hollow scraped in the ground and generally without intentional lining of any kind. The mother woodcock often sits very hard on her eggs, especially if incubation be far advanced, for she relies on the close harmonization of her plumage with her surroundings. Sometimes I have been able to approach to within a few feet of such a bird, and by not the slightest movement did she betray that she was alive. As the result of her early nesting, the woodcock has sometimes to cover her eggs when snow lies around to a considerable depth.

Rev. Henry H. Slater (1898) says that the nest is "often at the foot of a young Scotch fir, or other tree."

Eggs.—The European woodcock usually lays four eggs, but as many as six and even eight have been found in a nest, probably the product of two birds. These are much like large eggs of the American woodcock. They are about ovate in shape and have a slight gloss. The ground colors vary from "deep olive buff" to "cream buff." They are usually sparingly, but sometimes quite heavily, marked with irregular spots and small blotches. The underlying markings, in light shades of drab are numerous and quite conspicuous. Over these are varying amounts of spots and blotches of light browns, ranging in color from "snuff brown" to "clay color." Occasionally there are a few spots or scrawls of "bister" or "clove brown" about the larger end. Herbert Massey (1913) describes the eggs as follows:

The ground color ranges from the palest cream (nearly white) through deeper cream to pale buff, yellow-buff, and the deepest brown buff (many of the eggs of this latter type having a distinct pink tone), speckled and spotted and blotched with yellow-brown, dark brown, and purplish gray. As a rule, the eggs in the same set are fairly uniform in the pattern of the markings, but occasionally you get a set with one egg much more marked than the other three, and in many cases you find two distinct shades of ground color in the same set.

The measurements of 100 eggs, furnished by F. C. R. Jourdain, average 43.8 by 33.6 millimeters; the eggs showing the four extremes measure 49 by 34.8, 44.9 by 36.4, 40.2 by 34, and 43.1 by 31.6 millimeters.

Young.—Incubation lasts for 20 or 21 days and is performed by the female only. The young remain in the nest but a short time, where they are brooded by their mother and carefully tended by both parents. Several good observers have seen the mother bird carry her young away between her legs. Dresser (1871) quotes John J. Dalgleish as follows:

I have had on three occasions the good fortune to see the woodcock in the act of carrying her young. On the first occasion the bird rose from my feet

one day in the month of June, in a thick coppice cover in Argyllshire, and flew
with her strange burden carried between her thighs for about 30 yards, in the
manner well described in a note in Mr. Gray's Birds of the West of Scotland.
On following her she again rose, still carrying the young one, and flew into some
thick cover. On this and the next occasion, which was in Perthshire, the
birds uttered no cry; but the last time I witnessed this curious habit, which
was on the 5th of May last, the bird made the peculiar cry alluded to in the
note in Mr. Gray's work. On this occasion I could observe the bird more
distinctly, as it was in an old oak cover, with very little underwood, where I
discovered her. On rising she flew from 35 to 40 yards, calling as above mentioned, and then, alighting among some grass, seemed to flutter along, still
retaining hold of the chick. On raising her again, the same maneuver was
repeated, only that the distance flown each time was greater, but always in
the segment of a circle, as if she were unwilling to leave the rest of the brood.
On returning to the spot where she rose at first, I discovered one of these,
which was more than half grown, the quill feathers being well formed, and
must altogether have formed rather a heavy burden. On taking it up, it
uttered a cry, which was at once responded to by the parent bird, although
the latter did not again take to wing from the bushes into which it had
ultimately flown.

Abel Chapman (1924) writes:

For many years a question used to be discussed as to woodcocks carrying
their young; but the matter never specially interested me, until, on August 3,
1915, I happened to see it with my own eyes. This was in Houxty wood, and
since then I have witnessed the performance on many occasions. During the
war this wood was largely felled for military purposes and the area thus
cleared, and subsequently replanted, has become a specially favored resort
of our long-billed friends. The annexed sketch, made there on June 15, 1920,
shows exactly how the feat is accomplished. That particular woodcock rose
on the hillside a trifle above me, slowly flapping by close in front, and looking
back at me over her shoulder. What first struck my attention was the curiously
depressed tail, held almost vertical; then the mother's feet, hanging down
below; finally the youngster, with its very short beak, pressed between its
parent's thighs. Since then I have witnessed many similar exhibitions; indeed,
in summer they are almost daily on view.

Plumages.—The downy young of the European woodcock is thus
described in Witherby's (1920) Handbook:

Forehead and broad band over eye to nape light ochraceous buff, a russet
median streak from base of upper mandible to crown; crown russet intermixed
with light ochraceous buff, centre of nape russet, sides light ochraceous buff;
an irregular and interrupted russet band from nape to uropygial tuft, another
across wing; rest of upper parts and sides of body with irregular bands and
patches of ochraceous buff and russet; from base of upper mandible to eye
a broad black-brown streak; a small patch of same behind eye; a patch of
russet on lower throat; rest of under parts light ochraceous buff.

The juvenal plumage is therein fully described. It is much like
the adult, differing only in minor details, but can easily be recognized
by the looser or softer structure of the feathers. Practically all
of this plumage, except the primaries and secondaries, is replaced
in the fall by the first winter plumage, which is indistinguishable

from the adult. Adults have a complete postnuptial molt from July to December and a partial prenuptial molt, involving nearly everything but the wings, from February to May.

Food.—Mr. Gordon (1915) refers to the feeding habits of the woodcock as follows:

It feeds mainly by night on wet, boggy ground, and eats an enormous quantity of worms; indeed, it may swallow almost its own weight of food in the course of a single day. When the blackberries have ripened the woodcock betake themselves to the hillsides and consume great quantities of the fruit.

Mr. Slater (1898) says:

I have occasionally flushed woodcocks at night from wet rushy fields, where they were doubtless probing the ground for worms and larvae, occasionally turning over the droppings of cattle for concealed beetles. But they also feed in woods to a certain extent, turning the dead leaves over to find insects, etc. The accounts of the extent of their appetites and of the amount of worms, etc., which they will put away at a sitting are surprising. These they find in the earth with their bills, which are modified into a very delicate organ of touch.

If the horny epidermis be removed, a number of small pits of a hexagonal shape will be seen in the bone at the end of the bill, remotely suggesting an incipient honey comb. In each one of these pits a minute fibril of the olfactory nerve has its termination, and by this means, when the bill is thrust into the soft, wet soil, the slightest wriggle of the least living creature is instantly telegraphed to the woodcock's sensibilities.

Witherby's Handbook (1920) includes the following items in its food: Earthworms; also insects (coleoptera and their larvae, orthoptera (*Forficula*) larvae of lepidoptera, etc.); small mollusca, etc. Grains of maize recorded on one occasion in stomach, and mussels (*Mytilus*) also said to be eaten, as well as small crustacea.

Behavior.—Mr. Gordon (1915) says:

During its flight the bill of the woodcock is pointed downwards, and the wings are not extended to their full stretch. It seldom makes sustained flights, however, except on migration. During a shoot at Alnick a woodcock was seen to alight on the ground and then to throw leaves over its back, presumably to hide itself from the guns. If so, it would seem that the woodcock is one of the most sagacious of birds.

Selby (1833) writes:

The haunts selected by these birds, for their residence during the daytime, are usually the closest brakes of birch and other brushy underwood, and where the ground, from the deep shade, is nearly free from herbage; and, for this reason, thick fir plantations of 10 or 12 years' growth are a favorite resort. In woods that are very extensive they are generally found, and abound most in thickets by the sides of open glades, or where roads intersect, as by these they pass to and from their feeding ground at evening and in the dawn of the morning. Unless disturbed, they remain quietly at roost upon the ground during the whole day, but as soon as the sun is wholly below the horizon, they are in full activity, and taking flight nearly at the same instant.

leave the woods and cover for the adjoining meadows, or open land, over which they disperse themselves, and are fully engaged in search of food during the whole night.

Mr. Slater (1898) observes:

It is well known that woodcocks follow certain routes to their favorite feeding grounds in the evening, as they also have preferences for certain woods and certain parts of woods to lie in during the day. In short, they are very peculiar and fanciful in their tastes, and are guided by circumstances not apparent to us in their liking for one place rather than for another which seems to our eyes to offer the same advantages. A wood above my father's late house, in Northumberland, was a regular passing place for cocks, and at dusk on any April or May evening a sight of half a dozen at least was a certainty, as they passed rapidly above the trees, announced, long before they themselves were visible, by their peculiar half squeak, half whistle. I have here seen them "tilting" in the air in the manner described by St. John and others. It has been suggested that this tilting (at which time they tumble and twirl about in the air in pairs and threes, apparently prodding at one another with their bills) is connected with pairing, but I can not think so, as I have witnessed it as late as the end of May. I rather think it is pure playfulness, as of children just out of school, after lying concealed and quiet most of the day.

According to Yarrell (1871), woodcocks sometimes become exhausted and fall into the sea on their migrations; but they do not always perish, for he says:

A woodcock when flushed on the coast has been known to settle on the sea, and when again disturbed rose without difficulty and flew away. Numerous instances are recorded of woodcocks alighting on the decks of ships in the English Channel and elsewhere. The rapidity of flight of this bird is at times so great that a pane of plate glass more than three-eighths of an inch thick has been smashed by the contact, and one was actually impaled on the weather cock of one of the churches in Ipswich.

Fall.—Mr. Slater (1898), writing of the fall migration in Great Britain, says:

Though many breed with us, there is a large migration from the North in the late autumn. If the moon is full about the end of October, they appear to come in a big "rush" then, but sometimes in driblets as early as the end of September, as late as mid-November. But their movements are largely influenced by the wind and atmosphere as well as the moon; if the weather is foggy or they are exhausted by a heavy contrary wind, they drop on the coast as soon as they touch it, and large bags are sometimes made on the sand hills by those on the lookout for them. If the wind is light and weather clear, they seem to pass inland at once to favorite and suitable covers. Should frost come—which drives the worms down, and also prevents the birds from probing—cock move south and west. Therefore, it is in our southwest counties, Wales and West Ireland, where, owing to the Gulf stream frost and cold are seldom severe, that the best woodcock shooting is to be had, after the seasonal migration is over. Though they travel as a rule at night, and chiefly at the time of the full moon, this is not invariably the case; on October 28, 1881, I saw a woodcock come straight in from the sea, 20 yards high, and pitch on a bare patch of shingle; this was shortly before midday, and I thought it such an unusual circumstance that I skinned the bird for my collection.

Winter.—The woodcock is a winter resident as well as a migrant in Great Britain. Dresser (1871) writes:

Their numbers are, of course, greatly augmented in the winter, large numbers of immigrants being added to those which breed (as after mentioned); indeed I am not sure whether all of those we have in winter are immigrants, and that those which breed with us move further south in pursuance of their migratory instinct; but this is a point very difficult to discover. In the district I now allude to, their numbers are much diminished on the appearance of severe, frosty weather, when they appear to go to the coast, where they find the feeding grounds more open; if, however, the frost be slight, they remain.

On the west coast of Argyllshire they are found in greater numbers, and are not so much confined to covers, being found in open weather scattered through all the sheltered glens where there is any brushwood or even bracken. On the occurrence of frost, however, they all gather to the low-lying covers near the sea, where its influence serves to keep open the springs; and in such weather very large bags are often made, as they seem to come not only from the outlying spots above mentioned, but from the inland districts, where the frost has sealed up every one of their usual haunts.

DISTRIBUTION

Breeding range.—Northern Europe and Asia. North in Scandinavia to latitude 67°, in Lapland and Finland, in western Russia to 65°, and in eastern Russia to 64°. East to the Sea of Okhotsk. West to the British Isles. South to the Azores, Canaries, and Madeira (where it is resident), the Pyrenees, Alps, Transylvania, Carpathians, Himalayas (up to 10,000 feet), Mongolia, and Japan.

Winter range.—Great Britain, the Mediterranean basin, northern Africa and southern Asia, Persia, India, Burma, China, Japan, and occasionally Ceylon.

Casual records.—Casual in the Faeroes, Spitsbergen, Greenland, and North America. Prof. Wells W. Cooke (1912) says:

It wanders occasionally to eastern North America, and has occurred in Loudoun County, Va., in 1873 (Coues); Chester County, Pa., the end of November, 1886 (Stone); one was taken near Shrewsbury, N. J., December 6, 1859 (Lawrence); one, September, 1889, somewhere in New Jersey (Warren); one, probably of this species, near Newport, R. I. (Baird, Brewer, and Ridgway); one at Chambly, Quebec, November 11, 1882 (Wintle); and one at St. John, Newfoundland, January 9, 1862 (Sclater).

Egg dates.—Great Britain: 29 records, March 9 to August 5; 15 records, April 18 to June 22.

RUBICOLA MINOR (Gmelin)

AMERICAN WOODCOCK

HABITS

This mysterious hermit of the alders, this recluse of the boggy thickets, this wood nymph of crepuscular habits is a common bird and well distributed in our Eastern States, widely known, but not intimately known. Its quiet retiring habits do not lead to human intimacy. It may live almost in our midst unnoticed. Its needs are modest, its habitat is circumscribed, and it clings with tenacity to its favorite haunts even when closely encroached upon by civilization. The banks of a stream running through my place, close to the heart of the city, were once famous woodcock covers in which the birds persisted long after the surroundings were built up; and even within recent years I have had a pair of woodcocks living in the shrubbery along the stream for a week or two at a time.

Who knows where to look for woodcocks? Their haunts are so varied that one may not be surprised to find them almost anywhere, especially on migrations. Flight birds are here to-day and gone to-morrow. Their favorite resorts are alder thickets along the banks of meandering streams or spring-fed boggy runs; rich bottom lands or scrubby hollows, overgrown with willows, maples, alders, and poison sumac; or the scrubby edges of damp, second-growth woods, mixed with birches; any such place will suit them where they can find moist soil, not too wet or too sour, well supplied with earthworms. During the hot, sultry weather of July and August, the molting season, they seek the seclusion of cool, moist, leafy woods or dense thickets; or they may resort to the cool hillside or mountain bogs, fed by cool springs; or, if the weather is very dry, they may be found in the wet grassy meadows. Woodcocks do not like too much water and, after heavy rains, they may be driven from their usual covers to well-drained hillsides, sparsely covered with small birches, maples, locusts, and cedars. Sometimes they are found on the tops of mountains; George B. Sennett (1887) saw a pair on the top of Roan Mountain in North Carolina, at an elevation of 6,000 feet, "in a clump of balsams; the overflow from numerous springs which had their sources at this spot formed an open, adjoining marsh of several acres."

Woodcocks often appear in unexpected places, such as city parks, yards, gardens, orchards, or even lawns. John T. Nichols writes to me:

A neighbor (Mr. W. S. Dana) called for me at about 10 o'clock in the morning of a sparklingly clear, rather cool summer's day, to show me a woodcock that was feeding on his lawn, which slopes down to an almost fresh water arm of Moriches Bay. We found the bird still busily engaged where he had left it. It was out in the bright sunlight, crouched, walking about slowly but continuously. It held its body in an unsteady wavering manner, and was picking and digging about the roots of the short grass stubble, apparently obtaining some food too small for us to determine. The piece of lawn where the bird was operating was low and flat, adjacent to the edge of the water where protected by a low bulkhead. The ground was slightly moist, perhaps from seepage, which may have accounted for its presence. It was remarkably unsuspicious, allowing us to crawl within 2 or 3 yards, before flying back to alight under the shade of near-by trees; but was a full-grown bird, strong on the wing.

I have, more than once, seen a woodcock crouching in the short grass beside a country road, quite unconcerned as I drove past. I have frequently seen one in my yard about the shrubbery and I remember seeing my father stand on his front piazza and shoot one that was standing under an arborvitae hedge. Moist cornfields are often favorite resorts for woodcocks in summer.

Spring.—The woodcock is the first of our waders to migrate north and one of the earliest of all our migrants, coming with the bluebirds and the robins, as soon as winter has begun to loosen its grip. The date depends on the weather and is very variable, for the bird must wait for a thaw to unlock its food supply in the bogs and spring holes. Walter H. Rich (1907) has known the woodcock to arrive in Maine as early as February 10, and says that early birds find a living about the big ant hills, until the alder covers are ready for them.

In Audubon's (1840) time the migration must have been very heavy, for he says:

At the time when the woodcocks are traveling from the south toward all parts of the United States, on their way to their breeding places, these birds, although they migrate singly, follow each other with such rapidity, that they may be said to arrive in flocks, the one coming directly in the wake of the other. This is particularly observable by a person standing on the eastern banks of the Mississippi or the Ohio, in the evening dusk, from the middle of March to that of April, when almost every instant there whizzes past him a woodcock, with a velocity equaling that of our swiftest birds. See them flying across and low over the broad stream; the sound produced by the action of their wings reaches your ear as they approach, and gradually dies away after they have passed and again entered the woods.

No such flights can be seen to-day, but we occasionally have a comparatively heavy migration; such a flight occurred in 1923 and is thus described in some notes from Edward H. Forbush:

The most remarkable occurrence of the past two months was the prevalence of migrating woodcocks over a large part of southern New England and along the coastal regions to Nova Scotia. The first woodcock was reported in Massachusetts the last week in February and from the first week in March onward woodcocks were noted in slowly increasing numbers over a large part of New England. From March 22 to the first week in April the number of these birds scattered through Connecticut and eastern Massachusetts was remarkable. At evening one could find them almost anywhere. They were seen in the most unlikely places even in daylight. They were in all the towns around Boston and in the suburbs of the city itself, and west at least to the Connecticut Valley they were even more numerous in the woods and swamps. In southern New England at this time a large part of the snow had gone and in going had thawed the ground so that no frost remained and the woodcocks could find earthworms almost everywhere. Farther north there was not only frost in the ground but there was deep snow and the birds could find no food.

Courtship.—The woodcock may be found by those who seek him and know his haunts, but it is only for a short time during the breeding season, that he comes out into the open and makes himself conspicuous. His spectacular evening song-flight has been seen by many observers, and numerous writers have referred to it or described it more or less fully. William Brewster (1894) has given us the best and most complete account of it, but it is too long to quote in full here. I prefer to give my own version of it. The time to look and listen for it is during the laying and incubation period— say the month of April in Massachusetts, earlier farther south, even December and January in the Gulf States. The performance usually begins soon after sunset, as twilight approaches. On dark nights it ceases about when the afterglow finally disappears in the western sky; and it begins again in the morning twilight, lasting from dawn to broad daylight. On moonlight nights it is often continued through much or all of the night. The woodcock's nest is usually in some swampy thicket or on the edge of the woods, near an open pasture, field, or clearing; and here in the nearest open space, preferably on some knoll or low hillside within hearing of his sitting mate, the male woodcock entertains her with his thrilling performance. Sometimes, but not always, he struts around on the ground, with tail erect and spread, and with bill pointing downwards and resting on his chest. More often he stands still, or walks about slowly in a normal attitude, producing at intervals of a few seconds two very different notes—a loud, rasping, emphatic *zeeip*—which might be mistaken for the note of the nighthawk, and a soft guttural note, audible at only a short distance, like the croak of a frog or the cluck of a hen. Suddenly he rises, and flies off at a rising angle, circling higher and higher, in increasing spirals, until he looks like a mere speck in the sky, mounting to a height of 200 or 300 feet; during the upward flight he whistles continuously, twittering musical notes, like *twitter, itter, itter, itter,* repeated without a break. These notes may be caused by the whistling of his wings, but it seems to me that they are vocal. Then comes his true love song—a loud, musical, three-syllable note—sounding to me like *chicharee, chicharee, chicharee* uttered three times with only a slight interval between the outbursts; this song is given as the bird flutters downward, circling, zigzagging, and finally volplaning down to the ground at or near his starting point. He soon begins again on the *zeeip* notes and the whole act is repeated again and again. Sometimes two, or even three, birds may be performing within sight or hearing; occasionally one is seen to drive another away.

The performance has been similarly described by several others with slight variations. Mr. Brewster (1894) refers to what I have called the *zeeip* note as *paap* and the soft guttural note as *p'tul*, and says that—

"Each *paap* was closely preceded by a *p'tul*, so closely at times that the two sounds were nearly merged."

He counted the *paaps* as "uttered consecutively 31, 21, 37, 29, and 28 times."

Describing the action in detail, he says:

At each utterance of the *paap* the neck was slightly lengthened, the head was thrown upward and backward (much in the manner of a least flycatcher's while singing), the bill was opened wide and raised to a horizontal position, the wings were jerked out from the body. All these movements were abrupt and convulsive, indicating considerable muscular effort on the part of the bird. There was perhaps also a slight twitching of the tail, but this member was not perceptibly raised or expanded. The return of the several parts to their respective normal positions was quite as sudden as were the initial movements. The forward recovery of the head was well marked. The opening and shutting of the bill strongly suggested that of a pair of tongs. During the emission of the *paap* the throat swelled and its plumage was ruffled, but neither effect was more marked than with any of our small birds while in the act of singing.

The mouth opened to such an extent that I could look directly down the bird's throat, which appeared large enough to admit the end of one's forefinger. The lateral distension of the mouth was especially striking.

Referring to the song flight, he says: "Two flights, which I timed from the start to the finish, lasted, respectively, 57 and 59 seconds, the song 11 and 12 seconds, respectively." During the flight he followed him with a glass and "made out distinctly that while singing he alternately flapped his wings (several times in succession) and held them extended and motionless."

Francis H. Allen has sent me the following notes on his impression of the song:

In all that has been written of this wonderful performance of the woodcock's, I do not remember to have seen any full description of the song itself; the peeping, or *peenting*, on the ground, with the alternating water-dropping sounds and the accompaniment of head-jerking and wing-lifting has been described at length, as well as the remarkable spiral ascent into the air on whistling wings; but the character of the actual song, which is uttered at the summit of the ascent and as the bird comes down, is worth a little more attention. It begins in a confused series of chipping whistles which convey the impression of coming from at least three birds at once. These soon resolve themselves into groups of four to six—usually four in my experience—descending notes, the groups alternating with groups of high-pitched wing-whistles. These song notes vary in sweetness with different individuals, but are often very clear and musical. Not the least interesting aspect of the woodcock's evening hymn is the fact that so stolid appearing a bird should be moved by the fervor of courtship to execute so elaborate and exciting a performance. The excitement attending the affair as far as the spectator, or rather listener, is concerned lies to great extent in the wing whistling. When the woodcock first rises, the whistle is comparatively low, but as he mounts, the pitch rises and the rapidity of production increases. It is a steady succession of very short whistling notes for some time, but, when the bird and the whistle both reach their height, it comes in short groups of extremely rapid whistles alternating with brief intervals of motionless wings, as if the performer were breathless with excitement and effort and could not sustain his flight for long ·at a time. This is the effect, I mean. Probably the bird finds it easy enough, for he makes his flight at comparatively short intervals and during his periods of rest he is hard at work producing his harsh and unmusical nighthawklike *peent* notes which involve a deal of muscular effort.

Lynds Jones (1909) says that "the bird floats downward by a crooked path, the while calling in coaxing tones *p chuck tuck cuck oo*, *p chuck tuck cuckoo*, uttered more slowly at first, regularly increasing in rapidity until the notes are almost a wheedling call." Isador S. Trostler (1893) describes a feature of the courtship which I have not seen mentioned elsewhere; he writes:

The birds often play in a very droll manner, running round and round each other in a small circle, their feathers ruffled, their wings lifted, and their long bills pointing nearly directly upward, with their heads resting on their backs.

Sometimes they will hop on one foot, holding the other at a queer angle, as if it had been broken or hurt. The male bird utters a low indescribable sound during all the playing, and the sight of these queer antics is worth more than to have seen Modjeska or Barrett in their celebrated plays.

Nesting.—The nesting sites of the woodcock are almost as varied as its haunts at other times. I have never known how or where to look for its nest; in over 40 years of field work I have seen but one nest with eggs. That was shown to me by Mrs. Mary M. Kaan, in Chestnut Hill, Massachusetts, on June 2, 1924. It was located where I should never have thought of looking for one, in an open, rocky hollow in open woods, within 50 feet of a bridle path on one side and about the same distance from a swampy ravine and brook on the other side. The nest was on a little hummock, surrounded by herbage about a foot high; it was a mere hollow in the ground lined with dead leaves. Although it was in fairly plain sight, it was a long time before I could see the sitting bird, even when it was pointed out to me. The bird sat like a rock, as this species usually does, while I took a series of photographs of it, moving gradually nearer. I even removed two leaves which were resting on her bill, and Mrs. Kaan stroked her on the back before she left. The nest held only three eggs, which were probably a second laying.

The usual nesting sites are in alder runs, swampy thickets, brushy corners in pastures, or in underbrush or tall weeds along the edges of woods. Woodcocks are early breeders and it sometimes happens that nests are buried under late falls of snow; in such cases the birds continue to sit as long as it is possible to do so. The nest is often placed at the foot of a small tree or bush, occasionally beside a log or stump or even under fallen brush. An abundance of fallen leaves seems to be an essential requirement, of which the nest is usually made and among which the bird relies on its protective coloration for concealment; but its big black eyes sometimes reveal it.

L. Whitney Watkins (1894) found a nest near Manchester, Michigan, in heavy timber, and within a few feet of a reed-bordered, springy spot, it was within 2 feet of an ovenbird's nest. Another nest he describes as follows:

The old bird, curiously enough, had selected for her nesting site an open spot where some fallen boughs had partially decayed, and within 5 feet of a picket fence enclosing an open pasture field. Opposite her on the other side, were ash, elm, oak, and other trees, of no considerable size, and round about were many frost-dried stems of aster and goldenrod, interspersed with the fallen leaves of the previous summer. Little of green was near.

E. G. Taber (1904) found a nest that was situated in a swampy corner of a field planted with corn, only 6 feet from the open, on a slightly raised portion of the ground. This corner was overgrown with black ash, soft maple, tag alders, and ferns, mingled with poison ivy. Mr. Brewster (1925) describes two, of several, nests found near Umbagog Lake, Maine, as follows:

One, containing four eggs, incubated perhaps as many days, was in the face of a low mound partially overarched by balsam shrubs surrounded on every side by pools of water, and some 80 yards from the lake shore near the middle of swampy, second-growth woods made up chiefly of aspen, red cherry, and yellow birch trees, 20 or 30 feet in height, beneath which grew alders rather abundantly. The female woodcock flew up from her eggs at least 15 feet in advance of me, and whistling faintly soared off over the tree tops to be seen no more. I flushed a male about 50 yards from this nest.

Of the other he says:

It was at the edge of a little fern-grown opening, on a mound covered with brakes flattened and bleached by winter snows, beneath a balsam scarce 2 feet high, and not dense enough to afford much concealment for the eggs which, indeed, caught my eye when I was 15 feet away, there being no bird on them.

Mr. Trostler (1893) writes:

Finding a nest one day, I disturbed the setting bird three times, and again four times on the next day, and on the morning of the third day I found that the birds had removed the eggs during the night and placed them in a new nest about 8 feet away, where I found the eggs. I had marked the eggs to avoid any mistake. The second nest was a mere hollow in the mossy ground, and was in the middle of an open place in tall marsh grass, while the first was neatly cupped and lined with the above-mentioned vegetable down.

Another singular habit of the woodcock that I have never seen noted is that of both birds setting upon the nest in wet or cold weather. In doing this they huddle very close together and face in opposite directions, and I have always noted that they have their heads thrown back and their bills elevated to an angle of about forty-five degrees.

Mr. Nichols writes to me:

On Long Island there is a favorite nesting station for woodcock, where the woodland gives place to broad fields, separated by narrow stands of big trees with a sparse tangled undergrowth of shrubbery and catbriar, and where here and there a short fresh-water creek extends inland from the not distant bay.

Several writers have stated or implied that the woodcock raises two broods in a season. This would be an exception to the rule among waders. I believe that it normally nests early and that the late nests are merely second attempts at raising a brood, where the first nest has been destroyed.

An interesting case of nest-protecting display is thus described by Dr. Robert Cushman Murphy (1926):

She (assuming that it was the female) would allow us to come within a few feet before leaving her well-concealed position. Then she would spring from the nest, pitch on the ground close by, and, standing with the tail toward us, would raise and spread it so as to show to full advantage the double row of glistening white spots at the ends of the rectrices and under coverts. Next, flashing this striking banner slowly, she would move off among the trees in the attitude of a strutting turkey cock, stopping when we refused to follow, and then tripping ahead for a few steps, all the while bleating softly. The effect was astonishing; the ordinary low visibility of a woodcock against the forest floor no longer held, for the spotted fan of the tail had become a most conspicuous and arresting mark.

Eggs.—The American woodcock lays four eggs, sometimes only three, and rarely five. They vary in shape from ovate to rounded ovate and have a moderate gloss. The ordinary ground colors vary from " pinkish buff " to " cartridge buff " and in certain brown types from " pinkish buff " to " cinnamon." They are usually rather sparingly and more or less evenly marked with small spots, but sometimes these spots are concentrated about the larger end. In the lighter types, which are the most common, there are often many large blotches of light shades of " vinaceous drab " or " brownish drab "; these are conspicuous and often predominate. Mixed with them are numerous small spots of light browns, " cinnamon," " clay color," or " tawny olive." In the brown types these spots are in richer browns, " hazel," " russet," or " cinnamon brown," with the drab spots less conspicuous. The measurements of 53 eggs, in the United States National Museum, average 38 by 29 millimeters; the eggs showing the four extremes measure **41** by **30** and **35** by **27.5** millimeters.

Young.—The period of incubation is 20 or 21 days. Both sexes assist in this and in the care of the young. An incubating woodcock is notorious as a close sitter and can not usually be flushed from the nest unless nearly trodden upon; often it can be touched or even lifted from the eggs. The young are rather feeble when first hatched and are brooded by the parent bird much of the time for the first day or two. If flushed from her brood of young the female flutters away for a short distance as if hardly able to fly, with dangling legs and tail depressed and spread. If the young are strong enough to walk, she calls to them making a clucking sound, to which they respond with a faint peeping sound, as they run toward her; having gathered them under her wings, she covers them again trusting to her concealing coloration. If the young are too young and feeble to run, she may return when she thinks it safe, and carry them off between her legs, one at a time. Several reliable and accurate observers have testified to seeing this done; some who have not seen it have doubted it. The following account by Edwyn Sandys (1904) seems convincing:

The nest in question was on a bit of level ground amid tall trees. The sole suggestion of cover was a lot of flattened leaves which lay as the snow had left them. Perhaps 10 yards away was an old rail fence about waisthigh, and on the farther side of it was a clump of tall saplings. A man coming out of the wood told me he had just flushed a woodcock and had seen her brood, recently hatched and pointed out where they were. I went in to investigate, and located one young bird crouched on the leaves. It ran a few steps and again crouched, evidently not yet strong enough for any sustained effort. I went off, and hid behind a stump, to await developments. From this shelter the young bird was visible and it made no attempt to move. Presently the old one came fluttering back, alighted near the youngster, and walked to it. In a few moments she rose and flew low and heavily, merely clearing the fence, and dropping perhaps 10 yards within the thicket. Her legs appeared to be half bent, and so far as I could determine the youngster was held between them. Something about her appearance reminded me of a thing often seen—a shrike carrying off a small bird. I carefully marked her down, then glanced toward where the youngster had been. It was no longer there; and a few moments later it, or its mate, was found exactly where the mother had gone down. She flushed and made off in the usual summer flight.

William H. Fisher writes to me:

On May 16, 1903, I flushed an old bird at upper end of the Eagle Woods. She left three young on the ground, they remaining very quiet, cuddled in the dead leaves. In a few minutes she returned and alighted by them took one *between her legs*, holding it tight up to her belly, and flew off into a thicket. I sat and watched the other two young for about 15 minutes, hoping and expecting the mother bird would return, but, she not doing so, I got tired and left. As the usual set of eggs is four, I wonder if the old bird carried off one when she first flushed.

John T. Nichols tells, in his notes, of a brood found on Long Island:

This brood was found early in the morning by working painstakingly in a narrow stand of trees where a nest was suspected. The parent bird rose from almost under foot and fluttered away, as is customary in such cases, with tail spread, pointing down, legs dangling wide apart. It was perhaps a minute before the eye could pick out four young lying motionless side by side, so inconspicuous was their color against the background. For another couple of minutes they lay motionless. Then of one accord rolled to their feet and spreading their baby wings aloft, as though to balance, walked deliberately away with fine, scarcely audible cheeping, each in a slightly different direction. Apparently reliable reports are current of the woodcock carrying its young, but the characteristic peculiar labored flight, with deflected tail and widespread legs, just described, may also easily give such an impression erroneously.

Again he writes:

Just after sunrise on a clear morning I came upon 3 birds in an open field. Two of them flew in different directions, one swiftly and silently quickly disappeared, the other in the peculiar fluttering manner characteristic of a parent when surprised with young. As I reached the point where the two had risen the presence of helpless young was confirmed by the actions of a bird on the ground some 75 yards away, at the edge of the trees to which the parent had flown. Its head up, watching me, both wings were extended to the side, flapping feebly.

I had stood a couple of minutes scrutinizing the ground about, when my eye alighted on a fledgling. At the same instant it rose to its feet, raised and extended its wings to the side, and began to walk rapidly away, calling a high-pitched *seep*! Its wings were fully feathered, though little grown, feathers extending narrowly between them across the back, sides of its lower parts feathered, feathers not quite meeting in the center, otherwise in down. Contrast its helplessness with the young bobwhite which flies at a much earlier stage.

Audubon (1840) describes the actions of the anxious mother in the following well-chosen words:

She scarcely limps, nor does she often flutter along the ground, on such occasions; but with half extended wings, inclining her head to one side, and uttering a soft murmur, she moves to and fro, urging her young to hasten towards some secure spot beyond the reach of their enemies. Regardless of her own danger, she would to all appearance gladly suffer herself to be seized, could she be assured that by such a sacrifice she might ensure the safety of her brood. On an occasion of this kind, I saw a female woodcock lay herself down on the middle of a road, as if she were dead, while her little ones, five in number, were endeavoring on feeble legs to escape from a pack of naughty boys, who had already caught one of them, and were kicking it over the dust in barbarous sport. The mother might have shared the same fate, had I not happened to issue from the thicket, and interpose in her behalf.

Plumages.—The downy young woodcock, when newly hatched, is conspicuously and handsomely marked; the upper parts are " warm buff " or " light ochraceous buff," distinctively marked with rich " seal brown"; these markings consist (with some individual variation) of a large, central crown patch, extending in a stripe down the forehead, a large occipital patch, a stripe from the bill through the eye to the occiput, a broad stripe down the center and one down each side of the back, a patch on each wing and each thigh and irregular markings on the sides of the head and neck; the under parts are more rufous, " pinkish cinnamon " or " cinnamon buff," and unmarked.

The juvenal plumage appears at an early age, coming in first on the back and wings; the wings grow rapidly, and the young bird can fly long before it is fully grown. This plumage is much like that of the adult, but it can be distinguished during the first summer by its looser texture and by broader brown edgings on the wing coverts, scapulars, and tertials. A prolonged postnuptial molt of the body plumage during late summer and fall produces a first winter plumage which is nearly adult. At the first prenuptial molt, in late winter and spring, young birds become indistinguishable from adults.

Adults have an incomplete prenuptial molt, involving the body plumage, some wing coverts, scapulars, and tertials, in late winter and early spring, and a complete postnuptial molt in July and August. Fall birds are much more richly colored than spring adults.

Food.—The woodcock is a voracious feeder; its principal food is earthworms or angleworms, of which it has been known to eat more than its own weight in 24 hours. It is said to feed mainly at night or during the hours of twilight or dusk. The worms are obtained by probing in mud or damp earth in any place where worms are to be found, including gardens and cultivated fields. The long bill of the woodcock is well supplied with sensitive nerves, in which the sense of touch is highly developed; it can detect the movements of a worm in the soil and capture it by probing. Numerous borings are often seen close together, indicating that the bird does not always strike the worm at the first stab. Probably its keen ears also help to locate its prey. It is said to beat the soft ground with its feet or wings, which is supposed to suggest the effect of pattering rain and draw the worms toward the surface.

C. J. Maynard (1896) made the following observations on a captive bird:

The floor of its house was covered to the depth of four or five inches with dark-colored loam, in which I planted a quantity of weeds, beneath which the woodcock could hide. I would drop a number of worms on this soil, which, as the bird was too shy to feed at first, had ample time to bury themselves. At times, however, I was able to watch the bird unseen by it; then the woodcock, which had remained hidden in the corner behind the sheltering weeds, would emerge cautiously and walk over the ground, slowly and deliberately, pausing every instant or two as if listening intently. Then he would stamp with one foot, giving several sharp, quick blows, after which he would bow his head near the ground and again listen. Then suddenly he would turn either to the right or left or take a step or two forward, plunge his bill into the earth, and draw out a worm, which he would swallow, then repeat this performance until all the worms were eaten.

During dry spells, when the worms have returned to the subsoil, the woodcock must seek other foods. It then resorts to the woods, where it turns over the leaves in search of grubs, slugs, insects, and larvae. It has even been known to eat grasshoppers. Mr. Rich (1907) says that in early spring, before the alder covers are open, it feeds on ants. Frederick S. Webster (1887) reports a singular case, where the crop of a woodcock was crammed full of leaves of a common fern.

Behavior.—The woodcock is so nocturnal or crepuscular in its habits that it remains quietly hidden in its favorite covers during the day and is seldom seen to fly unless disturbed, when it flutters up through the trees with a weak, irregular, or zig-zag flight, dodging the branches. When clear of obstructions, it flies more swiftly and directly, but usually for only a short distance, and soon pitches down into the cover again. One can usually follow it and flush it again and again. Toward dusk it becomes much more active, and its shadowy form is often seen flying over the tree tops and across open places to its feeding grounds. At such times its flight is steady and direct, with regular wing strokes; its chunky form with its long bill pointing downward is easily recognized. While traveling at night its flight is quite swift. When rising in flight the woodcock produces, usually but not always, a distinct whistling or twittering sound. This has led to much discussion and differences of opinion, as to whether the sound is produced by the wings or is vocal. I am inclined to the latter theory, for I have often seen a woodcock fly without whistling, and many others have referred to such a flight.

Few of us have ever seen a woodcock alight in a tree, but Mr. Rich (1907) refers to several instances where the bird has been seen to do this by reliable witnesses. Once he himself shot one in the act.

Voice.—Except during the spectacular song-flight and courtship performance, the woodcock is a very silent bird, unless we regard the twittering heard when it rises as vocal. Mr. Nichols says in his notes:

The quality of the twitter of a rising woodcock corresponds more or less to the character of its flight. When, as is frequently the case, the bird merely flutters a short distance to drop again behind the screen of undergrowth, it amounts to little more than the chirping of crickets. On one occasion when I observed an individual barely escape the attack of an *Accipiter*, this sound, as it rose, was less shrill and loud than often, but more rapid and sustained, with an incisive quality suggesting a rattle snake's alarm. When a woodcock rises through thick brush or brambles its wings make a whirring sound not unlike that of the bob white, accompanied by a slight twitter.

Mr. Brewster (1925) writes:

Many years ago I expressed in print a belief that the whistling sound made by a rising woodcock is produced by the bird's wings. This conviction has since been confirmed by field experience at the lake with woodcock killed during the first half of September, and in varying conditions of moult. Such of them as still retained or had just renewed the attenuated outer primaries, almost always whistled when flushed, whereas no sound other than a dull fluttering one was ever heard from any of those not thus equipped. Hence I continue to hold firmly to the opinion that the woodcock's clear, silvery whistle emanates from these "whistling quills", as sportsmen fitly term them, and not from the bird's throat. There are, however, certain sounds, not very unlike those which combine to form the usual characteristic whistle, but more disconnected and twittering, which may be of vocal origin. One hears them oftenest from the woodcock hovering, just before alighting, or flitting low over the ground for trifling distances, beating their wings rather listlessly. This comparatively slow pulsation of the wings might account for the interrupted sequence of the sounds, but not perhaps, for their seemingly throaty quality.

Edward H. Forbush (1925) quotes three observers, as follows:

Mr. W. H. Harris asserts that he held a woodcock by the bill which whistled three times with a rotary motion of body and wings. Mr. J. M. Dinsmore held a woodcock by the body and wings to prevent movement of these parts, and he says that this bird whistled through its mouth and throat. Mr. H. Austin avers that he flushed a woodcock that did not whistle, marked the bird and put him up again when he whistled, which indicates that the bird may have made the sound with its vocal equipment.

Fall.—The following from the pen of Mr. Forbush (1912) illustrates the conditions which affect the fall flight:

The flights of birds from the North have not diminished in number so much as have the native birds. Occasionally a large flight stops here, as in early November, 1908, when woodcock were plentiful here, and when some gunners in Connecticut secured from 20 to 40 birds each in a day. This flight did not denote such an increase in the number of these birds, however, as generally was believed. The explanation is that they all came at once. The birds in Maine and the Provinces had a good breeding season, and they must have had a plentiful supply of food, for the autumn weather was mild, and they mostly remained in their northern homes until nearly the 1st of November. Flight birds were rare in Massachusetts up to that time, and the bags were small. The fall had been warm and dry, but on October 29 and 30 New England and the Provinces experienced a severe northeast storm along the seaboard, followed by a cold northwest wind, which probably froze up the northern feeding grounds, if the storm had not already buried them in snow. Either or both of these conditions drove the woodcock into southern New England. My correspondence shows that this flight landed in every county of Massachusetts except Dukes and Nantucket. As usual, comparatively few were seen in Barnstable County. Connecticut covers harbored many woodcock from about November 12 to November 20. There were many in Rhode Island, and the flight was noted as far south as Delaware.

Game.—It is as a game bird that the woodcock is best known, most beloved, and most popular, for it is a prince among game birds, and its flesh is a delight to the palate of an epicure. What sportsman will not stop in his pursuit of other game to hunt some favorite corner, some woodland border, or some brushy hillside where he has flushed this bird of mystery before? And what a thrill he gets as the brown ball of feathers suddenly flutters up from almost underfoot among the crisp autumn leaves, dodging up through the branches with a whistled note of warning, and flies away over the treetops! Perhaps he was too surprised at first to shoot; but, if he marked it down, he can soon flush it again, for it has not gone far; then, if he is quick and true at snap shooting, he may pick up the coveted prize, admire the soft, warm, ruddy breast, the pretty pattern of woodland lights and shades, the delicate long bill, and the big liquid eyes. An aristocrat among game birds!

In the early days, when I first began shooting, summer woodcock shooting was regularly practiced; the season opened in July, when the young birds of late broods were not large enough to furnish good sport and were not fit for the table. Moreover, the weather was often hot and the foliage was dense, making it unsatisfactory for the sportsmen. The only excuse for it was that it allowed some shooting in certain sections where local birds departed early and where flight birds seldom occurred. It went far towards exterminating local breeding birds in Massachusetts; it was bad for all concerned, and it is well that it was abandoned.

From the above and other causes woodcocks have decreased alarmingly during the past 50 years. One gets an impressive idea of the former abundance of the birds by reading the quaint shooting tales of Frank Forester, in which he boasts of having shot with a friend 125 birds in one day and 70 the next day before noon, and this with the old-fashioned muzzle-loading guns. His hunting trips were joyous occasions, in which the noonday luncheon, washed down with ample draughts of applejack, held a prominent place.

By far the best shooting is to be had on flight birds, which are big and fat and strong on the wing. In warm weather they frequent the black alder thickets where there are bunches of grass and weeds, or the vicinity of brooks or springs where there is a growth of alders, willows, and birches. On crisp, cold days in October they may be found on sunny hillsides or ridges, among birches, bayberries, or huckleberries, on the sunny edges of the woods, in cedar pastures, in locust scrub, or even in old scrubby orchards. For shooting in thick cover a light short-barreled gun that scatters well is desirable, for snapshots at short range are often necessary. I prefer a light charge of fine shot, which scatters more and does not tear the birds so badly. A good dog adds much to the pleasure of hunting and is very helpful in locating or retrieving birds. The birds will sometimes run for short distances before a setter or pointer, and it is often necessary for the shooter to flush his own bird, which may place him in a poor position to shoot. Therefore a well-trained spaniel, which runs around close to the shooter and flushes the birds, is generally more satisfactory.

For those who have no dog, or prefer to hunt without one, there is another method of shooting woodcocks which can be practiced successfully by one who is sufficiently familiar with their haunts and habits. From their haunts on the uplands, where they rest during the day, the birds fly through the open just before dark to their favorite feeding place along some swampy run or boggy thicket, resorting regularly to the same spot night after night. If the shooter knows of such a place, where the birds are fairly plentiful, he can station himself there about sunset and feel reasonably sure of a few shots during the brief time that the birds are coming in. But increasing darkness soon makes shooting difficult.

Enemies.—Like other ground nesting birds, woodcocks undoubtedly have many natural enemies among the predatory animals and birds; but these have always existed without detriment to the species. As has often been said, predatory birds and animals destroy mainly the weak and diseased individuals, which are the most easily caught; the stronger and more vigorous individuals are more likely to escape and perpetuate a hardier race, better fitted to survive.

The natural elements often take their toll in a wholesale destruction. Arthur T. Wayne (1910) relates the effect of a cold wave on the coast of South Carolina, February 13 and 14, 1899, when the thermometer dropped to 14° and the ground was covered with deep snow; he writes:

The woodcock arrived in countless thousands. Prior to their arrival I had seen but two birds the entire winter. They were everywhere and were completely bewildered. Tens of thousands were killed by would-be sportsmen, and thousands were frozen to death. The great majority were so emaciated that they were practically feathers and of course were unable to withstand the cold. One man killed 200 pairs in a few hours, I shot a dozen birds. Late Tuesday afternoon I easily caught several birds on the snow and put them into a thawed spot on the edge of a swift running stream in order that they would not perish, but upon going to the place the next morning I found one frozen. These were fearfully emaciated and could scarcely fly. Two birds were killed in Charleston in Broad Street. It will be many years before this fine bird can establish itself under most favorable conditions.

Telegraph and other wires cause the death of thousands of birds. Woodcocks migrate at night and fly low; if they strike head, bill, or breast against a wire it means almost certain death. Many dead birds are picked up under wires. Wires are increasing all the time and it is to be hoped that the birds will learn to avoid them.

But the main cause of the woodcock's disappearance is excessive hunting of a bird too easily killed, summer shooting in the North, and wholesale slaughter during a long winter season in the South. A good account of the barbarous sport, called fire hunting, as practiced in Louisiana, is given by Dr. E. J. Lewis (1885), as follows:

The shooter, armed with a double-barreled gun, and decked with a broad-brimmed palmetto hat, sallies forth on a foggy night to the "ridge," where the cocks are now feeding in wonderful numbers. His companion on these expeditions is generally a stout-built negro, bearing before him a species of old-fashioned warming pan, in which is deposited a goodly supply of pine knots. Having arrived on the ground, the cocks are soon heard whizzing about on every side; the pine knots are quickly kindled into a flame, and carried over the head of the negro. The shooter keeps as much as possible in the shade, with his broad-brimmed palmetto protecting his eyes from the glare, and follows close after the torch bearer, who walks slowly ahead. The cocks are soon seen sitting about on the ground, staring widely around in mute astonishment, not knowing what to do, and are easily knocked over with a slight pop of the gun, or more scientifically brought to the ground as they go booming off to the marshes.

The lurid glare of the torch only extends to a distance of 20 yards or so around the negro; the sportsman must, therefore, be on the *qui vive* to knock the birds over as they rise, otherwise they will immediately be shrouded in the impenetrable darkness of night.

These excursions are carried on with great spirit, sometimes continue the whole night through, and the slaughter of the cocks is often very great; with an experienced "fire hunter" it is no unusual occurrence to bag in this way 50 couple before morning.

DISTRIBUTION

Range.—The eastern United States and Canada.

Breeding range.—North to southern Manitoba (Brandon, Portage la Prairie, and Winnipeg); northern Michigan (Palmer, Sheldrake Lake, and Mackinac Island); southern Ontario (Bracebridge, Madoc, and Ottawa); southern Quebec (Montreal); southern New Brunswick (Grand Falls and North River); and Nova Scotia (Pictou). East to Nova Scotia (Pictou, Halifax, and Yarmouth); Maine (Rockland and Portland); Massachusetts (Winchendon and Boston); Rhode Island (Newport); Connecticut (Saybrook); New Jersey (Morristown, Laurenceville, Tuckerton, and Sea Isle City); Maryland (Baltimore, and Cecil, Dorchester, and Worcester Counties); District of Columbia (Washington); Virginia (Locustville, Norfolk, and Lake Drummond); North Carolina (Walke and New Bern); South Carolina (Summerville and Capers Island); Georgia (Savannah, Blackbeard Island, Okefinokee Swamp, and St. Marys); and Florida (Jacksonville and Micanopy). South to Florida (Micanopy and Tallahassee); Alabama (Autaugaville and Pleasant Hill); Mississippi (Cedar Grove); Louisiana (Covington); and Texas (Sour Lake). West to Texas (Sour Lake); Arkansas (Clinton and Newport); eastern Kansas (Neosho Falls); eastern Nebraska (London and West Point); southeastern South Dakota (Vermilion); probably western Minnesota (Ortonville); eastern North Dakota (Larimore and Bathgate); and southern Manitoba (Portage la Prairie).

Casual in summer west to Colorado (Boulder and Denver); Wyoming (Fort Bridger); and Alberta (Edmonton). A chick also was reported as seen near Indian Head, Newfoundland (Howe).

Winter range.—North to northeastern Texas (Jefferson); Arkansas (Stuttgart); probably Kentucky (Hickman); and rarely, North Carolina (Raleigh). East to rarely North Carolina (Raleigh); South Carolina (Charleston); and Florida (Gainesville, Fruitland Park, Lake Harney, and Orlando). South to Florida (Orlando, Panasoffkee Lake, and Tallahassee); Alabama (Autauga County); Mississippi (Biloxi); Louisiana (Covington, Abbeville, and Mermenton); and southern Texas (Beaumont and Victoria). West to Texas (Victoria, Hallettsville, and Jefferson).

Casual in winter north to Illinois (Mount Carmel); Indiana (Vincennes); Ohio (New Bremen); Virginia (Falls Church); Maryland (Mardela); New Jersey (Cape May, Haddonfield, and Plainfield); New York (Sing Sing and Collins); Connecticut (Bridgeport, New Haven, and New London County); and Massachusetts (Boston).

Spring migration.—Early dates of arrival are District of Columbia, Washington, February 6; Maryland, Barron Springs, February 5, and Mardela Springs, February 14; Pennsylvania, Carlisle, February 27, Nauvoo, March 4, Waynesburg, March 5, Port Province, March 7, Columbia, March 9, Bristol, March 10, Norristown, March 11, Renovo, March 13, Harrisburg, March 14, Philadelphia, March 15, Chambersburg, March 18, Coatesville, March 21, and Erie, March 23; New Jersey, Maurice River Light, February 15, Plainfield, February 22, Englewood, February 23, and Morristown, February 28; New York, Middletown, March 1, New York City, March 10, Shelter Island, March 10, Orient Point, March 12, Great West Bay Light, March 12, Branchport, March 13, Stephentown, March 17, Lansing, March 20, and Virgil, March 21; Connecticut, Portland, February 15, Plantsville, February 24, Bridgeport, February 27, Norwich, March 1, Middletown, March 3, Unionville, March 10, and Fairfield, March 14; Massachusetts, Groton, February 22, Rockdale, March 8, East Templeton, March 11, and Rehoboth, March 15; Vermont, Rutland, March 7, and Hydeville, March 25; New Hampshire, Monadnock, March 14, Manchester, March 20, Peterboro, March 25, and Durham, April 1; Maine, Portland 13, Farmington, March 16, Augusta, March 23, East Hebron, March 25, Ellsworth, March 28, Lewiston, March 29, and Norway, April 5; Quebec, Quebec, April 4, Neilsonville, April 15, and Montreal, April 21; New Brunswick,

St. John, March 21, Scotch Lake, March 29, and St. Andrews, April 3; Nova Scotia, Halifax, March 10, and Wolfville, March 21; Tennessee, Nashville, February 28, and Athens, March 1; Kentucky, Eubank, February 15, Versailles, February 29, and Alexander Station, March 15; Illinois, Odin, February 23, Quincy, March 3, Shawneetown, March 4, Evanston, March 13, Olney, March 13, Rockford, March 15, Fernwood, March 20, and Chicago, March 22; Indiana, Holman, February 16, Frankfort, February 16, Bicknell, February 16, Waterloo, March 1, Terre Haute, March 1, Red Key, March 9, Sedan, March 9, and Greencastle, March 10; Ohio, Cleveland, February 21, New Middleton, February 26, Hillsboro, March 2, Granville, March 7, East Rockport, March 8, Columbus, March 8, Oberlin, March 10, Lakewood, March 11, Sandusky, March 13; Michigan, Petersburg, March 2, Battle Creek, March 9, Ann Arbor, March 17, Detroit, March 24, and Norvell, March 31; Ontario, London, March 30, Dunneville, March 21, Toronto, March 25, Yarker, March 29, St. Thomas, March 30, and Sault Ste. Marie, April 3: Iowa, Keokuk, March 12, Mount Pleasant, March 13, and Hillsboro, March 15; Wisconsin, Racine, March 25, Wauwatosa, March 26, and Milwaukee, March 24; Minnesota, Leech Lake, March 30; and Kansas, North Topeka, March 21, and Lawrence, April 17.

Fall migration.—Late dates of fall departure are: Kansas, North Topeka, December 3; Minnesota, Hutchinson, November 3; Wisconsin, Greenbush, November 2, and Delavan, November 6; Iowa, Sigourney, November 3, Keokuk, November 16, Grinnell, November 27, and Ogden, December 30; Ontario, Guelph, October 30, Ottawa, October 31, St. Thomas, November 2, Plover Mills, November 5, Dunnville, November 6, and Toronto, November 11; Michigan, Manchester, October 19, Vicksburg, November 2, Livonia, November 11, and Ann Arbor, November 20; Ohio, Sandusky, November 1, Huron, November 2, Kingsville, November 7, Cleveland, November 8, Austinburg, November 10, and Grand Reservoir, November 15; Indiana, Roanoke, November 10, and Greensburg, November 10; Illinois, Lake Forest, October 20, Odin, October 28, La Grange, November 8, and Rantoul, December 6; Kentucky, Bardstown, November 18; Nova Scotia, Pictou, October 29, Halifax, November 6, and Yarmouth, November 15; New Brunswick, St. John, November 13; Quebec, Montreal, November 4; Maine, East Hebron, October 20, Skowhegan, October 26, Lewiston, October 27, Waterville, October 30, Winthrop, November 4, and Westbrook, November 23; New Hampshire, Tilton, October 22; Vermont, Rutland, November 3; Massachusetts, Rockdale, November 5, Boston, November 20, Watertown, November 29, and Cambridge, December 8; Connecticut, Middletown, November 16, Meriden, November 23, Hartford, November

24, New Haven, November 26, and Portland, November 28; New York, Shelter Island, November 10, Stephentown, November 16, Plattsburg, November 20, Brooklyn, November 25, Wyandance, December 1, and Lawrence, December 8; New Jersey, Camden, November 8, Demarest, November 17, Englewood, November 24, Mahwah, November 26, Morristown, November 29, and Bloomfield, November 30; Pennsylvania, Renovo, October 23, Erie, November 14, Beaver, November 28, and Berwyn, December 6; Maryland, Barron Springs, November 27, and Cumberland, December 12; and District of Columbia, Washington, December 30.

Casual records.—The woodcock has been detected outside of its regular range on a few occasions, as follows: Bermuda, Hamilton, October 1842 and probably one at Hungry Bay, a few years later; Keewatin, York Factory, last of August; northern Saskatchewan, Black River, August, 1892; and Montana, Billings, October 23, 1917.

Egg dates.—New York: 20 records, April 4 to May 29; 10 records, April 11 to 25. Pennsylvania and New Jersey; 22 records, March 23 to May 1; 11 records, March 30 to April 17. Indiana and Illinois: 26 records March 26 to May 30; 13 records April 15 to 28. North Carolina: 2 records February 18 and March 29. Texas: 1 record January 20.

CAPELLA GALLINAGO GALLINAGO (Linnaeus)

EUROPEAN SNIPE

HABITS

The European bird is so closely related to, being regarded now as only subspecifically distinct from, our Wilson snipe that I shall not attempt to write its full life history. The two birds resemble each other so closely in all their habits that this would involve useless repetition of much that I have written about the American bird.

The European snipe owes its place on our list to its occurrence, probably casually, in Greenland. There is a specimen in the British Museum that is supposed to have come from Canada, but its history is doubtful. The snipe that breeds in Iceland and the Faroe Islands has been separated, under the name *faeroeensis*, as subspecifically distinct from the bird breeding in Great Britain and in continental Europe. It seems quite likely that the Greenland records should be referred to this form.

Courtship.—Much study has been given to this subject by European observers and differences of opinion still exist as to how the curious winnowing sound or bleating is produced. While the normal time for hearing this is during the spring months, it has been heard in February, during the summer and even occasionally in the fall. Rev. Henry H. Slater (1898) writes:

Opinions differ widely as to the means by which this curious sound is produced. Meves declared that the tail feathers were the instrument, and claimed to have produced it artificially by the snipe's tail feathers fastened to the end of a long stick and swung through the air. Others hold that the tremulous motion of the tense wing feathers is the agency; a third theory is that the sound is vocal. The reader is at liberty to take his choice. I incline to the last, from analogy. I have seen the great snipe go through exactly the same evolutions at the nest, including the tremulous wings on the descending movement, and in perfect silence; I have watched the wood, the green, the broad-billed sandpipers, the Kentish plover, Temmick's and the little stint, and the red-necked phalarope, go through the same movements also at the nest, but in these cases the noise which accompanied the descending stage of the performance was unmistakably vocal.

Dr. Leonhard Stejneger (1885) was also much inclined to the vocal theory when he wrote:

Not only this power of the sound, but even more so the nature of the tune itself convinced me that it originates from the throat and not in any way either from the tail or the wing feathers, as suggested by many European writers. It is true that the wings are in a state of very rapid vibration during the oblique descent when the note is uttered, but this circumstance does not testify only in favor of the theory of the sound being produced by the wing, as the vibration most conclusively accounts for the quivering throat sound. Anybody stretching his arms out as if flying, and moving them rapidly up and down and simultaneously uttering any sound is bound to "bleat." Having heard, however, from my early days, of the wing or tail theories as the only orthodox ones, I did not feel convinced of the correctness of my own opinion until one evening I heard another bird of the same family produce a very similar note *while sitting on the ground*. Referring to the observation recorded under *Arquatella coucsi*, I here only remark that the sound was so similar as to leave no doubt whatever in my mind that it had a similar origin in both cases. It may be that a snipe has never been observed bleating on the ground, but the fact that a so nearly allied bird is capable of producing essentially the same sound while in that position is an argument in favor of the more natural explanation of the sound originating from the organ which in almost all other instances is adapted to that purpose.

John M. Boraston (1903) gives an excellent account of this nuptial flight, as follows:

Another bird which the buoyant spirits of the breeding season urge into unusual prominence is the common snipe. About the pairing time, at the beginning of April, he may for some weeks be observed on the wing frequently throughout the day. At such times he describes great circles in the air at a considerable height, the rapidly beating wings carrying him round at a high speed. At regular intervals during this great circling flight the wings are laid out flat, the one inside the great circle the bird is describing being tilted up and that outside depressed. At the same moment the tail feathers are opened out so that the sky may be seen between them as between the fingers of an open hand. Immediately the wings and tail are so set, the tips of the former begin to vibrate, the tail feathers remaining rigid, and the bird strikes off at a tangent, curving outward and slipping downward from the normal path of its circular flight. It is this recurring tangential deviation which causes the circle of the snipe's flight to become so vast. During the outward curving, downward flight the snipe's strange humming note is heard, synchronizing precisely with the vibration of the tips of its wings. The bill is closed when the note is being emitted. The bird's great circular flight is thus made up of two subordinate flights—the plain flight and the humming flight—in regular succession. After having described three or four great circles, the snipe reverses its course and proceeds in the opposite direction; but it is to be observed that in its "humming" flight it still works always on its "outer edge," the wing outside the great circle being invariably the one to be depressed and the one upon which the bird turns in performing the tangential, outward curving, downward flight. The sound made by the snipe may be nearly imitated by laughing in the throat with the lips closed, and associates itself in my mind with that made by the puffin when returning laden with fish to his burrow. It is like hollow, mirthless laughter; the expression of a wild earnest joy by sounds which to human ears seem mournful rather than joyous, and therefore unnatural, uncanny, weird. The snipe has another amusing trick in flight; he will suddenly jerk himself to one side, throw his wings halfway back, and allow himself to fall like a lopsided shuttlecock, until, as suddenly recovering himself, he sets off again on his circular career.

Seton Gordon (1915) gives the following good description of the snipe's tail, by which the sound is probably made:

The tail feathers of the snipe are of so peculiar formation that it may be well to give here a description of them: In the first outer tail feather the shaft is exceptionally stiff and shaped like a saber. The rays of the web are strongly bound together and are very long—the longest, in fact, reaching nearly three-quarters of the whole length of the web. The rays lie along the shaft of the feather like the strings of a musical instrument. Other species of snipe possess four drumming feathers, and one species has no fewer than eight. The drumming feathers of the hen snipe are not as strong as those of the male.

Eggs.—The European snipe normally lays four eggs, rarely five. These are indistinguishable from eggs of our Wilson snipe. The measurements of 100 eggs, furnished by Rev. F. C. R. Jourdain, averaged 39.4 by 28.7 millimeters; the eggs showing the four extremes measure 42.7 by 29, 39.3 by 30.3, 35 by 28.4 and 36.3 by 26.7 millimeters.

Young.—The period of incubation is about 20 days. Several observers have reported seeing the snipe carry off her young between her legs, as the woodcock is known to do.

Mr. Gordon (1915) writes:

Although eminent authorities have stated that a snipe with a brood by her feigns lameness to distract attention, I have never found this to be the case, the bird invariably flying off as she does when sitting on her eggs.

One warm July day I witnessed a very charming spectacle in a field bordering on a wide expanse of moorland. A kindred ornithologist and myself were seated at the edge of a wall overlooking the field when he became aware that a snipe was standing fearlessly in the long herbage a few yards from us. As we watched her, the bird came forward, and disappeared among some rushes bordering the wall. For the space of a minute or so she remained hidden, and we thought she had gone there to shelter, but presently she emerged from her obscurity, and following her closely were two small chicks. By comparison with the green grass these little people appeared almost black, so dark was their downy plumage. Their mother realized that danger was near, for she led them quickly away, but never turned to see whether her children were following her. They kept their position close behind her, although the pace for them was a quick one, and they were soon lost to sight behind a ridge. One realized how wonderfully obedient the chicks were: they were left in the rushes at the approach of danger, their mother having evidently enjoined them to remain concealed and without movement until she returned for them.

Behavior.—An interesting account of the habits of a tame snipe, reared in captivity, is published by Hugh Wormald (1909) to which I would refer the reader.

DISTRIBUTION

Breeding range.—Much of Europe and Asia. From Great Britain and Scandinavia (up to 70° N.) throughout northern Europe and Siberia. South, mainly in the mountains, to the Pyrenees, Alps, northern Italy, southern Russia, Turkestan, Yarkand, and south-eastern Mongolia. A few breed in the Azores, northwestern Africa, and India. Replaced by allied forms in Iceland, the Faroes, in tropical Africa, and in northeastern Asia.

Winter range.—Great Britain, the Mediterranean basin, Madeira, Canaries, Azores, Africa (south to Senegambia on the west and Abyssinia on the east), Arabia, Sokotra, southern Asia, Japan, Borneo, Formosa, and the Philippine Islands.

Casual records.—The only North American record, a specimen said to have been taken in Canada, is very doubtful. This and the Greenland and Bermuda records are probably referrable to the Iceland form, *faeroeensis*.

Egg dates.—Great Britain: 70 records, March 3 to August 21; 35 records, April 29 to May 25. Iceland: 16 records, May 10 to June 6; 8 records, May 26 to June 3.

CAPELLA GALLINAGO DELICATA (Ord)

WILSON SNIPE

HABITS

The above species, with its several varieties, enjoys a world-wide distribution and is universally well known. The American sub-species is widely distributed from coast to coast and occurs more or less commonly, at one season or another, in nearly every part of North America. It was formerly exceedingly abundant, but its numbers have been sadly depleted during the past 50 years by excessive shooting. Alexander Wilson first called attention to the characters, size, and number of tail feathers, which distinguished our bird from the European. But they are so much alike that it seems best to regard them as subspecies, rather than as distinct species.

Spring.—The snipe is an early migrant, leaving its winter quarters just below the frost line, just as soon as the northern frost goes out of the ground, about as early as the woodcock. When the warm spring rains have softened the meadows, when the hylas have thawed out and are peeping in the pond holes, when the cheerful *okalee* of the redwings is heard in the marshes and when the herring are running up the streams to spawn, then we need not look in vain for the coming of the snipe. Low, moist meadow lands, or wet pastures frequented by cattle, are favorite haunts, where their splashings and borings are frequently seen among the cow tracks. They are also found in high, bushy, wet pastures, or in the vicinity of spring-fed brooks among scattered clumps of willows, huckleberries or alders.

Courtship.—On the wings of the south wind comes the first wisp of snipe, the will-o-the-wisp of the marshes, here to-day and gone to-morrow, coming and going under the cover of darkness. All through the spring migration and all through the nesting season we may hear the weird winnowing sound of the snipe's courtship flight, a tremulous humming sound, loud and penetrating, audible at a long distance. One is both thrilled and puzzled when he hears it for the first time, for it seems like a disembodied sound, the sighing of some wandering spirit, until the author is discovered, a mere speck, sweeping across the sky. The sound resembles the noise made by a duck's wings in rapid flight, a rapidly pulsating series of notes, *who, who, who, who, who, who, who, who*, increasing and then decreasing again in intensity. It has been termed the "bleating" of the snipe, but this does not seem to describe it so well as "winnowing." J. R. Whitaker, with whom I hunted snipe in Newfoundland, told me that both sexes indulge in this performance and George M. Sutton (1923) suggested the possibility of it.

Dr. Joseph Grinnell (1900) gives the best account of this courtship flight, as follows:

I was in a broad grassy swale, studded here and there with scrub spruces and bordered by taller timber, when my attention was attracted by a curious far-off song which puzzled me for some time. Finally I descried the producer, a Wilson's snipe, so far overhead as to be scarcely discernible against the clear sky. It was flying slowly in a broad circle with a diameter of perhaps 600 yards, so that the direction of the sound was ever shifting, thus confusing me until I caught sight of its author. This lofty flight was not continuously on the same level, but consisted of a series of lengthy undulations or swoops. At the end of each swoop the bird would mount up to its former level. The drop at the beginning of the downward dive was with partly closed, quivering wings, but the succeeding rise was accomplished by a succession of rapid wing beats. The peculiar resonant song was a rolling series of syllables uttered during the downward swoop, and just before this drop merged into the following rise a rumbling and whirring sound became audible, accompanying the

latter part of the song and finishing it. This curious song flight was kept up
for 15 minutes, ending with a downward dash. But before the bird reached the
ground and was yet some 20 yards above it there was apparently a complete
collapse. The bird dropped as if shot for several feet, but abruptly recovered
itself to fly a short distance farther and repeat this new maneuver. By a
succession of these collapses, falls, recoveries, and short flights the acrobatically
inclined bird finally reached the ground, alighting in the grass near me.

All of the early American writers, and many others since then,
supposed that the winnowing sound was made by the bird's wings,
although many European observers long ago argued that it was made
by the two pairs of outer tail feathers, which are widely spread and
held downward at right angles to the axis of the body during the
downward swoops and vibrate as the air rushes through them. W. L.
Dawson (1923) says that—

the body of the sound is produced by the impact of the air upon the sharp
lateral feathers of the tail, held stiffly, while the pulsations of sound are
produced by the wings. At least it is certain that the pulsations of sound
are synchronous with the wing beats. The sound begins gradually, as while
the tail is expanding, and closes with a smooth diminuendo as the tail is
closing and while the wings are sailing.

N. S. Goss (1891) gives a different account of the courtship, as
follows:

In courtship, the male struts with drooping wings and widespread tail
around his mate, in a most captivating manner, often at such times rising
spirallike with quickly beating wings high in air, dropping back in a wavy
graceful circle, uttering at the same time his jarring cackling love note, which,
with the vibration of the wings upon the air, makes a rather pleasing sound.

Mr. Sutton (1923) noted some peculiar flight performances, which
may be connected with the courtship; he says:

On April 29 two birds were repeatedly flushed together; not always the
same two individuals necessarily, I presume, and not certainly of opposite
sex. But these birds often sailed gracefully over the cattails, in wide sweeping undulations, with wings set in a manner suggesting chimney swifts, a type
of flight totally different from any previously observed. The same stunt was
many times observed in the male bird of the pair whose nest was located.
In fact this type of display, if it were display, was so common that the usual
twitching, erratic flight was only rarely seen. I have wondered if this may
not have been a pair of birds, possibly recently mated, though not actually
nesting there.

On May 3, in a portion of the swamp near town, a new antic was observed.
A snipe, subsequently determined as a male, sprang up close at hand, and after
a few energetic, direct wing beats, put his wings high above his body and,
describing a graceful arc, dropped toward the ground, his legs trailing, only to
rise again to repeat the performance. Never during this exhibition did he
actually touch the ground with his feet, so far as I could see, but it gave that
impression. He was clearly excited, and I now know that such antics are a
certain indication of nesting activity. At such times the male gave forth several short notes which may accurately be termed "bleats." Occasionally the
bird, after performing this novel antic would drop to the grass some distance

away, and then fly up after a time, considerably nearer me, making it evident that he was attempting to lure me away. Then again, after trying these antics for a time, he would suddenly mount to the sky, and there would follow a season of the weird wind music—always delightful.

Aretas A. Saunders, in his notes, says that—

After the eggs are laid the female often answers this sound with a long call *okee okee okee* repeated 8 or 10 times and resembling the "buckwheat" call of the guinea hen. I believe the female is sitting on the eggs when she calls this way, for I have found the nest by locating the position of the sound at night and returning in the morning. The nest is usually in about the center of the male's circle of flight.

Nesting.—As with the woodcock my personal experience with the nesting of the Wilson snipe has been limited to one nest, found in the Magdalen Islands on June 18, 1904. The nest was found by watching the bird go to it in the East Point marshes. It was on dry ground in a little clump of grass, under some low and rather open bayberry bushes, on the edge of a boggy arm of the marsh, which extended up into the woods; it was built up about 2 inches above the ground and was made of short, dead straws and dead bayberry leaves; it measured 6 inches in outside and 3 inches in inside diameter. The four eggs which it contained blended perfectly with their surroundings and although in plain sight, they were not easily seen. P. B. Philipp (1925), who has found many snipe's nests in the Magdalen Islands, where he says the species is increasing, writes:

The nesting begins in the last 10 days of May, and is a simple affair. Usually wet marshy ground is selected, preferably with low brush and grass with lumps or tussocks rising above the bog water. The nest is a shallow hollow made in the grass or moss of one of these lumps, lined with broken bits of dead grass and sometimes with dead leaves.

William L. Kells (1906) gives a graphic account of finding a nest of the Wilson snipe in southern Ontario, as follows:

On the 17th of May, 1905, as I was passing through a patch of low ground overgrown with second growth willows, a rather large-sized bird flushed from a spot a few feet from where I had jumped over a neck of water. I did not see the exact place from which the bird had flown, but the fluttering sound of her wing caught my ear, and looking ahead I saw the creature, who with outspread tail and wings, was fluttering on the damp earth, and with her long bill down in the mud, was giving vent to a series of squeaking sounds. I knew at once that this bird had flushed from a nest, and that the object of her actions was to draw my attention from something that she was very desirous to conceal; but a little research revealed a nest containing four beautiful eggs. A clump of willows a little elevated stood about 6 feet from the pool over which the bird had flown, and midway between the water and the willows, which overhung it the nest was placed. This was simply a slight depression made by the bird in the moss and dry grass, and except from its concealed situation and being a little more expanded, there was no particular distinction between it and those of the more familiar killdeer plover and spotted sandpiper, though the lining was probably of a warmer texture, being of fine dry grass, while the eggs, as in the case of all the ground nesting waders, were arranged with the small ends inward.

A Colorado nest is thus described by Robert B. Rockwell (1912):

This nest was located on (and above) the surface of slightly damp ground at the edge of a good-sized area of very soft, boggy land formed by the seepage under the dyke of the Big Barr Lake. It was built in the center of a tussock of grass about 8 inches in length and was a very neat, well-shaped, and cupped nest composed entirely of fine dry grass. In construction it was far superior to any shore bird's nest I have ever seen, being so compactly and strongly put together that it was possible to remove it from the nesting site without injury. In general appearance the nest itself is not unlike certain sparrows' nests.

A nest photographed for me by F. Seymour Hersey, near the mouth of the Yukon River, Alaska, was in a very wet spot on the border of a marsh; it was a deep hollow prettily arched over with dry grasses at the base of a small willow bush.

The Wilson snipe is often a close sitter and sometimes will not leave the nest until nearly trodden upon. W. J. Brown (1912) tells of a case where he stroked the bird on the back and had to lift her off the nest to photograph the eggs.

Mr. Sutton (1923) has published a full and very interesting account of the breeding habits of the Wilson snipe in Crawford County, Pennsylvania, where he found several nests in a large, wet swamp among cat-tails and grasses; of the first nest he says:

The nest was beautifully situated in the center of a clump of dried fern stalks—a clump similar to hundreds of just such little islands near at hand but certainly admirably suited to such a nesting site, for the eggs were almost completely surrounded at the short distance of 4 inches by a paling of dead fern stalks. The eggs were about 9 inches above water at this time, although the water's depth changed constantly with every rainfall, and five days later the outer rim of the nest was only 2 inches above water level. Another was built upon a bit of decayed, sunken log and was composed entirely of grass stems rather carefully laid together. The eggs were but a few inches above the surface of the water, and although grass stems connected the nesting site with other vegetation the nest was virtually on an island surrounded by water 18 inches deep.

And of still another he says:

This nest was the only snipe nest I have seen which had any real protection from above. The nest was so placed under a dead willow branch and some leaning cat-tail stalks that it was really difficult to see it. The grasses composing the nest had been placed with care and were somewhat woven about the cat-tail stalks and other grasses standing near.

Eggs.—Four eggs is the normal number laid by the snipe; rarely five eggs are laid. They are about ovate pyriform in shape and slightly glossy. The ground colors vary from " buckthorn brown " or " Isabella color " in the darkest types to " deep olive buff " or " dark olive buff " in the lighter types, which are much commoner.

As a rule the eggs are boldly spotted and blotched, chiefly about the larger end; but often they are spotted more or less evenly over the entire surface. The markings are in dark shades of brown, "burnt umber," "bister," or "bone brown." Often there are splashes or scrawls of brownish black, or black, at the larger end. "Snuff brown," "vinaceous drab," or "brownish drab" under spots or blotches often occur. The measurements of 57 eggs average 38.6 by 28.1 millimeters; the eggs showing the four extremes measure 42.4 by 29.5, 36.1 by 29.9, and 37.5 by 25.5 millimeters.

Young.—The period of incubation is from 18 to 20 days, and it is shared by both sexes. Mr. Philipp (1925) says that three birds taken from the nest were all males. The young leave the nest soon after they are hatched, and wander about in the long grass, where their concealing coloration makes them very hard to find. One day, while watching snipe with J. R. Whitaker on a large marsh near the mouth of Sandy River in Newfoundland, I saw a snipe several times go down into the grass at a certain place. Thinking to find a nest there I made a careful search, and finally found one small downy young; but not another one could I find in a long hunt. This moist meadow full of grassy hummocks is a great breeding place for snipe. Here we frequently saw snipe sitting in trees, bushes, or on telegraph poles, uttering their loud *kep kep kep* notes of protest. On the girders of a steel bridge that spans the river at this point Mr. Whitaker has seen as many as five snipe perched at one time.

Mr. Sutton (1923) describes the behavior of an anxious mother as follows:

The mother's antics so claimed my attention that I did not keep close enough watch of the young, and eventually was unable to find them. I hesitated to tramp about much at the time for fear of stepping upon them. The mother bird grunted and clucked incessantly and fell upon her side uttering weird cries, and beating her wings pitiably. At times she would dart into the air and circle about in great haste, very close to me and alight in the tall grass, whence she would run gracefully away until she was again plainly in view. As she ran about her head was held rather stiffly, and it seemed that moving it from side to side much caused her inconvenience. In fact once or twice a definite impression was given that she was carrying something in her mouth, her head was held at such a strained angle.

Plumages.—The young snipe in its dark and richly-colored natal down is one of the handsomest of the young waders. The upper parts, including the crown, back, wings, and thighs, are variegated or marbled with velvetty black, "bay," "chestnut," and "amber brown"; the down is mainly black at the base and brown-tipped; the entire upper parts are spotted with small round white spots at the tips of some of the down filaments, producing a beautiful effect of color contrasts and a surprisingly protective coloration. The head is distinctively marked with a white spot on the forehead, a black crescent above it and a black triangle below it, partially concealed by brown tips; there is a distinct black loral stripe, extending faintly beyond the eye, and a less distinct black malar stripe; between these two is a conspicuous, large, white, cheek patch. The chin and upper throat are "light ochraceous buff"; below this on the lower throat is a large sooty-black area, partially concealed by brown tips, these "tawny" brown tips predominating on the breast and flanks, and shading off to "pale pinkish cinnamon" on the belly.

The juvenal plumage appears first on the back and scapulars, then on the breast and wing coverts. A bird in my collection, about half grown has the above parts well feathered and the remiges one-third grown; but the head and rump are still downy and the rectrices have not yet started. The juvenal plumage is like the adult, except that the buff edgings of the feathers on the sides of the back and the scapulars, forming the stripes, are narrower and paler, sometimes almost white on the outer webs. The body feathers and some of the scapulars and tertials are molted during the fall, making the young bird almost indistinguishable from the adult.

Both young birds and adults have a partial prenuptial molt in the late winter and early spring, involving the contour feathers, wing coverts, tertials, and the tail. Adults have a complete molt between July and October. The spring and fall plumages are alike except that the fresh fall plumage is somewhat more richly colored.

Food.—The feeding habits of the Wilson snipe are much like those of the woodcock, except that it often feeds in much wetter places and is somewhat less nocturnal. Benjamin T. Gault (1902) discovered by observation that snipe occasionally resort to open mud flats, unmindful of the cover of darkness and that they feed at all hours of the day. He describes their method of feeding as follows:

The snipe seemed to select as special feeding grounds the water line just bordering the flats, where the mud was soft and into which they delighted in sinking their bills to the fullest depth. And in withdrawing them they never elevated their necks in true sandpiper style. On the contrary they kept their heads well "chucked down," so to speak, and in moving about from place to place, which they seldom did, however, continue to hold them in the same fashion.

In some respect their probing methods resembled the rooting of swine—a simple, up and down forward movement, and if remembered rightly, without lateral twists or side thrusts of any kind, and at times exposing fully one-half of the bill.

Whether the Wilson snipe actually do resort to the so-called "suction" method of procuring their food is a question still undetermined in my mind. The glasses however brought out the important information that the probing or feeling movements of the bill were accompanied every now and then with a guttural or swallowing motion of the throat, which at times developed into a decided gulp, as though large morsels of some kind were being taken down, and this *without the removal of the bill from the muck.*

Henry W. Henshaw (1875) describes an entirely different method of feeding; he says:

In migrating, however, especially in Arizona and New Mexico, did it depend wholly upon its usual methods of obtaining sustenance, it would fare badly, since, in some sections, there is a total lack of meadow and marsh, and then it may be seen in bróad midday running along the sandy borders of the streams, and picking up from among the pebbles and *débris* any tidbits in the shape of insects it can find. It retains, however, even under these adverse conditions, its habit of squatting, and, when approached closely I have seen it lower its body close to the ground, shrink as it were into as little space as possible, and so remain till I was within a few feet, when it would get up with its well known *scaip, scaip,* and, following the turns and sinuosities of the streams, endeavor to find some little covered nook into which it could drop out of sight.

M. P. Skinner watched a snipe feeding on the muddy shore of a pond in the Yellowstone Valley; he says in his notes:

He was about 6 inches from shore and at each stroke his bill went in up to his eyes. The strokes were rapid like those of a woodpecker. He covered a space perhaps 4 inches wide and 15 feet long in an hour, getting something every half dozen strokes or so. He was very busy there for two hours at least.

Earthworms probably constitute the principle food of the Wilson snipe, but it also eats cutworms, wireworms, leaches, grasshoppers, locusts, beetles, mosquitoes, other insects and their larvæ, and some seeds of marsh plants.

Behavior.—Snipe are notorious for their erratic flight and they often, probably usually, do dodge and zigzag when they first flush in alarm, but not always; I have seen them fly away as steadily as any other shore bird. Snipe usually lie closely crouched on the ground trusting to their excellent protective coloration, and do not flush until nearly trodden upon; so that in their hurry to get away their flight is erratic. When well under way their flight is steady and swift with the occasional turnings common to all shore birds. When first flushed they generally fly low, but when flying from one part of a marsh to another, or when migrating, they fly very high. When alighting they pitch down suddenly from a great height and then flutter down slowly into the grass or drop straight down with wings elevated and bill pointing upwards. They are less gregarious than other waders; they usually flush singly, but often within a few yards of each other if plentiful. They are seldom seen in flocks. John T. Nichols tells me in his notes of a flock of seven which he saw on Long Island:

They were flying high from the east to west, the regular southward lane for shore birds, and bunched up like dowitchers or yellowlegs as they circled over the marsh, then slanted down obliquely (as these other birds would have done) to alight on a piece of dead stubble. By the time I reached them they had scattered somewhat; four (scattered) and three (bunched) flushed from this spot in close succession, and went off into the southwest. The migration of the snipe may be mostly by night; it certainly flies to some extent along the coast by day.

And Harry S. Swarth (1922) says:

While the usual manner of occurrence was for a single bird to be flushed, or perhaps two or three within a few square yards, there were times when snipe were noted in small flocks, almost like sandpipers in their actions. Groups of 10 or 12 individuals were seen circling about through the air in close formation and wheeling or turning in perfect unison. At such times almost the only thing to betray the identity of the birds was the call note, uttered at frequent intervals. At no time, however, did birds flushed from the ground depart in flock formation.

On the ground the snipe moves about deliberately with bill pointing downwards. If alarmed it squats for concealment before jumping into flight when hard pressed; the longitudinal stripes on its back and head so closely resemble prostrate stems of dead grass that the bird is difficult to distinguish. Mr. Skinner " saw one alight and run rapidly along the ground for 20 feet, erect with head high, like a running bob white." C. J. Pennock watched one standing on a bare mud flat with " a continued up and down rythmic movement of the entire body." E. H. Forbush (1925) writes:

The snipe can swim and dive and uses both wings and feet under water in its efforts to escape. Mr. Will H. Parsons writes that he shot one that fell into a little clear streamlet where later he found it dead, under water, grasping a rootlet in its bill. Later, on the Scioto River, as he relates, he shot another whch fell into the river, and, turning, swam back toward the shore. On seeing him approach it dived, and he saw it grasp a weed with its bill. Wading in he secured the bird " stone dead."

Voice.—Eliminating the winnowing flight notes, which are unquestionably instrumental, the Wilson snipe has a variety of vocal notes. The one most often heard is the familiar *scaipe* note, a note of alarm and warning, given as the bird rises in hurried flight. This note has been variously expressed in writing, perhaps best by the word " escape ", which the snipe often does, unless the sportsman is smart enough to say " no you don't," and prove it. On the breeding grounds we frequently hear its loud notes of protest, uttered while it is flying about or perched on some tree or post; these are in the form of a loud clear whistle, like *wheat wheat wheat wheat* or more subdued in tone like *whuck whuck whuck whuck;* they are always rapidly uttered and usually consist of four or five notes. E. W. Nelson (1887) refers to a similar note heard on the breeding grounds, as *yak yak yak yak* in quick, energetic, explosive syllables. At the time when the bird is uttering its note, it flies along within a short distance of the ground with a peculiar jerky movement of the body and wings as every note is uttered."

Mr. Nichols says in his notes:

When a bird gets up almost from underfoot, the *scape* is at times replaced by a series of short, hurried notes of similar character. It is interesting to find in the Wilson's snipe this imperfect differentiation of a note uttered at the moment of taking wing from one uttered when in or approaching full flight—as it is a condition slightly different from the calls of other more social shore birds which trust comparatively little to concealment, take wing while danger is still at a distance with hurried minor notes, so soft as to readily escape notice, and have each a loud diagnostic flight call of much service in their identification.

The *scape* of the snipe has sufficient resemblance to the woodcock's *peent*, which forms a part of the nuptial performance of that species, to leave little doubt that the two are homologous (that is, of the same derivation), if we assume snipe and woodcock to be related. It is, however, more analogous (that is, of corresponding place or purpose) with the wing twitter of the woodcock. Its harsh quality is in keeping with the voices of unrelated denizens of marsh and swamp, herons, rails, frogs, etc., and the discords of close-by bog sounds continually in its ears. The quality of the snipe's call contrasts sharply with the peculiarly clear, mellow whistle of the black-breasted plover, for instance, and ringing calls of species of similar habit, with carrying power over the open distances of their haunts. The connecting series of limicoline voices, through the reedy calls of such marsh-loving birds as the pectoral sandpiper, leaves little doubt that there is a correlation between habitat and quality of voice.

In some notes from Alaska, he writes:

July 17, on the slope of a low, gentle, tundra hill a little way back from the shore, ahead of me a snipe fluttered up a short distance, then down; up, then down; accompanying this performance with *chup chup chup chup chup chew chew chew chew chew*. It alighted in a comparatively open space with a couple of small bog holes of water, surrounded with a circle of scrub willows, and here I presently flushed it again. It rose with a *chape* note, more muffled and reedy than the ordinary Wilson snipe *scape*, and, curving downwind, rose higher, attaining considerable elevation in the distance, as I followed it with my glass. It now began to zigzag up and down, maintaining approximately its position in the sky to leeward. Meanwhile I heard an unfamiliar more or less whistled *peep-er-weep* once or twice, and an intermittent winnowing sound, *wish wish wish wish wish*, etc. Being uncertain as to whether these sounds came from the distant snipe, or from some other bird closer at hand in the air, I took my glasses off the former to look about me, and as I feared I should do, lost track of it in the sky. Presently the winnowing ceased and I began to hear a continuous harsh *cuta-cuta-cuta-cuta* from over the brow of the hill, which turned out to be a snipe, presumably the same one which had returned, standing on top of the only stake thereabouts.

Field marks.—The Wilson snipe should be easily recognized by its long bill, its erratic flight, its conspicuous stripes, and the rufous near the end of its tail. The harsh *scaipe* note is diagnostic. It might be confused with the dowitcher, but the flight, notes, and usual haunts of the latter are different. I have often thought that the pectoral sandpiper resembles the snipe, as it rises from the grass, but it lacks the long bill, and is not so conspicuously striped on the back.

Fall.—The fall migration of snipe is dependent on the weather, the first early frosts are apt to start them along; when the brilliant red leaves of the swamp maples add their touch of color to the marshes, and when the vegetation in the meadows begins to take on the rich hues of autumn, then we may look for the coming of the snipe. They are by no means confined to fresh-water marshes at this season. I have occasionally flushed a Wilson snipe on the salt marshes of Cape Cod, and have frequently found them on the dry grassy shores of islands in inland ponds.

Wells W. Cooke (1914) says:

They seem reluctant to return south in fall, even though they can have no appreciation of the constant persecution which awaits them during the six months' sojourn in their winter home. A few migrants appear in the northern part of the United States in early September, and, moving slowly southward, reach the southern part of the Gulf States shortly after the middle of October. Soon the main body of the birds follows, and all normally keep south of the line of frozen ground. Yet every winter some laggards remain much farther north, feeding about springs or streams. A few can usually be found on Cape Cod, Mass., while in the Rocky Mountains, near Sweetwater Lake, Colorado, the presence of warm springs has enabled snipe to remain throughout an entire winter, though the air temperature fell to 30° F. below zero.

Mr. Brewster (1906) writes:

During exceptionally wet autumns snipe occasionally resort in large numbers to the highly cultivated truck farms of Arlington and Belmont. An interesting instance of this happened in September, 1875, when a flight, larger than any that I have known to occur in the Cambridge region before or since, settled in some water-soaked fields covered with crops of corn, potatoes, cabbages, etc., on the Hittinger farm, Belmont. Learning of the presence of these birds about a week after their arirval, I visited the place early the next morning, but all save 10 or a dozen of them had departed, owing no doubt, to the fact that there had been a hard frost during the preceding night. The borings and other signs which they had left convinced me, however, that the statement made to me at the time by Mr. Jacob Hittinger, to the effect that he had started *four or five hundred snipe* there only the day before, was probably not an exaggeration of the truth.

Game.—The Wilson snipe, improperly called "jack snipe," but more properly called "English snipe," is one of our most popular game birds. Probably more snipe have been killed by sportsmen than any other game bird. It ranks ahead of all other shore birds and upland game birds except, possibly, the woodcock, ruffed grouse, and quail. When the startling cry of the snipe arouses the sportsman to instant action he realizes that he is up against a real gamey proposition. He must be a good shot indeed to make a creditable score against such quick erratic flyers. A tramp over the open meadows, brown, red, and golden in their autumn livery, with one or two good dogs quartering the ground in plain sight and with an occasional shot at a swiftly flying bird, is one of the delights of a crisp autumn day. The birds will lie closely on a calm day, but on a windy, blustering day they are restless and wild. It is well to hunt down wind as the birds usually rise against the wind and will fly towards and then quartering away from the shooter. When two men hunt along a narrow marsh, the man on the windward side will get most of the shooting. Snipe are usually shot on wet meadows or marshes, but that they are often found in other places is shown by the following quotations from Dwight W. Huntington (1903):

Audubon says the snipe is never found in the woods, but Forester mentions finding it in wild, windy weather early in the season in the skirts of moist woodlands under sheltered lee sides of young plantations, among willow, alder, and brier brakes, and, in short, wherever there is good, soft, springy feeding ground perfectly sheltered and protected from the wind by trees and shrubbery.

Abbott says: "During the autumn I have found them along neglected meadow ditches overhung by large willow trees, and again hidden in the reeds along the banks of creeks. I have shot them repeatedly in wet woodland meadows. I have often found snipe in bushy tracts and among the swamp willows, but I have never seen them in the forest, and believe they so rarely resort to the woods that it would not be worth while to seek them there."

Snipe must have been exceedingly abundant 50 or 60 years ago, as the oft-quoted achievements of James J. Pringle (1899) will illustrate. He was not a market hunter but a gentleman (?) sportsman, who shot for the fun of it and gave the birds away to his friends. His excuses for excessive slaughter and his apologies for not killing more are interesting; he writes:

The birds being such great migrants, and only in the country for a short time, I had no mercy on them and killed all I could, for a snipe once missed might never be seen again.

I shot with only one gun at a time; had no loader, but loaded my gun myself; had I shot with two guns and had a loader I would, of course, have killed a great many more birds, but in those days and in those parts it was impossible to get a man that could be trusted to load.

During the 20 years from 1867 to 1887 he shot, on his favorite hunting grounds in Louisiana, 69,087 snipe and a total of 71,859 of all game birds; but his shooting fell off during the next 10 years for he increased his grand total of snipe to only 78,602 and of all game birds to only 82,101! His best day, undoubtedly a world's record, was December 11, 1877, when he shot in six hours 366 snipe and 8 other birds. On his best seven consecutive shooting days, alternate days in December, 1877, he killed 1,943 snipe and 25 other birds. During the winter of 1874–75 he killed 6,615 snipe. Captain Bogardus, the famous trap shot, killed, with the help of a friend, 340 snipe on one day in Illinois, and seldom got less than 150 on good days. With such excessive shooting all through the fall, winter, and spring, is it to be wondered at that the snipe have decreased in numbers?

Winter.—As mentioned above snipe spend the winters in small numbers as far north as they can find unfrozen marshes and spring holes, but their main winter resorts are in the Southern States, the West Indies, and northern South America. They were formerly enormously abundant in the marshes and savannas of Florida and the other Gulf States, where they are still common in winter. C. J. Pennock tells me that they are still abundant all winter about St. Marks, Florida, his earliest and latest dates being September 12 and May 10. Arthur T. Wayne (1910) says that, in South Carolina, the snipe "are most abundant during the months of February and March, and at that time multitudes frequent the rice plantations, provided the water is not too deep over the land." J. H. Bowles (1918) says that in Washington "cold weather does not seem to bother them much. On January 1, 1916, when all freshwater marshes were frozen over, large numbers of them gathered on the Tacoma Flats." Mr. Skinner writes to me that in Yellowstone Park they are found in winter along creeks and rivers kept open by warm springs and on ground overflowed by warm water from the hot springs.

Aiken and Warren (1914) tell of the winter habits of the Wilson snipe, in El Paso County, Colorado, as follows:

Fountain Creek rarely freezes over entirely below its exit from the mountains, and along its banks there are many places where water that runs through the sand comes to the surface and forms springy holes and marshy meadows which are warmer than surface water. These become the winter feeding grounds for the snipe and one or a pair often content themselves with a very small area of muck. But at times of severe cold many of the smaller holes freeze and then the snipe concentrate at places where a larger flow of water keeps the holes open. On January 15, 1908, with 6 inches of snow on the ground and below zero weather Aiken visited a small beaver pond on the Skinner ranch 6 miles south of Colorado Springs. A bit of marsh above the pond and a short stretch of ooze along the outlet below remained open, and in this small area of one-fourth of an acre were 25 to 30 snipe. Some years ago a snipe was found running upon the ice when everything in the vicinity was frozen solid. A few snipe winter along banks of streams in the mountains.

That snipe know enough to protect themselves from storms may be illustrated by narrating here one of Aiken's experiences in Utah about 20 years ago. He was beating a snipe marsh near one edge of which extended a narrow arroyo or gully in which were some trees and bushes. The weather had been fair until without warning a heavy snow storm set in. At once snipe began to rise wildly from different parts of the marsh and one after another directed their flight toward the same point in the arroyo and dove between its banks. Upon investigation 8 or 10 snipe were found together in a little cave in the side of the arroyo that was partly hidden by bushes so that they were well protected from any storm. We conclude this was not the first time the snipe had resorted to this friendly shelter since they knew so well where to go.

DISTRIBUTION

Range.—North America, Central America, the West Indies, and northern South America. Accidental in the Hawaiian Islands.

Breeding range.—North to Alaska (Shumagin Islands, Bethel, St. Michael, Nome, Kowak River, Cape Smith, and Fort Yukon); Mackenzie (La Pierre House, Fort Anderson, Dease River, and Fort Smith); northeastern Manitoba (Fort Churchill); northern Ontario (Cape Henrietta Maria); Ungava (Fort George and Great Whale River); Labrador (Nain); and Newfoundland (Halls Bay, Grand Lake, and St. Johns). East to Labrador (Nain); Newfoundland (St. Johns); eastern Quebec (Magdalen Islands); Nova Scotia (Baddeck and Halifax); Maine (Calais and Waldo County); Massachusetts (Salem and Brookline); Connecticut (Portland); New York (Croton Falls); New Jersey (Newfoundland, Norristown, Trenton); and southeastern Pennsylvania (Mill Grove). South to southeastern Pennsylvania (Mill Grove); northwestern Pennsylvania (Meadville); northern Ohio (Fremont); northern Indiana (Miami, English Lake, and Cedar Lake); northern Illinois (Hinsdale and Winnebago); Iowa (Sabula, Grinnell, and Boone); Colorado (Estes Park, Barr, San Luis Lake, and Silverton); Utah (Parleys Park and Fairfield); southwestern Idaho (Nampa); and northern California (Sierra Valley and Shasta Valley). West to northern California (Shasta Valley); Oregon (Fort Klamath, Corvallis, and Salem); Washington (Yakima and Olympia); British Columbia (Chilliwack, Vancouver, and Metlakatla); and Alaska (Sitka, Kodiak, Nushagak, and Shumagin Islands).

Wilson's snipe also have been detected in summer north to Chimo, Ungava, Hopedale, Labrador, and Sandwich Bay, Quebec, and have been found lingering (probably non-breeders) south to Chloride, New Mexico, and Corpus Christi and San Angelo, Texas, while there is one breeding record for northern Los Angeles County, California (Mailliard, 1914).

Winter range.—The Wilson snipe winters regularly north to Washington (Tacoma); British Columbia (Chilliwack and Okanagan Landing); Wyoming (Yellowstone Park); Colorado (El Paso County); southern Arizona (Tucson and Fort Huachuca); southern New Mexico (Rio Mimbres); Texas (Austin, Kerrville, and Bonham); Oklahoma (Caddo); Arkansas (Fayetteville and Stuttgart); Alabama (Coosada and Montgomery County); central North Carolina (Raleigh); and southeastern Virginia (Virginia Beach); eastern North Carolina (Pea Islands); Bermuda; South Carolina (Charleston); Georgia (Savannah and Blackbeard Island); Florida (Canaveral, Orlando, Kissimmee, and Royal Palm

Hammock); Bahama Islands (New Providence, Watling Islands, and Great Inagua); Porto Rico (Guanica Lagoon); and the Lesser Antilles (Antigua, St. Vincent, Barbados, Grenada, and Trinidad). South to the Lesser Antilles (Trinidad); northern Venezuela (Caracas); Brazil (Rio de Janeiro); Colombia (Medellin and Puerto Berrio); and Panama (Frijole and Chitra). West to Panama (Chitra and the Canal Zone); Costa Rica (San Jose); Nicaragua (Greytown and the Escondido River); Honduras (Comayagua and Manatee Lagoon); Guatemala (Duenas and Atitlan); Mexico (Guanajuato, Escuinapa, Mazatlan, San Jose del Cabo, and Colonia Diaz); California (Salton Sea, Santa Barbara, San Francisco, and Eureka); and Washington (Tacoma).

It also has been known to winter (where warm springs or other factors assure open water) north to Nevada (Paradise), Utah (Provo), Montana (Terry, Helena, and near Bozeman), Wyoming(Como and Cody), Colorado (Fountain Creek, Sweetwater Lake, Clear Creek near Denver, and near Julesburg), Nebraska (Holt, Sioux, Dawes, and Cherry Counties, and along the Missouri River), North Dakota (Fort Yates), Iowa (Hancock County), Wisconsin (Milwaukee), Michigan (Grand Rapids), southern Ontario (Barrie), Ohio (Granville), New York (Oneida, Onondaga Lake, Poughkeepsie, Ithaca, New York City, and Long Island), Connecticut (Portland and New Haven), Massachusetts (Jamaica Plain, near Boston, Peabody, Hancock, and Cape Cod), and Nova Scotia (Wolfville). It has been detected in Alaska at Wrangell, on November 11, 1920, and at Craig, on December 7, 1919.

Spring migration.—Early dates of arrival in the spring are: District of Columbia, Washington, February 17; Pennsylvania, Philadelphia, March 7, Harrisburg, March 11, Carlisle, March 18, Berwyn, March 21, and Meadville, March 22; New Jersey, Fort Mott, March 16, and Pennsville, March 20; New York, Syracuse, February 26, Branchport, March 5, Orient Point, March 12, Buffalo, March 13, Brockport, March 18, Lansing, March 29, Oswego, April 1, and Ithaca, April 3; Connecticut, Portland, March 18, and New Haven, March 19; Massachusetts, Lynn, March 2, Newburyport, March 8, Boston, March 19, Somerset, March 21, and Salem, March 21; Vermont, Rutland, April 2; Maine, Farmington, April 6, and Lewiston, April 8; Quebec, Quebec, April 18, Montreal, April 19, and Godbout, May 5; New Brunswick, Scotch Lake, April 5, Petitcodiac, April 27, and Chatham, April 28; Nova Scotia, Halifax, April 5, Pictou, April 11, and Kentville, April 19; Kentucky, Bowling Green, February 24, Guthrie, February 25, and Russellville, February 26; Missouri, St. Louis, February 17, Old Orchard, February 20, Chillicothe, March 2, Jonesburg, March 11, and Kansas City, March 14; Illinois, Lebanon, February 11, Odin, March 6, Addison, March 10, Carlinville, March 11, Englewood, March 15, Morgan Park, March 17, Rockford, March 19, and Wheaton, March 26; Indiana, Bicknell, February 13, Greensburg, February 28, Frankfort, March 4, Greencastle, March 5, Bloomington, March 6, Brookville, March 7, Terre Haute, March 9, Vincennes, March 11, and Waterloo, March 12; Ohio, Granville, March 3, Cleveland, March 4, Columbus, March 8, Hudson, March 11, Sandusky, March 13, Oberlin, March 15, and New Bremen, March 18; Michigan, Ann Arbor, March 6, Vicksburg, March 18, Hillsdale, March 21, Kalamazoo, March 22, Battle Creek, March 24, Manchester, March 25, and Detroit, March 28; Ontario, Dunnville, March 24, Madoc, March 29, Queensboro, March 30, and Listowel, April 1; Iowa, Sabula, March 15, Boone, March 17, Grinnell, March 18, Keokuk, March 18, Coralville, March 19, Wall Lake, March 22, Cedar Rapids, March 23, and Sioux City, March 28; Wisconsin. Hillside, March 16, Madison, March 18, Elkhorn, March 19, Waukesha, March 20, Delavan, March 23, and Racine, March 24; Minnesota, Hutchinson, March 30, Minneapolis, March 29, Heron Lake, April 1, and Elk River, April 2; Oklahoma, Copan, March 8; Kansas, Emporia, March 14, Independence, March 19, and Wichita, March 19; Nebraska, Falls City, March 15, and Badger, March 25; South Dakota, Forestburg, March 12, Huron, March 15, and Sioux Falls, March 15; North Dakota, Fargo, April 15, Larimore, April 16, Lisbon, April 18, and Grafton, April 19; Manitoba, Greenridge, April 2, Dalton, April 8, Reaburn, April 9, Margaret, April 10, Aweme, April 14, and Shell River, April 16; Saskatchewan, Qu'-Appelle, April 9, and Indian Head, April 20; Colorado, Denver, March 10, Boulder, March 19, and Sweetwater Lake, March 26; Wyoming, Yellowstone Park, March 16; Idaho, Neeley, March 24, Meridian, April 9, and Payette Lake, April 17; Montana, Missoula, March 4, Helena, March 12, and Columbia Falls, March 27; Alberta, Onoway, April 13, Carvel, April 15, and Edmonton, April 21; and Mackenzie, Fort Providence, May 2, and Fort Simpson, May 10.

Late dates of departure in the spring are: Costa Rica, February 16; Haiti, April 13; Florida, Tallahassee, April 10, Fruitland Park, April 10, Gainesville, April 15, and St. Marks, May 10; Georgia, Cumberland, April 14, and Savannah, April 15; South Carolina, Columbia, April 19, and Charleston, May 1; Chihuahua, Lake Palomas, April 8; Lower California, Colnett, April 8, and Salton River, April 19; and Texas, Kerrville, April 11, Bonham, April 30, and Austin, April 30.

Fall migration.—Early dates of arrival in the fall are: Texas, Tivoli, August 19; Lower California, San Jose del Cabo, August 28; Chihuahua, Janos River, September 5, and Chuechupa, Septem-

ber 19; Sonora, August 19; South Carolina, Frogmore, September
10; Georgia, Savannah, September 15; Florida, St. Marks, September 12; Lesser Antilles, St. Croix, September 24, and Barbadoes,
October 11; Porto Rico, Guanica Lagoon, September 29; Costa
Rica, October 9; and Panama, Canal Zone, October 7.

Late dates of departure in the fall are: Montana, Big Sandy, October 24, and Missoula, December 5; Idaho, Meridian, November 21,
and Ketchum, December 20; Wyoming, Sundance, November 25, and
Yellowstone Park, December 9; Utah, Provo, November 25; Colorado, Greeley, November 3, and Boulder, December 24; Manitoba,
Killarney, October 24, Aweme, November 5, and Margaret, November
10; North Dakota, Chase Lake, October 21, Westhope, November 3,
and Marstonmoor, November 3; South Dakota, Harrison, October 24,
and Sioux Falls, November 22; Nebraska, Falls City, November 20,
Crawford, December 7, and Broken Bow, December 12; Kansas,
Independence, December 13; Minnesota, Elk River, November 1,
Jackson, November 6, Parkers Prairie, November 7, Fort Snelling,
November 13, and Heron Lake, November 14; Wisconsin, Unity,
November 3, Madison, November 6, Elkhorn, November 8, Shiocton,
November 13, North Freedom, November 14, and Milwaukee, Novem-
ber 15; Iowa, Davenport, November 2, Grinnell, November 4, Hills-
boro, November 11, Indianola, November 15, Marshalltown, Novem-
ber 18, Wall Lake, November 28, and Keokuk, November 28; Ontario, Toronto, October 29, Longpoint, November 2, Windsor, Novem-
ber 9, Kingston, November 12, Ottawa, November 17, and Point
Pelee, November 21; Michigan, Hillsdale, November 3, Ann Arbor,
November 5, Manistee, November 7, Manchester, November 12, Detroit, November 15, and Vicksburg, December 30; Ohio, Scio, Novem-
ber 6, Salem, November 16, Oberlin, November 22, Youngstown, No-
vember 21, Sandusky, December 2, and Cleveland, December 29; Indiana, Bloomington, October 24, Bicknell, November 9, and Lyons,
November 25; Illinois, Glen Ellyn, November 4, Canton, November
8, Fernwood, November 13, Lawrenceville, November 15, Elgin, November 17, and La Grange, November 23; Missouri, St. Louis,
November 21, and St. Charles County, December 14; Nova Scotia,
Pictou, October 24, and Halifax, December 3; New Brunswick,
Scotch Lake, October 20, and St. John, November 5; Quebec, Quebec,
November 5, and Montreal, November 13; Maine, Lewiston, Novem-
ber 5, Ellsworth, November 8, and Portland, November 15; Massachusetts, East Templeton, November 23, Salem, November 25, Lynn,
December 20, and Belchertown, December 20; Rhode Island, New-
port, December 3; Connecticut, New Haven, December 1, Portland,
December 7, and Lakeville, December 28; New York, Geneva, November 3, West Winfield, November 13, Fair Haven Light, November
17, Branchport, November 24, Shelter Island, November 29, Madi-

son County, December 10, and Orient Point, December 20; New Jersey, Bloomfield, November 1, Camden, November 7, Egg Island, November 8, and Pennsville, December 1; Pennsylvania, Berwyn, November 1, and Erie, November 21; and District of Columbia, Washington, December 22.

Casual records.—A Wilson's snipe was killed at Naaleho Plantation, Kau, Hawaiian Islands, several years prior to 1900 and a second was reported as seen in the same locality in the fall of the same year (Henshaw, 1902). It also has been reported as taken in Great Britain, but the record is too doubtful to warrant serious consideration.

Egg dates.—Magdalen Islands: 36 records, June 1 to 27; 18 records, June 3 to 14. Alberta: 39 records, May 16 to July; 20 records, May 28 to June 10. Utah: 48 records, May 8 to July 24; 24 records, May 12 to June 2.

CAPELLA MEDIA (Latham)

GREAT SNIPE

Contributed by Francis Charles Robert Jourdain

HABITS

The claim of this species to a place on the American list rests on a specimen obtained from the Hudson's Bay Company in Canada many years ago and now in the collection of the British Museum. Its breeding home is in Northern Europe and Asia, but on migration and during the winter months it has been met with in the British Isles, throughout southern Europe and Africa south to the Cape Province, as well as southern Asia from India westward. Unlike the common snipe, it frequently occurs singly and is by no means confined to marshy spots, but may be met with on rough pastures, moorlands, and fields. To this characteristic it owes its name of "solitary snipe."

Spring.—On the northward migration it is of very rare occurrence in the British Isles, and has only been recorded on a few occasions in Morocco, but of regular occurrence in south Spain; but is not uncommon on passage in Malta in April and May and occurs in small numbers in Italy in April and May and in Corfu and Epirus in March, also migrating in greater numbers along the west coast of the Black Sea. Probably the majority of the birds which visit South Africa make their way northward along the east side of the Continent. The northerly movement begins in Natal in January or February, so that it extends over a period of four or five months.

Courtship.—Observations on the courtship of this species are not numerous, for it is nocturnal in its habits and, except during the mating season, decidedly unsociable. In western Europe there has been a great diminution of the breeding stock of late years. Jutland, which was at one time a well-known breeding place, has long been entirely deserted, and it is necessary to visit the morasses of Scandinavia and Esthonia or Finland and Russia before one can make the acquaintance of this species in any numbers on its nesting ground. Unlike the common and jack snipe, there are no aerial evolutions to call attention to the display, but the whole is conducted on the ground between sunset and sunrise; and as the notes of the birds are not loud, it may well be imagined that it may readily be overlooked. The number of birds which attend at the "Spil," as it is called in Norway, or "Tok" (Russian), varies from eight to a dozen pairs to twenty or more in districts where the birds are comparatively common. Here late in May the males may be heard uttering low warbling notes, producing also sounds which have been compared to those made by running the nail along the teeth of a comb, and snapping their bills together, evidently in defiance. The display consists in expanding the tail like a fan and turning it over toward the back, the white outer feathers standing out conspicuously, with drooping wings and depressed and retracted head. In this attitude they perform a kind of dance, slowly at first, but becoming more and more rapid, and generally culminating in a series of fights between the rivals.

R. Collett, who furnished a long and detailed description of the procedure at one of these "leks" to Dresser (1871), is of opinion that the fighting is not of a serious character and consists chiefly of feeble slashes with the wings, but the Russian naturalist Alphéraky, a translation of whose interesting paper on the subject appeared in the Field for 1906 (p. 1075) with an illustration of the display, describes the ground as often strewn with feathers after these encounters. In the more northern latitudes there is of course little darkness, but there is a consensus of opinion that the display dies down about midnight and commences again as it becomes lighter. Alphéraky ascribes this to the arrival of the females on the scene. Clear and bright nights are most favorable for this performance, which seems to have some points of resemblance to that of the ruff and some to that of the black grouse (*Lyrurus tetrix*), but a series of observations are required before we can reconcile the discrepancies and fill up the gaps in the descriptions. According to Collett there is a period in the display when the bird is in a kind of ecstasy and produces a series of varied notes beginning with a whistle or two, followed by a snapping noise with five or six notes in rapid succession, then a hissing sound, followed by a rolling *sbirrrr*, which becomes deeper as uttered. A number of birds displaying at the same time produces a low continuous chorus of varied sounds. This is the more remarkable as the great snipe is at other seasons a particularly silent bird, and indeed is rarely heard to utter a sound of any kind, usually rising in silence.

Nesting.—The sites vary according to locality. In Jutland they were usually on grassy flats, but in Scandinavia generally on broken ground with birch scrub here and there. Here the female scratches a hollow among the moss and deposits her four handsome eggs. F. and P. Godman (1861), who found several nests in the Bodö district, Norway, discovered one which had an incomplete set of two eggs. On returning two days later to the spot nothing was visible but some disarranged bits of moss. Alarmed by their approach the bird flew off, leaving a hole in the moss through which the eggs were visible. On a third visit the bird was found incubating the two eggs, which were on the point of hatching, and was covered with fragments of moss which she had evidently torn up and thrown over herself. None of the other nests found were concealed in any way.

Eggs.—These are normally four in number, though occasionally three may be met with. They are pyriform in shape with a pale stone colored ground and boldly spotted and blotched with dark umber, shading into black and numerous ashy gray shell markings. The markings are usually denser and more concentrated at the big end, often with a tendency to a zone. The measurements of 100 eggs from northern Europe (69 by the writer, 19 by Goebel, and 12 by Rey) average 45.3 by 31.8 millimeters; the eggs showing the four extremes measure **48.8** by 31.9, 46.2 by **33.3**, **41.2** by 31.7, and 46.5 by **29.5** millimeters. Rey (1905) gives the average weight as 1.107 g. and Goebel as 1.035 g.

Young.—As to the share of the sexes in incubation our information is scanty; but, such as it is, goes to prove that it is conducted by the female alone. Naumann (1887) gives the period as 17 to 18 days and states that as soon as the young are dried they leave the nest and take to the long grass which effectually conceals them.

Plumages.—The reader is referred to A Practical Handbook of British Birds, edited by H. F. Witherby (1920), where a complete account of the plumages and molts of this species is given.

Food.—Naumann (1887) records small worms, insect larvae, small snails, coleoptera, water insects, and larvae of Phryganeidae. Yarrell (1871) includes larvae of insects, especially Tipulidae, and small slugs as well as worms. These last seem to form the staple diet.

Behavior.—The family parties soon break up and from late autumn to its arrival on the breeding grounds it is more likely to be met with singly than in company. Its flight is not so rapid as that of the common snipe, but slower and more direct, while instead of uttering the well known *scape*, it either rises in silence or merely utters a guttural croaking note.

Fall.—More frequently met with in the British Isles on the autumn migration from the end of July to mid-November than in spring, but probably frequently overlooked. By the beginning of August the young are full grown normally, and gradually make their way from the high north in Norway southward, the majority of migrants taking an easterly course and only a small proportion moving southwestward to the winter quarters.

DISTRIBUTION

Breeding range.—Norway, north to Tromsö, Sweden, to latitude 65° N., formerly in Denmark but now extinct, as also in Schleswig. It is said to have bred formerly in Holland and still does so in East Prussia and eastward to Estonia, Finland, Russia, according to Buturlin, up to latitude 63° near the Great Lakes, 65½° on the White Sea, and 67½° in the Petchora, while southward it is said to breed in Bessarabia (Rumania) and in the Governments of Kieff, Poltava, Kharkoff, and Voronsh, and to 51½° N. in the Urals as well as in the Caucasus. In Asia it breeds near Omsk, in the Altai and the tributaries of the Ob, but not beyond the Yenesei or in East Siberia.

Winter range.—Cape Province, Natal, Transvaal (September to March), Damara Land, Bechuana Land, Portuguese East Africa, Southwest Africa, Persia, Turkestan, and India (once).

Migration.—River Zambesi, Egypt (not uncommon), Alexandria, etc., Algeria, Greece (April 23, May 7), Cyprus, Corfu (March), Malta (March 30), Naples, Corsica (March 25), Valencia (October 9), Montenegro (April 15, 24), Asia Minor (May 9, Sept. 21), Fao, Persian Gulf, Iraq (April, Aug., Sept.).

Egg dates.—Formerly in Denmark from May 6 to June 8 (12 records), occasionally in July; in Scandinavia from end of May to middle of July (10 records, June 13 to July 15).

LYMNOCRYPTES MINIMUS (Brünnich)

JACK SNIPE

Contributed by Francis Charles Robert Jourdain

HABITS

Sometime during the spring of 1919, probably in April, a specimen of this snipe was taken by a native on St. Paul Island, Pribilof Islands, Alaska, and presented to G. Dallas Hanna. The bird is now in the collection of the California Academy of Sciences, and constitutes the only record for North America. It is, however, a widely distributed species, breeding not only in Arctic Europe, but also across the greater part of northern Asia, and wintering south to north Africa and southern Asia.

Courtship.—Of the courtship actions in the strict sense of the words we have practically no observations, as this species has rarely been kept in captivity and then singly and for short periods. The nuptial flight is, however, more conspicuous and was described in the oft-quoted letter of John Wolley, written from Muoniovara on November 27th, 1853, to W. C. Hewitson (1856), and published in the third edition of "Coloured Illustrations of the Eggs of British Birds" by that writer. To Wolley belongs the credit of being the first to discover and bring to the knowledge of naturalists the eggs of this species, for the eggs previously ascribed to this species from localities much farther south were not by any means satisfactorily authenticated. Wolley had been for some time at his headquarters on the borders of Sweden and what is now Finland, when, on June 17th, 1853, while working the great marsh at Muonioniska, he first heard the jack snipe, though as he states:

At the time I could not at all guess what it was—an extraordinary sound unlike anything I had heard before. I could not tell from what direction it came, and it filled me with a curious suspense. My Finnish interpreter thought it was a Capercally (*Tetrao urogallus*) and at the time I could not contradict him; but soon I found that it was a small bird gliding at a wild pace at a great height over the marsh. I know not how better to describe the noise than by likening it to the cantering of a horse in the distance over a hard hollow road; it came in fours with a similar cadence and a like clear, yet hollow, sound. The same day we found a nest which seemed of a kind unknown to me. The next morning I went to Kharto-uoma with a good strength of beaters. I kept them as well as I could in line, myself in the middle, my Swedish traveling companion on one side, and the Finn talker on the other. Whenever a bird was put off its nest the man who saw it was to pass on the word and the whole line was to stand whilst I went to examine the eggs and take them at once or observe the bearings of the spot for another visit as might be necessary. We had not been many hours in the marsh when I saw a bird get up before Herr Saloman, and I marked it down. In the meantime the nest was found and when I came up the owner was declared to have appeared striped on the back and not white over the tail. A sight of the eggs, as they lay untouched, raised my expectations to the highest pitch. I went to the spot where I had marked the bird, put it up again, found that it was indeed a jack snipe, and again saw it after a short, low flight drop suddenly into cover; once more it rose a few feet from where it had settled, I fired and in a minute had in my hand a true jacksnipe, the undoubted parent of the nest of eggs. In the course of the day and night I found three more nests and examined the birds of each. One allowed me to touch it with my hand before it rose, and another only got up when my foot was within 6 inches of it. It was very fortunate that I was thus able satisfactorily to identify so fine a series of eggs, for they differ considerably from one another.

The great German ornithologist Naumann (1887) also describes the nuptial flight, as observed by him in still weather on spring evenings, as scarcely audible at over a hundred paces and recalling the tapping noise made by the death-watch beetle. He writes the sound as "*Tettettettettett*," etc., and says each note lasts six seconds at a time, as the bird sweeps over the marsh now rising and then falling in tone as it is uttered.

V. Russon, the Estonian ornithologist, also observed the flight on a marsh near Kurkull, in Estonia, and noticed that the snipe rose high in the air and gradually descended again after a flight of several hundred yards. He compares the sound to the words: "*Lok-toggi, lok-toggi, lok-toggi*," which certainly agree with the impression given by Wolley's graphic description. He says the local names current in the district are derived from the resemblance the bird's notes bear to the rattle of a dilapidated wagon wheel. In the night the jack snipe is silent, but the display begins again with the first glimmering of dawn, but does not as a rule last long. The note described by Naumann he only heard on two occasions just before the bird settled in the swamp and believed it to be caused by rapid snapping of the bill.

Nesting.—Like the common snipe, the jack snipe breeds in the marshes, choosing a slight hollow in a fairly dry, grassy, or sedge-grown spot, but close to open swamp. Wolley describes the five nests seen by him as being all alike in structure, "made loosely of little pieces of grass and equisetum not at all woven together, with a few old leaves of the dwarf birch." It is an extremely close sitter, not stirring from its eggs till almost trodden on, while one bird actually allowed Wolley to touch it with his hand before it flew. The breeding season is late, for eggs are rarely met with before mid-June and have been recorded throughout July and even in August.

Ralph Chislett (1927) has published his recent experience with the nesting habits of the jack snipe, from which the following is quoted:

The wide marsh stretched for a number of miles between the birch-clad slopes of some low hills. From the hillsides, at intervals, open sheets of water of varying dimensions could be seen, and a fringe of the birch forest stretched almost down to a small, peaty pool. Through the woodland fringe a stream hurried, clear and cold with melted snow from the hill. Leaving the stream at a place where yellow globe-flowers grew in profusion, we followed the ridges of soft ground which intersected the marsh. Progress was impeded by scrub-willow, while hummocks of moss and mounds of crowberry and vaccinium overlay the peat foundation of the ridge, many of the hummocks being white with cloudberry blooms. Between the ridges in the marshy tracts grass grew thinly through the moss, and still more thinly in the centers, where our feet were brought up firmly at a depth of eighteen inches by the still frozen bottom. Later in the summer the marshes would probably be deeper.

Not more than two hundred yards from the wood, a ridge sank and allowed the surplus water from one flattened area of grassy marsh to drain through to

the next. On the north side of the trickle the ground rose slowly to the full
height of the ridge again, perhaps a yard above the marsh-level. Midway up
the little slope, on a dry bit of ground, a few stalks of scrub-birch partially
shielded the jack snipe from view as it sat on the nest by the side of a cloudberry plant. Not that shelter was needed. The nest would never have been
found had my foot not happened to drop within a few inches of it. Then
away the bird flew, with a low, almost direct flight, without any sudden twists
for some twenty yards, then down into the marsh. When flushed it disappeared
from view into the marsh and was not seen again until within a few feet of the
nest. Once, when spotted a couple of yards away, it covered that short distance
a foot at a time, crouching down for a few seconds between each very short
journey; then, still crouching, it covered the eggs and remained motionless.

The nest was found on June 12th, 1926, and it then contained four eggs.
The last time I inspected it was on July 6th, when the eggs were cracking at
their larger ends.

Eggs.—The eggs are extraordinarily large for the size of the bird,
being but little smaller than those of the common snipe (*Capella
gallinago*). They are, as a rule, more or less distinctly pyriform and
are normally four in number. The ordinary types vary in ground
color from " chamois " to " cream buff " in the buff types and " olive-
lake " or " corn-olive " to " olive-buff " in the green types. As a rule,
the markings are somewhat smaller and more uniformly distributed
than in common snipes' eggs. They are in some shade of light or
dark brown, such as " tawny," " russet-vinaceous," " chocolate,"
" liver," or " chestnut brown "; the underlying markings, which are
numerous and conspicuous in some cases, are in various shades of
" purple drab " or " drab-grey." The spiral smears, so frequently
found in common snipes' eggs, seem to be absent from those of the
jack snipe, and, though there are some cases of wide variation in
coloring, a series will be found to be browner and less bold in markings than a corresponding number of the common species. The measurements of 146 eggs average 38.53 by 27.37 millimeters; the eggs
showing the four extremes measure **44.5** by 28.5, 40 by **30, 35** by 27 and
38 by **25.5** millimeters. Rey (1905) states that the shells are somewhat thinner and lighter than with the common snipe and gives the
average weight as 660 grams.

Plumages.—The downy plumage is described by Dresser (1871) as
follows, from a nestling obtained at Muonioniska:

Entire upper parts richly varied, deep rufous and black, dotted here and
there with white; a buffy white streak passes from the forehead over the eye;
below this is a dark-brown streak covering the lores to the eye; from the base
of the lower mandible another white streak passes below the eye and one also
from the chin (which is buffy white) along the side of the head to the nape;
underparts dark-reddish brown, slightly varied with blackish brown; bill and
legs much developed.

For descriptions of subsequent plumages and molts the reader is
referred to "A Practical Handbook of British Birds," edited by H. F.
Witherby (1920).

Food.—Probably consists mainly of worms, with a considerable mixture of insects and some vegetable matter (seeds, etc.). Naumann (1887) remarks that he has several times found grass seeds in stomachs and believes that vegetable matter is taken as well as insects and worms. Newstead records Coleoptera (3 cases), Mollusca (*Tellina* and *Helix*, 2 cases), vegetable matter (grass, etc.), sand, and pebbles. Cordeaux found fragments of fresh-water shells and a few bivalves (*Pisidia*), while Saxby met with plant fibers and mud.

Behavior and voice.—The jack snipe is an extremely silent bird, and to a great extent, solitary, outside the breeding season. The noises made during the nuptial flight have already been dealt with, but it is characteristic of the species that when flushed, unlike the common snipe, it nearly always rises in silence. Naumann, however, writes that on rare occasions, generally toward evening, a weak, high-pitched note may be uttered, like "*Kitz*" or "*Kutz*," which he compares to a bat's squeak. One may, however, put up twenty birds one after another without hearing anything, though very rarely a single "*ahtch*" is uttered, much more softly than the corresponding note of the common snipe. On being flushed it dashes off quickly with unsteady flight, but pitches again before rising to any height, and, except on migration or on its breeding ground, usually flies low.

Field marks.—Its solitary habits and small size are the best field characters, combined with the fact that it is not shy and usually rises at very short range, so that one gets a good view of it before it pitches again at no great distance, where it can be flushed again. The almost invariable absence of any note on rising is very characteristic.

DISTRIBUTION

Breeding range.—Scandinavian Lapland and Finland south to about latitude 64°. In Germany it is said to have bred in various localities from Schleswig Holstein to East Prussia, but there is no doubt that most of these records, if not all, are not, and can never be, satisfactorily authenticated. It does, however, breed in the Baltic Republics (Estonia and Latvia) and apparently in North Poland, while in Russia it breeds on the tundra south to the Governments of Perm, Kazan, Vologda, Jaroslav, Vladimir, Orel, Tula, and Tver. In Asia, though absent from the extreme north of Siberia, it is found in the Arctic Zone south to Tobolsk and north to the Boganida (lat. 70°), while eastward it ranges to the Kolyma delta.

Winter range.—While a few birds remain in favorable localities or mild weather at short distances south of their breeding quarters, the main body migrates through Europe south to the countries bordering the Mediterranean and its islands (Balearic Isles, Corsica, Sardinia, Malta, Sicily, Ionian Isles, Crete, Cyprus, etc.). In Africa

it is met with in all the countries on the northern littoral from
Morocco to Egypt; also up the Nile Valley to the Blue Nile (Lakes
Nakuru and Naivasha), and sparingly to Kenya Colony. In Asia
from West Palestine, South Iraq, Persia, Afghanistan, throughout
India, Ceylon, Burma, China (scarce), Formosa, and Japan. In the
Canaries it occurs only on passage in small numbers.

Spring migration.—In south Spain, end of February and early
March; Corsica, February (late date March 27); Greece, February
(late dates March 2 and 19); Italy, April and early May (latest date
beginning of June); Cyprus, end of March and early April (late
date April 16). In the British Isles the passage lasts from the end
of March to the third week of May (late date June, North Uist);
in Denmark, April; south Sweden from end of March to middle of
April; in Hungary they leave about the end of March; and have
been noted in Russia in the Caucasus, the Kirghis Steppes, and the
Urals. In Asia they remain in Iraq to April 7; Sind, early April.
Arrival noted on the Boganida June 8. In Africa, Morocco (February), Tunisia (February, March), Abyssinia (February), and
Egypt (March).

Fall migration.—In the British Isles from mid September to end
November (early dates, August 12, 1910, Norfolk; August 20, 1910,
Essex; August 1, Norfolk). Heligoland (September and October);
also met with in practically all European countries, reaching south
Spain (November, end October, or early November). In Asia recorded from Asia Minor, Transjordania (October), arriving Sind
(early October) and India (September–October).

Casual records.—Once recorded from the Faeroes (1910); also on
Madeira (March 15, 1889); Andaman Isles (once), as well as on the
Pribilof Isles.

Egg dates.—June 4 to 12 (2 records); 14 to 21 (8 records); 22 to
30 (2 records); July 1 to 14 (3 records); 15 to 28 (4 records); 29
to August 2 (2 records).

LIMNODROMUS GRISEUS GRISEUS (Gmelin)

EASTERN DOWITCHER

HABITS

The dowitcher, or, as I should prefer to see it called, the red-
breasted snipe, occurs as a species entirely across the American
continent. The long-billed dowitcher, the western form, was
originally described as a distinct, full species; it has since been reduced to the rank of a subspecies, because of very evident intergradation; and now some very good ornithologists are in doubt as to the
propriety of recognizing the two varieties in nomenclature at all,

because no distinctly different breeding ranges for the two forms have been established, and typical (so-called) eastern birds have never been found breeding anywhere. What few breeding birds have come from Alaska and northern Mackenzie all seem to be *scolopaceus*, but *griseus* may still be found breeding there when we have larger series. I have had considerable correspondence with Prof. William Rowan about the breeding dowitchers of Alberta, including interchange of specimens. He seems to think that the Alberta birds are constantly distinct from either *griseus* or *scolopaceus* and perhaps worthy of a name. It seems to me that they are strictly intermediate and should not be named. In a letter recently received from P. A. Taverner he seems inclined to recognize the Alberta bird as a " short-billed bird resembling the eastern most, but intermediate, and with spotting characters different from either."

On migrations, and in winter, both forms are found entirely across the continent. The best that can be said is that *griseus* is more common on the Atlantic and *scolopaceus* is more common on the Pacific coast. Dr. Louis B. Bishop, with whom I have discussed this question, is inclined to call one a mutant of the other; he has some 200 dowitchers in his collection, from all parts of the country, those from the Atlantic and Pacific coasts being about equally divided and the two forms being about equally represented. In analyzing his series, taking into account length of bill, length of wing and brightness of color, he finds that: of *griseus*, 86 per cent are from the Atlantic coast, 2 per cent from the interior, and 12 per cent from the Pacific coast; and of *scolopaceus*, 14 per cent are from the Atlantic coast, 30 per cent from the interior, and 56 per cent from the Pacific coast. While collecting near Pasadena, California, on April 25, 1923, he shot into a large flock of dowitchers and picked up nine birds, all but one of which were typical *griseus*, in bill, wing, and color.

Spring.—The last of the dowitchers which winter in Florida, or migrate through there, leave for the north during May, though a general northward movement has been going on during April. The earliest birds sometimes reach Massachusetts by May 1, but usually the main flight comes along about May 20 and lasts for about ten days. Audubon (1840) observed large numbers of this species flying eastward along the coasts of Louisiana and Texas during April. And Arthur T. Wayne (1910) says that " these birds migrate to their breeding grounds in the far north between May 1 and 15, and when the tide is low in the afternoon and a light southerly wind prevails, flock after flock can be seen migrating in a northwesterly direction. I have yet to see these birds migrate along the coast line in the spring." This would seem to indicate an overland route from South

Carolina, in addition to the Atlantic coast route referred to above. Professor Rowan writes to me that dowitchers are common on both migrations in Alberta, and says:

In a long series of spring and fall skins, there is every gradation from the supposed typical eastern form (*griscus*) to the so-called long-billed form (*scolopaceus*). Bill lengths and colors do not correspond as they are supposed to do. As far as this district is concerned, there is absolutely no evidence in support of the splitting of this species into two races. The only two really long-billed birds that have been taken, were deliberately collected from a flock as their bills were so obviously longer than those of their companions even in life. Intermediate lengths, forming a nicely graded series, have been secured. The colors and markings of the spring birds are infinite in variety, and do not correspond to the bill lengths that should go with them.

There is a northward migration through the interior, in which this form is undoubtedly represented, but to what extent it is hard to tell, as it is impossible to separate all the records. Both forms are recorded on migrations in California and British Columbia.

Courtship.—Richard C. Harlow has sent me some brief notes on the courtship of this species, as seen on its breeding grounds in Alberta. There were at least eight pairs of birds in the vicinity and they kept up their courtships until he left on June 9. The males apparently outnumber the females, for at least two females were seen surrounded by little groups of three or four males, frequently singing and displaying. "The male frequently strutted like a woodcock and displayed, and several times arose and gave his flight song, a clear, liquid, musical, contralto gurgle." Professor Rowan thinks that both sexes indulge in this song.

Nesting.—The breeding range of the eastern dowitcher is imperfectly known or not known at all, unless we include the birds which breed in Alberta under this form, where in my opinion they belong. Prof. Wells W. Cooke (1912) writes:

The nest and eggs of the dowitcher are not yet known to science, nor has the species been seen in summer at any place where it was probably breeding. The dowitcher is a common migrant on the coasts of New Jersey, New York, Rhode Island, and Massachusetts, and in fall is sometimes very abundant. Farther north its numbers decrease: New Hampshire, tolerably common in fall, no spring records; Maine, tolerably common spring and fall; Quebec, rare migrant; New Brunswick, no records; Nova Scotia, once (Sharpe); Prince Edward Island, once; Ungava, a few in August, 1860, at Henley Harbor (Coues), one June 10, 1883, at Fort Chimo (Turner). North of Ungava, the only record is that of a single accidental occurrence at Fiskenaes, Greenland (Reinhardt). Evidently the dowitcher does not breed in any numbers, on the eastern coast of Ungava. The probability that it does not breed there at all is strengthened by the fact that several first-class observers, who during the fall migration were in the Gulf of St. Lawrence, did not see any of the birds. It undoubtedly does not go into northeastern Keewatin and the islands of the Province of Franklin, for it is not reported by the various expeditions that have traveled and wintered in those districts, while the specimens taken on the west coast of Hudson Bay belong to the form called *scolopaceus*. The only district left for the breeding ground is the interior of Ungava and the eastern shore of Hudson Bay.

W. E. Clyde Todd, who has probably done more field work than anyone else on the east coast of Hudson Bay, writes to me:

Replying to your query about the dowitcher, it is my opinion that this species does not breed in the interior of northern Ungava, but I admit I have nothing to prove it one way or the other. It seems to me, though, that if it did breed there, it would be far more common than it is at the southern end of James Bay in migration, instead of being one of the rarer kinds. I never saw it anywhere north of this part, but then I have not been in northern Ungava in the breeding season.

Turner's record of a single bird at Fort Chimo, on June 10, 1883, seems to be the only peg on which to hang the Ungava theory; and this may have been a straggler. The Alberta birds are somewhat intermediate; and probably typical *griseus*, if there is any such thing, will be found breeding somewhere in the muskeg regions of central Canada between Alberta and Hudson Bay.

There are several sets of dowitcher's eggs in collections, from this general region, collected in 1903 and 1906, which have been looked upon with some suspicion; one came from Hayes River Flat, 25 miles north of 55°, one from just south of Little Slave Lake, and three from Little Red Deer River, Alberta. Now that the dowitcher has been definitely shown to breed in Alberta, these records look authentic.

To A. D. Henderson and his guests is due all the credit for recent positive evidence. On June 18, 1924, he found a pair of dowitchers with two young, only a day or two old, "near a small lake in a muskeg about 17 miles northeast of Fort Assiniboine." The following season he found dowitchers again at three different places in the same region, " probably a dozen pairs in all "; and on June 2, about 35 miles northeast of Fort Assiniboine, he took his first set of three fresh eggs. The nest was " in a muskeg in open growth of small tamarac trees about 125 yards from a lake "; he describes it as " a hollow in a lump of moss, scantily lined with a few tamarac twigs, leaves, and fine dry grass, at the root of a small dead alder about 12 inches high "; it measured 1¾ inches deep and 4 inches across; the top was 4 inches above standing water.

Mr. Harlow, who was with Mr. Henderson the next year, 1926, took two sets of four eggs each. One " nest was in an extensive tundralike muskeg, very quaking and wet, and the nest was in a small bunch of dwarf birch, not over 12 inches high, on the end of a little ridge of moss and completely surrounded on three sides by water." The male was seen " singing " near the nest. He joined the female after she had fluttered off the nest and the pair were seen feeding together; several times they stood erect and rubbed their bills together. After the eggs were taken a set of phalarope's eggs was placed in the nest; the dowitcher returned took one look at the eggs and then flew away and was never seen near the nest again.

Eggs.—One of Mr. Henderson's sets was apparently complete with three eggs, but four is the usual number. There is probably no constant difference between the eggs of this and its long-billed relative. One of Mr. Harlow's sets he describes as "light olive-green, rather lightly marked with pin points, spots, flecks, and a few blotches of dark umber and dark brown." The other set, he says, is slightly darker olive-green and is "much more heavily spotted and blotched with small and large spots of umber and brown and under shell markings of a lighter color." The measurements of 18 Alberta eggs average 40.8 by 29.2 millimeters; the eggs showing the four extremes measure **44** by 29.5, 41 by **30.3**, **38.2** by 28.5, and 38.7 by **27.7** millimeters.

Plumages.—The plumages and molts, which are the same in both forms, are fully described under the long-billed dowitcher.

Food.—The favorite feeding grounds of the dowitchers are the mud flats and sand flats in sheltered bays and estuaries, or the borders of shallow ponds on the marshes, where they associate freely with small plovers and sandpipers. Although not inclined to move about actively, their feeding motions are very rapid, as they probe in the mud or sand with quick, perpendicular strokes of their long bills, driving them in their full length again and again in rapid succession; while feeding in shallow water the whole head is frequently immersed and sometimes several strokes are made with the head under water. Dr. E. R. P. Janvrin writes to me:

Mr. J. T. Nichols and I watched three individuals feeding on the salt meadows late in the afternoon, continuing our observations until it was so dark that we could hardly distinguish the birds any longer; at which time the birds were still feeding. The question arose whether dowitchers might not be nocturnal in their feeding habits, as is the case with the woodcock and Wilson's snipe, since the sense of sight is certainly not essential to their probing for food.

Various observers have noted among the food items of the dowitcher grasshoppers, beetles, flies, maggots, marine worms, oyster worms, leeches, water bugs, fish eggs, small mollusks, seeds of aquatic plants, and the roots of eelgrass.

Behavior.—Dowitchers are the gentlest and most unsuspicious of shore birds, which has made them easy prey for the avaricious gunner. Their flight is swift and steady, often protracted and sometimes at a great elevation, when looking for feeding places. They usually fly in compact flocks by themselves, sometimes performing interesting evolutions high in the air. They often fly, however, in flocks with other small waders, but the dowitchers are generally bunched together in the flock; I once shot four dowitchers out of a mixed flock without hitting any of the smaller birds. When a flock of dowitchers alights the birds are closely bunched, but they soon scatter out and begin to feed. If a flock is shot into, the sympathetic and confiding birds return again and again to their fallen companions until only a pitiful remnant is left to finally escape. Such slaughter of the innocents well-nigh exterminated this gentle species; but, now that it is protected, it is beginning to increase again.

Although all shore birds can swim, the dowitcher seems to be especially adept at it. Doctor Coues (1874) writes:

Being partly web-footed, this snipe swims tolerably well for a little distance in an emergency, as when it may get for a moment beyond its depth in wading about, or when it may fall, broken-winged, on the water. On such an occasion as this last, I have seen one swim bravely for 20 or 30 yards, with a curious bobbing motion of the head and corresponding jerking of the tail, to a hiding place in the rank grass across the pool. When thus hidden they keep perfectly still, and may be picked up without resistance, except a weak flutter, and perhaps a low, pleading cry for pity on their pain and helplessness. When feeding at their ease, in consciousness of peace and security, few birds are of more pleasing appearance. Their movements are graceful and their attitudes often beautifully statuesque.

W. E. D. Scott (1881) says:

A curious habit of this species was noted at the mouth of the Withlacoochee, where I saw the birds alight in very deep water and swim about for considerable time. This occurred in every instance after a flock had been fired at, and I thought at first that the birds had been wounded, but after observing the occurrence a number of times and on watching the birds while in the water I concluded that such was not the case. Those I noted were generally solitary individuals, but twice I saw three, and once four, alight in the water, swim lightly and gracefully about, and, when disturbed, rise easily and fly away.

Voice.—John T. Nichols has sent me the following notes on the characteristic calls of this species.

The flight note of the dowitcher resembles that of the lesser yellowlegs but is recognizably different, less loud and more hurried, usually suggesting the bird's name: *dowitch*, or *dowitcher*, sometimes of a single syllable. This call is subject to considerable variation. When used as a regular flight or recognition note I believe it is most frequently two-syllabled, clear and full. When the call becomes more abrupt and emphatic and the last syllable is multiplied it seems to indicate that the bird is excited rather than to have other especial significance; thus, *dowicheche.*

This note appears to be identical in the eastern dowitcher and the longbilled race which I have studied in Florida. Other minor calls of the dowitcher are single, unloud, low-pitched *chups* with which a flock manœuvred about decoys (Long Island, August) resembling an analogous yellowleg note; a low rattle when dropping down to alight (Long Island, May) ; a mellow, ploverlike *cluee,* suggesting a call of single lesser yellowlegs when loath to leave a feeding ground, calling to other more restless individuals of their kind. This was heard from a single dowitcher on the ground when a flock of lesser yellowlegs was flushed a little way off. When these departed it took wing with more usual dowitcher calls and followed after (Long Island, July). I have on record also a startled *chee* from an extra tame long-billed dowitcher in Florida, flushed by being almost struck by something thrown at it.

While observing the shore bird migration on the coast of New Jersey, during the last week of May, with Dr. Harry C. Oberholser, we frequently heard the pretty and vivacious flight song of the dowitcher. It was a sibilant, whistling song, rather loud and with a staccato effect. Doctor Oberholser, whose ears are better than mine now are, wrote down his impressions of it for me. Three short notes were heard separately, *tililoo, tidilee* and *tichilee,* accented on the first syllable; the last two were commonest. The complete song sounded like *tidilee-ti-tscha-tscha-tscha* or *tichilee-ti-tsocha-tscha-tscha,* with numerous variations and combinations of the above notes, a very striking song. This is somewhat similar in form to the song of the long-billed dowitcher heard on its breeding grounds and described by Dr. E. W. Nelson (1887); it is probably a courtship song.

Field marks.—The dowitcher when standing is a fat, chunky bird, with short greenish legs and a very long bill, with which it probes perpendicularly. In flight it also appears stout and usually carries its long bill pointed slightly downward; in adult plumage it appears very dark colored. It has none of the slender appearance of the yellowlegs and its flight is steadier. When seen flying away from the observer the grayish white central band on its back is conspicuous, as are the black and white, barred tail feathers.

Fall.—The dowitcher is one of the earliest of the fall migrants; probably the first arrivals are birds that, for one reason or another, have failed to raise broods of young, for the time elapsing between the late-spring migration and the early-fall flight is not sufficient for successful breeding. The first adults arrive on Cape Cod early in July; my earliest date is July 4. Adults are common all through July, and I have seen them as late as August 16. The young birds come along later, from August 8 to September 25. While with us they frequent the mud flats and edges of muddy ponds or bays in the marshes; they are seldom seen on the sandy beaches or far out on the sand flats. They associate freely with the smaller sandpipers, least, and semipalmated, or with the semipalmated plover and turnstones. Often in the great flocks of these small sandpipers a number of dowitchers may be easily recognized by their much larger size and very dark appearance, also by their much longer bills. They are then often concentrated in compact groups or strung out in a long line, close to the edge of the water, probing in the soft mud with quick strokes of their long bills. They are easily approached at such times, as they are almost as tame and unsuspicious as the little peep. When the flats are covered at high tide these birds resort to the salt marshes or meadows, where they rest and sleep; in such places they often lie very close and flush singly, much after the manner of Wilson snipe.

Game.—Dowitchers, or " brown backs," as they are called on Cape Cod, have been popular game birds, and immense numbers have been shot in past years. Audubon (1840) says that " it is not at all uncommon to shoot 20 or 30 of them at once. I have been present when 127 were killed by discharging three barrels, and have heard of many dozens having been procured at a shot." Edward Sturtevant says that a market hunter near Newport, Rhode Island, shot 1,058 dowitchers during the years from 1867 to 1874. Their popularity and their tameness nearly caused the extermination of the species. Mr. John C. Cahoon (1888) wrote then:

> They have decreased very fast during the last five years, and where we saw a flock of several dozens then we now see them singly or in bunches not exceeding 10 or 12. They are the least shy of any of the shore birds, and it is due to this fact that they have decreased so fast. They are easily decoyed, and although they fly swiftly their motion is steady and they keep closely together. They alight in a compact bunch, and the gunner usually shoots into them before they scatter out. Many are killed by a single discharge, and those that remain spring up with a sharp whistle and fly a short distance away, when hearing what they think to be the call of a deserted comrade they wheel about and come skimming bravely back to the murderous spot where they were first shot at. Again they are shot at, and again the remaining half dozen are loath to leave their dead and dying companions, and return to share their fate. One or two may escape, and as they drop silently down on some lonely sand spit, sad relics of their departed companions, what sorrowful thoughts must be theirs as they wait for their comrades that will never come.

Since that time the species has been saved by removing it from the game-bird list, and it has increased considerably until now it is again a fairly common bird. Whey flying in flocks it is too easily killed to offer the sportsman much of a thrill, but when flushed singly on the meadows it has more of a sporting chance for its life.

DISTRIBUTION

Range.—Chiefly eastern North America, islands of the Caribbean Sea and central South America; casual in Greenland, Alaska, the British Isles, and France.

Breeding range.—The dowitchers which have been found breeding in Alberta, from Little Red Deer River to Fort Assiniboine, are intermediate between *griseus* and *scolopaceus*, but nearer the former. Eggs have also been taken at Hayes River Flat and just south of Little Slave Lake, which are probably of this form. The breeding range of typical *griseus* probably lies between these points and the west side of Hudson Bay and perhaps extends north to the Arctic coast.

Winter range.—North to Louisiana (State game preserve, and Marsh Island) and probably rarely to North Carolina (Fort Macon). East to rarely North Carolina (Fort Macon); South Carolina (near Charleston, and Frogmore); Georgia (Savannah and Blackbeard Island); Florida (Amelia Island, Orange Hammock, and Bassenger); Bahama Islands (Great Inagua); Jamaica; Lesser Antilles (Guadeloupe, Barbadoes and Grenada); Trinidad; and Brazil (Para and Bahia). South to Brazil (Bahia); and northern Peru (Tumbez). West to northern Peru (Tumbez); Colombia (Medellin); Cuba (Isle of Pines); western Florida (Key West, Fort Myers, Sarasota Bay, Tarpon Springs, and Pensacola); Louisiana (Marsh Island); and southern California.

Spring migration.—Early dates of spring arrival are: Virginia, Hog Island, April 15, Norfolk, April 17, and Locustville, April 25; New Jersey, Long Beach, May 6, New Brunswick, May 16; New York, Shinnecock Bay Light, May 15, and Long Island, April 19; Connecticut, Norwalk, May 15; Rhode Island, Newport, May 20; Massachusetts, Monomoy Island, May 1; Quebec, Green Island, May 25; Quebec, May 28, and Fort Chimo, June 10; and New Brunswick, Grand Manan, June 13.

Late dates of spring departure are: New Jersey, Long Beach, May 20, Cape May, May 20, New Brunswick, May 23, and Elizabeth, May 31; New York, New York City, May 30, Long Island, June 12, and Long Beach, June 23.

Fall migration.—Early dates of fall arrival are: Massachusetts, Edgartown, July 4, Dennis, July 13, Monomoy Island, July 13, Marthas Vineyard, July 24, and Harvard, July 26; Rhode Island, Newport, July 10; Connecticut, Meriden, July 23; New York, Long Island, June 29, and East Hampton, July 1; New Jersey, Long Beach, July 6, and Cape May, July 10; Virginia, Cobb Island, June 19, and Bone Island, July 14; Georgia, Savannah, September 23; and Mississippi, Bay St. Louis, August 24. A few individuals may be found throughout the summer on the coast of Florida and other Southern States, but they are not known to breed in these regions.

Late dates of fall departure are: New Brunswick, Tabusintoc, October 23; Quebec, Labrador, August 23, and Montreal, September 27; Maine, Portland, August 13; Massachusetts, Harvard, August 25, Edgartown, September 4, and Cape Cod, October 23; Rhode Island, Newport, October 20; New York, Rochester, September 13, Orient, September 21, New York City, October 31, and Great

West Bay Light, November 2; New Jersey, Long Beach, October 1; and Virginia, Hog Island, November 12.

Casual records.—The dowitcher has many times been taken outside of what appears to be its normal range, in fact there are so many records for the interior that it seems certain individuals regularly follow the flyway of the Mississippi Valley.

Among these records are Bermuda, Harris Bay, September 26, 1847, and August 21, 1848, Pearl Island, September 10, 1874, and Peniston Pond, September 17, 1875; District of Columbia, Washington, September 1879; Pennsylvania, Erie, July 19, 1892, and Carlisle, August 12, 1844, and September 12, 1844; Tennessee, Reelfoot Lake, November 27, 1875; Illinois, Mount Carmel, October 9, 1875, Calumet, October, 1881, South Chicago, May 6, 1893, and Grand Crossing, July 19, 1893; Indiana, Liverpool, September 9, 1892; Ohio, Pelee Island, August 10, 1924, and September 3, 1910, and Columbus, October 16, 1921; Michigan, Wayne County, July 16, 1906, August 26, 1905, and October 7, 1890; Ingham County, August 26, 1897, and East Lansing, August 14, 1908; Ontario, Toronto, August 1, 1894, August 24, 1891, and September 15, 1889, and Ottawa, May 9, 1890; Iowa, Burlington, August 6, 1893, and August 16, 1893, and Marshalltown, August 10, 1914; Wisconsin, Lake Koshkonong, August, 1886; Texas, Corpus Christi, May 18, 1886, San Patricio County, June 11, 1887, Fort Clarke, April 26, 1882, Padre Island, August 26 and 27, 1891, Aransas Bay, August 14, 1905, and Rockport, February 3, 1909; Idaho, St. Joseph Marshes, September 12, 1895 or 1896; Mackenzie, Fort Rae, June 9, 1893; Greenland, Fiskenaesset in 1854; Ungava, Fort Chimo, June 10, 1883; and Alaska, Nushagak, September 24, 1882, and June 9, 1884.

There also are 15 records of its occurrence in the British Isles; one each near Havre, and Picardy, France, and northeastern Siberia, near Jakutsk.

Egg dates.—Alberta: 9 records, June 1 to 16.

LIMNODROMUS GRISEUS SCOLOPACEUS (Say)

LONG-BILLED DOWITCHER

HABITS

This is supposed to be a western form of the species, characterized by an average larger size, a decidedly longer bill, and more uniformly rufous under parts in the adult spring plumage. It was first described and long regarded as a distinct species. but later developments have shown intergradation and it has been reduced to subspecific rank. The above characters seem to hold good in all specimens collected on their breeding grounds in Alaska and northwestern Mackenzie; and these characters are distinctive and well marked.

But in immature and winter plumages the form can be recognized only by size; and, as the measurements of the two forms overlap and intergrade, only the extremes can be positively named. The matter is further complicated by the fact that the migration and winter ranges of the two forms overlap. This form, *scolopaceus*, is by no means rare on the Atlantic coast, and *griseus* occurs regularly on the Pacific coast; intermediates are most abundant in the central valleys, but occur on both coasts.

Spring.—The long-billed dowitcher is a rather early spring migrant; the migration starts in March; the main flight through the United States is in April; and it reaches its northern breeding grounds in May. Dr. E. W. Nelson (1887) says of its arrival in northern Alaska:

In spring, the middle of May, as the snow disappears, and the first pale leaves of grass begin to thrust their spear-points through the dead vegetable mat on the ground, or as early as the 10th on some seasons, this peculiar snipe returns to its summer home. At the Yukon mouth I found them on May 12, when they were already engaged in love-making, though the ground was still, to a great extent, covered with snow, and only here and there appeared a thawed place where they could feed. Toward the end of this month they are plentiful, and their curious habits and loud notes make them among the most conspicuous denizens of the marshes.

Courtship.—Doctor Nelson (1887) writes:

These are very demonstrative birds in their love-making, and the last of May and first of June their loud cries are heard everywhere about their haunts, especially in morning and evening. Two or three males start in pursuit of a female and away they go twisting and turning, here and there, over marsh and stream, with marvelous swiftness and dexterity. At short intervals a male checks his flight for a moment to utter a strident *peet u weet; wee-too, wee-too;* then on he goes full tilt again. After they have mated, or when a solitary male pays his devotions, they rise 15 or 20 yards from the ground, where, hovering upon quivering wings, the bird pours forth a lisping but energetic and frequently musical song, which can be very imperfectly expressed by the syllables *peet-peet; pee-ter-wee-too; wee-too; pee-ter-wee-too; pee-ter-wee-too; wee-too; wee-too.* This is the complete song but frequently only fragments are sung, as when the bird is in pursuit of the female.

Herbert W. Brandt says in his notes:

The male longbilled dowitcher pours forth his wild musical song as he hovers in the air with raised vibrating wings, perhaps 50 feet above the object of his rapturous outburst. The female, from her retreat on the cozy border of a lowland pool, modestly watches the ardent lover as he renders his melodious homage. In common with many others of the shore dwellers, the most conspicuous courting action is the pursuit race by a number of males for their desired, but elusive, lady love. It is then that one marvels at the speed and agility displayed by apparently awkward birds, as they twist and dodge in their aerial wooing. Even during his swift flight the suitor tries, but with poor success, to continue his musical efforts for the benefit of his larger paramour.

Nesting.—MacFarlane's notes record brief descriptions of some half a dozen nests found in the Anderson River region and on the borders of the wooded country. These were all located on marshy ground near a swamp or small lake. One is described as " a mere depression in the midst of a tuft or decayed grass, lined with a few withered leaves." A set collected for me by F. S. Hersey, near St. Michael, Alaska, June 9, 1914, was taken from a hollow in the moss betweeen two clumps of grass on the tundra; the female was flushed and shot. Mr. Brandt says in his notes:

The nest of the long-billed dowitcher is a mere depression scratched out on a small eminence on a wet moss-covered meadow through which short sedges grow sparingly to a height of about six inches. The nest, the bottom of which was usually wet, was in every case surrounded by shallow fresh water and the basinlike cavity was meagerly lined with grass and small leaves. In two nests the eggs rested on the cold wet moss foundation still frozen a few inches underneath and the scanty nesting material was all deposited on the rim of the nest. In every instance the female was conducting the incubation, but the male was in close attendance. The bird is a very close sitter and must be almost trodden upon before it will rise, wings spread, from its duties.

Eggs.—Four eggs seems to be the invariable rule for the long-billed dowitcher. In shape they vary from ovate pyriform to sub-pyriform; some are quite rounded and others are decidedly pointed. They have only a slight gloss. Mr. Brandt in his notes describes his four sets, as follows:

The ground color has considerable variation and shows two distinct types: The commoner one, the brown type, of which we found three sets is " Saccardo's olive "; and the other type, represented by a single set, is "greenish," shading to "bluish glaucous." The markings are bold, slightly elongated and seldom confluent, so that blotched markings are unusual. The eggs are medium to heavily spotted, causing the ground color to be conspicuous, and, in consequence, the underlying markings are very noticeable. The primary spots are in various shades of brown, namely: "Vandyke brown," "seal brown," and "Saccardo's umber," which make the egg one of unusual beauty. The underlying spots are "drab gray" to "light grayish olive" and are larger and more numerous than are found on the other limicoline eggs we collected at Hooper Bay.

In my set the ground colors vary from " dark olive buff " to· " olive buff." Two of the eggs are irregularly spotted and blotched with spots of various sizes; one is quite evenly marked with small elongated spots; and another is sparingly spotted and blotched, chiefly about the larger end. The colors of the markings are " Saccardo's umber," " bister " and " warm sepia," with underlying markings of " deep " to " pale brownish drab." In other collections I have seen a number of sets that matched almost exactly certain types of heavily blotched eggs of the Wilson snipe; these may be within the normal range of dowitcher's eggs; but I have always been suspicious that some of them were wrongly identified. The measurements of

79 eggs average 41.8 by 28.9 millimeters; the eggs showing the four extremes measures **45.5** by 30.5, 44 by **32**, **37.5** by 29.2 and 39.4 by **26.3** millimeters.

Young.—H. B. Conover has sent me the following interesting notes:

Newly hatched young were found June 22nd. The incubation period seems to be about 20 days. A nest found by Murie on May 31 with two eggs, had four eggs on June 2, and on being visited the evening of June 22, was found to contain two young and two pipped eggs. The colors of the soft parts of a downy young several days old were as follows: Tarsus olive with blackish stripes down the sides, bill black, iris brown. In the newly hatched young the tarsus is much lighter. On June 23 while visiting the nest of a black-bellied plover, I came across a pair of dowitchers that from their actions appeared to have young. Not wishing to stop at the time, I passed on, but on returning several hours later, found them again in a marsh at the foot of a long, low hill. When I sat down to watch, one bird wheeled about me calling, and then flew off down the valley. The other bird at first I could not locate, but soon saw it flying about the hillside chirping. I noticed that as this bird passed over a certain spot, it would hover about 15 feet above the ground, giving a whistling trill. After a few minutes it dawned on me, that each time it hovered to give this call, it was a little farther up the hillside. When I moved up toward the top of the hill, the bird alighted close by, scolded for a while and then commenced the same performance as before. In this way in about half an hour the dowitcher and I had crossed the hill from one marsh to another, a distance of about 600 yards. During all this time its mate had appeared only twice, when it flew by calling and then disappeared again. Finally the bird I was following alighted in the marsh at the far side of the hill from where we had started, and began running short distances, stopping and then running on again. Watching through some field glasses, I soon saw a young one following at its heels. Rushing down suddenly, three downies were found hiding with their heads stuck into holes or depressions in the moss. They appeared to be several days old. Evidently the old dowitcher had led these young ones across the hill by simply hovering over or in front of them and calling. The bird was collected and proved to be a male. Just what the relation of the male and female to the eggs and young is in this species it is hard to say. From the experience above I believe the male does nine-tenths of the work in caring for the chicks. I think this will probably prove true as to the incubation of the eggs as well, but that the female takes some share in the hatching seems probable, as one collected in the vicinity of a nest showed incubation patches.

Plumages.—The downy young dowitcher somewhat resembles the young snipe, but has a somewhat different pattern of similar colors. The large central crown patch is black, clouded, or overcast, with " chestnut " tips and with two indefinite spots of whitish tips; the black extends down to the bill; a broad, black loral stripe extends from the eye to the bill, and a still broader postocular stripe from the eye to the nape; these two stripes are separated from the dark crown patch by a stripe which is " tawny " above the lores, buffy white over the eyes, and white around the posterior half of the crown. The chin is buffy white, and the throat and breast are "ochraceous tawny," becoming lighter and grayer on the belly. The upper parts are much like those of the snipe, variegated, or marbled, with black, "chestnut," and "umber brown," and spotted with small round white spots, terminal tufts, which are very thick on the wings and form roughly two rows down the back and two rows on each thigh.

In fresh juvenal plumage in July in Alaska, the crown, back, and scapulars are black, broadly edged with "cinnamon rufous" or "hazel"; the throat, breast, and flanks are gray, the feathers broadly tipped with "ochraceous tawny" and streaked with black or spotted with dusky; the tertials, innermost greater coverts, and the median coverts are edged with "cinnamon buff." These edgings are much browner in *scolopaceus* and paler buff in *griseus*.

A postjuvenal molt, beginning in September and lasting until December or later, involves a change of the body plumage, sometimes the tail and some of the wing coverts and scapulars. This produces the first winter plumage, which is like the adult winter plumage, except for the retained juvenal scapulars, tertials, and wing coverts. The first prenuptial molt is limited to a few scattering feathers in the body plumage, above and below, some of the scapulars and wing coverts, and the tail; these are like corresponding spring feathers of the adult. There is considerable individual variation in the amount of new feathers in this first nuptial plumage. I have seen birds in this plumage from March 28 to September 9. They do not go north to breed, but remain in the South during the summer. At the first postnuptial molt, in August, they assume the adult winter plumage. In some young birds the prenuptial molt seems to be omitted and the postnuptial molt seems to be a change from one winter plumage to another.

Adults have a partial prenuptial molt from February to May, involving all the body plumage, most of the scapulars, some of the tertials, the central pair of rectrices and the wing coverts. I have seen adults in full nuptial plumage as early as March 4 and as late as August 21. July and August birds are very black above, due to the wearing away of the buff edgings. There is much individual variation in the extent and intensity of the rufous and in the amount of black spotting on the breast. The complete postnuptial molt of adults begins in August and is often finished in September. I have seen several birds in which the primaries were being completely renewed during both months.

Food.—Preble and McAtee (1923) give the following report on the contents of two stomachs of long-billed dowitchers:

Two stomachs, of the two specimens last mentioned from St. Paul Island, have been examined and their contents were almost exclusively the larvae of midges (Chironomidae), of which there were more than 75 in one gizzard and

more than 100 in the other. Vegetable débris, amounting to 3 per cent by bulk
of the stomach contents, also was present, and it probably was picked up
incidentally with the midge larvae. Included in the vegetable matter were
seeds of bottle brush (*Hippuris vulgaris*), sedge (*Carex* sp.), and water chick-
weed (*Montia fontana*).

Behavior.—I have never been able to discover any differences in
behavior between the two forms of the dowitcher; their habits are
doubtless similar. Some gunners think that they can distinguish
the two forms by their notes, but the differences in notes are probably due to individual variations in a somewhat varied vocabulary.
John T. Nichols (1920) one of the closest students and best authorities on shore birds' notes, says " the chances are there is no significant
difference in the calls of the two races."

Fall.—S. F. Rathbun has sent me the following notes on the habits
of this bird on its migrations through the State of Washington:

The long-billed dowitcher will be found in the company of almost any of
the shore birds, in flocks of varying numbers, and even as single individuals,
but appears to show somewhat of a partiality for the company of the black-
bellied plover and the red-backed sandpiper. On this coast both its spring
and autumnal migrations seem to be somewhat prolonged, for in the case of
the former we have records from April 11 until late in May; and for the latter
from early August until into November. It will be found alike on the sandy
beaches and the muddy flats, seemingly showing no particular preference for
either. When the tide is at its ebb on the flats the birds oftimes become widely
scattered and single ones may be found in unexpected places. On one occasion
as we were walking across a grassy marsh the head and neck of a long-billed
dowitcher was seen exposed above the growth along the edge of one of the
little channels running through the marsh. As we approached the bird it
could be seen making attempts to rise, but this it was unable to do on account
of being impeded by the length of the grass, and we drove the bird ahead until
an open spot was reached when it then took wing, at this time being but a few
feet away.

On various occasions while we were watching flocks of the small sandpipers
about some bit of water, dowitchers would fly past and, being attracted by the
calls of other birds, they then after circling for a moment or two would alight
at the pool to feed. When thus engaged they give the impression of being
somewhat deliberate in their actions and as they moved about some would
frequently wade up to their breasts into the shallow water, often so remaining
until by some action they seemed to lose a footing and when this occurred
a retreat would be made into a more shallow part. Oftentimes one or more
birds would suddenly cease feeding and assume a posture of repose and when
this took place it was a common occurrence to see some standing on but one
leg, thus to remain motionless for a time.

Dowitchers do not appear to be very shy when found in the flocks of the
smaller sandpipers, but are the first birds to retreat as one approaches the
flock; and on such occasions it is generally the case that one or more of them
will suddenly take wing and put the entire flock in motion. They are swift-
flying birds and when on the wing have a somewhat harsh note that is given
from time to time. In their spring dress they are attractive, as at this time
their under parts are a rich buff color, and a flock of dowitchers seen at this
season with the light striking full on their breasts is indeed a handsome sight.

Winter.—Dowitchers occur in winter as far south as Ecuador and Peru. Dr. Frank M. Chapman (1926) referred the birds collected in Ecuador to *scolopaceus*. Nonbreeding birds, or immatures, remain there all summer, as they do in other parts of their winter range. I have taken both forms of dowitchers in Florida, where they winter regularly in small numbers.

DISTRIBUTION

Range.—North America, Central America, Cuba, and northwestern South America. Casual in Japan.

Breeding range.—North to probably eastern Siberia (Cape Wankarem); Alaska (Kuparuk River and Point Barrow); probably Yukon (Herschel Island); and Mackenzie (Franklin Bay). East to Mackenzie (Franklin Bay). South to Mackenzie (Fort Anderson); Yukon (Lapierre House); and Alaska (Point Dall). West to Alaska (Point Dall, Pastolik, St. Michael, and Kowak River); and probably eastern Siberia (Cape Wankarem).

Winter range.—North to California (Los Banos and Santa Ana); Texas (Corpus Christi); Louisiana (State Game Preserve); Florida (East Goose Creek, Kissimmee, and Cape Canaveral); and probably Cuba (Santiago de Vegas and San Fernando). East to probably Cuba (Santiago de Vegas); Costa Rica (Alajuela); and probably Panama, Colombia, and Ecuador. South to Ecuador. West to Guatemala; Tehuantepec (San Mateo); Jalisco (La Barca); Lower California (La Paz, San Jose Mission and San Quentin); and California (San Diego and Los Banos).

Spring migration.—Early dates of spring arrival are: South Carolina, near Charleston, April 30; New York, Long Island, March 20; Illinois, Cary's Station, April 24, and Chicago, April 28; Minnesota, Heron Lake, May 1; Kansas, Manhattan, April 21, and Wichita, April 28; Nebraska, Callaway, April 8, and Omaha, April 28; Iowa, Wall Lake, May 9; South Dakota, Brown County, April 14, and Harrison, April 15; North Dakota, Menoken, May 7; Manitoba, Shoal Lake, April 24, Pilot Mound, May 1, and Margaret, May 18; Colorado, Loveland, April 6, Denver, April 26, and Durango, April 30; Wyoming, Cheyenne, May 2, and Lake Como, May 5; central and northern California, Alameda, March 15, Palo Alto, April 17, Ballona, April 19, and Stockton, April 20; Oregon, Malheur Lake, April 20; Washington, Menlo, May 1, and Fort Steilacoom, May 5; British Columbia, Courtenay, April 28, and Chilliwack, May 8; and Alaska, Craig, May 2, Kuiu Island, May 3, Fort Kenai, May 4, and St. Michael, May 20.

Late dates of spring departure are: Louisiana, New Orleans, March 20; Texas, Corpus Christi, April 20; Chihuahua, Lake Palomas,

April 9; Lower California, Gardner's Lagoon, April 19; and southern California, Santa Barbara, May 2.

Fall migration.—Early dates of fall arrival are: British Columbia, Courtenay, July 7, and Okanagan Landing, July 19; California, Balboa Bay, July 6, Santa Barbara, July 18, and Fresno, August 6; Lower California, San Quentin, August 10, and San Jose del Cabo, August 28; Tehuantepec, San Mateo, August 12; Montana, Billings, July 31; Utah, Provo River, July 24; Saskatchewan, Hay Creek, July 3; Colorado, Barr, July 5, and Denver, July 24; North Dakota, Devil's Lake, July 20, and Mouse River, August 10; Texas, Brownsville, July 11; New York, Long Island, July 16; North Carolina, Pea and Brodie Islands, July 7; and South Carolina, near Charleston, July 20.

Late dates of fall departure are: British Columbia, Chilliwack, October 29; Washington, Seattle, October 9, and Point Chehalis, October 19; northern and central California, Easton, October 18, Alameda, October 29, and Stockton, November 5; Wyoming, Hutton's Lakes, October 14; Colorado, Denver, October 3; Manitoba, Margaret, October 10; South Dakota, Harrison, November 2; Nebraska, Valentine, October 28; Kansas, Lawrence, October 3; Minnesota, St. Vincent, October 9; Missouri, St. Louis, October 28; New York, Long Island, November 2; and South Carolina, September 10.

Casual records.—Occurrences of the long-billed dowitcher outside of its normal range must, of necessity be based upon the evidence of specimens, as it is frequently confused with the more common dowitcher of the Atlantic coast, from Maine to Florida. Seven were collected in the District of Columbia in April, 1884; one at North Haven, Connecticut, August 5, 1886; Hamilton, Ontario, August 21, 1891; Leighton, Alabama, May 15, 1891; Dauphin Island, Alabama (2), July 5, 1913; Detroit, Michigan, August 26, 1905; Yokohama, Japan, March 13; and Yezo, Japan, October 13.

Egg dates.—Arctic Canada: 18 records, June 6 to July 5; 9 records, June 21 to July 3. Alaska: 17 records, May 29 to July 1; 9 records, June 3 to 19.

MICROPALAMA HIMANTOPUS (Bonaparte)

STILT SANDPIPER

HABITS

Strangely enough I have never seen, or rather recognized, a stilt sandpiper in life. As it is often associated with the lesser yellowlegs and so easily mistaken for it, I may have overlooked it. It is a rare bird in the localities where most of my work on shorebirds has been done and it does not seem to be very common anywhere. It is more common on migrations in the Mississippi Valley than else-where, on its way to and from its restricted breeding range on the barren grounds and Arctic coast of Canada.

Spring.—The spring migration is almost directly north from the Gulf of Mexico to Great Slave Lake and then down the Mackenzie Valley and other valleys to the Arctic coast. It is rare in spring on the Atlantic coast. R. J. Longstreet writes to me that he saw three on May 4 and 5, and four on May 8, 1925, in Volusia County, Florida. C. G. Harrold tells me that it is a common spring migrant in Manitoba, "even abundant at times, a flock of nearly 300 being seen in May, 1924, at Whitewater Lake." A. G. Lawrence records it, at the same lake, as early as May 5 and as late as June 2; he calls it " uncommon to fairly common." At Beaver Lake, in northern Al-berta, William Rowan saw flocks of from 20 to 25 birds every day from May 20 to 28, 1924. P. L. Hatch (1892) says that, in Minne-sota, "they come in small flocks, and keep mostly about shallow ponds, and along the smaller streams flowing through the marshes," but he has " found them on the sandy beaches of some of the larger lakes on several occasions." He says "they are shy and exceedingly vigilant, making it no easy matter to get them."

Nesting.—Comparatively little is known about the nesting habits of the stilt sandpiper. Roderick MacFarlane (1891) found it " fairly abundant on the shores of Franklin Bay, where a number of nests with eggs and young were discovered. It is, however, very rare in the interior, only one nest having been taken at Rendezvous Lake on the borders of the wooded country east of Fort Anderson." A nest with three eggs, found on June 22, 1863, is described in his notes as " near a small lake and composed of a few decayed leaves placed in a depression in the ground, partly concealed by a tuft of grass;" the female was flushed off the nest and shot. The nest found at Rendezvous Lake is not described, but one found at Franklin Bay, on July 6 or 8, 1865, containing four fresh eggs, was " a mere depression in the ground, lined with a few withered leaves and grasses."

Eggs.—Four eggs is probably the usual number laid by the stilt sandpiper. They are ovate pyriform in shape. The only eggs I have been able to locate are the three sets in the United States Na-tional Museum, collected by MacFarlane. J. H. Riley has kindly sent me descriptions and measurements of these. In the set of four eggs the ground color is " ivory yellow " with large irregular blotches and spots of two shades of " mummy brown," and a few rather large shell markings of " hair brown," the latter mostly towards the larger end. The spots and blotches are a little heavier towards the larger end, also, but in no sense do they form a ring. Another set of two eggs is similar, but the spots and blotches are much smaller, more numerous, and more evenly distributed over the surface; some of the "mummy brown" spots are even becoming scrawls. The third set of two eggs are like the set of four, except that the ground color is "pale olive buff" and the "mummy brown" blotches are on the average smaller. The measurements of these 7 eggs average 35.5 by 25.1 millimeters; the eggs showing the four extremes **36** by 25, 35 by **26, 35** by 25 and 36 by **24.5** millimeters.

Young.—Mr. McFarlane (1891) says: "On one occasion we could not help admiring the courage and ingenuity displayed by both parents in defense of their young, which resulted in saving two of the latter from capture."

Plumages.—In natal down the stilt sandpiper closely resembles several of the other species of tundra-nesting sandpipers. It can generally be recognized by its relatively longer legs and by its longer bill, with a broader tip. The head markings are also a little different. The forehead, cheeks, and throat are dirty white, with a broad, black, median stripe from bill to crown, another (loral) from bill to eye, and a short one (malar) below it. The crown, back, wings, thighs, and rump are variegated or marbled with black (predominating) and dull browns, "tawny" to "ochraceous tawny," and profusely dotted with dull white terminal down tufts; these dots form a distinct circle around the crown patch, below which the whitish sides of the head are marked with "ochraceous tawny." The lower throat is washed with pale buff, and the rest of the under parts are white.

In the juvenal plumage in August the head and neck are streaked with gray and whitish; the crown is dusky, with buffy edgings; the mantle is brownish black and dusky, with "tawny" edgings on the blackest feathers in the back and scapulars, and with pale buff or whitish edgings on the rest of the mantle and tertials; the under parts are white, suffused with pale buff on the throat, breast, and flanks; the wing coverts are edged with pale buff or whitish; the upper tail coverts are white and but little marked; the central tail feathers are dusky, edged with white, and the others are white, margined with dusky. This plumage is not worn long, for the post-juvenal molt of the body plumage begins late in August and lasts through September, producing a first-winter plumage. This is similar to the winter plumage of adults, but can be recognized by the juvenal wing coverts, some scapulars, and tertials.

I have been unable to trace the first prenuptial molt of young birds, which is probably accomplished in South America, nor have I been able to recognize a first nuptial plumage. Possibly young birds may not come north during their first spring.

Adults have a partial prenuptial molt in April and May, involving the body plumage, most of the scapulars, and some of the wing coverts and tertials. The complete postnuptial molt begins sometimes during the first week in July and sometimes not until the last of that month, and is completed in about two months, including the wings. A specimen taken in Argentina on September 21 had renewed the wings and practically all of the body plumage. In winter plumage the upper parts are brownish gray, with narrow, light edgings; the sides of the head and the under parts are white, with little or no barring; there is a dark streak through the eye, but no rusty on the head.

Food.—Audubon (1840) watched a flock of about 30 stilt sandpipers feeding, of which he writes:

I saw a flock of about 30 long-legged sandpipers alight within 10 steps of me, near the water. They immediately scattered, following the margin of the retiring and advancing waves, in search of food, which I could see them procure by probing the wet sand in the manner of curlews, that is, to the full length of their bill, holding it for a short time in the sand, as if engaging in sucking up what they found. In this way they continued feeding on an extended line of shore of about 30 yards, and it was pleasing to see the alacrity with which they simultaneously advanced and retreated, according to the motions of the water. In about three-quarters of an hour, during all which time I had watched them with attention, they removed a few yards beyond the highest wash of the waves, huddled close together, and began to plume and cleanse themselves. In the stomachs of several individuals I found small worms, minute shellfish, and vegetable substances, among which were the hard seeds of plants unknown to me.

N. B. Moore watched a stilt sandpiper feeding in Florida and says in his notes:

It alighted within 20 feet of me and commenced feeding at once, in water that nearly covered the tarsi. I was surprised to see it slowly step along, carrying its bill immersed nearly up to the base, and sweeping it slowly from side to side, much in the manner of the roseate spoonbills, which were at the same moment feeding near by. I noticed no action like that of swallowing at any time, its motions being continuous—as described—until I shot it to make sure of the species.

Stuart T. Danforth (1925) says of the food of this species in Porto Rico:

Seven stomachs (five collected on August 20 and two on September 17) were available for examination. Animal matter composed 70.1 per cent of the food, and vegetable matter of 29.9 per cent. Bloodworms (Chironomid larvae) were the largest food item, forming 72.8 per cent of the animal food. From 150 to 600 bloodworms were found in all but two of the stomachs. Dytiscid larvae formed 15.5 per cent, small Planorbis snails 7.1 per cent, and mosquito larvae 0.8 per cent of the animal matter. The vegetable matter was composed of seeds. Seeds of *Persicaria* formed 80 per cent of the vegetable matter; seeds of *Sesban emerus* 7 per cent; seeds of Compositae 10.2 per cent, and rubbish 2.8 per cent.

Prof. William Rowan writes to me:

In very dirty weather, particularly if a gale is blowing, stilt sandpipers have been noted hunting for food high and dry on rough pasture. This is probably an exceptional performance correlated with this type of weather, for it has never been observed at other times.

John T. Nichols says in his notes:

Just how this species makes use of its somewhat peculiar bill is not very clear. I have seen it alighted on flooded dead marsh, wading in the puddles and picking at the projecting dead stubble about on its own level. Again I find in my journal reference to three birds which alighted in water to their thighs, and immediately began to feed, moving about close together, immersing the bill to the eyes for an instant or two.

Verdi Burtch (1925), referring to a bird he saw at Branchport, N. Y., says:

I saw it catch and with much effort swallow a small frog, after which it lost all interest in fishing. It walked off a few steps and stood on one foot, all humped up and with eyes closed; quite a contrast to the usual alert sandpiper pose.

Behavior.—Audubon (1840) writes:

The flight of these sandpipers is rapid and regular. They move compactly, and often when about to alight, or after being disturbed, incline their bodies to either side, showing alternately the upper and lower parts. On foot they move more like curlews than tringas, they being as it were more sedate in their deportment. At times, on the approach of a person, they squat on the ground, very much in the manner of the Esquimaux curlew, *Numenius borealis;* and their flesh is as delicate as that of the species just named.

Dr. Arthur A. Allen (1913), after referring to the companionship and resemblance between stilt sandpipers and lesser yellowlegs, says:

In their habits, however, the two species were quite different. The yellowlegs were always rangy birds and covered a great deal of ground while feeding. Even when resting they were conspicuous by the nervous jerking of the head and neck. In flight they usually formed fairly compact flocks but scattered upon alighting. The stilt sandpipers, on the other hand, were quiet birds and went about their search for food very systematically, gleaning everything in their way. They frequently fed in a space a few yards square for over an hour at a time. When at rest they showed none of the nervous traits of the yellowlegs, being much more sedate, neither jerking the head nor tilting the tail. In flight they were quite similar to the yellowlegs, but as soon as they alighted they bunched and frequently the whole flock fed with their bodies nearly touching. Like the yellowlegs, the stilt sandpipers were seldom seen upon the exposed mud but preferred wading where the water was from 1 to 3 inches in depth, so that the entire head and neck frequently disappeared beneath the surface of the water while feeding. The notes of the two birds, though similar in form, were wholly unlike in quality, that of the stilt sandpiper being mellower and lower in pitch.

Coues (1878) at first mistook birds of this species for dowitchers and did not recognize them until he had them in his hands. He says:

They gathered in the same compact groups, waded about in the same sedate, preoccupied manner, fed with the same motion of the head, probing obliquely in shallow water with the head submerged, were equally oblivious of my approach, and when wounded swam with equal facility. The close structural resemblances of the two species are evidently reflected in their general economy.

Mr. Nichols says in his notes:

On alighting the stilt sandpiper sometimes lifts its wings halfway for an instant, a mannerism characteristic of the tattler group, which it would seem to have acquired from its associate, the yellowlegs.

Voice.—Following are Mr. Nichols's notes on this subject:

The common flight note of the stilt sandpiper is very like the single whistled *whu* of the lesser yellowlegs, but recognizably lower pitched and hoarser, at times with a quaver, *whr-r-u*, and varying down to a shorter, less loud *whrug*. An unloud, reedy *sher* has been heard from two birds when flushing.

Though with different feeding habits, stilt sandpiper, dowitcher, and lesser yellowlegs frequent the same grounds, associate very freely on the wing, and all three have a very similar flight note, though sufficiently different for identification. Perhaps the very lack of close relationship in these birds has facilitated convergence of their habits and calls, and it is not unreasonable to suppose that close association, even imitation, has played some part in bringing about the likeness of their voices. The greater yellowlegs differs more from the lesser, both in flight note and flight habits, than do these other two unrelated species.

Field marks.—I quote again from Mr. Nichols's notes on field characters, as follows:

On the wing the stilt sandpiper resembles the lesser yellowlegs closely. Its smaller size is scarcely appreciable, even in a flock of yellowlegs, the members of which will usually be at slightly varying distances from the observer. Adults have appreciably darker (barred) lower parts, and young birds, particularly, are greyer above than yellowlegs at the same season in this latitude. The somewhat shorter legs do not project so far beyond the tail, but the proportionately longer bill (with slight apparent drop at its tip) is the stilt sandpiper's best field mark. Its bill is proportionately longer even than that of the greater yellowlegs, with which this species is unlikely to be confused, varying as it does away from the lesser yellowlegs in an opposite direction, both as regards size and in other subtle characters. The head and neck of a yellowlegs are more "shapely," differing in this respect somewhat as a black duck differs from sea ducks.

On the ground the stilt sandpiper stands lower than a yellowlegs, having decidedly shorter legs, and correspondingly higher than our other shore birds of the same size. The color of its legs, dull olive green, is usually diagnostic. The legs are sometimes yellowish, and very rarely yellow, only one such having come under the writer's personal notice, a young bird in southward migration. The name "greenleg" is often used for it by Long Island baymen, who also suspect it of being a cross between yellowlegs and dowitcher. At sufficiently close range the margination of the feathers of the upper parts is quite unlike the spotting of the yellowlegs' plumage.

The broad white stripe over the eye is conspicuous in any plumage and the whitish tail shows in flight, as different from the whitish triangle on the rump and back of the dowitcher or the white rump of the yellowlegs. Most of these field marks, however, are too subtle for easy recognition, unless seen under favorable circumstances.

Prof. William Rowan has sent me the following notes:

Identification marks of the stilt are excellent and it is quite an easy bird to spot in almost any circumstances. It has a rump pattern all to itself and is therefore readily detected in flight. The end of the tail is darker than that of a yellowlegs, but the white of the rump end, instead of forming a straight line across the back, is horseshoe shaped. Although the turnstone and semipalmated plovers are reminiscent, they are quite distinct and not to be confused. When wading—the birds prefer to be belly deep—the carriage of the head makes the species unmistakable. The bill is always held and thrust beneath the surface perpendicularly. This necessitates a straight neck. In profile the feeding individual can be mistaken for no other sandpiper, is quite distinct from the yellowlegs, and can really only be confused with a phalarope. The Wilson phalarope habitually wades in this part of the world, swimming only occasionally, but its markings are distinctive. A flock of stilts is the most characteristic sight and the species can be identified at a great distance. The curious position of the head just referred to and the crowding of the individuals into each other make a quite unmistakable combination. They feed practically shoulder to shoulder, seldom scattering. The yellowlegs of a flock are always scattered, and the general aspect of the individuals is entirely different. Stilts never bob their heads after the manner of yellowlegs.

Fall.—The fall migration of adults begins very early, coming along with the dowitchers and first summer yellowlegs. I have an adult female in my collection, taken on July 5, 1885, on Monomoy Island, Massachusetts. The main flight of adults comes along during the latter half of July and first half of August, in this State, and the young birds come through in August and September; but this is a rare bird here, and the flight generally lasts for only a few days.

Mr. Nichols tells me that:

On Long Island the stilt sandpiper is usually uncommon, occurring in small numbers often closely associated with lesser yellowlegs or dowitcher. Rarely it occurs in great waves or flights as on August 12, 1912. This flight was made up exclusively of adult birds, so far as the writer's observations went. For the remainder of that season the species was unusually common. If, in ordinary years, some 200 stilt sandpipers are present on Long Island in southward migration, there were probably 3,000 in 1912. The earliest I have seen this species south on Long Island is July 10, 1921, two or three or more individuals associated with 40 or 50 lesser yellowlegs.

In the interior this species is commoner than it is on the Atlantic coast. Mr. Harrold says that in Manitoba it is fairly common in the fall, adults being noted as early as July 5; the young birds are usually with the lesser yellowlegs in the fall. Mr. Hersey collected a series for me in Manitoba between July 18 and 29, 1913. Stilt sandpipers were formerly sold in the markets, mixed with bunches of summer yellowlegs, but their sale is now prohibited, and they are too small to be considered as game birds.

Winter.—The winter home of the stilt sandpiper seems to be in southern South America, Argentina, Paraguay, Uruguay, and Chile, but actual records substantiated by specimens are not numerous. Ernest Gibson (1920) shot some " out of a flock of over 100 " which " might easily have been 200, so closely were they massed." They " were feeding on marshy ground; and as the flock rose at " his " approach, circled and passed away, the white under surfaces were quite dazzling in the sunlight." This was near Cape San Antonio, Buenos Aires, on December 27, 1913.

Dr. Alexander Wetmore (1926) writes:

The stilt sandpiper was encountered only in the Chaco, west of Puerto Pinasco, Paraguay, though it has been said that it is common in some parts of the Province of Buenos Aires in winter. At kilometer 80, on September 20, 1920, the first arrivals, a flock of a dozen, were recorded at the border of a lagoon; as I watched they rose suddenly to whirl rapidly away to the southward. On the following day about 20 were seen, and an adult female was taken. At Kilometer 170, on September 24, a small flock passed down the nearly dry channel of an alkaline stream known as the Riacho Salado, while at Laguna Wall (kilometer 200) about 30 were seen September 24, and 40 on the day following. The birds were found in little flocks, often mingled with other waders that walked or waded through shallow water on muddy shores where they probed with their bills for food.

DISTRIBUTION

Range.—North America, south to southern South America. The stilt sandpiper is one of the rarer shore birds and but little is known of its range and migrations.

Breeding range.—North to probably northeastern Alaska (Demarcation Point); probably Yukon (Herschel Island); Mackenzie (Fort Anderson, Rendezvous Lake, Franklin Bay, and probably Kogaryuak River); and probably Keewatin (Cape Eskimo). East to probably Keewatin (Cape Eskimo); and probably Manitoba (Fort Churchill and York Factory). South to probably Manitoba (York Factory); and Mackenzie (Artillery Lake). West to Mackenzie (Artillery Lake); and probably Alaska (Demarcation Point). Eggs have been taken only in northern Mackenzie.

Winter range.—Imperfectly known, but probably north to Tepic (Acaponeta River); Zacatecas; Tamaulipas (Matamoros); rarely Texas (Corpus Christi); rarely Louisiana (State Game Preserve); and Cuba. East probably to Cuba; and Brazil (Ilha Grande). South probably to Brazil (Ilha Grande); Uruguay (Colonia); and Chile. West to Chile; Bolivia (Falls of the Madeira); central Peru (Chorillos and Yquitos); Ecuador (Babahoyo); Colombia (Cienaga); Nicaragua (Momotombo); Guatemala (Duenas);

Oaxaca (Tehuantepec); Jalisco (Manzanillo and La Barca); and
Tepic (Ocaponeta River).

Spring migration.—Early dates of arrival in the spring are:
Florida, Banana Creek, March 10, Smyrna, March 26, and Pensa-
cola, April 5; North Carolina, Cape Hatteras, May 19; New York,
Long Island, May 18; Connecticut, Westport, May 28, and West
Haven, May 30; Rhode Island, Sakonnet, May 9; Maine, Saco,
May 5; Missouri, Kansas City, April 30; Illinois, Chicago, May 26;
Iowa, Sioux City, May 7, Emmetsburg, May 10, and Wall Lake,
May 23; Wisconsin, Racine, April 10; Minnesota, Wilder, May 1,
and Waseca, May 14; Texas, Bonham, March 29; Kansas, McPher-
son, May 7; Nebraska, Kearney, May 6, and Neligh, May 10; South
Dakota, Harrison, May 5, Vermilion, May 9, and Sioux Falls, May
14; North Dakota, Harrisburg, May 1, and Sweetwater, May 5;
Manitoba, Whitewater Lake, May 12; Colorado, Barr, April 27,
Fort Lyon, May 2, Colorado Springs, May 14, and Loveland, May
20; Wyoming, Cheyenne, May 25; Alberta, Fort Chipewyan, June
6; Mackenzie, Fort Resolution, May 19, and Athabaska delta, June
4; and Alaska, Demarcation Point, May 23.

Stilt sandpipers also have been detected as late as April in Cuba
and Jamaica while a late date for their departure from Lake
Palomas, Mexico, is April 7, from Dummetts, Florida, April 14 and
Port Orange, Florida, May 5.

Fall migration.—Early dates of arrival for the species on its
return from the North are: Colorado, Barr, July 5; North Dakota,
Benson County, July 1, and Nelson's Lake, July 14; South Dakota,
Forestburg, July 7; Nebraska, Lincoln, July 19; Iowa, Sioux City,
July 12; Texas Corpus Christi, July 3; Ontario, Toronto, July 18;
Maine, Chebeague Island, July 19, and Scarboro, July 30; New
Hampshire, Rye, July 31; Massachusetts, Cape Cod, July 4, and
Needham, July 24; Rhode Island, Newport, July 6, and Block Is-
land, July 15; New York, East Hampton, July 11; North Carolina,
Churches Island, July 29; Bahama Islands, Fortune Island, August
5; Barbados, July; St. Batholomew, September; and Paraguay,
Kilometer 80, September 20.

Late dates of fall departure are: British Columbia, Sumas Lake,
September 19; Colorado, Fort Lyon, September 8, Larimer County,
September 9, and Barr, October 5; Mackenzie, Fort Simpson, August
19, and Lower Slave River, August 27; Manitoba, Carberry, August
29, and Qu'Appelle, September 16; Nebraska, Lincoln, November 11;
Kansas, Lawrence, September 19; Wisconsin, Kelley Brook, September 13; Iowa, Burlington, September 28; Ontario, Toronto, September 26; Ohio, Columbus, October 4; Illinois, Chicago, September
1, Grand Crossing, September 23, and Cantine Lake, September 28;
Missouri, St. Louis, September 12, and Kansas City, September 28;

Maine, Scarboro, September 16; Massachusetts, Chatham, September 20, and Cape Cod, September 29; Rhode Island, Newport, September 9; New York, Buffalo, September 16, Bronx, September 19, Cayuga, October 10, and Jamaica, November 28; New Jersey, Morristown, October 16; Maryland, Pawtuxent River, September 8; District of Columbia, Anacostia River, October 26; North Carolina, Churches Island, September 23; and Florida, Fernandina, October 10, and Key West, November 1.

Casual records.—The rarity of the stilt sandpiper makes it difficult to determine whether some occurrences should be listed as regular migrants or as accidentals. Some of the following cases may be on the regular migration route of the species: Bermuda, two early in August, 1848 and one in early September, 1875; Newfoundland, Cow Head, September, 1867; Nova Scotia, Sable Island, August 18, 1902; New Brunswick, Courtenay Bay, September 8, 1881; and Montana, Chief Mountain, August, 1874.

Egg dates.—Arctic Canada: 3 records, June 22 and 27 and July 8.

CALIDRIS CANUTUS RUFUS (Wilson)

AMERICAN KNOT

HABITS

This cosmopolitan species, with a circumpolar breeding range, has been split into two generally recognized forms occupying the two hemispheres, with a doubtful third form, *rodgersi*, said to occupy eastern Asia. Our American bird is well named *rufus* on account of its color.

The knot, or redbreast, as it is called on Cape Cod, was a very abundant migrant all along the Atlantic coast of North America during the past century. George H. Mackay (1893) writes:

On the Dennis marshes and flats, at Chatham, the Nauset, Wellfleet, and Billingsgate, Cape Cod, and on the flats around Tuckernuck and Muskeget Islands, Mass., they used to be more numerous than in all the rest of New England combined, and being very gregarious they would collect in those places in exceedingly large numbers, estimates of which were useless. This was previous to 1850 and when the Cape Cod Railroad was completed only to Sandwich. Often, when riding on the top of the stage coach on the cape beyond this point, immense numbers of these birds could be seen, as they rose up in clouds, during the period that they sojourned there. It was at this time that the vicious practice of "fire-lighting" them prevailed, and a very great number of them were thus killed on the flats at night in the vicinity of Billingsgate (near Wellfleet). The mode of procedure was for two men to start out after dark at half tide, one of them to carry a lighted lantern, the other to reach and seize the birds, bite their necks, and put them in a bag slung over the shoulder. When near a flock they would approach them on their hands and knees, the birds being almost invariably taken on the flats. This practice continued several years before it was finally prohibited by law. I have it directly from an excellent authority that he has seen in the spring, six barrels of these birds (all of which had been taken in this manner) at one time, on the deck of the Cape Cod packet for Boston. He has also seen barrels of them, which had spoiled during the voyage, thrown overboard in Boston Harbor on arrival of the packet. The price of these birds at that time was 10 cents per dozen; mixed with them would be turnstones and black-bellied plover. Not one of these birds had been shot, all having been taken with the aid of a " fire-light."

Arthur T. Wayne (1910) says:

On May 18, 1895, I saw, on Long Island beach, a flock of these birds which I estimated to contain fully fifteen hundred individuals, while on May 21 of the same year, I observed a flock that had alighted on the beach, and that comprised without a doubt more than 3,000 birds.

Excessive shooting, both in spring and fall, reduced this species to a pitiful remnant of its former numbers; but spring shooting was stopped before it was too late and afterwards this bird was wisely taken off the list of game birds; it has increased slowly since then, but it is far from abundant now and makes only a short stay on Cape Cod.

Spring.—The main migration route of the knot in spring is northward along the Atlantic coast. The first birds usually reach the United States from South America early in April. On the west coast of Florida, in 1925, I took my first birds on April 2, and they were commonest about the middle of April. I have found them very common on the coast of South Carolina as late as May 23. Mr. Mackay (1893) writes:

They are still found in greater or less numbers along the Atlantic coast south of Chesapeake Bay. Near Charleston, S. C., Mr. William Brewster noted about 150 knots on May 6 and 8, 1885, and saw a number of flocks on May 13. They were flying by, or were alighted, on Sullivan Island beach. On May 17, 1883, he noted about 100 of these birds in the same locality. In the spring they pass Charlotte Harbor, Florida, so I am informed, in large numbers, coming up the coast from the south (a flight on May 26, 1890), at which time they are very tame. They are also more or less numerous near Morehead City, North Carolina (where they are known as " beach robins "), from May 15 to 30, their flight being along the beach, just over the surf, at early morning, coming from the east in the neighborhood of Point Lookout, 10 or 12 miles away, where they probably resorted to roost. This indicates that these birds were living in that locality.

On the Massachusetts coast the spring flight comes in May. Mr. Mackay (1893) says:

The most favorable time to expect them at this season is during fine, soft, south to southwest weather, and formerly they could be expected to pass in numbers beween May 20 and June 5. In former times, when such conditions prevailed, thousands collected on Cape Cod, when they would remain for a few days to a week before resuming migration.

The knot is less common in the interior, but Prof. William Rowan evidently regards it as a regular migrant in Alberta during the latter part of May; his notes record a flock of about 200 on May 21 and one of over 150 on May 23.

It seems to be a comparatively rare migrant on the coast of California, where it never was abundant. But it still occurs in large numbers on the coast of Washington. In some notes from Gray's Harbor, sent to me by D. E. Brown, he mentions a flock of over 500 birds seen on May 14, 1920. And S. F. Rathbun has sent me the following notes:

Late on the afternoon of May 16, 1921, we were on the south side of Gray's Harbor, Washington, on a marsh meadow bordered by the tide flats. At this hour the tide was nearly at its full, and the many shore birds that had been feeding on the flats were forced to retreat before the incoming waters and in consequence were driven close to the edge of the meadow. Not far from where we lay concealed a very large number of these had assembled on a somewhat elevated stretch of ground near the meadows border, among them being several hundred of the knots, these in two or three compact flocks all the individuals of which were facing the wind. The knots were resting quietly although there was much movement going on among the shore birds. We could easily by the aid of our glasses, see many turnstones, a few greater yellow-legs, these keeping by themselves, and in the shallow water at the edge of the flats a very large number of red-backed sandpipers and long-billed dowitchers, flanked by an immense flock of the smaller sandpipers. At this time the sun was low in the west and its almost horizontal rays fell full on the breasts of the knots, for in facing the wind they happened to be turned toward the sun, whose light intensified the pale cinnamon of their breasts, this making a beautiful sight.

Without any warning nearly all of this mass of birds suddenly took wing. As they rose, the knots keeping by themselves separated into three compact flocks and rising high in the air then flew directly towards the north giving their calls as they did so, and this appears to be a habit of the species when taking wing. Again, the knot does not appear to fly aimlessly about as do many other of the shore birds, and is generally to be seen in flocks, the individuals of which are closely associated, although at times scattering birds will be observed; and in flight by the seeming course a flock will pursue, we always receive an impression that it has some objective point in view.

Dr. W. E. Ekblaw has sent me some very full notes on the habits of the knot in northwestern Greenland in which he says:

The knot is one of the commoner shore birds of northwest Greenland, but even so, not numerous anywhere. It arrives in the land as early as the end of May, for early in the spring of 1915 when my two Eskimos, Esayoo and Etukashoo, and I were encamped at Fort Conger on Discovery Harbor in latitude 81° 45′ N., we heard the keen call of the knots flying over our camp the afternoon of May 30. The first knots that come are generally in small flocks, but they soon mate and scatter to their nesting places, only a few coming together from time to time near the favorite feeding places. If the weather of early June be inclement the flocks do not scatter so soon, but remain together until the conditions become favorable for mating and nesting. It is quite

likely that some of the pairs are already mated when they arrive, for the
sex organs are fully developed and ready to function upon their arrival.

In northeastern Greenland the time of arrival is about the same,
for A. L. Manniche (1910) writes:

The knots arrived at the Stormkap territory in couples at exactly the same
time as did the other waders; in two summers, respectively, on June 2 and
May 28. While the sanderlings, dunlins, turnstones, and ringed plovers immediately took to the sparsely occurring spots free from snow, the knots would
prefer to go to the still snow-covered hollows in the marshes and moors,
where I saw them running on the snow eagerly occupied in picking up the
seed of *Carex*- and *Luzula*-tufts the ends of which here and there appeared
over the snow. This sandpiper more than its relatives, feeds on plants at
certain seasons. In the first days I also observed now and then a couple
of knots on snowless spots on elevated table-lands and even on the top of
the high gravel banks at Stormkap. These may, however, have settled there
in order to rest after the voyage and not to search food. As soon as ponds of
melting snow and fresh-water beaches free from ice were to be found, the
knots would resort to these, and here the birds wading or swimming looked
for animal diet. In this season the knot did not appear on the salt-water
shore like other waders. Gradually as more extensive stretches of low-lying
table-land became free from snow, the knots occurred more frequently here
in their real nesting quarters; they would, however, still for a while often visit
moors and marshes with a rich vegetation of *Cyperaceae*.

Courtship.—Doctor Ekblaw describes this as follows:

The courtship is brief but ardent. Whether it is the females that woo the
males, as among the phalaropes, or as normally the males that woo the females, it is difficult to determine, for the breeding plumages of the two sexes
are quite indistinguishable. On June 3, 1916, I observed closely the courtship
of three knots high up on one of the plateaus of Numataksuah, back of North
Star Bay. Two males (?) were evidently pursuing one female (?), she leading, they winging rapidly in her wake, contending as they flew; apparently
all uttered the shrill piercing call to which the knots so frequently give voice
during the mating and nesting season of early summer, and which one rarely,
if ever, hears after the young are hatched. In great circles they flew, now
and then stooping to a zigzag pirouetting and dodging, again rising in wide
circles until they disappeared from sight in the bright sky, though their shrill
calls came to earth as sharp and clear as ever.

In the ecstasy of the mating season a single bird may indulge himself (?)
in a kind of dance flight alone. He rises high above the hills, sweeping the
sky in great graceful circles not unlike the stately flight of the sparrow hawk,
so smooth and calm it seems. From time to time he utters the shrill, clarion
call of the mating season, or the soft *coo-yee* that is most common about the
nesting grounds. Then suddenly he drops wildly, tumbling and tossing like
a night jar at sunset, as suddenly to break his fall and soar for miles on still,
outstretched wings, not a movement noticeable.

Mr. Manniche (1910) refers to it as follows:

The male suddenly gets up from the snow-clad ground, and producing the
most beautiful flutelike notes, following an oblique line with rapid wing strokes,
mounts to an enormous height often so high that he can not be followed with
the naked eye. Up here in the clear frosty air he flies around in large circles
on quivering wings and his melodious far-sounding notes are heard far and

wide over the country, bringing joy to other birds of his own kin. The song sounds now more distant, now nearer, when three or four males are singing at the same time. Now and then the bird slides slowly downwards on stiff wings with the tail feathers spread; then again he makes himself invisible in the higher regions of the air, mounting on wings quivering even faster than before. Only now and then the observer—guided by the continuing song—succeeds for a moment in discerning the bird at a certain attitude of flight, when the strong sunlight falls upon his golden-colored breast or light wings. Gradually, as in increasing excitement he executes the convulsive vibrations of his wings, his song changes to single deeper notes—following quickly after each other—at last to die out while the bird at the same time drops to the earth on stiff wings strongly bent upward. This fine pairing song may be heard for more than a month everywhere at the breeding places, and it wonderfully enlivens this generally so desolate and silent nature. The song will at certain stages remind of the fluting call note of the curlew (*Numenius arquatus*), but it varies so much with the temper of the bird that it can hardly be expressed or compared with anything else.

Nesting.—The nesting habits of the knot long remained unknown; Arctic explorers were baffled in their attempts to find the nest; and the eggs were among the greatest desiderata of collectors. This is not to be wondered at, however, when we consider the remoteness of its far northern breeding grounds, its choice of its nesting sites on high inland plains, its widely scattered nests, and its habit of sitting very closely on its eggs and not returning to them after flushing. Col. H. W. Feilden (1879) writes:

Night after night I passed out on the hills trying to find the nest of the knot. Not a day passed without my seeing them feeding in small flocks; but they were very wild, rising with shrill cries when one approached within a quarter of a mile of the mud flats on which they were feeding. It is very extraordinary, considering the hundreds of miles traversed by myself and my companions—all of us on the lookout for this bird's eggs, and several of us experienced bird's-nesters—that we found no trace of its breeding until the young in down were discovered.

Some of the earlier records of knot's nests are open to doubt, but there can be no doubt about the two nests found by Peary in 1909. Referring to his own failure and Peary's success, Colonel Feilden (1920) says:

The nests and eggs of the knot were obtained by Peary in the vicinity of Floeberg Beach where the "Nares" expedition of 1875–76 wintered on the exposed coast of Grinnell Land north of 82° N. lat., and where Peary, on the *Roosevelt*, wintered in 1908 and 1909 at Cape Sheridan some 3 or 4 miles farther north, and which was the base for his ever-memorable adventure to the North Pole. Probably the reason why we failed in 1876 to obtain the eggs was due to our ignorance of the localities selected by the birds for nesting. We saw the birds circling over and feeding around the small pools of water left by the melted snow, which here and there were surrounded by sparse tufts of vegetation, and we gave too much of our scanty time to the searching of the marshy spots. Peary's photographs show that in Grinnell Land the knot has its nests on the more elevated slopes and surfaces covered by frost-riven rocks and shales. The finding of a knot's nest in Grinnell Land is not an easy

task, and it is highly commendable that Peary on his return from the North
Pole to Cape Sheridan, and in the midst of his engrossing and more important
duties found occasions to take the unique photographs here reproduced.

Two nests with eggs were found by the Crockerland expedition in
northwestern Greenland, of which Doctor Ekblaw has sent me the
following account:

Though level lands along the shores and the river valleys, or about the pools
constitute the feeding grounds of the knots, the high plateaus far back among
the hills, covered with glacial gravel or frost-riven rubble, furnish their nesting
sites. By this rather anomalous choice of nesting site, the knot was long able
to keep its nest and eggs a secret, and it was not until the members of the
Crockerland Arctic Expedition persistently ran down every clue that two full
clutches of eggs in the nests were discovered in June, 1916, on a high flat-
topped ridge back of North Star Bay, at least 3 miles from shore.

The nests are placed in shallow depressions among the brown clumps of
Dryas integrifolia and *Elyna bellardi* which grow among the rubbles and
gravel of the high ridges. The nest is merely a small hollow, apparently rudely
shaped by the nesting bird. The bird in the nest is so like the terrane about
her, that she is well-nigh indistinguishable from it, even to one who knows
exactly where she is sitting. Trusting to her effective concealment, the
mother bird does not flush from the nest until almost pushed from it. When
I placed a camera only a foot from the sitting bird she did not leave it.
Though frightened so sorely that she panted and her heart beat visibly, she
stuck to her precious eggs. Her head turned to the wind, she crouched flat
upon the eggs, her feathers ruffled wide to hide them. When finally I placed
my hand upon her, she broke away, trying by the well-known shore-bird device
of feigning injury and inability to fly to draw the intruders away. The bird did
not appear at all shy and when she failed to draw us away, remained near us,
evidently anxious, but trying to appear unconcerned. Now and then she uttered a soft, but sharply pleading call, more plaint than protest. One nesting
bird did not leave her eggs until Doctor Hunt pushed her, protesting plaintively
quite away from the nest, with the stock of his rifle.

A set of four eggs in Edward Arnold's collection was taken by
Capt. Joseph Bernard, July 1, 1918, on Taylor Island, Victoria Land.
The nest was in a dry spot in a wet marsh; there was a snow bank
50 yards from the nest and a pond on the south side of the nest 100
yards away. He watched the nest for three or four hours, from a
hill 500 yards away, but did not see the bird again.

Eggs.—The knot lays four eggs, perhaps sometimes only three.
The eggs are ovate pyriform in shape, with a slight gloss. In the
set of three eggs, taken by the Crockerland expedition and now in
Col. John E. Thayer's collection, the ground colors vary from " pale
olive buff " to " olive buff "; they are spotted all over, but more
thickly at the larger end, with small spots or scrawls of " sepia,"
" Saccardo's umber," and " Vandyke brown," with underlying spots
of " pallid " and " pale brownish drab."

The other set of four eggs, from the same source and now in the
American Museum of Natural History, is thus described for me by
Ludlow Griscom:

Ground color varying from white with the faintest tinge of light olive (1 egg) to "olive buff" (2 eggs) and deep "olive buff" (1 egg); clouded and spotted, especially at the larger end, with shades of color varying from "dark olive buff" to "olive brownish," the intensity varying in direct proportion to the intensity of the ground color; where the spots coalesce into blotches at the larger end of the darkest egg, the color is blackish brown; the spotting is scant at the smaller end.

Referring in his notes to the same two sets of eggs, Doctor Ekblaw describes the ground colors as varying from very light pea-green, almost gray, to dark pea-green, "with brown, umber, and almost black dots and blotches of varying size and shape over the green, and faint subcrustal lavender blotches showing through." Other eggs which I have seen figured or described would fit these descriptions fairly well. The measurements of 42 eggs average 43.1 by 29.6 millimeters; the eggs showing the four extremes measure **49.8 by 33.8, 39.9 by 29.7 and 41.5 by 27.7** millimeters.

Young.—The period of incubation is said to be between 20 and 25 days. Both sexes have been taken with incubation patches, so this duty is doubtless shared by both. I quote from Doctor Ekblaw's notes again:

Though we found but two clutches of eggs, we discovered many families of young birds. They are able to leave the nest as soon as hatched, little gray downy chicks with faint blotches of brown, so like the dried tufts of *dryas* as to be quite undiscoverable when hidden among them. Three or four, or rarely five, chicks constitute the group. Their faint plaintive "cheeps" are so ventriloquistic and illusory that it is impossible to distinguish the direction from which they come. When an intruder approaches the little fellows squat at the signal from the parent bird wherever they happen to be at the time, and remain immovable as the pebbles and tufts of *dryas* until the danger is over, even though it be hours before the safety seems assured. Even the tiniest of these downy fledglings seem able to look after themselves. They run eagerly and constantly about independently pursuing the moths, crane flies, and flies upon which they feed, often 40 or 50 feet from their mother. The first signal from the mother, a mellow, solicitous *coo-ee* transforms them into immovable pebbles or tufts of *dryas*. When they are discovered and realize that their concealment is no longer effective, they scatter panic stricken like a flock of little chickens, chirping appealingly to their "mother" who dashes valiantly to their defense, quite beside "herself" with concern, fear, and anger.

Whenever the jaegers, relentless brigands of birdland, appear, the old knots do not hesitate to attack. In combining their forces, they drive full into the bigger birds, striking them from beneath again and again, until they chase them away. The young grow fast. In three weeks after hatching they are almost full grown and half-clothed in feathers, quite capable of taking care of themselves. They stay until they leave among the interior plains and plateaus, coming down to shore only when they are able to fly—and then the southward migration begins at once.

Apparently, the knots, like the phalaropes, reverse part of their secondary sex characteristics, for all the birds caring for the young that I collected were males, beyond doubt. When I examined the first bird that I collected with its young, I was surprised to find that the supposed "mother," who had so valiantly and zealously shielded "her" little ones, was actually father. I thought then that perhaps the mother bird had been killed and that in the emergency the father had assumed the responsibility for the youngsters; but later I became convinced by examination of many birds, that invariably it is the male that cares for the fledglings after they are hatched. The female incubates the eggs, but the male relieves her of further care in bringing up the family.

Plumages.—In its natal down the young knot can be easily recognized by the grayish, mottled colors on the upper parts and the absence of browns and bright buffs. The shape of the bill, characteristic of the species, is also diagnostic. The crown, back, rump, wings, and thighs are finely mottled or spotted with black, white, gray and dull "cinnamon buff," the last being the basal color. The forehead, the sides of the head, the throat, and the entire under parts are dull white, tinged with grayish on the flanks and crissum. There is a broad median stripe on the forehead, a broad loral stripe from the bill to the eye and a narrower rictal stripe of black.

The juvenal plumage appears first on the wings, scapulars, and sides of the breast; the primaries burst their sheaths before the young bird is half grown. In the juvenal plumage, as seen on migration in August, the crown is heavily streaked with blackish brown, the feathers being edged with light buff; the feathers of the back and scapulars have an outer border of light buff, then a black border, then another buff, and sometimes a faint black border inside of that; the greater and median wing coverts have a terminal buff and a subterminal black border; the tail feathers are edged with buff and the under parts are more or less suffused with pale buff. Probably the buff is brighter and deeper in fresh plumage and it fades out to white before this plumage is molted.

A postjuvenal molt takes place, between September and December, of the body plumage, some scapulars and some wing coverts. This produces the first winter plumage, which is like that of the adult, except for the retained juvenal scapulars and wing coverts. I have seen birds in this plumage as early as September 30. A partial prenuptial molt, similar to that of the adult, produces during the spring a first nuptial plumage in which young birds can be distinguished from adults by varying amounts of retained winter feathers. At the next complete molt, the first postnuptial young birds assume the fully adult winter plumage.

Adults have a partial prenuptial molt between February and June, involving most of the body plumage, but not all of the scapulars, wing coverts, and tertials. There is much individual variation in the time of this molt. I have seen birds in full nuptial plumage as early as March 21 and in full winter plumage as late as May 13. The complete postnuptial molt begins in July with the body molt, which is usually completed before October. I have seen adults in full nuptial plumage as late as September 6. The red-breasted birds reported by Mr. Mackay (1893) as shot on Cape Cod in December and February must have been exceptional cases of delayed or omitted molt; the February birds may have been cases of early spring molt.

Food.—Doctor Ekblaw says:

Their food when they first come to the North is scarce, and when the weather is unduly unfavorable they are hard put to it to find enough to live. They probe about the grasses and sedges on the wet moors and along the swales and pools, and sometimes wade breast deep into the water to pick out the small but abundant life that swarms in some of the pools, mostly crustacea and larvae. The upper mandible is relatively soft and pliant. Sometimes they search the tide pools left at low water, or poke about the rocks and gravel along shore.

Other Arctic explorers have referred to the scanty food of the knot in the north; H. Chichester Hart (1880) says that " of a number of knots' stomachs examined, only one contained any food; this consisted of two caterpillars, one bee, and pieces of an Alga; " Colonel Feilden (1879) saw knots " feeding eagerly on the buds of *Saxifraga oppositifolia;* " Mr. Manniche (1910) " saw them running on the snow eagerly occupied in picking up the seed of *Carex* and *Lazula* tufts, the ends of which here and there appeared over the snow." Later on, when the ponds and marshes are teeming with animal life, they have plenty of food.

With us, on migrations, the knots feed mainly on the sandy and stony beaches, moving deliberately along in compact groups close to the water's edge, probing in the sand for minute mollusks and small crustaceans. On the sandy beaches on the west coast of Florida, the wet sand is filled with minute shellfish known as *Coquinas*, on which the knots seemed to be feeding. They also feed to some extent on the mud flats and sand flats with the black-bellied plover, where they find marine insects and their larvae. Mr. Mackay (1893) says "they also eat the larvae of one of the cutworms (Noctuidae) which they obtain on the marshes," some of which he has found in their throats when shot. Edward H. Forbush (1912) says: "They are fond of the spawn of the horsefoot crab, which, often in company with the turnstone, they dig out of the sand, sometimes fighting the former birds before they can claim their share." W. L. McAtee (1911) says that they also feed on grasshoppers and on marine worms of the genus *Nereis*.

Behavior.—The knots fly swiftly in compact flocks, twisting and turning in unison like the smaller sandpipers, for which they might easily be mistaken at a distance. On the ground they are rather deliberate in their movements, generally grouped in compact bunches and all moving along together; they are less likely to scatter over

their feeding grounds than other waders.   When resting on the high
beaches between tides they stand quietly in close groups, all facing
the wind; their grey plumage renders them quite inconspicuous at
such times.   F. H. Allen tells me that he has seen half a dozen of
them hopping about on one leg in shallow water; this may be a sort
of game, frequently indulged in by many small waders.

Mr. Manniche (1910) says:

Peculiar to this species is its restless character. The resident couples
would every day make long excursions, not only to seek food, but probably
also for pleasure. Their great power of flight makes them able to do this
without difficulty. In rapid high flight they are now here and now there.
I often saw them set out in a northern direction high over the summits of
the mountains or in a southern far out over the ice in the firths, to return after
a short while.

In the breeding season the male is pugnacious and quarrelsome against birds
of its own kin as well as against other small birds, which appear within his
domain. Uttering a short cry he will fly up and pursue the intruder in the most
violent manner and often he would follow it so far away, that I could not see
them, even through my field glass. He would soon return, and having—triumphantly fluting—circled around several times, go down to his mate. I have
seen the knot pursue even skuas.

Mr. Mackay (1893) writes:

On the ground they are sluggish and not given to moving about much;
unless very much harrassed they are not nearly so vigilant as their companions, the black-bellied plover, but when they have become shy they are
exceedingly wary and always on the alert for danger. When the incoming
tide drives the knots from the flats they seek the marshes or some shoal
which is sufficiently elevated to remain uncovered during high water; they
also frequent the crest of the beaches. Here they generally remain quiet until
the tide has fallen sufficiently to permit them to return again to the flats to
feed. When on the marshes during high water they occupy some of the time
in feeding, showing they are by no means dependent on the flats for all their
food. They associate and mingle freely with the turnstone (*Arenaria interpres*),
black-bellied plover (*Charadrius squatarola*), and red-backed sandpiper
(*Tringa alpina pacifica*) as with their own kind, and apparently evince the
same friendship toward the two former birds as prevails between the American
golden plover (*Charadrius dominicus*) and the Eskimo curlew (*Numenius
borealis*). I have heard of but one instance (at Revere, Mass., during a storm)
of the knot being noted in the same flock with adult American golden plover.
At this time there were three, one of which was shot. I have heard, however,
of both adult and young knots mingling with young American golden plover, or
" pale-bellies," as they are locally called.

Voice.—The same writer says:

They make two notes. One is soft, of two articulations, and sounds like
the word " Wah-quoit " (by which name it is sometimes known on Cape Cod) ;
although uttered low, it can be heard quite a distance. This note is particularly noticeable when flocks are coming to the decoys; it has a faint rolling
sound similar to the note of the American golden plover (*Charadrius dominicus*) under the same conditions, only more subdued and faint. The other

is a single note resembling a little honk. These birds will also respond to the note of the black-bellied plover (*Charadrius squatarola*) as readily as to their own when it is given with a whistle.

Roland C. Ross (1924) gives the following graphic description of the croaking note:

The common call is a low-pitched, hoarse "skeuk," the lowest and heaviest voice on the flats. It struck me as a dull croak, coming pretty regularly from the feeding birds, and especially strong when they took wing. A lone bird in joining the flock would croak his coming. The sound can be imitated in quality and form but in a higher pitch. Make the facial contortions necessary to "cluck" to a horse, but don't "cluck"; make it "skeuk," and locate it in the wisdom teeth on the side being dislocated. Pitch it low; it will still be two tones too high. At a distance the sucking or harsh quality is lost. A softer, more musical rendition is given when the birds are well bunched and feeding, which came to my ear as "chook."

John T. Nichols (1920) says: "The flight note of the knot is a low-pitched whistle, frequently in two parts, with a peculiar lisp or buzz in it, *tlu tlu*."

Doctor Ekblaw describes the notes heard on the breeding grounds as follows:

Four distinct calls characterize the mating and nesting season. Most common are two piercingly shrill calls uttered generally on the wing, one of them resembling *wah-quoi* and the other *wee-a-whit*, easily distinguished, but somewhat alike. The long-drawn-out *coo-a-hee*, or *coo-hee*, is a soft, flutelike call also given in flight, but nearly always back among the hills, far from the shore where the nests are hidden. This flutelike call appears to be a signal or recognition call. The fourth call is a sharp, querulous *whit, whit, whit*, almost like a cluck, often given singly, but more often many times repeated. When their nesting haunts are invaded or their feeding grounds disturbed this call expresses their displeasure.

Field marks.—In spring plumage the knot is easily recognized by its reddish breast, which, however, is not as conspicuous as might be expected. In immature and winter plumage the best character is the absence of any conspicuous field mark. Even in flight it seems to be a plain gray bird; the rump and tail appear but little lighter than the rest of the upper parts and the faint white line in the wings is hardly noticeable. Its larger size will hardly distinguish it from the smaller sandpipers except by direct comparison. Its short, greenish yellow legs and its prominent bill might help one to recognize it under favorable circumstances.

Fall.—Doctor Ekblaw says:

As soon as the water begins to grow cold, when insect and other small life becomes scarce, and when the midnight sun approaches the horizon, the knots abandon the northland, plump and strong from their summer stay in the Arctic, and wend their way to the southland. Not even a belated straggler can be found after August 1.

The adults begin to arrive on Cape Cod about the middle of July; the height of their abundance comes about the first week in August and most of them disappear during that month, although Mr. Mackay (1893) has recorded them in October, December, and February. The young birds begin to arrive there about August 20, but the main flight of "graybacks," as the young are called on this coast, comes along in September and early October, stragglers sometimes lingering into November. When with us, knots frequent the beaches; although they are found on both sandy and stony beaches, I have sometimes thought that they preferred the pebbly beaches, feeding close to the water line, where they are often surprisingly invisible among the variously colored stones. They are not shy, as a rule, and generally allow a close approach before they fly off swiftly, uttering their characteristic notes. At high tide, when their feeding grounds are covered, they resort to the high beaches to rest, preen their plumage, and sleep.

By July 20 the first birds have reached South Carolina, where some remain until October 15. We saw what was probably the last of the migration on the west coast of Florida in 1924. The knots were there when we arrived on November 11. During a northerly gale and after a heavy rain on the 21st I saw several small flocks on the high and dry sand of an exposed beach, huddled together in compact bunches and reluctant to move. The last birds were seen on the 26th.

In the interior the knot seems to be even rarer in the fall than in the spring, but on the Pacific coast the reverse seems to be the case. It is regarded as rather rare in Alaska, but F. S. Hersey collected a small series for me at St. Michael on August 4 and 8, 1915, and H. B. Conover took two at Golovin Bay on August 14, 1924. D. E. Brown's notes record them at Grays Harbor, Washington, from August 21 to November 2, 1917.

Game.—Although no longer on the game-bird list, the knot is a good game bird. It flies in compact flocks, comes well to the decoys when attracted by the whistle of an experienced caller, flies rather swiftly, and makes a good table bird, for it is of good size and usually fat. It was always included in the list of what we used to call "big birds." On Cape Cod knots in all plumages are called "redbreasts" by the gunners, though the name "grayback" is often applied to the young birds. Mr. Mackay (1893) says:

When shy and coming to decoys to alight, they barely touch their feet to the sand before they discover their mistake and are off in an instant. They fly quickly and closely together and, when coming to decoys, usually pass by them down wind, most of the flock whistling, then suddenly wheeling with heads to the wind, and up to the decoys. At such times many are killed at one discharge.

Dr. L. C. Sanford (1903) writes:

One of my pleasant recollections of shore-bird shooting is associated with this bird. I give the date with some hesitation, for it was May 10, near Cobb Island. During several days previous redbreast had been flying, but the tides were not suitable, and it was useless to try for them. Here the flight is along the outer beach, at the edge of the surf, the birds stopping to feed on the mud flats exposed by the falling tide. The sun was not up and the water still high as we set the decoys off one of the points along the beach, close to the breaking waves; the blind was of seaweed, and before we were settled the first flock passed by high up, but a pair of birds dropped out of it and hovered in front of us; another minute and 10 more swung in. Flock after flock, from a few birds to hundreds, passed in the same line, coming into sight over the ocean, striking the beach and following its edge—now low just over the surf, now high up—the first light of sunrise giving them a black appearance. The undulating character of the flight was unmistakable and was in evidence when the dark line first appeared—now distinct on the horizon, presently out of sight in the waves, all of a sudden rising up over the decoys to circle in. Our chance lasted only a few minutes, for when the flat was exposed the birds all passed by out of range; occasionally we whistled in an odd one, but the flocks shied off. As we carried back our basket of birds it did not occur to us that the experience of that morning would be our last flight of redbreast, but it was.

DISTRIBUTION

Breeding range.—The breeding range of the knot in North America is imperfectly known, but appears to extend north to Franklin (Winter Harbor, Victoria Land, and Goose Fiord), and Grinnell Land (Fort Conger). East to Greenland (Floeberg Beach, Cape Sheridan, North Star Bay, Tuctoo Valley, Bowdoin Bay, and Disco Bay). South to southwestern Greenland (Disco Bay) and southern Franklin (Igloolik, Winter Island, and Cambridge Bay). West to Franklin (Cambridge Bay and Winter Harbor). Birds breeding in northeast Greenland may be the European form.

It has also been detected in summer in Alaska at Point Barrow, Point Hope, St. Michael, and other localities, where it may possibly breed.

Winter range.—Not well known but in the Western Hemisphere, seemingly most of South America, from Patagonia (Tierra del Fuego) and Argentina (Barracus al Sud and Cape San Antonio) on the south, Peru (Santa Luzia and probably Tumbez) on the west, Brazil (Iguape) on the east, to possibly Jamaica, Barbados, rarely Louisiana (Vermilion Bay), and Florida (St. Marks).

Spring migration.—Early dates of spring arrival on the Atlantic coast are: South Carolina, Frogmore, April 8, and Egg Bank, April 16; North Carolina, Pea and Brodie Islands, April 18; Virginia Locustville, April 10; New Jersey, Absecon Bay, April 21; New York, Long Beach, Long Island, April 29, and Canandaigua Lake,

May 23; Connecticut, Norwalk, May 24, Fairfield, May 29, and West-
port, May 30; Massachusetts, Tuckernuck Island, May 11, Franklin,
Igloolik, June 14; and Greenland, Jacobshaven, June 3, and Cape
Union, June 5.

On the Pacific coast, early dates are: California, Alameda, April
25; Washington, Destruction Island Light, May 6, and Willapa Harbor, May 11 [once at Dungeness, on February 25, 1915 (Cantwell)];
British Colombia, Fort Simpson, May 13; and Alaska, Nulato, May
10, Craig, May 13, Admiralty Island, May 14, St. Michael, May 29,
and Point Barrow, May 30.

Late dates of spring departure are: South Carolina, near Charleston, June 5; Virginia, Cape Charles, June 10, Cobb Island, June 25,
and Wallop's Island, June 27; New Jersey, Cape May County, June
3, and Elizabeth, June 11; New York, Amityville, May 31, and
Geneva, June 8; and Massachusetts, Cape Cod, June 13, Harvard,
June 19, Marthas Vineyard, June 24, and Monomoy Island, June 28.

Fall migration.—Early dates of arrival in fall migration are:
Washington, Lake Oxette, July 12; California, Alameda, August 1,
Monterey, August 7, and Santa Barbara, August 21; Massachusetts,
Cape Cod, July 15, Marthas Vineyard, July 24, Dennis, July 27, and
Monomoy Island, July 30; Rhode Island, Newport, August 1; Con-
necticut, Saybrook, August 21; New York, East Hampton, July 27,
Dutchess County, July 30, Rockaway, August 12, Montauk Point
Light, August 14, and Amityville, August 23; New Jersey, Tucker-
ton, July 3; Virginia, Wallops Island, August 12; North Carolina,
Pea and Brodie Islands, July 8; South Carolina, near Charleston,
July 20; Florida, Marco, July 1, and Lesser Antilles, Barbados,
September 6.

Late dates of fall departure are: Alaska, St. Michael, August 14,
Point Barrow, August 17, and Homer, August 23; Washington,
Grays Harbor, November 2; California, Anaheim Landing, October
3, and San Diego, October 9; Greenland, Discovery Bay, August 25;
Franklin, Winter Island, August 17; Prince Edward Island, Alex-
andra, September 24; Quebec, Godbout, August 7, Henley Harbor,
August 23, and Old Fort Island, September 30; Massachusetts,
Marthas Vineyard, October 8, and Monomoy Island, October 28;
Rhode Island, South Auburn, September 3, and Newport, September
14; Connecticut, Saybrook, September 25; New York, Shinnecock
Bay, September 16, Freeport, September 26, Penn Yan, October 15,
and Amityville, October 16; Virginia, Wallops Island, September
29; North Carolina, Church's Island, September 30; South Carolina,
near Charleston, October 15; Georgia, Savannah, September 24; and
Lesser Antilles, Barbados, December 27.

Casual records.—The knot has on numerous occasions been detected in the Central or Western States or other points outside of its normal range. Among these are Vera Cruz, Rivera, April 13, 1904; Texas, Corpus Christi, July 1 to 10, 1887; Kansas, Hamilton, September 19, 1911, and Lawrence, April 17, 1871; Nebraska, Omaha, September 30, 1893, and Lincoln, May 16, 1896, and August 27, 1896; Indiana, near Millers, August 24, 1896; Minnesota, Lanesboro, September 7, 1885; and Montana, Lake Bowdoin, October 4, 1915; Ohio, Sandusky River, spring of 1894, and Licking Reservoir, May 27, 1878; Ontario (occasionally common in spring), Point Pelee, September 15, 1906, and May 30, 1907, and Ottawa, June 4, 1890; Michigan, Port Austin, September 4, 1899, Benton Harbor, June 23, 1904, Forestville, June 20, 1903, Charity Island, September 1, 1910, and Oak Point, August 20–21, 1908; and Alberta, Beaverhill Lake, May 19–23, 1924.

Egg dates.—Greenland: 3 records, June 22 and 30, and July 9. Victoria Land: 3 records, July 1, 9, and 22. Grinnell Land: 2 records, June 26 and 27.

CALIDRIS TENUIROSTRIS (Horsfield)

EASTERN ASIATIC KNOT

The only North American record for this little known Asiatic species was established by Alfred M. Bailey (1925), when he captured a single specimen in northwestern Alaska on May 28, 1922. He says:

One specimen of this species, an adult male in light plumage, was taken at Cape Prince of Wales on May 28. At this date the tundra was still covered with snow, but the higher benches of the cape were becoming bare. The first arrivals of many species were just making their appearance, using these high exposed spots as resting places. Among these numerous migrants I took this one straggler. It was so tame I collected it with my .32 aux.

It is larger than our knot and is also known as the Japanese knot. Seebohm (1888) says:

It is the only *Tringa* with white on the upper tail coverts which has a straight bill more than an inch and a half long. In summer plumage it has no chestnut on the under parts, and the chestnut on the upper parts is principally confined to the scapulars. In winter plumage the two knots scarcely differ except in size. It is very closely allied to the common knot.

The breeding grounds of the Japanese knot are unknown, but Middendorff observed it during the whole summer on the southern shores of the Sea of Okhotsk, though he obtained no evidence of its nesting there. It has occurred on migration in the valley of the Ussuri, on the coasts of Japan and China, and on most of the islands of the Malay Archipelago. It winters on the coast of Australia, has occurred on the Andaman Islands, and in considerable numbers on the coast of Scinde.

ARQUATELLA MARITIMA (Brünnich)

PURPLE SANDPIPER

HABITS

This hardy northern bird has well been called "winter snipe" and "rock snipe," for it is known to us only as a winter visitor on rocky shores. Although it does not breed quite as far north as some species, it migrates for a shorter distance and winters farther north than any other wader; in fact, the southern limit of its winter range is far north of the normal winter range of any other. A. L. V. Manniche (1910) saw only three purple sandpipers during three seasons in northeastern Greenland, and the Crockerland expedition saw only one in northwestern Greenland in four years. Both expeditions were probably north of its normal breeding range.

Spring.—As soon as spring asserts itself the purple sandpipers begin to desert their main winter range on the coast of New England, some leaving in March and only a very few stragglers lingering into May. On May 29, 1909, we saw a few late migrants on the south coast of Labrador, where I secured one in full nuptial plumage. Ludwig Kumlien (1879) says that the purple sandpiper is the first wader to arrive in the spring at Cumberland Sound.

The 4th of June is the earliest date I met them at Annanactook; this was during a heavy snowstorm, and the earliest date possible that they could have found any of the rocks bare at low tide. The flock lit on the top of one of the small islands in the harbor and sheltered themselves from the storm by creeping behind and underneath ledges of rocks; they then huddled together like a flock of quails in winter. I have often noticed the same habit with them in late autumn, while they were waiting for low tide.

Courtship.—The same writer refers to a courtship performance, as follows:

As the breeding season approaches the males have a peculiar cry, resembling somewhat that of *Actiturus bartramius*, but lower and not so prolonged. When this note is uttered they assume a very dignified strut, and often raise the wings up over the back and slowly fold them again, like the upland plover.

Aubyn Trevor-Battye (1897) says:

Like all sandpipers, they do much of their courtship on the wing, chasing one another in circles with rapid turns and shifts. On the ground I have seen the male bird approach the female with trailing wings, arched back, and head low down, occasionally hopping, like a courting pigeon.

This species seems to be rather rare in Baffin Land. I have two sets of eggs, given to me by Capt. Donald B. MacMillan, collected with the parent bird at Cape Dorset. J. Dewey Soper collected a female there, with enlarged ovaries, on June 8; but he saw only three birds during "the spring and summer of 1926 along the south coast of Baffin Island." He says in his notes:

The first sandpiper observed by me the following spring was of this species, a solitary male collected on June 2, 1925, at Nettilling Lake. The lakes were still icebound and the land mostly covered with snow, but here and there were small open pools. Along the border of one of these the bird was feeding in the thin layer of thawed mud among the grassy hummocks. On June 11, in the same locality near the Takuirbing River, several were observed and collected. When flushed they emit a grating *ick-ick-ick* and when not too hard pressed will often light again a few yards away. They flush sluggishly, and when not come upon too abruptly will frequently elevate the wings leisurely above the back, as though stretching them before taking flight. On the whole, at this time, they were comparatively fearless and permitted close approach. Only one was observed giving a vocal performance on the wing. It rose slowly from the ground to a height of 15 or 20 feet and leisurely flying over the tundra gave a series of low, musical staccato notes resembling *to-wit-to-wit-to-wit-to-wit*, etc. The performance continues unbrokenly while the bird remains in the air over a distance of 25 or 30 yards.

Nesting.—Rev. Henry H. Slater (1898) says:

In the extreme north the nest is often quite close to the sea, little above high-water mark. But in Iceland and at the southern borders of its breeding range generally the purple sandpiper usually nests on the fells. My first nest, from which I shot the female mentioned above, was near the top of a high ridge in north Iceland, nearly 1,600 feet above sea level, on a small bare patch of recently uncovered ground amongst snow fields; it was a slight hollow in a withered tuft of *Dryas octopetala*, and rather a substantial nest for a wader, consisting of a good handful of leaves of *Dryas* and *Salix lanata*, a little short grass, two white ptarmigan's feathers and a few of the parents'.

W. C. Hewitson (1856) quotes Mr. Wolley as saying that in the Faeroes, "it breeds sparingly on the very tops of high mountains, where I found its young at the end of June still unable to fly."

Messrs. E. Evans and W. Sturge (1859) found the purple sandpiper breeding in Spitsbergen; they say:

The purple sandpiper (*Tringa maritina*, Brünn.) was very abundant in Coal Bay (on the south side of Ice Sound, so named on account of a small quantity of poor coal being found there), and we found four of their nests on the high field. Beautiful little nests they were, deep in the ground, and lined with stalks of grass and leaves of the dwarf birch (*Betula nana*, L.), containing mostly four eggs of an olive green, handsomely mottled with purplish brown, chiefly at the larger end. We watched this elegant little bird—the only one of the *Grallatores* we saw—with much interest as it waded into some pool of snow water or ran along the shingle, every now and then raising its wings over its back and exhibiting the delicate tint of the under side, at the same time uttering its loud shrill whistle.

No recent accounts of the nesting habits of this species seem to have been published and the data on eggs in collections seem to be rather scanty. I have never found a nest myself. Both sexes are said to incubate the eggs and share in the care of the young. The period of incubation is over 20 days.

Eggs.—A very good description of the eggs is given by Seebohm (1884) as follows:

The eggs of the purple sandpiper are four in number and remarkably handsome. They vary in ground color from pale olive to pale buffish brown, boldly mottled, blotched, and streaked with reddish brown and very dark blackish brown. On some eggs the blotches are large, and chiefly distributed in an oblique direction round the large end; on others they are more evenly distributed over the entire surface; and on many a few very dark scratches, spots, or streaks are scattered here and there amongst the brown markings. The underlying markings are numerous and conspicuous, and are pale violet gray or grayish brown in color.

Frank Poynting's (1895) colored plate of 12 selected eggs well illustrates the great variation in the beautiful eggs of this species. There are two distinct types of ground color, green and buff. In the green types the colors vary from "yellowish glaucous" to a light shade of "grape green"; and in the buff types from "cream buff" to "dark olive buff." They are sometimes evenly, but more often irregularly, spotted and blotched with various shades of brown, "sepia," "bister," and "snuff brown," sometimes boldly marked with "chocolate" and "burnt umber" and sometimes with great splashes of "vinaceous brown" overlaid with blotches of "chestnut brown" and "bay," a handsome combination. The measurements of 100 eggs, supplied by Rev. F. C. R. Jourdain, average 37.3 by 26.5 millimeters; the eggs showing the four extremes measure 40 by 28, 35.1 by 26.6 and 37.3 by 24.8 millimeters.

Plumages.—The nestling is described in Witherby's Handbook (1920) as follows:

Fore part of crown warm buff; black-brown median line from base of upper mandible to crown; crown and upper parts velvety black-brown, down with numerous cream and warm buff tips; nape light buff, down with sooty-brown bases; from base of upper mandible above eye to nape a black-brown streak, another short one from base of lower mandible, ear coverts as crown; cheeks warm or light buff, down with black-brown tips; remaining under parts grayish white, down sooty brown toward base.

The juvenal plumage is much like that of the summer adult, except that the feathers of the crown are tipped with creamy white, as are also the central tail feathers; the feathers of the mantle and scapulars are edged with buffy white; and the wing coverts and tertials are broadly edged with the same color or tipped with pale pinkish buff. The juvenal body plumage is usually molted before the birds reach us on migration, when young birds, in first winter plumage, can be recognized by the broad white edgings of the median coverts and by a few retained scapulars and tertials. Some of these juvenal feathers are retained through the next, the partial prenuptial molt. Subsequent molts and plumages are as in the adult.

Adults have a complete postnuptial molt between August and November and a partial prenuptial molt from January to May; this latter involves most of the body plumage, but not all of the scapulars, back, rump, or upper tail coverts.

Food.—The favorite feeding places of purple sandpipers are the wave-washed rocky shores of islands or promontories along the seashore, with a decided preference for islands. Here, where the rocks are fringed with rockweed, waving in the restless waves, or coverèd with barnacles and various slimy products of the sea, these sure-footed little birds are quite at home on the slippery rocks, as they glean abundant food at the water's edge and skillfully avoid being washed away. Yarrell (1871) says that—

it may be seen busily employed turning over stones and searching among seaweed for the smaller shrimps and sandhoppers which are to be found there, and it also feeds on young crabs, marine insects, and the soft bodies of animals inhabiting small shells.

Witherby's Handbook (1920) gives its food as—

varied, including insects: coleoptera (*Otiorhynchus*), diptera (larvae of *Chironomus*), also spiders, *Thysanura* (or *Collembola*), annelida and crustacea (*Amphipoda, Isopoda, Orchestia, Idotea, Gammarus,* and *Podocerus*) as well as mollusca (*Mytilus, Littorina, Purpura,* etc.). Vegetable matter is also eaten including algae, grasses, moss, buds, and leaves of phanerogams and remains of cryptogams. Seeds of *Cochlearia* have been identified and small fish (*Gobius*) nearly 1 inch long, as well as ova of lumpsucker.

Behavior.—The flight of the purple sandpiper suggests at times that of the spotted sandpiper, for when disturbed singly along the shore it is apt to fly out over the water with rapid downward wing strokes and, describing a large semicircle, return to the shore some distance ahead. When flying in a flock the birds are often closely bunched, the whole flock wheeling and turning in unison, showing alternately their dark bodies and their white bellies, in true sandpiper fashion. As a rule they do not make very long flights or fly very high. Their migrations are short and deliberate. They are rather sedentary birds and can generally be found in certain favorite localities all winter and year after year. But, as they show a decided preference for the outer sides of surf-swept ledges, they are not often seen from the land. They can swim almost as well as phalaropes and in calm weather they will often alight on half submerged seaweed or on the surface of the water. Dr. Charles W. Townsend (1905), who watched a flock on an island off Cape Ann, describes their actions as follows:

They finally alighted on a steeply sloping rock close to the water's edge on the northeastern point of the island so that they could be watched with binoculars and telescope from the shore. Fifty-eight birds were in sight and there were fully half as many more on the other side of the rock, hidden from view, except when they jumped up from time to time. The flock must have numbered 75. The tide was high and the birds were evidently trying to kill time until low water, when they could gather their food from the seaweed covered rocks. Most of them were resting, squatting on the rock with head to the wind, their dark purplish-gray backs contrasting strongly with their white bellies. Others were slowly raising their wings over their backs, showing the white under surfaces. Again they were chasing each other, making the sleepy ones jump suddenly, or running up the rock to escape an unusually high wave, fluttering with their wings to help themselves. From time to time they were joined by bunches of from 5 to 10 others.

Voice.—This species is a rather silent bird, but John T. Nichols says in his notes: " When about to take wing a flock of purple sand-pipers is rather noisy, keeping up a swallowlike chatter, each single-syllabled note suggestive of the *flip* of the tree swallow and of the *kip* of the sanderling."

Field marks.—A sandpiper seen on a rocky shore in New England in winter is likely to be a purple sandpiper. Mr. Nichols suggests the following field characters:

The purple sandpiper is a stockily built bird, which stands low and has a moderately long bill. Its breast and upper parts of a dark purplish gray match admirably the rocks on which it lives, and although darker are not very differ-ent in tone from the coloring of the red-backed sandpiper in fall, with which species it might possibly be confused. Both have a white line in the wing shown in flight, but in the purple sandpiper this broadens to a more con-spicuous wedge of white backward on the inner secondaries and extends across the bases of the primaries as narrow edging to their coverts, rather than turning the bend of the wing into the primaries. The best field character is the color of legs and feet, which are of a dull but strong yellow, appreciable at a consider-able distance. The basal third of the bill is of the same, but tinged with orange.

Fall.—The fall migration of the purple sandpiper is a gradual southward movement along the Atlantic coast. It disappears from its breeding grounds early in September, but the main flight does not reach New England until November or December. What few strag-glers have been seen on the Great Lakes were probably migrants from Hudson Bay. E. W. Hadeler writes to me that he observed one on the shore of Lake Erie, Painesville, Ohio, from October 22 to November 12, 1916, and again from October 24 to November 11, 1922. It is interesting to note the uniformity of the dates and the fact that the species was seen always on a stone breakwater, apparently feeding exclusively on the water-washed stones.

Winter.—The purple sandpiper is the " winter snipe " of the New England coast, where flocks of from 25 to 75 or more may be found regularly on certain outlying rocky ledges. Here they seek shelter among the rocks from the flying spray and from the wintry blasts; and here they find their food washed up by the waves or hidden in the half floating beds of rockweed. On December 10, 1913, while we were shooting eiders on one of the outer ledges in Jericho Bay,

Maine, a flock of about 50 of these hardy little birds seemed out of place in our rough surroundings. It was a cold, blustering day; the surf was breaking over the rocks and the sea was white with combing breakers; even the hardy sea ducks sought the shelter of the ledges; but these plump little birds seemed quite happy and contented as they huddled together in a compact flock on the slippery rocks. They were very tame and confiding; even the reports of our guns served only to make them circle out around the ledge a few times and then return to its shelter. Evidently this was their winter home. We did not have the heart to shoot any of them.

Mr. Nichols tells me that " very occasionally in winter, early spring or late fall, one finds single birds on the sandy beaches of New York or New Jersey south of the rocks."

DISTRIBUTION

Range.—Europe, Asia, and northeastern North America.

Breeding range.—In the Old World the purple sandpiper breeds in the Arctic regions from Iceland, Norway, and Spitsbergen east to Nova Zembla and the Taimyr Peninsula. In North America the breeding range extends north to Franklin (Igloolik); and Greenland (Hare Island, and Shannon Islands). East to Greenland (Shannon Islands and Ivimiut). South to Greenland (Ivimiut and Ivigtut); and Franklin (southern Baffin Island, Cumberland Sound, and Winter Island). West to Franklin (Winter Island and Igloolik). It has been detected in summer still farther north; Franklin (Mercy Bay, Fury Point, Boothia Felix, and Possession Bay); and Greenland (Bowdoin Bay, Thank God Harbor, North Star Bay, and Fort Conger).

Winter range.—The purple sandpiper winters farther north than any other shore bird. North and east to southern Greenland (Ivigtut); eastern Nova Scotia (St. Peter's Island); Massachusetts (Rockport, Westport, and Boston); Rhode Island (Cormorant Rock); Connecticut (Saybrook and Faulkner Island); and rarely New York (Gull Island, Montauk, and Amityville). South to New York (Amityville). West to New York (Amityville); Connecticut (New Haven); Maine (Cumberland County, Matinicus Island, and Washington County); New Brunswick (Grand Manan and the Bay of Fundy); Prince Edward Island; and southern Greenland (Ivigtut).

Spring migration.—Early dates of spring arrival are: Franklin, Annanactook, June 4, Winter Island, June 10, Cambridge Bay, June 10, and Igloolik, June 14; Greenland, about 72° north latitude, May 29; and Baffin Island, Cape Dorset, May 30.

Late dates of spring departure are: New York, Sag Harbor, April 18, and Long Beach, May 4, Rhode Island, Sachuest Point,

May 15; Massachusetts, Dennis, May 5; and Quebec, Prince of Wales Sound, May 27, Quatachoo, May 29, and Mingan Islands, May 29.

Fall migration.—Early dates of fall arrival are Quebec, Bras d'Or, August 4; New Brunswick, Grand Manan, August 13; Ontario, Toronto, October 27, Ottawa, October 29, and Hamilton, October 31; Maine, Metinic Green Island, August 6, Saddleback Ledge, August 19; Massachusetts, Cape Cod, September 6, Chatham, September 8, and Nahant, October 13; Rhode Island, Sachuest Point, September 13; and New York, Montauk, November 1, Orient, November 1, and Long Beach, November 2.

Late dates of fall departure are: Greenland, Possession Bay, September 1, and Thank God Harbor, September 3; Mackenzie, Great Bear Lake, September 16; and Franklin, Wellington Channel, August 28, Kingwah Fjord, September 6, Cumberland Gulf, September 13, and Pangnirtung Fjord, October 21.

Casual records.—The purple sandpiper has been reported as seen at the entrance to St. George Harbor, Bermuda, and there are a few records for the south Atlantic coast and the interior, among which are: New Jersey, Delaware Bay (specimen in British Museum), Beach Haven, October 31, 1896, and one found dead at the Absecon Lighthouse; Georgia, one in the Sennett collection taken, March 5, 1874; Florida, Key Biscayne, October 29, 1857, and Gordan's Pass, November 1, 1886; Missouri, Boonville, between April 16 and May 31, 1854; Illinois, near Chicago, November 7, 1871; Ohio, Sandusky, November 19, 1925, and Painesville, October 22, 1916, and October 24, 1922; and Wisconsin, Door County, May, 1881.

Egg dates.—Greenland: 18 records, May 16 to June 30; 9 records, June 1 to 19. Iceland: 6 records, May 21 to June 17. Baffin Island; 2 records, July 21 and 28.

ARQUATELLA PTILOCNEMIS PTILOCNEMIS (Coues)

PRIBILOF SANDPIPER

HABITS

As explained under the Aleutian sandpiper, this bird is probably not a subspecies of the purple sandpiper; so the name *maritima* can not be used for either *ptilocnemis* or *couesi*. I have therefore thought it best to follow Ridgway (1919) in the use of his names for the Pribilof and Aleutian sandpipers, rather than use the Check List names.

The Pribilof sandpiper has the most restricted distribution of any North American sandpiper. In summer it is confined to the chilly and foggy uplands of the Pribilof Islands, the equally cool, damp lowlands of St. Matthew Island, Hall Island, and perhaps St. Lawrence Island, all in Bering Sea. And its known migration range is limited to a few localities on the mainland of Alaska and in the Aleutian Islands, where it probably winters. It may breed more extensively on St. Lawrence Island than it is now known to do, but it has not yet been found breeding anywhere on the mainland. G. Dallas Hanna (1921) says:

I strongly suspect that the birds have some other extensive breeding ground than St. George, St. Paul, and St. Matthew Islands, because in September and October large flocks come to the two former islands; these appear to contain many more individuals than are in existence on all three. Whether St. Lawrence Island supplies the extra number or not remains for future determination. The winter range of the species is practically unknown, the only records being from Portage Bay, southeast Alaska, and Lynn Canal, between Alaska and British Columbia. The appearance of the birds at the former locality in flocks in spring (if identifications were correct) indicates that they wintered farther south, probably on Vancouver and other islands of British Columbia. They could hardly have come from beyond these localities and have remained undiscovered.

Spring.—The same writer says:

Spring migration takes place the latter part of April and the first half of May. My earliest record for St. Paul Island is April 15 (1915) when a flock appeared at Northeast Point. The height of migration is a little later than that date and may usually be expected from the 1st to the 15th of May. Birds are almost invariably paired upon arrival. Very few spring flocks have been seen on the Pribilofs, and they do not tarry by the beaches, but go directly to the upland nesting sites. It seems to be uncommon for more than the resident population to land upon an island in spring. The birds seem to go directly to the chosen breeding grounds, wherever they may be. This fact is of wide application among the northern shore birds. Only rare stragglers of such species as golden plovers, turnstones, and pectoral and sharp-tailed sandpipers stop at the Pribilofs on their way north, but large numbers of some of them come in fall.

Courtship.—Dr. E. W. Nelson (1887) writes:

The male of the pair seen by me on St. Lawrence Island in June kept flying up some 10 or 15 yards, its wings beating with a rapid vibrating or tremulous motion, while the bird thus poised trilled forth a clear, rather musical and liquid but hard, whistling note, which is probably the same note which Elliott likens to the trill of the tree frog. The short song ended, the musician glides to the ground upon stiffened wings and resumes his feeding or stands silently for a time on a projecting rock or knoll.

Nesting.—We found Pribilof sandpipers very common in July on the low tundra at the south end of St. Matthew Island, where they were evidently breeding just back of the beaches. They were also common in the interior at the north end of this island and on the highlands of Hall Island. We collected a few specimens of the birds, but had no time to hunt for nests. We are indebted to Mr. Hanna (1921) for his excellent account of the nesting habits of this bird, from which I quote as follows:

On St. George Island the high upland tundra has been chosen for breeding ground. Here, among the reindeer "mosses" and light gray, lichen-covered rocks the sandpipers reign supreme in the fog. Some speculating may be indulged in to find a reason for so unusual a choice of locality. Elevations up to 500 feet are sought. Perhaps they shun the seacoasts on account of the presence there of large numbers of foxes. During all history this has been a greater fox island than either St. Paul or St. Matthew. On the latter island in June and July the birds may be found in large numbers around and back of the drift-wood piles. If it were not for this fact being known, we might suspect that on St. George the light gray tundra was selected for protective purposes, the birds themselves being distinguished chiefly by their light colors. St. Paul Island, for some unaccountable reason, is not chosen as a breeding ground except by a very few pairs. In 1919 not over a dozen were found during the entire nesting season, when almost all of the available areas were seen.

On the breeding grounds of St. George and St. Matthew the birds are very common, and from one to a dozen are in almost constant attendance upon the visitor. They sight him from afar and fly to meet him. Some bird will almost always try to lead him astray. If followed, it flies from knoll to knoll, often not more than 20 yards away. It remains in front of the visitor regardless of the direction he may take; whether toward or from the nest, makes no difference. After several minutes of this a sudden flight, with the familiar "song," is taken to some distant hill and the searcher for a nest is left confused and confounded.

A search for the nest will exhaust the patience of any except the most persistent collector. Messrs. Compton and Partch have been more successful than anyone else in locating them, and all of us agree that when a bird flies to meet the visitor, as just described, it is a pure waste of time to watch or follow it. Every method known to us of locating nests by watching the actions of the parents has failed. We have located nests and then endeavored to establish rules for guidance with others, but no definite facts could be determined. It was finally agreed that it was useless to watch a bird under any circumstances more than 15 minutes. If the location of the nest is not disclosed in that time, it is safe to assume that the mate is on it, and it might be hours before the guard would go there. In the meantime it may fly half a mile away and forget to come back, even to tease the hopeful collector lying concealed in the mist and fog behind some cheerless rock. No definite range can be ascribed to any one pair of birds, because those off the nests mingle indiscriminately. Very often a bird will fly completely out of the range of vision in the fog.

The action of a bird leaving a nest is unmistakable, and can always be recognized, once it is learned. It is a quick, excited, jerky flight, very close to the ground, and the bird goes but a very few yards until it feigns injury in its endeavor to entice the intruder away. It will always flutter in front of a person, even though he walk directly toward the nest. When the bird is seen to fly, the eggs are even more inconspicuous and difficult to find unless the exact spot from which it flew be located. Crompton thus flushed a bird which he knew had a nest, but he was at a loss to find it. At last he left his cane as nearly as possible where the nest should have been and repaired to a near-by rock to watch and wait. In a few minutes the bird returned to the eggs, which were located about a yard from the stick. When the bird is flushed from a nest it seldom happens that the other parent is near.

The nest is a mere depression about three and a half inches wide by two and a half inches deep. Most of the material is removed, but it is evidently packed down to a certain extent. No foreign material is carried at all. The nest is usually, but not necessarily, on some very slightly elevated ground and among the lichens called "reindeer moss." Some nests have been found where there was an admixture of *Hypnum* moss and again where the dwarf willows creep, rootlike, beneath the surface.

Eggs.—I can not do better than to quote again from Mr. Hanna (1921); he writes:

The normal set of eggs consists of four. A greater number has never been found, and a less number only when it was uncertain if the full set had been laid. As much as three days may intervene between egg laying, but usually the four are deposited on successive days. When one set of eggs is taken, another will be laid. But the same nest is not used the second time, the contentions of some natives to the contrary notwithstanding. A set of eggs found as late as July 24, 1917, certainly indicated that two may be laid in the same season on rare occasions. One set is the rule.

The color of the eggs is, as would be expected, somewhat variable. The lightest set examined in connection with this report has the ground color "greenish glaucous." From this there is perfect gradation through "court gray" and "light olive gray" to "deep olive buff" in the darkest set. Variation in any particular set is very slight. Spots are large and bold as a rule. They vary in size from 15 millimeters to less than one, and they are usually massed about the larger end. In one case the eggs are uniformly spotted with small spots all over. In none is the spotting heaviest on the smaller end (reversed eggs). Spots are usually inclined to be round, but occasionally they are in the form of streaks arranged roughly in spiral form. Only rarely are they banded about the larger end. In two cases a narrow black line was produced spirally on the larger end. The coloration of the spots varies from "snuff brown" to "sepia" and from "cinnamon brown" to "mummy brown." In some cases they are "raw umber." The darkest shades occur where the spots overlap and some deep-seated ones are "pale aniline lilac" or "pale" to "deep quaker drab." Only rarely is the outline of a spot not sharp.

The average dimensions derived from the above series of 72 eggs are: Length, 39.473 and breadth 27.468. Those which showed the extreme measurements were 42.0 by 27.8; 35 by 27.4; 37.6 by 39, and 39.1 by 26.4.

Young.—The period of incubation is said to be about 20 days, in which both sexes share. William Palmer (1899) says:

The young leave the nest soon after hatching and are thoroughly well concealed by their mimicry of the confusing mixture of mosses, lichens, and other forms of vegetation which abounds and are so well intermingled on these islands. It requires much patience and a close scrutiny to detect a crouching young, even when it is directly within reach. Obedient to their mother's cries they flatten themselves with head and neck extended; with each yard of the ground precisely similar in pattern and color with every other yard, and the parents, especially the female, trying their best to coax us in other directions, and the uncertainty as to the exact location of the young, all combine against the collector, so that few specimens reward a tramp that seems exasperatingly needless. The young will not move, though one stands with the foot touching them, but when once handled and released they scamper off with all the quickness their long legs can give them. When we invade the vicinity of a nest or young it is amusing to watch the antics of the female. She invariably flies in front and flutters with feigned lameness but a few feet away. If the ground is rough it is more amusing to watch the precipitancy of her flight until she disappears in a hollow, to reappear in a moment on the other side, cautiously turning round and eying us to see if we are following. She always keeps in front of us, no matter which way we turn, and will continue thus for several hundred yards, when she will suddenly fly off to some distance and after waiting awhile will return to the vicinity of the nest or young.

Mr. Hanna (1921) writes:

So far as known, the food of both old and young consists of beetles and flies while the birds remain on the highlands; when they move to the ponds and sea-shores they eat copepods, amphipods, etc. As soon as the young birds are well able to fly they resort to the tide pools and small ponds near the sea. Later the older birds join them and the flocks increase in size to several hundred in favorable places. This takes place in August and September in such localities as the Salt Lagoon of St. Paul Island.

Plumages.—The color pattern of the downy young Pribilof sandpiper is similar to that of the Aleutian, but the colors are different, much duller. The bright browns and buffs of the upper parts are replaced by "burnt umber," "snuff brown," "clay color," and "cinnamon buff," and the black markings are largely replaced by dark browns; the black patch in the center of the back is about as in the Aleutian. The under parts are less pure white, always suffused with pale buff on the throat and flanks and sometimes largely so on the breast also.

Mr. Palmer's (1899) studies of the molts and plumages indicate that they are similar to those of the Aleutian sandpiper; he writes:

The downy young are beautiful little things, silvery white beneath, bright, rich ocherous above, variegated with black and dots of white. The general color above lacks the grayness of the similar age of *maritimus*. The white dots are interesting under the microscope. They are composed of a bunch of highly specialized down, in which the radii near the tip are crowded and colorless. As they grow older the first feathers appear on the sides of the breast, on the back and scapulars; then the primaries and larger wing coverts appear. The feathering continues until the breast and under parts are covered, when the tail appears. At this time there are no feathers on the rump or on the head or neck. In the next stage feathers have appeared on the occiput and on the auriculars and are also extending up the neck. At the same time the tips of the back feathers have become somewhat worn, so that the colored margins are narrower and the black more prominent. The wing coverts are also to some extent worn on their tips. When the bill is an inch long the down has nearly all disappeared, and when it has entirely gone the birds appear in small flocks on the beaches, the young generally keeping together. Then another change takes place, for the entire plumage now gives way to another, that in which the bird passes the winter. A few late July, immature birds show the beginning, for No. 118832, im. ♂, July 29, has a few new feathers on the middle of the back and on the scapulars. They soon extend all over the back, so that specimens collected up to August 10 have many of the new whitish feathers on that region. The contrast is striking between these feathers, the latest being of an almost even shade of pale plumbean with darker centers and generally with a narrow white margin. There are no specimens to show the complete change, but it is probable that these young birds remain on the islands until it is completed. By the middle of June the adults have fully changed to the breeding plumage, but on some specimens a few feathers of the previous winter's plumage persist much later. Thus on many specimens some alternate feathers of the scapulars and tertials are of the previous winter's well-worn plumage. In fact, few specimens are free from these old feathers. Soon after the middle of July the new plumage of the next winter begins to appear. At first a few feathers show about the breast, then on the scapulars, thence up the neck and over the head, so that by the 10th of August they have changed one-half. It would thus appear that before this species leaves the islands they assume entirely their new dress. And at this season, August 10, old and young flock together for the first time, and confine themselves to the sand beaches and surf margins about the islands for a few weeks, when they take flight by the 1st or 5th of September, and disappear until the opening of the new season.

The Pribilof sandpiper is much paler in the juvenal plumage and grayer in the winter plumage than the Aleutian.

Food.—Preble and McAtee (1923) report on the contents of 192 stomachs, as follows:

The articles of food composing more than 1 per cent of the total were: Mollusks, 32.63 per cent; crustaceans, 29.15 per cent; flies (Diptera), 23.49 per cent; beetles, 10.29 per cent; marine worms, 1.27 per cent; and vegetable matter, chiefly algae, 1.21 per cent. The vegetable matter, besides algae, included bits of moss and a few seeds of grass, lupine, violet, crowberry, and bottle brush.

Behavior.—Referring to the habits of Pribilof sandpipers, Mr. Palmer (1899) says:

They appear stupid when solitary and without a family, and will stand perfectly still, eying one from a little eminence. Occasionally we are startled by a loud *druuett* from the side of a sand dune, and I was at a loss for some time to discover the owner of this most unmusical sound, which finally turned out to be an individual of this species standing motionless and watching us. It would seem impossible for this sound to have issued from this bird if I had not seen it in the act. These sandpipers have the habit in common with others of their kind of suddenly elevating the wing directly over the back. Often when alighting on the tundra, as soon as they stopped up went one wing, followed soon after, perhaps, by the other. Often while watching a flock on the lagoon beach first one would elevate a wing, then another; it was always the near wing which went up first. I never saw a bird elevate the off wing first. I know of no reason for their doing so. They are tame. I have walked up to a flock of about 50, and with care could drive them before me for some distance before they took flight, being but a few feet away. They are often seen feeding in the water up to their breasts, and seem to take delight in it. They swim readily, but not often. On June 30 I saw one fly out to a stone in a pool, and after gathering all the food possible it deliberately swam to another, and having visited each stone in the same way flew back to the shore and then bathed itself, occasionally taking a swim.

Voice.—Mr. Hanna (1921) describes the notes of this bird as follows:

If a person climbs to the sandpiper country on St. George during May or June one of his first surprises will be a series of notes very much like those of the flicker, a full deep whistle repeated in the same pitch about a dozen times in quick succession. The bird utters this while on the wing, most likely when it is coming toward the intruder with great speed. When close by it wheels and settles lightly on a nearby hummock or "niggerhead." One wing will be held vertically extended for a few seconds after alighting and may be flashed at short intervals thereafter. Another note for which I have no descriptive language always reminded me of the sound of tree frogs. It is the note usually given when the birds are on the ground. While neither can be called a song they are very attractive and pleasant to the listener and most surprising to one familiar with the "peep peep" of sandpipers in winter.

Field marks.—In winter the Pribilof sandpiper looks much like the purple sandpiper; it frequents similar haunts and has much the same habits. But its summer plumage, with its rufous upper parts and mottled under parts, is strikingly different. It resembles the Aleutian sandpiper in all plumages, but it is decidedly larger and, in summer, its upper parts are lighter rufous and there is more white in the under parts.

Fall.—According to Preble and McAtee (1923):

About the middle of July, when the nesting birds are freed from family cares, they begin to resort to the beaches to feed, and at night gather in flocks to roost on some favorite rocky point. Later the young join the adults and the flocks increase in size through August. About August 9 the birds began to be common about the beaches, the flocks there apparently being in excess of the number breeding on the islands, and in all probability, therefore, comprised in part of migrants from other breeding stations. They continued to be abundant until my departure on the last of August.

The Pribilof sandpiper is too rare and beautiful to be treated as a game bird, but Mr. Hanna (1921) writes:

The birds possess some economic importance to the natives of the Pribilofs, and they have occasionally been eaten in the officers' messes. Their habit of congregating in fairly compact flocks and their fearless unassuming nature make them easy targets. For this reason close watch should be kept of the numbers returning annually, and should any noticeable diminution take place strict prohibitive measures can and should be invoked. This is possible because the islands are under strict governmental control as regards all wild life. Because of its limited range it would not be a difficult matter to completely exterminate the species. Special protective measures at this time, however, are not believed to be essential because there is even less hunting now than there has been for fifty or more years. The introduction of livestock and reindeer for fresh food removes in large measure the necessity for shooting, and the native is ordinarily too indolent to hunt unless he has to do so for food.

DISTRIBUTION

Range.—Known only from the islands in Bering Sea and the coast of Alaska.

Breeding range.—The Pribilof sandpiper breeds on the Pribilof Islands (St. Paul and St. George Islands) and north in Bering Sea to St. Matthew Island, Hall Island, and St. Lawrence Island.

Winter range.—The winter range is imperfectly known, but it has been taken in this season at Portage Bay, Alaska, and probably occupies much of the Alaskan coast southeastward to (rarely) the Lynn Canal.

Migration.—They have been noted in spring to arrive at St. Paul Island March 5; Nushagak, Alaska, April 1 to 14; St. George Island April 23; at St. Paul Island April 24; and Point Dall, Alaska, May 23.

Late departures in the fall have been observed at St. George Island, October 3; and St. Paul Island November 16.

Early fall arrivals have been noted on the Alaskan coast at Igiak Bay, July 23; Tigalda Island, August 5; Unimak, August 14; and Dexter, Norton Sound, August 29.

Egg dates.—Pribilof Island: 32 records, May 6 to July 2; 16 records, May 30 to June 11.

ARQUATELLA PTILOCNEMIS COUESI (Ridgway)

ALEUTIAN SANDPIPER

HABITS

I prefer the above scientific name to the Check List name, because I can not believe that the Aleutian sandpiper is a subspecies of the purple sandpiper. The Aleutian sandpiper was originally described by Robert Ridgway (1880) as a distinct species. Later it was treated, and still stands on our Check List, as a subspecies of the purple sandpiper, because it somewhat resembles it in its winter plumage. In Mr. Ridgway's (1919) latest work, he treats it as a subspecies of the Pribilof sandpiper, a closely related form, which had been previously described; he there describes it as "similar to *A. p. ptilocnemis* but decidedly smaller and much darker in color; the summer plumage with blackish and rusty or cinnamon-rufous predominating on back and scapulars, and all the colors much darker and more extended. Very similar in winter plumage to *A. maritima*, but summer plumage and young very different, both being conspicuously marked with rusty on back and scapulars, and the summer plumage with breast conspicuously blotched or clouded with dusky."

Among a series of 11 birds of this species, which we collected on Attu Island, at the extreme western end of the Aleutian Chain, on June 23, 1911, are two birds which closely resemble *ptilocnemis* in color, but in size are typical of *couesi*. At least one of them was a breeding bird, the parent of a brood of downy young, and doubtless both of them were summer resident birds. Dr. Ernst Hartert (1920) has described the resident bird of the Commander Islands as a distinct subspecies, under the name *Erolia maritima quarta*, of which he says: "In full summer plumage the feather-edgings are broader than in any other form and brighter, more rusty red, so that the rusty red seems to predominate on the whole of the upper parts." This description seems to fit our two birds from Attu Island very well; so that, if *quarta* is a recognizable form, as it seems to be, this subspecies should be added to our North American list. The birds could easily fly across from the Commander Islands to Attu Island and establish themselves there.

Spring.—The spring migration of this sandpiper is not extensive. Many birds have remained all winter on or near their breeding grounds in the Aleutian Islands; others have wintered along the coast as far south as Washington. D. E. Brown tells me that they remain on Destruction Island until May 1 and that they have been seen on Forrester Island as late as June 15. H. S. Swarth (1911) found them "very abundant" on Kuiu Island during his stay there from April 25 to May 6; he writes:

In company with the black turnstone and some other waders, they frequented the broad mud flats, which, at low tide, extend over hundreds of acres at this point. As the tide advanced their feeding grounds became more and more restricted, until, as the last available spot was covered, the whole flock departed, with roar of wings, to some jutting rocks at the mouth of the bay, there to remain, preening their plumage and resting, until the receding waters again exposed the mud banks. The flocks seen at this place comprised many hundred individuals, and it is curious that the species was observed absolutely nowhere else.

Herbert W. Brandt says in his notes from Hooper Bay:

The Aleutian sandpiper is a common transient visitor in the vicinity of Point Dall and is said by the natives to be a breeding bird in the mountain fastnesses of Cape Romanzoff. This species was first identified by us on May 18, but it may have arrived a few days earlier because up to that time we did not suspect its presence. It associated itself with the red-backed sandpiper, to which in the field it has a marked superficial resemblance and in consequence we may have overlooked it. These birds at that time travelled in bands of from 20 to 40 individuals and at low tide fed on the ice-bound sea beach that was then exposed, but when the high water came in and up to the wall of shore ice, thus covering their feeding grounds, they moved back along the open river margins and marshy pond borders. From May 23 to May 28 they were very common, when suddenly they departed, only to reappear in early July. The natives are very positive in their assertions that this island dweller breeds in the rugged mountains about Cape Romanzoff, but as we did not visit that area we could not authenticate their statements, nor did we learn anything of its nidification.

Lucien M. Turner (1886) writes:

The Aleutian sandpiper arrives at St. Michaels early in May of each year, and in considerable numbers, being generally, on their arrival, in the dark plumage, which is changed for the summer by the first of June on this locality. On their appearance they are strictly littoral-maritime, resorting to the larger bowlders and rocky shelves covered with seaweed, among which these birds industriously search for slugs and other marine worms. Usually several birds are together, rarely singly, and seldom over 8 or 10 in a flock.

Dr. Leonhard Stejneger (1885) says that, in the Commander Islands:

In March their ranks are reinforced by newcomers which have wintered on more hospitable shores, and in the latter part of the month enormous flocks of 500 or more swarm along the beach, especially on the north shore. About one month later the great flocks dissolve into small companies, which, following the water courses, disperse over the whole island, settling in pairs on suitable places at the beaches, on the tundras, or on the mountain plateaus, this bird being in fact one of the most numerous and the most equally distributed species of land birds on the islands.

Courtship.—We frequently observed the charming song flight of this sandpiper in the Aleutian Islands. The birds were especially abundant on Tanaga Island, where we found them nesting on the little knolls or hummocks on the tundra in a large alluvial plain back of the beach hillocks. The males were very active and noisy, indulging in their hovering song flights, rising 30 or 40 feet in the air and fluttering down while pouring out a delightful twittering song. Also, while flying about or while standing on some prominent hummock, they gave their loud, musical melodious calls of the upland plover; these loud notes were not heard anywhere except on their breeding grounds and were probably notes of greeting or of warning to their mates. Doctor Stejneger (1885) writes:

It was in the late afternoon of the 28th of April, 1883, that I first witnessed this singing performance of the sandpiper. The bird rose from the *Rhododendron* tundra on the northern slope of Kamennij Valley, and while flying about on quivering wings, sometimes remaining quite still in the air, it uttered a loud, agreeable, and melodious twitter, which really must be called a "song," whereupon, with outstretched wings, it descended obliquely, seating itself upon the top of a tussock. Sitting there, with puffed plumage and pendant wings, it produced a loud "bleating," so much like that of *Gallinago gallinago* as to completely convince me that the analogous note of the latter is produced by the throat in exactly the same manner. During the "bleating" the whole bird was quivering with a tremulous motion as if in a high state of excitement. The voice was slightly more melodious than that of the snipe.

Nesting.—While wandering over the foothills of Kiska Island on June 17, 1911, I found my first nest of the Aleutian sandpiper. I was crossing a flat place, high up on a hill, covered with moss and scanty growth of grass, when the bird fluttered off almost underfoot, feigning lameness. The nest was a deep hollow in the moss, 3 inches in diameter and fully 2 inches deep, partially concealed by a few blades of scanty grass, and lined with dead leaves, a few straws, and a few feathers of the bird. The four eggs were only slightly incubated. I found a similar nest, containing three small, downy young, on Attu Island on June 23; the nest was on a little hummock on a hillside, a deep hollow, lined with dead leaves and bits of straw. It was the male bird that flew from the nest in both cases.

Austin H. Clark (1910) found a nest on Attu Island on the side of a mountain, 700 feet or more above the valley and near an extensive patch of snow. Alfred M. Bailey (1925) found a nest at Emma Harbor, Siberia, on July 4, 1921, containing three young and an egg; the nest was "on the shores of the bay, in gravel along the beach." He also found several nests the following season near Wales, Alaska; "the nesting sites varied from exposed depressions in the moss to well-concealed dried grass." A set of eggs in Edward Arnold's collection, taken by Sheldon and Lamont on Montague Island, Alaska, June 22, 1916, came from a nest "on débris just above tidewater."

Eggs.—The Aleutian sandpiper almost invariably lays four eggs, although five have been found. These are ovate pyriform in shape and have a slight gloss. The ground color is " olive buff " or " deep olive buff." They are heavily, boldly, and irregularly blotched, chiefly about the larger end, with a few scattering smaller spots. The markings are in dark browns, "chestnut brown," " burnt umber," and "seal brown," varying with the thickness of the pigment. There are underlying blotches of "brownish drab," producing very handsome eggs. They can not always be distinguished with certainty from eggs of the Pribilof sandpiper, as they vary greatly in size; they average smaller, but the measurements overlap widely. The measurements of 50 eggs average 38 by 26.6 millimeters; the eggs showing the four extremes measure 43.2 by 26.8, 39.4 by 28, 35 by 26.3, and 37.3 by 24.1 millimeters.

Young.—Incubation is apparently performed by both sexes, and both assist in the care of the young. The birds that I flushed from my two nests, one with eggs and one with young, both proved to be males. Mr. Turner (1886) says:

The males are much devoted to their mates while incubating, and I have every reason to believe that the male does the greater part of the labor of incubating, as they were the ones generally found either on or near the nests. When alighting near the nest either sex has the habit of raising its wings perpendicularly and slowly folding them, all the while uttering a trilling peep, continued for several seconds.

The parents are very devoted to their young, employing the usual tactics to divert the attention of the intruder, stumbling and fluttering over the ground, as if both legs and wings were broken. The young leave the nest as soon as they are strong enough to run, but remain with their parents until they are fully fledged in their first winter or juvenal plumage and ready to fly in August.

Plumages.—The downy young Aleutian resembles, in color pattern, the young purple sandpiper, but can easily be recognized by its warmer and richer browns. The upper half of the head is " warm buff," shading off to " pale buff " on the lores and cheeks and to pure white on the throat and neck. A median black stripe is broad on the crown, tapering to a point at the bill; loral and malar black stripes converge at the bill; the rest of the upper head is spotted or striped with black. The nape is a mixture of dull buff and dusky. The back, wings, and thighs are variegated with black, " ochraceous tawny " and " warm buff," everywhere sprinkled with conspicuous dots, terminal tufts, of buffy white in an irregular pattern; there is a more or less well-defined black patch in the center of the back, varying in different individuals, centrally veiled with " burnt sienna " tips. The entire under parts are pure white.

In the juvenal plumage the center of the crown is blackish brown, with " ochraceous tawny " edgings; the rest of the crown and nape are " deep mouse gray "; the feathers of the back are brownish black, broadly edged with "tawny " or " ochraceous tawny "; the scapulars and all the wing coverts are deep sepia, broadly edged with colors varying from " tawny " to buffy white, whitest on the coverts; the under parts are white, with a broad band of pale buff across the throat and breast; the flanks are somewhat tinged with the same color; the throat, breast, and flanks are more or less heavily marked with median dusky streaks. This plumage is worn through July and part, or all, of August. The postjuvenal molt of the body plumage begins in some birds about the 1st of August, but in others not until two or three weeks later. This produces a first winter plumage similar to that of the adult, but distinguishable by the faded juvenal wing coverts and a few retained scapulars and tertials.

The partial prenuptial molt of both young birds and adults comes rather late in the spring, April and May, and involves the body plumage and some of the wing coverts and scapulars. Adults also have a complete postnuptial molt, beginning in August and lasting until October. The winter plumage is similar to that of the purple sandpiper, but it is conspicuously marked on the breast and flanks with large triangular or circular spots of dusky, whereas the purple sandpiper usually has a plain gray breast in winter.

Food.—Very little seems to be known about the food of the Aleutian sandpiper, but probably its diet is very similar to that of the purple sandpiper, which has similar feeding habits. Both species are fond of frequenting rocky shores and stony beaches, where they seem to be gleaning food. Doctor Stejneger (1885) has seen them "at low water eagerly picking up Gammarids among the stones close to the breakers." Bernard J. Bretherton (1896) writes:

Large flocks of these birds were seen during February, 1893, but were not met with during other winters. They were met with on a low sand bar, after a protracted storm which had thrown up millions of sand fleas, upon which they were feeding so industriously as to be easily approached and to which feast they returned several times, even after their ranks had been thinned by raking charges of fine shot.

Behavior.—In many ways the Aleutian sandpiper reminds one of its near relative, the purple sandpiper, but it is even tamer, less suspicious, and quieter in its movements. We had plenty of chances to get acquainted with it in the Aleutian Islands. We met it, and collected the first specimen of it, on the first island that we landed on, Akun Island, and after that we saw it on every island we visited, though it was much more abundant on the more western islands. These bleak islands, with their forbidding, rocky shores and stony beaches, washed with cold spray or enveloped in chilly fog, are the summer home of this hardy little "beach snipe," as it is called by the natives. It moves about so quietly and deliberately, and its colors match its surroundings so well, that we were constantly coming upon it unexpectedly. It was usually so intent on feeding that it paid no attention to passers-by; it was often necessary to back off to a reasonable distance before shooting one, and I shot several with squib charges in an auxiliary barrel. It is the tamest and most unsuspicious shore bird I have ever seen. On this point Mr. Turner (1886) says:

It is not at all shy, depending more on its color to hide by squatting among the crevices of the dark lava rocks and thus be unobserved. When cautiously approached, these birds generally run to the highest part of the rock or bowlder which they are on, then huddle together before taking flight the moment after. This habit allows them to be nearly all killed at a single discharge of the gun. The native boys, having observed this habit of these birds, procure a club about two feet long, and when the birds huddle together before taking flight the club is hurled in such manner as to sweep all the birds off the rock. This manner of procuring these birds is practiced by the western Aleut boys to a great degree.

Dr. E. W. Nelson (1887) writes:

A pair were found feeding on a series of bare, jagged rocks, over which the spray flew in a dense cloud as every wave beat at the foot of the rocky shore. I shot one of them, and the survivor merely flew up and stood eyeing me silently from the top of a low cliff 20 or 25 feet overhead until it, too, fell a victim. Later in the day another was seen near the border of a small lake in the interior of the island. It ran nimbly on before me, over the mossy hillocks, stopping every few feet and half turning to watch my movements, just as a spotted sandpiper would do under the circumstances. When driven to take wing, it flew a short distance, with the same peculiar down-curved wings and style of flight as has the spotted sandpiper.

Hamilton M. Laing (1925) says that "on one occasion one was seen to swim nimbly from one rock to another rather than fly."

Voice.—Except on its breeding grounds, we considered the Aleutian sandpiper a very quiet and silent bird. Its twittering flight song is a part of the nuptial ceremony, and it was only on its nesting grounds that we heard the loud, musical, flutelike, whistling notes so suggestive of the melodious calls of the upland plover. Doctor Nelson (1887) describes what may be the same notes, as follows:

While on the wing it uttered a rather low but clear and musical *tweo-tweo-tweo.* When feeding it had a note something like a call of the *Colaptes auratus,* and which may be represented by the syllables *clu-clu-clu.*

Mr. Clark (1910) also says:

The cry is loud and clear, bearing a striking resemblance to the call of the flicker.

Field marks.—In winter the Aleutian sandpiper might easily be mistaken for a purple sandpiper, which it closely resembles in appearance, haunts, and behavior, but the winter ranges of the two species are widely separated. From the Pribilof sandpiper it differs in being decidedly smaller, and in summer it is much darker, with less rufous above and more black below.

Fall.—The Aleutian sandpiper withdraws in the fall from the northern portions of its breeding range in Alaska and Siberia, and it may be that the birds which breed farthest north are the ones which migrate farthest south to spend the winter, for the species is resident throughout the year in the Aleutian Islands. In the Norton Sound region it evidently occurs only as a migrant from northern Alaska and Siberia. Doctor Nelson (1887) says:

Early in August, however, I was pleased to find it abundant in parties of from five to thirty or forty about outlying islets and along rugged portions of the shore. During each of the four succeeding seasons the same experience was repeated, and the last of July or first of August I was certain to find the numbers of them in the situations mentioned, where earlier in the season not one was to be found. They always remained until the middle of October, when the beaches became covered with ice and they were forced to seek a milder climate. The 1st of October, as the first snowstorms begin, these birds desert the more exposed islets and beaches for the inner bays and sandy beaches, where their habits are like those of other sandpipers in similar situations.

Winter.—This hardy sandpiper is well known to winter regularly and abundantly in the Aleutian and Commander Islands. According to notes received from D. E. Brown, it reaches the coast of Washington as early as October 1, where it spends the winter in

Grays Harbor and Jefferson Counties and on the outer islands.   Carl
Lien's notes, from Destruction Island, give it as a " common winter
resident. A flock of probably 50 spend the winter.   Nearly always
found in company with turnstones and surfbirds, and together with
these birds confine themselves entirely to the reefs."

DISTRIBUTION

Range.—The northeastern corner of Siberia, west coast of Alaska
and adjacent islands, including the Aleutians, south (rarely) to
northwestern Oregon.

Breeding range.—The breeding range of the Aleutian sandpiper
extends north to eastern Siberia (Emma Harbor) and Alaska (Cape
Prince of Wales).   East to Alaska (Cape Prince of Wales, Colville
River, and Port Moller); and the Shumagin Islands.   South to the
Shumagin Islands; the western part of the Alaskan Peninsula
(Muller Bay and Morzhovia Bay); and the Aleutian Islands (Una-
laska, Atka, Tanaga, Kiska, Agutta, and Attu Islands).   West to
the Aleutian Islands (Attu) and eastern Siberia (Emma Harbor).
The species also has been detected in summer at St. Lawrence and
St. Matthew Islands and at other points on the mainland of Alaska
(Point Dall, Pastolik, St. Michael, Nulato, and Port Clarence).

Winter range.—Resident throughout much of its range, but also
south in winter, along the Alaskan and British Columbian coasts
and as far as Washington (Destruction Island).

Migration.—The migrations performed by the Aleutian sandpiper
are very limited.   In the vicinity of St. Michael, Alaska, flocks will
appear as early as August 15, occasionally remaining until October
15.   They have been noted on the Asiatic side of Bering Sea at
Providence Bay in June, at East Cape in July, at Plover Bay in
September, and on Bering Island as late as October 24.

Spring migrants have been observed to reach Point Etolin, Alaska,
as early as April 8 and Bering Island April 24.   Spring departures
from the southern part of the winter range have been noted as late
as: Destruction Island, May 1; Forrester Island, May 7; and Admiralty Island, May 14.   An early fall arrival at Craig, Alaska, is
August 6 and at Destruction Island October 1.

Casual records.—This species has been collected or observed outside of its known normal range on a few occasions: Washington,
Point Chehalis, November 6, 1917, and Dungeness Spit, March 4,
1916; Oregon, Cape Meares, December 31, 1912, and March 18, 1913;
these may prove to be regular winter resorts.

Egg dates.—Alaska: 18 records, June 3 to July 24; 9 records,
June 15 to 22.

PISOBIA ACUMINATA (Horsfield)

SHARP-TAILED SANDPIPER

HABITS

This is a bird which few of us have been privileged to see. From its summer home in northeastern Siberia it migrates south to Japan, the Malay Archipelago, Australia, and New Zealand. On the fall migration it visits the coast of northwestern Alaska frequently, perhaps regularly, and often commonly. It occurs regularly, sometimes abundantly, on the Pribilof Islands in the fall. In southern Alaska and farther south it occurs only as a rare straggler. A. W. Anthony (1922) took a young male near San Diego, California, on September 16, 1921.

Some European writers have called it the Siberian pectoral sandpiper, which its resemblance to our common bird of that name seems to warrant. It is so much like our pectoral sandpiper in appearance, behavior, and haunts, that it has probably often been overlooked; it may therefore occur on our northwestern coast much oftener than we suspect.

Nesting.—The sharp-tailed sandpiper is supposed to breed in Mongolia and eastern Siberia; it has been seen and collected on its breeding grounds in northeastern Siberia, Cape Wankarem, the Chuckchi Peninsula, and the Kolyma Delta, but apparently its nest has never been found and its eggs are entirely unknown.

Plumages.—The downy young is entirely unknown. This sandpiper is handsomely and richly colored in any plumage, but the rich buff and bright browns of the juvenal plumage are particularly noticeable. The body plumage is molted in the fall, the wings and tail in late winter, and the body plumage is partially molted again in the spring. The plumages are well described in the manuals.

Food.—Preble and McAtee (1923) report on the food of this species, as follows:

Eight well-filled and one nearly empty stomach of the sharp-tailed sandpiper are available to illustrate the food habits. This number is too small to furnish reliable results, and too great dependence must not be placed in data as to the relative ranks of food items as here stated. The percentages found for the limited material, then, are flies (Diptera), 39.1 per cent; crustaceans, 18.1 per cent; mollusks, 14.2 per cent; caddisflies, 11.8 per cent; beetles, 8.8 per cent; Hymenoptera, 1.8 per cent; and vegetable matter, 3.9 per cent. Mr. Hanna notes that flocks of this species frequent the seal-killing fields, feeding on fly maggots, a statement receiving confirmation from stomach analysis.

Behavior.—Dr. E. W. Nelson (1887) tells us a little about the habits of this rare species, as follows:

They were nearly always associated with *maculata*, whose habits they shared to a great extent. When congregated about their feeding places they united into flocks of from ten into fifty, but single birds were frequently flushed from grassy spots. Their motions on the wing are very similar to those of the latter, and they were rarely shy. On October 1, 1880, they were found scattered singly over the marsh, and arose 30 to 40 yards in advance, and made off with a twisting flight, uttering at the same time a short, soft, metallic *pleep, pleep*, and pursuing an erratic, circuitous flight for a time they generally returned and settled near the spot whence they started. On the shore of Siberia, near North Cape, we found these birds very common, scattered over damp grass flats near the coast, the 1st of August, 1881. The ground was covered with reindeer tracks, and among these the sharp-tailed snipe were seen seeking their food. They were very unsuspicious and allowed us to pass close to them, or circled close about us. From their movements and other circumstances I judged that this district formed part of their breeding grounds, whence they reach the neighboring coast of Alaska in fall.

Field marks.—The sharp-tailed sandpiper most closely resembles the pectoral sandpiper, but it can often be recognized in the field by the more ruddy color of the upper parts. Most of the feathers of the shoulders, scapulars and secondaries are broadly edged with chestnut; these edgings are paler in winter. The bright chestnut crown, streaked with black, and the ruddy brown suffusion on the chest and sides, might be recognized under favorable circumstances.

Fall.—Not much seems to be known about the spring migration, but the fall migration is fairly well marked. Doctor Nelson (1887) says:

They usually make their first appearance on the shore of Norton Sound the last of August, and in a few days become very common. They sometimes remain up to the 12th of October, and I have seen them searching for food along the tide line when the ground was covered with 2 inches of snow. When feeding along the edges of the tide-creeks they may almost be knocked over with a paddle, and when a flock is fired into it returns again and again.

It is a regular fall migrant in the Pribilof Islands, between August 17 and November 9, where it associates in large flocks with the pectoral sandpiper on the seal-killing fields.

Doctor Stejneger (1885) writes:

Of this species I only obtained young specimens on Bering Island during the autumnal migration of 1882. From the middle of September and during the following three weeks they were observed both on the tundra near the great lake and on the rocky beach of the ocean searching for Gammarids. They were very shy and mostly single or in small families. Larger flocks were never seen.

From the Commander Islands the main flight continues on down the Asiatic coast, through Japan, China, and the Malay Archipelago, to New Zealand and Australia, where it spends the winter.

Winter.—W. B. Alexander writes to me that this is—

One of the commonest northern breeding birds which visits Australia. My earliest record of their arrival is August 31, 1925, at Cairns, North Queensland, and my latest record April 21, 1922, at Rockhampton, Queensland. From September to March they are to be found in small flocks throughout the coastal districts of Australia on the shores of estuaries and lakes and in fresh-water swamps. In October, 1922, I saw a flock of four on the open country near a dam on Alice Downs Station, near Blackall, central Queensland, a locality about 350 miles from the coast. Mr. D. W. Gaukrodger subsequently secured an excellent photograph of three of these birds at the same dam.

DISTRIBUTION

Range.—The sharp-tailed sandpiper breeds in the northeastern part of Asia—so far as known, in northeastern Siberia—wintering south to New Guinea, Tonga Islands, Australia, and New Zealand. Occurs in migration in Kamchatka, China, and Japan.

During fall migration it is of regular though rare occurrence in Alaska (Hotham Inlet, September 1, 1880; Port Clarence, September 9, 1880; Nome, September 2 to 16, 1910; St. Michael, September 16, 1877, August 29 and September 11, 1879, September 18, 21, and 24, 1899; Bethel, September 30 and October 1, 1914; St. Paul Island, August 17, 1897, September 7 and 13, 1910, September 14 and 20 and October 12, 1914; St. George Island, October 3, 1899; and Valdez, September 18, 1908).

Casual records.—The species is accidental in British Columbia (Massett, December 27, 1897, and Comox, October 4, 1903); Washington (mouth of the Nooksack River, September 2, 1892); England (Breydon, Norfolk, August, 1892, and Yarmouth, September, 1848 [?]); and the Hawaiian Islands (Laysan [specimen in museum at Bremen], a second specimen near Honolulu, a third specimen was collected on Maui [Henshaw], and Bartsch secured two specimens and saw others on Sand Island, November 8, 1907). One was taken near San Diego, Calif., on September 16, 1921.

PISOBIA MACULATA (Vieillot)

PECTORAL SANDPIPER

HABITS

This familiar sandpiper is well known as a migrant throughout most of North America, especially east of the Rocky Mountains, as it travels on its long journeys between the Arctic tundras, where it breeds, and its winter home in southern South America. It is more popular among gunners than the other small sandpipers, to whom it is known by several names. It is called "jack snipe" on account of its resemblance in appearance and habits to the Wilson snipe. It deserves the name, "grass bird," because it usually frequents grassy meadows. The name, "creaker," "creeker," or "Krieker," may have been derived from its reedy notes, from its haunts along the muddy banks of creeks, or from the German word *Kriecher*, on account of its crouching habits.

Spring.—The northward migration must start from Argentina in February, for it reaches Texas and Louisiana early in March, and I have seen it in Florida as early as March 14. On the other hand it has been taken at Mendoza, Argentina, as late as March 26. The main flight passes through the United States during March and April, but I have seen it in Texas as late as May 17. During May the migration is at its height in Canada and before the end of that month it reaches its summer home. William Rowan tells me that it is always very abundant in Alberta during May and that the males come alone at first, then mixed flocks, and finally only females. H. B. Conover writes to me that " these sandpipers seemed to arrive at Point Dall (Alaska) all at once. Up to May 20 none had been seen, but on the 21st they were found to be common all over the tundra. Immediately on arrival the males started their booming courtship." John Murdoch (1885) says that, at Point Barrow:

They arrive about the end of May or early in June, and frequent the small ponds and marshy portions of the tundra along the shore, sometimes associated with other small waders, especially with the buff-breasted sandpipers on the high banks of Nunava. Early in the season they are frequently in large-sized flocks feeding together around and in the Eskimo village at Cape Smythe, but later become thoroughly scattered all over the tundra.

Courtship.—The wonderful and curious courtship of the pectoral sandpiper has been well described by several writers. Dr. E. W. Nelson's (1887) pleasing and graphic account of it is well worth quoting in full; he writes:

The night of May 24 I lay wrapped in my blanket, and from the raised flap of the tent looked out over as dreary a cloud-covered landscape as can be imagined. The silence was unbroken save by the tinkle and clinking of the disintegrating ice in the river, and at intervals by the wild notes of some restless loon, which arose in a hoarse reverberating cry and died away in a strange gurgling sound. As my eyelids began to droop and the scene to become indistinct, suddenly a low, hollow, booming note struck my ear and sent my thoughts back to a spring morning in northern Illinois, and to the loud vibrating tones of the prairie chickens. Again the sound arose nearer and more distinct, and with an effort I brought myself back to the reality of my position and, resting upon one elbow, listened. A few seconds passed and again arose the note; a moment later and, gun in hand, I stood outside the tent. The open flat extended away on all sides, with apparently not a living creature near. Once again the note was repeated close by, and a glance revealed its author. Standing in the thin grasses 10 or 15 yards from me, with its throat inflated until it was as large as the rest of the bird, was a male *A. maculata*. The succeeding days afforded opportunity to observe the bird as it uttered its singular notes under a variety of situations and at various hours of the day or during the light Arctic night. The note is deep, hollow, and resonant, but at the same time liquid and musical, and may be represented by a repetition of the syllables *too-u, too-u, too-u, too-u, too-u, too-u, too-u, too-u.* Before the bird utters these notes it fills its esophagus with air to such an extent that the breast and throat is inflated to twice or more its natural size, and the great air sac thus formed gives the peculiar resonant quality to the note. The skin of the throat and breast becomes very flabby and loose at this season, and its inner surface is covered with small globular masses of fat. When not inflated, the skin loaded with this extra weight and with a slightly serous suffusion which is present hangs down in a pendulous flap or fold exactly like a dewlap, about an inch and a half wide. The esophagus is very loose and becomes remarkably soft and distensible, but is easily ruptured in this state, as I found by dissection. In the plate accompanying this report the extent and character of this inflation, unique at least among American waders, is shown. The bird may frequently be seen running along the ground close to the female, its enormous sac inflated, and its head drawn back and the bill pointing directly forward, or, filled with spring-time vigor, the bird flits with slow but energetic wingstrokes close along the ground, its head raised high over the shoulders and the tail hanging almost directly down. As it thus flies it utters a succession of the hollow, booming notes, which have a strange ventriloquial quality. At times the male rises 20 or 30 yards in the air and inflating its throat glides down to the ground with its sac hanging below, as is shown in the accompanying plate. Again he crosses back and forth in front of the female, puffing his breast out and bowing from side to side, running here and there, as if intoxicated with passion. Whenever he pursues his love-making, his rather low but pervading note swells and dies in musical cadences, which form a striking part of the great bird chorus heard at this season in the north.

Mr. Conover (notes) adds the following:

When the male rises in the air to boom, in sailing to the ground he throws his wings up over his back, much in the same manner as tame pigeons when descending from a height; also a male which flew by with pouch extended was noticed to jerk his head up and down as he gave his call. The bill was partly open and he gave the appearance of swallowing air to inflate his throat. As it is the esophagus which is inflated and not the windpipe, this in all probability is what he does.

S. A. Buturlin (1907) gives a somewhat different account of it, as observed by him in Siberia, as follows:

One would every now and then stretch both wings right over its back, and afterwards commence a grotesque sort of dance, hopping alternately on each leg; another would inflate its gular pouch and run about, crouching down to the ground, or would fly up to about a hundred feet in the air, then inflate its pouch and descend slowly and obliquely to the ground on extended wings. All these performances were accompanied by a strange hollow sound, not very loud when near, but audible at some distance, even as far as 500 yards. These notes are very difficult to locate, and vary according to the distance. When near they are tremulous booming sounds something like the notes of a frog, and end in clear sounds like those caused by the bursting of water bubbles in a copper vessel.

Nesting.—Mr. Murdoch (1885) says:

The nest is always built in the grass, with a decided preference for high and dry localities like the banks of gulleys and streams. It was sometimes placed at the edge of a small pool, but always in grass and in a dry place, never in the black clay and moss, like the plover and buff-breasted sandpipers, or in the marsh, like the phalaropes. The nest was like that of the other waders, a depression in the ground lined with a little dry grass.

A set in my collection, taken by F. S. Hersey, near St. Michael, Alaska, was in a slight hollow on the open tundra with no concealment. And a set in the Herbert Massey collection, taken near Point Barrow by E. A. McIlhenny, came from " a slight hollow lined with dry grass, in the dry, gray moss of the tundra."

Herbert W. Brandt in his manuscript notes says:

The pectoral sandpiper usually chooses for its homesite the upland rolling tundra, but an occasional isolated pair was found on the dry grass lands of the tide flats. This species builds the most substantial of any of the shore-birds nests that we met with at Hooper Bay, for even after it was removed from the grassy cavity in which it was built the nest would often hold firmly together. The birds showed exceptional skill in the concealment of their homes and consequently they were very difficult to find for they chose a tract where the curly bunch grass grew abundantly and under its domed protection they constructed an excavation deep in the moss. Here a substantial nest is fashioned of grasses and tediously lined or rather filled with small crisp leaves of the low perennial plants that there, in a dwarf creeping form, are the only representatives of the great inland forests. The dimensions vary between the following extremes: Inside diameter 3 to 3½ inches; depth 1¾ to 2½ inches; and outside depth 3½ to 5 inches. We never observed other than the female carrying on the loving duties of incubation and seldom indeed was the male even in close attendance. The female is very difficult to approach on the nest because she invariably leaves it before the ornithologist draws near and consequently we spent many hours endeavoring to watch the shy bird return to her nest.

The behavior of parent birds about the nests seems to be variable. W. Sprague Brooks (1915) says:

On approaching the vicinity of the nest the bird would leave it quietly and walk slowly about feeding and showing no excitement whatever. This happened several times until I decided to watch the bird and see if by any chance she might have a nest. In a short time she walked to a bunch of grass a few feet from me and settled on the nest. Even while I was packing away the eggs she showed no concern. I had precisely the same experience with the other two nests.

On the other hand, Alfred M. Bailey (1926) writes:

On July 3 Hendee flushed a female from a set of four slightly incubated eggs. "The nest," he states, "was in a patch of marsh grass, similar to the location usually chosen by the phalaropes, except that the ground was not wet. The female fluttered away to a distance of about 30 feet and went through a remarkable performance in her attempt to decoy me from the nest. She crept about among the hummocks in a very unbirdlike fashion, uttering all the time a mouselike squeaking."

Eggs.—Mr. Brandt in his manuscript notes has described the eggs so well that I can not do better than to quote him, as follows:

The eggs of the pectoral sandpiper are of particular interest because they are perhaps the most beautiful of the many handsome shore-bird eggs that are found in the Hooper Bay region. Their rich and contrasting colors, their bold splashed markings, and high luster make them veritable gems of oological perfection. In all nests that came under our observation four eggs constituted the complement, and these generally nestled points together amid the crisp leafy lining of their birthplace, standing most often at an obtuse angle to the horizontal. In outline they range from subpyriform to ovate pyriform. The exterior of the shell has a smooth, almost polished surface that reflects in many eggs a high luster. The ground color varies considerably from dull white to "cream buff" and even to "deep olive buff," but in all sets I have seen the ground color and markings follow the same shades and types in the same set of eggs. The surface markings are bold and individual, and appear as if they were daubed with a paint brush. These large rich spots are elongated and are placed parallel to the long axis of the egg, showing but little tendency to spiral. The heaviest markings are at the larger end, often merging into a large "chocolate" blotch, and in one case this rich blot of color covered more than a fourth of the egg. The color of the markings ranges from "walnut brown" and "sepia" to "chocolate" and "blackish brown," with "chocolate" the predominating shade. The underlying spots are prominent and numerous on some eggs, while on others they are almost wanting. They vary from "pearl gray" to "violet gray," with an occasional egg inclined to "Isabella color." In fact, each different clutch of eggs exhibits some individual interesting peculiarity.

My only set, taken for me by Mr. Hersey, would fit the above description very well, but it is not particularly handsome. The ground color is dull white or "pale olive buff," which is more or less evenly marked with small blotches and spots of "bister" and "bone brown." Mr. Murdoch (1885) says that they "may be distinguished from those of the buff-breasted sandpiper, which they closely resemble, by their warmer color." The measurements of 116 eggs, in the United States National Museum and in Mr. Brandt's collection, average 36.5 by 25 millimeters; the eggs showing the four extremes measure **38.5** by 25, 38 by **27**, **34** by 24.9, and **35.5** by **24.5** millimeters.

Young.—Mr. Conover writes to me as follows:

The incubation period seems to run from 21. to 23 days. A nest found May 31 with the complete set of four eggs was hatched on the morning of June 21. Another nest containing four eggs, from which the old bird was flushed, was found on June 2 and hatched on June 25. The first young were found on June 21. Contrary to their habits when there were only eggs in the nest, the mothers now showed great concern for their young. At one time Murie caught some newly hatched young, and holding his hand containing them extended on the ground, induced the old bird to come up and brood the chicks. She was so tame that he caught and banded her without difficulty. The male seems to take no part on the incubation or care of the young. He was often seen to join a hen driven from the nest, but only for purposes of courtship, as he would start booming immediately and chase her about. Before the eggs began to hatch, male birds seemed to disappear from the tundra. There was never more than one bird seen with the young. Thirty days seemed to be about the time necessary for the chicks to mature, as by July 20 fully fledged young were seen commonly about the tundra.

Mr. Buturlin (1907) says:

When I approached the breeding ground the old birds flew to meet me, one after another, and wheeled around uttering low tremulous notes of various kinds. These calls were evidently meant for the young and had different meanings. When the female is with them (and you must sit watching for an hour or more to observe this), the little ones are somewhat shy and take refuge under her. If you make the slightest movement she flies up, uttering the usual *kirip*, and kicks the young forwards, never backwards, until they tumble head over heels 5 or 6 inches away. There they lie as if dead, but with open eyes, and the mother flies around uttering a low tremulous *kirip, kirip, trip, trrrrrr*, evidently meaning "lie quite still." Then she alights near the young and runs about feigning lameness, while trying in every way to make you attempt to capture her. If, however, you keep quite quiet she becomes reassured, approaches near to where her young are, and utters with tender modulations, *day-day-day, day-day-day*, which means evidently "all right, come here." Then the chicks commence to chirp *peep, peep, peeyp*, and run to their mother. On one occasion I observed all this at a distance of about 10 paces, and once I was only about 3 paces from them. The downy young know their mother's call *day-day-day* so well that on one occasion a young bird, which I was taking home in my butterfly net, when it heard a female call quite close to me, climbed out of the net to rejoin her.

Mr. Brandt in his manuscript notes writes:

The potential energy stored up in the small richly colored eggs of this northern sandpiper is almost beyond comprehension. The downy chicks, as soon as they are out of the shell, show wonderful activity. When they are but 30 minutes old, their apparently slight legs carry them over the ground with great rapidity. They know at birth how to hide among the hummocks and vegetation so as to defy the sharpest eyes. In three weeks they are awing and six weeks later they are off on their long journey to the south, crossing mighty mountain ridges, great stretches of land and of sea.

According to W. H. Hudson (1920), the pectoral sandpiper arrives in the La Plata region, in southern South America, about the end of August, and he writes:

Among these first comers there are some young birds, so immature, with threads of yellow down still adhering to the feathers of the head, and altogether weak in appearance, that one can scarcely credit the fact that so soon after being hatched they have actually performed the stupendous journey from the northern extremity of the North American continent to the Buenos-Ayrean pampas.

Plumages.—The young pectoral in down is a beauty and is distinctively colored. The forehead, back to the eyes, lores, sides of the head and neck, and the breast are from "cinnamon buff" to "cream buff," paling to white or grayish white on the throat and belly. There is a broad, black, median stripe from the crown to the bill, a narrow, black loral stripe, which is joined by another, still narrower, malar stripe under the eye, extending to the auriculars; below the ear is a dark-brown spot. In the center of the crown is a black spot, surrounded by a circle of buffy white dots; around this the crown is a mixture of black and "burnt sienna," bordered with buffy white, except in front; and around this border, or along each side of it, is a narrow stripe of blackish brown above the buffy superciliary stripe. The nape is grizzly brown, buff, and whitish. The back, wings, and thighs are variegated with black, "chestnut," and "burnt sienna," and decorated with small dots of buffy white in an irregular pattern.

The juvenal plumage is much like that of the summer adult, except that the feathers of the mantle, scapulars, and the median and lesser wing coverts are edged with brighter colors, "tawny," "ochraceous-buff," and creamy white; and the breast is more buffy or yellowish. This plumage is apparently worn all through the fall and winter or until the first prenuptial molt in February and March, when the body plumage is renewed. At the first postnuptial molt, the next summer, the young bird becomes indistinguishable from the adult, having molted the entire plumage.

Adults have a partial prenuptial molt in the spring, from February to June, which involves the body plumage, except the back and rump and some of the scapulars, tertials, and wing coverts. The complete postnuptial molt of adults is much prolonged; the body molt begins in August, but the wings are not molted until the bird reaches its winter home, beginning in October and often lasting until February. Two adult females taken by Doctor Wetmore (1926) on September 9 in Paraguay "were in worn breeding plumage with no indication of molt." And one shot in Uruguay February 8 had renewed all but a few feathers of the entire plumage, while a male taken the same day was molting its primaries. There is very little difference between the summer and winter plumages; the feather edgings of the upper parts are more rufous in summer and more ashy in winter.

Food.—According to Preble and McAtee (1923), the contents of 21 well-filled gizzards of this species consisted principally of "flies (Diptera), 54.5 per cent; amphipods, 22.3 per cent; vegetable matter, chiefly algae, 10.5 per cent; beetles, 8 per cent; Hymenoptera, 2.1 per cent; and bugs (Hemiptera), 1.3 per cent." Other things eaten were mites, spiders, and caddis fly larvae and a few seeds of grass, lupine, and violet. P. L. Hatch (1892) says that "their food is principally crickets in spring, interlarded with various dry-land larvae, small bettles, and ground worms. In the fall the grasshoppers are first chosen, after which crickets and whatever other insects prevail at this season." Birds taken by B. S. Bowdish (1902) in Porto Rico had eaten fiddler crabs. Pectoral sandpipers feed mainly in grassy meadows, more or less dry, and their food is chiefly insects.

Behavior.—On the grassy salt meadows, where we usually find it, I have often been impressed with the resemblance of this sandpiper and the Wilson snipe, both in appearance and in behavior. It is often found in wisps or scattered flocks, the individuals widely separated and crouching in the grass. Often it flushes close at hand with a startling harsh cry and dashes hurriedly away with a zig-zag flight. Sometimes it flutters away for only a short distance and drops quickly into the grass. Again it makes a long flight, circling high in the air and then pitches down suddenly in some distant part of the marsh, or perhaps near the starting point. Though erratic at first, the flight is swift and direct when well under way. They sometimes fly in flocks like other sandpipers, but more often they are flushed singly. They usually flock by themselves but are sometimes associated, purely fortuitously I believe, with other species that frequent similar feeding grounds, such as Wilson snipe, Baird, least or semipalmated sandpipers.

The pectoral sandpiper has another snipe-like habit of standing motionless in the grass, relying on its concealing coloration, where its striped plumage renders it almost invisible, even in plain sight. It moves about slowly while feeding, probing in the mud with rapid strokes. Often it stands perfectly still with its head held high, watching an intruder; the dark markings on its neck end abruptly on the white breast, breaking up the outline and helping the bird to fade into the background. It is occasionally seen swimming across a narrow creek or channel.

Voice.—This is a rather noisy bird, especially so on its breeding ground, and its short, sharp flight notes are quite characteristic of the "creaker." Mr. Nichols contributes the following good description of them:

The notes of the pectoral sandpiper have a reedy character, intermediate in tone between the clearer calls of most shore birds and the hoarse cry of the Wilson's snipe. This is in keeping with its habits. Its characteristic flight note is a loud reedy *kerr*, resembling that of the semipalmated sandpiper (*cherk*) more closely than any other shore bird call, but recognizably heavier. Rarely in flight, the *kerr* varies into or is replaced by a near-whistled *krru*. On being flushed it often has hoarse, hurried cheeping notes, analogous with similar harsher notes of the Wilson's snipe. When in a flock of its own kind, alert and on the move, it has a short, snappy flocking note, a chorus of *tcheps* or *chips*. To my ear its flushing note is more or less a combination of flight note and flocking note, and it may reasonably be so. The flocking note communicates alertness to near-by members of a flock; the flight note is used more emphatically by birds separated from their companions or in active flight and disposed for companionship, whereas on being flushed the bird is signalling to possible companions; but as it has been feeding singly, concealed from such others as there may be by the grass, their distance is uncertain.

Field marks.—The pale-gray, almost white, tail with its dark, almost black, center and rump, is conspicuous in flight; a pale stripe in the wing is less noticeable. The snipelike colors of the upper parts, the dark, heavily streaked breast, contrasted sharply with the white under parts, and the short olive-yellow legs are good field marks when the bird is standing. The males are much larger than the females, which is unusual among shore birds.

Fall.—Regarding their departure from their breeding grounds, Murdoch (1885) says:

After the breeding season, they keep very quiet and retired, like the rest of the waders, and the adults appear to slip quietly away without collecting into flocks, as soon as the young are able to take care of themselves. As soon as the young have assumed the complete fall plumage, that is about the 10th of August, they gather in large flocks with the other young waders, especially about the small ponds on the high land below Cape Smythe, and stay for several days before they take their departure for the South. Stray birds remain as late as the first week of September.

On the New England coast the pectoral is both an early and a late migrant; a few adults sometimes appear in July and more come in August; but the main flight, mostly young birds, comes in September and October; they are often abundant in the latter month and I have seen them as late as October 31. When with us it is seldom seen on the sandy flats or beaches, but frequents the wet, fresh and salt meadows, preferably where the grass has been cut and which after a rain are covered with shallow pools of water. Here and along the margins of marshy creeks are its favorite feeding grounds. It does not decoy well and is no longer considered a game bird, but it has been popular with sportsmen for its gamy qualities and for the excellence of its flesh.

There is a marked southeastward trend in the fall migration of this species; from its breeding grounds in northern Alaska and northeastern Siberia its main flight seems to be towards the Atlantic coast of the United States; it is not abundant and rather irregular on the Pacific coast south of Alaska; it is common at times in the interior of Canada and usually abundant in New England. It occasionally occurs in enormous numbers in Bermuda and seems to be always rare in Florida; these facts would seem to indicate an ocean route to South America.

Winter.—The winter home of the pectoral sandpiper is in southern South America. Arthur II. Holland (1891) says that in the Argentine Republic, it is "usually found in marshy land with long water weeds abounding, frequenting the same spot for weeks together." Between September and March 26, Doctor Wetmore (1926) recorded it as "fairly common" at various places in Paraguay, Argentina, and Uruguay. It evidently spends over half the year in its winter home and makes very rapid flights to and from its Arctic breeding grounds, where it makes a short visit of about two months.

DISTRIBUTION

Range.—Northeastern Siberia, and North and South America; accidental in the Hawaiian Islands and the British Isles.

Breeding range.—The pectoral sandpiper breeds mainly on the Arctic coasts of Alaska and Mackenzie. North to Siberia (Kolyma Delta); Alaska (Cape Lisburne, Cape Smythe, Point Barrow, Colville delta, Collinson Point, Barter Island, and Demarcation Point); Yukon (Herschel Island); northeastern Mackenzie (Cambridge Bay); and northeastern Manitoba (York Factory). East to northeastern Manitoba (York Factory). South to Manitoba (York Factory); Mackenzie (Clinton-Colden Lake and Lac de Gras); and Alaska (Tacotna Forks and Hooper Bay). West to Alaska (Hooper Bay, Fort Clarence, Point Hope, and Cape Lisburne); and northeastern Siberia (Kolyma Delta). It has also been reported in summer at Fort Anderson and Bernard Harbor, Mackenzie, and in northwestern Greenland (Cape Hatherton).

Summer occurrence outside the range above outlined are Keewatin (Cape Eskimo); Manitoba (Button Bay); southwestern Alaska (Nushagak); and northeastern Siberia (Cape Serdze, and Nijni Kolymsk).

Winter range.—South America. North to Ecuador (near Quito); Bolivia (Falls of the Madeira, San Luis, and Caiza); and Paraguay (Colonia Risso). East to Uruguay (Santa Elena); and Argentina (Buenos Aires, La Plata, Barracas, Chubut Valley, Port Desire, and Colonia Rouquand). South and west to Argentina (Colonia Rouquand). West also to Chile (Santiago, Huasco, Antofagasta, Atacama, and Tarapaca); Peru (Chorillos and Junin); and Ecuador (near Quito).

Spring migration.—Early dates of arrival are: Florida, Fort De Soto, February 22, and Orange Hammock, February 25; Alabama, Greensboro, March 20; South Carolina, Frogmore, March 20; North Carolina, Raleigh, March 21; District of Columbia, Washington, March 26; Pennsylvania, Carlisle, March 28, Beaver, April 1, and Harrisburg, April 7; New York, Canandaigua, April 14, Buffalo, April 18, Gaines, May 5, and Orient, May 7; Massachusetts, Thompson's Island, March 30, Monomoy Island, April 11, and Dennis, April 16; Maine, Scarboro, April 13; Quebec, Quebec, May 2; Louisiana, Lake Borgne, March 12, New Orleans, March 18, and Baton Rouge Parish, March 19; Mississippi, Biloxi, February 28; Arkansas, Glenwood, March 27; Kentucky, Bowling Green, April 29; Missouri, St. Louis, March 2, Warrenburg, March 11, Fayette, March 16, and Independence, March 18; Illinois, Englewood, March 9, Rantoul, March 14, Mount Carmel, March 15, Canton, March 26, and Chicago, March 29; Indiana, Bloomington, March 15, Terre Haute, March 17, Bicknell, March 18, and Greencastle, March 22; Ohio, Columbus, March 1, New Bremen, March 24, Columbus, March 25, Oberlin, March 25, Cincinnati, March 28, and Youngstown, March 31; Michigan, Ann Arbor, April 8, and Detroit, April 12; Ontario,

Ottawa, April 27, and Fort Williams, May 10; Iowa, Keokuk, March 14, La Porte, March 25, Sigourney, March 26, and Des Moines, March 31; Wisconsin, Milwaukee, March 26, and Madison, March 31; Minnesota, Heron Lake, April 1, Hutchinson, April 5, and Wilder, April 6; Texas, Santa Maria, February 28, Houston, March 7, and Hidalgo, March 16; Oklahoma, Ponca City, March 31; Kansas, Topeka, March 29, and McPherson, April 9; Nebraska, Lincoln, March 10; South Dakota, Sioux Falls, April 10, and Forestburg, April 20; North Dakota, Charlson, April 27; Manitoba, Pilot Mound, May 1, Reaburn, May 9, and Margaret, May 9; Saskatchewan, Lake Johnston, May 9; Mackenzie, Sturgeon River, May 12, Fort Providence, May 14, Fort Simpson, May 16, and Fort Resolution, May 19; Colorado, Denver, April 21; Montana, Fergus County, April 22; Washington, Menlo, April 1; Yukon, Fortymile, May 16, and Dawson, May 19; and Alaska, Bethel, May 4, St. Michael, May 15, Demarcation Point, May 23, Kowak River, May 27, and Point Barrow, May 30.

Late dates of spring departure are: Costa Rica, Buenos Aires de Terrabe, May 29, and San Jose, May 19; Florida, Fort De Soto, May 20; Pennsylvania, Doylestown, May 27; New Jersey, Elizabeth, May 30; New York, Canandaigua, May 24; Massachusetts, near Boston, June 3; Louisiana, New Orleans, May 20; Mississippi, Bay St. Louis, May 10; Arkansas, Arkansas City, May 15; Kentucky, Bowling Green, May 11; Missouri, Lake Taney Como, May 7, St. Louis, May 11, and Columbia, May 15; Illinois, Elgin, May 12, Addison, May 17, La Grange, May 17, Havana, May 24, and Chicago, June 18; Indiana, Greencastle, May 4, Lyons, May 6, Crawfordsville, May 8, and Bloomington, May 9; Ohio, Tiffin, May 15, Oberlin, May 20, Columbus, May 21, and Youngstown, May 24; Michigan, Detroit, May 13, Hillsdale, May 17, and Ann Arbor, May 19; Ontario, Ottawa, May 25; Iowa, Lake Okoboji, May 27, Emmetsburg, May 28, Sioux City, May 30, and Forest City, May 31; Wisconsin, Elkhorn, May 14, and Madison, May 19; Minnesota, Heron Lake, May 16, Minneapolis, May 18, Hutchinson, May 19, and Hallock, May 28; Texas, Sweetwater, May 8, Corpus Christi, May 11, and Decatur, May 19; Kansas, Fort Riley, May 24, and Onaga, May 24; Nebraska, Valentine, May 17, and Neligh, May 26; South Dakota, Vermilion, May 12, and Sioux Falls, June 11; North Dakota, Charlson, May 11; Manitoba, Winnipeg, May 24, and Shoal Lake, June 2; Montana, Big Sandy, May 18; and Washington, Fort Steilacoom, May 5.

Fall migration.—Early dates of fall arrivals are: British Columbia, Okanagan Landing, July 16; Washington, Tacoma, August 17; California, Redwood City, August 22; Montana, Sweetgrass Hills, August 11; Wyoming, Yellowstone Park, July 19; Colorado, Denver, July 28; Mackenzie, Fort Wrigley, July 19; Saskatchewan,

Milk River, July 16, and Big Stick Lake, July 18; Manitoba, Moose-
jaw, July 7; North Dakota, Charlson, July 20; South Dakota, Forestburg, July 8, Huron, July 15; Nebraska, Valentine, August 8;
Texas, Brownsville, August 2, Tivoli, August 8; Minnesota, Minneapolis, July 15, Lanesboro, July 18, and St. Vincent, July 24; Wisconsin, Madison, July 22, North Freedom, July 25, and Racine, July
30; Iowa, Marshalltown, July 8, and Wall Lake, July 23; Ontario,
Toronto, July 14, and Todmorden, July 23; Michigan, Detroit, July
14, and Charity Islands, July 27; Ohio, Dayton, July 20, Bay Point,
July 24, Painesville, July 25, and North Lima, July 27; Illinois,
Chicago, July 2, and La Grange, July 27; Mississippi, Bay St. Louis,
July 15, and Beauvoir, July 26; Nova Scotia, Digby, July 26; New
Brunswick, Scotch Lake, August 9; Maine, Pittsfield, July 26; Massa-
chusetts, Marthas Vineyard, July 11; New York, Syracuse, July 2,
Orient, July 4, Rochester, July 10, and East Hampton, July 11; New
Jersey, Elizabeth, July 14, and Camden, August 16; Pennsylvania,
Beaver, August 6; District of Columbia, Washington, August 10;
Virginia, Chincoteague, August 1; South Carolina, Mount Pleasant,
July 21, and Frogmore, August 1; Alabama, Leighton, July 24;
Florida, Fort De Soto, July 25, and Key West, July 26; Bermuda,
Penistons Pond, August 3; Bahama Islands, Fortune Island, August
5; Porto Rico, Guayanilla, August 24; West Indies, Barbados,
August 16, Guadeloupe, September 2, and St. Croix, September 14;
Lower California, San Jose del Cabo, September 2; Guatemala,
Duenas, September 2; Costa Rica, San Jose, September 7; and
Colombia, Santa Marta, September 14.

Late dates of fall departure are: Alaska, St. George Island, October 3, Unalaska, October 5, St. Paul Island, October 8, and Nushagak, October 15; British Columbia, Comox, October 15, Chilliwak,
October 19, and Okanagan Landing, November 5; Washington,
Nisqually Flats, November 6, and Simiahmoo, November 1; Oregon,
Cold Springs Bird Reserve, October 27; California, Oakland, October 8; Lower California, San Jose del Cabo, October 24; Costa Rica,
La Estrella de Cartago, November 5; Montana, Flathead Lake, October 20, and Terry, October 21; Idaho, Deer Flat, November 1; Colo-
rado, Barr, October 5; Mackenzie, Slave River, September 29, and
Blackwater, October 7; Manitoba, Winnipeg, October 18, and Win-
nipeg, October 29; South Dakota Wall Lake, October 14, and Sioux
Falls, November 5; Nebraska, Lincoln, November 4; Minnesota, Hallock, October 16, and St. Vincent, October 25; Wisconsin, Madison,
October 11; Iowa, Marshalltown, November 18, and Keokuk, November 24; Ontario, London, October 16, Toronto, October 27, and
Ottawa, November 5; Michigan, Hillsdale, October 6, Bay City,
October 21, and Detroit, October 29; Ohio, Youngstown, November
5, Dayton, November 18, and Columbus, November 28; Indiana,

Lafayette, October 5. and Bicknell, November 1; Illinois, Chicago, October 3, and Lawrenceville, November 13; Quebec, Montreal, November 1, Quebec, November 10, and Anticosti Island, November 12; Maine, Lewiston, October 13, and Pittsfield, November 10; Massachusetts, Lynn, October 28, Harvard, October 30, and Monomoy Island, November 1; New York, Long Beach, November 7, Keuka, November 12, and Branchport, November 23; New Jersey, Camden, November 8; Pennsylvania, Erie, October 31, and Carlisle, November 2; District of Columbia, Anacostia, November 1; North Carolina, Raleigh, November 15; Florida, Lake Jackson, November 22, and Palma Sola, November 29; and Bermuda, St. George, October 9.

Casual records.—The pectoral sandpiper has been taken twice in the Hawaiian Islands, Koahualu, August 6, 1900, and October 14, 1900; once at Hopedale, Labrador; and several times in Greenland, in summer and fall. Observed in Labrador, Rigolet, June 24 to July 8, 1882, and Davis Inlet, July 18, 1883. In Europe it has apparently been detected only in the British Isles, where there are several records from Scotland and Ireland and the southern counties of England.

Egg dates.—Alaska: 16 records, May 27 to July 3; 8 records, June 2 to 18. Arctic Canada: 3 records, June 10 to 30.

PISOBIA FUSCICOLLIS (Vieillot)

WHITE-RUMPED SANDPIPER

HABITS

The white-rumped, or Bonaparte, sandpiper is a great traveller; it breeds in a limited area on the Arctic coast of North America and winters in extreme southern South America.

Spring.—From its winter home in South America, this sandpiper makes an early start; Dr. Alexander Wetmore (1926) writes:

At Guamini, Buenos Aires, from March 3 to 8, white-rumped sandpipers were encountered in northward migration from a winter range in Patagonia. The species was fairly common on March 3 and increased greatly in abundance on the two days that followed. The northward journey was apparently as concerted as the movement that carried the birds southward, as on March 6 there was a noticeable decrease in their numbers, and by March 8, though the birds were still common, the bulk of individuals had passed. They arrived in flocks from the southward, often of several hundred individuals, that whirled in and circled back and forth along the lake shore to decoy to birds feeding on the strand or to rise again and continue swiftly northward. Those that paused kept up a busy search for food along the muddy beaches in or near shallow water, or in company with little parties of buff-breasted sandpipers on the drier alkaline flats back of the shore line. In early morning they were especially active and were in continual movement. Occasionally they worked out into comparatively deep water where in feeding it is necessary to immerse the head over the eyes nearly to the ear openings. When disturbed flocks rose with soft notes that resembled *tseet tseet* or *tseup* to circle to new feeding grounds on the lake shore.

The spring migration route is apparently northward along the Atlantic coast of South America and through the West Indies to the United States. Only a few migrate along our Atlantic coast, as the main flight is northward through the interior, during May and the first few days of June. Many reach their breeding grounds before the end of May.

Courtship.—Doctor Wetmore (1926) gives an attractive account of what seems to be a beginning of courtship in Argentina; he writes:

Occasional parties of males, animated by the approaching breeding season, broke into soft songs and called and twittered, often for several minutes, in a musical chorus in low tones that had so little carrying power that they merged in the strong wind, and it was some time before I succeeded in picking out the sweet individual songs *tsep a tsep a tsep a* or *twee twee tee tee ty tee* given as the head was bobbed rapidly up and down. Occasionally when the fall sunlight came warmly I sat in the mud and let little bands of white rumps work up around me until they were feeding and calling within a meter or so, eyeing me sharply for any cause of alarm. At such times their twittering choruses came sweetly and pleasantly, clearly audible above the lap of waves and the rush of the inevitable winds of the pampas. Between songs the search for food continued without cessation. At short intervals, activated by the warmth of the sun, they suddenly indulged in dozens of combats with their fellows, bloodless affrays, of bluff and retreat, where they lowered their heads and with open mouths ran at one another pugnaciously. The one attacked sidled quickly away or fluttered off for a short distance, save where two of equal temperament chanced to clash when first one and then the other threatened with raised wings in alternate advance and retreat until the fray was concluded to their mutual satisfaction. At such times the movements of these otherwise plain little birds were sprightly and vivacious to a degree. Their loquacity at this season was marked as it contrasted strikingly with their silence and quiet during the resting period of southern summer. Flocks frequently rose to perform intricate evolutions and then returned with a rush to sweep along the shore and join less ambitious comrades. As they passed the white rump flashed plainly, certain advertisement of the species. At times the chattering of these active flocks reminded me of the twittering of swallows.

J. Dewey Soper found this species quite common at various places on Baffin Island, and has sent me some very full notes on it, from which I quote as follows:

The species was encountered at Nettilling Lake, June 10, 1925, when a mated pair was flushed from a marshy upland near the Takuirbing River. The sexual organs in both were fully developed, the female being almost on the point of laying. By the 14th the species had become quite common. The males practised their vocal performance on the wing immediately upon arrival. They rise to a height of about 60 feet above the tundra and there they hover with rapidly beating wings giving utterance to their nuptial song in notes so weak that when a wind is blowing nothing may be heard of it even at comparatively close range. It is given in a very low tone and slow tempo; the notes are weak and inclined to be squeaky, with a weird dripping quality like the sound of water oozing and dropping in a small cavern. The species appears to flush silently.

Nesting.—Very little seems to be known and still less has been published about the nesting habits of the white-rumped sandpiper. In MacFarlane's notes I find brief records of seven nests found by his party on the barren grounds and Arctic coast of Canada, from 1862 to 1865. One nest was found on June 21, 1862, 50 miles east of Fort Anderson; the female and three eggs were taken; the nest consisted of a few leaves in a small hole in the ground near a small lake. Another found on June 29, 1863, on the barren grounds, is described as "a mere depression in the ground lined with a few decayed leaves"; the female and four eggs were taken. There is a set of four eggs in the Herbert Massey collection, taken with the parent bird by E. A. McIllhenny at Point Barrow, Alaska, on June 25, 1898; the nest is described as "a hollow in the moss on top of a ridge on the tundra, lined with dry grass and partly arched over." This is farther west than the species is supposed to breed, but there are several birds in the Philadelphia Academy of Sciences collected there in June, which are in full breeding plumage.

Mr. Soper found a number of nests near Nettilling Lake, Baffin Island, on which he has sent me the following notes:

A nest containing four eggs was found on a grassy hummock on the tundra bordering the lake on June 16. Many were subsequently found. The nest is merely a shallow depression on the crown of a tussock of grass and mosses a few inches above the surrounding mud and water of the tundra. It is sparingly lined with blades of old grass and dead leaves of the dwarf arctic willow. Some are lined exclusively with the dried, oval leaves of *Salix herbacea*. According to collecting data, both sexes arrive together, with the female almost, if not quite, ready for immediate reproduction, as evidenced by the condition of the ovaries. The nest of four eggs found on June 16 was but four days after the first observed arrivals of the species.

The female upon one's approach plays the familiar artifice of simulating a prostrated condition, limping and dragging herself along the ground in an effort to attract one's attention from the nest. In this they are bold and fearless; and when one sits beside the nest they will frequently run up to within a foot or less of the observer. In photographing nests from a distance of only a few feet, the female will often return to her eggs while one's head is under the dark cloth adjusting the focus. One was so devoted to her eggs that she would run up and peck at my fingers and run over my hand as I extended it toward the nest. This species, when one approaches the nest, usually leaves it when one is 20 to 25 yards distant and runs along the ground, either directly toward the intruder or a little to one side. Because of its remarkable similarity to the covering of the tundra at this time, this first movement often escapes one, and consequently when the bird is first observed fluttering along the ground one naturally imagines himself near the nest, when, in reality, it may be 20 or 30 yards away. This ruse is a clever one, and no doubt would often save the nest from violation. The nests are easily found by retiring and watching the female with the glasses. They usually return to the nest with little

artifice or delay; in fact, often within two or three minutes. The above procedure is not an invariable practice, as one female I knew would flush directly
from the nest to begin her tactics only when there was danger of the nest
being actually trodden upon.

Eggs.—The four eggs usually laid by the white-rumped sandpiper are ovate pyriform in shape; all that I have seen are uniform
in shape and have characteristic colors and markings. One of the
two sets in the United States National Museum has a "deep olive
buff" ground color, and the eggs are heavily blotched about the
larger end, sparingly spotted elsewhere with "wood brown," "warm
sepia," and "benzo brown," and with a few underlying spots of
various shades of "brownish drab"; an egg from this set is well
figured by Frank Poynting (1895). The other set differs from this
one in having the ground color lighter, "olive buff," and the spots
finer, more scrawly, and lighter in color; the underlying drab markings are also more numerous.

There is also a set of four eggs in the Thayer collection, taken with
the parent bird by Alfred H. Anderson on Taylor Island, Victoria
Land, July 7, 1919. These eggs are much like the egg figured by
Mr. Poynting, except that in one or two of the eggs the ground
color is more greenish.

One of the three sets taken by J. Dewey Soper on Baffin Island
looks much like a miniature set of long-billed curlew's eggs. In
three of the eggs the ground color is "mignonette green," covered
with small spots, more thickly at the larger end, of "bister" and
"snuff brown"; the other has a "deep lichen green" ground color
and is irregularly blotched near the larger end, finely speckled elsewhere with "bister" and "brownish drab."

The measurements of 34 eggs average 33.7 by 24 millimeters; the
eggs showing the four extremes measure 36.1 by 23.6, 34.2 by 27.7,
31.5 by 23.5, and 35 by 22.8 millimeters.

Young.—Mr. Soper's notes on the young are as follows:

The first juveniles, about a day old, were seen and collected on July 11.
They were exceedingly active, a good example of precocial young. These were
ashy below, buffy above, with black markings, and the down over the lower
back and rump tipped with small spots of white. This species is much more
demonstrative and less artful in the concealment of young than Baird's sandpiper. The adults come within a few feet of the intruder, and by their
action advertise much more clearly the position of the young. The parent birds
keep up a continual fine twittering cry of alarm, the female louder and more
pronounced. The male comes on the scene only at intervals with a mouse-
like squeaking note. The young are adepts in the art of concealment, "freez-
ing" flat to the ground with warning notes from the adults. They will lie in
this fashion as though dead until actually picked up in the hand. When
they realize the game is up they then become wild and frantically struggle
to escape. When allowed to do so they will run rapidly away and either
hide again or attempt to reach the mother bird, whose frantic cries come
from but a few yards away.

A young white rump about two-thirds grown and almost on the point of flight was captured on August 1. Others seen a few days later on the shore of Kuksunittuk Bay were capable of short flights. As an experiment, I tried several times to keep individual young alive at my base tent on the Takuirbing River, but they invariably died within about 24 hours regardless of the best care.

Plumages.—The downy young white rumped is much like the downy young of other tundra nesting species of sandpipers. From the stilt sandpiper it can be distinguished by its much shorter legs and shorter and slenderer bill, from the Baird by its more buffy face and breast, these parts being pure white in *bairdi*, and from the least by paler and duller browns in the upper parts and by white, instead of buffy terminal tuft spots. The crown, back, rump, wings, and thighs are variegated or marbled with "Sanford's brown," or "tawny," and black, dotted, except on the front half of the crown, which is mainly bright brown, with whitish terminal tufts. The forehead, a broad superciliary stripe, the sides of the head, throat, and breast are pale buff or buffy white; the remaining under parts are grayish white. A median frontal stripe of black terminates in "tawny" toward the bill; there are extensive black areas on either side of the crown and on the occiput. The nape is grizzly, buff, gray and dusky.

In juvenal plumage the crown is sepia with "tawny" edgings; the back, rump, tertials, and scapulars are sepia, with "tawny" edges, and some of the feathers of the mantle and scapulars are also white tipped; the under parts are white, but the breast is suffused with light buff and narrowly streaked with dusky; the median and lesser wing coverts are broadly edged with light buff or whitish.

The postjuvenal molt of the body plumage usually occurs in September and October, mainly in the latter month, but sometimes not until November. The upper body plumage is not all molted, so that first winter birds can be distinguished by tawny or buffy edged feathers in the mantle and by the juvenal wing coverts. The next partial prenuptial molt apparently removes all traces of immaturity.

Adults have a prenuptial molt, beginning in March, of the underbody plumage, most of the upper-body plumage, sometimes the tail, and some of the wing coverts. But this is almost immediately preceded by the delayed molt of the remiges in January and February, so that it seems to be a nearly complete prenuptial molt, which is barely finished before the birds start on their long northward migration. The postnuptial molt of adults, beginning in August and often lasting into October, involves only the body plumage, the tail, and some scapulars, tertials, and wing coverts. The gray winter plumage, so different from the brightly colored spring plumage, is seldom seen in its completeness before the birds go south.

Food.—Very little seems to have been published on the food of the white-rumped sandpiper, but W. L. McAtee (1911) gives it credit for eating some injurious insects and worms, such as grasshoppers, the clover-root curculio, which is injurious to clover, and marine worms (*Nereis*), which prey on oysters.

Stuart T. Danforth (1925) says that four collected in Porto Rico—

had eaten 77.7 per cent of animal food and 22.3 per cent of vegetable matter. Fifty per cent of the animal matter consisted of bloodworms, 25 per cent of *Planorbis* snails, and 5 per cent of *Corixa reticulata*. The vegetable matter consisted entirely of seeds, of which those of Compositae formed 33.3 per cent, *Sesban emerus* 30 per cent, and *Persicaria portoricensis* 36.7 per cent. In addition to food, the stomachs contained mineral matter (coarse red sand) forming 32.5 per cent of the stomach contents.

Behavior.—Lucien M. Turner, who has had abundant opportunity to observe this species in Ungava, writes in his notes:

The flight of these birds is remarkably firm and swift, generally in an undulatory manner and swerving to the right or left often with the body inclined to one side, the wing nearly perpendicular, alternately presenting the upper and lower surface of the body. Just before alighting the wings are raised until the tips nearly touch over the back and for a moment held outstretched and then slowly folded. The bird is quite active while searching for food and seldom remains more than a few seconds in a spot, where it constantly picks here and there for the minute organisms which form its food. During this time all is activity and quite in contrast to the interval while the tide is high and the bird is on the high land resting and digesting its food. Here it is more sleepy and less easily disturbed. The eyesight of these sandpipers is certainly very acute, as they are able to detect the presence of a person at a long distance and give a twittering, snipey note, otherwise regardless of approaching danger. In all their doings the utmost harmony seems to prevail. The only object of their lives seems to be to gather food. No sooner does the water begin to ebb than a few of these birds will swish over some point of land with merry twittering, eagerly scanning the bank for the least appearance of mud now being exposed. By the time the tide has half ebbed myriads of these birds are sweeping back and forth along the river. As the water shallows over well known bars, and scarcely has the water shoaled enough to permit the birds to alight without swimming, than as many sandpipers as can collect on the place eagerly alight and begin probing the ooze for food. The lowering water is followed by the thronging birds to the last inch.

The flowing tide begins and the birds retreat carefully seizing every object of food that the rising water brings to the surface. Often they are so eager in their search that many birds are crowded into the deeper water and save themselves only by flight. This or that place is quickly covered over by the water and again the birds collect into larger flocks which now sway to the right or left, alternately, exposing their silvery white underparts which gleam in the sunshine like a stream of silver. The gray or brown of their backs relieving the color as the long stream of birds pass by. They partially halt their flight and become a compact flock, whereupon they separate into smaller flocks which, as the water gradually rises and covers their feeding grounds, now betake themselves to the higher lands of the banks above. Here, around the pools on the highlands, or among the grassy margins of

the lakes, they collect to wash themselves and digest the food they L
obtained from the salt-water mud.

As a person approaches one of these pools, in the latter part of Augu
little suspecting that anything will be found near them, these birds turn thei.
backs, which so closely resemble the lichen covered granite as to render the
birds indistinguishable. A nearer approach and they present their white
breasts which afford a striking contrast with the surroundings. In a moment
they run together and huddle into a compact flock before they take wing.
I have, by firing at the proper moment, secured every individual composing
a flock of over a dozen birds. If they fly they take to their wings with a
sudden impulse and fly in a zigzag movement for a few yards then swerve
to right or left continuing until another locality is reached, where they sit
quietly until approached. This is repeated every tide and, as the birds are
crepuscular also in their habits, their opportunities for becoming fat are
nearly doubled. They acquire the fat in a short time. The thickness of the
layer is often one-fourth of an inch and completely envelops the body. The
least abrasion of the skin or a shot hole soon fills the surrounding parts
with oil which has exuded from the wound, making the preparation of skins
for specimens a very difficult matter. The flesh of these birds is peculiarly
tender and richly flavored. At times I have gone out to shoot these birds
for the table and with five discharges (of half an ounce of No. 12 shot) I
secured on one occasion 82 birds. A heavy stick thrown in among them as
they wade along the water's edge also knocks many of them over, for these
birds seem so intent on procuring food that but little heed is given to the
hunter.

William Brewster (1925) says:

Invariably among the tamest and most confiding of our so-called shore birds,
they will usually permit one to approach, either on foot or in a boat, within
5 or 6 yards, while I have known a gun to be discharged into a flock with
fatal effect, but without causing any of the birds which escaped injury to
take wing. Like most obese creatures they are habitually sluggish, confining
their wanderings afoot to limited areas, and exploiting these very deliberately,
walking slowly and sedately in crouching attitudes, with measured steps, frequently stopping to thrust their bills listlessly a little way into the soft
ground, or to pick up small morsels of food from the surface. Occasionally,
however, one may see them running to and fro over the mud quite briskly
and ceaselessly, perhaps incited to this comparatively unusual behavior by the
example of other waders feeding close about them, for they are by no means
averse to the companionship of several of the lesser kinds, such as semipalmated plover and sandpipers, grass-birds, dunlins, etc. Although somewhat loath to take wing, even when threatened by obvious danger, they are
likely to fly swiftly and far, when once started, doubling and circling over the
marshes in much the same manner as other small sandpipers.

John T. Nichols, says in his notes:

When startled, a bird has been seen to crouch down concealing the bulk of
its white underparts and practically disappear against the brightly lighted mud
flat on which it had been feeding. This is a habit shared by its close relatives
the pectoral and least sandpipers.

Voice.—The white-rumped sandpiper is ordinarily a rather silent
bird, but its short, sharp flight note is characteristic of the species

d serves to distinguish it readily in the field. To me it sounds like *eep* or *tzip;* Mr. Nichols calls it " a squeaky mouse-like *jeet* "; Mr. Brewster (1925) describes it as " a feeble lisping *zip* or *tsip*, fringilline, rather than limicoline, in character "; and Doctor Townsend (1905) thinks that " it suggests at times the call note of the pipit." C. J. Maynard (1896) refers to " one cry in particular, being loudly given and greatly prolonged, resembling the scream of a rapacious bird more than the whistle of a sandpiper."

Field marks.—The best field mark for this species is the white rump, or rather upper tail-coverts; this is conspicuous in flight but is usually concealed by the wings when the bird is on the ground. I have noticed that, while the bird is standing with its side toward me, the gray of the upper parts extend down on the sides of the neck as far as the bend of the wing, whereas in the semipalmated sandpiper, with which it might be confused, there is a decided white space in front of the wing.

Mr. Nichols says in his notes:

This bird is a size larger than least or semipalmated sandpipers, and at favorable angles shows a diagnostic white patch crossing above the rather dark tail. This white patch is a good example of color which apparently functions as a recognition mark. If the same were fortuitous one would not expect the tail to be darker than in related species, as is the case, causing the white rump to show more prominently. Straight bill, (or with slight decurviture at the tip, like that of the pectoral sandpiper) and as a rule finely and sharply streaked head and breast prevent chance of confusion with the European curlew sandpiper, of casual occurrence on our Atlantic coast.

Fall.—The beginning of the fall flight is apparently southeastward from its breeding grounds west of Hudson Bay and perhaps southward from Baffin Island, where it breeds. Mr. Turner's Ungava notes give a very good idea of this first step in the migration and a good impression of the great abundance of this species; he writes:

As I proceeded farther northward I did not observe a single one of these sandpipers until we came to anchor off the mouth of Georges River (July 31) where quite a number were seen on the pebbly beach, seeking their food among the rocks and shingle as the tide receded. At this date quite a number, in fact fully three-fourths, of those seen were birds of the year as was fully attested by traces of downy plumage yet among the feathers of the body and especially on the head and neck. The sizes of the flocks varied from three or four to nearly a dozen, doubtless consisting of a single brood or, in the case of the larger flocks, of two or more broods with their parents. Some of the younger members of the flocks had the wing quills not fully developed while others were considerably farther advanced. Such a variation of plumage both in age and coloration was exhibited that I presumed there must be two weeks difference in the ages of the different young.

By the 10th of August all the young are well able to fly and make protracted flights in search of food. By this date they assemble in flocks, amount-

ing at times, to thousands of individuals, resorting to the mud flats left
by the receding tide. The mouth of the Koksoak and the cove to the westwa
of it present excellent tracts of mud deposited in the little indentations. I
the middle of September these birds begin to depart to the south. Many of ther
ascended the Koksoak and others doubtless followed the windings of the coast
down the Atlantic. I have seen numerous flocks over a hundred miles from
the mouth of the river as late as October 12th, and an occasional single bird
as late as the 20th of that month. I have observed, at the mouth of the
Koksoak River, flocks of these birds often numbering over a hundred individuals
suddenly appear from high in the air. These I suspected to be birds coming
from the regions to the northward of the strait for they always came from
the sea.

Thence there is an overland flight to the Atlantic coast. Mr.
Brewster (1925) says:

White-rumped sandpipers visit Lake Umbagog regularly and not infrequently, if rather sparingly, in autumn, appearing oftenest during the month
of October. Those arriving early in the season are mostly adult birds which
occur singly or two or three together; those coming later are of various ages and
sometimes in flocks containing as many as eight or nine members each, but
rarely, if ever, a greater number. Bonaparte's sandpipers are hardy birds.
They may be seen at the lake when its bordering marshes are stiff with
frost. Once (October 26, 1883) I found nine of them near the mouth of
Cambridge River two days after the entire region had been covered with
snow to a depth of 7 inches.

This bird is a regular, but never an abundant, migrant on the coast
of Massachusetts in the fall. The vast numbers which Turner saw
in Ungava must seek some other route; the species is never abundant
in the interior in the fall and it seems to be rather rare on the
Atlantic coast south of New England; the natural inference is that
it migrates at sea from Maine or Nova Scotia directly to South
America or the West Indies. It is abundant at times in Bermuda.

The adults begin to reach Cape Cod in August, but the main
flight comes in September, consisting partially of young birds; most
of the young birds come in October and some linger as late as November 10. While with us the white-rumped sandpiper frequents the
wet meadows and marshes near the shore, as well as the sand flats,
mud flats, and beaches, feeding at low tide singly or in small flocks
and usually associated with pectoral, semipalmated, or least sandpipers. During high tides, while the flats are covered, this species
may be seen on the high sandy beaches, mixed in with the vast
flocks of small shorebirds, sleeping, or resting, or preening their
plumage, while waiting for feeding time to come again; if the wind
is blowing, all the birds are facing it; many are crouching on the
sand and others are standing on one leg with the bill tucked under
the scapulars. These flocks often contain hundreds and sometimes
thousands of birds, mainly semipalmated sandpipers, semipalmated

over, and sanderlings. They are not all asleep, however, for if approached too closely, they all rise and whirl away in a vast shimmering cloud, flashing now white and now dark as they turn, and settle on the beach again at no great distance.

Winter.—August finds the white-rumped sandpiper migrating along the coast of Brazil and it has been known to reach Cape Horn as early as September 9. Doctor Wetmore (1926) writes:

The white-rumped sandpiper was the most abundant of the migrant shore birds in the regions visited in southern South America. The species was not recorded until September 6, 1920, when it appeared in abundance in southward migration on the lagoons at kilometer 80, west of Puerto Pinasco, Paraguay. The first flocks from which specimens were taken were adult females, and two taken on the date when they were first recorded had laid eggs a few weeks previous as was shown by the appearance of the ovaries. The southward migration came with a rush as the birds passed through the night as witnessed by their calls. The flight continued until September 21, when a dozen, the last seen here, were recorded. The birds circled about lagoons in small compact flocks or walked along on muddy shores, where they fed with head down, probing rapidly in the soft mud; anything edible encountered was seized and swallowed and the bird continued without delay in its search for more.

Farther south this species was encountered in abundance in its winter range on the pampa. Ten were recorded at Dolores, Buenos Aires, October 21, and from October 22 to November 15 the species was found in numbers on the coastal mud flats on the Bay of Samborombom. A few were seen at pools of water in the sand dunes below Cape San Antonio. Along the Rio Ajo white-rumped sandpipers were encountered in flocks of hundreds that came upstream to search the mud flats at low tide or were concentrated on bars at the mouth when the water was high. In early morning there was a steady flight of them passing to suitable feeding grounds. The birds flew swiftly, with soft notes, from 3 to 15 feet from the earth. In feeding they scattered out in little groups that covered the bare mud systematically. It was not unusual to record as many as 2,000 in a day. About two hundred were observed in the bay at Ingeniero White, the port of Bahia Blanca, on December 13, and at Carhue, Buenos Aires, from December 16 to 18, white-rumped sandpipers were noted in fair numbers on inundated ground back of the shore of Lake Epiquen or about fresh-water ponds on the pampa inland. None were found in Uruguay during February.

Ernest Gibson (1920) says of this species, at Cape San Antonio, Buenos Aires:

This is certainly our commonest wader, and is found everywhere in flocks, from, say, the end of October to the middle or end of March. The number in these gatherings is only restricted by the area of the feeding ground; hence, when large mud flats are available in the vicinity of our fresh or salt water lagunas and cangrejales, or at the subsidence of a flood, the flocks are sometimes of enormous size. The observer may see many acres of ground which look to be in continuous movement, the surface being alive with the restless throng of sandpipers running about and chasing each other, feeding, or taking constant short flights.

DISTRIBUTION

Range.—North and South America; casual in Europe.

Breeding range.—Although the white-rumped sandpiper has been noted in summer from Wainwright, Alaska, east to southern Greenland (Julianshaab), the only places where eggs have been taken are Point Barrow, Alaska; Herschel Island, Yukon; Taylor Island, Victoria Land; Fort Anderson and Rendezvous Lake, Mackenzie; and the southeast shore of Lake Nettilling, Baffin Island.

Winter range.—North to Paraguay (Rio Pilcomayo and Rio Parana); and Uruguay (Montevideo). East to Uruguay (Montevideo); Argentina (La Plata, Cape San Antonio, Bahia Blanca, Rio Chubut, and Puerto San Julian); the Falkland Islands; and Tierra del Fuego. South to Tierra Fuego; and southern Chile (Straits of Magellan). West to Chile (Straits of Magellan and Santiago); and Paraguay (Rio Pilcomayo).

Spring migration.—Early dates of spring arrival are: Florida, De Funiak Springs, May 12; Georgia, Savannah, May 17; South Carolina, Mount Pleasant, May 7, Frogmore, May 7, and Charleston, May 16; North Carolina, Cape Hatteras, May 2, Churchs Island, May 6, and Pea and Brodie Islands, May 15; Virginia, Smith's Island, May 14; District of Columbia, Washington, May 11; New Jersey, Long Beach, May 9, Trenton, May 12, and Bernardsville, May 14; New York, Mastic, May 11, Canandaigua, May 19, Rockaway Beach, May 21, and Freeport, May 22; Connecticut, Middletown, May 10, and New Haven, May 19; Rhode Island, Block Island, May 16; Massachusetts, Melrose, May 9, and Harvard, May 20; Vermont, Woodstock, May 14, Brattleboro, May 18, and Rutland, May 19; Maine, Scarboro, May 29; Quebec, Godbout, May 24, and Quebec City, May 27; Louisiana, Lobdell, May 14; Kentucky, Bowling Green, April 27; Missouri, Jacks Fork, May 15, and Sand Ridge, May 16; Illinois, De Kalb, May 8, and Elgin, May 11; Ohio, Canton, May 8, Berlin Center, May 11, and Youngstown, May 17; Michigan, Detroit, May 6; Ontario, Toronto, May 26; Iowa, Marshalltown, May 4, and Sioux City, May 7; Wisconsin, Whitewater, April 28; Minnesota, Wilder, May 5, Jackson, May 13, and Heron Lake, May 19; Texas, Brownsville, April 11, and Ingram, May 8; Kansas, Emporia, May 4, Lawrence, May 5, and Topeka, May 7; Nebraska, Neligh, May 1, and Peru, May 13; South Dakota, Sioux Falls, May 5, and Vermilion, May 9; Manitoba, Whitewater Lake, May 12; Saskatchewan, Ravenscrag, May 13; and Mackenzie, Fort Resolution, May 19, and Fort Simpson, May 26.

Late dates of spring departure from the wintering grounds are: Argentina, French Bay, March 7, and Guamini, March 8. In North America, late dates are: South Carolina, Mount Pleasant, May 30, and Frogmore, May 31; North Carolina, Raleigh, May 24, and Lake Ellis, June 15; Virginia, Smith's Island, June 7; Delaware, Lewes, June 8; Pennsylvania, Erie, June 4; New Jersey, Bernardsville, May 24, and Camden, May 24; New York, Castleton, June 2, and Long Beach, June 20; Massachusetts, Harvard, June 4; Illinois, Waukegan, June 9; Ohio, Painesville, June 14, and Lakeside, June 25; Ontario, Toronto, June 21; Iowa, Sioux City, May 30, and Keokuk, June 5; Wisconsin, Madison, May 30; Minnesota, Hallock, June 8; Texas, Lomita, May 22, and Gainesville, May 24; Kansas, Fort Riley, May 22 and Stafford County, June 6; Nebraska, Lincoln, May 20, Republican Fork, May 25, and Valentine, May 25; South Dakota, Forestburg, May 27, and Vermilion, June 5; North Dakota, Charlson, June 1; Manitoba, Reaburn, June 6, Duck Mountain, June 8, and Shoal Lake, June 20; and Saskatchewan, Kutanajan Lake, June 9, and Quill Lake, June 10.

Fall migration.—Early fall arrivals are: Saskatchewan, Indian Head, July 1; Texas, Tivoli, August 17; Minnesota, St. Vincent, August 4; Wisconsin, Lake Koshkonong, August 1; Iowa, Marshalltown, August 19, and Keokuk, August 21; Ontario, Toronto, August 23; Michigan, Lansing, July 29; Massachusetts, Marthas Vineyard, July 16, and Ipswich, July 24; Rhode Island, Providence, July 18, and Block Island, July 27; New York, Orient, July 24; New Jersey, Long Beach, July 7; Pennsylvania, Erie, August 29; Florida, Palma Sola, August 27; Paraguay, near Puerto Pinasco, September 6; and Patagonia, Orange Bay, September 9.

Late departures in the fall are: Mackenzie, Slave River, October 1; Saskatchewan, Eastend, September 12; Manitoba, Shoal Lake, September 21; Minnesota, Hallock, October 16; Iowa, Marshalltown, November 7; Ontario, Toronto, November 2, and Ottawa, November 5; Ohio, Columbus, October 28, and North Lima, October 29; Ungava, Koksoak River, October 20; Baffin Island, Pangnirtung Fiord, September 25; Labrador, Battle Harbor, October 29; and Quebec, Montreal, October 31; Maine, Lake Umbagog, October 14, and Bangor, October 23; Massachusetts, Lynn, October 12, Boston, October 22, Harvard, October 24, and Cape Cod, November 10; Connecticut, Branford, October 23, and East Hartford, October 30; New York, Ithaca, October 16, Quogue, October 30, Shinnecock Bay, October 30, Oneida Lake, November 3, and Canandaigua, November 4; Pennsylvania, Philadelphia, October 10, and Erie, October 29; District of Columbia, Anacostia, October 24; Virginia, Lake Drummond, November 5; Ohio, Columbus, November 15; North Carolina, Church's Island, October 7, and Raleigh, December 7; South Carolina, Mount Pleasant, October 17, and Frogmore, October 24; Georgia, Savannah, October 9; and Florida, St. Augustine, December 2.

Casual records.—Although probably on the migrational highwa．
records of the white-rumped sandpiper in Central America, the Wes
Indies, and Lesser Antilles are so few that in these places it can
only be considered as a casual visitor. Specimens are in the British
Museum from Lion Hill, Panama; Momotombo, Nicaragua; and
Tizimin and Cozumel Island, Mexico. It also has been observed
or taken on the islands of Barbados (September 20 and 22, year ?);
Dominica (November 5, 1904); St. Lucia; Guadeloupe; Martinique;
Trinidad; Porto Rico (Mayaguez, October 2, 1900, and Culebrita,
April 15, 1912); Cuba; the Bahamas (Inagua, May 27, 1879, and
Fortune Island, August 5, 1876); and the Bermuda Islands. Ex-
amples were reported from the Yellowstone River, Montana, August
8 to 13, 1878; it has been taken at Laramie, Wyo.; in New Mexico
(Fort Fillmore, October, 1852, and Zuni Mountains, September 16,
1851); and there are several records for eastern Colorado. The
specimen reported from Oakland, Calif., was probably the Pectoral
sandpiper, *P. maculata.* One was taken at Hopedale, Labrador.

White-rumped sandpipers have been reported in the British Isles
fourteen or fifteen times and a specimen was taken in Franz Josef
Land on June 28 (year unknown, but prior to 1898).

Egg dates.—Arctic Canada: 14 records, June 15 to July 24; 7 rec-
cords, June 30 to July 12. Alaska: 2 records, June 25.

PISOBIA BAIRDI (Coues)

BAIRD SANDPIPER

HABITS

Spring.—This sandpiper belongs to that class of birds which
Abel Chapman (1924) so aptly terms "globe spanners," for on its
migrations its traverses the whole length of both American continents twice a year. From its wintering grounds in Patagonia
it must start north even earlier than the preceding species or else
it must travel faster. Dr. Alexander Wetmore (1926) observed it
migrating past Buenos Aires on March 5 in company with white-
rumped sandpipers, and it has been known to reach Texas early
in March. From there its course seems to be northward between
the Mississippi River and the Rocky Mountains. A. G. Lawrence
tells me that it passes through Manitoba between April 28 and May
29; and J. A. Munro gives me, as his spring dates for southern
British Columbia, April 30 to May 10. Prof. William Rowan
(Mss.) calls it extremely abundant in Alberta about the middle of
May and usually gone by the 24th. It is very rare east of the
Mississippi in the spring. E. A. Preble (1908) saw large flocks
foraging on floating ice at Lake Athabaska on May 25. Dr. Joseph

Grinnell (1900) records it at the Kowak River, Alaska, on May 20. Joseph Dixon (1917) says:

On May 31, 1914, at Griffin Point, Arctic Alaska, the first pair of Baird sandpipers for the season were noted feeding along the rim of a frozen tundra pond. The weather had turned bitterly cold during the previous night, and as a result the newly formed ice on the ponds was thick enough to support a man. Strictly speaking, there was no night at this date, for the two months of continuous daylight had already begun; so in a short time the sandpipers were bustling about picking up the mosquito and other pupae which were being washed out by a newly-born stream that gurgled under the snow and ice on its way down to the frozen lagoon.

Courtship.—Two somewhat different accounts of the courtship of this species have been published. W. Sprague Brooks (1915), who found this bird breeding at Demarcation Point, Alaska, writes:

Only once did I note any courtship activity. On this occasion (May 24), the male would fly a few feet above the female, while she rested on the ground, with quick erratic wing strokes suggesting a nighthawk. Frequently he would alight and raise the wings high over the back as a gull does before folding them. Then with the forearms perpendicular, the primaries would be slowly raised and lowered like a pump handle, generally lowered to right angles with the forearms, sometimes lower. Not a sound was uttered.

Alfred M. Bailey (1926), whose observations were made at Cape Prince of Wales, Alaska, says:

Cutting down the opposite side of the ridge, I heard many calls which reminded me of home in the early spring, for the combined totals sounded like the singing of many little grass frogs in a meadow pond. It was the call, or rather the "spring song," of the Baird sandpiper. I soon flushed a little female, which fluttered away uttering cries of alarm. I concealed myself, and she soon returned, the male also hovering about, making his little froglike peep. At times he would rise high in the air, in the way so characteristic of male sandpipers, give forth his song, and sail down to perch.

Nesting.—MacFarlane's notes mention seven nests found in the vicinity of Franklin Bay, but very few data were given; "on June 24, 1864, a nest containing four eggs was found in the Barren Grounds, in a swampy tract between two small lakes, and was composed of a few decayed leaves placed in a small cavity or depression in the ground, shaded by a tuft of grass." John Murdoch (1885) says:

The nest was always well hidden in the grass and never placed in marshy ground or on the bare black parts of tundra, and consists merely of a slight depression in the ground, thinly lined with dried grass. All the eggs we found were obtained from the last week in June to the first week of July, a trifle later than the other waders. The sitting female when disturbed exhibits the greatest solicitude, running about with drooping, outspread wings, and loud outcry, and uses every possible wile to attract the intruder from the eggs. The nest is so well concealed and forms so inconspicuous an object that the only practical way to secure the eggs is to withdraw to one side and allow the sitting bird to return, carefully marking where she alights. Having done

this on one occasion and failing to find the eggs, after flushing the bird
or three times I discovered that I had walked on the eggs, though I had
looking for them most carefully.

Mr. Brooks (1915) writes:

Two nests were found, each containing four eggs and about one quarter incubated on June 12 and 14, 1914. Murdoch found them nesting rather later
than other waders at Point Barrow, but my experience at Demarcation Point
was quite the opposite, for here they were the first to breed. A female taken
June 2, had a fully formed and colored egg about ready to lay. Both of the
above nests were on dry, well-drained tundra near the bases of knolls. The
nests were like the other sandpipers, and lined with dry willow leaves, but the
cavities were less deep than those of the semipalmated sandpiper.

The female was on one nest and the male on the other. The former left the
nest when I was some distance away and flying directly toward me alighted
within a few feet. While I was at the nest she walked hurriedly about close
by constantly uttering a plaintive *weet-weet-weet* always repeated three times.
Occasionally she would take a short flight about me and utter a note very
similar to the rattling call of the pectoral sandpiper. The male when disturbed
acted quite differently. He sat closer and on leaving the nest showed the
greatest concern, dragging a " broken " wing in the most distressing manner.
In neither case was the mate about as frequently occurs with the semipalmated
sandpiper.

Mr. Dixon (1917) says:

At Griffin Point, less than 50 miles to the eastward of Demarcation Point,
the first set of eggs (fresh) was taken on June 24. The last set was found
July 11, with the four eggs nearly ready to hatch. Murdoch speaks of the
nests being well concealed and always hidden in the grass. In those nests
which we found, no attempt had been made at such concealment, as they were
placed absolutely in the open, with nothing to cover or conceal the eggs at all,
and the nests so shallow that the tops of the eggs were almost or quite level
with the surrounding grass. Far from being conspicuously exposed thereby,
however, the eggs were shielded from discovery in the most effective manner
possible, for in color and markings they blended so perfectly with the brown
tundra that a person could easily look directly at them from a distance of 6
feet and still not be able to see them.

This method of nesting seems to be the most effective way of escaping one
great danger at least, namely, the notice of the countless jaegers, both parasitic
and pomarine. These robbers subsist almost entirely during the breeding period
on the young and eggs of other birds, and cruise continually back and forth
over the sandpipers' nesting ground, looking for the least telltale feather, bit of
wind-blown down, or other object which might afford a clue to the whereabouts
of a nest.

Herbert W. Brandt found only one nest of the Baird sandpiper
near Hooper Bay, Alaska, which he tells me—

Was on a dry mossy ridge amid the dunes and was partially concealed by the
surrounding curly grass. It was flimsily constructed of grass stems and filled
with a scant handful of small leaves of the dwarf birch and blueberry, together
with a few adjacent reindeer-moss stems. The measurements of this nest were:
Inside diameter 3 inches, and depth perhaps 2 inches.

gs.—The Baird sandpiper lays ordinarily four eggs, occasionally y three. These vary in shape from ovate or ovate pyriform to ovate, and they have a slight gloss. In color they often resemble ertain types of western sandpipers' eggs, as they are usually of a decidedly reddish tone; but they are considerably larger. The ground color varies from "pinkish buff" to "pale pinkish buff" or from "olive buff" to "cartridge buff." Three quite different types are represented in my collection. In the western sandpiper type the "pinkish buff" ground color is quite evenly covered over the whole egg with small, elongated spots, somewhat thicker at the larger end and having a spiral tendency, of "Hay's russet" and "chestnut brown," with a few underlying spots of "brownish drab." Another set has a "cartridge buff" ground color, which is unevenly covered, chiefly at the larger end, with small spots of duller browns, "bister," "Saccardo's umber," and light shades of "brownish drab." This seems to be the commonest type. An unusually beautiful set has a "pinkish buff" ground color, sparingly sprinkled with minute brown dots and boldly blotched with great, irregular splashes of deep, rich browns, "chestnut," "chocolate," and "liver brown," overlying large splashes of various shades of "vinaceous gray." The measurements of 54 eggs average 33.1 by 23.8 millimeters; the eggs showing the four extremes measure 33.5 by 24.4, 34.3 by 24.6 and 30 by 22 millimeters.

Young.—Incubation is shared by both sexes, but we have no data as to its duration. Mr. Dixon (1917) found the male bird covering the eggs more often than the female, and others have reported finding the male caring for the young. Mr. Dixon (1917) says of the young:

The young sandpipers were found feeding in the shallower pools, where the water was less than 1 inch deep. At times as many as five were noted in an area 1 yard square. They congregated along the water's edge, picking up, as the tide slowly receded, many bits of food. The nature of this provender I could not make out, although the young birds would often come within 20 feet of me when I remained motionless for a few minutes. The old birds were much more shy, often taking flight or retreating to distant gravel bars upon my approach. Considerable time was spent by both young and old in making short flights about the harbor. These flights alternated with periods of food getting, and were seemingly in preparation for the fall migration. It was only a few days then until the bulk of the species left on their southward journey.

Plumages.—The downy young Baird sandpiper is well colored to escape detection on the brown tundra moss. The crown and upper parts are variegated with black and "tawny" in an irregular pattern and dotted with white terminal tufts; the crown is centrally "tawny," with a median black stripe, and is bordered with black; the forehead, back to eyes, sides of the head and all under parts are pure white; there is a black spot in the center of the forehead, a black stripe from the bill, through the eye, to the occiput and another below it and parallel to it; there is a white superciliary stripe and some white mottling on the back of the head and neck.

The juvenal plumage is equally concealing. The crown is sepia with buffy edgings; the back and scapulars are dark sepia with broad white edgings; the wing is like the adult except that the coverts and tertials are edged with "pinkish buff" and tipped with white; the under parts are like the adult but the breast is more pinkish buff and more faintly streaked. A partial postjuvenal molt, including most of the body plumage and some of the scapulars, wing coverts, and tertials and takes place in October or later. I have seen birds in full juvenal plumage as late as October 3; young birds migrate in this plumage. At the first prenuptial molt the following spring young birds become indistinguishable from adults.

Adults have a partial prenuptial molt in April and May, including only part of the body plumage. The postnuptial molt begins in July, when the body plumage is molted before the birds migrate; the wings are molted after the birds reach their winter home, from December to February, not long before they started to migrate north again. I have seen birds in full nuptial plumage as early as May 1 and as late as July 29, and in full winter plumage as late as April 5. The adult nuptial and winter plumages are somewhat different; the colors are brighter and richer in the spring and the markings are more distinct; in the fall the upper parts are nearly uniformly buffy brownish with dusky shaft streaks; the chest and sides of the breast are dull brownish buff and not distinctly streaked.

Food.—Preble and McAtee (1923) found in the stomachs of three Baird sandpipers, taken on the Pribilof Islands, amphipods, algae, ground beetles, and a weevil. Mr. McAtee (1911) includes this species among those that eat mosquito larvae, crane-fly larvae, grasshoppers, and the clover-root curculio, all injurious insects. It feeds on the open mud flats with other species of sandpipers, but seems to prefer to feed about the edges of the shallow inland pools or where the muddy flats are partially overgrown with grass. William Brewster (1925) watched some of them feeding, of which he says:

On first noticing me draw near they stood erect, with upstretched necks, regarding me intently and distrustfully, but their feeding operations were resumed soon after I ceased to advance. By successive runs, 8 or 10 feet in length and often executed very swiftly, they moved about quickly in various directions over soft mud or through shallow water, frequently stooping to pick up small morsels of food, but not once using their bills for probing under ground or water.

Voice.—Dr. Charles W. Townsend (1905) says that the note, which he heard several times, seemed to him "exactly like that of the semipalmated sandpiper, a rather shrill, trilling whistle." Mr. Brewster (1925) says that—

the *kreep* call they utter in flight is sufficiently unlike that of any other wader of similar size and general coloring to be of service as a means of field identification when the birds are seen on wing. It is appreciably different from the call of any other sandpiper known to me, although not so very unlike that of the sanderling.

Field marks.—The Baird sandpiper is one of the most difficult of all this group to recognize in the field, because it has no prominent distinguishing field marks peculiar to itself. It has characters in common with any one of several small sandpipers. In color and general appearance it is most like the least sandpiper; it is decidedly larger, but size is of little value unless the two are side by side for comparison; it is lighter colored above, more extensively buffy on the breast, and has darker legs. It is a size larger than the semipalmated and western sandpipers, more buffy on the breast than either, and has a shorter bill in proportion to its size than the latter. It is about the size of the white-rumped sandpiper, but is less distinctly streaked on the crown and back; the buff breast of the Baird will distinguish it when standing or even in flight; and the white rump of *fuscicollis* is a sure flight mark when visible. From the red-backed sandpiper, about the same size, it can be distinguished by its shorter and straighter bill and by marked color differences. It might be mistaken for a female pectoral, but the latter is more conspicuously striped above, more like a snipe in this respect, the crown is darker, more contrasted, and the breast is darker, more abruptly separated from the white belly, and more sharply streaked with dusky; when flying the pectoral shows more white in the wings. The Baird is but slightly smaller than the buff-breasted sandpiper and very much like it; but Prof. William Rowan (MSS.) has pointed out some differences. The patterns of the backs are very similar, but the buff breasted has a much paler crown and lacks the white throat and eye stripe, as well as the clear-cut white sides and black center of the rump of the Baird. The buff breasted has yellow legs and the Baird has black. The Baird shows no white in the wings in flight. Young Bairds in juvenal plumage are easily recognized by the scaled appearance of the mantle produced by dark feathers with broad white edges.

Fall.—Baird sandpipers leave their northern breeding grounds rather early. Mr. Murdoch (1885) reported the last one seen at Point Barrow on August 12, and Mr. Dixon (1917) saw none after August 15 in northern Alaska. E. A. Preble (1908) saw several flocks on migration at Great Slave Lake as early as July 10.

The main flight seems to be directly south through the Mackenzie Valley and between the Rocky Mountains and the Mississippi River to Mexico and South America, where it probably migrates down the west coast to its winter home. But the route is also extended both east and west in the fall. Some birds fly southeastward, through the Great Lakes, to the coast of New England, whence they apparently migrate over the ocean to South America. Others migrate southward through the extreme western States.

Mr. Brewster (1925) says that they "visit Lake Umbagog (Maine) early in September, appearing oftenest during the first week in the month." My Massachusetts dates run from August 7 to September 15. E. W. Hadeler records it in his Ohio notes from September 2 to October 11; and Edward S. Thomas has seen it there as early as August 12. It is an abundant migrant in Manitoba; we collected adults there on July 29; and C. G. Harrold tells me that birds passing through in August and September are practically all juveniles. Professor Rowan refers to it as probably the most plentiful wader in Alberta in the first half of September; he has taken it there as late as November 8. J. A. Munro calls it a regular fall migrant at Okanagan Landing, British Columbia; his earliest and latest dates are July 16 and September 18. J. H. Bowles (1918) observed it on the Tacoma Flats, Washington, from July 26 to September 5, and says:

They were found in singles, pairs, or trios, most often associating with the semipalmated plover (*Aegialitis semipalmata*) when any were to be found. When flying with a company of the other small sandpipers they would separate as soon as the flock alighted to feed, the Baird's going to comparatively dry ground for their food while the others waded about in the water and at the water's edge. They could not have been called common, but from one to three or four were to be found on almost any day.

John T. Nichols has observed Baird sandpipers on the Pacific Ocean and writes to me as follows:

August 6, 1926, 52° 19' N., 137° 42' W., three to six birds of this species came about a ship bound southeast for Seattle, flying with and parallel to her course. One, apparently misjudging her speed, was killed by striking the rigging forward. Perhaps the Baird sandpiper is comparatively scarce on the Pacific coast due to an offshore migration route.

Winter.—According to Prof. Wells W. Cooke (1912) this sandpiper reaches its winter home in September. Chile seems to be its principal winter home, where it has been taken repeatedly in the high mountains at 10,000 to 12,000 feet and once at over 13,000.

DISTRIBUTION

Range.—Northeastern Asia and North and South America; accidental in England.

Breeding range.—North to the northeastern coast of Siberia (probably Koliutschin Island and Cape Serdze Kamen); northern Alaska (Wainwright, Point Barrow, Camden Bay, Barter Island, and Demarcation Point); Yukon (Herschel Island); Mackenzie (Franklin Bay, Baillie Island, and Cambridge Bay); and southern Baffin

Island. East to Baffin Island and probably Greenland (Etah). South to Mackenzie (Cambridge Bay, Bernard Harbor, Fort Anderson, and Peel River); and Alaska (Cape Prince of Wales and Point Dall). West to Alaska (Cape Prince of Wales and Point Dall); and northeastern Siberia (probably Koliutschin Island).

Winter range.—North to Chile (Tarapaca); and Argentina (Tucuman, Cordoba, and Buenos Aires). East to Argentina (Buenos Aires). South to Argentina (Buenos Aires); and Chile (Talcahuano). West to Chile (Talcahuano, Huasco, and Tarapaca).

Spring migration.—In spring the Baird sandpiper is practically unknown on the Atlantic coast, the route being up the Mississippi Valley, the plains States, and (to a lesser degree) the Pacific coast. Early dates of arrival are: Missouri, Monteer, March 20, and near Boonville, April 16; Ohio, Painesville, April 25, Oberlin, April 28, and Cleveland, May 8; Michigan, Vicksburg, April 15; Iowa, Sioux City, April 9, Mason City, April 19, and Marshalltown, April 25; Minnesota, Waseca, May 10, and Hutchinson, May 18; Texas, Boerne, March 16, and Electra, April 9; Kansas, Emporia, March 27; Nebraska, Gibbon, March 19, Lincoln, March 23, and Callaway, April 7; South Dakota, Forestburg, April 6, and Brown County, April 18; North Dakota, Jamestown, May 1, and Charlson, May 4; Saskatchewan, Indian Head, May 9, and Orestwynd, May 10; Mackenzie, Fort Resolution, May 19, Fort Simpson, May 20, and Fort Providence, May 26; Arizona, Fort Verde, May 5; Colorado, Loveland, March 29; Wyoming, Cheyenne, April 8, and Laramie, April 23; Montana, Knowlton, May 12, and Bitterroot Valley, May 18; Alberta, Flagstaff, April 16, Alliance, April 24, and Fort Chipewyan, May 24; California, Santa Barbara, April 27; Washington, Dayton, April 11; British Columbia, Chilliwack, April 29, and Okanagan Landing, April 30; and Alaska, Admiralty Island, May 12, Kowak River, May 20, Demarcation Point, May 23, Nulato, May 27, Cape Prince of Wales, May 28, and Point Barrow, May 29.

Late dates of spring departure are: Mexico, city of Mexico, May 19; Guerrero, Iguala, June 1; Ohio, Youngstown, June 2; Michigan, Detroit, May 24; Iowa, Sioux City, June 6; Texas, San Angelo, May 15, and Ingram, May 26; Kansas, Wichita, May 20; Nebraska, Neligh, May 26, and Valentine, May 30; South Dakota, Vermilion, May 24, and Sioux Falls, June 11; North Dakota, Charlson, May 22, and Jamestown, June 4; Saskatchewan, Indian Head, June 2, and Quill Lake, June 16; Wyoming, Yellowstone Park, June 3; Alberta, Fort Chipewyan, June 1; and British Columbia, Okanagan Landing, May 10, Vaseaux Lake, May 18, and Sumas, May 19.

Fall migration.—Early dates of fall arrival are: British Columbia, Okanagan Landing, July 7; Washington, Wrights Peak, July 21, Blaine, August 4, and Tacoma, August 6; California, Santa Barbara,

July 25; Lower California, San Jose del Cabo, September 3; Alberta, Strathmore, July 31; Wyoming, Toltec, July 27; Colorado, Denver, July 21, Boulder County, July 27, and El Paso County, July 29; Saskatchewan, Maple Creek, July 17; Manitoba, Oak Lake, July 12, and Red Deer River, July 23; South Dakota, Forestburg, July 25; Nebraska, Callaway, August 4, and Lincoln, August 9; Texas, San Angelo, July 20; Ontario, Toronto, July 28; Michigan, Charity Island, July 9; Ohio, Bay Point, July 3; Illinois, Chicago, July 2; Massachusetts, Monomoy Island, July 14; New York, Montauk, August 14, Locust Grove, August 18, Onondaga Lake, August 27; Pennsylvania, Beaver, August 21, Erie, August 22; Mexico, Zacatecas, August 16, Colonia Garcia, September 4, and Janos River, September 5; and Patagonia, Arroyo Seco, Rio Negro, September 6, and Huanuluan, September 12.

Late dates of fall departures are: Alaska, Point Barrow, September 4; British Columbia, Comox, September 15, and Okanagan Landing, October 18; Washington, Tacoma, September 27; Oregon, Netarts Bay, September 12; California, Monterey, October 24; Colorado, Boulder County, September 25, and Barr, October 5; Saskatchewan, Indian Head, September 21; Manitoba, Oak Lake, September 5, and Shoal Lake, September 14; North Dakota, Charlson, September 21; Nebraska, Valentine, October 10, and Lincoln, November 3; Kansas, Lawrence, October 26; Texas, Tom Green and Concho Counties, October 20; Iowa, Burlington, October 2, and Keokuk, October 14; Ontario, St. Thomas, October 3, Toronto, October 10, and Plover Mills, October 20; Ohio, Painesville, October 11, and New Bremen, October 28; Illinois, Chicago, October 2; Missouri, Independence, October 13; Maine, Warren Island, September 20, and Bangor, November 1; Massachusetts, Cambridge, October 30; Connecticut, West Haven, October 28, and Stratford, November 3; New York, Shinnecock Bay, October 31, and Canandaigua, November 20; and Pennsylvania, Erie, October 6.

Casual records.—The Baird sandpiper has several times been taken or observed in various parts of Mexico so that it seems reasonable to believe that at least a part of the birds migrate over that country. In other Central American countries and in the West Indies it is rare. Among the records are: Costa Rica (Cerro de la Candelaria, October 1900, Volcano Irazu, June 8, 1894, La Estrella de Cartago, November 5, 1907, and San Jose, September 18); and Cuba (Cocos Island). It also has been detected on the Galapagos Islands (Barrington Island, October 6, 1897); Lesser Antilles (Dominica, October 1, 1904); Virginia (Four-mile Run, September 3 and 25, 1894); New Jersey (Stone Harbor, September 5, 1898); Quebec (Montreal,

September 17, 1892) ; New Brunswick (St. Andrews, September 10, 1901) ; and England (Rye Harbor, Sussex, November 11, 1900).

Egg dates.—Alaska: 27 records, June 9 to August 24; 14 records, June 19 to July 2. Arctic Canada: 20 records, June 10 to July 21; 10 records, June 19 to 26.

PISOBIA MINUTILLA (Vieillot)

LEAST SANDPIPER

HABITS

Contributed by Charles Wendell Townsend

This least of all our sandpipers is so little smaller than the semipalmated sandpiper and differs so slightly from it in other ways that the two are generally confused in life. Their small size and their notes have given them the familiar name of "peep," but near New York they are also called "oxeye." Who has not been gladdened by the sight of flocks of these gentle little birds scampering along the beach or diligently feeding in the tidal flats and in the salt marshes!

Spring.—The duration of the spring migration is much more brief than that of the autumnal one. The birds are hastening to their breeding grounds and the least sandpiper is only a month in passing through. In New England this is from about May 5 to June 7. At this time the birds are more apt to be found on the beaches than in the fall, although they are found in greatest abundance in the marshes.

Courtship.—The most noticeable part of the courtship of the least sandpiper is the song. I have observed it on the breeding grounds in Nova Scotia and in Labrador, as well as during the spring migration in New England. The bird springs up into the air on quivering, down-curved wings and circles about, now lower, now higher, reaching at times a height of 50 or more yards. In the air it emits a short sweet trill which is rapidly repeated, and with each song burst the wings are rapidly vibrated. On one occasion in Labrador the bird remained in the air circling and repeatedly trilling for five minutes by the watch, and continued to trill after it had reached the ground. Immediately it was up again, trilling, and, as I left the bog, it followed me, still trilling.

This courtship song has been described at great length and with much appreciation by Robert T. Moore (1912) from intimate studies made by him on five nesting birds in the Magdalen Islands, and he has recorded these songs in musical notation. He ranks it high among bird songs and dwells on its tremulous and pathetic qualities. He observed one that rendered its entire song from the ground within a foot of his hand. " It consisted of a series of trills, which ascended just one octave on a minor chord. The tone quality was pure and sweet and rendered pathetic by the minor chord, which served as its medium." He says of the records he made of the flight songs of three birds that—

Each in its notes, progressions, and even time is totally different from the others, yet, without sight of the bird, I would instantly recognize them as songs of the least sandpiper. This is due to the fact that the quality of tone is constant in all, being pure and sweet, the tempo is always extremely fast, the notes being delivered with great rapidity, and the pitch high. Trills and runs are characteristic and make an additional recognition quality.

All these observations were made on birds that were both incubating and singing. On one occasion only did he see two birds together.

This flight song piped overhead and was sung over and over again with a tremulous zest. Alternating with it, was repeated for long intervals an excited call of two notes. We glanced up and for the first time beheld two adult least sandpipers together. Alternately they flapped and soared and circled about in rapturous fashion. For several minutes the alternation of song and call continued without break of any kind. Sometimes the song was given three times consecutively and followed by as many as 30 or 40 repetitions of the call, this in turn to be followed by the song again.

W. E. Saunders (1902) has recorded the courtship as observed by him at Sable Island. He was there between May 16 and 23, too early for nesting. He says: " I found them invariably in pairs, evidently mated, and often sitting so close together that two could be obtained at a single shot if desired." To his ear the song notes resembled somewhat those of the spotted sandpiper. He says of the courtship flight:

Sometimes both birds would be in the air at once, but whether the female gave the note as well as the male, I could not definitely ascertain without shooting the birds, which I was very loath to do. The note would be given continuously for perhaps three or four minutes, during which time the bird flies slowly with steady flapping of the wings, mounting in the air gradually until, when watching them in the evening, one loses sight of them in the gloom.

Nesting.—The least sandpiper makes its nest either in wet grassy or sphagnum bogs close to a pond or tidal water, or on dry uplands, often among low bushes. In either case the nest is a simple affair. P. B. Philipp (1925) describes its method of construction as observed by him in the Magdalen Islands:

The bird picks out a spot in the wet moss of a bog or in the dry leaves of a ridge, and scratches a shallow hollow in which it sits, and, by rapidly turning, molds a depression of the required depth. Which of the pair does this I have never determined, but the other bird is usually present, standing close to the nest-builder and offering encouragement by a low, rapid twittering.

The nest depression in the moss is generally lined with dry leaves, although these may be very few in number, and a little dried grass.

The internal dimensions of the nest as given by Audubon (1840) are: Diameter, 2½ inches; depth, 1¼ inches.

J. R. Whitaker writes, in his notes on these birds at Grand Lake, Newfoundland, that the nest is nearly always amongst a labyrinth of pools of water, and is usually on the side or the top of a hummock of sphagnum moss, but I have found them on flat ground amongst reindeer moss. When on a moss hummock, the scratch is about 2 inches deep and there is always an inch or so of material in the bottom usually composed of cranberry leaves and short bits of cotton grass stems.

Eggs.—[*Author's note:* Four eggs is the rule with the least sandpiper. They vary in shape from ovate pyriform (the usual shape) to subpyriform, and they have only a slight gloss. The ground colors vary from " deep olive buff " to " pale olive buff," or from " pale pinkish buff " to " cartridge buff." There are two extreme types of markings, the boldly blotched and the finely sprinkled type, with many intergradations between them. Some eggs are more or less evenly covered, usually more thickly about the larger end, with a mixture of dots, small spots, and small, irregular blotches. In some the blotches are larger, more elongated, often spirally arranged and often confluent at the larger end. In still others the whole egg is evenly covered with very fine dots and small markings. There are two sets from Labrador of the latter type in my collection; one has a pinkish ground color, covered uniformly with a fine sprinkling of reddish brown markings, exactly like certain eggs of the western sandpiper; the other set is similarly marked, but the ground color is " olive buff " and the markings are in darker browns. At the other end of the range of variation I have a particularly handsome egg, which has an " olive buff " ground color, with a few large splashes of " vinaceous drab," overlaid, chiefly around the larger end, with a few great splashes of " liver brown," " chestnut brown," and " bone brown." The ordinary markings are in various shades of dark, rich browns, " bay," " liver brown," " chestnut," and " hazel," deepening to blackish brown where the pigment is thickest. The underlying spots are in pale shades of " vinaceous drab." The measurements of 65 eggs in the United States National Museum average 29 by 21 millimeters; the eggs showing the four extremes measure 31 by 21, 30 by 22, 26.5 by 20, and 28 by 19 millimeters.]

Young.—Incubation is believed to be performed largely by the male. Mr. Philipp (1925):

Collected four birds from the nests and all proved to be males on dissection. Also a bird which was accidentally stepped on while it was shielding four young or " downies " was a male. In fact, after the eggs are laid both birds are seldom seen around the nest. The incubating bird is most solicitous about its nest. It sits very closely and, when flushed, half runs, half flutters for a few feet as if trying to lead the intruder away. If you are not deceived

by these actions but remain quiet, the bird soon returns and walks daintily
about, uttering a quickly repeated *peep, peep, peep,* often with such vehemence
that the saliva fairly runs from its bill.

Mr. Moore (1912), however, shot a bird which he thought was
both incubating and singing, and it proved to be a female.

Sometimes both parents show solicitude for the young as in the
following case in the Yukon region, reported by Dr. Louis B.
Bishop (1900):

I came upon a female surrounded by four downy young. Both parents
tried time and again the well known wounded-bird tactics to lure me from
the spot where the young were hidden in the bunches of grass, and finding
this a failure, would circle around me only a few yards off, uttering a plaintive
twitter.

Plumages.—[*Author's note:* The tiny chick of the least sandpiper
is prettily colored as are the young of all the tundra nesting species.
The upper parts, crown, back, wings, and thighs, are quite uniformly
variegated with rich browns, "bay," "chestnut" and "Sanford's
brown," through which the black basal down shows in places; this
is spotted irregularly, from crown to rump, with small round spots,
terminal tufts, of yellowish buff. The forehead and sides of the
head and neck are pale buff, with narrow, black frontal, loral and
malar stripes. The under parts are pure white.

Young birds are in juvenal plumage when they arrive here in
August and generally do not show much signs of molting before they
leave here in September. This plumage is darker and more richly
colored above than in the spring adult; the feathers of the crown,
back, scapulars and all wing coverts are broadly edged with rich,
bright browns, "hazel" or "cinnamon rufous," broadest and brightest on the back and scapulars; some scapulars are tipped with white;
the throat is often faintly, but sometimes not at all, streaked with
dusky. A partial postjuvenal molt in the fall, involving the body
plumage and some of the scapulars and tertials, produces a first
winter plumage which can be distinguished from the adult by the
retained juvenal wing coverts, scapulars, and tertials. At the first
prenuptial molt the next spring young birds become indistinguishable
from adults, except for some of the old juvenal wing coverts.

The complete postnuptial molt of adults begins in August and is
mainly accomplished after the birds have migrated. At a partial prenuptial molt, mainly in April and May, the adult renews the body
plumage and tail and some of the tertials and wing coverts. Adults
in spring are more brightly colored, with more rufous and buffy
edgings, and the breast is more distinctly streaked than in fall.]

Food.—These birds appear to be feeding on small crustaceans and
worms on the beaches and on insects and their larvae in the marshes.
It is to be hoped that with the increase of the birds the pest of

green-head flies and of mosquitoes in the salt marshes may diminish. E. A. Preble (1923) examined two stomachs from birds shot in the Pribilof Islands and found that one of them contained amphipods exclusively, the other the following items: "23 seeds of bottle brush (*Hippuris vulgaris*), 50 per cent; bits of hydroid stems, 40 per cent; and chitin from the blue mussel (*Mytilus edulis*), 10 per cent." A. H. Howell (1924) reports as follows: " Of the 19 stomachs of this bird collected in Alabama, practically all contained larvae or pupae of small flies (Chironomidae) in a few bits of aquatic beetles were found." Dr. Alexander Wetmore (1916) found in the stomach of a bird taken in Porto Rico " the heads of more than 100 minute fly larvae (75 per cent) and fragments of small beetles (*Hetercerus* sp.) (25 per cent)."

Behavior.—The least sandpiper has always been a confiding and an unsuspicious bird, and these characteristics have increased since it has been protected at all seasons. So diligent are they in their search for food that they appear to take no notice of man if he remain quiet, and they run about almost at his feet. They are fascinating birds to watch. Not only are they gregarious, collecting in large and small flocks on the migrations, but they are also of a sociable disposition and associate amicably with other shore birds, large and small. They run around among yellow legs like pigmies among giants. A mixed company of several kinds of sandpipers and of plovers feeding together is a common sight. In flight the different species, although in company, generally, but not always, keep by themselves.

In the marshes—which are their preferred feeding grounds, although, as stated above, they are sometimes found on the beaches, especially in the spring—they scatter widely, and one may flush one bird after another, previously unseen in the grass. They soon unite in a flock, however, and after circling about and turning now this way, now that, with great nicety of evolution, drop down again suddenly, often near the spot from which they sprang. A single bird flushed generally darts off in irregular zigzags, very much after the manner of a Wilson snipe, calling as it goes.

In feeding in marshes they frequent the short grass and also the open sloughs or mud holes. Here they snap up insects or probe diligently for larvae in the mud and shallow water. They are fond of the mud and sand flats in the tidal estuaries at low water where they appear to find plenty of food, and they run about on the eel grass. In all these places they spread out in an irregular fashion when feeding. Such gluttons are they that they are generally loaded with fat on the southward migration and they are often very fat in the spring. Notwithstanding this, their wind seems to be excellent and their flight as swift. They are fond of bathing like most birds, and of this Mr. Nichols writes in his notes as follows:

It squats in shallow water, ducking the head under, throwing the water back and fluttering the wings, and at the end of the bath jumps an inch or two into the air with a flutter, apparently to shake the water out of its feathers. Afterwards it usually stands quietly and gives its plumage a thorough preening.

Voice.—The nuptial song has been described under courtship, but the bird has also a variety of call notes from a simple *weep* or *peep*, from which, doubtless, it gets its common name, to a succession of notes more or less complicated. John T. Nichols (1920) has written at length on the voices of shore birds, and has kindly furnished the following for this article:

The identification flight-call is a loud diagnostic *kreep*, distinguished by the ēē sound from any note of the semipalmated sandpiper . . . In flushing, a least sandpiper sometimes utters a string of short unloud notes with or without the ēē sound, *quee-quee-quee-que* or *queque* to be followed almost immediately by some variation of the flight call, as it gets more fully under way. The flight note varies down to a *che* and *cher*, not readily, if at all, distinguishable from similar calls of the semipalmated sandpiper . . . When a flock are up and wheeling about a feeding spot to alight there again almost at once, they have sometimes a confiding little note *chu chu chu chu*, etc. It has also a whinny, a little less clearly enunciated than that of the semipalmated but almost identical with the same.

Field marks.—The small size of the least sandpiper distinguishes it readily from all the other sandpipers in this country except the semipalmated, with two exceptions to be noted later. As the least is more frequently found on tidal flats in the estuaries and in salt marshes, it is sometimes called the "mud peep," while the semipalmated, which especially delights in the sand beaches is called the "sand peep." Unfortunately this rule, although of general value, is far from absolute, and the birds often exchange places. The least sandpiper is more often found on the beach in the spring than in the fall. The semipalmation is, of course, a diagnostic mark in the hand, but only under exceptional circumstances can it be seen in the field. The color of the tarsus, however, is distinctive and can be made out in favorable light at a considerable distance. I have always thought it absolutely distinctive, but the published descriptions and plates of these two birds are often inaccurate. I have, therefore, compared the legs of both these species, freshly collected, with Ridgway's (1912) "Color Standards and Color Nomenclature." In the semipalmated sandpiper the tarsi of the adults are black and this is also the case in the juvenals except that there is a slight greenish tinge to be seen on close inspection. In the adult least sandpiper the tarsi are distinctly yellow with a faint greenish cast. They correspond best to the *sulphine yellow* of Ridgway, while the toes, which shade off a little darker, are *citrine*. In the juvenal, there is more of a greenish tinge, and I have put the tarsi down as *oil yellow*, the toes shading into *yellowish oil green*. In deciding on these colors I have had the advice of an artist. The richer brown plumage of the back and the darker streakings and wash of the breast help to distinguish the least from the lighter and grayer semipalmated bird, but in the fall these distinctions are less marked in the adult. Even at this season, however, a least sandpiper on the beach in a flock of semipalmated stands out by its browner colors, and, in the marsh, a semipalmated in a flock of least looks very gray. The least sandpiper is a little smaller than the other bird, but this character as well as the color of the plumage are of slight value without the presence of both birds for comparison.

Another point, which at times can be satisfactorily made out in the field, is that the bill of the least sandpiper is slightly decurved, while that of the semipalmated is straight and stouter. It has been noted by Coues (1861) and by others independently, that the least sandpiper is a perfect miniature of the pectoral sandpiper even to the color of its legs. The great difference in size, however, prevents any confusion.

Two other sandpipers, referred to above, may, however, be mistaken for least or semipalmated sandpipers, although they are somewhat larger. Gunners at Ipswich used to call them "bull peep." I refer to the white-rumped and the Baird sandpipers. The white rump of the former is diagnostic and is easily seen in flight, but is generally covered by the wings when the birds are running on the sand. The plumage of both Baird and white-rumped sandpipers is dark in front of the bend of the wing, while in the semipalmated and juvenal least it is light. This is a fine point that I have found of great value.

Fall.—The last migrant for the north has scarcely gone before wisps of returning sandpipers appear. The regular northward migration in Massachusetts ceases about June 7, although an occasional nonbreeding bird may remain, and the migrants begin to return about July 4. A surprisingly large number of early fall migrants appeared at Ipswich on July 3, 1911. A flock of at least 50 whirled about and alighted near me on the marsh. One must suppose that the early migrants in the spring are the early ones to return in the fall. They are generally all gone from the New England coast by the end of the first week in September, although stragglers may be found in October. They migrate both by day and by night.

Carl Lien writes in his notes from Destruction Island, Washington, that the least sandpiper—

Constitutes, with the western sandpiper, the great body of migratory birds, and if the nights are a little misty the numbers that circle around the light at nigh resemble a snow storm, and they continue until daybreak when they apparently get their bearings, and continue their journey. The spring movement begins about the middle of April or a little later, and lasts until about the 10th of May, beginning again the first week in July and lasting until the middle of September.

Game.—Fortunately this bird has been removed from the list of game by the Federal law, and we may be sure it will never be replaced. In the absence of larger birds—too frequently the case—the gunner used to shoot these tiny birds in large numbers, and it must be admitted they were delicious eating. At his blind near a slough or mud hole in the salt marshes he would arrange his flock of tin or wooden decoys, generally made to represent yellowlegs, within easy reach of his gun, and he would call down with his tin whistle any passing flock. A projecting spit of mud extending out into the little pool afforded a convenient alighting place for the " peep," and their death trap, for here they could conveniently be raked by gun fire from the blind. The terrified and bewildered survivors spring into the air, and circling about over their dead and dying companions afford several more effective shots, which shower the victims down into the mud and water. Only a remnant of the flock escapes, to fall victims, perhaps, to their easy credulity at a neighboring blind. Sometimes the gunner in his greed would wait for the birds to bunch together closely on the spit, but before this took place to his satisfaction the alarm calls of a tattler or yellowlegs might ring out over the marsh and every bird would spring into the air and be off, much to his chagrin. Fortunately this destruction has not been carried too far. The law has stepped in before it is too late, as alas! may be the case with some of the larger shore birds. The increase of this species since the Federal law went into effect in 1913 is very striking. Mr. Philipp (1925) says there is " a large increase in this dainty shore bird. In 1907 an exhaustive search for breeding birds in the Magdalens resulted in finding 11 pairs. In 1923 in the same territory over 50 pairs were located with eggs or young."

DISTRIBUTION

Range.—North and South America; casual in Europe and Asia.

Breeding Range.—The least sandpiper breeds north to Alaska (Cape Blossom and the Kowak River); probably Yukon (Herschel Island); Mackenzie (Peel River, Fort Anderson, Rendezvous Lake, and Franklin Bay); southern Franklin (Cambridge Bay); Keewatin (Cape Fullerton); Labrador (Ramah); and Newfoundland (Quarry and Gaff Topsail). East to Labrador (Ramah, Okak, and Nain); Newfoundland (Quarry); and Nova Scotia (Sable Island). South to Nova Scotia (Sable Island); Quebec (Magdalen Islands); Keewatin (probably Fort Churchill); probably Saskatchewan (Isle de la Crosse); southern Mackenzie (probably Fort Simpson); south-

ern Yukon (Teslin River and Lake Marsh); and southern Alaska
(probably Gustavus Bay, and probably Kodiak). West to Alaska
(probably Kodiak, Nushagak, Lake Aleknagik, and Cape Blossom).

Winter Range.—North to California (San Francisco Bay, Owens
Lake, and Salton Sea); rarely Arizona (Mellen); Texas (Lomita
and Decatur); rarely Louisiana (Vermilion Bay); Alabama
(Dauphin Island); and rarely North Carolina (Pea Island). East
to rarely North Carolina (Pea Island); South Carolina (near
Charleston); Georgia (Savannah, Darien, and St. Marys); the
Bahama Islands (Abaco, New Providence, San Salvador, Acklin, and
Great Inagua Islands); probably the Lesser Antilles (St. Chris-
topher); French Guiana (Cayenne); and Brazil (Para, Pernambuco,
and Bahia). South to Brazil (Bahia and Cuyaba); and Peru
(Chorillos and Tumbez). West to Peru (Tumbez); Ecuador (Santa
Elena); the Galapagos Islands (Indefatigable Island); Costa Rica
(La Estrella de Cartago and Puntarenas); Honduras (Chame-
licon); Guatemala (Lake Atitlan and Chiapam); Jalisco (Zapotlan,
La Barca, and Guadalajara); Sinaloa (Mazatlan); Lower California
(San Jose del Cabo and Carmen Island); and California (Santa
Barbara and San Francisco Bay).

Spring migration.—Early dates of arrival are: Virginia, Back
Bay, April 18; District of Columbia, Washington, April 19; Mary-
land, Cambridge, May 1; Pennsylvania, Mercer County, April 18,
Butler, April 27, Cataract, May 2, Erie, May 8, and Pittsburgh, May
9; New Jersey, Cape May, April 4, Caldwell, April 7, Princeton,
April 30, and Camden, May 4; New York, Orient, April 21, New
York City, April 25, Auburn, April 29, Canandaigua, May 4, and
Rochester, May 9; Connecticut, Saybrook, May 3, and New Haven,
May 8; Massachusetts, Woods Hole, April 23, Ipswich, April 24,
Rehoboth, April 29, and Monomoy Island, May 6; Vermont, St.
Johnsbury, May 6; Maine, Saco, May 5; Quebec, Quebec City, April
28, and Godbout, May 12; Nova Scotia, Halifax, April 20; Kentucky,
Bowling Green, April 23, and Lexington, May 7; Missouri, Courte-
nay, April 1, Corning, April 5, and Independence, April 15; Illinois,
De Kalb, April 6, Rantoul, April 9, and Milford, April 13; Indiana,
Jeffersonville, April 5, Richmond, April 21, and Fort Wayne, April
22; Ohio, New Bremen, April 19, Painesville, April 30, and Oberlin,
May 5; Michigan, Vicksburg, April 30, Battle Creek, May 3, and
Detroit, May 4; Ontario, Listowel, May 3, Toronto, May 4, Hamilton,
May 8, and Ottawa, May 10; Iowa, Marshalltown, April 25, Emmets-
burg, April 27, and Forest City, April 30; Wisconsin, Beloit, April
18, Whitewater, April 28, and Madison, May 7; Minnesota, Lake
Wilson, April 18, Heron Lake, April 24, and Waseca, April 30;
Kansas, McPherson, April 9, Lawrence, April 24, and Wichita, April
28; Nebraska, Lincoln, March 21, Valentine, April 6, and Alda,

April 10; South Dakota, Huron, April 8, Vermilion, April 20, and
Pitrodie, April 22; North Dakota, Stump Lake, April 28, James-
town, May 1, and Grafton, May 3; Manitoba, Gimli, May 6, and
Shoal Lake, May 15; Saskatchewan, Orestwynd, May 7, Indian
Head, May 12, and Dinsmore, May 14; Mackenzie, Fort Providence,
May 15, Fort Simpson, May 17, and Fort Resolution, May 19; Colo-
rado, Durango, April 12, Loveland, April 19, and Barr, April 26;
Utah, Bear River Marshes, May 10; Wyoming, Cheyenne, April 23,
and Laramie, April 23; Montana, Great Falls, April 16; Alberta,
Carvel, May 6, and Flagstaff, May 9; Oregon, Narrows, April 16,
Newport, April 21, and Klamath Lake, April 30; Washington,
Tacoma, April 28, and Grays Harbor, April 30; British Columbia,
Comox, April 20, Chilliwack, April 21, and Courtenay, April 22;
and Alaska, Craig, May 2, Juneau, May 4, Bethel, May 6, and Kowak
River, May 15.

Late dates of spring departure are: Porto Rico, Laguna de
Guanica, May 26; Cuba, Mariel, May 10, and Santiago de las Vegas,
May 14; the Bahama Islands, April 25; Florida, Punta Rassa, May
13, and St. Marks, May 28; Alabama, Bayou Labatre, May 16;
Georgia, Savannah, May 17; South Carolina, Lady Island, May 12,
and Aiken, May 14; North Carolina, Lake Ellis, May 18, and
Raleigh, May 22; Pennsylvania, Erie, May 24, and Beaver, May 28;
New Jersey, Bernardsville, May 20, Bloomfield, May 23, and Eliza-
beth, May 30; New York, Pine Plains, May 30, Rochester, May 31,
and Orient, June 4; Connecticut, Norwalk, May 30, and New Haven,
June 5; Massachusetts, Dennis, June 2, Harvard, June 9, and Pitts-
field, June 16; Vermont, St. Johnsbury, June 6; New Hampshire,
Manchester, June 3; Maine, Fryeburg, May 30, and Lewiston, June
6; Kentucky, Lexington, May 23; Chicago, May 23, and Port Byron,
June 15; Indiana, Greencastle, May 26, and Lake County, June 1;
Ohio, Columbus, May 21, Oberlin, May 23, and Youngstown, June
11; Michigan, Detroit, May 23, Sault Ste. Marie, May 26, and Man-
chester, May 29; Ontario, Listowel, May 23, Point Pelee, May 30,
London, June 1, and Brighton, June 10; Iowa, Sioux City, May 30,
Forest City, May 31, and Keokuk, June 2; Wisconsin, Berlin, May
24, Tomahawk, May 27, and Green Bay, June 4; Minnesota, Elk
River, May 23, and Walker, June 6; Texas, Seadrift, May 8, Ingram,
May 10, and San Angelo, May 16; Kansas, Emporia, May 15,
Wichita, May 18, and Lawrence, May 21; Nebraska, Peru, May 15,
Neligh, May 16, and Badger, May 18; South Dakota, Forestburg,
May 21, Huron, May 23, and Yankton, May 25; North Dakota,
Cando, May 24, and Charlson, June 1; Manitoba, Margaret, June 4,
Reaburn, June 15, and Shoal Lake, June 20; Saskatchewan, Indian
Head, May 23, and Osler, June 19; Colorado, Fort Lyon, May 29,
and Barr, June 19; Wyoming, Cheyenne, May 27; Montana, Terry,

May 21, and Great Falls, June 3; Alberta, Flagstaff, June 1; Tepic, Las Penas Islands, May 5; Lower California, Rivera, April 21, and Gardners Lagoon, April 23; California, Santa Barbara, May 10, Alameda, May 13, and Los Angeles, May 19; Oregon, Newport, May 20; Washington, Chelan, May 21, and Seattle, May 31; and British Columbia, Okanagan Landing, May 19.

Fall migration.—Early dates of fall arrival are: British Columbia, Atlin, June 29, Chilliwack, July 2, Okanagan Landing, July 3, and Courtenay, July 7; Washington, North Dalles, July 4, and Clallam Bay, July 17; Oregon, Silver Lake, July 1; California, Santa Barbara, July 18, and Bakersfield, July 19; Lower California, San Quentin, August 10; Alberta, Onoway, July 1; Wyoming, Fort Bridger, July 13, Utah, Provo, July 26; Colorado, Barr, July 5, Chihuahua, Pochaco, August 3; Saskatchewan, Isle de la Crosse, July 18; Manitoba, Victoria Beach, July 7, and Shoal Lake, July 27; North Dakota, Pembina, July 17, and Turtle Mountain, July 30; South Dakota, Forestburg, July 5, and Sioux Falls, July 24; Nebraska, Lincoln, July 14; Kansas, Emporia, August 6, and Osawatomie, August 31; Texas, Tom Green, and Concho Counties, July 20, and Tivoli, July 30; Minnesota, North Pacific Junction, July 8, Lanesboro, July 15, and St. Vincent, July 30; Wisconsin, Madison, July 11, North Freedom, July 14, and Madison, July 24; Iowa, Marshalltown, July 8, and Sioux City, July 17; Ontario, Toronto, July 4; Michigan, Detroit, July 7, and Charity Island, July 10; Ohio, Bay Point, July 3, Painesville, July 8, and Youngstown, July 27; Illinois, Chicago, July 2, and Peoria, July 13; Kentucky, Lexington, July 16; Maine, Portland, July 23; New Hampshire, Manchester, July 10; Vermont, St. Johnsbury, July 16, and Rutland, July 19; Massachusetts, Cape Cod, July 1, Ponkapog, July 16, and Dennis, July 25; Connecticut, New Haven, July 14, and Niantic, July 22; New York, Long Beach, July 3, Mastic, July 4, and Rochester, July 21; New Jersey, Tuckerton, July 3, Camden, July 7, and North Branch, July 8; Pennsylvania, Renovo, August 3, Beaver, August 11, Erie, August 13, and Pittsburgh, August 15; Maryland, Chesapeake Beach, August 16; South Carolina, Bulls Point, July 30; Georgia, Savannah, July 23; Alabama, Leighton, July 26; Florida, Palma Sola, July 9, James Island, July 20, and Pensacola, July 26; Bahama Islands, Long Island, July 16, Great Bahama, July 18, and Inagua, July 28; Cuba, Guantanamo, August 15, and Batabano, August 26; Jamaica, Port Henderson, August 2; Porto Rico, Mona Island, August 9, and Joyuda, August 28; Lesser Antilles, Barbuda, August 14, St. Vincent, August 20, and Trinidad, August 22; and Venezuela, Bonaire, July 23, Macuto, August 2, and La Guaira, August 10.

Late dates of fall departure are: Alaska, St. Paul Island, September 14; British Columbia, Chilliwack, September 11, and Okanagan

Landing, September 15; Washington, Nisqually Flats, November 14;
Oregon, Portland, September 7, Netarts Bay, September 11, and Tilla-
mook, September 15; Montana, Corvallis, September 7; Utah, Ogden,
October 8; Colorado, Denver, October 3, and Barr, October 5; Sas-
katchewan, Indian Head, September 4, and Rosetown, September 6;
Manitoba, Aweme, September 26, and Margaret, October 3; North
Dakota, Grafton, September 22; South Dakota, Forestburg, Septem-
ber 21, and Lacreek, September 29; Nebraska, Nebraska City, Octo-
ber 10, and Lincoln, November 11; Oklahoma, Copan, October 16;
Minnesota, Lanesboro, September 15; Iowa, Emmetsburg, September
23, Keokuk, September 24, and Marshalltown, October 12; Ontario,
Kingston, September 29, Ottawa, October 12, and Point Pelee, Octo-
ber 15; Michigan, Detroit, October 6; Ohio, Columbus, October 22,
Youngstown, October 29, and Cleveland, November 9; Illinois, De
Kalb, October 9; Missouri, Courtenay, November 9; Tennessee, Octo-
ber 23; Nova Scotia, Pictou, October 8; Quebec, Montreal, October
20; Maine, Lewiston, October 16; Massachusetts, Lynn, October 4,
Taunton, October 7, and Woods Hole, October 30; New York, Say-
ville, October 6, Ithaca, October 12, Canandaigua, October 14, and
Branchport, October 28; Maryland, Back River, November 3; and
District of Columbia, Anacostia River, November 27.

Casual records.—The least sandpiper has on a few occasions been
detected outside of its normal range. Among these occurrences are:
Chile (no definite locality [Salvin]); Greenland (Disko Fjord, August, 1878, Noursoak Peninsula, spring of 1867, and Frederikshaab,
July, 1857); England (Cornwall, October 1853, and September, 1890,
and Devonshire, September, 1869, and August, 1892); and northeastern Siberia (Belkoffsky, July 23, 1880, and Plover Bay, August
13, 1880).

Egg dates.—Magdalen Islands: 79 records, June 3 to 30; 40 records, June 8 to 17. Labrador and Newfoundland: 13 records, June
7 to July 1; 7 records, June 15 to 25. Arctic Canada: 14 records,
June 14 to July 8; 7 records, June 27 to July 1.

PISOBIA SUBMINUTA (Middendorff)

LONG-TOED STINT

HABITS

I prefer the above name, as adopted by Robert Ridgway (1919),
to the Check List name, *damacensis*, as it seems to have more certain application. The status of the species and its nomenclature is
fully discussed by Dr. Leonhard Stejneger (1885).

This is one of several Asiatic species that have gained places on
our list as stragglers to Alaska. A specimen of the long-toed stint
was taken by Dr. Charles H. Townsend on Otter Island, in the

Pribilofs, on June 8, 1885, constituting the only North American record. As the species migrates regularly through the Commander Islands to Kamchatka, it would not be surprising if careful collecting in the western Aleutians showed it to occur frequently in North American territory. Its close resemblance to some other small sandpipers might easily cause it to be overlooked. Very little seems to be known about its habits.

Spring.—Doctor Stejneger (1885) says:

The long-toed stint arrives at Bering Island in large flocks during the latter part of May, and are then met with on sandy beaches, where the surf has thrown up large masses of seaweed, busily engaged in picking up the numerous small crustaceans, etc., with which the weeds abound. Most of the birds stay only a few days, going further north, while a small number remain over summer, breeding sparingly on the large swamp behind the village. My efforts to find the nests were unsuccessful, but I shot birds near Zapornaja Reschka on the 17th and 22d of June, and on the 7th of August.

W. Sprague Brooks (1915) reports birds seen or taken at points in Kamchatka on May 21 and 25, 1913, which probably were just arriving on their breeding grounds.

Eggs.—I can find no description of the nesting habits of the long-toed stint in print and have located only one set of eggs. This is in Col. John E. Thayer's collection and has very scanty data. It was taken by O. Bernhaner at Lake Baikal, Siberia, on June 18, 1902; the nest was "placed on the ground." The four eggs in this set are ovate pyriform in shape and have hardly any gloss. The ground colors vary from " olive buff " to " deep olive buff." They are spotted, chiefly at the larger end, with " snuff brown," " sepia," and " warm sepia," with a few underlying spots of " pale brownish drab." They measure 28.3 by 20, 28 by 19.7, 28.5 by 20.7 and 28.3 by 20 millimeters.

Plumages.—The downy young seems to be entirely unknown. I have not seen enough specimens to add anything to our knowledge of the molts. Mr. Ridgway (1919) has described the immature and seasonal plumages quite fully.

DISTRIBUTION

Breeding range.—Said to breed in eastern Siberia, the shores of the Sea of Okhotsk, Kamchatka, Bering Island, and south to the Kurile Islands. Eggs have been taken at Lake Baikal, Siberia, and it probably breeds in the valley of the Lena River, south of the Arctic Circle.

Winter range.—The Malay Archipelago, India, Burma, Ceylon, the Philippines, and Australia.

Migration.—It arrives on Bering Island during the latter part of May and on Kamchatka as early as May 21. Fall migrants reach the Philippines as early as August 10.

Casual record.—Accidental on the Pribilof Islands, Otter Island, June 8, 1885.

Egg date.—Siberia: 1 record, June 18.

PISOBIA RUFICOLLIS (Pallas)

RUFOUS-NECKED SANDPIPER

HABITS

A long time ago Col. John E. Thayer (1909) added this species to the North American list. In a lot of birds which he received from A. H. Dunham were a pair of adults and two young of the rufous-necked sandpiper, or eastern least stint, as it is also called. They were collected at Nome, Alaska, on July 10, 1908, where they had evidently bred. This record was discredited, however, and the species was placed on the hypothetical list. But the species was firmly established as a North American bird by Alfred M. Bailey (1926), who reported the capture of two specimens in Alaska, an adult female at Cape Prince of Wales on June 11, and a bird of the year at Wainwright on August 15, 1922. The birds were breeding in that vicinity, an offshoot from the main breeding range of the species in northeastern Siberia.

Spring.—The main migration route is northward from southern Asia, the Philippine Islands, and even Australia, through the Kurile and Commander Islands and Kamchatka to its breeding grounds. Dr. Leonhard Stejneger (1885) says:

This species arrives at Bering Island late in May in rather large flocks, but does not stay long. None were met with during the whole summer, until, in the first half of September, they took a short rest on the shores of our island before continuing their long travel to the southward.

A large series of these birds was collected by the Jesup North Pacific expedition in northeastern Siberia. Dr. J. A. Allen (1905) quotes from the field notes of N. G. Buxton as follows:

Abundant spring and fall migrant, and some breed at Kooshka, but the majority move farther inland during the breeding season. First birds arrived May 28, and were common on the 30th in large flocks and in company with the red backed. By June 5 they have paired or passed on, and are not common again until the second week of July. They have mostly gone by September 11. In habits similar to *Pelidna alpina.*

Nesting.—Mr. Bailey (1926) was fortunate enough to see a pair building their nest, along a stream bed on the high tundra at the base of Wales Mountain, Alaska; in his notes for June 14, 1922, he wrote:

With my glasses I watched a pair of little pink-necked sandpipers as they worked around the grass at the foot of the hill. The male would give up his searching among the dried grass stalks to demonstrate his love for his little partner, upon which she would take to wing and circle about. Finally she entered a little tussock of grass, standing on her "nose" fluttering her tail and wings. Soon the male pushed his way inside, too, and after a few more rustling about, they took to wing. I looked in the grass and found a little cavity which they were just lining with leaves. Upon examining their nesting clump, I found a small pit, exactly similar to the nest of the western sandpiper, in which they had deposited about 20 small willow leaves. I marked the spot carefully, but upon my return found the nest abandoned.

W. Sprague Brooks (1915) found a few pairs breeding at the head of Providence Bay, northeastern Siberia; he writes:

Two sets of fresh eggs, numbering three and four, respectively, were taken on June 11, 1913; the male incubating one and the female the other. Both birds when disturbed fluttered off the nest like other sandpipers. The nests were cavities on small mounds of tundra lined with dry willow leaves.

Eggs.—I have been unable to locate any eggs of the rufous-necked sandpiper and do not know what became of the two sets referred to above. Joseph Dixon (1918) implies that the eggs resemble those of the spoonbill sandpiper.

Plumages.—In the downy young the crown and upper parts are variegated with black, "tawny" and "warm buff"; the forehead, superciliary stripe and sides of the head and neck are "warm buff"; the under parts are white, washed on the breast with pale buff; a narrow median stripe on the forehead and a broader loral stripe are black. The specimen described above was taken at Cape Serdze, Siberia, on July 16, and shows the beginning of the juvenal plumage: the back and scapulars are well covered with young feathers and the wings are well started, though the bird is still very small and mostly downy. The feathers of the back and scapulars are black, broadly edged with "hazel," and the scapulars are tipped with white.

Older young and subsequent plumages are well described by Robert Ridgway (1919). The molts are apparently similar to those of other species in the genus. The postnuptial molt of the body plumage occurs mainly in August and the wings and tail are molted in January and February. I have seen birds in winter plumage as early as August 13 and as late as March 15. Probably the prenuptial molt of the body plumage takes place in April. In fresh nuptial plumage the bright colors of the upper parts are veiled with "drab-gray" tips, which soon wear away. There is much individual variation in the amount of rufous on the head, neck, and breast. Mr. Dixon (1918) says that in this plumage the rufous-necked sandpiper looks very much like the spoonbill sandpiper; and, as its behavior is similar, it might easily be mistaken for it.

DISTRIBUTION

Breeding range.—Northeastern Siberia (probably the delta of of the Lena River and the shores of the Sea of Okhotsk, certainly at Providence Bay, Kooshka, and Cape Serdze); and northwestern Alaska (Cape Prince of Wales, Wainwright, and probably Nome.)

Winter range.—The Malay Archipelago, the Philippines, and Australia.

Migrations.—First arrivals reach Gichiga, Siberia, May 28, and they are mostly gone by September 11. They pass Bering Island late in May and again during the first half of September. One taken by G. Dallas Hanna on St. Paul Island, August 27, 1920. They have been taken in the Philippines as early as August 13. Japan, China, and Lake Baikal are included in the migration route.

PELIDNA ALPINA ALPINA (Linnaeus)

DUNLIN

HABITS

The well-known European dunlin has occurred occasionally as a straggler on our eastern coasts, Massachusetts and New York. It has probably occurred here more often than is known, for it closely resembles our red-backed sandpiper, especially in winter plumage. There is no reason why it should not occur here more often, for it is now known to breed regularly on the east coast of Greenland.

Thayer and Bangs (1914) thought, at one time, that we should recognize three races of the dunlin, which they designated as follows:

Pelidna alpina alpina (Linn.), western Europe. Small, with shortest, straightest bill; upper parts darker with less reddish; heavily spotted (sometimes almost streaked) with dusky below, between throat and black breast patch.

Pelidna alpina pacifica Coues. North America. Much larger, with much longer, more curved bill; upper parts paler with much more reddish; much less heavily spotted with dusky below, between throat and black breast patch.

Pelidna alpina sakhalina (Vieill.) East Siberia. Size and length and shape of bill intermediate between that of the other two forms; colors much paler than in either; upper parts very pale reddish, much mixed with gray; back of neck and top of head nearly wholly pale gray; below very slightly spotted with dusky, between throat and black breast patch (much less so, even than in *pacifica*).

Recently, Mr. Bangs tells me, he has come to the conclusion that the Siberian bird should not be separated from the American, as the characters are too slight and rather intermediate. This seems like a wise decision, as the naming of intermediates is undesirable.

Much has been published on the habits of the dunlin, but, as they differ but little from those of our birds, it seems superfluous to write its full life history.

Nesting.—Comparatively few of the great hosts of dunlins which visit England in fall and winter breed on the mainland of Great Britain. Macgillivray (1852) gives a good account of their nesting habits in Scotland, as follows:

The dunlins, in fact, breed in great numbers on the heaths of many parts of Scotland and its larger islands, where they may be found scattered in the haunts selected by the golden plovers, with which they are so frequently seen in company that they have popularly obtained the name of plovers' pages. Sometimes about the middle of April, but always before that of May, they are seen dispersed over the moors in pairs like the birds just named, which at this season they greatly resemble in manners. From this period until the end of August none are to be found along the shores of the sea, instead of searching which, they now seek for insects and worms, in the shallow pools, soft ground, and by the edges of lakes and marshes. The male frequently flies up to a person intruding upon his haunts, and sometimes endeavours to entice him away by feigning lameness.

Rev. Henry H. Slater (1898) says that the nest "is usually in a tussock of grass, a roughly made hollow, inartistically lined with grass, but often carefully concealed in the herbage."

A. L. V. Manniche (1910) found the dunlin a common breeding bird on the northeast coast of Greenland. He writes:

The nests are most frequently built on hillocks with long grass. I found, however, not seldom nests of dunlins on small islets covered with short grass, but always near to or surrounded by shallow water. The dunlin's nest is often placed on similar spots, and has the same exterior as that of the phalarope, but it can easily be distinguished, as the bottom of the dunlin's nest is always lined with a few withered leaves of *Salix arctica*, while the phalarope uses bent straws as layer for its eggs. On spots where many dunlins nest several newly scratched but half-finished nests may always be found; they are probably left because the birds have found the ground too wet. The dunlins like to nest on moors and bogs partly irrigated by melted snow streaming down from the rocks. On such places I found many nests with eggs and newborn downy young, which were lying close together in broods carefully guarded by the old female, on isolated larger hillocks surrounded by the ice-cold snow water. When the flood of melting snow is unusually strong, such localities may be completely inundated, and then not only the eggs but also the frail young ones, which are not yet able to save themselves by swimming through the cold water to dry spots, will be destroyed.

Eggs.—The great amount of variation in the beautiful eggs of the dunlin is well illustrated in Frank Poynting's (1895) fine colored plate of 12 eggs. Herbert Massey (1913) gives a better description of the eggs than I can give, so I quote him, as follows:

The eggs of this species resemble those of *G. gallinago* very closely in color, but in comparing a series (74 sets or 296 eggs) with that of *G. gallinago* one is struck by the greater proportion of the lighter ground colors in the dunlin, the very deep olives and the very dark browns being almost absent. On the other hand, the beautiful light blue-green and the pale buff are rare in *G. gallinago*. The surface spots are chiefly two shades of brown, a rich red and a dark brown, with, in many cases, spots of violet gray. In *T. alpina* it is rare to find the two shades of brown in the same egg, as is often the case with *G. gallinago*. The markings are very varied, some eggs dusted all over with tiny specks, others with specks and fair-sized spots, and again others with great blotches of color, chiefly at the larger end. The pattern markings on the eggs of the same set are often very dissimilar. Many of the eggs of this species show the spiral arrangement of the spots. The eggs are very glossy, and on this account have a brighter appearance than eggs of *G. gallinago*. I have only one set entirely without gloss.

The number of eggs is normally four, occasionally only three, and as many as five and even six have been found in a nest. The measurements of 100 eggs, furnished by Rev. F. C. R. Jourdain, average 34.3 by 24.4 millimeters; the eggs showing the four extremes measure **38.3** by 25.4, 35 by **25.8**, **31.3** by 23.2, and 32 by **23** millimeters.

Young.—Incubation is shared by both sexes and requires 22 days. Macgillivray (1852) says of the young:

Like those of the golden plover and lapwing, they leave the nest immediately after exclusion from the egg, run about, and when alarmed conceal themselves by sitting close to the ground and remaining motionless. If at this period a person approaches their retreat, the male especially, but frequently the female also, flies up to meet the intruder and uses the same artifices for deceiving him as many other birds of this family. After they are able to shift for themselves the young remain several weeks on the moors with their parents, both collecting into small flocks, which are often intermingled with those of the golden plover, and often in the evenings uniting into larger. They rest at night on the smoother parts of the heath, and both species, when resting by day, either stand or lie on the ground. When one advances within a hundred yards of such a flock it is pleasant to see them stretch up their wings, as if preparing for flight, utter a few low notes, and immediately stand on the alert, or run a short way; but at this season they are not at all shy.

Seton Gordon (1915), after giving a charming account of the breeding haunts of the dunlin in Scotland, has this to say about the solicitude of a devoted mother.

It was about this time that I saw the hen in precisely the same locality as before. She showed much more anxiety than the cock, uttering almost incessantly two alarm notes as she walked round me. One of these notes was the characteristic trill, unlike, I think, any other cry in the bird world; the other, which appeared to be the note of extra alarm, was a harsh cry reminding me much of the alarm note of the lesser tern. In order to observe the effect, I called several times, imitating the cry of one of her chicks. The effect was striking and instantaneous; the bird rushed up in alarm and literally rolled herself about on the ground with feathers ruffled. She, indeed, presented such an appearance that it was quite impossible to see her head or feet emerging from the disheveled bundle into which she rolled herself. Evidently her tactics were quite different—considerably less elegant, but perhaps equally forcible—to those used by the dotterel under similar circumstances. After a time she began to realize that her deception was producing no effect on the object of her mistrust, and moved anxiously round me.

Plumages.—In natal down the young dunlin is similar to the young red-backed sandpiper, but is paler in color, more buffy, and less rufous. The subsequent molts and plumages are similar to those of our American bird. They are well described in Witherby's (1920) Handbook.

Food.—Macgillivray (1852) made some careful observations on the feeding habits of dunlins, which are well worth quoting, as follows:

> Being in a muddy place, which probably afforded a good supply of food, they did not run much, but yet moved quickly about, with their legs a little bent, the body horizontal, the head a little declined, and the bill directed forward toward the ground at an angle of about 45°. I observed that they seemed in general merely to touch the surface, but also sometimes to introduce their bill into the mud for about a fourth of its length; but this was always with a rapid tapping and somewhat wriggling movement, and not by thrusting it in sedately. This flock having flown away, I observed another of about 12 individuals alight at a little distance on the other side of the mill stream. Being very intent on tapping the mud, they allowed me to approach within 10 paces, so that I could see them very distinctly. I examined the marks made by them in the mud. Although it was soft, very few footmarks were left, but the place was covered with numberless small holes made by their bills, and forming little groups, as if made by the individual birds separately. Of these impressions very many were mere hollows not much larger than those on a thimble, and not a twelfth of an inch deep; others scarcely perceptible, while a few were larger, extending to a depth of two-twelfths; and here and there one or two to the depth of nearly half an inch. On scraping the mud, I could perceive no worms or shells. It is thus clear that they search by gently tapping, and it appears that they discover the object of their search rather by the kind of resistance which it yields than by touch like that of the human skin.

Witherby's (1920) Handbook says that the food is mainly animal and includes mollusks, worms, crustaceans (shrimps and sandhoppers), insects (beetles, flies, etc.), and spiders.

Behavior.—The habits of the European dunlin seem to be the same as those of our bird. It is equally tame and confiding, unless shot at too much, and it has the same habit of flying in large, closely bunched flocks. John T. Nichols tells me that some that he saw near Liverpool in September, " when on the ground, moved about very actively for the most part (contrasted with the sluggishness of the redback as we know it in migration) and presented a low, hunch-shouldered figure." Abel Chapman (1924) says:

> On one occasion, on May 14, seeing three small waders floating on the mirror-like surface of the tide and quite 200 yards offshore, we punted out to them in full anticipation of having at last fallen in with phalaropes. Curiously, the trio proved to be dunlins, a species I can not recall having seen contentedly swimming in deep water on any other occasion.

DISTRIBUTION

Breeding range.—Northern Europe: Iceland, the Faroes, British Isles, northern coasts of Germany, northern Russia east to Kolguev, Spitzbergen, and probably Nova Zembla. South to Holland and rarely to northern Spain and northern Italy. Replaced by one or more other forms in Siberia, to which Asiatic migrants probably belong.

Winter range.—Great Britain, Madeira, the Canaries, the Mediterranean, northern and eastern Africa as far south as Zanzibar, the Red Sea, and perhaps India.

Casual records.—Accidental in North America; Shinnecock Bay, Long Island, New York, September 15, 1892; Chatham, Massachusetts, August 11, 1900. It has probably been many times overlooked.

Egg dates.—Orkney Islands: 50 records, May 12 to June 27; 25 records, May 20 to June 2. Iceland: 16 records, May 18 to June 16; 8 records, June 3 to 12.

PELIDNA ALPINA SAKHALINA (Vieillot)

RED-BACKED SANDPIPER

HABITS

Although this sandpiper is certainly red-backed enough to deserve the name, it seems to me that American dunlin would be a better name, as it is only subspecifically distinct from the well-known European dunlin. The doubtful question as to whether a third subspecies should be recognized on the Pacific coast has been referred to under the preceding form.

Spring.—It is a hardy bird and perhaps a lazy bird for it winters farther north than most of its tribe and makes shorter migrations than any of the waders that breed in Arctic regions. From its winter range well within the United States it migrates northward from Florida and the Carolinas along the Atlantic coast to the Middle States, rarely to New England, through the Great Lakes region, and along the west coast of Hudson Bay to its summer home on the barren grounds. C. J. Pennock tells me he has seen it in Florida, Wakulla County, as late as May 26; I found it very abundant and in fine spring plumage on the coastal islands of South Carolina on May 22 and 23; and I have seen it near Corpus Christi, Texas, as late as May 29. These are all late dates, however, for the migration starts in April and is generally completed in May. A single bird which I saw on the coast of Louisiana on June 22, 1910, was a nonbreeding loiterer. A. G. Lawrence and C. G. Harrold both record it in their notes as common in Manitoba from the middle to the last of May (12 to 29). William Rowan, however, finds it rare in Alberta.

There is a heavy northward migration along the Pacific coast. In some notes sent to me by D. E. Brown from Grays Harbor, Washington, he says:

This bird, next to the western sandpiper, was by far the most abundant of all the shore birds. It was noted in immense flocks the day of my arrival,

May 3, and was very common when I left, May 24.   Mixed flocks of this species and western sandpipers must have contained 6,000 or 7,000 birds.

Herbert W. Brandt in his manuscript notes says:

The red-backed sandpiper is one of the most abundant shore birds inhabiting the Hooper Bay region, confining itself almost entirely to the low-lying flats. The Eskimos first reported this hardy species on May 10 and two days later we collected our first specimen at Point Dall. They were common in loose flocks by May 15 and abundant by May 20. At that time they were often associated with the Aleutian sandpiper, to which, in the field, they bear a marked resemblance. Soon after the later date the flocks disintegrated into mated couples and they then repaired to their lowland breeding haunts.

Courtship.—Dr. E. W. Nelson (1887) gives an attractive account of the courtship of this species, as follows:

Soon after they arrive in spring they are engaged in pairing, and the males may be seen upon quivering wings flying after the female and uttering a musical, trilling note, which falls upon the ear like the mellow tinkle of large water drops falling rapidly into a partly filled vessel. Imagine the sounds thus produced by the water run together into a steady and rapid trill some 5 to 10 seconds in length, and the note of this sandpiper is represented. It is not loud but has a rich full tone, difficult to describe, but pleasant to hear among the discordant notes of the various waterfowl whose hoarse cries arise on all sides. As the lover's suit approaches its end the handsome suitor becomes exalted, and in his moments of excitement he rises 15 or 20 yards, and, hovering on tremulous wings over the object of his passion, pours forth a perfect gush of music, until he glides back to earth exhausted, but ready to repeat the effort a few minutes later. The female coyly retreats before the advances of the male, but after various mishaps each bird finds its partner for the summer and they start off house hunting in all the ardor of a rising honeymoon.

Mr. Brandt in his manuscript notes describes it a little differently, thus:

The red-backed sandpiper, often called the American dunlin, arrives in flocks, the individuals of which are apparently not all mated. A female will jump up and be immediately pursued by two to five males, and as they all twist about, in and out, twittering all the time, the alternate flashing of their reddish backs and black lower parts seems like the signals of the telegraphic code. The males appear never to catch the females, but to try to keep as close to them as possible. When they alight again in the flock whence they started they at once resume feeding without further display. The thrilling song of this dainty bird is delivered while hovering with quivering wing beats in mid-air. It appears as if both male and female carry on the vocal effort, which sounds something like the cheery tinkling of ice in a glass, and ends with a real lover's note *dear, dear, dear.* This is repeated again and again and is one of the pleasant characteristic songs of the marshy grass-woven flats, where the discords of waterfowl prevail. After the fastest male has captured his elusive sweetheart the two retire to their chosen place on the flats to take up their more serious duties. Here the female lays her eggs, often in a situation that is moist, and never very far from a small pond or slough.

Nesting.—The same observer says of the nest:

The home of the red-backed sandpiper is almost always found on a dry eminence in the widespread grassy tidelands, where, near some pool under the damp matted vegetation of the previous year, sufficient concealment is afforded. Here in a mere depression in the ground, still frozen underneath, a fragile nest is hurriedly made of dry grass stems and filled, rather than lined, with the tiny crisp leaves of the berry-bearing plants, that are deposited by the flood tides of autumn in this area. The range of measurements of 25 nests is: Inside diameter, 3½ to 4 inches; inside depth 2 to 3 inches; total depth, 3 to 5 inches.

This sandpiper is among the early nesters, we having taken the first completed set of eggs on May 29, while by June 1 we had discovered 75. The middle of June found the downy young bursting forth, dainty creatures clad in black and brown with markings similar to those of the other sandpiper chicks.

Dr. Joseph Grinnell (1900) found this species breeding on the Arctic coast of Alaska, about 20 miles northeast of Cape Prince of Wales, on June 27 and 28; he writes:

The birds were found scattered out on the tundras whence they could be flushed from their nests or from where they had been feeding. One nest was a cup-shaped cavity slightly lined with grasses and sunk into the top of a hummock of moss surrounded by marshy ground. The two others found were similarly located except that they were embedded in clumps of grass, and mostly hidden from view by the surrounding blades. Each nest contained four eggs. One was fresh but the other two were considerably incubated.

Prof. Wells W. Cooke (1912) made the statement that this species has two breeding areas " separated by nearly 1,500 miles of Arctic coast, from Point Barrow to the Boothia Peninsula," where "there seems to be no certain record of the occurrence of the red-backed sandpiper." This is far from true, for it is well known to breed there and eggs have been taken at many places along the Arctic coast.

Eggs. Herbert W. Brandt (Mss.) describes his series of 120 eggs of this sandpiper very well, as follows:

The four eggs of the red-backed sandpiper, which is their complement, are very handsome and show more variation than the eggs of most of the other shore birds breeding in the Hooper Bay region. In shape they are subpyriform to ovate pyriform and rest amid the leafy nest lining with the small ends together often so placed that the sitting bird during incubation touches only the larger ends. The shell is not as strong as many shore-bird eggs of the same size but they are not fragile by any means and they have considerable luster. As was true of many of the limicoline eggs found along that Bering Sea coast, there were two general types of ground color—the one, the greenish, that predominated by a ratio of about 15 to 1—and the other was the brownish type. The ground color ranges from "pale glaucous green "— that is the most common type—to "glaucous green," while the brownish-tinged eggs shade from "olive buff" to "dark olive buff." The surface markings are conspicuous and vary greatly, for on some types the spots are small and well scattered over the eggs; on others they are large, irregular, and bold; while on still other specimens they are confluent on the larger end and form a blotch that completely decorates that part of the egg. These spots are irregular in shape, but are inclined to be elongated with their axis twisting to the right, so that when a series of eggs is viewed looking toward the larger end, the spots produce a clockwise spiral. Some of these spots are more twisted than others, but on a few eggs there are no spiral tendencies at all. The surface spots are quite variable in color, dependent largely on the thickness of the pigment deposited, for where the latter is thin the true color is observable, but when the decoration is liberal, the blot becomes opaque and the color is lost. These spots range from " auburn " and " raw umber " to " chestnut brown " and " blackish brown." The underlying spots are well hidden by the boldness of the surface markings and inclined to be small and regular and are often more or less numerous. Their shades are delicate, ranging from " pallid gray " to " mouse gray." An occasional egg exhibits scattering insignificant additional markings of deep " blackish brown."

The measurements of 145 eggs average 36.3 by 25.3 millimeters; the eggs showing the four extremes measure **40.1** by **25.9**, **39.2** by **26.5**, **34** by 25, and 34.5 by **23.5** millimeters.

Young.—Both sexes incubate and are rather close sitters, as well as devoted and bold in the defense of their young. The period of incubation is probably the same as for the European dunlin, 22 days. John Murdoch (1885) says:

Both parents share in the work of incubation, though we happened to obtain more males than females with the eggs. The young are pretty generally hatched by the first week in July, and both adults and young keep pretty well out of sight till the 1st of August, when they begin to show about the lagoons and occasionally about the beach, many of the young birds still downy about the head. The autumn flight of young birds appears about the middle of August, associating with the young *A. maculata* and *M. griseus scolopaceus*, in good-sized flocks, particularly about the pools on the high tundra below Cape Smythe. They continue plenty in these localities, sometimes appearing along the beach, for about a week, when the greater part of them depart, leaving only a few stragglers that stay till the first few days of September.

Plumages.—The downy young red-backed is much paler and more buffy than that of the least sandpiper. The crown, back, wings, and thighs are variegated with brownish black, " ochraceous tawny " and " hazel," except at the base of the down on the back, there is no rich, deep brown; the above parts are quite thickly sprinkled, especially on the back, with minute, round spots, terminal tufts of pale buff; a distinct stripe of these nearly encircles the posterior half of the crown. The black of the crown extends nearly to the bill and there is a black loral stripe; the rest of the head and a band across the lower throat are " warm buff." The rest of the under parts are white. The nape is a grizzly mixture of dull buff and dusky.

The juvenal plumage, as seen in Alaska in August, is strikingly handsome and quite distinctive. The feathers of the crown are dusky, edged with " ochraceous tawny "; the sides of the head and nape are " drab-gray," streaked with dusky; the feathers of the back are black, broadly edged with three colors in different areas,

" ochraceous tawny," " hazel," and buffy white; the scapulars are black, edged with "light ochraceous buff"; the wing coverts are gray, tipped with pale buff; the rump and upper tail coverts are "hair brown" to " drab"; the breast is tinged with grayish and pale buff and streaked with dusky; the throat and rest of the under parts are white, conspicuously and more or less heavily spotted with dusky on the sides of the belly. This beautiful plumage is worn for only a short time and is molted before the birds leave their northern breeding grounds. The postjuvenal molt begins in August and is generally finished before October; it involves nearly all of the body plumage, nearly all of the scapulars, and some of the tertials, but not the rump, upper tail coverts, or flight feathers.

In first winter plumage young birds are much like adults, but the ashy brown upper parts are usually somewhat paler, and they can always be recognized by the juvenal wing coverts and a few retained scapulars and tertials. A partial prenuptial molt, similar to that of the adult, produces a first nuptial plumage, in which young birds can be distinguished only by the retained juvenal wing coverts. In fresh plumage the black belly patch is veiled with white tips, which soon wear away and leave this area clear black.

The first postnuptial molt of young birds and the corresponding molt of adults produce adult winter plumages. The molt is complete and begins in July or even late in June; the wings are apparently molted first in July, and are entirely renewed before the birds start to migrate; the body molt begins in August and lasts through September; there are usually traces of the old nuptial plumage left when the birds arrive here on migration. The partial prenuptial molt of adults comes in April and May and involves the body plumage, but not all the scapulars or rump or wing coverts.

Food.—Red-backed sandpipers obtain their food on the ocean beaches at low tide, on sandy flats or on mud flats, often feeding in company with sanderlings, or with other small shore birds. Some writers have referred to them as nervous and active running about in a lively manner while feeding, but I have usually found them rather sluggish and inactive at such times, easily approached and unsuspicious. Their food consists of small mollusks, sand fleas, and other small crustaceans, amphipods, flies and other insects and their larvae, diving and other aquatic beetles, marine worms, and occasionally a few seeds of aquatic plants. They are apt to gather where fish cleanings and other offal are thrown out, to feed on the flies and other insects that abound there. Dr. Charles W. Townsend (1905) writes:

In feeding they frequently plunge the bill, slightly open to its base in the soft sand or mud, appear to work it about and when successful draw forth an amphipod or a worm. Several times on one occasion I saw one draw a worm to the water close at hand as if to wash it before swallowing it. On another occasion a couple of dunlins were so tame that it was possible to approach within 5 feet of them. They were diligently probing in the sandy mud, wading in water up to their bellies. At this depth it was necessary for them to immerse their heads entirely, and I could see them shut their eyes as they went under water. Whether the eyes were afterwards opened or not I am unable to say. When disturbed they flew but a short way, and if they happened to alight in water too deep for their legs, they swam readily, as do all shore birds. When disturbed the dunlin utters a short *kuk*. Their call note is distinctive, and resembles somewhat the word *purre*, by which name the European species is called. The note is plaintive and sometimes melodious, and recalls, without its harshness, the cry of the common tern.

Behavior.—The earlier writers refer to this as an active, restless bird. Audubon (1840) says:

There seems to be a kind of impatience in this bird that prevents it from remaining any length of time in the same place, and you may see it scarcely alighted on a sand bar, fly off without any apparent reason to another, where it settles, runs for a few moments, and again starts off on wing.

Giraud (1844) writes:

It is a restless active bird and gleans its food with great nimbleness, and seems to be fond of continually changing its position. Soon after alighting they collect together and make a short excursion over the water, again alighting a short distance from where they had previously taken wing. During their aerial excursions, when whirling about, they crowd so close together that many are killed at a single shot. On one of these occasions Mr. Brasher informs me that he killed 52 by discharging both barrels into a flock. This number is greater than I ever before heard of; but from 10 to 15 is not unusual.

Wilson (1832), writing when shore birds were abundant, says of this flocking habit:

These birds, in conjunction with several others, sometimes collect together in such flocks, as to seem, at a distance, a large cloud of thick smoke, varying in form and appearance every instant, while it performs its evolutions in air. As this cloud descends and courses along the shores of the ocean, with great rapidity, in a kind of waving, serpentine flight, alternately throwing its dark and white plumage to the eye, it forms a very grand and interesting appearance. At such times the gunners make prodigious slaughter among them; while, as the showers of their companions fall, the whole body often alight, or descend to the surface with them, till the sportsman is completely satiated with destruction.

Suckley (1860) found them equally abundant in the Puget Sound region, for he writes:

Early in the season, before they have been rendered wild by being much shot at, I have observed that upon a volley being fired into a flock the unharmed birds in terror sweep around in several circles, and hovering " *bunch*," as the sportsmen say, over their wounded companions, and sometimes realight with them. At the moment of their hovering in a compact body over the wounded is the time generally seized to fire the reserved barrels; two or three shots will frequently bring down from 30 to 60 birds; and I have known one instance where an officer of the Army bagged 96 birds from one discharge of his fowling piece. After being fired into once or twice the flocks, learning to avoid sympathizing with their dead and wounded, become shy and wary.

Several observers have remarked on the remarkable tameness of the red-backed sandpiper. William Brewster (1925) spent two hours photographing five of these birds within 8 feet of his boat on an open mud flat; they paid no attention to his movements, the click of the camera, or the flapping of the focusing cloth; "during much of the time they were apparently asleep;" he even had difficulty in frightening them away until he splashed water on them. I have frequently walked up to within a few feet of feeding birds and had some difficulty in inducing them to fly more than a short distance.

Their eyesight is keen enough, however, as shown by an incident related by W. E. Saunders (1896). A bird which had been feeding near him for about an hour, stopped, looked steadily, as if afraid, and "shrank down flat on the ground, where he lay perfectly still." After some time Mr. Saunders discovered an eagle approaching, so far away that he could hardly see him. After the eagle had passed the sandpiper resumed his feeding.

Voice.—The red-backed sandpiper is usually silent when on the ground. John T. Nichols, in his notes, calls the "flushing note of a single bird a fine *chit-l-it*. Its flight note is an emphatic near-whistled *chu* or *chru*, resembling some of the calls of the pectoral and semipalmated sandpipers, but quite diagnostic when one is sufficiently familiar with it. This call may also be phonetically suggested by the syllable *purre*, which is a colloquial name of the European dunlin, of which it is a race."

Doctor Townsend (1905) says: "The note is plaintive and sometimes melodious, and recalls, without its harshness, the cry of the common tern." Mr. Murdoch (1885) and others have noticed that the rolling call, heard on the breeding grounds in June, "reminds one of the notes of the frogs in New England in spring." A bird which Mr. Brewster (1925) flushed "uttered a peculiarly mellow *tweet-twel-l-l-ut* just as it rose on wing."

Field marks.—In spring plumage the American dunlin deserves the name red backed, for its back is even redder than that of its European relative; at that season the black patch on the belly is very conspicuous, even at a long distance, so that the species is easily recognized. It is a short-legged, rather stocky bird, about the size of the sanderling, and can be identified in the fall by its rather long and somewhat curved bill and its dull, mouse-colored back. A narrow white stripe in the wing can be seen in flight.

Fall.—Of their departure from Alaska, Doctor Nelson (1887) writes:

The young are mostly on the wing toward the end of July, and the birds begin to gather into flocks along the muddy edges of the brackish pools and the banks of tide creeks. Very soon after this they begin to lose their summer plumage, and the molt continues until the last of September or first of

October. During the first of October they are very common in flocks and
singly among the lakes and streams; a little later and the borders of these
situations are edged with ice and most of the birds leave for the south, but
some of the hardier ones betake themselves to the seashore, where they join
with Coues's sandpiper and remain as late as the 12th or 13th of the month.

The southward migration separates into two widely divergent
main routes, with only stragglers between. One route is southward
along the Pacific coast and one southeastward along the west coast
of Hudson Bay, through the eastern Great Lakes, and to the coast
of New England and farther south. E. A. Preble (1902) saw them
on the west coast of Hudson Bay, just commencing the migration,
on July 19, and "present by thousands" south of Cape Eskimo
on August 3 to 13. It seems to be a rare bird in the interior Provinces of Canada; my Manitoba correspondents have no fall records,
and Professor Rowan has only one for Alberta. Mr. Brewster
(1925) saw it regularly at Lake Umbagog, Maine, in October; and
W. E. Clyde Todd (1904) calls it common in Erie County, Pennsylvania; probably these two points represent the north and south limits
of the eastward route. Mr. Todd (1904) quotes from Samuel E.
Bacon's notes as follows:

In former years extensive flights took place about the 1st of November,
upon which occasions bushels of them are said to have fallen to a single gun.
During these great flights the flocks were accustomed to follow the outside beach
of the peninsula (having presumably come directly across the lake) to its
southeastern extremity, thence crossing over to the sand beach east of the mouth
of Mill Creek, where, after having been sadly depleted by dozens of guns, they
would finally rise high in the air and pass southward over the mainland, flock
following flock, all day long. I know this by hearsay only, but am positive that
this is the bird that used to arrive in such numbers late in the fall. On October
29, 1897, I killed 53 of these birds out of two flocks, comprising in all perhaps
as many more, and this is the nearest approach to a flight that has occurred of
late years.

The redbacks do not reach the Massachusetts coast in any numbers until the last week in September and the main flight comes in
October, with some lingering into November and a few remain all
winter occasionally. While with us they frequent the ocean beaches
and salt-water mud flats, where they associate with sanderlings,
ringnecks, peep, and turnstones. During high tides they rest on the
high, sandy beaches in the large flocks of other small waders. They
fly in close flocks, low over the water. The adults which come first,
have nearly completed the body molt when they arrive here.

Winter.—It is only a short flight farther to their winter homes on
our southern coast. Dr. Louis B. Bishop (1901) found this to be
"the most abundant sandpiper" on Pea Island, North Carolina, in
winter. Arthur T. Wayne (1910) says that it usually arrives in South
Carolina about the first week in October and remains until May 25.
"With the exception of the western sandpiper, this species is the

most common of all the waders that winter on the coast. It is a very hardy bird and is apparently not inconvenienced by a temperature of 6° above zero." We found it common all winter on the coastal islands and mud flats on the west coast of Florida. Mr. Nichols says in his notes:

Where met with on its winter range in northwest Florida it apparently shifted its feeding grounds with high or low water, at the particular locality in mind, more or less dependent on the wind. When offshore winds caused low tides and extensive mud flats, it was less numerous; when the water was high, numbers were seen flying over the bay. They were present on inundated landward flats, and, as the tide receded, fed along the edge of the bay near by, wading in the water and often immersing most of the head as they probed.

According to J. Hooper Bowles (1918) they winter farther north on the Pacific coast than on this side. He writes:

These birds are among the last of the Limicolae to arrive in the fall migration, often reaching Washington after many of the other species have left for the South. They make up for it, however, by staying with us all winter and late into the spring. On the Nisqually Flats I have seen them in flocks of hundreds when the marsh was a solid pack of snow and ice, the rise and fall of the tide making sufficient feeding grounds to keep them fat and strong.

DISTRIBUTION

Range.—North America and eastern Asia; casual in Central America and the West Indies.

Breeding range.—North to northeastern Siberia (Taimyr Peninsula, Nijni Kolymsk, Cape Wankarem, and East Cape); Alaska (Cape Prince of Wales, Point Barrow, Colville Delta, and Camden Bay); Mackenzie (Cape Bathurst, Mackenzie Bay, Franklin Bay, and Baillie Island); and Franklin (Port Kennedy). East to Franklin (Port Kennedy and Felix Harbor); and probably eastern Keewatin (Cape Fullerton). South to probably eastern Keewatin (Cape Fullerton); northwestern Mackenzie (Great Slave Lake and Peel River); and Alaska (probably Nushagak and Ugashik). West to Alaska (Ugashik, Pastolik, Hooper Bay, and St. Michael); and northeastern Siberia (Cape Serdze, Plover Bay, and Taimyr Peninsula). The species also has been recorded as breeding in Greenland, and on the coast of Labrador (Okak), but the records are indefinite or otherwise unsatisfactory.

Winter range.—North to Washington (Dungeness Spit); Texas (Refugio County); Louisiana (Freshwater Bayou and New Orleans); and southern New Jersey (Anglesea). East to southern New Jersey (Anglesea, and Five-mile Beach); Virginia (Wallops, Cobbs, Sandy, and Hog Islands); North Carolina (Pea Island and Fort Macon); South Carolina (Port Royal and Frogmore); Georgia (Savannah and Darien); and Florida (Amelia Island, Tarpon

Springs, and Fort Myers). South to Florida (Fort Myers); Texas (probably Brownsville); and Lower California (La Paz). West to Lower California (La Paz); California (San Diego, Alamitas Bay, Los Banos, San Francisco Bay, and Humboldt Bay); Oregon (Yaquina Bay); and Washington (Nisqually Flats, Tacoma, and Dungeness Spit).

It also has been noted in winter north to the mouth of the Fraser River, British Columbia (specimen in U. S. National Museum); Barnstable, Massachusetts (Howe, December 23, 1903); Long Island, New York (Fleischer, December 25, 1914); and south to Great Inagua, Bahama Islands (Worthington, February 3, 1909).

Spring migration.—Early dates of arrival in the spring are: New York, Long Island, April 3, Canandaigua, April 20, and Orient, May 7; Rhode Island, Block Island, May 12; Massachusetts, Monomoy Island, April 13, Rehoboth, May 2, and Boston, May 4; Quebec, Quebec, May 2; Illinois, Addison, May 9; Ohio, Youngstown, April 18, Cedar Point, May 8, Tiffin, May 10, and Oberlin, May 11; Michigan, Jackson, May 4, Detroit, May 13, and Ann Arbor, May 14; Ontario, Toronto, May 12, and Point Pelee, May 13; Iowa, Sigourney, May 13; Wisconsin, Whitewater, May 1, Madison, May 10, and Elkhorn, May 13; Minnesota, Heron Lake, May 11, Waseca, May 14, and Hutchinson, May 18; eastern Nebraska, Lincoln, May 7; South Dakota, Vermilion, April 29, and Huron, May 6; North Dakota, Sweetwater, May 10; Manitoba, Whitewater Lake, May 12, and Shoal Lake, May 22; British Columbia, Courtenay, April 18, Chilliwak, April 25, and Metlakatla, April 29; Yukon, Dawson, May 24; Alaska, Howcan, April 2, Kuiu Island, April 28, Craig, May 1, mouth of the Yukon River, May 10, Admiralty Island, May 14, Fort Kenai, May 16, and Point Barrow, May 31; and Siberia, Bering Island, May 26, and Nijni Kólymsk, May 28.

Late dates of spring departure are: Florida, Gasparilla Island, May 24, St. Marks, May 26, and New Smyrna, May 26; Georgia, Savannah, May 29; South Carolina, Mount Pleasant, May 29; North Carolina, Fort Macon, May 22, and Churchs Island, May 26; Virginia, Pig Island, May 28; New Jersey, Anglesea, May 20; New York, Canandaigua, May 26, New York City, May 30, Rockaway, June 3, and Geneva, June 7; Massachusetts, Cape Cod, May 22, and Ipswich, May 30; Maine, Scarboro, June 2; Quebec, Quebec City, May 28; Illinois, Waukegan, May 27, Riverdale, May 31, and Chicago, June 5; Ohio, Painesville, May 27, Oberlin, June 1, and Lakeside, June 16; Michigan, Sault Ste. Marie, May 29, Detroit, May 30, and Neebish Island, June 3; Ontario, Mitchell's Bay, June 1, Hamilton, June 3, Point Pelee, June 10, and Toronto, June 13; Iowa, Emmetsburg, May 25, Storm Lake, May 26, and Sioux City, June 4; Wisconsin, Madison, May 27, and Green Bay, June 4; Minnesota,

Lanesboro, May 30, Heron Lake, June 2, and Wilder, June 10;
Texas, Fort Brown, May 16, Dallas, May 20, and Corpus Christi,
May 29; eastern Nebraska, Lincoln, June 9; South Dakota, Ver-
milion, May 24, and Forestburg, May 30; North Dakota, Jerusalem,
June 1; Manitoba, Killarney, May 28, and Shoal Lake, June 5;
California, Fresno, May 15, Santa Barbara, May 17, and Alameda,
May 21; Oregon, Beaver Creek, Lincoln County, May 18, and Silver
Lake, June 4; and British Columbia, Cowickan, May 18.

Fall migration.—Early dates of fall arrival are: Washington,
Smith Island, August 14, and Point Chehalis, August 20; California,
Santa Barbara, September 9, Alameda, September 19, and Hayward,
September 20; Manitoba, Gimli, August 20; South Dakota, Forest-
burg, July 30; eastern Nebraska, Lincoln, September 1; Minnesota,
Wilder, September 16; Ontario, Brighton, July 31, and Ottawa,
August 21; Michigan, Saginaw Bay, August 20, and Ann Arbor,
September 21; Ohio, Youngstown, August 10, Pelee Island, August
15, and Cleveland, August 22; Illinois, Chicago, July 22; Quebec,
Godbout, September 7; Massachusetts, Norton, August 26, and Taunton, September 1; New York, Orient, August 11, Canandaigua, September 14, and Ithaca, September 24; Pennsylvania, Erie, September
25; Maryland, Lock Raven, September 3; District of Columbia,
Washington, September 25; Virginia, Smiths Island, September 28;
and South Carolina, Mount Pleasant, September 30.

Late dates of fall departures are: Siberia, Bering Island,
October 25; Alaska, Sitka, October 10, mouth of the Yukon River,
October 13, and St. Paul Island, October 30; British Columbia,
Comox, October 22, and Chilliwack, November 29; Manitoba, Lake
Winnipeg, October 31; eastern Nebraska, Lincoln, November 7;
Minnesota, Hallock, October 16; Wisconsin, Madison, November 15;
Iowa, Keokuk, October 4, and Marshalltown, October 12; Ontario,
Ottawa, October 29, and Long Point, November 2; Michigan,
Detroit, October 11, Sault Ste. Marie, October 22, and St. Clair
Flats, November 20; Ohio, Huron, November 5, Youngstown, Novem-
ber 8, and Columbus, November 28; Illinois, Chicago, October 31,
Lake Forest, November 3, and La Grange, November 6; Maine,
Lewiston, October 12, and Portland, November 25; Massachusetts,
Lynn, November 3, Boston, November 10, and Monomoy Island,
November 14; Rhode Island, Block Island, November 16; Connecti-
cut, Fairfield, November 29; New York, Orient, November 12, and
Long Beach, December 25; and Pennsylvania, Erie, November 3.

Casual records.—Accidental occurrences of the red-backed sandpiper have been reported mostly from the Rocky Mountain States.
Among these are: Arizona, near Tucson, April, 1883; Nevada,
Pyramid Lake, May, 1868; and Utah, Ogden and Salt Lake City
(reported in September by Allen). It also has been reported as

detected at Dominica, West Indies, October 1, 1904; and at Momotombo, Nicaragua, on May 23. (This last record represented by a
specimen in the British Museum.)

Egg dates.—Alaska: 83 records, May 26 to July 8; 42 records,
June 4 to 30. Arctic Canada: 15 records, June 5 to July 7; 8
records, June 26 to July 3.

EROLIA FERRUGINEA (Brünnich)

CURLEW SANDPIPER

Contributed by Francis Charles Robert Jourdain

HABITS

The curlew sandpiper is only an occasional visitor to America, and
with the exception of a single record from Point Barrow all the
recorded instances have been reported from the eastern side of the
Continent. It has been met with in Canada on two occasions, about
ten times in the Eastern States, twice in the West Indies and once in
Patagonia.

Courtship.—Very few observations on this species have been made
on its breeding grounds in eastern Siberia, so our information as to
its courtship is still very defective. The late Dr. H. Walter, during
his enforced detention on the Taimyr Peninsula, from September,
1900, to August, 1901, while frozen in on board the exploring ship
"Sarja," noted that they arrived on the Peninsula on June 13, and
from that date onward were to be met with chasing one another in
little parties of three or four over the tundra. There is no mention
of any song flight (as in *Crocethia alba*, *Erolia temminchii*, *Arquatella maritima*, *Calidris canutus*, etc.).

Nesting.—The usual nesting place is on the gentle slope of the
drier tundra, where the reindeer moss is interspersed with tufts of
wiry grass and allowing a wide field of view over the neighborhood.
Miss Haviland (1915a) noted that the actual nest hollow was rather
deep, so that the pointed ends of the eggs were pointed downwards
almost vertically. Walter describes them as shallow depressions,
lined with a few dry bents, but H. L. Popham (1898) also remarks
that "the nest was a rather deep hollow amongst the reindeer moss in
an open space on a ridge of ground, somewhat drier than the surrounding swampy tundra, in much the same sort of place as that
generally chosen by a grey plover."

Although Middendorff undoubtedly met with birds about to breed,
and indeed extracted a partly developed egg from the oviduct of a
female which he had shot on the Boganida River in latitude 74°
N., no one had actually found the nest of this species till Mr. H.
Leyborne Popham (1898) visited the lower reaches of the Yenesei

in 1897. Two years previously (August, 1895), he had met with family parties on the delta and had shot young which must have been reared in the neighborhood. On July 3, 1897, finding the way below Golchika blocked by the ice, he turned back to explore an island of soft tundra with a rocky shore. One of his men called out that he had seen a sandpiper and at once, according to his own words:

I sent the other two men away and lay down to watch the bird, which stood still for some time, then flew some distance away and I lost sight of it among some turnstones. We again saw the bird near the same spot, so Hansen and I lay down to watch while the mosquitoes did their worst. The bird stood for some time watching us and then began running about; it was very difficult to keep it in sight for it took advantage of every little hollow to run in and every little ridge to hide behind. It then flew to another place and did the same thing again, so I asked Hansen to get up and walk away. The bird remained quite motionless, watching him go, and then ran backwards and forwards and finally stopped still behind a small tuft of grass. After waiting for some minutes I raised my head slightly; the bird instantly flew off and stood watching, but, as it saw nothing moving, it began running about again and settled down in the same spot; then I felt sure I had a nest safe, but to make doubly sure I went through the same performance again, a shower of rain no doubt hastening matters, and this time I distinctly saw the bird shuffle the eggs under it. I jumped up, shot the bird as it ran away, and soon had the pleasure of looking at the first authentic eggs of the curlew sandpiper. The bird, which proved to be the female, remained silent throughout; at one time I thought I heard it make a sound like a dunlin, but, as I afterwards saw dunlins close by, I was probably mistaken.

The next news comes from the Russian explorers who wintered on the coast of the Taimyr Peninsula in 1900–1901. In Doctor Walter's posthumous notes he writes that the curlew sandpiper nested in numbers near his winter quarters. The nests were placed in grassy places and by mid-June (old style) contained full clutches. On the approach of anyone the sitting birds, warned by their mates, left the nests quickly and both birds remained very passive and un-obtrusive. Usually a long wait was necessary before the female returned to the nest, and often the watch resulted in failure. Some individuals also wander about in flocks through the breeding season, and later on young and old collect in large flocks and stay till late in the autumn. Doctor Walter collected three clutches of eggs here, and another Russian naturalist, Dr. Katin Jartzew, also took several on Kotelni Island, in the New Siberian Isles, in 1902. Since that date the only information we have received is that furnished by Miss Haviland (Mrs. Brindley), who visited the delta of the Yenesei in 1914. In her account (1915) of her travels she writes:

On July 6, as I was returning from a long round over the tundra that lay in the northern angle of the Yenesei and Golchika Rivers, all at once I saw a little rufous curlew, which was standing on a tussock about 20 yards away, watching me quietly. When I stopped she flew away, but soon alighted again and looked at me. Full of excitement, but still rather skeptical as to the likelihood of finding eggs, I lay down and watched her, but at the end of an hour and a half I could come to no conclusion, for the bird only strolled about and preened herself nonchalantly. I was not even certain of her sex, and her solitude and her quiet behavior made me doubt whether, after all, she might not be a nonbreeding bird. Nevertheless, I marked the place and turned homeward, meaning to come back next day. On the morrow I turned out early and tramped over 8 swampy miles of tundra. The second pair of sandpipers were not to be seen, but the first bird was still pottering round the same spot. To-day she was a little more demonstrative and flew about uneasily. Once she uttered a sharp, anxious note, *wick-wick-wick*, two or three times repeated. By this time I was convinced that the nest was close at hand, but it was difficult to locate it, for although the bird could dodge me successfully enough behind tussocks of moss only 6 inches high, my person unfortunately was too bulky for these, the only available hiding places. The ground was on a very gradual slope. On the right hand and on the left were two small tarns, still covered with blue ice. In the distance grazed some herds of reindeer, and once a Samoyede sledge glided swiftly over a ridge. Heavy drifts of snow still lay in the sheltered hollow, and the sleet showers that came slapping over the tundra made me glad to wrap myself up in my Burberry coat.

The bird had whirled away round the tarn at my approach, so I hid myself as well as I could behind a tussock and settled down to wait for her return. Twenty minutes passed—half an hour. "It's time she was coming back," thought I, and turned my head carefully to reconnoiter. And lo and behold, not 30 yards behind, the sandpiper stood and studied me contemptuously! She had been watching all the time. "What a fool!" doubtless would have been her comment if she could have spoken. It is no use to try and gull the waders; up to a certain point I believe that they can almost see you *think!*

I retired abashed to another hiding place about 50 yards farther up the slope. The bird at once showed her appreciation of this move by flying toward the spot where I had first seen her. She was so small that it was very difficult to mark her as she tripped between the tussocks. When I thought that she must be settled on her eggs I jumped up quickly. She took wing at once, but when I went to the place whence she had risen there was no sign of the nest. This happened twice; but as she returned to the same spot each time, I knew that the treasure was there all right and that patience would win it. I marked the bird down by a dodge that I used when looking for gray plover's eggs under similar circumstances and which is described elsewhere; but each time that I flushed her she seemed to jump up from a different place. She was so little and so nimble that she could run over the moss for some yards before she was seen. The next time I gave her ample time to settle down and lay still in the wet, sucking lumps of sugar until I nearly fell asleep. Then all at once a Buffon's skua came overhead, flying low in the squally wind. I snatched my gun and shot him as he flew by, and as he fell I saw the sandpiper spring up from a spot where I had marked her once before. I left the skua and ran up to the place. The bird began to call again and drooped a wing to decoy me away. Half a minute's search and there was the nest at my feet.

Eggs.—The clutch consists of four eggs normally, blunt pyriform in shape with slight gloss. Walter describes the ground as pale yellowish white with greenish tinge and large and small blackish-brown spots, more confluent at large end. There are also a few pale violet-gray shell marks. They are snipelike in character, and the markings are rich and handsome, sometimes ranging to deep rufous brown in color. Their small size, combined with bold type of markings, renders them readily recognizable. The measurements of 20 eggs average 36.26 by 25.67 millimeters, the eggs showing the four extremes measure **39.6** by 25.6, 37.5 by **26.4**, **33.3** by 25.3, and 36.6 by **25** millimeters.

Incubation.—The bird which Popham shot from the eggs was a female, but both males and females were obtained from the nests by the Russian ornithologists, so that apparently the duty is shared by both sexes.

Plumages.—The molts and plumages are fully described in "A Practical Handbook of British Birds," edited by H. F. Witherby (1920), to which the reader is referred.

Food.—On its breeding grounds the main food of this species consists of insects. Cordeaux has found remains of Coleoptera and Diptera and their larvae in stomachs. Worms are also freely taken, but on migration it is a coastal species and subsists chiefly on marine forms, such as the small crustacea (Gammaridae) which are found in vast numbers on the shore, minute mollusca, and vegetable matter.

Behavior.—Even in the breeding season this species shows signs of a sociable disposition, several pairs breeding frequently at no great distance apart. When the young are fledged they assemble in flocks before leaving for the south and during the winter months may be found on the mud flats of our estuaries and flat coasts, as well as occasionally on reservoirs and sewage farms inland. During the breeding season it appears to be a silent bird, only a shrill alarm note, *wick-wick-wick*, being noted, while the shore haunting flocks keep up a long twitter.

Fall.—The migrations of this species are very extensive, reaching over practically the whole of the Old World. To the British Isles it is a passage migrant, arriving from the end of July to late October and occasionally November. In Denmark the old birds are said to arrive in August and the birds of the year in September, leaving in September-October. On the shores of the Baltic it occurs commonly, but seems to avoid the extreme west of Europe on its way south, though passing Tangier in September and occurring in small numbers in Portugal. It is also met with on passage in all the Mediterranean countries, as well as north Africa and passes the Canaries on migration. It ranges on the west side of Africa to Gaboon, Liberia, the Gold Coast, Princes Island, Loango, and south to Cape Province. While on the east side it is recorded from the Nile Valley, the Red Sea, Sudan, Mozambique, Zanzibar, Nyassaland, Madagascar, etc., and it occurs regularly on Mauritius. In Asia it ranges across the continent to the Indian Ocean, the Mekran coast, Sind, Yarkand, India, Ceylon, the Andamans Nicobars, Burmese coast, Malacca Peninsula, Hainan, Formosa, and East China. Further, it has been recorded from the Malay Archipelago, Java, Borneo, New Guinea, the Philippines, Moluccas, and has also been found in Australia (West Australia and New South Wales), Tasmania, and New Zealand. In America there are two Canadian records, one from Toronto and one from Nova Scotia; while in the Eastern States it has occurred in Maine, Massachusetts, New Jersey, and Long Island, and has been recorded from Grenada and Carriacou, Lesser Antilles, and also in Patagonia. In Alaska it has once been obtained at Point Barrow.

DISTRIBUTION

Breeding range.—The supposed instances of breeding in western Greenland are now discredited, and the only definitely known breeding places are in eastern Siberia, from the delta of the Yenesei to latitude 74° on the Taimyr Peninsula and northward, as well as on the Liakhof Isles and other islands of the New Siberian group.

Spring migration.—Dates: Rio de Oro (N. W. Africa), April 27; Gibraltar, April 24; Egypt, May 8; Barcelona and Santander, May; Malaga, May 9; Corsica, May 7, 8, and 16; Italy, April 1–June 5; Malta, May 7, 12, 13, 27; Greece, April 15, 28, but chiefly May; Corfu. passage lasts till end of May; Transylvania, May 29; Cyprus, May 20, 24; Lake Baikal, May; Allaliabad, May 17; Amoy, China, May 16; Archangel, June 18; Boganida River, May 27; arrives North Taimyr, June 4.

Fall migration.—Dates: Belfast, Ireland, August 25 to end of September; Portugal, September; Italy, September 15–October 30; Cyprus, September 2; Greece, arrives September; Tangier, September; Yarkand, August–September; Karachi, September; Gilgit, August–September; Selangor, August; Mergui Archipelago, November 6; Ceylon, October; Lower Pegu, August; Transvaal, November 24; Natal, October 18.

Casual records.—Aldabra Island, Madagascar, November 6; Madeira, April 30, September 22 and October 7 and November 27. New Zealand, Canterbury, February 3, 1902; April 5, 1903 (2); Otago, March, 1903; Grenada (Wells); Bering Island (Steller). There are several records for this species for North America, some dating back to the earlier days of American ornithology. In some cases the details are indefinite and can not be considered as absolutely trustworthy. Among the occurrences recorded are: Lesser Antilles, Grenada (Cory, 1892), and Carriacou (Clark, 1905); New Jersey, Great Egg Harbor, two in the spring of 1829, Long Beach, Barnegat Bay, July 29, 1904, and Tuckerton and Cape May (Stone, according to C.

C. Abbott, 1868); New York, nearly a dozen specimens at Fulton market secured on Long Island (Giraud, 1844), Long Island (?) June 9, 1891; Shinnecock Bay, May 24, 1883; Connecticut, near Hartford, October 3, 1859, New Haven, August 30, 1886, and June, 1874; Massachusetts, Cape Ann, fall of 1865, East Boston, early May, 1866, Nahant, about 1869, Ipswich, about 1875, Cape Cod, about May 10, 1878, and Chatham, August 26, 1889; Maine, Scarboro, September 9, 1875 (?), and Pine Point, September 15, 1881; New Brunswick, Grand Manan; Nova Scotia, Halifax, October, 1864, and September, 1868; Ontario, Toronto, about 1886 (Fleming); and Alaska, Point Barrow, June 6, 1883.

Egg dates.—Full clutches on North Taimyr, June 24; Liakhof Isles, June 24; Taimyr, July 1 (incubated) and July 6 (fresh); Yenesei delta, July 3 and July 7.

EURYNORHYNCHUS PYGMEUS (Linnaeus)

SPOON-BILL SANDPIPER

HABITS

This unique little sandpiper has a very restricted breeding range in extreme northeastern Siberia, whence it migrates to southern Asia and wanders very rarely to extreme northwestern Alaska. Joseph Dixon (1918) says: " There are but three specimens claimed to have been taken in North America, as far as known to the author, with some doubt attached to the locality of capture of one of these." He has shown that the bird supposed to have been taken on the Choris Peninsula, Kotzebue Sound, Alaska, by Captain Moore, of the British ship " Plover," was really taken in northeastern Asia in 1849, and that no authentic record for North America· has been established since that time until 1914. He says further:

The only well-established occurrence of the spoon-billed sandpiper in America is that vouched for by Fred Granville, of Los Angeles, California, who, on August 15, 1914, took two specimens at Wainwright Inlet, on the Arctic coast of Alaska. One of these specimens, a female, is now number 3552 in the collection of A. B. Howell, of Covina, California, while the other, a male, is number 1698 in the collection of G. Willett, of Los Angeles.

Referring to the capture of these two birds, he quotes from Mr. Granville's letter of January 9, 1918, as follows:

On August 15, 1914, I and my assistant hiked back of Wainwright to what I judged to be a distance of about 10 miles, traveling in a northerly direction. The tundra where I found the spoonbills was interlaced as far as the eye could see with little lagoons and long channels of water, and in this territory I collected the two spoonbills. These birds were shot out of a flock of possibly 10. I followed them for about an hour before I could get a shot at them. The birds would run along the tundra en masse and were undoubtedly gleaning food from the moss. The minute they would catch sight of me they would fly out of shotgun range. There were about six birds that looked to me through field glasses to be in markedly different plumage from the birds I shot. These six birds, immature as I supposed, seemed to be of a solid color, and that a dark gray. On the first shot fired, with which I got two, the birds flew across a lake and I lost track of them, though I spent four or five hours looking for some more. I believe that these birds breed in the neighborhood of Wainwright and hope that at some close future date some one will bear out my statement.

Spring.—There is an adult male in nuptial plumage in the British Museum, which was taken at Shanghai, China, in April. The only other information we have about the spring migration is the following brief statement by Dr. E. W. Nelson (1883):

On the northeast coast of Siberia Nordenskiold records this bird as occurring in such numbers that on two occasions in spring it was served upon their mess table on board the "Vega" while they were lying frozen in at their winter quarters. It arrived in spring at Tapkau, with the first bare spots, early in June, and disappeared in July. To the westward, in the same vicinity, during the summer of 1881, I saw several of these birds, and at Plover Bay, on the Bering Sea shore of the same coast, secured a fine adult female in breeding plumage, taken on June 26. Nothing peculiar was observed in its habits, and I approached the bird without difficulty or its showing the slightest concern as it stood on the flat at that place. The bird was first seen feeding in the shallow water at the edge of a pool, and then stood with its head drawn back and without paying the slightest attention to me until it was shot.

Courtship.—Mr. Dixon (1918) has made a thorough study of this species and has given us a fine account of its interesting song flight, illustrated by a diagram, from which I quote, as follows:

The song and nuptial flight of the male spoonbill, attractive as they were to the collector, in sight of such rare birds at last, were as elusive as a will-o'-the-wisp. In fact we were never able to locate a female spoonbill on the nest, and I have always believed that our lack of success in this regard was due to the warning given by the male. Upon approaching the nest site, while we were yet afar off, we were greeted by the male in full song. This song, ventriloquial, pulsating, and cicadalike in quality, seemed to come first from one and then from another point in the heaven above. Sometimes we searched the sky altogether in vain, but usually the bird was discovered in rapid flight at an altitude of two or three hundred feet above the earth. The nuptial flight consists of momentary poises alternating with rapid dips. When the bird hovers or poises, the rapid beating of the wings is accompanied by a fine, rhythmical, pulsating, buzzing trill, *zee-e-e, zee-e-e, zee-e-e,* rapidly repeated. Following this the bird approaches the intruder, swinging down in a sharp curve until 10 feet lower than the previous hovering point, where he again poises on rapidly beating wings, pouring forth anew his insistent, musical trill. After repeating this performance four or five times the songster sweeps down in a long graceful curve until he almost touches the earth near his brooding mate, then curving off, he turns and rises rapidly and almost perpendicularly until almost out of sight. From this new point of vantage the whole performance is repeated. After four or five such excursions, in each of which the intruder is approached from a different direction, the guardian of the nest descends by raising his wings nearly vertically until they form in anterior outline the letter V. The bird thus gliding on motionless wings drops lightly but quickly to earth, uttering the *zee-e-e* in a richer yet more subdued tone. As soon as he touches the earth the song ceases and the silent bird trots quietly off over the moss, where his trim form blends with the lichen and mossy tussocks, so that, upon remaining motionless, he disappears with amazing rapidity. Time and time again we thus lost sight of the birds, which we later discovered by the aid of binoculars to be standing or squatting motionless within 50 feet of us. Although this "fading out" method of exit is commonly employed by many shore birds, in the case of the spoonbilled sandpiper it seems to have been developed to an extreme degree.

Nesting.—To F. E. Kleinschmidt is due the credit for finding the first nest of the spoonbill sandpiper near Cape Serdze, northeastern Siberia, on July 15, 1910. The nest and the four eggs, which were nearly hatched, are now in the collection of Col. John E. Thayer. The following extract from Captain Kleinschmidt's letter in regard to it was published by Colonel Thayer (1911):

I was in hopes that I could get five or six clutches of the spoonbills, so I took all kinds of chances with my boat in the ice on the Siberian coast. I found, however, but one set of eggs and they were just ready to hatch. The male is the parent bird of the eggs, but the female belongs to neither eggs nor downies, simply because the habits of this sandpiper are similar to those of the phalarope. The male has to stay at home, keep house, and attend to the young, while the female thinks she has done all that is necessary by merely fulfilling the duties nature demands of her, namely, the laying of the eggs. I shot the female in close proximity of the nest, but we never found a female with the downies. It was always the male. Although our observations were limited to but a few, still I believe the male solely attends to the hatching and the rearing of the young. The female also is larger than the male. The nest as well as the downies were found on the gentle slope of the tundra, bordering small fresh-water ponds. The nest was a rounded hollow in the moss, thickly lined with dry willow leaves. The downies blend so perfectly with the color of the moss that the closest scrutiny will scarcely reveal their hiding place.

Mr. Dixon (1918) found a nest, with two fresh eggs, near Providence Bay, Siberia, on June 22, 1913, and one, with three young just hatched, near Cape Serdze, on July 17, 1913. Regarding his experience with it, he writes:

The two nests of this bird that came under the author's observation were discovered through flushing the brooding male. The birds were very shy, and as there was no cover other than a thin growth of grass about 6 inches high approach by stealth was difficult. The birds usually sneaked off while the observer was 40 or 50 yards distant, and in order to find the nest it was necessary to hide, as best one could, near the place where the sandpiper had flushed, until it returned again to the nest. In one instance a depression partly filled with water was the only available hiding place. Fortunately for the watcher the water was not cold and the male bird returned in 12 minutes to the nest, which contained two *fresh* eggs. The nest of this sandpiper was found to be merely a cavity scratched out among the dead grass blades. It was a shallow affair placed where the grass grew thickest. On June 22, 1913, at Providence Bay, the writer witnessed the construction of a nest from a distance of about 40 feet. The bird, a male, scratched and then picked at the dead and matted grass blades and moss until he had dug out quite a hole. Then he squatted down in the depression and twisted about, pressing against the moss that formed the sides of the nest, until a cavity about 3½ inches in diameter and an inch deep was formed. Dead leaves from a creeping Arctic willow that grew in the moss nearby were used to line the nest.

There are two sets of eggs, one of three and one of two, in the United States National Museum, taken by Louis L. Lane, at Cape Serdze in June, 1912, but no further data came with them.

Eggs.—The small sets referred to above were probably incomplete; doubtless four eggs is the normal set. The six eggs in the Thayer collection are subpyriform in shape and have a slight gloss. The ground color is uniform in all of them; it is between " cinnamon buff " and "dark olive buff," or a warm shade of the latter. Three eggs are finely speckled all over, only a little more thickly at the larger end, with light browns, "tawny" and "snuff brown"; one egg is heavily blotched at the larger end with " Verona brown " and "warm sepia," and only sparingly spotted elsewhere.

J. H. Riley tells me that the eggs taken by Louis Lane vary in ground color from a warm tint of " dark olive buff " to " deep olive buff." The set of two is rather evenly but not heavily marked over the surface with small blotches, dots, and scrawls of two shades of "bister," with a few shell markings of " drab " here and there over the surface. One egg of the set has the " bister " markings larger and thicker on the large end. The other set has the spots larger and heavier at the large end, and in two eggs they are darker, " clove brown " or even " blackish brown." The shape is subpyriform.

The measurements of these 11 eggs average 30.4 by 21.8 millimeters; the eggs showing the four extremes measure **33** by 22.8, 30.5 by **23.3**, **28.7** by 20.8, and 29.3 by **20.3** millimeters.

Young.—Regarding incubation and care of the young, Mr. Dixon (1918) writes:

Regarding the time required for incubation, we have only circumstantial evidence to offer, but our observations lead us to believe that about 18 or 20 days elapse between the time the last egg is laid and the first young hatched. The most striking fact in the domestic life of the spoonbilled sandpiper is that the major portion of the household duties, aside from the actual laying of the eggs, is performed by the male and not the female bird. In addition to our own observations, Kleinschmidt also has found this to be the case. In the author's experience, none of the several females taken were found on or within 50 feet of the nest. It is possible, however, that they may have been warned by the male birds and had sneaked off before we were close enough to detect their leaving. In the unequal division of domestic duties conditions among the spoonbills are similar to those among the phalaropes, where the male, after he has been courted and won by the larger and more brilliant female, takes upon himself almost all of the household cares. However, in the case of the spoonbilled sandpiper there is nothing to show that the female does the courting, although she is the larger of the two. The female spoonbill is thus seemingly content to merely lay the eggs, while she lets the male build the nest, incubate the eggs, and take care of the young. In corroboration of the latter statements, the author observed a male bird building a nest at Providence Bay, Siberia, June 22, 1913; another male was flushed repeatedly from a nest containing two fresh eggs near the same place, on the same day, while a third male was found tending three downy young at Cape Serdze, Siberia, on July 17, 1913.

On July 17, 1913, at Cape Serdze, Siberia, while strolling along the spongy green turf beside a fresh-water pond, my attention was attracted by the "broken wing" antics of a spoon-billed sandpiper. Although my eyes remained "glued" on the spot from which the bird arose, no nest or sign of young could be found when I reached the place. Soon a second bird, presumably the female, arrived on the scene. Both appeared much concerned, and from their actions I felt sure that there were young near by. A careful search of the short grass, which was not over 2 inches high, failed to reveal any living creature. I therefore retired to a grassy mound about 20 yards away and awaited developments. Both parent birds, giving their alarm notes, circled about overhead, where they were soon joined by a pair each of Eastern least and Temminck's stints. The two pairs of stints were later found to have broods of downy young in the grass on the opposite shore of the lagoon near by. Soon both spoonbills flew off across the lagoon and disappeared, but the male returned promptly, alighting quietly near the margin of the pond. Here he stood motionless for nearly a minute, and then trotted through the grass directly to the spot from which I had first flushed him. At this point he stood still for another full minute, during which time he looked all around, seemingly to make sure that the coast was clear. Having satisfied himself that no active enemy was in sight he stepped forward and bending over uttered a soft call in a low tone, *plee-plee-plee*. This call was repeated a second time, and instantly there arose directly in front of him a tiny mouse-like brown form, seemingly rising from out of the very ground. With tottering unsteady steps the downy young sandpiper stumbled and fell toward the parent, who continued calling and encouraging it. Upon my sudden appearance the old bird gave a quick warning note and at this signal the youngster squatted motionless with neck stretched forward on the ground. Although I knew the exact spot where it disappeared, it was some time before I was able to locate the tiny form, so well did it blend with the clump of reddish moss upon which it had squatted. A careful search revealed no other young sandpipers, so I returned to my hiding place. This time I had to wait longer for the male to return, and while I was waiting a second sandpiper, which I believed to be the female, arrived but did not go near or call the young. Two or three minutes elapsed this time between the return of the male and the giving of the low call notes, when, as before, another downy young quickly arose at the signal and toddled over to its parent. After this second experience I was forced to change my hiding place, as the male sandpiper refused to return to the young until I moved. He seemed much concerned upon this last visit, probably realizing that it was high time the young should be hovered and warmed.

I could not understand why all the young had not risen at once in answer to the parent's call, but I noticed that he had in each case gone up to within less than two feet of the one in hiding, and then with lowered head facing the chick, gave the call note. In each case it was the youngster thus directly addressed that responded to the signal and arose. The note of the young was a low rusty squeak, scarcely audible to human ears. It was very similar to the note of the young semipalmated sandpiper. As far as my observations went, there was no attempt on the part of the parent to feed the young, and it is my belief that from the time they are hatched the young spoonbills hunt their own food. The exercise thus gained was found in the case of young semipalmated sandpipers to be essential to the health of the chicks. In addition to keeping warm by running about the young spoonbills are hovered and warmed at regular intervals by the parent. The brood mentioned above had survived a fairly severe snowstorm on the preceding day.

Plumages.—The most remarkable thing about the downy young spoonbill sandpiper is the well developed spoon-shaped bill, even when first hatched. As will be seen by referring to Colonel Thayer's (1911) excellent colored plate, this is much shorter than the adult bill and the spatulate tip is more oval. The crown, back, rump, wings, and thighs are variegated with black, white, "ochraceous tawny" and paler buffs, dotted with white terminal tufts on the head, which form two white stripes from the eyes to the nape; and dotted with both white and buff tufts on the back and rump; the forehead, a superciliary stripe, the sides of the head, the throat, and the neck are "warm buff"; the rest of the under parts are white; a median frontal stripe, a loral stripe, and a malar spot are black.

The juvenal plumage I have never seen. Birds collected on the southward migration are apparently all in winter plumages; young birds are distinguishable from adults at this age. For descriptions of first winter and subsequent plumages I would refer the reader to Ridgway's Birds of North and Middle America. I have not studied sufficient material to work out the seasonal molts, but they are apparently similar to those of other small sandpipers of the genus *Pisobia.*

Food.—The food of the spoonbill sandpiper seems not to have been definitely determined, but Mr. Dixon (1918) watched a pair feeding, of which he says:

Our observations disclosed no peculiar advantage attending the singular shape of this sandpiper's bill, though careful watch was kept to see just how this member was used. On July 17, 1913, a pair of spoon-billed sandpipers was watched for half an hour as the two birds fed within 50 feet of the observer, concealed behind a sandy dune. Their favorite feeding ground was a fresh-water pond with a fringe of green algae about the sandy border. Under these conditions the birds used their bills, as any other sandpipers would, as probes to pick out insects or larvae from the algae. Occasionally one would hesitate a moment, when the vascular tip of the mandible quivered slightly as though the bird were straining something out of the green algae. At this time the bill was held at nearly right angles to the surface of the water; it was never used as a scoop along the surface.

Behavior.—I must again quote from Mr. Dixon (1918), who has furnished most of our information about this little known species. Referring to behavior and recognition marks he writes:

In color, size, and actions the spoon-billed sandpiper closely resembles the Eastern least stint (*Pisobia minuta ruficollis*), the marked similarity between them resulting in both the author and his fellow collector W. S. Brooks, failing to distinguish between the two species until June 20, after we had been among them for some days. Although the spatulate tip of this bird's bill is very noticeable when viewed from directly above or below, it is not a character which can be advantageously used to identify the species in the field, for the simple reason that in nearly all close views of the living bird only lateral or frontal aspects of the bill are obtained. Even when a bird was feeding, and the bill was observed under the most favorable conditions, the peculiar shape was not nearly as conspicuous as one would expect. In the author's experience, the most reliable method of identifying the bird in the field was by noting the glint of light that was reflected from the broad tip of the upper mandible when the sunlight struck the bill at a certain angle. Even in flight the bird could often be identified by this faint beam of reflected light. We found that the sandpiper had a decided preference for the grassy margins of fresh-water ponds, while single birds were frequently found feeding along the algae-bordered rims of tundra pools. Sandy lagoons where rivers entered the bay were favored by them as well.

Fall.—The same writer outlines the fall migration, based on birds in the British Museum, as follows:

An adult male, still in summer plumage, was taken August 8, at the mouth of the Amur River in southwestern Russia. An immature was secured on October 8 at Hakodadi (Hakodate), Japan, while an adult female was collected at Rangoon, India, on December 1.

Winter.—In their winter home in India, according to Doctor Nelson (1887) " these birds frequent the muddy flats at the mouths of rivers, sand bars, and the seashore, where, with the various species of *Tringa*, they always find an abundant harvest of food deposited by the receding tide."

DISTRIBUTION

Range.—Eastern Siberia, south in winter to southern China and India; casual in Alaska.

Breeding range.—The spoon-billed sandpiper has been found breeding only along the Arctic coast of northeast Siberia (Cape Wankarem, Pithkaj, Cape Serdze, near Koliuchin Island, and Providence Bay).

Winter range.—The winter range of this species appears to be mainly on the coasts of India (Rangoon, Akyab, Tenasserim, and the Arakan coast).

Migration.—Specimens have been collected at Shanghai, China, in April and it seems to arrive on its breeding grounds early in June (Emma Harbor, Siberia, June 6). An early date of fall arrival is indicated by a specimen from the mouth of the Amur River, southwestern Russia, taken on August 8, while a late date of fall departure is October 8, at Hakodadi, Japan.

Casual records.—A specimen of this sandpiper has been reported as taken on the Choris Peninsula, Alaska, in 1849 (Harting, 1871), but subsequent investigation (Dixon, 1918) indicates that the bird was probably taken on the Siberian side of Bering Strait. Two specimens were, however, taken near Wainwright Inlet, on August 15, 1914 (Dixon, 1918).

Egg dates.—Siberia: 2 records, June 22 and July 15.

EREUNETES PUSILLUS (Linnaeus)

SEMIPALMATED SANDPIPER

HABITS

Contributed by Charles Wendell Townsend

This little sandy colored sandpiper, appropriately called the " sand peep," seems most at home on the sea beaches, but it also frequents the sand flats of tidal estuaries, and to a less extent, the salt marshes, and is even found on the shores of inland lakes during the migrations.

Courtship.—Although I have never seen this bird on its northern breeding grounds, I have been so fortunate as to have heard many times the courtship song during the migrations on the New England coast, and to have witnessed some, at least, of its posturing on the ground. This sandpiper is more of a musician than the least, and his song is well worth hearing. I can but repeat what I have already published on the subject (1905):

Rising on quivering wings to about 30 feet from the ground, the bird advances with rapid wing beats, curving the pinions strongly downward, pouring forth a succession of musical notes—a continuous quavering trill—and ending with a few very sweet notes that recall those of a goldfinch. He then descends to the ground where one may be lucky enough, if near at hand, to hear a low musical *cluck* from the excited bird. This is, I suppose, the full love flight song, and is not often heard in its entirety, but the first quavering trill is not uncommon, a single bird or member of a flock singing this as he flies over.

Dr. Joseph Grinnell (1900) writes as follows of this species at Cape Blossom, Alaska, in July:

A few were to be found in the interior on damp, grassy flats, but the strip of low meadow bordering the lagoon back of the mission was by far the most popular resort. Here the grass was short and smooth as a lawn, with occasional narrow branches from the main slough cutting their way back toward the higher ground. In one part of this stretch of tide flats the sandpipers were so numerous that as many as a dozen pairs were in sight at once, and their twittering notes were to be heard on all sides. They were flying back and forth over the meadows chasing one another, with shrill, rolling notes uttered so continuously as to become almost inaudible from their monotony. At times in an individual case this trilling would become so intensified as to remind one of the shrill notes of the white throated swift.

Joseph Dixon (1917*a*), writing of a bird that sang at an elevation of about 50 feet above the nest says: " His song seemed to come from every direction, and this illusion was difficult to account for even by the unusual location of the songster." Whether the *whinny* heard from birds, many of which are posturing on the sand is a modification of the nuptial song or rather a partial reproduction of it, I do not know, but I am inclined to think it is. Many of these musicians appear on close scrutiny to be young birds, which would explain the imperfection of the song. The posturing is often in the nature of mock fighting—I have never seen any real blows exchanged—when two, facing each other, crouch almost flat on the sand, and then suddenly spring at each other with wings outspread. Again, two would slowly walk toward each other with neck and body almost touching the ground and with head up. This act is often performed with tail cocked up over the back, displaying a white triangle of tail coverts, and every now and then the birds would run at each other with outspread wings. All birds acting thus appeared to be uttering a series of rolling notes, which, emitted from a number of birds scattered over the flats, produces a considerable volume of sound. I have described this partial song as a *whinny*, and have tried to reduce it to syllables—*eh, eh, eh*, or *what-er, what-er*.

Lucien M. Turner in his Ungava notes records two individuals that " ran back and forth, uttering a purring twitter, holding their wings over their back with the head and neck depressed, while the posterior portion of the body was somewhat elevated. The throat was at times inflated and at other times every feather of the body was nearly reversed, presenting a strange sight."

Herbert W. Brandt supplies the following from observations in Alaska:

The semipalmated sandpiper flies high into the air, often almost out of sight, and pours forth a sustained tinkling song, which sounds like its native name uttered as a high-pitched trill—"la-v-la-v-la-v." As it sings it rapidly fans the air with short wing beats, at the same time moving at considerable speed continuously back and forth over a distance of 50 yards or more. Four of the birds which I took to be males were rather noisy, twittering, and purling, and occasionally one of them rushed at another as if he seriously intended to wage mortal combat. The feathers on his dainty neck stood out in an angered ruff; his wings were half spread, showing their light markings; and when the little warrior was just about to strike he folded his wings and elevated his tail until it was almost vertical above his long wing tips. There was, however, no real fight, for each one seemed to know his superior and gave way, after a little display, like a weaker rooster in a well-regulated barnyard.

Nesting.—H. W. Brandt contributes the following:

The semipalmated sandpiper nests amid the short herbage on the grassy dunes near the moaning breakers of Point Dall, where it selects a site quite exposed to view. Among the creeping berry vines the bird simply scratches a depression in the sand, and this it lines with a few disconnected grass stems, stiff moss stems, and a handful of tiny, crisp-dried leaves of the cranberry, willow, or dwarf birch. The range of measurements of five nests is: Inside diameter, 2 to 2½ inches; inside depth, 1½ to 2 inches; total depth, 2½ to 3¼ inches. The nest is very fragile and breaks up at once if disturbed. Like all shore birds that nest in the open, the brooding bird is anything but a close sitter, and in consequence the nest must be found by diligent search. An incubating female was collected as it departed from the nest.

Roderick Macfarlane, who found many nests of this species in the Barren Grounds, describes two of them as follows:

Nest was found between two small lakes—a few withered grasses and leaves in a shallow hole or depression, partly shaded from view by a tuft of grass. The nest was a mere depression in the midst of some hay and lined therewith, as well as with a few withered leaves.

Winthrop Sprague Brooks (1915) relates his experience in Alaska as follows:

Thirteen nests were found, the first, a set of three fresh eggs, being taken on June 12. All the nests were essentially alike—mere cavities in damp tundra close to a pool, and lined with dry willow leaves. On seven nests the female was found, and the male on six. Although the male seems to take about an equal share in brooding on the eggs and taking care of the young, I could not see that he did this at any particular time, for I could find either sex on the nest at midnight or midday. Neither sex showed any more concern than the other when an intruder was at the nest. In most cases the bird disturbed would flutter along a few yards and then remain walking quietly and watching. On one occasion a female made a great disturbance. Semipalmated sandpipers on the breeding ground are the most gentle and interesting birds of the North.

Eggs.—[*Author's note:* Four eggs seems to be the invariable rule with the semipalmated sandpiper. They are usually ovate pyriform in shape with a tendency to become subpyriform. The shell is somewhat glossy. The eggs can not with certainty be distinguished from those of the least sandpiper on one hand or the western sandpiper on the other hand; the measurements overlap with both and the colors and markings intergrade with both. I have 11 sets of semipalmated, and I can match nearly every one of them with sets from my series of the other two species. In series, however, they much more closely resemble the least sandpiper.

Herbert W. Brandt has sent me a description of his sets taken in Alaska, which are probably of the normal type, as follows:

In the six sets before me the ground color is uniformly dull white and is conspicuous. The markings are bold and individual, with most of them round instead of elongate, although there is a slight spiral tendency. These spots are dark, ranging from "claret brown" to "burnt lake," producing a deep red effect when examined in series. The underlying spots are numerous and rather conspicuous, due to the whitish ground color. They shade from "light Quaker drab" to "Quaker drab."

Less than half of my sets, all from Alaska, would fit his description; the ground colors in most of mine vary from " pale olive buff " to " olive buff "; in some it is " deep olive buff," and in one " Isabella color." The colors of the markings run from "liver brown" to "chestnut brown" in the darkest and from "hazel" to "cinnamon brown" in the lightest. There are comparatively few underlying drab markings. The eggs show the same variations in shape and arrangement of markings as eggs of the least sandpiper. I have two sets from Point Barrow, taken with the parent bird, which are almost exactly like eggs of the western sandpiper in color and style of markings but smaller, and several other sets approaching them in appearance. There are 10 sets of eggs in the Museum of Comparative Zoology in Cambridge collected by W. Sprague Brooks near Demarcation Point, Alaska, with the parent bird in each case. Three of these are of the western sandpiper type, and three others are similarly marked with different shades of brown. The measurements of 52 eggs average 30.2 by 21.2 millimeters; the eggs showing the four extremes measure 32 by 21, 30 by 22, 27.7 by 21.3, and 31.5 by 20 millimeters.]

Young.—According to Mr. Dixon (1917*a*), incubation lasts 17 days. It is performed equally by the male and female, as is shown by Mr. Brooks's very conclusive report quoted above. Mr. Dixon (1917*a*), writing of birds observed in Alaska says the young so exactly match the surroundings that they are invisible at 3 feet. He relates the case of a snowy owl that sailed from its perch in the direction of a brood of young which flattened and froze obedient to the alarm cry of the mother. The owl poised directly over them, but evidently failed to see them and flew away. On another occasion two parasitic jaegers flew by; the young flattened, and all escaped but one that began to move before the second jaeger had passed and was promptly snapped up.

He says:

It was found that the parents made no effort to feed the young. It was soon seen, however, that such care was not necessary. The young would stumble about and pick up minute gnats and flies with great dexterity, and the shallow algae-rimmed pools furnished them many a juicy " wriggler." The gait of the young sandpipers was a stumbling toddle, while their large feet and legs were all out of proportion to the rest of their slender bodies. By dropping and extending their wings they were able to use them as crutches, which often kept them from falling.

In about a month they were fully fledged, and a week later the sandpipers were leaving for the south.

Plumages.—[*Author's note:* In natal down the young semipalmated most closely resembles the young western sandpiper, but it is generally paler, with less brown or rufous. The forehead, sides of the head, and all under parts are white, faintly washed on the cheeks and upper breast with pale buff; a median stripe on the forehead, reaching only halfway to the bill, a broad loral stripe, and a malar spot are black; there is a black spot in the center of the crown, broken by a few very small white dots, surrounded by "hazel" and bordered with black; a short stripe over the eye and an auricular patch are black and "hazel" mixed; between these and the crown patch there is a broad band of white dots, terminal tufts; the back, rump, wings, and thighs are variegated "hazel" and black, with numerous small white dots, terminal tufts. The bill is broad at the tip.

Young birds are in juvenal plumage when they reach the United States on the fall migration. They can be distinguished from adults by the buffy edgings above and by the absence of dusky streaks on the throat and upper breast. The feathers of the crown are edged with sandy buff and those of the back and scapulars with "ochraceous buff" or creamy white; the wing coverts are edged with pale buff; the upper breast is washed with buff and the rest of the under parts are white. This plumage is partially molted during September and October, producing a first winter plumage, which is like the adult winter plumage, except for the juvenal wing coverts, some scapulars, and a few body feathers, which are retained. At the first prenuptial molt, the next spring, young birds become practically adult.

Adults have a complete molt from July to November, the body plumage being molted first and the wings last, the latter sometimes not until winter. Their partial prenuptial molt involves the body plumage, sometimes the tail and some wing coverts; it begins in February and lasts into May. The freshly molted spring plumage, in early May, has a "drab-gray" appearance, due to broad drab-gray tips on the feathers of the mantle; these tips soon wear away, revealing the bright colors of the nuptial plumage before the end of May.]

Food.—I have recorded the following found by me in the stomachs of this species taken on the New England coast; insects of various kinds, including beetles, small mollusks (*Littorina*), worms and crustaceans (*Gammarus orchestia*), bits of seaweed and sand. Dr. Alexander Wetmore (1916) records the contents of six stomachs from birds taken in Porto Rico in August; 99.16 per cent was animal matter, 0.84 per cent vegetable matter.

Beetles, bugs, fly pupae, and small mollusks form the bulk of the food. Small water scavenger beetles (*Hydrophilidae*) were found in four stomachs and amount to 27 per cent. Two ground beetles (*Bembidium* sp.) amount to 5 per cent and miscellaneous beetles to 3.34 per cent. One bird had eaten nothing but four back swimmers (*Notonecta* sp.), and these made 16.66 per cent. Fly pupae figure largely in two stomachs, forming 21.66 per cent of the total, and snails (*Planorbis* sp.) 13 per cent, while miscellaneous animal matter amounts to 12.50 per cent. The small quantity of vegetable matter present was rubbish. The numbers of Diptera eaten speak well for this sandpiper.

Preble and McAtee (1923) found in the stomach of a bird shot in the Pribilof Islands " remains of the beach beetle (*Aegialites californicus*), 10 per cent; fragments of small flies (Diptera), 85 per cent; and two seeds (not identified), 5 per cent."

Arthur H. Howell (1924) says, " Two stomachs of this birds from Alabama contained the remains of small mollusks, fly larvae and beetles. This species is known to feed on marine worms and mosquitoes."

Behavior.—Semipalmated sandpipers are fascinating birds to watch. When feeding on the beaches, they run along in a scattered flock just above the wave line, retreating rapidly as the wave advances, but sometimes being forced to flutter above it, all the time eagerly seeking for choice morsels. With head down, not held up as is the case with its companions the semipalmated plovers, it runs along dabbling here and there irregularly, and occasionally probing with its bill in the sand. These probings are not so deep nor so systematic as those of the sanderling, which makes a series of six to a dozen holes in succession throwing up the sand on either side. In its greediness the semipalmated sandpiper sometimes attempts to swallow too large a morsel for its small round mouth, which is much out of proportion to the stretch of the end of the bill, and many shakings of the head are needed to get a large morsel past the sticking point. I have seen one try several times to swallow a large beach flea (*Talorchestia megalophthalma*), and then fly off with it in its bill.

On a rocky shore I have seen them hunting for insects at high tide on the smooth rocks, and at low tide, running among the rocks covered with seaweed (*Fucus vesiculsus*) and on the floating weed, fluttering their wings from time to time to keep from sinking. Here they find plenty of food in the small mollusks and crustaceans, *Littorina* and *Gammarus*. On an August day on the coast of Maine I saw one searching about on floating rockweed several miles from land. Shore birds doubtless often rest in this way in their long journeys over sea.

In flight, semipalmated sandpipers in flocks, large and small, often move as one bird, twisting and turning with military precision, alternately displaying their light breasts and darker backs—flashing white and then almost disappearing. The method which enables shore birds, or, indeed, any flocking bird, to accomplish these evolutions is obscure. In the case of the semipalmated sandpiper these evolutions appear often to be made in silence, although it is of course possible that signals, not audible to the human observer, may be given. It has been suggested that telepathy or even that "a common soul" dominating the flock may be the interpretation, but both of these explanations are at present, at least, outside of scientific ken. 1 have noticed that birds who do not habitually execute evolutions, like English sparrows and the young of those that are skillful in this direction when adult, as for example, starlings, are much less proficient at this, and it seems to me possible that the whole thing may be accounted for by quickness of observation and of reaction, inherited and acquired.

Semipalmated sandpipers like other shore birds often stand on one leg and even hop along on it in feeding and they also sleep in this attitude. It is difficult to distinguish these from cripples, and one is easily deceived; the cripples seem as happy and tireless in feeding as the others.

William Brewster (1925) thus charmingly describes the habits of this bird in the wet and soft ground at Lake Umbagog:

Here they trot to and fro, almost as actively and ceaselessly as so many ants, picking up the inconspicuous worms or larvae from the surface of the ground and seeking them beneath it by thrusting down their sensitive bills quite to the nostrils, after the manner of boring snipe, but less quickly, vigorously, and persistently. They are also given to wading out into shallow water where they pull up good sized masses of aquatic plants, such as *Utricularia*. By shaking and piercing these with their bills they evidently obtain from them food of some kind, perhaps insect larvae or small *Crustacea*.

At high tide on the beaches, when the wet sand with its bountiful food supply is covered, great flocks of this species, together with the least sandpiper, the sanderling, and the semipalmated plover, often spend an hour or more huddled together on the dry sand. Each species keeps more or less separate. The birds generally face the wind, but sometimes they arrange themselves in the lee of bits of driftwood or other obstructions, and "tail out" down wind in long streamers as it were, each sheltered by the one next to windward. They sleep standing on one or both legs with the bill tucked under the feathers of the back—not "under the wing" as in poems—or they squat down, resting their breasts on the sand. They occasionally seem to yawn by stretching one wing over a leg. They also spread both wings above the back as do many other shore birds, and they flirt the bill nervously from side to side, to relieve their ennui, perhaps shaking the head at the same time.

Voice.—The varied courtship songs and notes have been described above. Their call note, to my ears, is very much like that of the least sandpiper, but shriller and less melodious. A harsh rasping note and a peeping sound are also given and a low, rolling gossipy note is often emitted when they approach other birds or decoys, a note that used to be imitated with deadly effect by gunners. John T. Nichols (1920) says:

The flight note of the semipalmated sandpiper is a rather loud "cherk," softer and less reedy than the analogous krieker "kerr." It is commonly modified to a softer "cher" or "che," which with much variation becomes the conversational twittering of members of a feeding flock. Soft short, snappy "chips" are characteristic of flocks maneuvering about decoys * * * Hurried cheeping notes ("ki-i-ip") on being flushed, are suggestive of the same note of the krieker.

Field marks.—These have been discussed at length under least sandpiper to which the reader is referred, but may be summed up here as follows: a little larger than the least sandpiper, grayer, bill stouter and straight, tarsi and feet black, semipalmated. The young can be distinguished from the old in the field by their nearly white breasts washed with a smoky tint. In the hand their tarsi are seen to be black with a slight greenish hue.

Game.—The fact that so many of these birds could be easily killed at one shot, and the fact that they were so fat and palatable broiled or cooked in a pie, made them always much sought after by the pot hunter. As large shore birds grew scarcer and it became more and more difficult for the gunner to fill his bag with them, " peep " shooting, even by sportsmen, was in vogue. The Federal law has now wisely removed this species from the list of game birds and prevented its extinction. The bird has responded to this protection in a marked degree, and flocks of 500 or more are common and pleasing sights on our beaches where one-tenth of this number was once rare.

The shooting of semipalmated sandpipers occurred largely on the beaches. The gunner dug a hole in the sand, banked it up, and put brush and driftwood, often reinforced with seaweed, on the ramparts. At a convenient distance decoys of wood or tin were placed, arranged like a flock of birds with their heads pointing to the wind. Occasionally large clamshells were stuck in the sand, simulating very well a flock of peep. Much depended on the skill of the gunner in calling down the birds as they flew along, by cunningly imitating their notes and by his care in keeping concealed and motionless until the moment that he delivered his fire. To bring down a score of birds from a closely packed flock required but little skill, where, to pick off a single peep, flying erratically and swiftly by, called for well-seasoned judgment; but the chances for these birds were small indeed when the beaches were lined with inviting decoys and concealed whistling gunners.

Fall.—On the New England coast the semipalmated sandpiper is a little later in migration than its colleague, the least sandpiper.

July 10 to October 30 are the usual dates, but few are seen after September 20. The adults come first, but after the middle of August the young appear, to be distinguished by their nearly white breasts washed with a smoky tint, and by their more unsuspecting ways.

The extraordinary abundance of this species at certain times on migration is well illustrated by what Stuart T. Danforth (1925) says of it in Porto Rico. He writes:

The semipalmated sandpiper is by far the most abundant shore bird at Cartagena Lagoon, though it occurs only as a fall migrant. I have records from August 13 to October 20, 1924. During the latter part of August they are present in almost unbelievable numbers. I hardly dare estimate their numbers, but on August 26, when they were at the height of their abundance, I am sure that 100,000 would have been a low estimate of their numbers. They simply swarmed over the mud flats. On this date, although I was trying to avoid shooting them, I got 16 while shooting other birds. They were so abundant that stray shots could not help killing numbers of them. On other days many were also unintentionally shot in the same manner. In fact, all but 4 of the 36 that I collected were shot in this way. This species prefers the mud flats, but when they were so excessively abundant some were forced to feed in the sedge and grass associations, and when the fall rains came a little later practically all of them were forced to the sedges and grasses and even to the cane fields. But within a few days after this most of them left for parts unknown.

DISTRIBUTION

Range.—North America, South America, the West Indies, and northeastern Siberia; accidental in Europe.

Breeding range.—The semipalmated sandpiper breeds north to the northeastern coast of Siberia (Plover Bay); Alaska (Point Hope, Point Barrow, Barter Island, Camden Bay, and Demarcation Point); Yukon (probably Herschel Island); Mackenzie (Franklin Bay), Victoria Land; northern Keewatin (Cape Fullerton); Labrador (Okak); and Newfoundland. East to Labrador (Okak). South to Labrador (Okak); Newfoundland; northern Quebec (Fort George); southern Keewatin (Severn River); probably eastern Manitoba (York Factory and Fort Churchill); Mackenzie (Fort Anderson); and Alaska (Pastolik). West to Alaska (Pastolik, Hooper Bay, St. Michael, probably Nome, Port Clarence, Kowak River, probably Cape Blossom, and Point Hope); and northeastern Siberia (Plover Bay).

Winter range.—North to Sonora (Hermosillo); Texas (Fort Brown, Corpus Christi, and Refugio County); Louisiana (State Game Preserve, Marsh Island, False River, and Hog Bayou); and South Carolina (Bulls Point). East to South Carolina (Bulls Point, Sea Islands, Frogmore, and Port Royal); Georgia (Chatham County, Blackbeard Island, Darien, and St. Marys); Florida (Mosquito Inlet

and St. Lucie); Bahama Islands (Great Inagua); Haiti (Monte
Christi and Sanchez); Porto Rico; Lesser Antilles (Antigua, Bar-
bados, Carriacou, Grenada, and Trinidad); French Guiana (Cay-
enne); and Brazil (Island Mexiana, Island Cajetuba, and Bahia).
South to Brazil (Bahia); rarely Patagonia (Nuevo Gulf); and Peru
(Parecas Bay). West to Peru (Parecas Bay); Colombia (Cartagena
and Sabanillo); Guatemala (San Jose); Valley of Mexico; Sinaloa
(Mazatlan); and Sonora (Hermosillo).

Spring migration.—Early dates of arrival in the spring are: North
Carolina, Highlands, April 12, and Raleigh, April 13; Virginia,
Cobb Island, May 14, and Smiths Island, May 16; District of Colum-
bia, Washington, May 10; Pennsylvania, Grove City, May 3, and
Milford, May 9; New Jersey, Elizabeth, May 6; New York, Orient,
April 16, Canandaigua, April 26, Geneva, May 5, and Rochester,
May 7; Connecticut, Saybrook, May 9, and Norwalk, May 11; Mas-
sachusetts, Monomoy Island, April 22, Ipswich, April 24; Maine,
Lewiston, May 6; Quebec, May 2; Missouri, Appleton City, April 3,
and Boonville, April 16; Illinois, Springfield, April 25, Quincy, May
3; Indiana, Camden, April 18, Bicknell, April 24, and Bloomington,
April 26; Ohio, Lakeside, May 3, New Bremen, May 5, and Oberlin,
May 7; Michigan, Ann Arbor, April 1; Ontario, Toronto, May 14,
and Ottawa, May 14; Iowa, Keokuk, April 19, Emmetsburg, April
27, and Sioux City, May 2; Wisconsin, Elkhorn, May 1, and Madison, May 7; Minnesota, Wilder, April 19, Jackson, April 24, and
Hallock, May 9; Kansas, McPherson, April 15, Lawrence, May 5,
and Emporia, May 9; Nebraska, Neligh, April 30, Omaha, May 4,
and Lincoln, May 5; South Dakota, Sioux Falls, May 5, and Harrison, May 8; Manitoba, Gimli, May 10, and Shoal Lake, May 19;
Saskatchewan, Dinsmore, May 13, and Indian Head, May 19; and
Mackenzie, Fort Chipewyan, May 24, and Fort Simpson, May 26.

Late dates of spring departure are: Cuba, Guantanamo, May 8,
and Mariel, May 10; the Bahama Islands, Hog Island, April 27,
Salt Key, May 5, and Inagua, May 27; Florida, Whitfield, May 11,
Fort De Soto, May 25, and St. Marks, May 26; Georgia, Savannah,
May 22; South Carolina, Ladys Island, May 26; North Carolina,
Fort Macon, May 17, Cape Hatteras, May 20, and Raleigh, May 22;
Virginia, Smiths Island, May 22, and Cape Charles, May 27; Dis-
trict of Columbia, Washington, May 22; Pennsylvania, Warren,
May 24, and Erie, June 4; New Jersey, Camden, May 25, Long
Beach, June 1, and Elizabeth, June 18; New York, Rochester, June
2, Syracuse, June 4, Poughkeepsie, June 5, Geneva, June 8, and New
York City, June 15; Connecticut, Norwalk, May 30, and Fairfield,
June 9; Rhode Island, Sakonnet Point, June 4; Massachusetts,
Dennis, May 30, Lynn, June 2, and Harvard, June 9; Maine, Port-
land, June 3; Louisiana, Lobdell, May 28; Missouri, Boonville, May

31; Illinois, Oak Park, May 26, Shawneetown, May 27, and Chicago, June 13; Ohio, Oberlin, June 1, Port Clinton, June 3, and Lakeside, June 10; Michigan, Sault Ste. Marie, May 31, and Detroit, June 2; Ontario, Toronto, June 2, Hamilton, June 5, and Todmorden, June 13; Iowa, Clear Lake, May 20, Mason City, May 27, and Sioux City, May 30; Wisconsin, Madison, May 31; Minnesota, Leech Lake, May 27, Minneapolis, June 1, and Lanesboro, June 3; Texas, Texas City, May 17, Point Isabel, May 19, and Gainesville, May 24; Kansas, Fort Riley, May 22, Republican Fork, May 25, Emporia, May 27, and Stafford County, June 6; Nebraska, Long Pine, May 25, Valentine, May 30, and Lincoln, June 8; South Dakota, Faulkton, May 27, Forestburg, June 2, and Harrison, June 3; Manitoba, May 31, Dominion City, June 1, and Shoal Lake, June 14; and Saskatchewan, Quill Lake, June 11, and Kutanajan Lake, June 13.

Fall migration.—Early dates of fall arrival are: British Columbia, Okanagan Landing, July 15, Atlin, July 16, and Courtenay, July 24; Colorado, Larimer County, July 18; Saskatchewan, Quill Lake, July 4, and Kiddleston, July 16; Manitoba, Russell, July 11, Red Deer River, July 23, and Shoal Lake, August 3; North Dakota, Mouse River, August 10; South Dakota, Forestburg, August 2; Kansas, Emporia, August 31; Texas, Brownsville, October 1, and Lake Worth, October 19; Minnesota, St. Vincent, July 24; Iowa, Sioux City, July 12, and Winnebago County, July 29; Ontario, Todmorden, July 21, and Amherstburg-Colchester, July 29; Michigan, Charity Island, July 9, and Detroit, July 22; Ohio, Columbus, July 12, Bay Point, July 16, and Painesville, July 19; Illinois, Chicago, July 2; Missouri, St. Louis, August 6; Mississippi, Biloxi, July 10, Beauvoir, July 18, and Bay St. Louis, July 21; Nova Scotia, Wolfville, July 10; Maine, Portland, July 23, and Pittsfield, July 24; Massachusetts, Monomoy Island, July 3, Marthas Vineyard, July 8, and Ipswich, July 10; Rhode Island, Newport, July 14, and Providence, July 22; Connecticut, Milford, July 28, and New Haven, July 30; New York, Orient, July 4, East Hampton, July 8, Freeport, July 12, and Rochester, July 12; New Jersey, Long Beach, July 7, and Cape May, July 14; Pennsylvania, Carlisle, July 27; District of Columbia, Washington, August 10; Virginia, Cobb Island, July 15; South Carolina, Frogmore, July 22; Florida, Palma Sola, July 8, Fernandina, July 14, Pensacola, July 16, and Fort De Soto, July 17; Cuba, Guantanamo, August 15, and Batabano, August 26; Porto Rico, Mona Island, August 11, and Cabo Rojo, August 24; and the Lesser Antilles, St. Croix, August 14, and Barbados, August 18.

Late dates of departure in the fall are: British Columbia, Lake Teslin, September 12, and Okanagan Landing, September 16; Saskatchewan, Ravine Bank, August 25; Manitoba, Winnipeg, Septem-

ber 13; Nebraska, Lincoln, October 30; Kansas, Topeka, September
15; Minnesota, Lanesboro, September 15; Wisconsin, Racine, October
1; Iowa, Marshalltown, October 12, and Burlington, October 15;
Ontario, Ottawa, October 5, London, October 16, and Point Pelee,
November 15; Michigan, Sault Ste. Marie, October 1, and Detroit,
October 15; Ohio, Salem, October 9, Youngstown, October 26, and
Dayton, November 16; Illinois, Chicago, October 9, and Cantine,
October 17; Missouri, St. Louis, October 17; Prince Edward Island,
North River, October 27; Nova Scotia, Wolfville, September 24;
Quebec, Montreal, October 18; Maine, Lewiston, October 17; Mas-
sachusetts, Dennis, October 21, Boston, October 23, Harvard, October
24, and Lynn, October 25; Connecticut, Middleton, October 7, and
New Haven, October 23; New York, Canandaigua, October 14, Sing
Sing, October 20, New York City, October 24, Shinnecock Bay, Oc-
tober 30, and Ithaca, November 1; New Jersey, Morristown, September 24, Cape May, October 2, and Elizabeth, October 16; Pennsylvania, Beaver, October 3; and District of Columbia, Washington,
October 26.

Casual records.—The semipalmated sandpiper is not common in
Colorado and Utah, although in both of these States it has been
taken on several occasions. Other casual records are Wyoming,
Horse Creek, 1859, and Alkali Lake, October 31, 1897; Montana,
Fort Keogh, May 15 and 16, 1889, Sweetgrass Hills, August 11,
1874, Billings, August 12, 1900, and Miles City, August 14 and 15,
1900; Washington, Blaine, August 4 to 8, 1900, Puget Sound, July
15, 1857, Shoalwater Bay, May 3, 1854, and Simiahmoo, May,
1858; and Pribilof Islands, St. Paul Island, June 12, 1890.

There also are at least three records for the British Isles: Romney
Marsh, Kent, September, 1907, Marazion Marsh, Cornwall, October
10, 1853, and Northam Burrows, Devon, September, 1869.

Egg dates.—Arctic Canada: 70 records, June 12 to July 24; 35
records, July 3 to 6. Alaska: 33 records, June 2 to July 5; 17
records, June 6 to 18.

EREUNETES MAURI Cabanis

WESTERN SANDPIPER

HABITS

Spring.—The western sandpiper has an unique distribution and
peculiar migrations. It occupies a very restricted breeding range in
the coastal regions of northwestern Alaska, but is spread out over a
wide winter range, entirely across the continent in southern North
America, in Central America, and in northern South America. But
we know very little about its migration routes between these two

seasonal ranges. I have not a single spring record for it from any of my correspondents in the interior. Undoubtedly it has been generally overlooked on account of its close resemblance to the semipalmated sandpiper, an abundant species which few collectors bother to shoot. Its northward migration along the Pacific coast, in April and May, is well known; this flight is mainly coastwise and the birds are often extremely abundant. D. E. Brown, in some notes sent to me from Westport, Washington, refers to this species as easily outnumbering all other shorebirds combined; they were associated with red-backs, but outnumbered them 10 to 1. Dr. E. W. Nelson (1887) says of the arrival of these birds in Alaska:

As the snow disappears on the low ground about Norton Sound, from the 10th to the 15th of May each year, and the ponds, still ice-covered, are bordered by a ring of water, these gentle birds arrive on the shore of Bering Sea, in the vicinity of Saint Michael and the Yukon mouth. The advancing season finds their numbers continually augmented until, toward the end of May, they are extremely common and are found scattered everywhere over the mossy flats and low hillsides. Their gentle character and trusting ways render them very attractive to the frequenter of their territory at this season.

Courtship.—The same gifted writer describes the courtship of this gentle little sandpiper as follows:

The warm days toward the end of May cause the brown slopes and flats to assume a shade of green, and among the pretty bird romances going on under our eyes none is more charming than the courtship of this delicate sandpiper. They have forsaken the borders of icy pools, and, in twos and threes, are found scattered over the tundra, showing a preference for small dry knolls and the drier tussock-covered parts of the country in the vicinity of damp spots and small ponds. Here the gentle birds may be seen at all times tripping daintily over the moss or in and out among the tufts of grass, conversing with each other in low, pleasant, twittering notes, and never showing any sign of the wrangling so frequent with their kind at this season. The female modestly avoids the male as he pays his homage, running back and forth before her as though anxious to exhibit his tiny form to the best advantage. At times his heart beats high with pride and he trails his wings, elevates and partly spreads his tail, and struts in front of his lady fair in all the pompous vanity of a pigmy turkey-cock; or his blood courses in a fiery stream until, filled with ecstatic joy, the sanguine lover springs from the earth, and, rising upon vibrating wings, some 10 or 15 yards, he poises, hovering in the same position, sometimes nearly a minute, while he pours forth a rapid, uniform series of rather musical trills, which vary in strength as they gradually rise and fall, producing pleasant cadences. The wings of the songster meanwhile vibrate with such rapid motion that they appear to keep time with the rapidly trilling notes, which can only be likened to the running down of a small spring and may be represented by the syllables *tzr-r-e-e-e, zr-e-e-e-, zr-e-e-e,* in a fine high-pitched tone, with an impetus at each "z." This part of the song ended, the bird raises its wings above its back, thus forming a V, and glides slowly to the ground, uttering at the same time, in a trill, but with a deeper and richer tone, a series of notes which may be likened to the syllables *tzur-r-r-r, tzur-r-r-r.* The word "throaty" may be applied to these latter notes as distinguished from the high-pitched key of the first part of the song.

Nesting.—Herbert W. Brandt, who has had extensive experience with the nesting habits of this species, says in his manuscript notes:

The gentle little western sandpiper is the most abundant and most widely distributed shore bird occurring in the Hooper Bay region. Throughout the area, wherever dry ground is found, it is plentiful, and it even occurs on the lower mountain slopes of the Askinuk Range. Before the tundra had discarded its snowy mantle the first birds of this species had responded to the lure of early spring, for they arrived on May 14, and two days later they were common, while on May 20 they were abundant, carrying on everywhere their dainty aerial butterfly courtship. The western sandpiper is usually found in large scattering colonies especially on the upland tundra where for large areas they average one or two pairs to the acre. Isolated couples, however, are occasionally encountered.

The nest of the western sandpiper is well concealed from view by the surrounding curly bunch-grass that everywhere in the dryer areas forces its way up amid the moss. Under this protection a depression is made and scantily lined with grass, and usually in addition with considerable tiny leaves of the prostrate berry-bearing vines, of the dwarf birch, and of the reindeer moss stems. In consequence, the nest is very fragile and loosely made, but before it is disturbed it is neatly cup-shaped. The range of measurements of 32 nests is: Inside diameter, 2 to 3 inches; depth of cavity, 1½ to 3 inches; and total depth, 2½ to 4 inches. Both male and female share in the tender duties of incubation and are often very loath to forsake their nest, so that when crossing their chosen haunts an incubating bird, by fluttering up before one's very feet, will occasionally unwittingly betray its well-concealed abode.

These charming little creatures are most brave, even eager in defense of their homes, often charging with puffed-out feathers and head drawn against the body to make themselves look as formidable as possible. Their tameness and familiarity are remarkable. Often after we had removed the eggs the parent would go to the empty nest, sit on it for a little while, then come out, her little body a-purr with agitation, and inquire in her thin incessant voice what had become of the eggs. It is little wonder that I shot very few specimens for identification purposes. This tiny sandpiper had won too deep a place in my affections.

The confiding nature of these birds is referred to by other writers. Doctor Nelson (1887) tells how one of his men lay on the ground with his outstretched hand close beside a nest; but the bird soon returned, crossed his arm and settled on the nest, where she was caught with turn of his hand and released. Alfred M. Bailey (1926) placed his " hat over one set of eggs, leaving just room for the parent bird to crawl under, which she immediately proceeded to do."

Eggs.—Herbert W. Brandt has given me the following good description of his 120 eggs of this species, collected by him at Hooper Bay, Alaska:

Four eggs always constitute a complete set with the western sandpiper, but occasionally late nests with three eggs in each were observed, which were probably second layings. They are pyriform to subpyriform in shape and are placed in the nest with the small ends together and pointed downward, snuggling amid the loose interior contents of the nest. The shell is smooth, has a slight luster, and is strongly constructed. The markings on the same set of eggs always follow the same type in color, and likewise the ground color is always the same shade. In the series of eggs the prevalent ground color is "cream color," but the shades vary from dull white, which is very rare, to equally rare "wood brown." The ground color is often almost obliterated by the profuseness of the markings, especially on the larger two-thirds of the egg. The color of the surface markings is usually "Kaiser brown," but they show considerable variation, dependent upon the amount of pigment deposited, ranging from "brick red" to "chestnut brown." The spots are somewhat elongated and vary from small pin points to large blotches that may completely cover the larger end of the egg. These have a decided tendency to spiral from left to right. The underlying markings are inconspicuous and are only visible on eggs having a pale background and then they are of small size and indistinct. The eggs are generally flecked with additional markings consisting of a few intense irregular spots or fine lines of slate black to black. These blackbird-like markings are almost always on the larger end, although on many eggs they are entirely wanting. In series the eggs of the western sandpiper have a decidedly bright red appearance, and are thus distinct from any eggs occurring in the Hooper Bay region.

The western sandpiper has been known to lay five eggs.

The measurements of 120 eggs, furnished by Mr. Brandt, average 30.8 by 21.9 millimeters; the eggs showing the four extremes measure **32.5** by 22.3, 32 by **22.8, 28.7** by 21.6, and 30.3 by **21.1** millimeters..

Young.—H. B. Conover tells me that both sexes incubate, at least both had incubation patches. He says in his notes:

On June 15 the first newly hatched young were found. The parents were very solicitous and flew about twittering anxiously. Soon other old birds joined them and seemed just as anxious as if the young were their own. This habit of these sandpipers in joining forces to help their neighbors was very noticeable both before and after the eggs had hatched. By June 30 half-grown young that could already fly for a few yards were being seen. Western sandpipers with their chicks were everywhere, and during a walk around the tundra you had a constant attendance of anxious mothers and fathers wheeling about. Eggs were still being found on July 5. By July 18 the mud flats were covered with fully fledged young of this species.

The incubation period for this species seems to be about 21 days. A nest found on May 26 with four eggs hatched on June 15 late in the evening. Another found on May 29 with three eggs in it, had four eggs on May 30, and three young and a pipped egg on the evening of June 19. The rapidity with which these birds lay and hatch their eggs and raise their young is very remarkable. In 60 days from their arrival on the nesting grounds the young are full grown and taking care of themselves.

Mr. Brandt in his manuscript says:

It seemed to us as if every western sandpiper about Hooper Bay must have deposited its first egg on practically the same day, because the four days following May 26 more than 50 nests were recorded, and after June 15 the beautiful brown and black mottled young all of the same size were to be found everywhere. These newly born bird mites are not long abed, however, for in one case an hour after hatching their cradle was empty.

Plumages.—The downy young western sandpiper, when first hatched, is richly colored in warm, bright browns and buffs, quite different in appearance from the young semipalmated sandpiper. Behind a broad " cinnamon buff " forehead is a large, rounded crown patch extending from above the eyes to the nape, in which the down is basally black, but deeply tipped " burnt sienna "; in the center of this a cluster of buffy down tips produces a spot, which is divided by a blackish median stripe extending down to the bill; a band of pale buff, produced by down tips, encircles the sides and rear of the crown patch; there is a loral stripe and a short malar stripe of black; the sides of the head and neck are " cinnamon buff "; and a variable pattern of " burnt sienna " decorates the auricular region, behind and above the eye. The remainder of the upper parts, back, wings, rump, and thighs are a mixture of black and dark, rich browns, " bay," " burnt sienna," and " amber brown," sprinkled, in an irregular pattern, in the darker portions with tiny buff tips. The under parts vary from pale buff on the breast to buffy white on the throat and to white on the belly. The bright colors fade to dull browns and grayish as the chick grows older. The first of the juvenal plumage appears on the scapulars and then on the sides of the breast.

In fresh juvenal plumage, as seen in Alaska in June, the crown is " sepia " with " pinkish cinnamon " edgings; the nape is " drab-gray," streaked with dusky; the feathers of the mantle are brownish black, edged with " tawny " on the back and broadly edged with " tawny " and white on the scapulars; the rump, upper tail coverts, and central tail feathers are " sepia "; the other rectrices are " light mouse gray "; the wing coverts are " mouse gray," tipped with " tawny " or lighter buff; the throat and under parts are white, washed on the breast with " light cinnamon-drab," and streaked on the sides of the breast with dusky. This plumage fades somewhat during migration and the body plumage is mostly all molted before October. In their first winter plumage young birds can be distinguished from adults only by the wing coverts and a few retained scapulars and tertials. At the first prenuptial molt they become practically adult.

Adults have a complete postnuptial molt in the summer and fall, molting the body plumage in July and August and the wings and tail in November or later. The prenuptial molt in March and April involves only the body plumage. The fresh plumage, in April, is veiled with " drab-gray " tips, which soon wear away, revealing the bright nuptial colors.

Food.—Very little has been published on the food of the western sandpiper, but it probably feeds on the same things as the other small sandpipers with which it associates.   Arthur H. Howell (1924) says:

Six stomachs of this bird collected in Alabama showed its food to be minute fly larvae, aquatic beetles and bugs, marine worms, and small snails.

Stuart T. Danforth (1925) found 150 bloodworms and a Hydrophilid larva in the stomach of one taken in Porto Rico.

Behavior.—S. F. Rathbun has sent me the following notes on the habits of the western sandpiper on the coast of Washington:

This is one of the small sandpipers of this region that will be found common at the time of the migration periods along the ocean beaches and on the tide flats.   It occurs in flocks of varying sizes, some of which contain an exceedingly large number of birds.   At times if care is used one can approach a flock quite closely, often within 15 or 20 feet, and it is of interest to watch the actions of the individuals.   They are active birds, being constantly on the move as they feed, and while thus engaged keep up a continual conversation, as it were, this being of the nature of a soft, rolling whistle which is pleasant to hear.   These sandpipers seem to prefer to feed at or near the waters edge, particularly where there is an ebb and flow, being very active in following up the water as it recedes and equally so in avoiding its incoming, but always at the very edge as it were.   They secure their food by a skimming like movement of the bill over the surface of the mud that has just been covered by the water, and as the birds advance or retreat in following the flow it is quite amusing to observe the seeming pains taken to avoid coming into contact with it.   And still at times individuals may be seen in some of the very shallow spots.   It is a fine sight to see a flock of these sandpipers suddenly take alarm as they are feeding; all quickly spring into the air as if moved by the same impulse at exactly the same moment, and then form a compact body that will execute a variety of evolutions in perfect harmony.   The flock will rise and fall and wheel and turn, and at times may split into several smaller ones, these to again reunite, and should one happen to stand where the light falls directly on the birds the white of their underparts as they turn is very striking.   These actions may be repeated a number of times, and then without warning the flock of birds will alight and quickly scatter in search of food. Scenes like this are what give an enlightenment to the waste places and fortunately, under the protection now afforded the species, are likely to continue to be enacted in the future.   But large as the numbers of the western sandpiper still appear to be, they are not comparable to those of fifteen or twenty years ago, and the cause of this decrease in their numbers is the same old story. It seems hardly possible that a bird so small could have been regarded as game and its hunting come under the name of sport, but such was the case and it brought about the logical result.   One may be thankful, however, that this no longer can be done, and hope that the lapse of time may bring about somewhat of an increase in the number of these birds.

Voice.—John T. Nichols contributes the following on the calls of this species:

The most common loud call of the western sandpiper has the *ee* sound found in the *kreep* of the least sandpiper, a plaintive quality as in the voice of the sanderling, and suggests somewhat the squawk of a young robin.   It is variable and may be written *chee-rp*, *cheep*, or *chir-eep*.   It seems to be the flight note of the species, corresponding to the *cherk* of the semipalmated sandpiper, and is also used by a bird on the ground calling to others in the air which alight with it, as such flight notes sometimes are. Its closest resemblance with a note of the semipalmated is to the *serup* sometimes heard from that bird when flushing.

Some of the calls of the western are apparently indistinguishable from those of the semipalmated sandpiper, but as studied on the northwest coast of Florida, where it greatly outnumbered the other form, more seemed different. Birds took wing with a *sirp*, or at another time a *chir-ir-ip*, which heard also in a medley of variations from a flock already on the wing, suggesting the notes of the horned lark, may be more or less analogous with the short flocking note of the semipalmated sandpiper.

Field marks.—It is most difficult and often impossible to distinguish between the western and the semipalmated sandpipers in life; and I have experienced difficulty in distinguishing between them even in the hand. The western has a longer bill, and I believe that the bill measurements of corresponding sexes do not overlap, though they approach very closely; but the longest-billed female semipalmated may have a longer bill than the shortest-billed male western. In spring and summer plumages the western shows much more rufous in the upper parts and is more conspicuously and more heavily streaked on the breast, but in winter plumage the two species are very much alike. Mr. Nichols has given me a few characters by which this species can be recognized even in winter; he calls it "a somewhat larger, rangier, paler, grayer bird " than the semipalmated; it also has " better developed white stripes over the eyes which meet more broadly on the forehead, the top of the head is not so dark, its dark auricular area is not so prominent, the markings on the top, and particularly on the sides, of the head and neck are finer.

As to the bills, he says:

There is a subtle difference in their bills, however, which I have frequently noticed in life and once or twice checked by taking specimens. The bill of a long-billed semipalmated sandpiper is quite straight and becomes slender toward the end; that of a short-billed western is not so slender toward the end and with just an appreciable downward bend before its tip. In long-billed individuals of the western sandpiper the bill becomes slender toward the end and frequently has a decided drop at the tip. Such birds are unmistakably different to anyone thoroughly familiar with the semipalmated sandpiper.

Fall.—Like many other waders, these little sandpipers begin to move off their breeding grounds at a very early date. As early as June 21, 1914, F. S. Hersey saw western sandpipers flocking at the mouth of the Yukon River, Alaska. Some of the flocks contained from 40 to 60 birds. The larger flocks were all of this species, but the smaller flocks often contained one long-billed dowitcher.

Doctor Nelson (1887) says, of its fall wanderings:

Early in July the young are on the wing and begin to gather in flocks toward the 1st of August. The last of these birds are seen on the coast of Norton

Sound and the Yukon mouth the 1st of October. Although it is not recorded from the Seal and Aleutian Islands, I have seen the bird at St. Lawrence Island, south of Bering Straits, and at several points along the northeastern coast of Siberia, and it frequents the Arctic coasts of Alaska in addition to being found throughout the interior along streams where suitable flats occur. Murdoch notes it as a fall visitor at Point Barrow. It has been found in abundance on the southeast coast of the Territory, where it occurs during the migrations.

On the coast of British Columbia and farther south it is an abundant fall migrant, but it is rare or casual inland; the first arrivals sometimes reach California before the middle of July. Migration records for the great interior are almost entirely lacking and how it reaches the Atlantic coast, where it is so abundant in fall and winter, is a mystery.

Mr. Nichols wrote to me as follows:

The occurrence of this bird on the North Atlantic coast of the United States is irregular. At times it is really numerous on Long Island over periods of several years, and then it becomes rare again. In the 1912 southward migration the western was carefully looked for among the abundant semipalmated sandpiper but no evidence of its presence was found. In 1913 a single bird with a very white head and a peculiar note suggesting a young robin was, I now feel confident, a western sandpiper, at the time it passed as unidentified. The following year one of the white-headed long-billed juvenal westerns was picked out in a flock of semipalmated in August and collected. Later several others, all well-marked birds were identified in flocks of the semipalmated. In 1916 and 1917 the species was still more numerous. On October 12, 1917, at Long Beach with R. C. Murphy it was estimated that about one-half the *Ereunetes* were this, one-half the common eastern form. Specimens of each were obtained from gunners present. The following year (1918) a flock on the beach in late spring (June 2) were predominatingly western; the species returned again from the north in early July (July 4). During this or the immediately succeeding southward migrations the semipalmated fell off in numbers, and furthermore, a great many birds thought to be western were indeterminate. Mr. E. P. Bicknell met the same condition which I found at Mastic further west at Long Beach. I remember a letter wherein he spoke of the semipalmated being replaced by the western, but I did not take just that view of it. For a year or two I have no real idea how common either species was. I saw numerous birds that seemed to be western, but mostly indeterminate, and took no specimens. Later the standard semipalmated reestablished its usually large numbers and this season (1925) probably for the first time the western was again common among them, about as in 1916, some of this latter form easily identifiable birds (in life).

Winter.—Arthur T. Wayne (1910) says:

The western sandpiper is the most abundant of all the waders that winter on this coast. It is not unusual to see thousands of these birds any day during the winter months. It can almost be considered a permanent resident, as it is only absent from May 20 until July 8. The adults arrive in worn breeding plumage and immediately begin to moult the feathers of the head and throat. By the first week in August they have acquired their autumn plumage.

Among the big flocks of small sandpipers that we saw all winter frequenting the extensive mud flats in the vicinity of Tampa Bay,

Florida, I am satisfied that this species was well represented, if not the predominating species. I confess that I can not identify in life more than a very small percentage of these little "peep," and then only when seen under most favorable circumstances. One dislikes to shoot any number of the gentle little birds for identification. But what few we shot proved to be western sandpipers, and I am inclined to think that most of them were. Mr. Nichols writes to me:

In my limited experience *mauri* is commoner than *pusillus* on the west coast of Florida. In Wakulla County in March and September, 1919, most all the *Ereunetes* were western, only one or two among them definitely identified as *pusillus;* and in April, 1917, two or three western were identified with least sandpipers south of Sanibel Light.

DISTRIBUTION

Range.—North America, Central America, the West Indies, and northern South America.

Breeding range.—So far as known, the western sandpiper breeds only in Alaska. North to Cape Prince of Wales, Cape Blossom, Point Barrow, and Camden Bay. East to Camden Bay and St. Michael. South to St. Michael, Pastolik, and Hooper Bay. West to Hooper Bay, Nome, and Cape Prince of Wales. It has been taken in summer in northeastern Siberia at two points, East Cape on July 14, 1913, and Cape Serdze, on July 16, 1913.

Winter range.—The Pacific, Gulf, and South Atlantic coasts of the United States, the West Indies, Central America, and northern South America. North to Washington (Dungeness Spit, and Smith Island); Texas (Brownsville and Corpus Christi); Louisiana (Cameron and Vermilion Parishes); Alabama (Dauphin Island); and rarely, North Carolina (Pea Island). East to rarely, North Carolina (Pea Island and Fort Macon); South Carolina (Charleston); Georgia (Blackbeard Island); Florida (Amelia Island, and Fort Myers); Cuba (Guantanamo); and Trinidad. South to Trinidad; Venezuela (Margarita Island); probably northern Colombia (Sabanilla); probably Costa Rica (Barranca Puntarenas); Tehuantepec (Tehuantepec City); and Lower California (La Paz). West to Lower California (La Paz); California (San Diego County, Alameda, Oakland, and Berkeley); and Washington (Point Chehalis, Seattle, and Dungeness Spit). It also has been detected in winter on San Clemente Island, off the coast of southern California.

Spring migration.—The spring movement of birds that have wintered on the South Atlantic coast is imperfectly known, there being available no interior records that indicate the route by which they reach the breeding grounds. The species has been detected at Long Beach, New York, as early as April 25, and at Mastic, New

York, on May 12, while late spring departures from South Carolina have been noted at Charleston on May 8, and from Mastic, New York, on June 2.

Early dates of arrival in the West are: Arizona, Fort Verde, April 11, and San Pedro River, April 17; Colorado, Denver, May 2, and Loveland, May 9; Nevada, Smoky Creek, May 6; Idaho, Meridian, May 6; British Columbia, Sumas, April 20, and Chilliwack, April 26; and Alaska, Kuiu Island, April 28, Craig, May 2, Patterson's Bay, May 7, Admiralty Island, May 8, Fort Kenai, May 12, Hooper Bay, May 14, and Prince of Wales Island, May 15.

Late dates of spring departure at western points are: Texas, Somerest, May 5, San Angelo, May 6, Seadrift, May 8, and Tom Green and Concho Counties, May 12; Kansas, Lawrence, May 26; South Dakota, Vermilion, May 24, and Forestburg, May 26; lower California, San Quentin Bay, May 10; California, Fresno, May 12, Santa Barbara, May 16, Los Angeles, May 19, Alameda, May 21, and Owens Lake, June 1; Oregon, Mercer, May 14; Washington, Ilwaco, May 18, Neah Bay, May 24, Clallam Bay, May 25, and Quillayute Needles, May 30.

Fall migration.—Early dates of arrival in the fall are: British Columbia, Courtenay, July 7, Nootka Sound, July 23, and Okanagan Landing, July 28; Washington, Cape Flattery, July 2, Destruction Island, July 3, and Granville, July 4; Oregon, Cow Creek Lake, July 4; California, Santa Barbara, July 3, Fresno, July 5, and Tulare Lake, July 7; Lower California, San Quentin, August 24; Mexico, San Mateo, August 7; Idaho, Meridian, July 23, and Big Lost River, July 25; Wyoming, Fort Bridger, July 13; Oklahoma, Old Greer County, July 19; Arizona, Tucson, August 16, and San Bernardino Ranch, August 24; Texas, Mobeetie, July 27, Beaumont, August 5, Rockport, August 12, Hereford, August 18, and Padre Island, August 21; Massachusetts, Monomoy Island, July 19, and Nahant, August 4; New York, Mastic, July 4, and Freeport, July 16; South Carolina, Charleston, July 8; and Florida, James Island, July 20.

Late dates of fall departure are: Alaska, Craig, September 24, and St. Lazaria Island, September 29; British Columbia, Chilliwack, September 11, and Comox, September 26; Montana, Great Falls, September 4; New Mexico, Albuquerque, October 5; Massachusetts, North Truro, September 2, and Harvard, September 8; New York, Chateaugay, September 13, Amityville, September 17, and Long Beach, October 12; New Jersey, Cape May County, September 14; District of Columbia, Anacostia River, September 25; and Virginia, Four-mile Run, September 11.

Casual records.—Casual occurrences of the western sandpiper must, of course, be based upon specimen evidence, as this species is easily confused with the semipalmated sandpiper. For this reason several records are considered doubtful, while in other regions it may be more numerous than is now known. One was taken August 21, 1907, at Beaver, Pennsylvania, while two were collected at Burlington, Iowa, on October 15, 1895, and one at Columbus, Ohio, on September 12, 1925.

Egg dates.—Alaska: 159 records, May 23 to July 7: 80 records, May 29 to June 15.

CROCETHIA ALBA (Pallas)

SANDERLING

HABITS

Along the forearm of Cape Cod, from the elbow at Chatham to the wrist near Provincetown, extend about 30 miles of nearly continuous ocean beaches, to which we can add 10 more if we include that long, narrow strip of beach and marsh called Monomoy. Facing the broad Atlantic and exposed to all its furious storms, these beaches are swept clean and pounded to a hard surface by the ceaseless waves. Even in calm weather the restless ocean swells and surges up and down over these sloping sands, and the winter storms may make or wash away a mile or so of beach in a single season. Here on the ocean side of the beach, the "back side of the beach," as it is called on the cape, is the favorite resort of the little sanderlings in fair weather or in foul. They are well named "beach birds," for here they are seldom found anywhere except on the ocean beaches, and I believe that the same is true of the Pacific coast. They are particularly active and happy during stormy weather, for then a bountiful supply of food is cast up by the heavy surf. But at all times the surf line attracts them, where they nimbly follow the receding waves to snatch their morsels of food or skillfully dodge the advancing line of foam as it rolls up the beach.

Spring.—To the ends of the earth and back again extend the migrations of the sanderling, the cosmopolitan globe trotter; few species, if any, equal it in world-wide wanderings. Nesting in the Arctic regions of both hemispheres, it migrates through all of the continents, and many of the islands, to the southernmost limits of south America and Africa, and even to Australia.

The spring migration starts in March, though the last migrants may not leave their winter resorts until late in April; they have been noted in Chile from April 11 to 29, and even in May. The earliest migrants have been known to reach New England and Ohio before the end of March. The main flight passes through Massachusetts in May, a few birds lingering into June. In the interior and on the Pacific coast the dates are about the same. C. G. Harrold has taken it in Manitoba as early as April 29, but William Rowan (1926) says that the main flight comes along during the last week in May and the first few days of June, when it is abundant.

A. L. V. Manniche (1910) thus describes the arrival of the sanderling on its breeding grounds in northeastern Greenland:

The sanderling arrived at Stormkap singly or in couples respectively June 2, 1907, and May 28, 1908. In company with the other waders and large flocks of snow buntings, which arrived at the same time, the sanderlings would in the first days after their arrival resort to the few spots in the marshes and the surrounding stony plains, which were free from snow; here they led a miserable existence. Heavy snow storms and low temperature in connection with want of open water made the support of life difficult to the birds.

The temperature increased quickly and caused in a few days the places in which the birds could find food to extend very much. The areas free from snow grew larger and larger, and the ice along the beaches of small lakes and ponds with low water disappeared before the scorching sun; at the same time small ponds of melting snow were formed around in the field. Now the sanderlings would in couples retire from the party of other birds, and lead a quiet and tranquil life on the stony and dry plains. Now and then they would pay a visit to ponds of melting snow and beaches of fresh water lakes in order to bathe and seek food, and here they would join the party of other small waders as for instance *Tringa alpina* and *Ægialitis hiaticula*. According to my experience old birds would never resort to salt water shore.

Courtship.—The same observer tells us all we know about the courtship of the sanderling, as follows:

The pairing began toward the middle of June. The peculiar pairing flight of the male was to be seen and heard when the weather was fine, and especially in the evening. Uttering a snarling or slight neighing sound, he mounts to a height of some two meters from the surface of the ground on strongly vibrating wings, to continue at this height his flight for a short distance, most frequently in a straight line, but sometimes in small circles.

When excited he frequently sits on the top of a solitary large stone, his dorsal feathers blown out, his tail spread, and his wings half let down, producing his curious subdued pairing tones. He, however, soon returns to the female, which always keeps mute, and then he tries by slow, affected, almost creeping movements to induce her to pairing, until at last the act of pairing takes place; when effected, both birds rush away in rapid flight, to return soon after to the nesting place. I have also observed males in pairing flight without being able to discover any female in the neighborhood, and then, of course, without realizing the pairing as completing act. The male is in the pairing time very quarrelsome, and does not permit any strange bird to intrude on the selected domain. He seems to be most envious against birds of his own kin.

Nesting.—The sanderling breeds only in the far north, so far north that only very few Arctic explorers have found its nest. Strangely, however, the first recorded nest was found in a region where it rarely breeds and considerably south of its main breeding grounds. This was the nest found by Roderick MacFarlane (1908) on the barren grounds of northern Canada, of which he says:

On the 29th of June, 1864, we discovered a nest of this species in the barren grounds east of Fort Anderson. It contained four eggs, which we afterwards learnt were the first and only authenticated examples at that time known to American naturalists. The nest was composed of withered grasses and leaves placed in a small cavity or depression in the ground. The contents of the eggs were quite fresh, and they measured 1.44 inches by 0.95 to 0.99 in breadth, and their ground color was a brownish olive marked with faint spots and blotches of bister. These markings were very generally diffused, but were a little more numerous about the larger ends. They were of an oblong pyriform shape. The parent bird was snared on the nest. It is a very rare bird in the Anderson River country, and we failed to find another nest thereof.

The main breeding grounds of the sanderling are probably on the more northern Arctic islands, but not enough nests have ever been found anywhere to produce the hosts of birds which we see on migrations. Col. H. W. Feilden (1877) gives the following description of his discovery of the nest of this species:

I first observed this species in Grinnell Land on the 5th of June, 1876, flying in company with knots and turnstones; at this date it was feeding, like the other waders, on the buds of *Saxifraga oppositifolia*. This bird was by no means abundant along the coast of Grinnell Land, but I observed several pairs in the aggregate, and found a nest of this species containing two eggs in latitude 82° 33′ N. on June 24, 1876. This nest, from which I killed the male bird, was placed on a gravel ridge, at an altitude of several hundred feet above the sea, and the eggs were deposited in a slight depression in the center of a recumbent plant of Arctic willow, the lining of the nest consisting of a few withered leaves and some of the last year's catkins. August 8, 1876, along the shores of Robeson Channel, I saw several parties of young ones, three to four in number, following their parents, and led by the old birds, searching most diligently for insects. At this date they were in a very interesting stage of plumage, being just able to fly, but retaining some of the down on their feathers.

The best account we have of the home life of the sanderling is given to us by Mr. Manniche (1910), who found this species to be one of the commonest breeding birds in northeastern Greenland. He writes:

In the extensive moor and marsh stretches west of Stormkap are many smaller stony and clayey parts lying scattered like a sort of islands. As these "stone isles" are most restricted in size, I could without special difficulty realize the existence of the birds here, and I found several nestling sanderlings on such places. The problem was decidedly more difficult to me when the birds had their homes on the extensive table-lands farther inland; here it will depend on luck to meet with a couple of nestling sanderlings.

The laying began about June 20. The first nest found containing eggs dates from June 28; these had, however, already been brooded for some days. The clutch of eggs latest found dates from July 15; the eggs in this nest were very much incubated. The sanderling places its nest on the before mentioned dry clay-mixed stony plains sparsely covered with *Salix arctica*, *Dryas octopetala*, *Saxifraga oppositifolia*, and a few other scattered low growths. I only found the nest on places of this type, never on moors or plains entirely uncovered. The larger or smaller extent, the higher or lower position over the level of the sea and the distance from nearest shore of such locality is, according to my experience, of no consequence. It only seems, as if the sanderling prefers to nest on such places, which are situated not very far from fresh water—a lake or a pond—to the shores of which the young ones are often directed. Some nests found prove, however, that the birds do not insist upon this.

The situation of the nest is also extremely constant. At the edge—or rarer farther in—of a tuft of *Dryas*, the bird will form a cup-shaped not very deep nest hollow, the bottom of which is sparsely lined with withered leaves of *Salix arctica* or other plants growing in the neighbourhood. In size, and partly in shape the sanderling's nest resembles that of *Tringa alpina*. The striking likeness in color to the surroundings and the monotonous character of the landscape makes it extremely difficult to find the nest unless the bird itself shows the way to it. The number of eggs in a clutch is always four. I found eleven nests with eggs and some fifty hatches of downy young ones but none of these differed from the normal number.

By excellent tactics the breeding female understands to keep secret the hiding place of the nest. She will generally leave the nest so early and secretly, that even the most experienced and attentive eye does not perceive it. She rushes rapidly from the nest with her head pressed down against her back executing some peculiar creeping movements quite mute, and hidden between stones and plants; following natural hollows in the ground she will first appear in a distance of at least 100 meters from the nest. By means of short, snarling, and faint cries and now and then by flying up, she will then try to turn one's attention to herself. She will often settle for some moments on small stones, clods of earth, and similar places, from which she again will rush away with her dorsal feathers erected and her wings hanging down and always in a direction opposite to that in which her nest is situated.

H. E. Dresser (1904) gives a translation of notes on this species made by Dr. H. Walter in the Taimyr Peninsula, from which I quote as follows:

The nests, found late in June and early in July, contained four eggs each in three cases and three eggs in one case. The nest was placed, unlike that of the other waders, which affected the grass-covered portions of the tundra, between bare clay lumps on moss, and consisted of a shallow depression lined with a few dry straws and a white tangle. In two cases the male, and in two the female, was incubating. On the 16/29 July, when the young in down were taken, the male showed anxiety, but the female was not seen. During the breeding season some of these birds wandered about in small flocks. This species remained until the end of August.

Eggs.—The sanderling lays four eggs, sometimes only three. The eggs are very rare in collections and few are available for study, but they have been well described and fully illustrated. The eggs taken by Doctor Walter are described by Mr. Dresser (1904) as follows:

Blunt pyriform, fine grained, with a faint gloss. Ground color pale yellowish white, with a very pale greenish tinge and somewhat marked with small yellowish brown and dark brown spots; a few indistinct light violet gray markings; at the larger end a few blackish dots and streaks.

In the colored illustrations of 10 eggs before me, the shapes vary from ovate pyriform, the prevailing shape, to subpyriform. The prevailing ground colors are greenish olive, " ecru-olive," " lime green," or " grape green "; a few eggs are more buffy, " cream buff " to " deep olive buff." The markings are small, and often inconspicuous, spots, scattered quite evenly over the entire surface, but sometimes more thickly about the larger end. These are in dull shades of brown, " buffy brown," " snuff brown," or " sepia." They are not handsome or showy eggs. The measurements of 41 eggs, furnished by Rev. F. C. R. Jourdain, average 35.7 by 24.7 millimeters; the eggs showing the four extremes measure 38.2 by 24.7, 34.1 by 26.1, 33.1 by 24.4 and 35.3 by 23.5 millimeters.

Young.—Authorities seem to differ as to whether both sexes incubate or not. Both Feilden and Walter secured incubating males, but Manniche (1910) says:

Till the laying is finished both birds will faithfully accompany each other, but as soon as the brooding begins, the males will join in smaller flocks and wander around on the table lands and at the beaches of the fresh waters, often in company with *Tringa canutus* and *Strepsilas interpres*. They usually left the country some days before the middle of July. I secured several males for examination but never found the least sign of a breeding spot.

He gives the period of incubation as 23 to 24 days and says of the young:

The bursting of the egg shells will generally begin already some three days before the emergence of the young. The mother bird will immediately carefully carry the shells away from the nest in order not to attract the attention of ravens and skuas. Between the emergence of the young will elapse not more than a few hours; as soon as the latest born young one feels sufficiently strong; that is, when the down is dry, all the nestlings will leave the nest at the same time. If the old female considers the nearest surroundings of the nest to be unsafe or too difficult in food for the brood, she will immediately lead the young away. Thus I have met with newly hatched young ones, hardly one hour after their departure from the nest in a distance of 500 to 600 meters from this. In the cases concerned the disturbance by my frequent visits to the nests during the breeding may have caused the early departure.

In the following 12 to 14 days the chicks are guarded by their careful and extremely vigilant mother, who leads them over stony plains, by overflows of melted snow and fresh-water beaches; they are eagerly occupied in seeking food, which at this period exclusively consists of small insects and larvae and pupae of these. I have often observed that the chicks take shelter under the wings of their mother from the cold nights and the heavy showers. The chicks' power of resistance against cold and severe weather is relatively small.

When the sanderling wants to protect her young ones against hostile attacks she executes still more surprising systematic tactics than she does when brooding. Already when at a distance of some 200 to 300 meters from the young ones the old female would rush toward me and by all kinds of flapping and creeping movements in an opposite direction try to lead me astray; all the while she would squeak like a young one, and now growl angrily, striving to draw my attention toward herself only. Now and then she would rise very high in the air in a direct rapid flight, to disappear behind a rock on the opposite beach of a lake, etc. From quite another direction she soon appeared again just before my feet.

If I finally retired still farther away from the young ones and for a while kept myself hidden in the field, she would fly slowly, sometimes quite low, over the earth to the spot where the young still were lying motionless and mute, with their bodies pressed flat against the earth and their neck and head stretched out. When at last the female considers the danger to be over, she, flying or running close to the chicks, produces a short chirping song, at the tones of which all four young ones suddenly get up and begin to run about. Only in this case the sanderling produces its highly peculiar " sanderling song," which is very similar to the song of *Sylvia curruca*. As long as the young kept lying quiet on the ground in the before-mentioned attitude they were extremely difficult to find, if I had not from my ambush by aid of my field glass exactly marked down the spot where they last appeared. The young ones do not seek any real cover, as in hollows in the ground, under plants, behind stones, or similar natural hiding places. When I had found a single young one, which while I kept it in my hands began to chirp, it generally happened that the three other young, which had till then kept quiet, suddenly rose and, with the wings raised, uttered a quite fine mouse-like squeaking and hastily rushed away, while the old female, as if paralyzed, lay down before my feet, still squeaking exactly like the chicks.

Within 12 to 14 days the young ones are full grown and able to fly. Strange to say, the brood of the sanderling seems to suffer very little from hostile persecution, a fact which may be due to the accomplished vigilance and prudent behaviour of the old female and the young as well as the extremely suitably coloured clothing of these. I wonder that these defenceless small beings can avoid the Polar fox, which in this season more frequently than usual visits the domain of the waders, and which, as well known, has an excellent sense of smell.

Plumages.—The nestling sanderling is thus described in Witherby's Handbook (1920) :

Forehead buff with a median black line from base of upper mandible to crown; nape buff, down with dusky bases; rest of upper parts variegated light buff, warm buff and black and more or less spangled white; lores buff, two black lines across lores toward eye; under parts white, cheeks, chin and throat suffused light buff.

Mr. Manniche (1910) gives a colored plate showing four ages of downy young sanderlings, which the above description fits. A nestling 7 days old shows the remiges about one-third grown, while the body is still all downy. Another nearly fully grown only 11 days old is still downy on the head, neck, rump, and crissum, but is nearly fully feathered on the mantle and wings, partly feathered on the under parts and the wings extend beyond the stump of a tail; it must be close to the flight stage. Such is the rapid development of these little Arctic birds that Mr. Manniche (1910) says that they can fly when 14 days old.

In fresh juvenal plumage in the Arctic the feathers of the crown, mantle, wing coverts, scapulars, and tertials are blackish brown, broadly tipped, and all except those of the crown are also notched, with buff; the sides of the head, neck, and breast are washed with buff; before these birds reach us on migration these buff tints have mostly faded out to creamy yellow or white; the feathers of the lower back, rump, and upper tail coverts are ashy brown or grayish buff, each with a dusky shaft streak and narrowly tipped with dusky; as these feathers are not molted during the first winter they produce a peculiar rump pattern by which young birds can be easily recognized. Young birds are in juvenal plumage when they arrive here, with conspicuous black and white backs. But the postjuvenal molt begins in September and is generally completed before November; this molt involves the body plumage, except the rump, and some of the wing coverts and tertials. The first winter plumage is like that of the adult, plain gray above and white below, except for the retained juvenal feathers as indicated above.

A partial, or perhaps nearly complete, prenuptial molt takes place in young birds between March and May, involving the body plumage, sometimes the tail and most of the scapulars and wing coverts. In this first nuptial plumage young birds are much like adults, but can be recognized by some retained wing coverts and tertials; the latter are shorter than in adults, reaching not quite to the tip of the fourth primary in the folded wing; in the adult wing the tertials reach nearly to the tip of the third primary. At the next molt, the first postnuptial, the adult winter plumage is assumed.

Adults have a complete postnuptial molt from July to October or later. The body plumage is molted first, mainly in August and September, and the wings later, mainly in October; specimens have been seen with primaries in molt in February and March, but these are probably abnormal. The prenuptial molt of adults is incomplete, involving nearly all of the body plumage, but not all of the feathers of the back, scapulars, tertials, or wing coverts. The fresh nuptial plumage in early May is veiled with broad grayish white tips, which soon wear away. There is great individual variation in the amount of red assumed and in the molting date.

Food.—The sanderling obtains most of its food by probing in the wet sand of the seashore or by picking up what is washed up and left by the receding waves. The former method is well described by Dr. Charles W. Townsend (1920) as follows:

On the hard wet sand of the beaches one may see in places the characteristic probings of the sanderling without a trace of their foot marks, and these may be the cause of considerable mystery to the uninitiated. While the semipalmated sandpiper runs about with his head down dabbing irregularly here and there, the sanderling vigorously probes the sand in a series of holes a quarter of an inch to an inch apart in straight or curving lines a foot to 2 feet long. Sometimes the probings are so near together that the line is almost a continuous one like the furrow of a miniature plough. The sand is thrown up in advance so that one can tell in which direction the bird is going. A close inspection of the probings often reveals their double character, showing that the bill was introduced partly open. The probings are for the minute sand fleas and other crustaceans in the sand, their principal food. I have seen sanderlings running about nimbly on the beach, catching the sand fleas which were hopping on the surface. I have also seen them catching flies. I have a record of one I shot in 1884, whose stomach was stuffed with small specimens of the common mussel, *Mytilus edulis*.

The food consists mainly of sand fleas, shrimps, and other small crustaceans, small mollusks, marine worms, flies, fly larvae, and other insects, and sometimes a few seeds. Early in the season in the Arctic regions when animal life of all kinds is scarce the sanderling is said to subsist on the buds of saxifrage and other plants, as well as bits of moss and algae.

Behavior.—I have always loved to walk by the seashore alone with Nature, and especially to tramp for miles over the hard sands of our ocean beaches, where the heaving bosom of the restless sea sends its flood of foaming breakers rolling up the steep slopes, cut into hills and valleys by the action of the waves. From the crest of the beach above or from the lonely sand dunes beyond comes the mellow whistle of the plover, disturbed in his reveries; out over the blue waters a few terns are flitting about or screaming in anxiety for their, now well grown, young perched on the beach. Flocks of small shore birds hurry past well out over the breakers, flashing light or dark, as they wheel and turn; and high overhead the big gray gulls are circling. But right at our feet is one of the characteristic features of the ocean beach, a little flock of feeding sanderlings, confiding little fellows, apparently unmindful of our presence. They run along ahead of us as fast as we can walk, their little black legs fairly twinkling with rapid motion. They are intent only on picking up their little bits of food and most skillfully avoid the incoming wave by running up the beach just ahead of it; occasionally a wave overtakes one when it flutters above it; then as the wave recedes they run rapidly down with it, quickly picking up what food they find. If we force them to fly, which they seem reluctant to do, they circle out over the waves and settle on the beach again a short distance ahead of us; by repeating this maneuver again and again they lead us on and on up the beach, until, tired of being disturbed, they finally make a wide circle out over the water around us and alight on the beach far behind us. Their flight is swift, direct, and generally low over the water, with less of the twistings and turnings so common among shore birds. They usually flock by themselves, but are often associated in small numbers with knots, small plovers, or other beach-loving species. When satiated with food or tired of strenuous activity, they retire to the crest of the beach, or the broad sloping sand plains beyond it, to rest and doze or preen their plumage. Here they stand or squat on the sand, often in immense flocks, all facing the wind. Their colors match their surroundings so well that they are not conspicuous and I have often been surprised to see them rise. These large flocks are generally wary and not easily approached. But small parties or single birds feeding along the surf line are very tame and if we sit quietly on the beach, they will often run up quite close to us. Like many other shore birds, they are fond of standing on one leg or even hopping about on it for a long time, as if one leg were missing; often a number of birds will be seen all doing this at the same time, as if playing a sort of game; but if we watch them long enough, the other leg will come down, for they are not cripples.

Voice.—J. T. Nichols writes to me of the limited vocabulary of this bird, as follows:

The note of the sanderling is a soft *ket, ket, ket,* uttered singly or in series somewhat querulous in tone. It is at times used in taking wing, also with variations in the conversational twittering of a feeding flock. The sanderling is a rather silent bird at all times and seems to have a comparatively limited vocabulary.

Field Marks.—The sanderling is well named "whitey" or "whiting," for the large amount of white in its plumage, particularly in late summer, fall, and winter, is one of its best field marks. In winter it appears to be nearly all white while on the ground, against which the stiff black legs, the rather heavy black bill and a dark area at the bend of the wing stand out in sharp contrast. In flight the broad white stripe in the wing, contrasted with black, is diagnostic; and the tail appears white, or nearly so, with a dark center. Young birds in the fall can be recognized by the mottled black and white back. Its foot prints in the sand are recognizable, as well as the probings made by its bill.

Fall.—Mr. Manniche (1910) observed the flocking of the young sanderlings in Greenland, during August, prior to their departure about the end of that month; he writes:

The flocks of sanderlings every day increase in size till they culminate about August 20th. August 21st, 1906, I met on the shore at Hvalrosodden with a flock numbering at least 300 sanderlings. I walked there toward evening and, as the weather was unusualy fine, the birds were very lively; the imposingly large flock of birds executed evolutions in the air with incredible dexterity, now scattered and then in a compact column, now very high in the air and then close to the glassy level of the sea.

The first adults reach Massachusetts in July and are common or abundant during the latter part of that month and through August. The earlier arrivals are in worn spring plumage, but all stages of body molt are seen during their stay with us. The young birds come along in the latter part of August and are most abundant in September and October, after the adults have gone. The earlier migrants are generally in small flocks or little groups, but the late storms often bring along immense flocks, which settle on the beaches in dense masses or sweep along between the crests of the waves in great clouds.

The sanderling is a common migrant, sometimes abundant, throughout the interior east of the Rocky Mountains, coming along at about the same dates as on the Atlantic coast. Prof. William Rowan tells me of a bird he shot in Alberta on November 8, 1902, that was feeding with a Baird sandpiper "on the ice of a completely frozen lake." It is a common migrant on the Pacific coast at about the same dates as elsewhere. D. E. Brown (notes) records it at Grays Harbor, Washington, as late as December 20, 1917.

Game.—In the old days, before the shooting of small shore birds was prohibited by law, sanderlings ranked as game birds among the beach gunners. They were popular because they were so abundant and so tame that they could be shot in large numbers, especially when flying in large flocks. They are exceedingly fat in the fall and are delicious to eat. A favorite method of shooting them was to dig a hole in the sand of the beach, as near the water as practicable, in which the gunner could hide and shoot into the flocks as they flew by. Dr. Charles W. Townsend (1905) tells of a man who, in 1872, "saw two baskets, each holding half a bushel and rounded full of these birds," shot by one man between tides.

Winter.—The winter home of the sanderling is extensive. A few birds sometimes spend the winter as far north as Massachusetts. They are common on the Atlantic and Gulf coasts from North Carolino southward, as well as on the Pacific coast up to central California at least. From these northern points the winter range extends southward to central Argentina and Chile, and even farther south. On the west coast of Florida, where I spent the winter of 1924-25, sanderlings were common all winter, associating with redbacked sandpipers and other small waders on the extensive sand flats, or with knots and piping plovers on the beaches. It was interesting to note how tame they were on the protected bathing beaches and how wild they were elsewhere.

DISTRIBUTION

Range.—Cosmopolitan; breeding in Arctic or subarctic regions and wintering mainly south of 40 degrees north latitude.

Breeding range.—In North America the breeding range of the sanderling extends north to Alaska (Point Barrow); northern Franklin (Price of Wales Strait, Bay of Mercy, and probably Winter Harbor); northern Grant Land (Floeberg Beach); Grinnell Land; northern Greenland (Thank God Harbor, Stormkap, and

Shannon Island); and perhaps Iceland (Mickla Island). East to Iceland (Mickla Island); southern Greenland (Glacier Valley and Godthaab); and eastern Franklin (Igloolik and Winter Island). South to Franklin (Winter Island); Keewatin (Cape Fullerton); Mackenzie (Bernard Harbor and Franklin Bay); and Alaska (probably Barter Island and Point Barrow). West to Alaska (Point Barrow).

Winter range.—In the Western Hemisphere the sanderling ranges in winter north to: Washington (Dungeness Spit and Smith Island); southeastern California (Salton Sea); Texas (Corpus Christi, Aransas River, Refugio County, and Galveston); Louisiana (State Game Preserve); western Florida (probably Pensacola and Bagdad); and rarely Massachusetts (Plymouth County). East to rarely Massachusetts (Harvard, Dennis, Muskeget Island, and Nantucket); rarely New York (Long Beach); rarely New Jersey (Long Beach and Cape May); Virginia (Virginia Beach and Cobb Island); North Carolina (Pea Island, Cape Hatteras, and Fort Macon); Bermuda; South Carolina (Mount Pleasant and Frogmore); Georgia (Savannah and Darien); Florida (Amelia Island, Seabreeze, Mosquito Inlet, and Key West); Bahama Islands (Andros, Watling, and Fortune Islands); Jamaica; Lesser Antilles (probably Barbados); Brazil (Cajetuba Island and Iguape); and Argentina (Misiones, San Vicente, and Tombo Point). South to Argentina (Tombo Point); and Chile (Coquimbo Bay). West to Chile (Coquimbo Bay); Peru (mouth of the Tambo River and Chorillos); Ecuador (Santa Elena); Galapagos Islands (Bindloe and Albemarle Islands); probably Colombia (Carthagena). Vera Cruz (Barra de Santecomapan); Lower California (San Jose del Cabo, Santa Margarita Island, San Cristobal Bay, and Cedros Island); California (San Diego, San Clemente Island, Santa Barbara, San Francisco, Bolinas, and Point Reyes); Oregon (Netarts Bay); and Washington (Grays Harbor and Dungeness Spit).

Spring migration.—Early dates of arrival in the spring are: Maine, Augusta, April 11, and Saco, May 5; Franklin, Bay of Mercy, June 3, Prince of Wales Strait, June 7, Walker Bay, June 9, Winter Island, June 10, and Igloolik, June 16; Greenland, coast at about 72 degrees latitude, May 29, Cape Union, June 5; Kentucky, Bowling Green, May 1; Missouri, Kansas City, April 30; Illinois, Chicago, May 10; Ohio, Oberlin, April 6, Lakeside, April 17, and Columbus, May 10; Michigan, Detroit, May 16; Ontario, London, May 13, and Toronto, May 20; Minnesota, Goodhue, April 20; eastern Nebraska, Alliance, April 6; South Dakota, Vermilion, April 29; North Dakota, Harrisburg, May 20; Manitoba, Oak Lake, May 5; Saskatchewan, Orestwynd, May 23; Mackenzie, Fort Simpson May 29; Colorado, Loveland, May 12, and near Denver, May 16; Wyoming, Lake Como,

May 5, and Laramie, May 15; Alberta, Edmonton, April 29, and Fort Chipewyan, June 7; and Alaska, mouth of the Yukon River, May 10.

Late dates of spring departure are: Georgia, Cumberland, April 14; South Carolina, Sea Islands, April 23; North Carolina, Fort Macon, May 17, and Cape Hatteras, May 20; Virginia, Smiths Island, May 22, and Cobb Island, June 6; New Jersey, Cape May, June 13; New York, New York City, May 30, Geneva, June 3, and Sing Sing, June 5; Connecticut, Fairfield, May 31; Massachusetts, Harvard, June 4, Dennis, June 7, and Monomoy Island, June 27; Maine, Scarboro, May 30; Quebec, Quebec City, May 27, and Montreal, June 1; Kentucky, Bowling Green, May 22; Illinois, Waukegan, May 24, and Chicago, May 26; Ohio, Painesville, May 28, and Youngstown, June 2; Michigan, Detroit, May 28; Ontario, Point Pelee, June 1, Toronto, June 2, and Brighton, June 19; Iowa, Emmetsburg, May 25; Wisconsin, Madison, May 23; Minnesota, Walker, June 10; Texas, Point Isabel, May 3, and Corpus Christi, May 22; eastern Nebraska, Lincoln, May 21; South Dakota, Yankton, June 1; Manitoba, Lake Winnipeg, June 8, Shoal Lake, June 8, and Lake Manitoba, June 12; Saskatchewan, Hay Lake, June 9, and Quill Lake, June 10; Colorado, Denver, May 31; California, Santa Barbara, May 26; San Nicholas Island, May 30, Hyperion, May 31, and Redondo, June 4; and Washington, Quillayute Needles, May 30.

Fall migration.—Early dates of arrival in the fall are: British Columbia, Okanagan Landing, July 25, and Comox, August 15; Washington, Dungeness Spit, August 18, Clallam Bay, August 22, and Tacoma, August 23; California, Santa Barbara, July 29; Alberta, Strathmore, July 31; Montana, Flathead Lake, August 29; Saskatchewan, Big Stick Lake, July 19; Manitoba, Victoria Beach, July 11, Shoal Lake, August 8, and Oak Lake, August 17; South Dakota, Pine Ridge Reservation, July 12; eastern Nebraska, Lincoln, August 22; Texas, Tivoli, August 3, Brownsville, August 15, and Padre Island, August 21; Ontario, Toronto, July 16, and Ottawa, August 14; Michigan, Charity Island, July 19; Ohio, Lakeside, July 11, Cedar Point, July 21, and Painesville, July 25; Indiana, Millers, August 1; Illinois, Chicago, July 24; Massachusetts, Monomoy Island, July 1, Marthas Vineyard, July 8, and Dennis, July 12; New York, Brooklyn, July 6, Montauk Point, July 20, and Rochester, July 23; New Jersey, Cape May, July 20; Pennsylvania, Erie, July 27; Virginia, Chincoteague, August 1; North Carolina, Church's Island, July 29; South Carolina, Mount Pleasant, July 14; Florida, Bradentown, July 12, Pensacola, July 19, Fernandina, July 21, and Daytona Beach, July 28; Jamaica, Spanishtown, August 20; and Lesser Antilles, St. Croix, September 13.

Late dates of fall departure are: Alaska, Demarcation Point, August 30; Mackenzie, Fort Franklin, September 16; Alberta, Beaverhill Lake, November 8; Colorado, Loveland, September 30, and Pueblo, October 1; Manitoba, Margaret, October 20, and Lake Manitoba, November 7; North Dakota, Grafton, September 14; Nebraska, Lincoln, October 4; Wisconsin, Lake Mills, October 3; Iowa, Burlington, October 15, and National, October 29; Ontario, Kingston, October 15, Point Pelee, October 16, and Ottawa, October 22; Michigan, Ann Arbor, October 26, Portage Lake, November 5, and Forestville, November 24; Ohio, Cedar Point, October 21, Lakeside, October 29, and Columbus, November 7; Illinois, LaGrange, October 29, and Chicago, November 3; Franklin, Bay of Mercy, August 30; Prince Edward Island, North River, October 30; Quebec, Quebec City, November 12; and Maine, Portland, November 25.

Casual records.—In spite of its wide distribution the sanderling is not frequently detected outside of its normal range. Although but a short distance from the coast, there are only five records for the vicinity of Washington, D. C. (September, 1874, October 24, 1885, September 22, 1894, September 26–30, 1898, and September 27, 1898). It has been taken once in Kansas (Lawrence, October 7, 1874). There also is a record for the Hawaiian Islands (Hauai in October, 1900) and one in Haiti (Gaspar Hernandez, March 4, 1916).

Egg dates.—Greenland: six records, June 29 to July 7. Grinnell Land: one record, June 24. Arctic Canada: two records, June 18 and 29.

LIMOSA FEDOA (Linnaeus)

MARBLED GODWIT

HABITS

Next to the long-billed curlew and the oyster catchers, this is the largest of our shore birds. For that reason and for other reasons it is rapidly disappearing, and before many years it may join the ranks of those that are gone but not forgotten. Although shy at times, it is often foolishly tame and is then easily slaughtered. It is large enough to appeal to the sportsman as legitimate game and it makes a plump and toothsome morsel for the table. But, worst of all, its breeding grounds on the prairies and meadows of the central plains are becoming more and more restricted by the encroachments of agriculture; the wide-open solitudes will soon be only memories of the past.

In Audubon's (1840) time this was an abundant species and much more widely distributed than it is to-day. He writes:

On the 31st of May, 1832, I saw an immense number of these birds on an extensive mud bar bordering one of the Keys of Florida, about 6 miles south of Cape Sable. When I landed with my party the whole, amounting to some thousands, collected in the manner mentioned above. Four or five guns were fired at once, and the slaughter was such that I was quite satisfied with the number obtained, both for specimens and for food. For this reason we refrained from firing at them again, although the temptation was at times great, as they flew over and wheeled round us for awhile, until at length they alighted at some distance and began to feed.

The marbled godwit is a rare bird in Florida to-day; I saw only one during the five months of my last winter on the west coast. It was formerly abundant as a migrant on the Atlantic coast from New England southward, where now it is merely a straggler. It is still fairly common on the Pacific coast, where probably most of the birds now go. Even in Minnesota, close to its present breeding grounds, it has decreased enormously. Dr. Thomas S. Roberts (1919) writes:

When the writer, in company with Franklin Benner, went to Grant and Traverse Counties in June, 1879, to study the wild life of that region, the great marbled godwit was so abundant, so constant and insistent in its attentions to the traveler on the prairie, and so noisy that it became at times an actual nuisance. They were continually hovering about the team, perfectly fearless and nearly deafening us with their loud, harsh cries—" go-wit, go-wit." On getting out of the wagon to search for their nests, the birds became fairly frantic until we were fain to stop our ears to shut out the din. Now and then the birds would all disappear and peace would ensue for a brief period, but they had only retired to muster their forces anew, for shortly a great company would bear down upon us, flying low over the prairie, and spread out in wide array, all the birds silent, until, when almost upon us, they swerved suddenly upward over our heads and broke out again in a wild, discordant clamor. Once I counted 50 birds in one of these charging companies. This, to us, novel experience, went on from day to day in various places and has left a vivid impression that can never be effaced. Happenings of this sort have long since become things of the past in Minnesota. The godwits gradually disappeared before conditions associated with the advance of man into their domain until now it is doubtful that more than an occasional pair remains to nest in some remote part of the State.

The godwits have always been favorites with me and in my early days I had always longed to see them. The opportunity came at last when I visited North Dakota in 1901. We had been collecting for several days in some extensive sloughs bordering a large lake in Steele County, which we found exceedingly rich in bird life, when on June 12 I first made the acquaintance of this magnificent wader. The beautiful Wilson's phalaropes were flitting about among the tussocks, and it was while hunting for their nests that we noticed, among the numerous noisy killdeers and western willets flying over us, a strange hoarse note, strikingly different from either, as a large brown bird flew past, which we recognized as a godwit. All doubts were soon dispelled by collecting my first specimen of a species I had often longed to see, and I could not help pausing to examine and admire the beautiful markings of its richly colored wings. We saw only four of these birds that day, but on the following day they became more abundant. There were about 20 of them flying about over the meadows, showing considerable concern at our presence, constantly uttering their peculiar cries, and showing so little regard for their own safety that we were led to infer that they were breeding or intending to breed in that vicinity. We spent some time looking for their nests, but as we knew practically nothing about their nesting habits at that time, we were not successful in locating any nests.

Spring.—I can not find that the marbled godwit was ever common on the Atlantic coast north of Florida in the spring. It still migrates northward along the Pacific coast, mainly in April; D. E. Brown has seen it at Gray's Harbor, Washington, as early as April 9. The main migration route seems to be up the Mississippi Valley, mainly in April; it has been recorded in southern Saskatchewan as early as April 16.

Nesting.—In southwestern Saskatchewan, in 1905 and 1906, I became better acquainted with the marbled godwit on its breeding grounds. Along the lower courses of the streams, near the lakes, but sometimes extending for a mile or more back from the lake, are usually found broad, flat, alluvial plains, low enough to be flooded during periods of high water. These plains are more or less moist at all times, are exceedingly level, and are covered with short, thick grass only a few inches high. Such spots are the chosen breeding grounds of the marbled godwit, and, so far as our experience goes, the nests of this species are invariably placed on these grassy plains or meadows.

The godwit makes no attempt at concealment, the eggs being deposited in plain sight in a slight hollow in the short grass. We found, in all, four nests of this species with eggs, had two sets of eggs brought to us by ranchmen, and found two broods of young. The first nest was discovered on May 29, 1905. We had been hunting the shores of a large alkaline lake, where a colony of avocets were breeding on the mud flats near the outlet of a deep, sluggish stream, and it was while following along the banks of this stream, as it wound its devious course down through a series of broad, flat meadows, that I flushed a godwit out of the short grass only a few yards from the stream and about 100 yards from the lake. On investigation I found that she had flown from her nest, merely a slight hollow in the grass lined with dry grass, which had, apparently, been simply trodden down where it grew, without the addition of any new material brought in by the birds. Only two eggs had been laid, so we marked the spot for future reference and retired. On June 5 this nest was photographed, and the four eggs which it then contained were collected.

While driving across a low, wet meadow, toward a reedy lake, on June 8, 1905, and when about 200 yards from the lake, we were surprised to see a marbled godwit flutter out from directly under the horse, which was trotting along at a leisurely pace. We stopped as soon as possible and found that we had driven directly over its nest, which barely escaped destruction, for it lay between the wheel ruts and the horse's footprints, one of which was within a few inches of it. The nest was in every way similar to the first one, the bird having beaten down the short grass to form a slight hollow in which the four handsome eggs had been laid in plain sight.

On June 9, 1906, we visited the locality where the first nest was found, and I enjoyed a most interesting experience with an unusually tame individual of this normally shy species. While walking across the flat meadow near the creek, I happened to see a marbled godwit crouching on her nest beside a pile of horse droppings. She was conspicuous enough in spite of her protective coloration, for the nest was entirely devoid of concealment in the short grass. Though we stood within 10 feet of her, she showed no signs of flying away, which suggested the possibility of photographing her. My camera was half a mile away in our wagon, but I soon returned with it and began operations at a distance of 15 feet, setting up the camera on the tripod and focussing carefully. I moved up cautiously to within 10 feet and took another picture, repeating the performance again within 5 feet. She still sat like a rock, and I made bold to move still closer, spreading the legs of the tripod on either side of her and placing the camera within 3 feet of her; I hardly dared to breathe. moving very slowly as I used the focussing cloth, and changed my plate holders most cautiously; but she never offered to move and showed not the slightest signs of fear, while I exposed all the plates I had with me, photographing her from both sides and placing the lens within 2 feet of her. She sat there patiently, panting in the hot sun, apparently distressed by the heat, perhaps partially dazed by it, and much annoyed by the ants which were constantly crawling into her eyes and half open bill, causing her to wink or shake her head occasionally. I reached down carefully and stroked her on the back, but still she did not stir, and I was finally obliged to lift her off the nest in order to photograph the eggs.

Two nests found by Gerard A. Abbott (1919) in Benson County, North Dakota, were evidently better concealed than the nests we found. He writes:

I was certainly surprised to discover my first godwit's nest with the parent crouching beneath a little screen of woven grass blades on four heavily blotched eggs. Her general contour and the situation and design of the nest was suggestive of many king rails whose nests I have found, after noticing how the grass blades were woven together canopy like to shield the bird and her treasures. About a mile from this nest and screened on one side by willow sprouts sat another tame godwit. This time the grassy hollow held five boldly marked eggs. Incubation was one-half completed and the date was

June 8. These five eggs bear a general resemblance to each other and I believe they are all the product of the same bird.

Eggs.—The marbled godwit lays four eggs regularly, very rarely
three and still more rarely five. The eggs are ovate or ovate pyriform in shape, with a slight gloss. The ground colors usually run
from "pale olive buff " to "deep olive buff," in the greener types
from "dark olive buff " to "ecru olive," and in the brownest types
to "Isabella color." They are more or less sparingly and irregularly marked with small rounded spots, and with irregular, rarely
elongated blotches; these are often thicker at the larger end, but
seldom confluent. The markings are usually much more conspicuous than in other godwit's eggs, but they are in dull browns, such as
"Saccardo's umber," "warm sepia," and "bister." The underlying spots and blotches range in color from "pallid brownish drab "
to "deep brownish drab." Some of the greenish types are only
faintly spotted with "light brownish olive." One very handsome
egg has a "pale olive buff " ground color, conspicuously splashed
and blotched with "pale Quaker drab," overlaid with a few small
blotches and scrawls of "Saccardo's umber." The measurements of
64 eggs average 57 by 39.6 millimeters; the eggs showing the four
extremes measure **61** by 40.5, 59.5 by **42.5, 51** by 38.5, and 53.7 by
37.7 millimeters.

Young.—I have no data on the period of incubation and do not
know whether both sexes incubate or not. The only incubating bird
I collected was a female. Though we looked diligently for the
young we did not succeed in finding any until June 27, 1906. We
were driving across some extensive wet meadows, ideal breeding
grounds for marbled godwits, when we saw a godwit, about a hundred yards ahead of us, leading two of its young across a shallow
grassy pool; we drove toward them as fast as we could, but as we
drew near the old bird took wing and the young separated, moving
off into the grass in opposite directions. They had evidently been
well schooled in the art of hiding and were well fitted by their protective coloring to escape notice, for, though we secured one of them
readily enough while it was still running, the other disappeared
entirely right before our eyes and within 10 yards of us. Its disappearance seemed almost miraculous, for there was practically nothing there to conceal it, as the grass was quite short, and there were
no shrubs or herbaceous plants of any kind in the vicinity. We
searched the whole locality carefully and thoroughly, but in vain.
The youngster may have been crouching flat on the ground, relying
on its resemblance to its surroundings, or it may have taken advantage of some slight inequalities in the ground and skulked away
farther than we realized. Later in the day we found another pair
of godwits, in a similar locality, with two young, one of which we

secured. The young were in the downy stage, and apparently not over a week old. They showed unmistakable godwit characters, particularly in the shape of the head and bill, and the long legs and neck.

Plumages.—The downy young marbled godwit is in dull colors. The upper parts, including the posterior half of the crown. back rump, and wings are " bone brown " or " light seal brown," variegated on the back and rump with pale buff or grayish-white. The under parts, including the forehead, sides of the head, and neck, are " pink-ish-buff," deepest on the neck and flanks, almost white on the belly and head and pure white on the chin and cheeks. There is a narrow loral stripe, extending not quite to the eye, a spot behind the ear, and a short stripe in the middle of the lower forehead of blackish-brown. The shape of the head and bill is characteristic of the species.

The cinnamon juvenal plumage begins to appear on the flanks at an early stage and its development is rapid. Before the end of July the young bird is fully fledged and able to fly. The fresh juvénal plumage is much like that of the adult in winter; but the throat and the sides of the head and neck are plain cinnamon without dusky streaks; the feathers of the back and scapulars are more broadly edged or notched, with brighter cinnamon; the greater and median wing coverts are much more broadly bordered with or more extensively cinnamon; the greater coverts are almost clear cinnamon, with very few dusky markings; and the tail is more broadly barred with dusky.

Apparently only a very limited amount of molt takes place during the first year. I have seen birds in juvenal or first winter plumage in November, January, and May, though the last two may be exceptional cases. Perhaps some young birds assume the adult plumage at the first prenuptial molt, but certainly not later than the first postnuptial. More material is necessary to settle this point.

Adults have a complete postnuptial molt beginning in July and lasting well into the fall. This produces the winter plumage in which the breast is immaculate cinnamon and there is little, if any, barring on the flanks. At the prenuptial molt in February and March the body plumage, or most of it, and the tail are molted.

Food.—Doctor Roberts (1919) says of the feeding habits of the marbled godwit:

With their long, up-curved bills they probe the shallow water of sloughs and lake shores for aquatic insects and mollusks and also spend much of their time on meadows and low-lying prairies, where they devour grasshoppers and other insects of many kinds. These big birds, when they were as abundant as they once were, must have been an important factor in keeping in check the dangerous insect hordes of our State. But they, with others of their kind, are gone and man is left to fight conditions as he must with agencies of his own devising, less efficient, perhaps, than those provided by nature.

Audubon (1840) says: "While feeding on the banks, it appears to search for food between and under the oysters with singular care, at times pushing the bill sidewise into the soft mud beneath the shells." The sand beaches of California are favorite feeding grounds, where I have seen it associated with the long-billed curlew. I was interested to see with what dexterity these long-billed birds could pick up a small mollusk and swallow it; I could plainly see the small object gradually travel up the long bill and into the mouth of the bird. Other observers have recorded in the food of this godwit snails, crustaceans, insects and their larvae, worms, and leeches.

Behavior.—The flight of the marbled godwit is strong, rather swift and direct; the head is usually drawn in somewhat, the bill pointed straight forward, and the feet stretched out behind. Audubon (1840) says: "When flying to a considerable distance, or migrating, they usually proceed in extended lines, presenting an irregular front, which rarely preserves its continuity for any length of time, but undulates and breaks as the birds advance." Mrs. Florence M. Bailey (1916) writes:

In flight they often made a close flock, calling *queep, queep, queep, queep, queep,* affording a beautiful sight as the light struck them and warmed up the cinnamon wings that make such a good recognition mark. They soared down handsomely, showing the cinnamon, and as they alighted held their wings straight over their backs for a moment, the black shoulder straps showing in strong contract to the warm cinnamon.

Though the flocks were generally most amicable, occasionally one or two of their number would get to scrapping. Two got hold of each other's bills one day and held on, one or both crying lustily. In a group another day two came to blows, first just opening their bills at each other and talking argumentatively. Later one of them made passes at the other till the harried bird lifted his wings as if meditating escape, and finally when a pass was made at his long unprotected legs, flew away. When one was teased by a companion it often cried complainingly, *go-way, go-way, go-way, go-way.*

It was amusing to watch the birds feed. As a wave rolled up, combed over and broke, the white foam would chase them in, and as they ran before it, if it came on too fast, they would pick themselves up, open their wings till the cinnamon showed, and scoot in like excited children. But the instant the water began to recede they would right about face and trot back with it, splashing it up so that you could see it glisten. As they went their long bills— in the low afternoon sun strikingly coral red except for the black tip—were shoved ahead of them, feeding along through the wet sand, the light glinting from them; and if anything good was discovered deeper, the hunters would stop to probe, sometimes plunging the bill in up to the hilt, on rare occasions when the tidbit proved out of reach, actually crowding their heads down into the sand.

Like all of the shore birds, the marbled godwit is exceedingly demonstrative on its breeding grounds, flying out to meet the intruder as soon as he appears, making fully as much fuss at a distance from its nest as near it, and giving no clue as to its exact location. The cries of one pair of birds often attract others, and I have seen as many as eighteen birds flying about at one time in an especially favorable locality. It shows no signs of fear at such times, often alighting on the ground within ten or fifteen yards, standing for an instant with its beautifully marbled wings poised above it, a perfect picture of parental solicitude. Even while they were feeding on the shores of the lakes we could frequently walk up to within a few yards of them.

Hamilton M. Laing (1913), after describing how a snipe escaped from a duck hawk by diving into some rushes along a creek, tells of a similar trick played by a godwit, as follows:

In the second chase, the victim marked for death was a marbled godwit. Having often seen these birds swirling about at a dizzy pace and listened to the roar of their long knife wings as they smote the air in a playful descent, I felt assured that when the hawk started after them he would be very much outclassed. Yet in less than half a mile he was among them, had singled a victim and was stooping wickedly. Each time the godwit dodged, he emitted an angry or terrified cry, but the silent pursuer, with never a sign of fatigue, swooped and swooped and wore him down. Each time now the hawk overshot his mark a little less in the turnings. The last resort of the godwit was exactly that of the other snipe, but the former being over the big slough, dropped into the water. I saw the hairbreadth escape and the splash, but whether or not the godwit dived to get away, I could not tell. Some of the sandpipers can dive well, and probably the godwit escaped thus.

Voice.—The marbled godwit has a great variety of striking and characteristic notes. Its ordinary call note, when only slightly disturbed, sounds like *terwhit, terwhit, terwhit,* or *pert-wurrit, pert-wurrit,* or *godwit, godwit, godwit,* from which its name is probably derived; these notes are all strongly accented on the last syllable, and are uttered almost constantly while the birds are flying about over their breeding grounds. When considerably alarmed these notes are intensified, more rapidly given, and with even more emphasis, *kerweek, kerwee-eek,* or *kerreck, kreck, kreck, kerreck;* sometimes they are prolonged into a loud, long-drawn-out scream *quack, qua-a-ack,* or *quoick, quoi-i-ick,* somewhat between the loudest quacking of an excited duck and the scream of a red-shouldered hawk. There is also a more musical, whistling note, less often heard, sounding like the syllables *kor-koit* or *ker-kor-koit, korkoit,* the accent being on the *kor* in each case; this note seems to indicate a more satisfied frame of mind and is much more subdued in tone. All of these notes are subject to great individual variation, and, as the godwits are very noisy birds, we were given ample opportunities to study them, but to write them down in a satisfactory manner is not so easy.

P. A. Taverner (1926) writes: "Their loud exasperating *eradica-radica-radica-radica* varied with *Your-crazy-crazy-crazy* and confirmed by *Korect-korect* sets all the prairie on the alert."

John T. Nichols says in his notes:

A bird flying toward decoys gave a single unwhistled note, *hank*, likely the flight note of the species in migration. Alighted, it had a short, unloud note, a goose-like *honk*, especially when other shore birds flew past (Long Island, August). The few godwits of any species that I have seen in migration have mostly been silent.

Field marks.—The marbled godwit is so large and so well marked as a big brown bird that it is likely to be confused with only one other bird, the long-billed curlew. It nearly equals the curlew in size, and the rich cinnamon color in the wings is conspicuous in both species, but the long, curved bill of the curlew serves to distinguish it, even at a considerable distance, and the notes of the two birds are quite different. At short range the shape of the head, the long, slightly upturned bill, pinkish buff on its basal third, and the bluish-gray legs are distinctive marks.

Fall.—As soon as the breeding season is over, or even before all the broods are fledged, the marbled godwits begin to gather into flocks and become much more wary. Even as early as June 27, 1906, we saw as many as 36 birds in one flock, but as we did not see any young birds among them we inferred that these must have been birds whose eggs or young had been destroyed. As I have always had to leave for the East before the southward migration began I am unable to give any information on this subject from personal observation, but Dr. Louis B. Bishop has kindly placed at my disposal his notes relating to this movement.

At Stump Lake, North Dakota, in 1902, he noted on July 28 a flock of about 100 marbled godwits, chiefly adults, all that were taken being old birds; and on July 30 he saw a flock of about 50, which he assumed to be composed chiefly of young birds, all that were taken being in juvenile plumage. At the same locality in 1905 he saw on July 26 a flock of about 40, both adults and young, all that were collected being young birds; on August 2, *all* of these birds had disappeared. This exact locality, a sandy point at the western end of the lake, was visited only on the above dates. These birds were undoubtedly migrants, as they were not known to have bred in that vicinity.

After I had left Saskatchewan, Doctor Bishop visited the breeding grounds of the marbled godwits, and on July 3, 1906, found adult birds tolerably common, but they had all departed two days later. At Big Stick Lake, from July 18 to 21, 1906, he saw large flocks of adult godwits containing hundreds of birds, but on July 22 very few were left. He also writes that adults reach the North Carolina coast in the middle of July, as he has in his collection adults taken on July 11 and 27, 1904, and that young birds appear about a month later, as he has specimens taken August 10 and 19, 1904.

Evidently the godwits move off their breeding grounds as soon as the young are able to fly, those birds which have been unsuccessful in rearing their young being the first to leave, and forming the vanguard of the early migration in July. Probably most of the adults start on their southward migration before the end of July, and well in advance of the young, the later flight being composed almost entirely of young birds, and moving more deliberately.

The fall migration is or was very well marked and rather unique; many individuals formerly migrated almost due east from their breeding grounds in the interior to the Atlantic coast of New England. Others still continue to migrate westward to the Pacific coast and southward to the Gulf coast. All of the earlier writers indicate that this was an abundant migrant on the Atlantic coast from New England southward about the middle of the last century. The immense flocks which passed along our shores have been gradually disappearing until now only a few straggling birds are ever seen. Probably what comparatively few birds are left migrate to the Atlantic coast farther south or to the Gulf or Pacific coasts. Probably excessive shooting has driven them from their former haunts. They have always been popular with sportsmen and have been slaughtered unmercifully. They share with some other species the fatal habit, prompted by sympathy or curiosity, of circling back again and again over their fallen companions after a flock has been shot into, so that is is an easy matter for the gunners to kill them in large numbers.

Although it breeds and lives on the grassy meadows of the interior, the marbled godwit seems to prefer the seacoast on its migrations, frequenting more rarely the shores of large lakes. It is common as a migrant on the Pacific coast even as late as December, but it seems to be absent from California in January and February. Bradford Torrey (1913) says:

I have seen godwits and willets together lining the grassy edge of the flats for a long distance, and so densely massed that I mistook them at first for a border of some kind of herbage. Thousands there must have been; and when they rose at my approach, they made something like a cloud; gray birds and brown birds so contrasted in color as to be discriminated beyond risk of error, even when too far away for the staring white wing patches of the willets to be longer discernible.

As a flock there was no getting near them; I proved the fact to my dissatisfaction more than once; but sitting quietly on the same bay shore I have repeatedly known a single godwit or willet to feed carelessly past me within the distance of a rod or two.

Winter.—It is a comparatively short journey for this godwit to its winter home in the Gulf States and Central America. I have seen and collected a few godwits in Florida, but it is now impossible to see them in anything like the numbers mentioned by Audubon (1840) and Maynard (1896). The former says:

This fine bird is found during winter on all the large muddy flats of the coast of Florida that are intermixed with beds of racoon oysters. As the tide rises it approaches the shores, and betakes itself to the wet savannahs. At this season it is generally seen in flocks of five or six, searching for food in company with the telltale, the yellow shanks, the long-billed curlew, and the white ibis.

The latter writes:

The marbled godwits are very common in the South in winter, but they are particularly abundant in Florida. Back of Amelia Island, just south of St. Marys River, thus lying just on the extreme northern confines of the State, are extensive flats on which are pools that become partly dry during winter. These were the familiar resorts of the godwits, and flocks of hundreds would gather around them. They were quite wild while here, rising with deafening clamor when approached, but they had become so attached to the locality that they would merely circle about and alight on the borders of some neighboring pool. From this point, southward along the eastern coast as far as Merritts Island they were very numerous but were not common at Miami, and I did not see them on the Keys. On the west coast, however, they occurred in large numbers, especially on the muddy flats about Cedar Keys. On Indian River I found the godwits very unsuspicious, in so much so that I have frequently killed them with dust shot.

DISTRIBUTION

Range.—North and Central America. The range of the marbled godwit is now greatly restricted, the breeding areas being principally in North Dakota and central Saskatchewan and it is now extremely rare in winter anywhere on the Atlantic coast.

Breeding range.—North to Alberta (probably Edmonton) ; Saskatchewan (Osler and Crescent Lake) ; Manitoba (Winnipeg) ; and Wisconsin (Iron County). East to Wisconsin (Iron County, Stoughton, and Lake Koshkonong) ; and Iowa (Newton). South to Iowa (Newton and probably Sioux City) ; South Dakota (Miner County and probably Huron) ; and Montana (Billings). West to Montana (Billings and Strater) ; and Alberta (Medicine Hat and probably Edmonton). It also has been detected in summer at Okanagan, British Columbia, Pelican Narrows, Saskatchewan, Moose Lake, Manitoba, and York Factory, Manitoba.

Winter range.—North to Lower California (Magdalena Bay and La Paz) ; Sinaloa (Mazatlan) ; Oaxaca (Tehuantepec) ; western Yucatan ; probably Texas (Corpus Christi) ; probably Louisiana ; and Georgia (Savannah). East to Georgia (Savannah and Darien) ; Florida (Amelia Island, Tarpon Springs, Fort Myers, and Miami) ; eastern Yucatan (Cozumel Island) ; and British Honduras (Belize). South to British Honduras (Belize) ; and Guatemala (Chiapam). West to Guatemala (Chiapam) ; probably Colima (Manzanillo) ; and Lower California (Magdalena Bay). Marbled godwits formerly wintered north to southeastern South Carolina (Frogmore) and they are casual at this season in southern California (San Diego, Lake Elsinore, La Jolla, and Humboldt Bay).

Spring migration.—Early dates of arrival are: Missouri, St. Louis, April 13, Boonville, April 16, and Corning, April 18; Illinois, Warsaw, April 2, Calumet, April 4, and Rockford, April 8; Ohio, Lakeside, April 20, and Columbus, April 21; Michigan, Ann Arbor, May 5; Iowa, Emmetsburg, April 21, and Gilbert Station, April 23; Minnesota, Heron Lake, April 8, Wilder, April 19, and Goodhue, April 20; Nebraska, Lincoln, April 18; North Dakota, Bismarck, April 30, Jamestown, May 1, and Harrisburg, May 5; Manitoba, Oak Lake, April 25, Reaburn, May 2, Margaret, May 7, and Winnipeg, May 11; Saskatchewan, Indian Head, April 16, McLean, April 16, South Qu'Appelle, April 20, and Wiseton, April 24; Colorado, Loveland, April 20, Larimer County, April 26; Wyoming, Cheyenne, May 1, and Douglas, May 15; Montana, Milk River, May 18; Alberta, Flagstaff, May 10, and Alliance, May 11; California, Santa Barbara, April 27, San Buenaventura, April 28; and Washington, Grays Harbor, April 9.

Late dates of spring departure are: Florida, Amelia Island, May 15; Georgia, Wolf Island, April 30; South Carolina, Hilton Head, April 24; Missouri, Warrensburg, May 4, and Boonville, May 31; Illinois, Chicago, May 26; Nebraska, Valentine, May 16; Colorado, Durango, May 28, and Barr, May 30; Lower California, San Martin Island, April 10, and Turtle Bay, April 14; and California, Sandyland, June 9, Santa Barbara, June 15, and Los Angeles, June 16.

Fall migration.—Early dates of arrival in the fall are: California, Los Angeles, July 7; Lower California, San Quentin, August 6, and Cape San Lucas, September 9; Wyoming, Douglas, July 31; Colorado, Barr, June 24; Illinois, Chicago, July 22; Ohio, Pelee Island, July 24; Maine, near Portland, August 8; New Hampshire, Seabrook, August 17, and Rye Beach, August 27; Massachusetts, Eastham, August 10; Connecticut, West Haven, August 26; New York, Lawrence, July 21; North Carolina, Pea and Brodie Islands, July 11; South Carolina, Ladys Island, August 21, and Bay Point, August 24; and Florida, St. Marks, September 11.

Late dates of fall departure are: California, Nigger Slough, November 15, Humboldt Bay, December 7, and San Diego, December 12; Colorado, Denver, September 5, Boulder, September 18, and San Luis Lake, October 1; Saskatchewan, Ravine Bank, August 25, and Defoe-Guernsey Camp, August 26; Manitoba, Margaret, September 22; North Dakota, Charlson, September 16, and Westhope, September 24; Nebraska, Lincoln, October 16; Michigan, Newberry, September 23; Ohio, Sandusky Bay, October 12; Illinois, northeastern part, October 20; Quebec, Montreal, September 3; Maine, Popham Beach, September 13; Massachusetts, Newburyport, September 7; New York, Shinnecock Bay, September 15; New Jersey, Cape May, September 14; North Carolina, Beaufort, November 17; and South Carolina, Mount Pleasant, November 3.

Casual records.—The marbled godwit has on several occasions been recorded outside of its normal range principally to the south and east of its winter quarters. Among these are: Ecuador (Santa Rosa, 1877); Lesser Antilles (Grenada, August 29, 1881, and also from the islands of Carriacou and Trinidad); Porto Rico (recorded from Boqueron by Gundlach); and Cuba (recorded from Cardenas in September by Gundlach). It also has been noted from Alabama (near Greensboro, in 1880, and Dauphin Island, August 21, 1911); Ontario (Toronto, May 30, 1895, and June 7, 1890); Arizona (San Pedro River, January 27, 1886); and Alaska (Ugashik, July 16 and 18, 1881, Nelson Island, July 5, 1910, and Point Barrow, August 26, 1897).

Egg dates.—Saskatchewan: 38 records, May 15 to June 27; 19 records, May 30 to June 9. Minnesota and Dakotas: 16 records, May 10 to June 14; 8 records, May 25 to June 8.

LIMOSA LAPPONICA BAUERI Naumann

PACIFIC GODWIT

HABITS

The bar-tailed godwit of Europe is represented in eastern Siberia and western Alaska by this larger race, with a more spotted rump. From the above breeding grounds it migrates to a winter range in Australia, New Zealand, and many oceanic islands. South of Alaska it is a mere straggler in North America.

Spring.—On its spring migration the Pacific godwit passes through the Aleutian Islands and the Pribilof Islands on its way to its breeding grounds in northwestern Alaska. I saw two birds on Atka Island on June 13, 1911, probably belated migrants; it has been said to breed near Unalaska, but this seems hardly likely. William Palmer (1899) reported it as a migrant in the Pribilof Islands from early in May until June 13. Probably the main northward flight passes through the Kurile and Commander Islands to northeastern Siberia. Dr. E. W. Nelson (1887) says of its arrival in Alaska:

On May 26, 1877, while I was at Unalaska, a native brought in a half dozen of these birds, and on June 3 I obtained three others from the sandy beach of a small inner bay. They were very unsuspicious and easily killed. Although these birds appeared to be migrating, yet the following years I found them arriving at Saint Michael in flocks of from 25 to 200 from the 13th to 20th of May. These flocks were shy and kept in continual motion, wheeling and circling in rapid flight over the lowland, now alighting for a moment, then skimming away again in a close body. Their movements and habits at this season are similar to those of other godwits. By the last of May the flocks are broken up, and the birds are distributed in small parties over their breeding ground.

Herbert W. Brandt says in his notes:

For a large shore bird the dinful Pacific godwit is of common occurrence on the vast mossy upland tundra about Hooper Bay and is even more numerous in similar areas in the Igiak Bay region, including the lower slopes of the mountain sides. The vociferous guardian parents, however, make themselves so conspicuous by their clamorous agitation that they seem more plentiful than they are in reality. The first bird to arrive from afar, a beautiful ruddy specimen, was captured May 15, and by May 20 occasional bands of 20 or more birds were feeding along the overflow river margins. These flocks remained for some days and were apparently transients, for they passed elsewhere. One flock of 21 highly colored birds stayed with us until June. In the meanwhile the happy mated pairs had already taken charge of their respective upland domains, for on May 25 a nest with two eggs was found, which on May 28 held four eggs.

Courtship.—Doctor Nelson (1887) gives a brief account of this, as follows:

Their courtship begins by the 18th or 20th of May and is carried on in such a loud-voiced manner that every creature in the neighborhood knows all about it. The males continually utter a loud ringing *ku-wew, ku-wew, ku-wew,* which is repeated with great emphasis upon the last syllable, and the note may be heard for several hundred yards.

Nesting.—We are indebted to Mr. Brandt for practically all we know about the nesting habits of this rare species. I quote from his notes, as follows:

The Pacific godwit chooses an elevated dry site for its domicile, preferring the ridges on the rolling tundra and nests even occur on the lower mountain slopes. The nest is well concealed, for it is usually placed between clumps of bunch grass and is thus well screened from view by the standing vegetation. The structure is usually a simple depression in the moss and lichens and lined haphazardly with fragments of the surrounding reindeer moss, but occasionally a real nest is carefully fashioned with considerable grass woven in a circular manner and is thus rather substantially constructed. In one instance the bird added to the nesting material while the eggs were being laid. The range of measurements of 12 nests is: Inside diameter, 6 to 7 inches; inside depth, 3 to 4 inches; and total depth, 3 to 5 inches. I observed the female Pacific godwit alone to incubate, but the male was always near by. She is perhaps the closest brooder of any incubating shore bird we encountered, so much so that she often literally had to be almost stepped on before she arose. The alert male lookout meets the intruder at a considerable distance from the nest and with a loud tongue acts as an escort to the discomfort of the interloper. Thus but little clue can be had from the bird's actions as to the whereabouts of the brooding female, and in consequence, in spite of the number of nests in the region, relatively few are found, and those mostly by chance The peculiar contents of one nest were originally five eggs of the willow ptarmigan, on top of which four eggs of the Pacific godwit had been laid. Evidently the latter bird had driven the ptarmigan away from its nest, as there were but three godwit's eggs in it when first observed, the fourth egg having been deposited on the following day. The entire nestful was left to hatch in order to ascertain whether or not the ptarmigan would be reared by the incubating godwit, but this composite set was later deserted and then despoiled by jaegers.

Eggs.—Mr. Brandt was fortunate enough to collect 20 sets of eggs of this rare species, which he describes in his notes as follows:

The egg of the Pacific godwit is subpyriform to ovate pyriform in outline with the majority following the latter shape although one set is elongate ovate. The shell is strong, smooth, slightly granular with somewhat of a luster, yet an occasional surface is almost dull. There are two general types of ground color—the greenish, that is the rule, and the brownish type that we but rarely encountered. " Serpentine green," dull " citrine " to " yellowish glaucous " cover the range of greenish ground colors, while " snuff brown " matches the other type. The surface markings are not as numerous as on most shore-birds' eggs, and in consequence they are more scattered than usual. These spots are small in most instances, but in a few beautiful sets they are large and, more rarely, even convergent on the larger end so as to form a rich blotch. In a few rare instances there were no surface markings at all, the paler underlying spots being the only decoration. The primary markings are irregular to elongated without a spiral tendency. In color they are " cinnamon brown," " snuff brown," and " mummy brown " or " brownish olive," usually the latter if the ground color is decidedly greenish. The underlying spots are not very bold, although they are numerous and occasionally of considerable size. These neutral spots range from " light mouse gray " or " Quaker drab " to " deep olive gray " in color. Additional markings of grayish black slightly fleck some eggs while they are wanting on others. In a few cases these markings assume the form of pen scratches which usually encircle the larger end. The eggs, which were the rarest that we took on the trip, were always four in number, except for one set of three and one nest of five eggs, the only abnormally large set that I met with among the Alaska species of the entire shore-bird group.

The measurement of his 80 eggs average 55.3 by 38.2 millimeters; the eggs showing the four extremes measure 60.5 by 37.7, 52.6 by 40.7, 50.5 by 38.2, and 54.8 by 36.1 millimeters.

Young.—The same observer says:

Both birds share in the duties of incubation and are very zealous in defense of their treasures, especially when their pretty tawny brown chicks are first bursting forth. We saw the first downy young on June 18 when we came upon two and one hatching egg at an altitude of about 300 feet on the side of the Askinuk Mountains. These sturdy babies have little to fear from their marine enemies for their parents dominate the chosen domain with a vigor that no feathered creature can withstand. It is very interesting to watch the agitated father or mother running rapidly about, scolding, or wading in a pool of snow water, every now and then raising its long wings to a vertical position above its back, thus exhibiting the delicate tints of the underside, and then deliberately folding them one at a time.

Plumages.—The nestling Pacific godwit is warmly covered with long, thick, soft down, the prevailing colors of which are warm buff and sepia, in indistinct patterns; none of the markings are clearly defined, as in the sandpipers, but are soft and blended. The large circular crown patch is clear "warm sepia," extending in a median stripe down to the bill; there is a narrow loral stripe from the bill to the eye and a broader one, though less distinct, from the eye to the occiput, both "warm sepia"; above these, broad stripes of grayish buff extend from the lores to the occiput, nearly encircling the dark crown, from which a median stripe of the sepia extends down the neck. The back, wings, and thighs are softly variegated with "warm sepia," "wood brown," and "cinnamon buff." The under parts are largely "pinkish buff," suffused with "cinnamon buff" on the breast and fading out to nearly white on the chin. The down is all dusky or dark sepia at the base.

In fresh juvenal plumage, as seen in Alaska in August, the crown is streaked with sepia, the feathers edged with light buff; the feathers of the mantle, scapulars, tertials, and wing coverts are sepia or dusky, edged or notched with light buff; the rump and upper tail coverts are white, but much more heavily spotted with dusky than in the European form; the remiges are all conspicuously barred with dusky and light buff; the buff edgings fade out almost to white later on; the under parts are dull buffy whitish, shaded on the chest with deeper grayish buff. A postjuvenal molt begins in September, at which the body plumage is renewed, but not the remiges and few, if any, of the rectrices; most of the wing coverts are retained and some of the tertials. The resulting first winter plumage is like that of the adult except for the wings and tail.

At the first prenuptial molt the next spring the sexes begin to differentiate, the males being more richly colored with more cinnamon feathers in the white under parts, and the females have the throat and breast more or less streaked with sepia. This molt is incomplete and irregular, with much individual variation in the advance toward maturity. Sometimes there is very little or no molt, the worn winter plumage being retained until summer; sometimes new winter feathers are acquired; but usually some or many of the body feathers, the tail, and some tertials and wing coverts are molted and replaced with feathers like the adult. The new tail feathers of the first nuptial plumage are plain gray, unbarred. Birds in this plumage are found on their breeding grounds and probably breed at this age.

At the next molt, the first postnuptial, the adult winter plumage is assumed by a complete molt from July to December. Adults have a partial prenuptial molt, between February and May, which involves most of the body plumage, usually the tail, some of the tertails, and some of the wing coverts; they also have a complete postnuptial molt beginning with the body plumage in July or August. In the adult nuptial plumage the central pair of tail feathers are barred completely; the others are usually plain gray, but sometimes the outer pair or two are partially barred.

Food.—Very little has been published on this subject. William Palmer (1899) says:

In the ponds they feed by keeping their bills in the water and move invariably all in the same direction, heads to the wind. With care I could approach within a few feet. Much the greater part of the stomach contents of these birds consisted of hundreds of minute threadlike aquatic larvae of a midge (*Chironomis*). Pieces of mollusks' shell had been swallowed by several of the birds. Flies, closely related to our common house fly, and tiger beetles were detected in small quantities. Of the six godwits, five had been killed on St. Paul Island, and had fed for the most part upon midges, which were probably abundant in a fresh-water pond on the island. The sixth bird was taken on Walrus Island. It had caught over 500 specimens of a species of beetle (*Aegialites debilis*), the sole representative of a unique family of beetles, described some time ago and subsequently lost sight of until recently discovered again.

The above report on stomach contents was made by Dr. S. D. Judd and has been amended by Preble and McAtee (1923), who report that the items of food, ranked by bulk, are flies, 76.6 per cent; beetles, 17; mollusks, 3.6; marine worms, 1.3; and vegetable matter, 1 per cent. The jaws of marine worms (Nereidae) were mistaken for jaws of tiger beetles.

Behavior.—Doctor Nelson (1887) writes:

They frequent open grassy parts of the country and are quick to protest against an invasion of their territory. As a person approaches, one after the other of the birds arises and comes circling about, uttering a loud *ku-wew* with such energy as to make the ears fairly ring. If their nests are near, or they have young, they come closer and closer, some of the boldest swooping close by one's head and redoubling the din. This same note is heard upon all sides while the birds conduct their courtships, and it serves also to express their anger and alarm. At the mating season the males have a rolling whistle also like that of the ordinary field plover, but shorter. When the birds fly at this time they hold the wings decurved and stiffened and make a few rapid strokes, then glide for a short distance. On the ground it walks gracefully, its head well raised, and frequently pauses to raise its wings high over the back and then deliberately folds them. They may be decoyed when flying in flocks if their whistling note be imitated. If wounded and taken in hand, they utter a loud, harsh scream.

Mr. Brandt says in his notes:

The Pacific godwit has wonderful powers of flight, and, as it wheels about protesting against an intrusion, the slightest beat of its long, decurved wings seems, without perceptible effort, to drive it forward like an arrow from the bow. That its power of flight is extraordinary is shown by the fact that it spends the winter time of the north in southern Australia and New Zealand. It migrates along the eastern coast of Asia and is one of the interesting Old World birds that find their northeastern limit on the Alaskan shores of Bering Sea. During the love-making period, shortly after this godwit's arrival on May 15, it could be heard for an hour at a time high up in the air, as it circled about, uttering continuously its wild far-reaching cry, which was very distinctive among the medley of voices. The call of the male is often answered by the female with the syllables, *tut-tut*, not unlike a clucking chicken. The Pacific godwit differed from the other shore birds nesting at Hooper Bay in that individuals in immature plumage were breeding. Sometimes a gray-breasted immature female would be paired with a rich plumaged male, or again both mates would be in full color; but I encountered many pairs in which both parents showed the light grayish breast of adolescence. In fact, the immatures seemed to be in the majority. It is believed that this godwit does not assume its fully adult feathers until the beginning of the third year; but, like the bald eagle, it breeds during the second year. The earliest spring arrivals at Hooper Bay were immatures and they seemed to migrate in separate flocks. One group of about 20 richly cinnamon-breasted adults stayed in our vicinity for several days from May 20 onward. Perhaps they were resting and feeding in preparation for the final stage of their journey to more polar lands for they, as well as all the other large flocks of godwits no doubt passed on to the north. The birds that nested in the Hooper Bay region arrived in an inconspicuous manner, simply filtering into their chosen haunts and were already mated.

Field marks.—The Pacific godwit can be easily distinguished in the field from either of our two other American godwits. The marbled godwit has much more rufous in the upper parts, particularly in the wings, and has no white on the rump. The Hudsonian is very dark on the upper parts, almost black on the wings; it has a pure white rump and a black tail. The Pacific is dull brown above, with no rufous; it has a white rump, spotted with dusky, and a tail barred with dark gray and white.

Fall.—Doctor Nelson (1887) says:

These godwits are among the first of the waders to leave Alaska in fall. The young are flying by the middle of July and before the end of August not one of these birds, young or old, is to be found.

Young birds apparently wander northward and eastward before they start on their southward migration, for they have been taken in August at Wainwright and at Point Barrow in company with young dowitchers and red-backed sandpipers.

DISTRIBUTION

Range.—Alaska and eastern Asia south to Australia, New Zealand, and the Samoan Islands.

Breeding range.—The Pacific godwit breeds from northeastern Siberia (Taimyr Peninsula, Marcova, and Nijni Kolymsk); east to western Alaska (Unalaska Island, Hooper Bay, Kotlik, Pastolik, Cape Prince of Wales, Cape Blossom, and Kowak River).

Winter range.—The Malay Archipelago, Samoan and Fiji Islands, New Zealand, and Australia, and probably other islands of Oceanica.

Migration.—The migration route of this species is almost entirely in the Eastern Hemisphere, through the Commander Islands, Japan,

China, and the Philippines. They have been observed to arrive in
Siberia on May 10 (Bering Island) and May 30 (Nijni Kolymsk)
and in Alaska on May 15 (Hooper Bay), May 20 (St. Paul Island),
and May 29 (Unalaska). After the breeding season, individuals
have been known to wander north to the Colville delta and Point
Barrow. The latest date of fall departure noted for Point Barrow is
August 18 and for St. Michael September 10.

Casual records.—One specimen obtained at La Paz, Lower California (Belding), and recorded as this species is now regarded as a
marbled godwit, and there is one record from the island of Kauai, and
several from Laysan, Hawaiian Islands (Bryan). A specimen taken
on Cape Cod, Massachusetts, on September 16, 1907, is referable to
the European form *Limosa lapponica lapponica.*

Egg dates.—Alaska: 15 records, May 25 to July 9; 8 records, May
29 to June 5.

LIMOSA HAEMASTICA (Linnaeus)

HUDSONIAN GODWIT

HABITS

I can count on the fingers of one hand the red-letter days when I
have been privileged to see this rare and handsome wader. It has
always been among the great desiderata of bird collectors. Its eggs
are exceedingly rare in collections. Many ornithologists have never
seen it in life. I can find no evidence that it was ever common. All
the earlier writers reported it as uncommon or rare. Audubon
(1840) referred to it as "of rare occurrence in any part of the
United States." He never saw it in life and handled only a few
market specimens in the flesh.

Spring.—From its winter home in far southern South America
the Hudsonian godwit migrates in spring by some unknown route
to the coast of Texas, where it arrives in April. I saw three adults
and collected a pair in fine spring plumage near Aransas Pass on
May 17, 1923. From Texas and Louisiana it migrates northward
through the Mississippi Valley, central Canada and the Mackenzie
Valley to the Arctic coast. Prof. William Rowan in his notes refers
to it as a scarce, but regular, spring migrant in Alberta; his dates
are between April 29 and May 29. He and C. G. Harrold (1923)
recorded 24 birds between these dates in 1923. Their records are as
follows:

April 29, 2 flocks of 6 each (also 2 avocets on this date, although on the
30th it snowed all day) ; May 7, 2 Hudsonians at the lake and one with a party
of marbled godwits at a muddy slough a few miles away; May 8, a flock of
4 Hudsonian and 2 marbled ; May 15, flock of 3 Hudsonian, 2 marbled, and 1
Willet; May 22, a fine male Hudsonian with 8 or 9 marbled. One other
specimen was seen flying over about May 10.

At Whitewater Lake, in Manitoba, Mr. Harrold noted one each day on May 10 and 11, 1924, and 12 at the same place in 1925, practically all between May 13 and 20. I saw one at Lake Winnipegosis on June 5, 1913, a late date. On the Atlantic coast it is known only as a rare straggler in the spring and it is practically unknown on the Pacific coast.

Nesting.—Practically all of what little we know of the nesting habits of the Hudsonian godwit is contained in Roderick MacFarlane's notes. A female and four eggs were taken near Fort Anderson on June 9, 1862, from a nest on the ground made of a " few decayed leaves lying in a small hole scooped in the earth." Another nest on the Lower Anderson was "on the borders of a small lake " and was made of " a few withered leaves placed in a hole or depression in the ground."

A set of four eggs, in the Thayer collection, was collected by Bishop J. O. Stringer at Mackenzie Bay, June 30, 1897, from " a nest situated in a hollow in the grass." Edward Arnold also has a set of four eggs, taken by Bishop Stringer in the same locality on June 29, 1899; the nest was " in a tuft of grass on an island in Mackenzie Bay."

Eggs.—The Hudsonian godwit probably lays four eggs normally, though there are sets of three in collections. What few eggs I have seen, not over a baker's dozen, are ovate pyriform in shape and have little or no gloss. The ground colors vary from " dark olive buff " to " olive buff," or from " light brownish olive " to " ecrue olive." They are usually sparingly marked with rather obscure spots, irregularly distributed, but generally mostly around the larger end, in darker shades of similar colors, such as " buffy olive," " light brownish olive," " buffy brown," " bister," or " sepia." There are usually underlying spots of " hair brown " or shades of " drab," and some eggs have a few black dots at the larger end.

A set in the United States National Museum is thus described for me by J. H. Riley:

No two eggs in this set are alike. They vary in ground color from a little darker than " citrine drab," through " light brownish olive," to " dark olive buff." The darkest egg has a zone of " olive brown " spots at the larger end, with a few " clove brown " dots here and there, and a few scattered spots and blotches of " olive brown " over the rest of the egg. The next darkest egg is similar, but with the contrast between the ground color and the " olive brown " zone more pronounced and an increase in size and number of the " clove brown " spots. The lightest (" dark olive buff " ground) egg has a solid cap of " clove brown " at the larger end and quite numerous blotches, scrawls, and spots of " clove brown " and " olive brown," with a few shell markings of " drab " over the rest of the surface.

Some of the eggs I have seen are much like well-marked eggs of the black-tailed godwit. The measurements of 27 eggs average 55.2 by

38.1 millimeters; the eggs showing the four extremes measure **60.6** by **39.6**, **56** by **41.2**, and **51** by **35** millimeters.

Plumages.—I have never seen a downy young Hudsonian godwit nor any very young juvenals. The sexes are alike in the juvenal plumage and probably all through the first year. The plumages are alike in winter but the females are somewhat larger. A young female in juvenal plumage, taken in Maine in September, is similar to the winter adult, except that the crown is more streaked with dusky; the feathers of the mantle are "sepia," edged with "pinkish cinnamon"; the scapulars and tertials are edged, notched, or barred with "cinnamon," and the tail is tipped with buffy white. I have seen birds in this plumage up to October 13; but usually the partial postjuvenal molt of the body plumage and probably some of the scapulars and tertials begins in October. Material is lacking to illustrate the first prenuptial molt, which takes place in South America. Probably this molt is very limited in young birds. A female, taken on May 28 in Wisconsin, probably in first nuptial plumage, shows a mixture of fresh adult nuptial body feathers both above and below, and fresh tail feathers, but the primaries are worn. Probably at the next molt, the first postnuptial, which is complete, the adult winter plumage is assumed.

Adults have an extensive prenuptial molt, involving everything but the wings and perhaps the tail. This is accomplished during the late winter or early spring before the birds migrate. Dr. Alexander Wetmore (1926) says:

A male shot March 7 is in full winter plumage with worn primaries but newly grown tail feathers and lesser wing-coverts. Two females shot March 8 have renewed the flight feathers and tail and have the breeding plumage growing rapidly on the body.

The postnuptial molt is complete; the body molt begins in July and is well advanced towards completion when the birds reach our shores in August or September; the wings are apparently molted later, after the birds reach their winter homes in South America. There is a striking difference between the richly colored nuptial plumage and the dull and somber winter plumage, with the brownish gray upper parts and the pale grayish buff under parts.

Strangely enough, all the recent manuals that I have seen state or imply that the sexes are alike in nuptial plumage; and this in spite of the fact that many years ago Swainson and Richardson (1831) called attention to the striking difference between the two sexes, which are decidedly unlike. In the male the underparts are deep, rich brown, "Mikado brown" or "Kaiser brown," with much individual variation in the amount of black transverse barring, which is sometimes almost entirely lacking in the center of the breast. In the female, which is always somewhat larger, the under parts are barred

298 BULLETIN 142, UNITED STATES NATIONAL MUSEUM

with white, dusky, and brown; the feathers of the flanks are brown with three or four black or dusky bars and broad white tips; on the breast only the outer half of the feather is brown, the remainder is white, with two or three dusky bars and a broad white tip. Careless sexing may have caused the oft-repeated error.

Food.—Edward H. Forbush (1925) says that "the food of the Hudsonian godwit includes worms, many insects (including horseflies and mosquitoes), mollusks and crustaceans, and various small forms of marine life."

Behavior.—He also says:

While with us it seems to have a preference for sandy shores and sand spits, but it also frequents mud flats, beaches, and creeks in the salt marsh, and sometimes goes to the uplands after insects.

Dr. L. C. Sanford (1903), writing of the habits of the Hudsonian godwit in the Magdalen Islands, says:

On the islands where these birds congregate they frequent the large open lagoons where the low tide leaves exposed miles of sand bars. Here they follow the water's edge and wade in up to the full length of their long legs, feeding on animalculae and small larvae, for which their bill is peculiarly adapted, having the same flexible tip as that of the Wilson's snipe. With the rising water, first the small sandpipers, then the larger birds are driven from the flats; last of all, the godwit. They start in flocks of from 10 to 20 and keep well in the center of the lagoon, flying over the flooded flats, avoiding carefully all land, even the farthest points and islands.

The long black lines of birds undulating in their flight can readily be distinguished from any other shore bird. They have a very dark appearance. In a short half hour the last flocks have passed and there is no further flight until the next tide. At high water they congregate on the upper beaches, well out of reach of any disturber. For a long time it was impossible to arrange a blind in the range of the flight, but finally by piling up heaps of seaweed and staking them down far out in the shallow water, we managed to kill a small number. They quickly learned the danger, however, and would keep on their course just out of reach.

Dr. D. G. Elliot (1895) writes:

Like the other godwit, its larger relative, it is a shy bird during migration and keeps a watchful eye on an intruder in its domain, rising at a considerable distance and uttering its shrill cry. It sometimes decoys readily, setting its wings and sailing up to the wooden counterfeits, lured on by a close imitation of its note, but soon discovers the deception and either alights only for a moment or else wheels about over the decoys, and hastily departs, provided it escapes the rain of shot from the discharged gun of the concealed sportsman. About Hudson's Bay it is met with in large flocks, resorting to the beach when the tide is low, and feeding on the crustacea it discovers there, retiring to the marshes as the tide rises.

Professor Rowan writes to me:

Like the majority of waders, this godwit can swim with ease and has been observed swimming of its own accord when crossing from one sand ridge to another, and also when dropped into deep water after being shot in flight but not killed.

The flight of the species is distinctly "ploverish." The greater contrast, against its white parts, of its darker balance makes it distinguishable at considerable distance from the willet when in flight. They can easily be mistaken for each other if casually observed, especially in the grey plumage of young and fall adults.

In walking this godwit has much the same attitudes of the marbled, generally very ungraceful and altogether hunched up, neck closely drawn into the body. It is, however, altogether warier than the marbled and carries its neck stretched out more frequently.

On the whole it is an extremely silent species. I have seen dozens of birds but have only heard a call twice. This sounded like *ta-it* on both occasions, less raucous than the marbles call but in general quite reminiscent of it.

Doctor Wetmore (1926) says:

In plain gray winter plumage this godwit is as inconspicuous and nondescript in appearance as a willet. In general size it suggests a greater yellowlegs, but can be distinguished at any distance by its quiet carriage, for it does not practice the constant tilting that is the habit of the yellowlegs. These godwits sought company with scattered flocks of stilts or smaller shore birds, and in feeding walked rapidly, at times in water nearly to their bodies or again in the shallows. As they moved they probed rapidly and constantly in the mud with a nervous thrusting motion, often with the beak immersed clear to their eyes. Morsels of food that were encountered were passed rapidly up the length of the bill and swallowed. When their movements carried them too near the stilts the latter hustled them about, and made them run rapidly to escape their bills, but in spite of this discouragement the godwits remained in as close proximity as permitted to their belligerent neighbors, perhaps, because of similarity in feeding habit. Some Hudsonian godwit gave a low chattering call when flushed, a low *qua qua* that resembled one of the notes of *L. fedoa*. As they extend the wings to fly the dark axillars show as a patch of black and in flight the white tail, with black band across the tip is prominent. The birds are hunted to such an extent that they are exceedingly wary. When opportunity offered I took only a few for specimens.

Referring to their habits in Alberta, C. G. Harrold (1923) says:

The individuals in the parties seen on April 29 were feeding very close together like dowitchers. Not a single bird was seen on dry land and most of them were wading about in water 4 inches to 6 inches deep, one bird swimming after the manner of a yellowlegs which has waded out of its depth. Although the Hudsonian godwits associate with the marbled, the latter bully them considerably, chasing them away if they approach the marbled too closely when feeding.

Voice.—Mr. Harrold (1923) says that "their call note is a soft *chip* (very unlike the harsh notes of the vociferous marbled), and when alarmed they utter a low sandpiper-like chattering." They are usually very silent birds.

Field marks.—In spring plumage the Hudsonian godwit can be recognized easily at almost any distance by the rich brown underparts, almost black upper parts, white rump, and black tail; at a long distance it looks very black. On the wing in all plumages the white rump and black tail are conspicuous and the wings are diagnostic;

the axillars are jet black and the lining of the wing is black; the wings are nearly black, with a small, central white patch, much smaller than that of the willet. An immature bird while standing, might be mistaken for a willet, but it is a much slenderer bird and has a longer, slenderer bill.

Fall.—Hudsonian godwits gather in flocks on the western shores of Hudson Bay, preparing for their eastward migration to the Atlantic coasts of the Maritime Provinces and New England. The normal migration route is probably over the ocean from Nova Scotia to British Guiana or Brazil, the birds being seen in New England and Long Island only when driven in by severe storms.

E. A. Preble (1902) saw a number on the beach about 50 miles north of York Factory as early as July 19, and it was last seen by him below Cape Churchill on August 24, 1900. This was the beginning of the eastward migration from Hudson Bay. The species is practically unknown in the interior of southern Canada in the fall.

Doctor Sanford (1903) writes:

I have seen these birds on some of the islands in the Gulf of St. Lawrence in large flocks. They arrive late in July, the first comers being steadily augmented by new arrivals until by the first week of August their greatest abundance has been reached. From this time on the numbers rapidly decrease, and by the last of the month only odd birds are seen. The young appear about the middle of September, and until October 1 are common in the same locations. On the adjacent mainland and the shores farther south the birds are seldom met with, and then only as odd stragglers. Where they stop next and what their course is on departing is a mystery. Probably they keep well out to the open sea, and along with the golden plover wisely skip the United States in the fall flight south.

As indicated above, Hudsonian godwits evidently pass by New England far out at sea in fair weather, as they are strong, swift fliers, capable of a long, continuous flight. But during heavy easterly storms they are occasionally driven in and onto our coasts. The first one I shot was one of four birds taken on Monomoy Island, Massachusetts, September 5, 1892, after a severe northeast storm, which lasted for two days and brought in a heavy flight of shore birds. This was an adult. I have two other birds, both young birds, taken on Cape Cod on October 2 and 4. Mr. Forbush (1912) reports " a flock of about 50 birds seen at Ipswich on August 26, 1908, of which several were killed." He also says:

On August 13, 1903, a large flight occurred on the Long Island coast and many were killed, but little was heard of them to the southward. The only flight of godwits that is shown on the record of Chatham Beach Hotel for seven years is in August, 1903. No birds were taken on the 13th, when the great flight appeared on Long Island, for at Chatham the weather apparently was fair, with a west wind. One bird, perhaps a straggler from the Long Island flight, was picked up on the 20th after a southeast wind had blown for two days. On the 26th a northeast wind set in, and it blew from the east or northeast for six days. On the 29th seven godwits were killed. During the seven years for which the record was kept godwits were taken only singly or in pairs, with the above exception, and the record shows 42 killed all told. Twenty-four were taken during east, north, or northeast winds; eight in north-west winds; six in southwest winds; two in west winds; and only one in a south wind.

Mr. S. Prescott Fay (1911) reports an unusually heavy flight at Cape Cod from early in August until October 22, 1910, during which 25 birds were shot on 17 different dates. He saw a flock of 10 on August 15, but says:

In most cases they were lone birds and, contrary to their habits, were tame and decoyed readily. However, on September 5, during a heavy easterly storm with a downpour of rain, a flock of 30 to 35 birds went over our stand at Chatham. Instead of alighting, as we supposed they would do, for they appeared very much exhausted, they continued their slow flight and disappeared, going due south in the heaviest part of the storm. However, a man a short way below us shot three of these birds as we watched them go over him high up, and later we found some one else above us had shot one from the same flock only a minute or two earlier. One of these men estimated that the flock contained over 40 birds, so my figures may be too low or else, after he fired, the birds may have separated so that we might have seen only part of the original flock.

Winter.—The winter home of the Hudsonian godwit is in extreme southern South America, from Argentina and Chile south to the Straits of Magellan and the Falkland Islands.

A. H. Holland (1892) says that, in Argentina, it "appears in flocks late in the winter after heavy rains from July to August. They were met with both in summer and winter plumage." Ernest Gibson (1920) reported it as formerly " very abundant, in numerous flocks, some of apparently over 1,000," in the Province of Buenos Aires. He says that—

On more than one of these occasions several birds have dropped to my gun. The flock would then again and again sweep round and hover over the indi-viduals in the water, uttering loud cries of distress, quite regardless of my presence in the open and the renewed gunfire. Though the godwit is such an excellent table bird, I found myself unable to continue the slaughter under these circumstances. I might select my birds, but so closely were they packed together that the shots went practically "into the brown," and caused innumerable cripples.

Conditions have changed since then, for Doctor Wetmore (1926) writes:

Save for a record to be mentioned later, the Hudsonian godwit was first recorded on November 13, 1920, when four, in winter plumage, were found with small sandpipers on the tidal flats near the mouth of the Rio Ajo, below Lavalle, Buenos Aires. Two more were seen here on November 15. The species was not noted again until March 3, 1921, when two were seen along the Laguna del Morte in the outskirts of Guamini, Buenos Aires. Four more were found on March 4, one in brown dress and the others still in winter plumage. On March 5 eight were recorded, one only showing distinct signs of breeding plumage. On the day following three passed swiftly northward over the lake without pausing to alight, while on March 7 eight were seen together and a single bird later, and by a lucky shot I secured one, a male. March 8, 12 that fed in a small bay were so slow in rising that I secured 3. At dusk 12 more came to roost on a mud bar in company with golden plover. Though reported 50 years ago as found in great bands and among the most abundant of shore birds in this region, the small number that I have recorded here are all that were observed in continued field work throughout the winter range of the species. I was fortunate in seeing these, as by chance I found a spot where they tarried in northward migration from some point to the south.

The passing of this fine bird must be a cause for regret among sportsmen and nature lovers alike, to be attributed to the greed of gunners and to the fact that its large size and gregarious habit made it desirable to secure and when opportunity offered easy to kill in large numbers. There is little hope even under the most rigorous protection that the species can regain its former numbers. It would appear that the small number that remain winter mainly in Patagonia, as the species was encountered in any number only when in migration from that region.

DISTRIBUTION

Range.—North America, chiefly east of the Rocky Mountains to southern South America. Now almost extinct.

Breeding range.—The only eggs of this species that have been collected were taken at Mackenzie Bay and on the Anderson River, Mackenzie. It has been reported in summer from Alaska (Kenai, Nulato, Ugashik, mouth of the Yukon River, and Point Barrow); east to Prince Edward Island and the Magdalen Islands (Audubon); but in no case, save the one above mentioned, is there satisfactory evidence of breeding. Preble found it common on the Barren Grounds south of Cape Eskimo, during the early part of August, and it also was noted by him in the country north of York Factory, in the middle of July.

Winter range.—The Hudsonian godwit appears to winter only in southern South America. It has been taken or observed at this season in the Falkland Islands (Mare Harbor); Argentina (Chubut Valley, Lavalle, Azul, Buenos Aires, and La Plata); and Chile (Straits of Magellan, Ancud, and Valparaiso). MacFarlane (1887) reported them as abundant on the coast of Peru (San Juan) on November 9, 1883, but it seems unlikely that they were preparing to winter in that latitude.

Spring migration.—This species always has been apparently rare on the Atlantic coast in spring and but few records are available. Among these are Maryland, West River, May 6, 1886 (only record for the State); Delaware, Rehoboth, May 8, 1906; and New York,

Long Beach, May 23, 1925. Records of spring arrival for the interior are not much more numerous but among these are: Louisiana, Vinton, April 22; Missouri, April 19; Illinois, Albany, April 22; Ohio, New Bremen, April 22, and Youngstown, April 26; Michigan, Detroit, May 14; Ontario, Point Pelee, May 13; Iowa, Blue Lake, May 7; Minnesota, Heron Lake, April 19, and Grant County, April 25; Kansas, Lawrence, April 19; Nebraska, Lincoln, May 10; South Dakota, Vermilion, May 8; North Dakota, Harrisburg, May 6; Saskatchewan, Indian Head, May 11; Montana, Terry, May 10; Alberta, Beaverhill Lake, April 28; Mackenzie, Fort Anderson, June 7; and Alaska, Fort Kenai, May 5, Valdez, May 10, Lynn Canal, May 12, and St. Michael, May 22.

Late dates of spring departure are: Ontario, Toronto, June 13; Iowa, Sioux City, May 17; Wisconsin, Albion, June 3; Minnesota, Grant County, May 15, Hallock, May 17, Hallock, May 18, and Mankato, May 25; Nebraska, Lincoln, May 22, and Ceresco, June 12; South Dakota, Vermilion, May 24; North Dakota, Charlson, May 22; and Manitoba, Shoal Lake, May 29, and Lake Winnipegosis, June 5.

Fall migration.—Early dates of arrival in the fall are: Keewatin, York Factory, July 19; Manitoba, Big Stick Lake, July 21; South Dakota, Artesian, July 10; Iowa, Sioux City, August 12; Ontario, Rupert House, July 30, and Toronto, August 20; Ohio, Pelee Island, August 24; Illinois, Mount Carmel, August 29, and Aledo, September 9; Louisiana, New Orleans, September 27; Rhode Island, Newport, July 29; New York, Shinnecock, August 8, Mastic, August 21, South Oyster Bay, August 25, and Quogue, August 31; New Jersey, Anglesea, August 26; North Carolina, Pea Island, September 13, 1911 (only record for the State); and West Indies, Barbados, October 5, and Dominica, October 8.

Late dates of fall departures are: Keewatin, Cape Eskimo, August 14, and Fort Churchill, August 24; Minnesota, St. Vincent, September 15; Wisconsin, Racine, November 1; Ontario, Ottawa, October 11, and Toronto, October 20; Quebec, Montreal, October 11; Massachusetts, Monomoy Island, October 2, Ipswich, October 20, and Eastham, November 3; Connecticut, Little River marshes, October 11, and Lyme, October 30; Rhode Island, Newport, October 13; and New York, Onondaga Lake, October 13, Branchport, October 29, and Ithaca, November 5.

Casual records.—A specimen of the Hudsonian godwit was taken near St. George, Bermuda, in the fall of 1875.

Egg dates.—Arctic Canada: 8 records, June 9 to 30.

LIMOSA LIMOSA LIMOSA (Linnaeus)

BLACK-TAILED GODWIT

Contributed by Francis Charles Robert Jourdain

HABITS

The only claim this species has to a place in the North American fauna rests upon its accidental occurrence in Greenland, where it is said to have occurred twice. There is, however, an element of doubt about the records. The first is due to Fabricius, who states in his *Fauna Greenlandica* that he had seen a single specimen; the next occurrence is said to have taken place near Godthaab, or if Holböll's reference is to the same specimen, at the Kok Islands near Godthaab, and was recorded by Reinhardt, senior, in 1824. The skin was sent to the Museum at Copenhagen, but Dr. J. Reinhardt, junior, was unable to find it there, as he states in the *Ibis* 1861, page 11. Winge pertinently suggests that there may have been some confusion with *Limosa haemastica*, of which species several specimens were sent to Copenhagen from Greenland, including one from Godthaab, sent by Holböll. The distance from Iceland to Greenland is not very great, but one would expect stragglers from that direction to arrive on the east side of Greenland instead of on the west side, where the great majority of accidental visitors are of Nearctic origin.

Spring.—Fortunately we are now in possession of fairly full and complete descriptions of the courtship activities of this species on the arrival at its breeding grounds in Holland (Huxley and Montague 1926). Here it appears during the last days of March; in 1925 the first arrival took place on March 25, but up to March 31 a large proportion of the breeding stock had not yet put in an appearance. It is, however, interesting to note that many of the birds were not only on their breeding territories, but were obviously in pairs, although some unmated birds were also present and small flocks of newly arrived birds were also met with. Evidently the males do not migrate in advance of the females in order to "stake out their claims," as is the case with certain other species.

In the British Isles, where the black-tailed godwit has long ceased to breed, it is now only an irregular passage migrant chiefly from mid April to mid June, in small numbers along the south and southeast coasts. The Iceland breeding birds, however, pass through Ireland on their way north and reach their destination during the latter half of April or early in May in small flocks, but in these northern latitudes the breeding season is naturally later than in Central Europe and the eggs are not laid till late in May.

Courtship.—This is dealt with by Huxley and Montague (1926) in considerable detail and is divided into seven sections: (1) The ceremonial flight and its variations, (2) the joint flight, (3) the tail display, (4) the scrape ceremony, (5) the pursuit, (6) fighting, and (7) coition. Taking these consecutively, the ceremonial flight is much the commonest and most striking action during the courtship period and is confined to the male alone. He rises at a steep angle with quickly beating wings, uttering repeatedly a loud trisyllabic call, *tur-ee-tur*. When a height of some 150 or 200 feet has been gained the real ceremonial flight starts. The most obvious point about it is the change of call—the quick trisyllable is suddenly replaced by a lower-toned disyllable, which may be represented by the letter *ghru-toe* (or *grutto*, the Dutch name for godwit).

This change was inevitable; on no single occasion did we hear it in any way departed from. The change in flight is equally notable. The quick beat of the wings is suddenly slowed and is replaced by a succession of slow, clipping strokes; at the same time the wings are markedly bent downward just as those of the redshank in some of his courtship flights. The tail is spread to the full and is twisted round, first to one side and then to the other. Simultaneously the whole body is tilted over in the same direction as the tail and the bird flaps along with slow wing beats and body heeled over for 20 or 30 yards. Then the tail is screwed over toward the other side, and the body heels over correspondingly. Thus the performing bird flies along rolling from side to side and repeating the *grutto* call continuously. We are, on the whole, inclined to attribute it to the rudder action of the tail.

The flight generally takes place within a circle of 150 to 300 yards in diameter and about 200 feet up, but both direction and duration are variable and Huxley has seen one bird "rolling" for over a mile in a straight line, while another has come down after a dozen wing strokes. The descent is even more striking; the rolling flight and call stop simultaneously and the bird glides with rigid wings suddenly nose-diving downwards with almost closed wings till about 50 feet from the ground when the wings are opened and the godwit side-slips in all directions. Just before alighting the wings are opened and held vertically for a second or two afterwards. Another method, occasionally used, is to descend with the wings about two-thirds open, causing a loud roaring noise due to the wind passing through the separated primaries, and in this case the bird alights directly with spread wings and tail.

The "joint flight" is shared by both sexes and is normal in character, both birds (but especially the male) calling quickly as when rising for the ceremonial flight. The female is generally slightly in front of the male on these occasions. During the "tail display" the male struts round the hen with the tail fully expanded like a fan, but depressed to about an angle of 60° to 70° with the horizontal and tilts it from side to side so that the black and white surface is presented to the female. The "scrape ceremony" is chiefly confined to the male who runs to a depression and crouches down in it with slightly open wings, tail coverts puffed out and compressed tail pointing upwards, while he presses his breast against the ground as if smoothing off a scrape. Females were noticed to go through this action with appreciably spread tails and after some scratching with the feet.

Other godwits are always pursued with loud outcry, as well as harriers, lapwings, etc., but there is little real fighting between males, and what there is does not seem to be of a particularly vicious type. The opponents face each other and attempt to seize each other's bills, striking with their feet as they descend from the jump. Such sparring rarely lasts longer than two or, at the outside, three minutes. In coition the hen stands rigid with horizontal bill, the male standing about a foot behind her "with vibratory wings and spread tail, uttering a clear disyllabic note; then he rises and floats forward above the female with dangling legs and no apparent change in the rate of vibration of his wings. He poses for a moment upon her back, still calling with wings held stiffly upspread and vibrating tail. Immediately after pairing both birds usually continue feeding."

Nesting.—The breeding grounds of this species vary considerably in character. On the great heaths of Brabant one may come across a pair nesting in short, dry heather; in the dune country on the Dutch coast they breed among the sea buckthorn and sallow bushes on the sandhills; in Texel most pairs prefer the rectangular patches of rich grass in the "polders" (reclaimed marshes), while in Jutland and Iceland a few pairs breed on the vast expanses of quaking marsh near the coast. Nowhere have we met with it more plentifully than in the Dutch polders where I have seen as many as 13 nests with eggs in a single day. All were much alike; a saucerlike hollow in the ground where the grass was thickest and richest, lined with a thick pad of dead grass.

Eggs.—Here are laid the four pyriform eggs; five have been recorded once or twice, but the only case of six eggs which is known to me was probably due to two females sharing a nest. As a rule the eggs do not vary much, though sometimes a single egg may be found in which the ground color is pale bluish gray with blotches of deeper ashy gray and a few darker flecks. The great majority of eggs vary in color from greenish or olive green to olive brown and occasionally reddish brown in ground, with blotches or spots of darker brown or olive and a few ashy shell marks. The measurements of 100 eggs average 54.71 by 37.37 millimeters; the eggs showing the four extremes measure **59.8** by 37.8, 55.3 by **40.7**, **48.5** by 37.7, and 55 by **34** millimeters.

Young.—The only estimate of the incubation period known to me is that of Faber, who gives it as 24 days, but recent evidence on this point is lacking. Both sexes share in the work of incubation, according to von Wangelin, and this is confirmed by Huxley and Montague, who noticed that in the earlier stages the male spent, at least in one case, three hours on the nest to one by the female. This, however, applies only to the daytime. Hantzsch's statement, that apparently it is carried out by the hen alone, seems to be quite erroneous. The downy young as soon as dried are led out of the nest and are closely attended to by both parents. Only a single brood is reared in the season.

Plumages.—The molts and plumages are fully described in "A Practical Handbook of British Birds," edited by H. F. Witherby (1920), to which the reader is referred.

Food.—Naumann (1887) records insect larvae, worms, snails and slugs, fish and frog spawn, tadpoles; also insects (Coleoptera, Orthoptera, and Odonata). On migration, shells of small marine and fresh-water mollusca have been found in stomachs, also insects, small shore crustacea (Gammaridae) and the usual sand or gravel.

Behavior.—The godwits are striking looking birds, readily recognizable in summer plumage by the cinnamon pink of the neck and breast and the bold contrast of black and white in the tail, taken in connection with the long legs and straight, slightly upturned bill. The latter character at once distinguishes them from the whimbrels and curlews and their large size marks them out from most of the other European Limicolae. The loud, musical, disyllabic call of the male is also very characteristic. In winter the warm coloring is lost, but the godwits are noisy birds and at this time of year the breeding note is replaced by a monosyllabic *chut*. Moreover, their contour when flying overhead is peculiar, for the long legs are carried out beyond the tail and have somewhat the effect of long middle tail feathers not unlike those of the Arctic skua or jaeger.

Fall.—In the British Isles they begin to appear on our southeast coasts in August, though not in any numbers as a rule, and have generally left before the end of October. The Iceland birds assemble in flocks at the end of August and leave the island by the beginning of September, while in south Sweden, the Baltic republics, and Poland they desert their breeding grounds in the latter part of July and drift southwards to the North German coast. None stay in Holland after September, and gradually they work their way southward to the shores of the Mediterranean, where a certain number winter in favorable localities. The main streams of migration seem to be towards the Straits of Gibraltar on the west side and along the east side of the Balkan Peninsula, but along the west side of the peninsula they are much scarcer. Considerable numbers of west Asiatic birds migrate to the marshes of the Euphrates and winter there, while others pass into India and Burma.

Winter.—During the winter months these godwits either haunt the seashore, displaying special preference for low-lying coasts where extensive areas of mud flats are exposed at low tide, or else are to be found where there are large marshes along the edges of lakes, and less frequently by the banks of rivers. On the open coasts and the Spanish marismas they are subject to a good deal of persecution from the larger falcons, especially the peregrine, which greatly appreciates them as an article of diet. Lord Lilford describes the great flocks of these godwits on the lower reaches of the Guadalquiver as spreading out into long lines or gathering into dense masses like starlings or dunlins, when trying to avoid the attentions of their long-winged enemies.

DISTRIBUTION

Breeding range.—In Iceland it is very local, being confined to the low-lying country in the southwest (Arnes and Rangarvalla-Sysla), where it breeds in fair numbers; Faroes (only once definitely recorded); formerly in the British Isles from Yorkshire to Norfolk, but extinct as a breeding species since 1847, unless a possible Lincolnshire record for 1885 is accepted; Belgium, Holland, and its islands, West Jutland, North Germany, locally in South Sweden, Hungary, Poland, the Baltic Republics (Lithuania, Latvia, Estonia); in Russia, according to Buturlin, it breeds in the governments of St. Petersburg (Leningrad), Moscow, Riazan, on the Volga south to the mouth of the Kama, in the Ufa and Perm governments north to 60° N. In western Asia it nests in the Tobolsk government. The Irtysh Valley, Baraba Steppe, and locally in Turkestan, but the exact limits of this and the smaller eastern race (*L. l. melanuroides* Gould) are not yet defined.

Winter range.—The main winter quarters of this species are in the Mediterranean region, the coasts of North Africa, and the Nile Valley, the marshes of Iraq and the Indian Peninsula east of Burma. It has been recorded from the Azores, Maderia, and the Canaries; is common in suitable localities along the North African littoral from Morocco through Algeria and Tunisia to Egypt, and has been recorded from the Egyptian Sudan, Kordofan, and Abyssinia, and exceptionally as far South as Natal. In Asia it ranges to the Persian Gulf, the Indian Peninsular, but scarce in the south, Ceylon, Burma, etc., while the eastern race visits the islands of Malaysia and ranges to Australia.

Spring migration.—The northward movement from Morocco takes place in February and March and it appears in Andalusia in February (late date April 6). In Corsica it has been noted as late as April 23 and on passage, Malta, March 24–25. In Tunisia it is most plentiful in February and March, and does not stay in Egypt after March (late date April 7). It also stays in the plains of northern India until March (late date Delhi, May 25). It passes through Portugal in February and March; Italy in March and April; Greece (February 10, March 7, etc.); Montenegro, large flock March 17–25; Bulgaria (March 10–31, flock of 200 on April 1).

Fall migration.—The southward bound hosts arrive in Andalusia in August-September, but in Portugal, though a few appear in September, most pass in October. In north Italy the earliest arrival dates from the end of July, and in the Balkan Peninsular and the passage lasts from September to November (early date August 18, Bulgaria, late date November 13, Bulgaria), reaching Egypt in October. At the Euphrates marshes it arrives early in August and reaches India in October (early date, Nepal, September 7).

Egg dates.—In Holland and Germany the first eggs may be found in the last 10 days of April and early May, but as they are largely taken for the market at that time, many sets in collections are second and even third layings. Seven records, April 18–30; 10 records, May 1–10; 12 records, May 11–20; 8 records, May 21–25. In Jutland breeding is rather later; six records May 10–15; and still later in Iceland, six records, May 23-June 2.

GLOTTIS NEBULARIA (Gunnerus)

GREENSHANK

Contributed by Francis Charles Robert Jourdain

HABITS

The claim of this species to a place in the North American list dates back to Audubon, who obtained three specimens on Sand Key, near Cape Sable, Florida. Since that occurrence no other specimens have been obtained.

Courtship.—There are few species the study of whose family life is attended with greater difficulties than the greenshank. In the first place it is an exceedingly wary and keen-sighted bird, and furthermore, it is not sociable during the breeding season, each pair nesting apart from its fellows in some of the wildest and most desolate country imaginable. In the British Isles its main breeding grounds are on the vast expanse of sodden moorland, interspersed here and there by lochs and "flows" (stretches of water-logged ground with black peaty pools), which cover a great part of the Scottish counties of Sutherland, Caithness, and Ross. Further southward it also breeds on suitable ground in Inverness-shire and other parts, but here the country is more broken and varied and there are big stretches of old pine forest and more modern coniferous plantations. In both classes of country observation is attended with difficulties. On the open treeless moorlands houses are few and far between, the climate is anything but inviting in early May, rainstorms are frequent, varied by squalls of hail and fogs, while in some seasons heavy snowfalls take place from time to time. On the other hand the country is open, with few hills of any size, and the direction of the birds' flight can be marked for long distances, while further south, though the extent of possible breeding ground is infinitely smaller, it is far more difficult to follow a bird in flight as it skims over a belt of forest or round a shoulder of a hill. So it is little wonder that of the actual courtship of the greenshank we have hardly anything on record. What little we know may be classified under two heads; the wonderful song flight of the male and the ritual of the courtship itself. The song flight may be seen even after incubation has begun, though possibly only in the earlier stages, and has been noticed by several observers. The fullest and best description is that of Mr. J. Walpole Bond (1923), which may be summarized as follows:

When singing, the greenshank rises fairly high—sometimes very high—above the moor and starts by soaring, head to wind, of course. It may then remain soaring, looking very hawklike indeed, while it sings. Or else—and this generally happens—it varies the performance by proceeding in a succession of downward, inverted arcs of good size, though soaring is resumed for a few moments as the summit of each curve is reached. In this case "singing" only takes place on the downward portion of the curve; on the down curve, too, the wings are sometimes vibrated very rapidly. Sometimes also when the "song" itself is in progress the wings are flicked up and down with measured rhythm.

The song itself is a musical and moderately fast repeated dissyllable *tew-hoo*, a rich note, harmonizing with the desolate surroundings in which bird life, except for an occasional meadow pipit, (*Anthus pratensis*) is often almost entirely absent. Walpole Bond also notes a twanging and metallic *chuck*, *dock*, or *duk*, sometimes heard after each quick *tew-hoo*, and questions whether this latter sound is vocal or caused by wings or tail. Personally I have not noticed the latter sound, perhaps because I have generally heard the song at a great height and always at some distance. It should be added that this performance is often kept up for long periods. Gilroy (1922) mentions a case when it lasted for twenty minutes, and though I have not timed the birds, I have heard it more or less continually for ten or twelve minutes, ending with a precipitate dive earthwards. Of the actual courtship ritual I have seen no published record. The birds arrive on their breeding ground early in April. On an occasion when a heavy snowfall had practically wiped out all early nests on the Caithness-Sutherland moors, I saw two birds on a little sandy spit by the side of a small loch. The male was evidently pressing his attentions on his mate and approached her with high flapping wings, showing the underside almost as the redshank does, and actually raising his wing over the hen until at last coition took place. Both birds remained quiet for some little time afterwards and then rose together and flew away, calling all the time.

Nesting.—The information with regard to the nesting habits in all the older works is of the baldest and scantiest nature, but the last decade has seen a great advance in our knowledge and Mr. N. Gilroy (1922) in particular has published a fascinating little pamphlet on this bird in which his observations on over twenty nests examined between 1906 and 1922 are carefully coordinated, so that now the actions and movements of breeding birds are much better understood. The whole account is of the deepest interest, but as it extends to some twenty pages it is only possible here to give a short résumé of the present stage of our knowledge. The greenshank generally nests within easy reach of some small lochan, often a mere pool, to which the young can easily be led by the parents soon after they are hatched out. The nest itself is usually on dry ground. On the treeless moorlands of Southerland Caithness it is almost always made either close up against or actually on one of the many grey bits of rock lying amongst the heather. Exceptionally it has been found on the top of a hummock, but as a rule should be looked for within a few hundred yards of the feeding ground, sometimes quite exposed but difficult to see as the sitting bird exactly resembles in color the grey stones lying about and generally sits till almost trodden on. In the Inverness country the birds nest close to a mark, just as the Sutherland birds do, but here instead of a grey boulder it is usually a bit of bleached and dead pine, of which thousands of fragments lie scattered about. Exceptionally I have known a bird make use of an iron fence post as a mark. When a bird has been found standing about the edge of some tiny pool the probability is that his mate is sitting not far away, but the difficulty of finding her is vastly increased by the fact that the main feeding ground is generally by the side of a good-sized lake, which may be any distance from one to four miles away, and here one of the pair may spend the greater part of the day. Moreover, it is not uncommon to find that several pairs of birds use the same lakeside as their main resting and feeding ground. Even so, if the sexes changed duties at short intervals or behaved in exactly the same manner, it would not be a matter of great difficulty to trace a bird back to its nesting ground. But there seems to be considerable individual variation in this respect. There is, however, a very strong tendency to return to the same breeding place year after year. The classical case is T. E. Buckley's record of a nest found between two stones which was again occupied two seasons later presumably by the same bird, but there are innumerable cases where two or three nesting sites, used in as many years, lie within one hundred yards of one another. This makes the discovery of nests much easier if one can revisit the district for two or more years in succession. New nests are merely saucer-like depressions with a few heather stalks and some dead bents, but almost always some leaves of bay myrtle or bilberry in the hollow, and if the bird has begun to sit, some of its own small breast feathers.

Eggs.—Normally, four in number, occasionally only three, while five have occurred; second layings usually consist of three eggs. Larger numbers, such as eight, recorded by Booth, are probably due either to two hens laying together or one clutch spoilt by weather and a second laid subsequently. They are pyriform in shape and wonderfully handsome, the ground color varies from stone color to warm buff, marked sometimes sparingly and sometimes freely with irregular spots and blotches of deep red-brown, as well as ashy or purplish shell marks. In most eggs the markings are heavier at the large end. The measurements of 100 eggs average 51.41 by 34.80 millimeters; the eggs showing the four extremes measure 59.8 by 37.7, 45.8 by 35.4, and 50.4 by 32.4 millimeters.

Young.—That incubation is sometimes shared by both sexes is proved by the fact that both Walpole Bond and Seton Gordon have witnessed the change of duties and the latter has actually photographed the birds in the act of changing places. Yet Gilroy watched one bird from 10.45 a. m. to 7.50 p. m., which remained all the time at a loch side in Sutherland on May 16, although its mate was sitting on a clutch of fresh eggs. Evidently there is considerable individual variation in this respect.

Plumages.—The molts and plumages are fully described in "A Practical Handbook of British Birds," edited by H. F. Witherby (1920), to which the reader is referred.

Food.—During the breeding season the food consists chiefly of insects and their larvæ, but tadpoles and frog spawn are freely taken and Oswin Lee records a pair feeding busily for nearly an hour in the evening on them, and small water beetles. Fresh-water mollusca, such as *Planorbis*, are also taken and occasionally a small fish. Along insects the following genera of Coleoptera have been recorded: *Phyllopertha*, *Cneorhinus*, *Harpalus*, *Dytiscus*, *Gyrinus*, *Aphodius*, and *Ilybius*. Among Diptera, Tipula and their larvae; also *Notonecta glauca* and *Lestes nympha*. In the autumn and winter a great part of the food is picked up on the coast and includes worms, lug-worms, crustacea (*Palaemon*, *Crangon*, *Hippolyte*, *Squilla*, and in large numbers Gammaridae).

Behavior.—Although a large proportion of its breeding area is absolutely devoid of trees, the greenshank also nests in country intersected by belts of forest, and it is interesting to note that it perches readily on trees and makes good use of them as lookout posts. It is always wary and readily takes alarm, rising with loud outcry on the approach of danger. As MacGillivray notes, when searching for food it often wades out into the water until it reaches nearly to the tarsal joint and moves " with rapidity, running rather than walking and almost constantly vibrating its body." It is interesting to note the difference in the behavior of individual birds under similar circumstances. As a rule the incubating bird sits very closely and will sometimes allow herself to be touched before leaving the eggs. When flushed one bird will spring up and dart away with rapid flight and a single cry of alarm, another will for a minte or two fly about with deafening clamor, and in one case a bird dashed off but pitched about five yards away, yelping loudly and next minute flew straight at my head, with repeated cries of *Ip, chip, chip, ip, chip, chip*, etc. Just as it reached me it sheered off with its long green legs dangling, but returned to the charge again, repeating the process ten or twelve times, after which it settled on the ground and called vociferously, but after 10 minutes had passed flew away still calling. This behavior was, of course, quite exceptional.

N. Gilroy (1922) lays great stress on one note uttered when the bird is about to take its place on the eggs. This is a clear, piercing cry of *Tchook-tchook-tchook*, continually uttered till the bird settles down on the nest. It does not necessarily imply that the bird is rendered uneasy by the presence of a watcher and is apparently used even when the bird is quite undisturbed, so if one is lucky enough to be within earshot when it is uttered it forms a valuable clue to the position of the nest.

Fall.—When the young are fledged the family parties make their way to the coast. Here they frequent the " pools of brackish water at the heads of the sand fords and the shallow margins of the bays and creeks " as MacGillivray says. The same writer describes its flight as "rapid, gliding, and devious, it alights abruptly, runs to some distance, stands and vibrates." By September or October at the latest it leaves its haunts in Scotland and makes its way southward along the coast line.

Winter.—Although there are a few midwinter records even in the British Isles by far the greater proportion of these birds spend the winter from the Mediterranean southward and in southern Asia, the Malay Archipelago, Australia, etc. Here they are chiefly known as shore birds, only occasionally being found by the sides of inland lakes and marshes.

DISTRIBUTION

Breeding range.—Scotland, chiefly in the north, but has extended its range of late years; Norway, Sweden, Finland, Russia, south to the governments of St. Petersburg, Pskov, Tula, Riazan, Kazan,

and Ufa; across northern Asia to Kamchatka, south to latitude 55°
in the west and 54° in the east.

Winter range.—The Mediterranean countries and Africa, south to
Cape Province and Natal; in Asia, India, Ceylon, Burma, Siam,
China, Hainan, Formosa, and Japan; Sunda Islands, Moluccas,
Borneo, Java, Timor, Sumatra, Norfolk Island, Australia, and New
Zealand.

Spring migration.—From its winter quarters in South Africa it is
recorded from Morocco (Mogador) in May and near Gibraltar in
March, April, and May (late date May 22); passes Corsica in some
numbers (May 8), arrives in Greece, where some also winter, at the
end of March and in April, leaving in May (late date May 8);
leaves Egypt in March; passes Cyprus in April and leaves the
marshes of lower Iraq at the end of April, and also leaves India
about the same time. In France it arrives late in April or early May,
and in Spain has been observed as late as the third week of May,
even in the south. First arrivals reach South Russia in March and
pass through north Germany about mid-April, arriving on the British
coasts from the middle of April onward and in south Sweden in the
latter part of May.

Fall migration.—While the spring migration is usually noticed
only in small numbers, in pairs or even singly, the fall migration is
better marked. From mid-July to late in November they may be
met with on the British coasts, but most birds leave in September-
October, passing through Holland in August and September-October; in North France (early date mid-July), and reaching Spain in
September, crossing over the Straits of Gibraltar in October, and
Malta in September (occasionally in June, July, and August, probably nonbreeders). From Bulgaria it is reported in September
(early date August 20); Montenegro, September (early date July
19); Cyprus, October 3; and Greece, arrives in September. Some
birds reach the marshes of Iraq at the end of July, but mostly in
August, and in India from the middle to the end of September,
Pegu in October. Along the west coast of Africa they are noted
from Mogador (September), Gambia (September), Gold Coast (September 13), Cape Province and Natal (September–October).

Casual records.—Has occurred in Madeira, the Canaries, Azores,
Mauritius (once). Cape Verde Islands, Florida (Audubon), Norfolk Island, Chile, and Buenos Ayres.

Egg dates.—Some 39 dates from Scotland all fall in May. The
earliest date for a full clutch is May 9. From May 9 to 16 (22 dates),
17 to 23 (11 dates), 23 to 28 (5 dates).

TOTANUS TOTANUS (Linnaeus)

REDSHANK

Contributed by Francis Charles Robert Jourdain

HABITS

The redshank is a recent addition to the American list. Two specimens have been shot near Angmagsalik, in East Greenland, the first on May 29, 1902, and the second on April 24, 1909, and were recorded by the superintendent, Johan Petersen. Unfortunately, neither bird was sent to Copenhagen, so it remains uncertain whether they belong to the typical race or to the larger form described by Lehn Schiøler as *T. totanus robustus*. Doctor Coues suggested (1897) that the redshank should be included in the hypothetical list of North American birds on the ground of a specimen said to have been taken on Hudson Bay and transmitted to the British Museum, where, however, it is not to be found.

Courtship.—Fortunately we have very full accounts of the courtship and love song of this species from the observations of Messrs. E. Selous, W. Farren, and J. S. Huxley. Mr. Farren's (1910) account (incorporating much of Mr. Selous's notes) is as follows:

In courting, the male redshank approaches the female with his head erect and his body drawn up tall and straight. As he draws near he raises his wings high above his head for an instant as when alighting on the ground after a flight. Then allowing his wings gradually to droop he vibrates them and also his legs, the latter very rapidly, with a motion suggestion of a soldier "marking time." Mr. Selous (1906) has described this action, including the vibrating of the wings and legs, as follows: "The male bird, walking up to the female, raises his wings gracefully above his back. They are considerably elevated, and for a little he holds them aloft merely; but soon, drooping them to about half their former elevation, he flutters them tremulously and gracefully as though to please her." The female, as though unimpressed, turned from him and continued to feed, which did not greatly disturb her amorous wooer, as he also commenced to peck about as though feeding. But very soon he again walks up to the female "and now raising his wings to the fluttering height only, flutters them tremulously as before. He walks on a few steps and stops. He again approaches, and standing beside her—both being turned the same way—with his head and neck as it were curved over her, again trembles his wings, at the same time making a little rapid motion with his red legs on the ground as though he were walking fast, yet not advancing." This action occurs with fair frequency during the period before egg laying. I have witnessed it several times, having first been attracted by the raised wings of the male, rendered conspicuous by the white secondaries and undersides, without which I should probably not have seen the birds at all.

The habit of deliberately extending the wings upward on alighting, and thus exposing the light undersurface is one of the most characteristic actions of the redshank, and the white gleaming of the wing for a second or so before the wings are furled often enables one to identify the species even when the birds themselves are too far off to be recognized otherwise. Mr. Farren (1910) also adds:

Redshanks are fond of perching, either on horizontal branches of trees, on posts or rails; in the Cambridgeshire fens I have seen them displaying, as described by Stevenson, on the long low stacks of freshly dug peat, and also on the ground. A male may be seen running fussily about in front of the female, vibrating its body and drooping its wings and often uttering a note similar to the trilling song which accompanies the spring soaring flight.

J. S. Huxley (1912) gives a clearer and more complete picture of the courtship than any previous describer. The first stage consists in the pursuit of a hen by a male bird. Directly he stops feeding and runs after her, she runs away. Never in a straight line for any distance, but in a series of curves, often doubling back and sometimes describing a circle or even a figure of eight, while the cock follows her line a few yards behind. The cock's head is held sideways at an angle of quite 20 degrees with the line of his body in order to keep the hen in view, and his neck is stiffly stretched out. His pure white tail is expanded so that half is visible on each side of his folded wings. The chase often lasts for quite a long time, when the hen flies off leaving the male disconsolate, but sometimes she will stop and then the second stage begins.

The male may run on a yard or two, but soon stops.

He first unfolds his wings and raises them right above his back so as to expose their conspicuous undersurface of pure white, somewhat clouded or barred with grey. Then fluttering them tremulously but keeping them raised all the time he advances very, very slowly towards the hen, lifting his feet high in the air and often putting them down scarcely in advance of where they were before. Meantime as he steps on he stretches his neck a little forward, opens his mouth, and gives utterance to a single continuous note, wh.ch is changed into a long roll or rattle by the quick vibration of the lower mandible. The sound is quite like that of a nightjar, but higher and without any of the little breaks in the pitch of the note. So he advances closer and closer, the hen usually remaining motionless. Again at any time during this stage she may reject his suit by flying off, but if she is going to accept him, she simply stays still, often without moving a muscle the whole time. As the cock gets closer, he gets more and more exc.ted, vibrates his wings more and more rapidly, at length so fast that almost his whole weight is supported by them, though he still continues to execute the high stepping movements with his feet. At last when just behind the hen, he abandons the ground and flutters up on to her back on which he half alights. The period when he is there on her back is the third and last state of the courtship; it is very short and is of course in a sense nothing more than getting into the proper position for the actual pairing. Sometimes the hen, suddenly repugnant, gives a violent jerk or sideways twist and shakes him forcibly on to the ground, herself runn'ng or flying away. Occasionally, however, she apparently is satisfied; she spreads her tail diagonally and the cock with a quick and wonderfully graceful motion, half supported all the time by his fluttering wings, accomplishes the act of pairing. Then the hen gives the same violent twist that I have just mentioned, he gets shaken off, and they both begin quietly feeding, often side by side.

The love flight of the redshank is a very striking feature of the courtship and may be seen even after incubation has begun. J. S. Huxley (1912) describes it as follows:

A redshank rises up into the air, and there flies in a series of switchbacks. Just before the bottom of each switchback he gave very quick wing flaps, almost fluttering, one would call it, this made him start up again. He went on fluttering or flapping till he was about halfway up and for the rest of the upstroke of the switchback he soared up with the impetus he had gained. His wings now were set back and down; his neck and head thrown up in a beautiful proud attitude; his tail spread out. Then he turned the angle of his wings and glided down, still in the same attitude.

While flying thus he gives vent to what one may call a song—a series of pure, sweet single notes, never uttered on other occasions. The flight may be quite short, or may go on for several minutes. W. Farren (1910) writing of the same love-flight describes the song as " *Dhu-lee, dhu-lee, du-lee, du-lee, du-le, dle-dle-dle-dle,*" the latter part becoming shorted and quicker as it nears the end, when it may be continued to a vanishing point.

It should be noted that the nightjar-like note already referred to is only used on the second stage of the courtship, yet it was audible at all hours of the day and night from which Huxley deduced that, as only a fraction of the courtships were consummated and the total number of birds did not exceed 50, each bird must pair several times a day.

The contests between the males seem to be usually of a formal character, but Selous (1906) describes one case where two birds fought with determination, jumping at one another and each attempting to seize the mandibles of the other with its own.

Nesting.—The Iceland redshank has very similar habits to the ordinary European bird and haunts the swamps and morasses near the sea as well as the neighborhood of the larger lakes inland during the breeding season. Here it nests in colonies, varying in number from five or six to about twenty pairs. The nests are usually some distance apart, and generally well concealed, the sitting bird choosing a hollow where the vegetation grows thickest. In the British Isles the common redshank has greatly increased its breeding range during the last 25 years and has gradually made its way inland up the river valleys to many districts where it was previously quite unknown. Here it shares its breeding grounds with the lapwing (*Vanellus vanellus*), but the nest is not exposed like that of the latter but neatly hidden at the foot of some tall wisp of dead grass. The bird will even twist the dead grasses together to get the required protection and some nests are so artfully hidden that they can only be found by accidentally flushing the bird. In an East Anglian marsh a bird got up almost at my feet. There was a small flattened tussock of grass with long dead stalks growing up round it, but not a sign of nest or eggs, yet I felt certain that the bird had been incubating. On probing the solid-looking green tussock my fingers slipped into a hollow space beneath, where the four eggs were lying. The bird had been sitting in a neat cup of grass, completely roofed in above, and had slipped out by parting the growing grass at the side, which had closed up again. Exceptionally nests may be found, especially near the coast, quite exposed, but as a rule the bird takes advantage of every bit of cover available. On the level patches of short rich grass in the Dutch polders many pairs breed, and I have seen sixteen nests in a day. Narrow drains only a few inches wide are cut by the farmers in the turf, and here the grass is not cropped quite so close at the sides, so even under these disadvantageous conditions the redshanks avoid the open flats and prefer the partial concealment of the drain sides. In the great mud flats of the Marisma of the River Guadalquiver in South Spain, too, there is little in the way of cover, but the nests are never so exposed as those of the stilt or avocet. But wherever found, whether in Iceland, Holland, or Spain, there are the excited parents flying round and round with incessant and clamorous cries of *tu-e-too*, *tu-e-too*, alarming all the other breeding species and generally the first to give warning of danger.

The nest is substantially made of grasses and hollowed out by the pressure of the bird's breast and little in the way of extraneous matter is used, though occasionally, especially in open sites, quite a substantial cup may be built of stalks, grasses, bits of heath, moss, etc.

Eggs.—Normally four, rarely five, but in second or third layings three are not uncommon, and cases of six, seven, and eight eggs in a nest have been recorded, probably due to two hens laying together, though in some instances they may be due to a full clutch being laid after an interruption by snow or floods. The eggs are pyriform in shape and when large series are examined, show considerable variation, the ground color ranging from creamy white, stone color, to pale greenish gray or light purplish red and warm reddish ochreous. They are freely blotched and spotted with purple brown or rich red brown and ashy shell marks; sometimes a dark hair streak at the big end. In some eggs the blotches are very large, but others are more uniformly marked with small spots. In a series they show much richer and redder coloring than *Vanellus*, *Himantopus*, or *Recurvirostra*, and lack the distinctive green ground of *Tringa erythropus*. The measurements of 36 eggs from Iceland average 45.39 by 31.75 millimeters; the eggs showing the four extremes measure 49 by 32.4, 46.5 by 33.1, 42.3 by 31.3, and 43.7 by 30.5 millimeters. The measurements of 100 British eggs average 44.56 by

31.56 millimeters; the eggs showing the four extremes measure **48.4 by 32.4, 46.5 by 33.1,** and **41.5 by 28.5** millimeters. It would be seen from the above figures that Icelandic eggs (like the birds) are slightly larger than British specimens. The incubation period lasts 23 to 25 days and is apparently chiefly undertaken by the female, but J. Cunningham has shot the male from the eggs.

Plumages.—The molts and plumages are fully described in "A Practical Handbook of British Birds," edited by H. F. Witherby (1920), to which the reader is referred.

Food.—The redshank is a shore feeder to a great extent for the autumn months and often a riverside and marsh harvester in spring and summer. In the latter season its food consists chiefly of insects and their larvae, including Coleoptera (*Hyphidrus, Onthophagus,* etc.), Diptera, especially Tipulidae; also the larvae of Ephemeridae and Phryganeidae, spiders, worms (*Lumbrici*); and it is said small frogs and berries are also taken. In autumn crustacea (including Gammaridae, shrimps, and small crabs) are taken; also Mollusca (*Cardium*) and smaller marine univalves and annelids in addition to insect food when procurable; and small fish have been found in the stomach by Professor Patten.

Behavior.—The restless and wary nature of this very numerous species renders it very unpopular with the shore shooters, as its loud yelping cry of *Took took* alarms every bird within earshot. As they are poor eating and do not pay for shooting, they frequently escape, although a good many are shot. During the breeding season it is quite a common sight to see a redshank perched on a post, or tripping lightly along a rail with upraised wings, and it will at times even settle on a tree.

Fall.—As soon as the young are able to fly (for only one brood is reared in the season) the redshanks form into family parties or small flocks and work their way down the valleys toward the shore. On the British coasts large reinforcements arrive from the continent, but it is not possible to tell whether the birds which remain throughout the winter are visitors from the north or locally bred birds. In Iceland they leave about the end of September or early in October, and on the British coasts are most numerous from mid-July to mid-November.

Winter.—The main winter quarters of this species are in Africa, but it is of scarce occurrence in the south; and also in southwestern Asia; farther east in Asia it is replaced by other races, which winter in India, the Malay Peninsula, and the islands of Malaysia.

DISTRIBUTION

Breeding range.—In Iceland and the Faeroes the breeding race is *T. totanus robustus.* The typical race (*T. totanus totanus*) breeds

in suitable localities throughout the British Isles and the Continent of
Europe, north to latitude 71° in Norway, rare in North Finland,
and scarce in Russian Lapland, while it is absent from the islands off
the North Russian coast and reaches about latitude 58° N. in the
Urals and 56½° in West Siberia. Southward its range extends to
Andalusia, northern Italy, Sardinia, and in small numbers to Greece,
as well as at over 6,000 feet in the Caucasus. Probably it also nests
in Morocco, though this has not yet been proved, and perhaps also
in Tunisia, while in West Asia it breeds in Turkestan. East Asiatic
birds apparently belong to another race or races.

Winter range.—The Iceland race (*T. totanus robustus*) passes
through the British Isles and has been recorded from Morocco. The
typical race (*T. totanus totanus*) winters in small numbers in the
British Isles and also on the Scandinavian coast, but not in Central
Europe, crossing the Mediterranean and wintering in Africa, where
it has been recorded in Cape Province and Natal, but only in small
numbers, the majority evidently wintering in the Tropics. Eastward
it is found in the marshes of Iraq and the shores of the Persian Gulf,
but probably Indian birds and those which winter in Ceylon, the
Andamans, Malay Peninsula, China, Hainan, Borneo, Java, Sumatra,
Philippines, Celebes, Sunda Islands, and Japan belong to other races.

Spring migration.—The passage northward at the Straits of Gibraltar takes place in March and April, while in Tunisia most leave in
April, though specimens have been obtained in June (probably non-
breeders); and in Egypt it stays till April. In Abyssinia it has
been met with in March (March 12, Zoulla) and most leave the
marshes of Iraq in mid-May, though some stay till the end of the
month. It passes Malta in March and April, and nearly all have left
Greece by May, but passes Cyprus in April, arriving in Holland and
Denmark in April and Sweden late in that month and reaching
Finland early in May. Large numbers passed over St. Catherine's
Light in the Isle of Wight from 2.30 a. m. till dawn on April 3 and
4, 1910.

Fall migration.—In south Sweden it leaves in September and also
departs from Denmark and Holland about the same time. The passage at the Straits of Gibraltar takes place in September and October
and in Malta in September, while in the Iraq marshes the first
arrivals take place at the end of July, but the majority come in
August, and it is recorded from Fao in August and September, arriving in Egypt in September, while it has occurred as far south as the
River Niger in the same month.

Casual records.—It is an occasional visitor on passage to the
Canaries and has been met with on Madeira (March 15, April 20, 26,
September 24, October 24) as well as in East Greenland (Angmag-
salik April 24, May 29).

Egg dates.—In Iceland the eggs are laid from the end of May to early in June, May 28–June 8 (six dates), June 9–18 (five dates). In the British Isles the first eggs are laid at the end of March and through April and May, but late records in May, even in the north, are probably due to second layings: March 28 to April 16 (10 dates); April 17 to 25 (16 dates); April 26 to May 5 (10 dates). In the Shetlands Saxby records the first eggs on May 16. In Holland I have seen some 60 nests between May 11 and 31, but many were undoubtedly second layings. In Salonika eggs have been found as early as March 5.

TOTANUS MELANOLEUCUS (Gmelin)

GREATER YELLOW-LEGS

HABITS

The names, telltale and tattler, have long been applied to both of the yellow-legs, and deservedly so, for their noisy, talkative habits are their best known traits. They are always on the alert and ever vigilant to warn their less observant or more trusting companions by their loud, insistent cries of alarm that some danger is approaching. Every sportsman knows this trait and tries to avoid arousing this alarm when other, more desirable, game is likely to be frightened away. And many a yellow-legs has been shot by an angry gunner as a reward for his exasperating loquacity.

The two yellow-legs are still left on our list of game birds, because their numbers do not seem to decrease much in spite of the large numbers that are killed every year by sportsmen. William Brewster (1925) says that he has "failed to note any decided lessening of their numbers in New England during the past 30 or 40 years." This stability in numbers is probably more apparent than real. The birds have been driven from many of their former haunts by increased building of summer colonies, improvements in seashore resorts, draining and filling of marshes, and other changes; so that fewer birds can make the restricted localities seem as well populated as ever.

Spring.—The spring migration of the greater yellow-legs is well marked on both coasts and in the interior, a generally northward trend. It begins in March, reaches the northern States in April and extends through May or even into June, Although most of the birds are on their breeding grounds in May. The bulk of the flight passes through Massachusetts in May and through California in April. It seems to avoid the prairie regions of southern Canada; William Rowan tells me that he and C. G. Harrold regard it as "probably the scarcest of the regular waders. In years of steady collecting, during the height of the migration, spring and fall, he (Harrold) has seen the greater yellow-legs only half a dozen times." J. A. Munro tells me that in southern British Columbia, Okanagan Landing, it is much less common in spring than in fall; he has recorded it as early as March 23.

J. R. Whitaker writes to me from Newfoundland that he usually sees the first yellow-legs during early May: "On their first arrival the high tundras are still in the grip of winter and many of the ponds on the lower levels are partly covered with ice." John T. Nichols tells me that it is often abundant on Long Island in the spring. He says in his notes: "In May, 1919, the waters of a certain nontidal coastal creek, due to wind conditions, receded to an unprecedented lowness, leaving broad muddy shores exposed where almost always water stands. In what seemed almost a magical response to the unusual water conditions, about 100 greater yellowlegs assembled at the creek, the largest flock I have ever seen. Alighted, the birds were silent, and without the nervous *hikkuping* one associates with this species. Once all got up and circled in a compact flock to return to the mud and shallows again."

Courtship.—Mr. Whitaker writes to me:

The time for nesting varies as much as 10 days between the few pairs which frequent the lower levels and the bulk of the birds which nest on the high grounds. On the lowlands a pair of birds will take up their quarters near the place they intend to nest soon after their arrival and the cock bird may be seen high up in the air uttering his nesting song. He will sometimes be so high that he appears but a speck against the blue sky. His loud notes carry a long distance and sound like *tweda-tweda-tweda* uttered quickly and continually for quite a long time.

Dr. Charles W. Townsend (1920) writes:

The courtship song of the greater yellowlegs comes up from the marshes of Essex County throughout the month of May, but is heard in greater volume during the two middle weeks. It has a sweet and pleading character and seems to say *wull yer! wull yer!* Although it differs from the flickerlike call described in the original Memoir, which may be heard at the same time, it, too, has a decided flickerlike flavor. It is heard throughout the day, but in the evening until it is nearly dark the marshes often resound with the plaintive callings.

H. S. Swarth (1911) observed some greater yellow-legs on the wooded islands of southeastern Alaska in April, of which he says:

At this time the males were going through various courting antics, posing with upraised, quivering wings, or running in circles on the sand bars around the object of their attentions, and incessantly uttering the shrill whistle peculiar to the species.

Nesting.—Considering the fact that the greater yellow-legs is such a common and widely distributed bird, remarkably little has been published on its nesting habits, and comparatively few nests have been found, in spite of the fact that it does not go very far north to breed and its breeding grounds are fairly accessible. I know from personal experience with it that its nest is very hard to find. I have spent many hours hunting for its nest on the high tundras of central Newfoundland, where it breeds commonly, and secured only one set of eggs. The male bird is very noisy and solicitous, flying out to meet the intruder while he is a long way from the nest, alighting on any available spruce tree, stump, rock, or other eminince, pouring out a steady stream of invective cries and showing the greatest anxiety, but giving not the slightest clue as to the location of the nest. And the female sits so closely on the nest that it is only by the merest chance that she can be flushed. The high tundra around Gafftopsail and Quarry, Newfoundland, is an immense tract of boggy ground, full of small ponds and muddy splashes, interspersed with mossy hummocks and outcroppings of rocks. My set was taken there on June 9, 1912; it was in a mere hollow in the moss on a small hummock in a shallow, muddy pond hole; the female was flushed, and the four eggs were fresh.

Mr. Whitaker has sent me the following notes on the nesting habits of the greater yellow-legs in Newfoundland:

On June 17, 1919, whilst walking over a big tundra with a friend (Geo. H. Stuart, 3rd), a yellow-shank which flew up from the side of a water hole showed considerable excitement, there were a number of small ponds just there dotted with mossy islands; we beat all the ground between these ponds but could find nothing, however, we noticed that each time we approached the edge of the tundra where a stunted growth of scattered dead larch trees were, and where the wintergreen, laurel, and labrador tea bushes merged into the sphagnum of the tundra, the bird seemed more excited and flew close round our heads shrieking out his harsh notes *tee erk, tee erk, tee erk* more fiercely. We decided to hide away at some distance and watch, thinking this must be the hen bird and we would wait until she returned to the nest. We retired several hundred yards and hid in some spruces, the bird following part of the way and alighted on the top of a bush growing in the moss and there remained for upwards of an hour, then flew to a pond near, settling on an island, fed for a while, and after preening went to sleep; this seemed absolutely hopeless, so we decided to have another look over the ground. Each of us had a long pole with a handkerchief tied to the end, with these we covered all the ground which appeared suitable most thoroughly without any results. I then remembered hunting for green-shanks nests in the north of Scotland; there the nests were usually placed on a dry ridge, and seeing such a ridge near the edge of the tundra I suggested to my friend that we should go and look it over. We had not proceeded in its direction more than 10 yards when right in front of me and not more than 6 feet away on the top of a dry peat hummock amongst some scrubby tea plant squatted a yellow-shank with a downy young one on her back. I called my friend, who was only a few yards away; he came and we both watched the bird for some time before putting her up. When she did go there were four downy young in a very slight hollow without any trace of nesting material but a few leaves which had probably blown in. Amongst these we found some fragments of eggshell.

On June 6th of the following year I was out on that tundra again and worked my way towards where we had found the nest, but never saw or heard a sign of the bird. However, I went to the old nest and when within 3 feet to my astonishment saw a yellow-shank lying flat on the nest. I could hardly believe my eyes.. I watched her for some time as she sat there perfectly motionless; on putting her up, she began to scold loudly, sometimes flying close round my head and then she would perch on a dead bush near, bobbing her head, uttering *tee erk, tee erk, tee erk* all the time. Four beautiful eggs lay in the slight depression. I had been there fully 15 minutes when away in the far distance I heard another yellow-shank which quickly approached and was evidently the mate, for they both continued their abuse until I was out of sight. It very often happens that the male bird is not within miles of the incubating female, and under these conditions finding a nest is a mere fluke. There is one rule which holds good in all the nests I have found, and this is that a yellowlegs never nests on ground which is too soft to scratch in. There must be soil or dry, hard peat. I once found a nest on a boulder which had a thin covering of peat and reindeer moss on it, whilst the surrounding ground was wet and mossy, so being unsuitable for making a scratch. The nest is nearly always placed quite close to a flashet or pond of water; I have only twice seen a nest at a distance of 20 yards from any water hole.

William Brewster (1883) found the greater yellow-legs abundant on Anticosti Island in July and, although he found no eggs or young, he obtained "the strongest circumstantial evidence" that the birds were breeding there. The fact that this island has been for many years a protected sanctuary may have had some effect in keeping up the supply of these birds.

Fifty years or more ago Dr. E. W. Nelson (1877a) found several pairs of greater yellow-legs about the Calumet Marshes, which from their actions he felt sure were breeding there. He records a nest and four eggs found near Evanston, Illinois, in June, 1876; "the nest was situated in a slight depression at the base of a small hillock near the border of a prairie slough, and was composed of grass stems and blades."

Ernest S. Norman (1915) while driving over a soft and spongy spot in a swamp, in Manitoba, in which his team nearly became mired, was surprised to see a greater yellow-legs fly up from its nest within 1 foot of the front wheel of the wagon. The nest, which contained four heavily incubated eggs on June 24, is thus described:

The nest was just a depression in the moss, with a few bits of ivy grass as a lining. It had no shelter whatever, as a fire had swept over the place about a month previous to the finding of the nest so that there was not even grass growing anywhere near the nest.

Eggs.—The four eggs, usually comprising the set, of the greater yellow-legs are ovate pyriform in shape and have a slight gloss. They are rather handsomely marked and are practically indistinguishable from eggs of the European greenshank. The ordinary ground colors are pale buff, "light buff" to "cartridge buff." They are irregularly spotted and blotched, chiefly about the larger end, with dark browns, "bay," "liver brown," and "chestnut brown," and with conspicuous underlying spots and blotches of various shades of "purple-drab." An especially handsome set in my collection, one of the most beautiful sets of waders' eggs I have ever seen, is richly colored in reddish browns. The ground colors vary from "pinkish buff" to "orange-cinnamon" or "sayal brown." The four eggs are heavily and boldly marked with large, longitudinal blotches and splashes of rich browns, "claret brown," "mahogany red," and "bay," over underlying blotches, nearly concealed, of various shades of "purple drab." The measurements of 51 eggs average 48.9 by 33 millimeters; the eggs showing the four extremes measure **53.5** by 33.8, **51.8** by **35.1**, **43.7** by 31.5, and 44.9 by **30.8** millimeters.

Young.—We have no data as to the period of incubation or in what way the sexes share it. Both sexes share in the care of the young, which are brooded by the female for the first day. The young birds referred to by Mr. Whitaker had left the nest on the second day.

Plumages.—In the downy young greater yellow-legs a median stripe of "bone brown" extends from the bill upwards, increasing in width until it covers the whole of the occiput; a wide loral stripe of brownish black extends from the bill to the eye; the forehead and sides of the crown are silvery gray; and the cheeks and throat are silky white. The rest of the upper parts, hind neck to rump, are variegated or heavily blotched with "bone brown," "wood brown," and pale buff, the dark color predominating, especially on the rump. The under parts are grayish white, almost gray on the breast.

The juvenal plumage appears first on the scapulars and back and then on the breast. Two young birds, about half grown on June 30, are fully feathered on the mantle; the breast is well feathered, but covered with white downy tips, the wings are half grown, but the tail has not appeared; the crown is "bister," streaked with white; the feathers of the back, scapulars, and wing-coverts are "bister" or "warm sepia," spotted or notched with "pinkish buff" or buffy white, whitest on the upper back and most buffy on the scapulars; the sides of the neck and upper breast are streaked with and the flanks are barred with dusky; the rest of the under parts are white. This plumage is worn for three months or more, well into October. Young birds are in this plumage when they pass us on migration, but the buffy tints have mostly faded out to white.

Beginning in October a partial postjuvenal molt takes place involving the body plumage, most of the scapulars, and some of the wing coverts. This produces a first winter plumage which is similar to that of the adult, but the general tone of the upper parts is grayer and the feathers of the mantle are edged with dull white. The type of William Brewster's Lower California race, *frazari*, and most of his series of it are in this plumage.

A partial, first prenuptial molt, mainly in March and April, involving the body feathers, most scapulars, some wing coverts and usually the tail, produces a first nuptial plumage. Some adult nuptial plumage is acquired on the head, neck, and breast, but the head and neck are not so heavily streaked and there is less barring in lighter colors on the breast and flanks; but the mantle, back, and scapulars are very different from the adult winter or nuptial plumages; these feathers are more or less variegated, barred or spotted with ashy brown and dark sepia, and are notched, edged, or tipped with gray, grayish white or white, producing a rather evenly mottled appearance. This is apparently a nonbreeding plumage, for I have seen it only in birds taken far south of the breeding range. At the first postnuptial molt the following summer, which is complete, the adult winter plumage is assumed.

Adults have a partial prenuptial molt of the body plumage, usually the tail, scapulars, some tertials, and most wing coverts between February and May. In the nuptial plumage the crown is nearly all dark sepia; the mantle and scapulars are very dark sepia, almost black, notched or tipped with white spots; and the breast and flanks are heavily and irregularly barred with dark sepia. The white notches and tips wear away toward the end of the season. The complete postnuptial molt of the body plumage occurs in August and September, but the wings are not molted until winter. In adult winter plumage the crown is streaked with sepia and white about evenly; the breast and flanks are faintly marked, or peppered, with pale sepia; and the feathers of the back and scapulars are mainly plain " wood brown," with inconspicuous whitish edgings and notches.

Food.—The greater yellow-legs seems to prefer to feed in shallow water; its long legs enable it to wade in deeper water than most other waders, and it is often seen using them to their full extent in water up to its body. It moves about nimbly and gracefully, actively engaged in catching small minnows and water insects, delicately balanced on its long legs, bowing or nodding, as if its body were on a pivot, in a very pleasing manner. Much of its food seems to consist of small minnows, in pursuit of which it is very active and lively. Mr. Nichols has sent me the following notes on the subject:

The greater yellowlegs at times catches killifish up to as large a size as it can swallow, wading in water as deep as it can stand. Having secured a fish, it manipulates same up its long bill and into its mouth. Sometimes it catches a fish tangled in a mass of fine water weed, and in this case may either fiddle with and disengage it, or work it up to its mouth and swallow it before disengaging the bill from the weed. I have seen an unusually large fish, probably (*Fundulus heteroclitus*), worked up the bird's bill two or three times and turned head first to swallow, stick at the base of the bill, and drop into the water again. Finally, with a great bulging of face and throat, the fish slipped down.

Satisfied for the moment, the bird rose and flew to the leeward end of the pond hole where it had been feeding, alighted, walked up the bank, and stood in a tuft of partly dry grass at the edge of the water, quietly facing out into the breeze for some twenty minutes, although all the time alert and watchful. In this sheltered position it would not have been noticed unless known to be there.

Dr. Paul Bartsch (1899) found a greater yellow-legs in the Washington market whose throat was jammed full of top minnows. He says that many times he has " watched this bird wade out into the shallow water of the bars, moving along slowly with tilting gait, suddenly lower that long head and neck and proceed to run through the water at a speed which would have done credit to a college sprinter, quickly striking to right and left with his bill." Others have noted a similar performance.

I have occasionally seen greater yellow-legs on damp, grassy meadows where they were probably feeding on insects or their larvae, snails, worms, or crustaceans, all of which have been found in their stomachs. Lucien M. Turner refers in his notes to a bird he shot at the mouth of the Koksoak River, Ungava, on September 18, 1882, which had been feeding on the berries of *Empetrum nigrum.*

Three birds collected by Stuart T. Danforth (1925) had eaten exclusively animal matter: " The recognizable fragments were: Dragon-fly naiads, 65.33 per cent; aquatic Hemiptera (*Belostoma* species), 22 per cent; fish scales (*Poecilia vivipara*), 6.0 per cent; Dytiscid larvae, 0.66 per cent."

Behavior.—The flight of the greater yellow-legs is quite swift, strong, and well sustained on the downward and sweeping strokes of its long, pointed, dark-colored wings. Its long neck and bill extended forward and its long, yellow legs stretched out behind give it a slender, rakish appearance which is quite distinctive. It usually flies at a good elevation and when traveling it often flies at a great height. It scans the ground beneath, looking for a suitable place to feed or searching for desirable companions. It responds readily to the call of its own species and will often answer an imitation of its notes from a great distance; sometimes when it is too far away to be seen. When coming in from a distance it usually flies in wide circles around the caller several times until it is satisfied that it is safe to alight. It then comes zig-zagging or scaling down on downcurved wings and settles lightly near its would-be companions. On alighting it stands for a moment with its wings extended upward in a graceful attitude, folds them deliberately, gives a few jerky bows or upward nods, and then either begins to feed or settles down to rest. It is not very particular as to its companions; it associates freely with any of the smaller waders that frequent the mud flats, meadows, or shallow ponds; it seems to be particularly fond of the companionship of the teals when they are feeding in shallow water.

It is not as gregarious as the lesser yellow-legs; it is most often seen singly or in small parties, but I have counted as many as 40 in a flock on rare occasions.

When walking on the ground its movements are lively and its carriage is graceful, though its long legs seem to give it a somewhat jerky gait at times. On its breeding ground it often alights on the tops of spruce or larch trees, or on bushes or dead stubs, on which it balances rather awkwardly. It is normally a shy and wary species; large flocks are very difficult to approach; but sometimes single individuals seem to be absurdly tame in the presence of other tame species or among decoys. Some good photographs of it have been taken at short range. William Brewster (1925) tells of one that he approached in the open to within ten feet and then fired his gun directly over it without causing it to fly. Mr. Nichols suggests, in his notes:

It would seem almost as though these birds drew an abstract danger line, difficult to cross from the outside without alarming them, but once inside which, man became to them a mere harmless item of the landscape. I have had a greater yellowlegs, a bird of the year, come to decoys (under the impression that they were others of its kind) and as the water was too deep, alight and stand on one of the decoys, recognizing in it a piece of wood, meanwhile being remarkably tame, perhaps waiting for others of the flock (of decoys) to take alarm. Is not this pragmatic rather than rational philosophy which they possess, the weakness most in favor of the gunner who hunts shore birds with decoys?

He also adds the following notes on behavior:

I have seen the greater yellowlegs preen its plumage in leisurely manner without repeatedly dipping the bill in the water, as the lesser frequently does. It reached far back over its shoulder, lifted a wing slightly to pick under it, stretched its neck up to reach the breast with its bill, and scratched its chin deliberately with the right foot. On another occasion a bathing bird crouched down in shallow water, ducking the head and at the same time fluttering and splashing vigorously with the wings.

A resting bird stands at ease, neck hunched down, with slight alert movements of the head. From time to time it may turn its bill back and bury it in the feathers along the back with a little shake of same, one eye at least exposed and open though blinking sleepily. An interesting pose which may be assumed for two or three minutes is with the bill resting diagonally downward across the feathers of the breast. It may stand for a long time on one motionless straight leg, inclined so as to bring the foot under its center of gravity, the other leg raised and concealed by the feathers.

Though a wounded lesser yellowlegs will sometimes dive and swim under water, I have not seen the smaller species alight in spots too deep for wading. The greater yellowlegs on the other hand does so not infrequently. It swims gracefully with phalaropelike motion of the neck, held erect, stern tilted up like that of a gull. In shallow water over mud so soft and sticky that it made wading difficult I have seen a bird launch itself forward, swimming, as the easier method of propulsion.

Voice.—Mr. Nichols (1920) has published the results of a detailed study of the vocabularies of the two yellow-legs, which are noted for the variety of their calls. He has recognized and described nine different calls of the greater yellow-legs, as follows:

(1) The yodle (a rolling *toowhee toowhee*, etc.) is commonest in a flock from birds remaining in one locality, not traveling. I think I have heard it from a single bird in the fog. It is characteristically given in the air, generally with set wings, by birds which seem to contemplate alighting. It advertises birds tarrying in one general locality, and has probably the function of *location* notice. It is doubtless homologous with the gather call of the spotted sandpiper with which it has little analogy.

(2) Loud ringing 3, *wheu wheu wheu*. The characteristic cry of the species, spring and fall. It is commonly given by passing or leaving birds. It advertises the species—and a change of policy in the individual according to its loudness. Analogous with notes of other species spoken of as *flight notes* or identification notes; occasionally heard from an alighted bird. This call is subject to considerable variation, when heard from a bird about to drop down and join others feeding it is comparatively low-pitched and even, leaving or about to leave a feeding ground, highly modulated.

(3) Four *wheus*, heard as follows, seem to have a rather definite significance; low, hurried, descending, heard from a bird leaving companion; short, clear, four, by a following bird; loud, four, bird without intention of alighting, trying to flush decoys. This may be called a *recruiting* call.

(4) Twos (*wheu wheu*) seem to be characteristic of a *recruit*. A "gentle" bird which comes nicely to decoys is apt to call in twos when approaching and coming in.

(5) Rarely, in taking wing in the presence of an intruder, a single bird utters a string of unmodulated *wheus* which breaks up into threes or fours as it goes off. This is likely a note of *protest*, which would be more common in the breeding season.

(6) Conversational murmuring, from a flock dropping in, expresses *companionship* and confidence.

(7) Conversational *chup* notes from birds about to alight, also heard from birds alighted, moving about at ease. The *alighting* note.

(8) Unloud *chups* identical with the preceding but more hurried, given by a small flock of birds as they take wing. The *flushing* note.

(9) *Kyow*, common in spring, only rarely heard in southward migration; probably associated with the breeding season; seems to express *suspicion*.

Different renderings of some of the above notes have been given by others. Mr. Brewster (1883) describes a note heard on the breeding grounds as "an incessant *clack-clack-clack-clack*, which sounded very like the clatter of a mowing machine." He then goes on to say: "In addition to the cry already described, they uttered a rolling *pheu-pheu-phe*, *pheu-pheu-phe*, repeated a dozen times or more in quick succession; a mellow *pheu, pheu, pheu*, resembling the whistle of the fish hawk; and a soft, hollow *hoo, whoo, whoo*, very like the cooing of a dove. The latter note was given only when the bird perched on the top of some tall spruce."

Field marks.—The greater yellow-legs resembles the lesser so closely in color pattern that the two can not be readily distinguished except by direct comparison in size. The bill of the greater is relatively larger, and it is rather more boldly marked. The voices of the two are somewhat different. Other characters are referred to under the next species.

Fall.—Adults move off their breeding grounds at an early date and loiter along in a leisurely manner. The first migrants appear in the northern states in July, sometimes as early as the second or even the first week. Young birds come later; there is usually a heavy flight of them during the first half of October, and many linger in Massachusetts until the middle of November or later. Mr. Brewster (1925) says of the migration at Umbagog Lake, Maine:

We often saw them arriving and departing by day, usually in the early morning or late afternoon if the weather were fine, at almost any time if it were stormy. When seen approaching from farther north, they were commonly first sighted so high in the air that they looked no bigger than swallows. After circling twice or thrice over the lake on set wings, whistling loudly and volubly, they were likely to pitch headlong into the marshes to feed and rest there during the remainder of the day, if not for a considerably longer period, provided no gunner happened to fare that way. Some, however, kept straight on without stopping and perhaps without lowering their line of flight below the level of the mountain tops to the southward over which they were accustomed to pass."

Mr. Whitaker tells me that the last of the yellow-shanks move out of Newfoundland about the end of October; these are probably all young birds. And Edward S. Thomas sends me a record for Columbus, Ohio, of December 11, 1925. This bird well deserves the name of " winter yellowlegs."

Probably many migrate at sea, from Nova Scotia to the West Indies, for Capt. Savile G. Reid (1884) says that it is " more or less common " in Bermuda, " arriving early in August and remaining for a month or so," where it is " much in request among the energetic sportsmen."

Game.—The greater yellow-legs is a fine game bird; I can not say as much for the lesser yellow-legs. Large numbers have been shot in past years. Prof. Wells W. Cooke (1912) says: "A hunter near Newport, Rhode Island, shot 1,362 greater yellow-legs in the eight seasons, 1867–1874; his highest score, 419 birds, was in 1873, from August 19 to October 19." Dr. Charles W. Townsend (1905) reports that " 463 greater yellow-legs were sent from Newburyport and vicinity on one day, October 11, 1904, to a single stall in Boston market." I knew an old gunner who celebrated his eightieth birthday a few years ago by shooting 40 yellow-legs.

It is a pity that the delightful sport of bay-bird shooting, which was such a pleasant feature of our earlier shooting days, had to be gradually restricted. Hudsonian curlew, and black-bellied and golden plover and greater yellow-legs were all fine game birds. I could see no reason for cutting out the curlew, as it is well able to take care of itself; golden plover were sadly depleted in numbers and black-bellied plover and both yellow-legs were decreasing; perhaps it was wise to eliminate them all.

Those were glorious days that we used to spend on the marshes of Cape Cod. On the inner, or bay, side of Monomoy are extensive marshes, meadows, sand flats, and mud flats, 9 miles in length and nearly a mile wide in places at low tide. These were great feeding resorts for hosts of shore birds; and in the good old days, when there were shore birds to shoot and when we were allowed to shoot them, blinds were scattered all along the marshes and flats. On a dry sand spit or beach a hole was dug in the sand and seaweed was piled up around it high enough to conceal a sitting gunner; on a wet marsh a substantial blind was built of brush, with a seat in it for two men; in some places in the meadows, where the grass grew high, a box or a board to sit on was all the gunner needed. Wooden or tin decoys painted to imitate yellow-legs or plover were set up in the sand or mud, all facing the wind and within easy range. Here in a comfortable blind the hunter could lounge at ease, bask in the genial sun of early autumn, smoke his pipe and meditate, or watch the many interesting things about him, the rich autumn colors of the marsh vegetation, the ever-changing picture of sky and sea, the black terns and the swallows winnowing the meadows, the gulls and the terns over the sea and the flocks of small waders running over the mud flats. Suddenly he is awakened from his reveries by the well-known note of the winter yellow-legs and discerns a mere speck in the distant sky; he whistles an imitation of its note; the bird answers him and, looking for companionship, circles nearer; by judicious calling the bird is attracted within sight of the decoys and, after several cautious circlings, it sets its wings and scales down to the decoys, where it meets its fate. Perhaps a whole flock may slip in unexpectedly, wheel over the decoys and hurry away, giving the gunner only a hurried chance for a quick shot. Perhaps a curlew may fly over or a flock of beetle-heads fly swiftly by; the gunner must be ready for all such chances. There is an ever-changing panorama of bird life on the marshes, full of surprises and delights for the nature lover.

Winter.—The greater yellow-legs has a wide winter range, from the southern United States, where it is comparatively rare, to southern South America, where most of the birds seem to go. W. H. Hudson (1920) says:

The greater yellow-legs is best known as an Arctic-American species, descending south during migration, and arriving in La Plata at the end of September or early in October, singly or in pairs, and sometimes in small flocks. Without ever being abundant the bird is quite common, and one can seldom approach a pool or marsh on the pampas without seeing one or more individuals wading near the margin, and hearing their powerful alarm cry—a long, clear note repeated three times. These summer visitors leave us in March, and then, oddly enough, others arrive, presumably from the south to winter on the pampas, and remain from April to August. Thus, notwithstanding that the yellow-shanks does not breed on the pampas, we have it with us all the year 'round.

Dr. Alexander Wetmore (1926) saw it in Paraguay as early as September 8 and in Chile as late as April 26. He writes:

After their arrival in September greater yellow-legs were distributed throughout the open pampa wherever shallow ponds offered suitable feeding places. Occasionally 10 or 20 gathered in a flock, especially when northward migration was under way in March and April, but when on their wintering grounds it was usual to find two or three in company, seldom more. They are rather silent during the winter season but when the northward journey begins are as noisy as is their custom in the north. The species is large so that it is attractive to pot hunters and many are killed. I saw a number of crippled birds during the last two months of my stay in Argentina and consider that it is these injured individuals, unable to perform the necessary flight, or without desire to do so from their injuries, that are recorded on the pampas from May to August when all should be in the Northern Hemisphere. Reports of their breeding in Argentina, based on the presence of these laggards in migration are wholly unauthenticated.

I am inclined to think that most of the birds that remain in the South from April to September are one-year-old birds which are not ready to breed.

DISTRIBUTION

Range.—North and South America.

Breeding range.—The breeding range of the greater yellow-legs extends north to Alaska (Bethel); British Columbia (Fort St. James); Mackenzie (Peel River); Alberta (Island Lake); Manitoba (Kalcoala); Labrador (Whale River and Hopedale); and Newfoundland (Gaff Topsail). East to Newfoundland (Gaff Topsail). South to Newfoundland (Gaff Topsail); Quebec (Natashquan River, Anticosti Island, and near Mt. Laurier); probably formerly Illinois (Evanston); and British Columbia (Clinton). West to British Columbia (Clinton, Fort George, and Fort St. James).

They also appear to occur in summer with more or less regularity north to Alaska (St. Paul Island, Bethel, and Nome); Keewatin (near Cape Eskimo); and Franklin (Cumberland Sound); and non-breeding specimens have at this season been noted south to the Bahama Islands (Great Abaco); Florida (Key West, Sarasota Bay, and Ponce Park); Alabama (Leighton); Texas (Amarillo, Lipscomb, Pecos, and Corpus Christi); and California (Fresno, Santa Barbara, and Nigger Slough).

Winter range.—North rarely to Washington (Dungeness Spit);
rarely Arizona (Fort Verde and Bill Williams River); Texas (Tom
Green and Concho Counties, Boerne, San Antonio, and Refugio
County); Louisiana (Abbeville, Avery Island, and New Orleans);
and probably Virginia (Hog Island). East probably to Virginia
(Hog Island and Sandy Island); probably North Carolina (Corolla
and Pea Island); South Carolina (Ladys Island and Frogmore);
Georgia (Blackbeard Island, Darien, and St. Marys); Florida
(Amelia Island, Daytona Beach, Miakka, and the Florida Keys);
the Bahama Islands (Andros, New Providence, and Inagua Islands);
probably Porto Rico; the Lesser Antilles (Antigua, Barbados, and
Grenada); French Guiana (Cayenne); Brazil (Para, Cajetuba,
Iguape, Pelotas, and Rio Grande do Sul); Uruguay (Lazcano, San
Vicente, and Colonia); and Argentina (Buenos Aires, Azul, Carhue,
and Bahia Blanca). South to Argentina (Bahia Blanca); Chile
(Straits of Magellan, Valparaiso, Paposo, and Antofagasta); Peru
(Lake Titicaca, Tinta, and Chorillos); Ecuador (Cuenca, Canar, and
Quito); Colombia (Bogota, Medellin, and Cartagena); Costa Rica
(San Jose and Puntarenas); Guatemala (Lake Atitlan); Jalisco
(Guadalajara); Sinaloa (Escuinapa); Lower California (San Jose
del Cabo, La Paz, and San Quintin); California (San Diego, Long
Beach, Santa Barbara, and the San Joaquin Valley); and rarely
Washington (Dungeness Spit). Greater yellow-legs also have been
reported as wintering on the coast of British Columbia (Macoun).

Spring migration.—Early dates of spring arrival are: Maryland,
Patapsco Marsh, March 26; Pennsylvania, Carlisle, March 19, and
Erie, March 28; New Jersey, Cape May, March 18, and Camden,
April 4; New York, Jamaica, March 20, Lowville, March 22, and
Montauk Point, March 23; Connecticut, West Haven, March 25, and
Fairfield, April 9; Massachusetts, Taunton, April 4, and Cambridge,
April 15; Maine, Pittsfield, April 26; Quebec, Quebec, April 18,
Godbout, April 26, Montreal, May 4, and Lake Mistassini, May 7;
Missouri, Kansas City, March 2, Corning, March 19, and Jasper City,
March 24; Illinois, Englewood, March 19, Tampico, March 22, and
Lebanon, March 29; Indiana, Terre Haute, March 19, Indianapolis,
March 22, and Vincennes, March 30; Ohio, Waverly, March 14, and
Columbus, February 21; Michigan, Bay City, March 26, Ann Arbor,
March 30, and Hillsdale, March 31; Ontario, Ottawa, March 25,
Toronto, March 26, and Blair, April 10; Iowa, Storm Lake, March 20,
La Porte, March 21, and Keokuk, March 26; Wisconsin, Delavan,
March 30, Madison, April 3, and Milwaukee, April 10; Minnesota,
Wilder, March 30, and Waseca, April 10; Oklahoma, Caddo, March
11; Kansas, Manhattan, March 11, Emporia, March 26, and Wichita,
April 6; Nebraska, Falls City, March 22, Valentine, April 6, and
Lincoln April 10; South Dakota, Sioux Falls, March 27, and Harri-

son, April 7; North Dakota, Bathgate, April 15, and Grafton, April 19; Manitoba, Aweme, April 10, Ossowo, April 15, and Reaburn, April 16; Saskatchewan, McLean, April 29, and Indian Head, May 3; Mackenzie, Fort Simpson, May 16; Colorado, Barr, March 29, and Colorado Springs, April 10; Utah, Salt Lake, April 7; Wyoming, Fort Sanders, April 20, and Yellowstone Park, April 28; Idaho, Meridian, April 14, and Rupert, April 20; Montana, Great Falls, April 6, and Helena, April 9; Alberta, Onoway, April 13, Alliance, April 26, and Carvel, April 30; and British Columbia, Chilliwack, March 28, and Okanagan Landing, March 23.

Late dates of spring departures are: Argentina, Tucuman, April 5; Chile, Concon, April 26; Florida, Daytona Beach, April 10, Bassenger, April 16, Indian River, April 23, and Pensacola, May 2; Alabama, Leighton, May 15; Georgia, Cumberland, April 17 and Savannah, April 20; South Carolina, Chester, April 21, and Ladys Island, May 5; North Carolina, Lake Ellis, May 18, Cape Hatteras, May 20, and Raleigh, May 29; Virginia, Cobb Island, May 19, Wallops Island, May 26, and Cape Charles, May 27; Bermuda, June 5; District of Columbia, Washington, May 20; Pennsylvania, Erie, May 25, Tinicum, May 26, and Jeffersonville, May 27; New Jersey, Camden, May 25, mouth of Pensauken Creek, May 30, and Elizabeth, June 9; New York, Geneva, June 1, Orient Point, June 11, and Gardiners Island, June 18; Connecticut, Litchfield, June 9, Fairfield, June 12, and Hadlyme, June 15; Massachusetts, Marthas Vineyard, June 14, and Monomoy Island, June 16; Louisiana, New Orleans, April 27; Tennessee, Nashville, May 24; Illinois, Addison, May 23, and La Grange, May 25; Indiana, Richmond, May 20, and English Lake, June 3; Ohio, Columbus, May 27, and Berlin Center, May 27; Michigan, Neebish Island, May 20, and Detroit, May 25; Ontario, London, May 24, and Toronto, June 9; Iowa, Sioux City, May 19, and Keokuk, June 5; Wisconsin, North Freedom, May 24, and La Crosse, June 4; Minnesota, Lake Wilson, May 20, and Madison, May 31; Texas, Brownsville, April 28, and Point Isabel, May 14; Nebraska, Peru, May 15, Neligh, May 26, and Whitman, June 1; South Dakota, Forestburg, May 21, and Harrison, May 28; Manitoba, Reaburn, May 18, Winnipeg, May 20, and Whitewater Lake, June 5; Saskatchewan, McLean, May 18, South Qu'Appelle, May 27; Arizona, Fort Verde, May 3; Colorado, Durango, May 11, Barr, May 11; Wyoming, Laramie, May 29; Montana, Choteau, May 19, and Terry, May 27; Lower California, Hardy River, April 15; California, Santa Barbara, May 16, Los Angeles, May 19, and Buena Park, May 22; Oregon, Cold Spring Bird Reserve, May 12; and Washington, Clallam Bay, May 24.

Fall migration.—Early dates of arrival in the fall are: Washington, Tacoma, July 4, and Granville, July 7; Oregon, Malheur Lake,

July 1; California, Fresno, July 5, Santa Barbara, July 18, and Dunlap, July 30; Montana, Milk River, July 24; Wyoming, Laramie River, August 4, and Yellowstone Park, August 17; Utah, Utah Lake, July 26; Colorado, Barr, June 27; Arizona, Fort Verde, July 29; Chihuahua, Tachaco, July 30; Saskatchewan, Crane Lake, June 22, and McLean, July 5; Manitoba, Franklin, July 17, Margaret, July 30, and Oak Lake, August 4; South Dakota, Harding County, July 19, and Forestburg, July 22; Texas, Corpus Christi, July 3, and near Amarillo, July 27; Minnesota, Hallock, July 19, and St. Vincent, July 20; Wisconsin, Madison, July 29, and Racine, July 30; Iowa, Sioux City, August 14, and Winthrop, August 20; Ontario, Toronto, July 28; Michigan, Jackson, July 19, Isle Royale, August 1, Sault Ste. Marie, August 7, and Ann Arbor, August 14; Ohio, Columbus, July 12, Pelee Island, July 24, and Dayton, August 2; Illinois, Addison, July 19, Chicago, July 23, and Rantoul, July 26; Louisiana, Louisiana Branch, August 16; Maine, Pittsfield, July 26; Massachusetts, Cape Cod, July 11, and Marthas Vineyard, July 22; Rhode Island, Block Island, July 9; Connecticut, Milford, July 28; New York, Montauk Point, July 10, East Hampton, July 16, and Rochester, July 18; New Jersey, Barnegat Bay, July 13, and Five-mile Beach, July 15; Pennsylvania, Erie, July 28; District of Columbia, Washington, July 24; North Carolina, Pea and Bodie Islands, July 22; South Carolina, Ladys Island, July 21, and Frogmore, August 8; Alabama, Leighton, July 22; and Florida, Ponce Park, July 12, Palma Sola, August 2, and Key West, August 20. The southern part of the winter range is reached early in September; Paraguay, Puerto Pinasco, September 8.

Late dates of fall departure are: British Columbia, Comox, October 28, and Chilliwack, November 21; Nevada, Washoe Lake, November 6; Alberta, Fort Chipewyan, October 9, and Camrose, October 16; Montana, Great Falls, October 20; Idaho, Meridian, November 12; Wyoming, Fort Bridger, October 14, and Medicine Bow, October 24; Colorado, Denver, October 3, and Barr, October 29; Manitoba, Margaret, October 20, Oak Lake, October 27, and Aweme, November 5; North Dakota, Marstonmoor, October 27; South Dakota, Forestburg, October 22, and South Dakota, Forestburg, October 22, and Sioux Falls, October 29; Nebraska, Lincoln, November 14; Kansas, Emporia, October 12; Minnesota, Madison, October 22, St. Vincent, October 25, and Lanesboro, November 12; Wisconsin, Delavan, October 22, and North Freedom, November 8; Iowa, Emmetsburg, October 22, and Keokuk, November 9; Ontario, Ottawa November 15, Toronto, November 19, and Port Dover, November ? Michigan, Ann Arbor, October 22, Sault Ste. Marie, Novemb and Manchester, November 7; Ohio, Painesville, October 30, C bus, December 11, and Youngstown, November 12; Indiana, Lafay-ette, October 21; Illinois, Addison, October 22, and La Grange, October 28; Missouri, Independence, November 7; Kentucky, Bowling Green, November 22; Franklin, Arctic Island, Cumberland Sound, September 14; Quebec, Montreal, October 25; Maine, Skowhegan, October 24, and Scarboro, November 5; Massachusetts, Dennis, November 1, Monomoy Island, November 12, and Marthas Vineyard, November 20; Rhode Island, Newport, November 4; Connecticut, Fairfield, October 31, and Portland, December 11; New York, Orient, November 12, Montauk Point, November 20, and Branch-port, November 20; New Jersey, Elizabeth, October 30, and Five-mile Beach, November 7; Pennsylvania, Beaver, November 6; League Island, November 9, and State College, November 14; Maryland, Back River, November 13; District of Columbia, Washington, November 2; and Bermuda, November 10.

Casual records.—The greater yellow-legs has been detected outside of the range above outlined on but one occasion, a specimen taken at Tresco Abbey, Scilla Islands, England, on September 16, 1906.

Egg dates.—Newfoundland and Labrador: 9 records, June 9 to 20. British Columbia: 2 records, May 20 and 21.

TOTANUS FLAVIPES (Gmelin)

LESSER YELLOW-LEGS

HABITS

The lesser or "summer" yellow-legs is a smaller edition of the greater or "winter" yellow-legs, and both are quite similar in behavior. The lesser is more abundant and less shy, hence rather better known. The seasonal names, applied to them by gunners, have been well chosen, as the lesser comes to us in summer and the greater lingers with us almost into winter. Both have the exasperating telltale habit of arousing the neighborhood by their loud cries of alarm.

Spring.—The lesser yellow-legs is a rare bird in New England in the spring. The main flight from South America passes through the West Indies to the Southern States and then northward through the Mississippi Valley to the breeding grounds in central Canada. I have seen birds in Florida as early as February 27; these may have been wintering birds, for the main flight there comes during the latter part of March. I have seen birds in Texas as late as May 17. C. J. Pennock's migration dates for Delaware run from April 23 to May 29, where it is a regular spring migrant. Long Island marks about its northern limit on the Atlantic coast in spring. It usually arrives in southern Manitoba about the middle or last of April;

A. G. Lawrence sends me an unusually early record for Whitewater Lake, April 8, 1925. From the first to the middle of May it arrives on its breeding grounds in northern Alberta and farther north, as far as the limit of trees. Dr. Joseph Grinnell (1900) writes:

This proved to be a common bird in the Kowak Valley. Its arrival was noted in the vicinity of our winter camp on May 19, and from that day on its presence could hardly be overlooked, for as one approached their domains the yellowlegs would fly to meet him, uttering prolonged, monotonous cries. Besides these notes of alarm the males had a full, melodious warble, sung for minutes at a time as they flew slowly about overhead. Their favorite haunts appeared to be the meadows lying between strips of timber, especially if there was a shallow lake or pond in the vicinity.

Nesting.—MacFarlane recorded in his notes some 30 nests of this yellow-legs, found by him and his men in the wooded country about Fort Anderson and its vicinity from 1862 to 1866. He speaks of it as " a very noisy bird " that " will keep going before one, from tree to tree, for several hundred yards beyond its nest." One nest is described as "near a lake, a small hole in the ground, with a few decayed willow leaves underneath the eggs "; another nest was " about 150 yards from a lake, on a rising, thinly wooded piece of ground "; another was " on the face of a low hill, or rising ground, in the midst of a tuft of hay, or rather of a 'tête-de-femme,' made of a very few dead leaves in a depression "; others were "underneath or shaded by some stunted willows on the borders of a swampy tract, lined with a few withered grasses."

J. Fletcher Street (1923) has published an interesting account of the nesting habits of this species in Alberta, from which I quote as follows:

As Mr. Thomson had told us we found the chosen nesting site of the yellow-legs to be on relatively high ground at an elevation from a few feet to a possible 30 feet or more above the level of the ponds. Invariably the nests were found not closer than 100 feet from the water's edge and sometimes as far away as 200 yards. Generally a sloping bank, a ridge or a level plateau was chosen for the immediate nesting site. No nests were noted in the heavily forested area; all of those secured in the region about Belvedere being found among broken hills covered with burnt and fallen timber with a second growth largely of low poplars, the burnt stubs affording excellent perches for the birds. Therefore the assumption would be that amid normal conditions the species would select rather open and high woodlands with sparse, low undergrowth within a reasonable distance of marshy or grassy ponds.

It is not until the full clutch of eggs is laid that the birds show that degree of concern which leads to their undoing. Then there is great excitement on the nesting grounds. The female bird will fly about with drooping legs and tail, keeping up an incessant *kip, kip,* and alighting upon near-by stubs. In this the male will join her, but not to the same degree, frequently, after the initial rally, flying away to the lake. His darker breast markings and slightly larger size readily identify him. If the observer retires and conceals himself the excitement of the female will gradually subside, she will fly from stub to stub, at length become silent, look about inquiringly and take a short flight to the ground and run to the nest. After settling she may be approached within 4 feet before flushing which she does with a loud call of alarm. While on the nest she sits low and close.

The nest is a mere depression in the ground, lined with a few leaves or a small amount of dry grass, the cup having a diameter of 3.5 to 4 inches and a depth of 1.25 to 1.50 inches. It may be located next to a stub, along a prostrate log or in the open.

Richard C. Harlow, who collected with Mr. Street in the same region, tells me that this bird will sometimes scratch out several hollows within a radius of 50 or 75 yards and line some of them with dry aspen leaves before laying in the one selected. Three of the nests found by Mr. Harlow were close to or between fallen burnt logs and one was in a bushy situation in a clearing near the edge of some woods. The nests were lined with dry leaves of poplar and aspen and a few dry grasses. One set that he collected for me was at the base of a small bush on dry barrens, half a mile from water. Richard H. Rauch in the same general locality found a nest in what he calls an unusual location, 10 yards from the margin of a small lake in a very wet muskeg; the nest was a depression in the moss, lined with a few dry birch leaves.

Eggs.—The yellow-legs lays four eggs, occasionally only three. These are ovate pyriform in shape and have a slight gloss. The ground colors usually vary from "olive-buff" to "cream-buff" and rarely from "honey yellow" to "cartridge buff," or from "light pinkish cinnamon" to "pinkish buff." The more richly colored eggs are often boldly and handsomely marked. Some are quite evenly covered with small blotches and spots; others also have large, irregular blotches and splashes, chiefly about the larger end and often with a spiral trend. These markings are in dark rich browns, "chocolate," "liver brown," "bay," and "chestnut brown," sometimes deepening almost to black, where the pigment is thickest. Many large underlying blotches and spots of various shades of "purple-drab" and "ecru-drab" are conspicuous and add to the beauty of the eggs. There is an albino egg in the national collection, creamy white with only a few small pale brown spots. The measurements of 51 eggs average 42 by 28.9 millimeters; the eggs showing the four extremes measure **45** by **30, 42** by **30.5, 39.5** by 29.5, and 41 by **27.5** millimeters.

Young.—Incubation is shared by both sexes, but we have no information as to its duration. MacFarlane found a pair of yellowlegs with three recently hatched young "in a small watery swamp," where the young were able to conceal themselves in the short grass. Mr. Street (1923) says:

Young were found for the first time on June 4. Both male and female at this time were highly excited, the female approaching within 10 feet of us.

All the young had left the nest and had taken refuge in the shade of a log to escape the burning rays of the sun. No eggshells were found in the nest or near by. As we retired from the immediate locality the female flew down to the ground and softly "kipped" as if to rally the scattered young. On the succeeding day a nest was found which at 10 a. m. contained one young and two eggs. At 12.30 p. m. all the birds had hatched and had left the nest, being found quite a distance away. One bird was walking, readily indicating that the migration to the water must start within a few hours of the time that the young are out of the eggs.

After June 6 all the same excitement that characterized the action of the adult birds at the nesting site was transplanted to the meadow lands. One uninitiated in the ways of the species might easily suppose that he was now upon the breeding grounds, for the young keep well concealed and are difficult to discover. Perhaps the exhibition of the adults at this time and the secretive habits of the birds during the early days of the mating have tended to keep the nesting habits of the lesser yellowlegs so long a mystery.

Plumages.—In natal down the young yellow-legs is "pinkish buff" on the back, shading off to "cartridge buff" on the crown, to paler buff on the forehead and sides of the head and to pure white on the under parts; there is an indistinct frontal black stripe; the crown is heavily mottled with brownish black; a black stripe extends from the bill through the eye to the nape; and there are three broad bands on the center and sides of the back and large patches on the rump and thighs of brownish black.

Young birds develop rapidly, the juvenal plumage coming in first on the sides of the breast, scapulars, and wings. A young bird, taken July 10, is nearly fully grown; the crown and neck fully feathered, the breast nearly so, and the wings and tail nearly grown. In this fresh juvenal plumage the feathers of the crown are tipped with whitish, and those of the back, scapulars, and wing coverts are edged, tipped, or notched with pale buff to white.

Subsequent molts and plumages are similar to and very much like those of the greater yellow-legs. I have seen a number of birds in what I call the first nuptial plumage migrating northward; they may breed in this plumage. I have seen several adults molting their primaries in January and February.

Food.—The favorite feeding grounds of the yellow-legs are on flat marshes near the coast, where the grass is short and where the high course of tides or heavy rains leave the marshes partially covered, or dotted, with shallow pools or splashes; away from the coast it is equally at home in wet, short-grass marshes, mud flats, shallow ponds and even wet places in cultivated fields. In such places it walks about in an active manner, usually in shallow water, but often up to the full length of its long legs, gleaning most of its food from the surface of the water or mud and seldom probing for it. During one season on Monomoy large numbers of yellow-legs frequented the drier parts of the meadows where the long grass had been beaten down flat by the storms of the previous winter. These places seemed to hold some strong attraction for them, for they repeatedly returned after being driven off. While we remained partially concealed in some clumps of tall grass, they frequently alighted near us and ran nimbly about over the flattened grass, darting rapidly in various directions to pick up food. The grass was full of minute grasshoppers and other small insects on which they were feeding. Evidently this food was unusually abundant that season, for I have never seen them there in any numbers since 1921.

Arthur H. Howell (1924) says that, in Alabama, "this bird feeds mainly on insects, including ants, bugs, flies, and grasshoppers, and on small crustaceans, small fishes and worms." Dr. Alexander Wetmore (1916) reporting on the food of four birds, taken in Porto Rico, says that "water boatmen found in each of the four make 57.5 per cent, and two stomachs contained nothing else. Crustacean remains, among which were several crabs, were identified in two stomachs, and make the remainder, 42.5 per cent."

The contents of nine stomachs taken by Stuart T. Danforth (1925) in Porto Rico were examined:

Dytiscid larvae formed 26.6 per cent of the animal matter, and Hydrophilid larvae, 1.8 per cent; Bloodworms, 5.1 per cent; Planorbia snails, 5 per cent; Fleabeetles 1.1 per cent; Hydrophilid adults, 3.1 per cent; Dytiscid adult, 0.7 per cent; grasshoppers, 0.22 per cent; Bupestrid beetle, 0.55 per cent; Lycosid spider, 0.55 per cent; Notonectidae, 1 per cent; fish scales, 0.33 per cent; Carabid beetle (Stenous sp.), 0.55 per cent; and other beetles, 3.2 per cent.

Behavior.—Either in flight or on the ground the two yellow-legs are so much alike that one is often mistaken for the other, unless a direct comparison in size can be made. William Brewster (1925) has expressed it very well, as follows:

The summer yellow-legs seems an exact counterpart of the winter in respect to general appearance and behavior. It has the same firm, measured step, when walking about in quest of food; the same perfection of form and outlines, and grace of position, when standing erect and watchful; the same habit of tilting its body and alternately lengthening and shortening its neck with a bobbing motion, when suspicious of danger and about to take wing. Its flight, also, is essentially similar to that of its big cousin, but somewhat slower and more buoyant, and hence not so suggestive of momentum as that of the larger, heavier-bodied bird.

The lesser yellow-legs is more universally common than the greater and more apt to associate with other species of small waders, where it towers above them, as it stalks gracefully about on its long legs. It is more apt to be seen in large flocks, though the flocks are seldom compact and are usually much scattered, especially when feeding. And it is much less shy; although usually rather watchful and wary, not easily approached by a moving object, it is often surprisingly tame. If the observer is sitting down and motionless, even in plain sight, the birds will often fly back and forth over him or even alight on the ground near him.

I have often seen yellow-legs bathing, but Aretas A. Saunders (1926) describes it better than I can, as follows:

To do this a bird would go to the deeper, clearer water forming the mid-channel of the pond, the same spot where the black ducks bathed earlier in the morning. There it would sit down in the water, remaining still for a time. Then it would splash water over its back and wings, duck its head, and sit still again. When sitting thus in the water its tail was usually half spread, and resting on or just under the water surface. When the bath was over the bird would stand up, stretch its wings and then preen, taking care to go over carefully all the feathers of the back, wing, and breast and scratching with its toes those portions it could not reach with the bill.

He observed them fighting also and says:

Why they should fight at this season of the year, when the mating season was over and the food supply seemed abundant enough for all comers, is not easily explained. Yet it was a common thing to see two birds stand facing each other with heads and necks up, and bills tilted at an angle a little above the horizontal. After eyeing each other a short time, one would dart at the other, apparently trying to get its bill above its opponent's and strike at the latter's eyes. The second bird would dodge back and then return the attempted blow. They never actually struck each other, and after several such tiffs one bird would crouch down in front of the other, the yellowlegs' way of surrendering, and the other bird would stalk off and pick a fight with some other that had been peacefully feeding. Sometimes the fight varied from this form and the birds lowered their heads at the beginning like roosters and then fluttered up into the air as they went at each other.

The well-known bobbing habit is well described in some notes sent to me by Francis H. Allen, as follows:

Watched one on a slough for about an hour. Method of bobbing was to raise the head by stretching the neck and at the same time lower the tail, the whole body being held rigid, then lower the head with the bill pointing somewhat downward and raise the tail to normal. The body seems to turn on a pivot, but the lengthening of the neck is an independent movement.

Voice.—John T. Nichols has sent me some very elaborate notes on the varied calls of the yellow-legs, from which I quote as follows:

When on the ground in flocks the lesser yellow-legs is usually silent. The same is true frequently of single birds coming in. In the air it is more or less noisy and has two common, distinct notes—*wheu* and *kip* or *keup*, which seem to be used rather indiscriminately on various occasions and which vary into one another. Wandering singles and small companies seem to use the *wheu* more, often double. The combination *wheu hip* is frequent. From large companies, especially in uncertainty, one may hear a chorus of *kips*.

(1) The yodle probably corresponds in significance with that of the greater yellow-legs—*location*. It is certainly its homolog and scarcely, if at all, distinguishable from it. When a flock of a half dozen lesser yellow-legs came to

decoys, one bird alighted first, had a low-pitched, unfamiliar *too-dle-hoo-hoo,
too-dle-hoo-hoo, too-dle-hoo-hoo*, before the others, still on the wing, came back
and alighted with it.   Though probably of similar derivation, this note was
quite different from the yodle of the species, and is probably more of a gather
call (Long Island, August).

(2) The *wheu* is a regular *flight note*, likely advertisement.   Generally silent
birds alighted, sometimes call an occasional single *wheu* (at such times particularly soft and mellow) before others drop in to join them, as if in welcome.
When double this note of the lesser yellow-legs is at times clear and full,
difficult to differentiate from that of the larger species, and apparently likewise characteristic of a "gentle" bird, which will join decoys or others alighted.

(5) Whereas the *wheu* note of the lesser yellow-legs is most frequently
single and very seldom more than double, I have heard a variation of it in
series from one of an alighted flock (Mastic, July 13, 1919), *hyu-hyu-hyu-
hyu-hyu*, etc.   Presumably this was in protest at my presence, corresponding
to the similar note of the larger species.

(6) Soft, unloud murmuring of a flock in chorus, *yu yu yu*, etc., characteristically heard, as on August 10, 1919, from a flock moving leisurely over the
meadows, after having been flushed, to shortly alight again, expressive of
companionship and confidence.

(7) When dropping down to alight, often hovering over decoys, a flock of
lesser yellow-legs has soft short *cup, cup, cup*, etc., notes.

(8) At the instant of flushing almost the identical notes as above given
hurriedly with more emphasis.   This for the lesser yellow-legs is a rough
analog of the cheeping note of the pectoral sandpiper, but in view of the different habits of the two species, can not be said to be strictly analogous with same.

(10) An unloud chuckle or series of short notes suggesting a very distant
jack curlew, heard sometimes, not very frequently, when one or more birds take
wing.   Should probably be considered a flushing note or signal to take wing.
Seems like the attempt of one individual to reproduce the preceding, which
is often from several birds of a flock.

(11) The *kip* is likely one bird calling to another close-by.   It is typically a
flocking note, otherwise used almost exactly as is note No. 2.   A variation,
keup, with broader sound, approaching the *wheu*, expressing *attention*, is frequent.   It has been heard from a flock of birds which had been resting and
bathing, just before taking wing (Mastic, September 15, 1918).

(12) An infrequent note of quite different character from the lesser yellow-
legs' ordinary calls is very high and clear, *queep*.   It is subject to much variation, as *peep-quip, eep!* but is characterized by the high *ee* sound.   It has been
heard from birds alighted, more particularly when their companions, alarmed
or for some other reason, move on, and is thought of as the *tarrying individual's*
note.   On August 17, 1919, I had picked up decoys preparatory to leaving a
pool in the meadows when a single lesser yellow-legs came down to the pool
calling a similar *kee-a* on the wing, though I was in full view.   It went on without alighting with *wheu* notes characteristic of the species.   Probably this was
an individual which wanted to stay, from a small company which had left the
meadow.

(13) Wounded birds, on being pursued and captured, have a harsh scream
of fear, *cheerp*.   I have noticed this from birds of the year in southward migration only, not from adults under the same circumstances.

The above numbers indicate notes analogous with those of the
greater yellow-legs, similarly numbered.   Where the lesser has no

notes analogous with certain notes of the greater, these numbers are omitted.

Field marks.—There is no conspicuous character, except size, by which the lesser yellow-legs can be distinguished in life from the greater, unless one is expert enough to recognize the notes, which are varied and variable in both species. From nearly all other species it can be distinguished by its slender, shapely head and neck and by its long, conspicuously yellow legs. Its light, almost white, tail and rump contrast conspicuously with its uniformly dark back and wings; adults in worn nuptial plumage appear almost black on the upper parts; and there is no conspicuous white mark in the wings. The lesser yellow-legs is most likely to be confused with the long-legged stilt sandpiper in immature plumage; but the latter is somewhat smaller and has olive-colored legs instead of yellow. Adult stilt sandpipers, before they have entirely lost the barred under parts, can be recognized by these marks and by other characters described under that species.

Fall.—Adult summer yellow-legs in worn nuptial plumage reach New England in July, thus deserving the name. My earliest date is July 11, but they are often abundant before the end of that month. The young birds appear about a month later; the loose flocks are made up of both ages in August; the adults usually depart before the end of August, and few young birds are left after the middle of September.

Mr. Nichols says in his notes:

It has frequently been remarked by old shore-bird gunners on Long Island that the lesser yellowlegs and other species of shore birds in southward migration are abundant early in the season, and then after a period of comparative scarcity become again more numerous. The explanation most commonly advanced for this condition is two flights, first the old, then the young birds. It is unquestionable that the first birds to come south are adults, but beyond that fact this hypothesis will not hold.

The fluctuation in numbers of the shore birds on Long Island during the fall migration period may best be explained by supposing that the bulk of each species has a more or less definite late-summer range to which it travels from the breeding grounds and where, if conditions are favorable, it remains until autumn. Before the main flight, birds of each species are mostly adults, during it, mixed adults and young. To explain double abundance of most species in southward migration by first the passage of adults, then that of young, is pretty surely erroneous. Where such double abundance does occur it is probably first birds passing through, second birds stopping to feed.

There are not infrequent records of southbound lesser yellowlegs on Long Island the end of June (June 24, 1922, my earliest at Mastic), and I have seen a flock of 40 or 50 by July 10; July 31 is the earliest mention I chance to find in my notes of a bird of the year.

There is probably a considerable and regular migration at sea for Capt. Savile G. Reid (1884) says that in Bermuda this is " the most conspicuous and noisy of the August arrivals. It has been seen as early as July 13, but usually disappears toward the end of September. Considerable numbers fall victims to the gun, as they are not bad eating."

C. J. Pennock has noted it in Delaware as late as October 12, and has seen it in Florida as early as September 16. It is an abundant migrant in the interior. Edward S. Thomas tells me that in Ohio the average fall migration dates are between August 3 and October 16; he has a very late record of a specimen collected on November 29, 1923. From the prairie Provinces of Canada the main flight departs in August, but A. G. Lawrence gives me September 29, 1923, as his latest date.

J. A. Munro tells me that it is " an abundant autumn migrant " at Okanagan Landing, British Columbia; his dates run from July 9 to September 1. This species seems to be a rare migrant on the coasts of Washington and California.

Game.—The summer yellow-legs has always been a popular game bird and has always been counted in the class of "big birds." It is still fairly abundant, but occurs in nothing like its former numbers. Giraud (1844) was informed by a noted gunner "that he killed 106 yellow-shanks by discharging both barrels of his gun into a flock while they were sitting along the beach." No such flocks occur to-day. However, they are not all gone, for Stuart T. Danforth (1925) says that at Cartagena Lagoon, Porto Rico,

they occur in flocks of from 2 to 100. They reach their greatest abundance early in October. On October 7 and 11, 1924, I observed over 1,000, and on other days shortly before and after these dates from 500 to 800. Usually there are not over 100 present at once. They feed in the shallow open water, on the mud flats, and among the flooded grasses and sedges. They often associate with other sandpipers, especially the greater yellowlegs, stilt, and semipalmated sandpipers They are surprisingly tame while in Porto Rico, and it is slaughter, not sport, to shoot them. Sometimes the flocks are so densely packed that hunters kill as many as 20 at a single shot.

I have never felt that the summer yellow-legs should be in the game-bird class, though I must confess that it has some gamey qualities. It is, at times, absurdly tame; it decoys very easily, returns again and again to the slaughter, and its little body is so small that many lives must be sacrificed to make a decent bag. However, it *is* interesting sport to sit in a well-made blind on a marsh, with decoys skillfully arranged, and show one's skill in whistling up these lively and responsive little birds. After all, gunning is not so much a means of filling up the larder as an excuse for getting out to enjoy the beauties of nature and the ways of its wild creatures.

Mr. Nichols explains how it is done on Long Island, where this species has for many years furnished most of the shooting; he writes:

To the Long Island gunner the yellow-legs and its associates are known as "bay snipe." Various customs relating to their pursuit for sport (sniping) have arisen in the course of the generations that it has been in vogue. Imitation wooden birds ("stool") are set out as decoys in the marshes over which the birds may be expected to pass, and the gunner stations himself within range behind a blind usually constructed of bushes. There is opportunity for considerable skill in setting out the decoys, placing and constructing the blind, imitating the cries of the various species to draw them within range. Where possible the decoys are placed so as to be seen from every direction against a surface of water; if in a small pool scattered about, if in a larger water area, directly off some projecting point so as not to be blanketed by the land. The larger the show of decoys, the larger the flocks of birds that will be tempted to respond to them, and one attempts to scatter them so that each will stand apart, no three which are close together will be in line. They all face more or less directly into the wind as would alighted birds. Ideally the blind is placed to windward of the rig of decoys. Approaching birds maneuver toward it from down wind, and are so less likely to notice the gunner and take alarm before coming within range.

Winter.—Although a few lesser yellow-legs may spend the winter occasionally as far north as Louisiana and Florida, the main winter home is in southern South America and very few are to be found regularly north of that continent. A. H. Holland (1892) records it as fairly common throughout the year in Argentina but more numerous from October to February. Dr. Alexander Wetmore (1926), referring to the same general region, writes:

The lesser yellow-legs was widespread in distribution after October and was more abundant on the whole than *Totanus melanoleucus.* The birds frequented the shores of open lagoons, shallow pools, or coastal mud flats, and though found distributed singly or two or three together it was not unusual to encounter them in larger bands that might contain 100 individuals. On their wintering grounds they were rather silent, but with the opening of northward migration resumed their habit of uttering musical though noisy calls when disturbed in any manner. On the pampas they congregated during drier seasons about lagoons and flocks often sought refuge from the violent winds that swept the open plains behind scant screens of rushes. After any general rain these flocks dispersed to pools of rain water in the pastures, where insect food was easily available. The winter population was thus not stationary, but shifted constantly with changes in the weather. By the first of March the lesser yellow-legs had begun their northward movement and numbers were found near Guamini, where they paused to rest after a northward flight from Patagonia. In their case, as in that of other migrant species from North America, it was instructive to note that the migration southward came in September and October when the birds traveled southward with the unfolding of the southern spring and that the return northward was initiated by the approach of rigorous weather in faraway Patagonia. Migrant flocks, many of whose members offered sad evidence of inhospitable treatment at the hands of Argentine gunners in the shape of broken or missing legs, were noted on the plains of Mendoza, near the base of the Andes, in March. And during early April the migration became a veritable rush so that on the night of April 5, at Tucuman, the air was filled with the cries of these and other waders in steady flight northward above the city.

DISTRIBUTION

Range.—North and South America.

Breeding range.—The yellow-legs breeds north to Alaska (Kowak River and Fort Yukon); Mackenzie (Fort Anderson, Rendezvous Lake, and Horton River); and Ungava (Fort George and Whale River). East to Ungava (Whale River); and formerly New York (Phelps). South to formerly New York (Phelps); formerly Indiana (Lake County); formerly Illinois (near Chicago); Wisconsin (Lake Koshkonong); and central Alberta (Belvedere). West probably to northern British Columbia (Bennett and Telegraph Creek); Yukon (Lake Marsh); and Alaska (Eagle and Kowak River).

Nonbreeding individuals are frequently observed in summer south of the breeding range: Nebraska (Lincoln); Colorado (Barr, Loveland, and Las Animas); Wyoming (Albany County); Montana (Fort Keogh, and Terry); and Oregon (Corvallis and Malheur Lake).

Winter range.—North to Sinaloa (Mazatlan); the coast of Texas (Fort Brown and Refugio County); Louisiana (State Game Preserve); and Florida (Pensacola, Goose Creek, and Wilson). East to Florida (Wilson, and Royal Palm Hammock); Jamaica; the Bahama Islands; Porto Rico; rarely the Lesser Antilles (Barbuda and Carriacou); British Guiana (Bartica Grove, Camacusa, and Altagracia); French Guiana (Cayenne); Brazil (Mapa, Mexiana, Marajo, Cantagallo, and Novo Fribourgo); Uruguay (Lazcano and San Vicente); and Argentina (Buenos Aires, Azul, and the Chubut Valley). South to Argentina (Chubut Valley); and Chile (Gregory Bay, Straits of Magellan, Santiago, and Valparaiso). West to Chile (Valparaiso, Puerto del Huasco, Atacama, and Tarapaca); Peru (Chorillos, Junin, and Cajabamba); Ecuador (Canar, Babahoyo, and Quito); Colombia (Medellin and Cartagena); probably Panama (Culebra); Costa Rica (La Estrella de Cartago); probably Nicaragua (Escondido River); Jalisco (La Barca); and Sinaloa (Mazatlan).

Spring migration.—Early dates of spring arrival are: Georgia, Cumberland, March 12; South Carolina, Charleston, March 5, and Frogmore, March 20; North Carolina, Corolla, March 15, and Atlantic, March 19; District of Columbia, Washington, March 12; Maryland, Havre de Grace, March 15; Bermuda, April 26; Pennsylvania, State College, April 1; New Jersey, Cape May Court House, April 1, and Morristown, April 6; New York, Branchport, March 26, and Roslyn, April 3; Connecticut, Hartford, April 19; Massachusetts, Taunton, April 4, and Monomoy Island, April 29; Vermont, Hartford, April 28; Maine, Pittsfield, April 26, and Saco, May 1; Quebec, Montreal, April 30, and Godbout, May 5; New Brunswick,

Scotch Lake, May 2; Nova Scotia, Kentville, April 21; Mississippi, Bay St. Louis, March 13; Kentucky, Bowling Green, March 27; Missouri, Marionville, March 14, Corning, March 15, and Independence, March 25; Illinois, Lebanon, March 29, and Rantoul, March 31; Indiana, Bicknell, March 30, Greencastle, April 1, and Terre Haute, April 8; Ohio, Sandusky, March 18, and Oberlin, March 30; Michigan, Hillsdale, March 31, Ann Arbor, April 9, and Detroit, April 11; Ontario, Oshawa, April 19, Ottawa, April 25, and Reaboro, April 30; Iowa, Sioux City, March 11, and Iowa City, March 30; Wisconsin, Fox Lake, April 3, New London, April 7, and Milwaukee, April 8; Minnesota, Jackson, March 18, Heron Lake, March 24, and Lanesboro, April 7; central and northern Texas, San Antonio, March 20, Dallas, March 22, Bonham, March 23, and Electra, March 24; Oklahoma, Caddo, March 11, and Copan, March 28; Kansas, Leroy, March 12, and Manhattan, March 23; Nebraska, Falls City, March 23, Callaway, March 26, and Lincoln, March 27; South Dakota, Forestburg, April 1, Harrison, April 13, Sioux Falls, April 16; North Dakota, Westhope, April 10, and Charlson, April 18; Manitoba, Greenridge, April 7, Reaburn, April 13, and Margaret, April 15; Saskatchewan, Qu'Appelle, April 9, Lake Johnston, April 16, and Eastend, April 17; Mackenzie, Hay River, May 2, Fort Resolution, May 5, Fort Simpson, May 9, and Fort Reliance, May 13; New Mexico, Glenrio, April 15; Colorado, Durango, April 5, Denver, April 19, and Salida, April 25; Wyoming, Lake Como, May 5; Montana, Terry, May 6, and Choteau, May 8; Alberta, Onoway, April 13, Edmonton, April 17, Stony Plain, April 22, and Athabaska Landing, May 17; California, Fresno, April 10, and Santa Barbara, April 24; Oregon, Gaston, March 7, Malheur Lake, March 8, and Klamath Lake, March 31; Washington, Menlo, April 27; British Columbia, Okanagan Landing, March 23, and Courtenay, April 16; and Alaska, Nulato, April 29, and Chilcot River, May 12.

Late dates of spring departure are: Argentina, Tafi Viejo, April 15; Chile, Concepcion, April 14; Florida, Bradentown, May 1, and Pensacola, May 25; Georgia, Savannah, May 28; South Carolina, Charleston, May 26; North Carolina, Lake Ellis, May 10, Raleigh, May 18, and Cape Hatteras, May 20; Virginia, Chesapeake Bay, May 12, and Hog Island, May 16; District of Columbia, Washington, May 17; Maryland, Patapsco, May 17; Pennsylvania, State College, May 17, Doylestown, May 20, and Limerick, May 22; New Jersey, Hackettstown, May 16, and Morristown, May 19; New York, Amagansett, May 25, Rockaway, June 1, and Locust Grove, June 7; Connecticut, Norwalk, May 22; Massachusetts, Boston, May 20, and Woods Hole, May 24; Vermont, Wells River, June 3; Maine, Winthrop, June

1; Louisiana, Vermilion Bay, April 27; Mississippi, Bay St. Louis, May 10; Arkansas, Stuttgart, May 14; Illinois, Chicago, May 15, De Kalb, May 23, and Rantoul, May 26; Indiana, Terre Haute, May 12, Hobart, May 13, and Bicknell, May 18; Ohio, Painesville, May 26, Columbus, May 28, and Oberlin, May 30; Michigan, Manistee, May 20; Ontario, Modoc, May 28, and Ottawa, May 31; Iowa, Waterloo, May 30, Forest City, May 31, and Sioux City, June 4; Wisconsin, New Richmond, May 15, La Crosse, May 21, and Madison, May 27; Minnesota, Clarissa, May 23, and Jackson, May 27; Texas, Dallas, May 20, Brownsville, May 24, and Huntsville, May 28; Oklahoma, Copan, May 19; Kansas, Ellis, May 18, and Wichita, May 20; Nebraska, Long Pine, May 16, Badger, May 19, and Lincoln, May 20; South Dakota, Vermilion, May 28, Harrison, May 29, and Sioux Falls, June 11; North Dakota, Charlson, May 17, Bismarck, May 18, and Harrisburg, June 11; Manitoba, Aweme, May 20, Margaret, June 1, and Whitewater Lake, June 10; Saskatchewan, Indian Head, May 28, Touchwood Hills, May 30, and South Qu'Appelle, June 1; New Mexico, Glenrio, May 16; Colorado, Barr, May 17, and Boulder, May 20; Wyoming, Laramie River, June 1; Montana, Choteau, May 26, Corvallis, May 31, and Terry, June 12; California, Fresno, May 12; Oregon, Lawen, May 10, and Klamath Lake, May 18; and British Columbia, Mirror Lake, May 30.

Fall migration.—Early dates of fall arrival are: British Columbia, Okanagan Landing, July 9, and Atlin, July 12; Washington, Tacoma, July 7, Ozette Island, July 11, and The Olympiades, July 12; Oregon, Malheur Lake, July 1, and Corvallis, July 10; California, Goleta, August 11, and Santa Barbara, August 16; Montana, Milk River, July 25, and Billings, July 31; Wyoming, Camp Carling, July 28; Colorado, Barr, July 5, Boulder, July 9, and Sterling, July 22; Arizona, San Bernardino Ranch, August 2; New Mexico, Guadalupe Mountains, August 7, and State College, August 10; Saskatchewan, Quill Lake, July 5, and Kiddleston, July 7; Manitoba, Margaret, July 4, Oak Lake, July 12, and Shoal Lake, July 13; South Dakota, Forestburg, July 1, and Pine Ridge Reservation, July 12; Nebraska, Valentine, July 11, and Lincoln, July 14; Oklahoma, Copan, August 7; Minnesota, Hallock, July 6, and St. Vincent, July 23; Wisconsin, Madison, July 22, and North Freedom, July 28; Iowa, Winnebago, July 27, Sioux City, August 3, and Wall Lake, August 4; Ontario, Lac Seul, July 5, Port Dover, July 17, and Toronto, July 18; Michigan, Jackson, July 17; Ohio, Cedar Point, July 5, Bay Point, July 11, and Youngstown, July 27; Indiana, Hobart, July 9; Illinois, Chicago, July 2, La Grange, July 4, and Addison, July 19; Mississippi, Biloxi, July 12, and Bay St. Louis, July 13; Nova Scotia, Wolfville, July 27; Maine, Pittsfield, July 26; Vermont, Rutland, July 27; Massachusetts, Chatham, July 4, Harvard, July 13, and Cape Cod, July 15;

Connecticut, North Haven, July 21; New York, Mastic, June 24, East Hampton, July 8, and Geneva, July 16; New Jersey, Parkerton, July 1, Cape May, July 4, and Long Beach, July 9; Maryland, Ocean City, July 20; Bermuda, July 13; Virginia, Wallops Island, July 26; North Carolina, Currituck Sound, July 5, and Pea and Bodie Islands, July 8; South Carolina, Charleston, July 15; Florida, Ponce Park, July 12, Key West, July 16, and Pensacola, July 18; the Lesser Antilles, Barbados, July 4, Grenada, July 10, and St. Croix, July 26; and Argentina, Las Palmas, July 31.

Late dates of fall departure are: Alaska, St. George Island, October 18; Oregon, Klamath Lake, November 17; California, Red-wood City, November 28; Alberta, Dorenlee, October 3, and Nanton, October 5; Montana, Choteau, September 4; Colorado, Boulder, September 28, and Denver, October 3; Saskatchewan, South Qu'Appelle, October 16; Manitoba, Margaret, October 12, Oak Lake, October 13, and Reaburn, October 17; North Dakota, Harrisburg, October 26; South Dakota, Forestburg, October 25, and Fort Sisseton, October 28; Nebraska, Falls City, November 15, and Lincoln, November 17; Minnesota, St. Vincent, October 1, and Lanesboro, October 11; Wisconsin, North Freedom, October 6, Madison, October 7, and Meridian, November 1; Iowa, Gilbert Station, October 22, Marshalltown, November 1, and Emmetsburg, November 1; Ontario, London, October 14, and Ottawa, October 18; Michigan, Sault Ste. Marie, October 20, Ann Arbor, October 21, and Lansing, October 28; Ohio, Youngstown, October 27, Sandusky, November 4, and Columbus, November 29; Indiana, Indianapolis, October 23; Illinois, De Kalb, October 10, Rantoul, October 30, and Aledo, November 3; Missouri, Kansas City, November 23; Nova Scotia, Pictou, October 8; New Brunswick, Scotch Lake, October 28; Quebec, Montreal, October 7, and Koksoak River, October 8; Maine, Kennebec County, October 15, and Pittsfield, October 20; Massachusetts, Taunton, October 20, and Monomoy, November 11; New York, Orient, October 18, Branchport, October 21, and Ithaca, November 10; New Jersey, Sandy Hook, October 25; Pennsylvania, State College, October 28, and Waynesburg, November 2; Maryland, Cambridge, October 25; District of Columbia, Anacostia, November 1; Virginia, Hog Island, November 12; and South Carolina, Charleston, November 3.

Casual records.—The yellow-legs has been recorded from the Pribilof Islands (St. Paul Island, June 11, 1890); and three times from England (Nottinghamshire, about 1854, Cornwall, September, 1871, and Fair Isle, Shetland Islands, September, 1910). Moschler (1856) reported that in 1854 he received a specimen from Greenland.

Egg dates.—Alberta and Manitoba: 38 records, May 15 to June 16; 19 records, May 27 to June 4. Arctic Canada: 28 records, June 2 to July 1; 14 records, June 20 to 27. Labrador Peninsula: 7 records, June 3 to July 2.

REFERENCES TO BIBLIOGRAPHY

REFERENCES TO BIBLIOGRAPHY

ABBOTT, GERARD ALAN.

    1919—The Lure of the Godwit. The Wilson Bulletin, vol. 31, pp. 97–99.

AIKEN, CHARLES EDWARD HOWARD, and WARREN, EDWARD ROYAL.

    1914—The Birds of El Paso County, Colorado.

ALLEN, ARTHUR AUGUSTUS.

    1913—Stilt Sandpipers (*Micropalama himantopus*) at Ithaca, N. Y. The Auk, vol. 30, pp. 430–432.

ALLEN, JOEL ASAPH.

    1905—Report on the Birds Collected in Northeastern Siberia by the Jesup North Pacific Expedition. Bulletin of the American Museum of Natural History, vol. 21, p. 219.

ANTHONY, ALFRED WEBSTER.

    1922—The Sharp-tailed Sandpiper in Southern California. The Auk, vol. 39, p. 106.

AUDUBON, JOHN JAMES.

    1840—The Birds of America, 1840–44.

BAHR, PHILIP HEINRICH.

    1907—Some Observations on the Breeding Habits of the Red-necked Phalarope. British Birds, vol. 1, pp. 202–207.

BAILEY, ALFRED M.

    1925-6—A Report on the Birds of Northwestern Alaska and Regions Adjacent to Bering Strait. Part VI. The Condor, vol. 27, pp. 232–238.

BAILEY, FLORENCE MERRIAM.

    1916—A Populous Shore. The Condor, vol. 18, pp. 100–110.

BARTSCH, PAUL.

    1899—A Piscivorous Yellow-leg. The Wilson Bulletin, No. 24, p. 8.

BEST, MARY GERTRUDE S., and HAVILAND, MAUD D.

    1914—Notes on the Red-necked Phalarope in the Outer Hebrides. British Birds, vol. 8, pp. 9–12.

BISHOP, LOUIS BENNETT.

    1900—Birds of the Yukon Region. North American Fauna, No. 19.

    1901—The Winter Birds of Pea Island, North Carolina. The Auk, vol. 18, pp. 260–268.

BOND, J. WALPOLE.

    1923—Concerning the Greenshank. British Birds, vol. 16, pp. 208–213.

BORASTON, JOHN MACLAIR.

    1903—Birds by Land and Sea.

BOWDISH, BEECHER SCOVILLE.

    1902—Birds of Porto Rico. The Auk, vol. 19, pp. 356–366.

BOWLES, JOHN HOOPER.

    1918—The Limicolae of the State of Washington. The Auk, vol. 35, pp. 326–333.

BRETHERTON, BERNARD J.

    1896—Kadiak Island. A contribution to the Avifauna of Alaska. The Oregon Naturalist, vol. 3, pp. 45–49; 61–64; 77–79; 100–102.

BREWER, THOMAS MAYO.
    1878—Changes in our North American Fauna.   Bulletin of the Nuttall
        Ornithological Club, vol. 3, pp. 49–52.
BREWSTER, WILLIAM.
    1883—Notes on the Birds Observed during a Summer Cruise in the Gulf
        of St. Lawrence.   Proc. Bost. Soc. of Nat. Hist., vol. 22, p. 364.
    1894—Notes and Song-flight of the Woodcock (*Philohela minor*).   The
        Auk, vol. 11, pp. 291–298.
    1906—The Birds of the Cambridge Region of Massachusetts.   Memoirs of
        the Nuttall Ornithological Club, No. 4.
    1925—The Birds of the Lake Umbagog Region of Maine.   Bulletin of the
        Museum of Comparative Zoology at Harvard College, vol. 66, Part 2.
BROOKS, WINTHROP SPRAGUE.
    1915—Notes on Birds from East Siberia and Arctic Alaska.   Bulletin of
        the Museum of Comparative Zoology at Harvard College.
BROWN, WILLIAM JAMES.
    1012—Additional Notes on the Birds of Newfoundland.   The Ottawa
        Naturalist, vol. 26, pp. 93–98.
BURTCH, VERDI.
    1925—Some Notes on the Birds of the Branchport, N. Y. Region, 1923.
        The Auk, vol. 42, pp. 554–557.
BUTURLIN, SERGIUS ALEKSANDROVICH.
    1907—On the Breeding Habits of the Rosy Gull and the Pectoral Sandpiper.
        The Ibis, 1907, pp. 570–573.
CAHOON, JOHN CYRUS.
    1888—The Shore Birds of Cape Cod.   Ornithologist and Oologist, vol. 13,
        pp. 121–124, 129–132, 153–156.
CAMERON, EWEN SOMERLED.
    1907—The Birds of Custer and Dawson Counties, Montana.   The Auk,
        vol. 24, pp. 241–270.
CHAPMAN, ABEL.
    1924—The Borders and Beyond.
CHAPMAN, FRANK MICHLER.
    1891—On the birds observed near Corpus Christi, Texas, during parts of
        March and April, 1891.   Bulletin of the American Museum of
        Natural History, vol. 3, pp. 315–328.
    1908—Camps and Cruises of an Ornithologist.
    1926—The Distribution of Bird Life in Ecuador.
CHISLETT, RALPH.
    1927—Notes on the Breeding of the Jack Snipe.   British Birds, vol. 21,
        pp. 2–6.
CLARK, AUSTIN HOBART.
    1905—Birds of the Southern Lesser Antilles.   Proc. Boston Society Natural
        History, vol. 32, pp. 203–312.
COOKE, WELLS WOODBRIDGE.
    1912—Distribution and Migration of North American Shore Birds.   U. S.
        Dept. Agriculture, Biological Survey, Bulletin No. 35, Revised.
    1914—Our Shore Birds and Their Future.   Yearbook of Department of
        Agriculture for 1914, pp. 275–294.
COUES, ELLIOTT.
    1861—Notes on the Ornithology of Labrador.   Proceedings of the Phila-
        delphia Academy of Natural Sciences, 1861, pp. 215–257.
    1874—Birds of the Northwest.

COUES, ELLIOTT—Continued.

1878—Field Notes on Birds Observed in Dakota and Montana along the Forty-ninth Parallel during the Seasons of 1873–1874. Bulletin United States Geological Survey, No. 4, pp. 545–661.

1897—Status of the Redshank as a North American Bird. The Auk, vol. 14, pp. 211–212.

DANFORTH, STUART T.

1925—Birds of the Cartagena Lagoon, Porto Rico. Journal of the Department of Agriculture of Porto Rico, vol. 10, no. 1.

DAVIES, SUTTON A.

1895—In Quest of Birds on the Muonio River. Zoologist, ser. 3, vol. 19, pp. 326–335.

1905—On the Birds of the Upper Muonio River. The Ibis, 1905, pp. 67–85.

DAWSON, WILLIAM LEON.

1909—The Birds of Washington.

1923—The Birds of California.

DIXON, JOSEPH.

1917—The Home Life of the Baird Sandpiper. The Condor, vol. 19, pp. 77–84.

1917a—Children of the Midnight Sun. Bird Lore, vol. 19, pp. 185–192.

1918—The Nesting Grounds and Nesting Habits of the Spoon-billed Sandpiper. The Auk, vol. 35, pp. 387–404.

DRESSER, HENRY EELES.

1871—A History of the Birds of Europe.

1904—On the late Dr. Walter's Ornithological Researches in the Taimyr Peninsula. The Ibis, 1904, pp. 228–235.

EIFRIG, CHARLES WILLIAM GUSTAVE.

1905—Ornithological Results of the Canadian "Neptune" Expedition to Hudson Bay and Northward. The Auk, vol. 22, pp. 233–241.

ELLIOT, DANIEL GIRAUD.

1895—North American Shore Birds.

EVANS, EDWARD, and STURGE, WILSON.

1859—Notes on the Birds of Western Spitzbergen, as observed in 1855. The Ibis, 1859, p. 171.

FARREN, WILLIAM.

1910—Articles on "Redshank and Greenshank" (pp. 509–521).' "The Godwits" (pp. 521–528).

From "The British Bird Book." Edited by F. B. Kirkman. 1910–1913.

FAY, SAMUEL PRESCOTT.

1911—Hudsonian Godwit (*Limosa haemastica*) in Massachusetts. The Auk, vol. 28, pp. 257–258.

FEILDEN, HENRY WEMYSS.

1877—List of Birds Observed in Smith Sound and in the Polar Basin during the Arctic Expedition of 1875–76. The Ibis, 1877, p. 401.

1879—Notes from An Arctic Journal. Zoologist, 1879, p. 107.

1920—Breeding of the Knot in Grinnell Land. British Birds, vol. 13, pp. 278–282.

FORBUSH, EDWARD HOWE.

1912—A History of the Game Birds, Wild-Fowl and Shore Birds of Massachusetts and Adjacent States.

1925—Birds of Massachusetts and Other New England States.

GAULT, BENJAMIN TRUE.

1902—Food Habits of the Wilson Snipe. The Wilson Bulletin, vol. 9, pp. 7–10.

GIBSON, ERNEST.
  1920—Further Ornithological Notes from the Neighborhood of Cape San
      Antonio, Province of Buenos Ayres. The Ibis, 1920, pp. 1–97.

GILROY, NORMAN.
  1922—Field Notes and Observations on the Greenshank. British Birds,
      vol. 16, pp. 129–133.

GIRAUD, JACOB POST.
  1844—The Birds of Long Island.

GLADSTONE, HUGH STEUART.
  1907—The Red-necked Phalarope in Ireland. British Birds, vol. 1, pp.
      174–177.

GODMAN, FREDERICK DU CANE, and PERCY SANDON.
  1861—On the Birds observed at Bodo during the Spring and Summer of
      1857. The Ibis, 1861, pp. 87–89.

GOEBEL, H.
  Numerous articles on eggs of Russian and Siberian Birds, chiefly published
  in the Zeitschrift für Oologie (und Ornithologie).

GORDON, AUDREY.
  1921—A Note on the Nesting of the Red-necked Phalarope. British Birds,
      vol. 15, pp. 90–91.

GORDON, SETON.
  1915—Hill Birds of Scotland.

GOSS, NATHANIEL STICKNEY.
  1891—History of the Birds of Kansas.

GRINNELL, JOSEPH.
  1900—Birds of the Kotzebue Sound Region. Pacific Coast Avifauna No. 1.

GRINNELL, JOSEPH; BRYANT, HAROLD CHILD; and STORER, TRACY IRWIN.
  1918—The Game Birds of California.

HANCOCK, JOHN.
  1874—A Catalogue of the Birds of Northumberland and Durham. Nat-
      ural History Transactions of Northumberland & Durham, 1873,
      vol. 6, pp. xxvi, 178.

HANNA, G. DALLAS.
  1921—The Pribilof Sandpiper. The Condor, vol. 23, pp. 50–57.

HARROLD, C. G.
  1923—Notes on the Hudsonian Godwit in Alberta. The Canadian Field-
      Naturalist, vol. 37, pp. 138–139.

HART, H. CHICHESTER.
  1880—Notes on the Ornithology of the British Polar Expedition, 1875–6.
      Zoologist, 1880, p. 205.

HARTERT, ERNST.
  1920—Die Vögel der paläarktischen Fauna.

HATCH, PHILO LUOIS.
  1892—Notes on the Birds of Minnesota.

HAVILAND, MAUD D.
  1915—Notes on the Breeding Habits of the Grey Phalarope. British Birds,
      vol. 9, pp. 11–16.
  1915a—Notes on the Breeding Habits of the Curlew Sandpiper. British
      Birds, vol. 8, pp. 178–183.

HENSHAW, HENRY WETHERBEE.
  1875—Report upon the Ornithological Collections made in Portions of
      Nevada, Utah, California, Colorado, New Mexico, and Arizona dur-
      ing the years 1871, 1872, 1873, and 1874. Report upon Geographi-
      cal and Geological Explorations and Surveys West of the One
      Hundredth Meridian.
HEWITSON, WILLIAM CHAPMAN.
  1856—Eggs of British Birds, 3rd ed.
HOLLAND, ARTHUR H.
  1891—Further Notes on the Birds of the Argentine Republic. The Ibis,
      1891, pp. 16–20.
  1892—Short Notes on the Birds of Estancia Espartella, Argentine Repub-
      lic. The Ibis, 1892, p. 193–214.
HOWELL, ARTHUR HOLMES.
  1924—Birds of Alabama.
HUDSON, WILLIAM HENRY.
  1920—Birds of La Plata.
HUNTINGTON, DWIGHT WILLIAM.
  1903—Our Feathered Game.
HUXLEY, JULIAN S.
  1912—A first account of the Courtship of the Redshank. Proceedings of
      the Zoological Society of London, 1912, pp. 647–655.
  1925—The Absence of "Courtship" in the Avocet. British Birds, vol. 19,
      pp. 88–94.
HUXLEY, JULIAN S., and MONTAGUE, F. A.
  1926—Studies on the Courtship and Sexual Life of Birds. VI. The Black-
      tailed Godwit, Limosa limosa (L). The Ibis, 1926, pp. 1–25.
JONES, LYNDS.
  1909—The Birds of Cedar Point and Vicinity. The Wilson Bulletin, No.
      67, vol. 21, pp. 55–76, 115–131, 187–204; vol. 22, pp. 25–41, 97–115,
      172–182.
KELLS, WILLIAM L.
  1906—Nesting of Wilson's Snipe. The Ottawa Naturalist, vol. 20, pp.
      53–55.
KNIGHT, ORA WILLIS.
  1908—The Birds of Maine.
KUMLIEN, LUDWIG.
  1879—Contributions to the Natural History of Arctic America. Bulletin
      of the United States National Museum, No. 15.
LAING, HAMILTON M.
  1913—Out with the Birds.
  1925—Birds Collected and Observed during the Cruise of the Thiepval in
      the North Pacific, 1924. Victoria Memorial Museum Bulletin,
      No. 40.
LEWIS, ELISHA J.
  1885—The American Sportsman.
MACFARLANE, RODERICK ROSS.
  1908—List of Birds and Eggs Observed and Collected in the North-west
      Territories of Canada, between 1880 and 1894. In through the
      Mackenzie Basin, by Charles Mair.
MACGILLIVRAY, WILLIAM.
  1852—A History of British Birds.

MACKAY, GEORGE HENRY.
　　1893—Observations on the Knot (*Tringa canutus*). The Auk, vol. 10, pp. 25–35.
　　1894—Notes on Certain Water Birds in Massachusetts. The Auk, vol. 11, pp. 223–228.
MANNICHE, ARNER LUDVIG VALDEMAR.
　　1910—The Terrestrial Mammals and Birds of North-east Greenland. Medelelser om Gronland, Bd. 45.
MASSEY, HERBERT.
　　1913—Notes on the Eggs of the North American Limicolae, Referring Principally to the Accidental Visitors. The Condor, vol..15, pp. 193–198.
MAYNARD, CHARLES JOHNSON.
　　1896—The Birds of Eastern North America.
McATEE, WALDO LEE.
　　1911—Our Vanishing Shorebirds. Biological Survey Circular No. 79.
MOORE, ROBERT THOMAS.
　　1912—The Least Sandpiper during the Nesting Season in the Magdalen Islands. The Auk, vol. 29, pp. 210–223.
MURDOCH, JOHN.
　　1885—Report of the International Polar Expedition to Point Barrow, Alaska. Part 4, Natural History.
MURPHY, ROBERT CUSHMAN.
　　1926—Nest-Protecting Display of the Woodcock. Bird-Lore, vol. 28, pp. 265–266.
NAUMANN, JOHANN FRIEDRICH.
　　1887–1895—Naturgeschichte der Vögel Mitteleuropas. Edited by C. R. Hennicke.
NELSON, EDWARD WILLIAM.
　　1877—A Contribution to the Biography of Wilson's Phalarope. Bulletin of the Nuttall Ornithological Club, vol. 2, pp. 38–43.
　　1877a—Birds of Northeastern Illinois. Bulletin of the Essex Institute, vol. 8, pp. 90–155.
　　1883—The Birds of Bering Sea and the Arctic Ocean. Cruise of the Revenue Steamer Corwin in Alaska and the N. W. Arctic Ocean in 1881.
　　1887—Report upon Natural History Collections made in Alaska.
NEWTON, ALFRED.
　　1896—A Dictionary of Birds.
NICHOLS, JOHN TREADWELL.
　　1920.—Limicoline Voices. The Auk, vol. 37, pp. 519–540.
NORMAN, ERNEST S.
　　The Nesting of the Greater Yellowlegs in Manitoba. The Oologist, vol. 32, pp. 126–127.
OSGOOD, WILFRED HUDSON.
　　1909—Biological Investigations in Alaska and Yukon Territory. North American Fauna, No. 30.
PALMER, WILLIAM.
　　1890—Notes on the Birds Observed During the Cruise of the United States Fish Commission Schooner Grampus in the Summer of 1887. Proceedings of the United States National Museum, vol. 13, pp. 249–265.

PALMER, WILLIAM—Continued.

1899—The Avifauna of the Pribilof Islands. The Fur-Seals and Fur-Sea Islands of the North Pacific Ocean, part 3, pp. 355–431.

PEABODY, PUTNAM BURTON.

1903—Wilson's Phalarope. The Oologist, vol. 20, pp. 11–12.

PEARSON, HENRY JOHN.

1904—Three Summers Among the Birds of Russian Lapland.

PEARSON, THOMAS GILBERT.

1916—The Avocet. Educational Leaflet No. 88. Bird-Lore, vol. 18, pp. 342–345.

PHILIPP, PHILIP BERNARD.

1925—Notes on Some Summer Birds of the Magdalen Islands. The Canadian Field-Naturalist, vol. 39, pp. 75–78.

POPHAM, HUGH LEYBORNE.

1897—Notes on Birds Observed on the Yenesei River, Siberia in 1895. The Ibis, 1897, pp. 89–108.

1898—Further Notes on Birds Observed on the Yenesei River, Siberia. The Ibis, 1898, pp. 489–520.

1901—Supplementary Notes on the Birds of the Yenesei River. The Ibis, 1901, pp. 442–458.

POYNTING, FRANK.

1895–6—Eggs of British Birds.

PREBLE, EDWARD ALEXANDER.

1902—A Biological Investigation of the Hudson Bay Region. North American Fauna, No. 22.

1908—A Biological Investigation of the Athabasca-Mackenzie Region. North American Fauna, No. 27.

PREBLE, EDWARD ALEXANDER, and MCATEE, WALDO LEE.

1923—A Biological Survey of the Pribilof Islands, Alaska. North American Fauna, No. 46.

PRINGLE, JAMES J.

1899—Twenty Years of Snipe Shooting.

REID, PHILIP SAVILE GREY.

1884—The Birds of Bermuda. Part 4 in Contributions to the Natural History of the Bermudas. Bulletin United States National Museum, No. 25.

REY, EUGENE.

1905—Die Eier der Vögel Mitteleuropas, 2 vols.

RICH, WALTER HERBERT.

1907—Feathered Game of the Northeast.

RIDGWAY, ROBERT.

1880—On a New Alaskan Sandpiper. Bulletin of the Nuttall Ornithological Club, vol. 5, pp. 160–163.

1919—The Birds of North and Middle America, part 8.

ROBERTS, THOMAS SADLER.

1919—Water Birds of Minnesota Past and Present. Biennial Report of the State Game and Fish Commission of Minnesota, for the Biennial Period Ending July 31, 1918.

ROCKWELL, ROBERT BLANCHARD.

1912—Notes on the Wading Birds of the Barr Lake Region, Colorado. The Condor, vol. 14, pp. 117–131.

ROSS, ROLAND CASE.

1922—Red Phalarope in Southern California. The Condor, vol. 24, pp. 66 and 67.

Ross, Roland Case—Continued.
    1924—Occurrence and Behavior of Certain Shorebirds in Southern Cali-
        fornia. The Condor, vol. 26, pp. 90–92.
Rowan, William.
    1926—Notes on Alberta Waders included in the British List. British
        Birds, vol. 20, pp. 2–10, 34–42, 82–90, 138–145, 186–192.
Sandys, Edwin.
    1904—Upland Game Birds.
Sanford, Leonard Cutler, Bishop, Louis Bennett, and Vandyke, Theodore
Strong.
    1903—The Waterfowl Family.
Saunders, Aretas Andrews.
    1926—The Summer Birds of Central New York Marshes. Roosevelt Wild
        Life Bulletin, vol. 3, pp. 335–475.
Saunders, William E.
    1896—Keen Sight of Birds. The Ottawa Naturalist, vol. 9, p. 214.
    1902—Birds of Sable Island, N. S. The Ottawa Naturalist, vol. 16,
        pp. 15–31.
Scott, William Earl Dodge.
    1881—On Birds Observed in Sumpter, Levy, and Hillsboro Counties,
        Florida. Bulletin of the Nuttall Ornithological Club, vol. 6,
        pp. 14–21.
Seebohm, Henry.
    1884—History of British Birds.
    1888—The Geographical Distribution of the Family Charadriidae, or the
        Plovers, Sandpipers, Snipes, and their Allies.
Selby, Prideaux John.
    1833—Illustrations of British Ornithology.
Selous, Edmund.
    1906—Observations Tending to Throw Light on the Question of Sexual
        Selection in Birds, etc. Zoologist, 1906, pp. 201–19, 285–94, 419–28.
Slater, Henry Horrocks.
    1898—British Birds with their Nests and Eggs. Order Limicolae.
Stejneger, Leonhard.
    1885—Results of Ornithological Explorations in the Commander Islands
        and in Kamtschatka. Bulletin of the United States National
        Museum, No. 29.
Stoddard, Herbert L.
    1923—Some Wisconsin Shore-bird Records. The Auk, vol. 40, pp. 319–321.
Street, J. Fletcher.
    1923—On the Nesting Grounds of the Solitary Sandpiper and the Lesser
        Yellowlegs. The Auk, vol. 40, pp. 577–583.
Suckley, George, and Cooper, James Graham.
    1860—The Natural History of Washington Territory and Oregon.
Sutton, George Miksch.
    1923—Notes on the Nesting of the Wilson's Snipe in Crawford County,
        Pennsylvania. The Wilson Bulletin, vol. 35, pp. 191–202.
Swainson, William, and Richardson, John.
    1831—Fauna Boreali-Americana, vol. 2, Birds.
Swarth, Harry Schelwaldt.
    1911—Birds and Mammals of the 1909 Alexander Alaska Expedition.
        University of California Publications in Zoology, vol. 7, pp. 9–172.
    1922—Birds and Mammals of the Stikine River Region of Northern
        British Columbia and Southeastern Alaska. University of Cali-
        fornia Publications in Zoology, vol. 24, pp. 125–314.

TABOR, E. G.
 1904—A Woodcock at Home. Bird-Lore, vol. 6, pp. 149–153.
TAVERNER, PERCY ALGERNON.
 1926—Birds of Western Canada.
TAYLOR, WALTER PENN.
 1912—Field Notes on Amphibians, Reptiles, and Birds of Northern Humboldt County, Nevada. University of California Publications in
  Zoology, vol. 7, pp. 319–436.
THAYER, JOHN ELIOT.
 1909—Limonites Ruficollis in Alaska. The Condor, vol. 11, p. 173.
 1911—Eggs of the Spoon-bill Sandpiper (*Eurynorhynchus pygmeus*). The
  Auk, vol. 28, pp. 153–155.
THAYER, JOHN ELIOT, and BANGS, OUTRAM.
 1914—Notes on the Birds and Mammals of the Arctic Coast of East
  Siberia. Birds. Proceedings of the New England Zoological Club,
  vol. 5, pp. 1–66.
TODD, WALTER EDMOND CLYDE.
 1904—The Birds of Erie and Presque Isle, Erie County, Pennsylvania.
  Annals of the Carnegie Museum, vol. 2, pp. 481–596.
TORREY, BRADFORD.
 1913—Field Days in California.
TOWNSEND, CHARLES WENDELL.
 1905—The Birds of Essex County, Massachusetts. Memoirs of the Nuttall
  Ornithological Club, No. 3.
 1920—Supplement to the Birds of Essex County, Massachusetts. Memoirs
  of the Nuttall Ornithological Club, No. 5.
TREVOR-BATTYE, AUBYN.
 1897—The Birds of Spitsbergen, as at Present Determined. The Ibis, 1897,
  pp. 574–600.
TROSTLER, ISADOR S.
 1893—The American Woodcock. The Oologist, vol. 10, pp. 278–279.
TURNER, LUCIEN MCSHAN.
 1886—Contributions to the Natural History of Alaska.
TYLER, JOHN G.
 1913—Some Birds of the Fresno District, California. Pacific Coast
  Avifauna, No. 9.
WATKINS, LUCIUS WHITNEY.
 1894—Mimicry in the Nesting of the American Woodcock. The Nidiologist,
  vol. 1, pp. 174–175.
WAYNE, ARTHUR TREZEVANT.
 1910—Birds of South Carolina. Contributions from the Charleston Museum, No. 1.
WEBSTER, FREDERIC SMITH.
 1887—A Fern-eating Woodcock. The Auk, vol. 4, pp. 73–74.
WELCH, L. W.
 1922—Vermilion Flycatcher and Red Phalarope at Long Beach, California.
  The Condor, vol. 24, p. 62.
WETMORE, ALEXANDER.
 1916—Birds of Porto Rico. United States Department of Agriculture
  Bulletin No. 326.
 1925—Food of American Phalaropes, Avocets, and Stilts. United States
  Department of Agriculture, Department Bulletin No. 1359.
 1926—Observations on the Birds of Argentina, Paraguay, Uruguay, and
  Chile. United States National Museum Bulletin 133.

WHEELWRIGHT, H. W.
    1864—"An Old Bushman." A Spring and Summer in Lapland.
    1865—Ten Years in Sweden.
WILSON, ALEXANDER.
    1832—American Ornithology.
WITHERBY, HARRY FORBES, and OTHERS.
    1920—A Practical Handbook of British Birds.
WORMALD, HUGH.
    1909—A Tame Snipe and Its Habits. British Birds, vol. 2, pp. 249–258.
YARRELL, WILLIAM.
    1871—History of British Birds, Fourth Edition, 1871–85. Revised and enlarged by Alfred Newton and Howard Saunders.

PLATES

PLATE 1. LESSER YELLOW-LEGS. Immature. Gimli, Manitoba, August, 1914; presented by Mr. A. G. Lawrence.

PLATE 2. RED PHALAROPE. *Upper:* Nest and eggs of red phalarope, Cape Prince of Wales, Alaska, July 1, 1922; presented by Mr. Alfred M. Bailey, by courtesy of the Colorado Museum of Natural History. *Lower:* Male red phalarope on his nest, Golchika Island, Yenisei River, Siberia, July, 1914; presented by Mrs. Maud D. (Haviland) Brindley, referred to on page 5.

PLATE 3. NORTHERN PHALAROPE. *Upper:* Pair of northern phalaropes, Outer Hebrides, June 11, 1913; presented by Mrs. Maud D. (Haviland) Brindley, referred to on page 23. *Lower:* Nesting site of northern phalarope, Unalakleet, Alaska, June 20, 1918; from a negative taken by Mr. T. L. Richardson for the author.

PLATE 4. NORTHERN PHALAROPE, *Upper:* Nest and eggs of northern phalarope, St. Michael, Alaska, June 9, 1914. *Lower:* Another nest, near the Yukon Delta, Alaska, June 16, 1914. Both photographs taken by Mr. F. S. Hersey for the author, referred to on page 19.

PLATE 5. WILSON PHALAROPE. *Upper:* Nesting site of Wilson phalarope, Reedy Lake, Saskatchewan, June 8, 1905. *Lower:* Nest and eggs of Wilson phalarope, Quill Lake, Saskatchewan, June 3, 1917. Both photographs taken by the author, referred to on page 30.

PLATE 6. WILSON PHALAROPE. *Upper:* Male Wilson phalarope on his nest, Barr Lake, Colorado; presented by Mr. Robert B. Rockwell. *Lower:* Young Wilson phalarope, Wolf Lake, Whiting, Indiana, June, 1925; presented by Mr. Edward S. Thomas.

PLATE 7. AMERICAN AVOCET. *Upper:* Nest and eggs of American avocet, Hay Lake, Saskatchewan, June 15, 1905. *Lower:* Another nest, Big Stick Lake, Saskatchewan, June 14, 1906. Both photographs by the author, referred to on page 38.

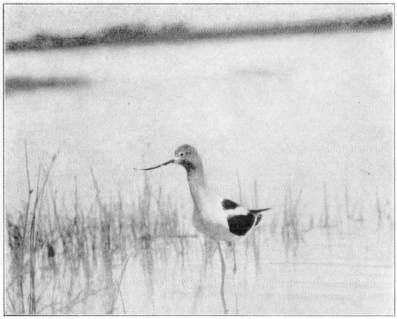

PLATE 8. AMERICAN AVOCET. *Upper:* Downy young American avocet. *Lower:* Adult American avocet. Both photographs presented by Mr. Jenness Richardson.

PLATE 9. AMERICAN AVOCET. *Upper:* Young American avocets, just hatched, Barr Lake, Colorado; presented by Mr. Robert B. Rockwell. *Lower:* Nest and eggs of American avocet, near Keysville, Utah; presented by Mr. Clark Blickensderfer.

PLATE 10. BLACK-NECKED STILT. *Upper:* Nesting site and nest of black-necked stilt, Lake Key, Florida, May 8, 1903. *Lower:* Another nest, same locality and date. Both photographs by the author, referred to on page 47.

PLATE 11. BLACK-NECKED STILT. *Upper:* Elevated nest of black-necked stilt, Firebaugh, California, June 30, 1923; presented by Mr. John G. Tyler. *Lower:* Typical nest of black-necked stilt, Fresno County, California, May 20, 1917; a photograph by Mr. J. A. Miles, presented by Mr. John G. Tyler.

PLATE 12. BLACK-NECKED STILT. *Upper:* Downy young black-necked stilts. *Lower:* Adult black-necked stilt on its nest. Both photographs presented by Dr. Frank M. Chapman, by courtesy of D. Appleton & Company.

PLATE 13. BLACK-NECKED STILT. Nest and eggs of black-necked stilt, near Salt Lake City, Utah; presented by Mr. Clark Blickensderfer.

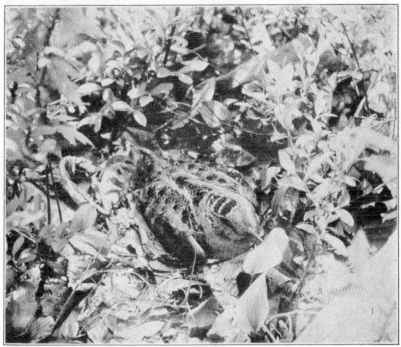

PLATE 14. AMERICAN WOODCOCK. *Upper:* American woodcock on its nest, Brookline, Massachusetts, June 2, 1924. *Lower:* Nearer view of the same bird. Both photographs by the author, referred to on page 65.

PLATE 15. AMERICAN WOODCOCK. American woodcock on its nest, Staten Island, New York, about 1900; presented by Mr. Howard H. Cleaves.

PLATE 16. AMERICAN WOODCOCK. *Upper:* Downy young of American woodcock, near Montreal, Quebec, May 11, 1924; presented by Mr. W. J. Brown. *Lower:* Nest and eggs of American woodcock, in a thicket on a hillside in a field of sedge, near Elkridge, Maryland, April 1, 1917; presented by Mr. William H. Fisher.

PLATE 17. WILSON SNIPE. *Upper:* Nest and eggs of Wilson snipe, Magdalen Islands, Quebec, June 18, 1904. *Lower:* Nearer view of same nest. Both photographs by the author, referred to on page 84.

PLATE 18. WILSON SNIPE. *Upper:* Wilson snipe on the nest shown on plate 17; presented by Mr. Herbert K. Job, referred to on page 84. *Lower:* Nest and eggs of Wilson snipe, Yukon Delta, Alaska, June 18, 1914; a photograph taken by Mr. F. Seymour Hersey for the author, referred to on page 85.

PLATE 19. DOWITCHER. *Upper:* Nesting site of dowitcher, nest under the bush in the centre, near Fort Assiniboine, Alberta, June 3, 1926. *Lower:* Nearer view of the nest. Both photographs presented by Mr. Richard H. Rauch, referred to on page 109.

PLATE 20. *Upper:* DOWITCHER. Dowitcher on the nest shown on plate 19, referred to on page 109. *Lower:* STILT SANDPIPER. Stilt sandpiper, immature, Ithaca, New York; presented by Dr. Arthur A. Allen.

PLATE 21. LONG-BILLED DOWITCHER. *Upper:* Nesting site of long-billed dowïtcher, Yukon Delta, Alaska, June 20, 1914; a photograph taken by Mr. F. Seymour Hersey for the author. *Lower:* Long-billed dowitcher, Monterey County, California, October 10, 1913; presented by Mr. W. Leon Dawson.

PLATE 22. LONG-BILLED DOWITCHER. *Upper:* Distant view of long-billed dowitcher's nest, St. Michael, Alaska, June 9, 1914. *Lower:* Nearer view of same nest. Both photographs taken by Mr. F. Seymour Hersey for the author, referred to on page 117.

PLATE 23. KNOT. *Upper:* Knot on its nest. *Lower:* Nest and eggs of knot. Both photographs taken by Dr. W. Elmer Ekblaw at North Star Bay, Greenland, in June, 1916; presented by him and by courtesy of the American Museum of Natural History, referred to on page 135.

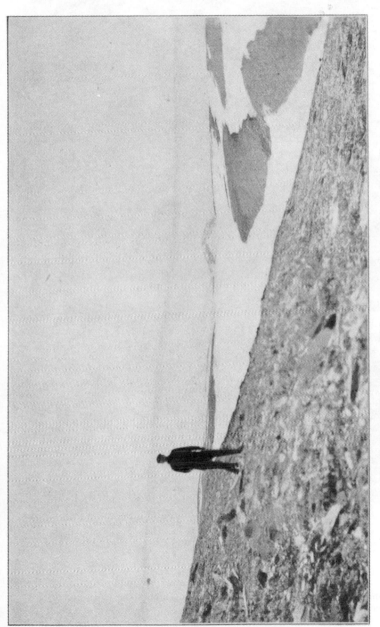

PLATE 24. KNOT. Nesting site of knot, near Sheridan River, Grinnell Land, June 27, 1909; a photograph taken by Admiral Robert E. Peary, loaned by Mr. H. F. Witherby, and published on the author's own responsibility, referred to on page 135.

PLATE 25. KNOT. *Upper:* Knot on its nest. *Lower:* Nest and eggs of knot, near Sheridan River, Grinnell Land, June 27, 1909. Both photographs taken by Admiral Peary and published under the same circumstances as plate 24, referred to on page 135.

PLATE 26. PURPLE SANDPIPER. *Upper:* Purple sandpiper on its nest, Spitsbergen, July 2, 1922; presented by Maj. W. M. Congreve. *Lower:* Purple sandpipers on the rocks at Scituate, Massachusetts, December 28, 1926; presented by Dr. John B. May.

PLATE 27. ALEUTIAN SANDPIPER. *Upper:* Nest and eggs of Aleutian sandpiper. *Lower:* Downy young of Aleutian sandpiper. Both photographs taken by Mr. Alfred M. Bailey at Emma Harbor, Providence Bay, Siberia, July 4, 1921; presented by him and by courtesy of the Colorado Museum of Natural History, referred to on page 162.

PLATE 28. ALEUTIAN SANDPIPER. *Upper:* Nesting site of Aleutian sandpiper. *Lower:* Nest and eggs of Aleutian sandpiper. Both photographs taken by the author on Kiska Island, Alaska, June 18, 1911, referred to on page 161.

PLATE 29. PECTORAL SANDPIPER. *Upper:* Nesting site of pectoral sandpiper. *Lower:* Nest and eggs of pectoral sandpiper. Both photographs taken by Mr. F. Seymour Hersey for the author at St. Michael, Alaska, June 9, 1914, referred to on page 172.

PLATE 30. PECTORAL SANDPIPER. *Upper:* Pectoral sandpiper, Buckeye Lake, Ohio, September, 1924; presented by Mr. Edward S. Thomas. *Lower:* Downy young pectoral sandpipers, St. Michael, Alaska, June 27, 1914; a photograph taken by Mr. F. Seymour Hersey for the author.

PLATE 31. WHITE-RUMPED SANDPIPER. *Upper:* Nest and eggs of white-rumped sandpiper, June 23, 1925. *Lower:* White-rumped sandpiper on its nest, June 21, 1925. Both photographs taken by Mr. J. Dewey Soper at Nettilling Lake, Baffin Island; presented by him, and by courtesy of the Department of Mines, Canada, referred to on page 183.

PLATE 32. *Upper:* SHARP-TAILED SANDPIPER. Sharp-tailed sandpipers, Alice Downs, Queensland, Australia; a photograph taken
by Mr. D. W. Gaukrodger and presented by Mr. W. B. Alexander. *Lower:*
WHITE-RUMPED SANDPIPER. Downy young white-rumped sandpiper, Nettilling Lake, Baffin Island, July 13, 1925; presented by Mr.
J. Dewey Soper and by courtesy of the Department of Mines, Canada.

PLATE 33. BAIRD SANDPIPER. *Upper:* Nest and eggs of Baird sandpiper, Griffin Point, Alaska, June 24, 1914. *Lower:* Baird sandpiper on above nest. Both photographs presented by Mr. Joseph Dixon, referred to on page 195.

PLATE 34. BAIRD SANDPIPER. *Upper:* Young Baird sandpiper,
Herschell Island, Yukon, July 30, 1914. *Lower:* Nest and eggs of Baird
sandpiper, Griffin Point, Alaska, July 11, 1914. Both photographs presented by Mr. Joseph Dixon.

PLATE 35. LEAST SANDPIPER. *Upper:* Least sandpiper incubating. *Lower:* Least sandpiper at its nest. Both photographs taken by **Mr.** Herbert K. Job, Magdalen Islands, Quebec, June 18, 1921, and presented by him.

PLATE 36. LEAST SANDPIPER. *Upper:* Least sandpiper feeding, Carpinteria, California, August 13, 1917; presented by Mr. W. Leon Dawson. *Lower:* Nest and eggs of least standiper, Magdalen Islands, Quebec; presented by Mr. P. B. Philipp.

PLATE 37. RED-BACKED SANDPIPER. *Upper:* Flock of red-backed sandpipers and one turnstone, Gimli, Manitoba, May 24, 1922; presented by Mr. A. G. Lawrence. *Lower:* Nest and eggs of red-backed sandpiper, Cape Prince of Wales, Alaska, June 25, 1922; presented by Mr. Alfred M. Bailey and by courtesy of the Colorado Museum of Natural History.

PLATE 38. CURLEW SANDPIPER. *Upper:* Nest and eggs of curlew sandpiper, near Golchika, Yenisei River, July 7, 1914. *Lower:* Site of above nest. Both photographs presented by Mrs. Maud D. (Haviland) Brindley, referred to on page 233.

PLATE 39. SPOON-BILL SANDPIPER. *Upper:* Nesting site of spoon-bill sandpiper, Providence Bay, Siberia, June 22, 1913. *Lower:* Nest and eggs of spoon-bill sandpiper, in above locality. Both photographs presented by Mr. Joseph Dixon, referred to on page 239.

PLATE 40. SEMIPALMATED SANDPIPER. *Upper:* Pair of semipalmated sandpipers, near their young, Griffin Point, Alaska, July 2, 1914. *Lower:* Nest and eggs of semipalmated sandpiper, Griffin Point, Alaska, July 12, 1914. Both photographs presented by Mr. Joseph Dixon.

PLATE 41. SEMIPALMATED SANDPIPER. Semipalmated sandpipers; presented by Mr. A. Brooker Klugh.

PLATE 42. WESTERN SANDPIPER. *Upper:* Nesting site of western sandpiper, Yukon Delta, Alaska. *Lower:* Nest and eggs of western sandpiper, Yukon Delta, Alaka, June 16, 1914. Both photographs taken by Mr. F. Seymour Hersey for the author.

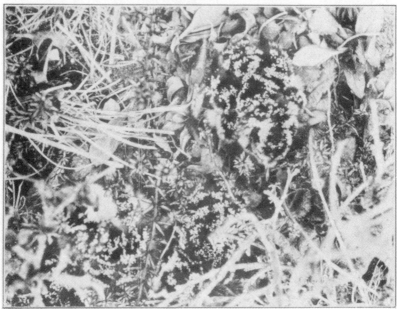

PLATE 43. WESTERN SANDPIPER. *Upper:* Nest and eggs of western sandpiper, Wales, Alaska, June 25, 1922; presented by Mr. Alfred M. Bailey and by courtesy of the Colorado Museum of Natural History. *Lower:* Downy young western sandpipers, Yukon Delta, Alaska, June 23, 1914; a photograph taken by Mr. F. Seymour Hersey for the author.

PLATE 44. SANDERLING. *Upper:* Nesting site of sanderling, north-eastern Greenland, July, 1908. *Lower:* Sanderling on its nest in above locality. Both photographs presented by Mr. A. L. V. Manniche, referred to on page 267.

PLATE 45. SANDERLING. *Upper:* Nest and eggs of sanderling, north-eastern Greenland, 77° north. *Lower:* Downy young sanderlings, 3, 7 and 11 days old. Both photographs presented by Mr. A. L. V. Manniche.

PLATE 46. SANDERLING. *Upper:* Sanderlings on the beach, Staten Island, New York, October 12, 1909; presented by Mr. Howard H. Cleaves. *Lower:* Immature sanderling, Ithaca, New York; presented by Dr. Arthur A. Allen.

PLATE 47. MARBLED GODWIT. *Upper:* Nest and eggs of marbled godwit, Reedy Lake, Saskatchewan, June 8, 1905. *Lower:* Another nest, Hay Lake, Saskatchewan, June 5, 1905. Both photographs taken by the author, referred to on page 279.

PLATE 48. MARBLED GODWIT. *Upper:* Distant view of marbled godwit on its nest, Hay Lake, Saskatchewan, June 9, 1906. *Lower:* Close up view of same bird. Both photographs taken by the author, referred to on page 280.

PLATE 49. MARBLED GODWIT. *Upper:* Marbled godwits on the beach at Santa Barbara, California, May 4, 1914; presented by Mr. W. Leon Dawson. *Lower:* Nest and eggs of marbled godwit, same as shown on plate 48, taken by the author.

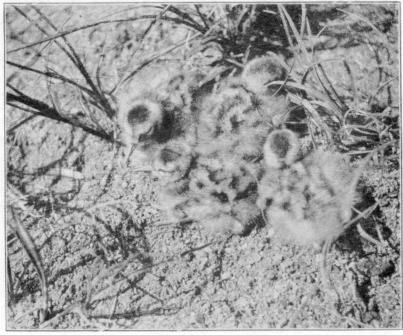

PLATE 50. PACIFIC GODWIT. *Upper:* Nest and eggs of Pacific god-wit, Hooper Bay, Alaska; presented by Mr. Herbert W. Brandt. *Lower:* Downy young Pacific godwits, Yukon Delta, Alaska, July 2, 1914; a photograph taken by Mr. F. Seymour Hersey, for the author.

PLATE 51. *Upper:* BLACK-TAILED GODWIT. Black-tailed godwit coming onto its nest; presented by Prof. Julian S. Huxley. *Lower:* RED-SHANK. Nest and eggs of redshank; presented by Mr. C. W. Colthrup.

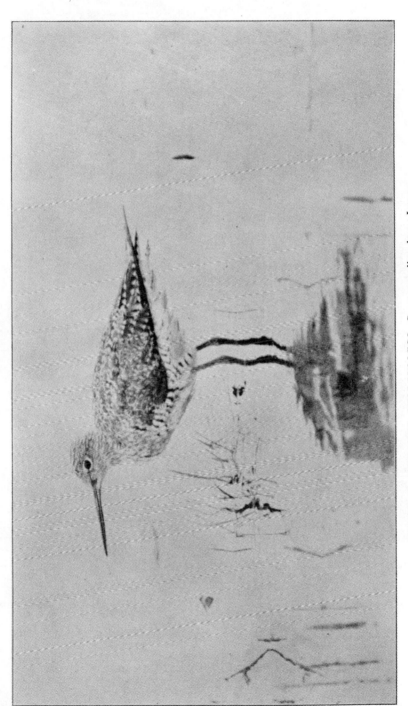

PLATE 52. GREATER YELLOW-LEGS. Greater yellow-legs, Lyon, Michigan, April 25, 1924; presented by Mr. Walter E. Hastings.

PLATE 53. LESSER YELLOW-LEGS. *Upper:* Nesting site of lesser yellow-legs, Belvedere, Alberta, June 3, 1923; presented by Mr. J. Fletcher Street. *Lower:* Nest and eggs of yellow-legs, Belvedere, Alberta, June 4, 1923; presented by Mr. George H. Stuart, 3rd. Both referred to on page 337.

PLATE 54. LESSER YELLOW-LEGS. *Upper:* Nesting site of lesser yellow-legs, near Belvedere, Alberta; presented by Mr. Richard C. Harlow. *Lower:* Nest and eggs of lesser yellow-legs in the same general locality; presented by Mr. Richard H. Rauch. Both referred to on page 338.

PLATE 55. LESSER YELLOW-LEGS. *Upper:* Lesser yellow-legs; presented by Mr. A. Brooker Klugh. *Lower:* Downy young lesser yellow-legs, Belvedere, Alberta; presented by Mr. J. Fletcher Street, referred to on page 338.

INDEX

A CATALOGUE OF SELECTED DOVER BOOKS
IN ALL FIELDS OF INTEREST

A CATALOGUE OF SELECTED DOVER BOOKS
IN ALL FIELDS OF INTEREST

AMERICA'S OLD MASTERS, James T. Flexner. Four men emerged unexpectedly from provincial 18th century America to leadership in European art: Benjamin West, J. S. Copley, C. R. Peale, Gilbert Stuart. Brilliant coverage of lives and contributions. Revised, 1967 edition. 69 plates. 365pp. of text.
21806-6 Paperbound $3.00

FIRST FLOWERS OF OUR WILDERNESS: AMERICAN PAINTING, THE COLONIAL PERIOD, James T. Flexner. Painters, and regional painting traditions from earliest Colonial times up to the emergence of Copley, West and Peale Sr., Foster, Gustavus Hesselius, Feke, John Smibert and many anonymous painters in the primitive manner. Engaging presentation, with 162 illustrations. xxii + 368pp.
22180-6 Paperbound $3.50

THE LIGHT OF DISTANT SKIES: AMERICAN PAINTING, 1760-1835, James T. Flexner. The great generation of early American painters goes to Europe to learn and to teach: West, Copley, Gilbert Stuart and others. Allston, Trumbull, Morse; also contemporary American painters—primitives, derivatives, academics—who remained in America. 102 illustrations. xiii + 306pp.
22179-2 Paperbound $3.50

A HISTORY OF THE RISE AND PROGRESS OF THE ARTS OF DESIGN IN THE UNITED STATES, William Dunlap. Much the richest mine of information on early American painters, sculptors, architects, engravers, miniaturists, etc. The only source of information for scores of artists, the major primary source for many others. Unabridged reprint of rare original 1834 edition, with new introduction by James T. Flexner, and 394 new illustrations. Edited by Rita Weiss. 6⅝ x 9⅝.
21695-0, 21696-9, 21697-7 Three volumes, Paperbound $15.00

EPOCHS OF CHINESE AND JAPANESE ART, Ernest F. Fenollosa. From primitive Chinese art to the 20th century, thorough history, explanation of every important art period and form, including Japanese woodcuts; main stress on China and Japan, but Tibet, Korea also included. Still unexcelled for its detailed, rich coverage of cultural background, aesthetic elements, diffusion studies, particularly of the historical period. 2nd, 1913 edition. 242 illustrations. lii + 439pp. of text.
20364-6, 20365-4 Two volumes, Paperbound $6.00

THE GENTLE ART OF MAKING ENEMIES, James A. M. Whistler. Greatest wit of his day deflates Oscar Wilde, Ruskin, Swinburne; strikes back at inane critics, exhibitions, art journalism; aesthetics of impressionist revolution in most striking form. Highly readable classic by great painter. Reproduction of edition designed by Whistler. Introduction by Alfred Werner. xxxvi + 334pp.
21875-9 Paperbound $3.00

VISUAL ILLUSIONS: THEIR CAUSES, CHARACTERISTICS, AND APPLICATIONS, Matthew Luckiesh. Thorough description and discussion of optical illusion, geometric and perspective, particularly; size and shape distortions, illusions of color, of motion; natural illusions; use of illusion in art and magic, industry, etc. Most useful today with op art, also for classical art. Scores of effects illustrated. Introduction by William H. Ittleson. 100 illustrations. xxi + 252pp.
21530-X Paperbound $2.00

A HANDBOOK OF ANATOMY FOR ART STUDENTS, Arthur Thomson. Thorough, virtually exhaustive coverage of skeletal structure, musculature, etc. Full text, supplemented by anatomical diagrams and drawings and by photographs of undraped figures. Unique in its comparison of male and female forms, pointing out differences of contour, texture, form. 211 figures, 40 drawings, 86 photographs. xx + 459pp. 5⅜ x 8⅜.
21163-0 Paperbound $3.50

150 MASTERPIECES OF DRAWING, Selected by Anthony Toney. Full page reproductions of drawings from the early 16th to the end of the 18th century, all beautifully reproduced: Rembrandt, Michelangelo, Dürer, Fragonard, Urs, Graf, Wouwerman, many others. First-rate browsing book, model book for artists. xviii + 150pp. 8⅜ x 11¼.
21032-4 Paperbound $2.50

THE LATER WORK OF AUBREY BEARDSLEY, Aubrey Beardsley. Exotic, erotic, ironic masterpieces in full maturity: Comedy Ballet, Venus and Tannhauser, Pierrot, Lysistrata, Rape of the Lock, Savoy material, Ali Baba, Volpone, etc. This material revolutionized the art world, and is still powerful, fresh, brilliant. With The Early Work, all Beardsley's finest work. 174 plates, 2 in color. xiv + 176pp. 8⅛ x 11.
21817-1 Paperbound $3.00

DRAWINGS OF REMBRANDT, Rembrandt van Rijn. Complete reproduction of fabulously rare edition by Lippmann and Hofstede de Groot, completely reedited, updated, improved by Prof. Seymour Slive, Fogg Museum. Portraits, Biblical sketches, landscapes, Oriental types, nudes, episodes from classical mythology—All Rembrandt's fertile genius. Also selection of drawings by his pupils and followers. "Stunning volumes," Saturday Review. 550 illustrations. lxxviii + 552pp. 9⅛ x 12¼.
21485-0, 21486-9 Two volumes, Paperbound $10.00

THE DISASTERS OF WAR, Francisco Goya. One of the masterpieces of Western civilization—83 etchings that record Goya's shattering, bitter reaction to the Napoleonic war that swept through Spain after the insurrection of 1808 and to war in general. Reprint of the first edition, with three additional plates from Boston's Museum of Fine Arts. All plates facsimile size. Introduction by Philip Hofer, Fogg Museum. v + 97pp. 9⅜ x 8¼.
21872-4 Paperbound $2.00

GRAPHIC WORKS OF ODILON REDON. Largest collection of Redon's graphic works ever assembled: 172 lithographs, 28 etchings and engravings, 9 drawings. These include some of his most famous works. All the plates from Odilon Redon: oeuvre graphique complet, plus additional plates. New introduction and caption translations by Alfred Werner. 209 illustrations. xxvii + 209pp. 9⅛ x 12¼.
21966-8 Paperbound $4.50

DESIGN BY ACCIDENT; A BOOK OF "ACCIDENTAL EFFECTS" FOR ARTISTS AND DESIGNERS, James F. O'Brien. Create your own unique, striking, imaginative effects by "controlled accident" interaction of materials: paints and lacquers, oil and water based paints, splatter, crackling materials, shatter, similar items. Everything you do will be different; first book on this limitless art, so useful to both fine artist and commercial artist. Full instructions. 192 plates showing "accidents," 8 in color. viii + 215pp. 8⅜ x 11¼. 21942-9 Paperbound $3.75

THE BOOK OF SIGNS, Rudolf Koch. Famed German type designer draws 493 beautiful symbols: religious, mystical, alchemical, imperial, property marks, runes, etc. Remarkable fusion of traditional and modern. Good for suggestions of timelessness, smartness, modernity. Text. vi + 104pp. 6⅛ x 9¼. 20162-7 Paperbound $1.25

HISTORY OF INDIAN AND INDONESIAN ART, Ananda K. Coomaraswamy. An unabridged republication of one of the finest books by a great scholar in Eastern art. Rich in descriptive material, history, social backgrounds; Sunga reliefs, Rajput paintings, Gupta temples, Burmese frescoes, textiles, jewelry, sculpture, etc. 400 photos. viii + 423pp. 6⅜ x 9¾. 21436-2 Paperbound $5.00

PRIMITIVE ART, Franz Boas. America's foremost anthropologist surveys textiles, ceramics, woodcarving, basketry, metalwork, etc.; patterns, technology, creation of symbols, style origins. All areas of world, but very full on Northwest Coast Indians. More than 350 illustrations of baskets, boxes, totem poles, weapons, etc. 378 pp. 20025-6 Paperbound $3.00

THE GENTLEMAN AND CABINET MAKER'S DIRECTOR, Thomas Chippendale. Full reprint (third edition, 1762) of most influential furniture book of all time, by master cabinetmaker. 200 plates, illustrating chairs, sofas, mirrors, tables, cabinets, plus 24 photographs of surviving pieces. Biographical introduction by N. Bienenstock. vi + 249pp. 9⅞ x 12¾. 21601-2 Paperbound $4.00

AMERICAN ANTIQUE FURNITURE, Edgar G. Miller, Jr. The basic coverage of all American furniture before 1840. Individual chapters cover type of furniture—clocks, tables, sideboards, etc.—chronologically, with inexhaustible wealth of data. More than 2100 photographs, all identified, commented on. Essential to all early American collectors. Introduction by H. E. Keyes. vi + 1106pp. 7⅞ x 10¾. 21599-7, 21600-4 Two volumes, Paperbound $11.00

PENNSYLVANIA DUTCH AMERICAN FOLK ART, Henry J. Kauffman. 279 photos, 28 drawings of tulipware, Fraktur script, painted tinware, toys, flowered furniture, quilts, samplers, hex signs, house interiors, etc. Full descriptive text. Excellent for tourist, rewarding for designer, collector. Map. 146pp. 7⅞ x 10¾. 21205-X Paperbound $2.50

EARLY NEW ENGLAND GRAVESTONE RUBBINGS, Edmund V. Gillon, Jr. 43 photographs, 226 carefully reproduced rubbings show heavily symbolic, sometimes macabre early gravestones, up to early 19th century. Remarkable early American primitive art, occasionally strikingly beautiful; always powerful. Text. xxvi + 207pp. 8⅜ x 11¼. 21380-3 Paperbound $3.50

ALPHABETS AND ORNAMENTS, Ernst Lehner. Well-known pictorial source for decorative alphabets, script examples, cartouches, frames, decorative title pages, calligraphic initials, borders, similar material. 14th to 19th century, mostly European. Useful in almost any graphic arts designing, varied styles. 750 illustrations. 256pp. 7 x 10. 21905-4 Paperbound $4.00

PAINTING: A CREATIVE APPROACH, Norman Colquhoun. For the beginner simple guide provides an instructive approach to painting: major stumbling blocks for beginner; overcoming them, technical points; paints and pigments; oil painting; watercolor and other media and color. New section on "plastic" paints. Glossary. Formerly *Paint Your Own Pictures.* 221pp. 22000-1 Paperbound $1.75

THE ENJOYMENT AND USE OF COLOR, Walter Sargent. Explanation of the relations between colors themselves and between colors in nature and art, including hundreds of little-known facts about color values, intensities, effects of high and low illumination, complementary colors. Many practical hints for painters, references to great masters. 7 color plates, 29 illustrations. x + 274pp.
20944-X Paperbound $2.75

THE NOTEBOOKS OF LEONARDO DA VINCI, compiled and edited by Jean Paul Richter. 1566 extracts from original manuscripts reveal the full range of Leonardo's versatile genius: all his writings on painting, sculpture, architecture, anatomy, astronomy, geography, topography, physiology, mining, music, etc., in both Italian and English, with 186 plates of manuscript pages and more than 500 additional drawings. Includes studies for the Last Supper, the lost Sforza monument, and other works. Total of xlvii + 866pp. 7⅞ x 10¾.
22572-0, 22573-9 Two volumes, Paperbound $11.00

MONTGOMERY WARD CATALOGUE OF 1895. Tea gowns, yards of flannel and pillow-case lace, stereoscopes, books of gospel hymns, the New Improved Singer Sewing Machine, side saddles, milk skimmers, straight-edged razors, high-button shoes, spittoons, and on and on . . . listing some 25,000 items, practically all illustrated. Essential to the shoppers of the 1890's, it is our truest record of the spirit of the period. Unaltered reprint of Issue No. 57, Spring and Summer 1895. Introduction by Boris Emmet. Innumerable illustrations. xiii + 624pp. 8½ x 11⅝.
22377-9 Paperbound $6.95

THE CRYSTAL PALACE EXHIBITION ILLUSTRATED CATALOGUE (LONDON, 1851). One of the wonders of the modern world—the Crystal Palace Exhibition in which all the nations of the civilized world exhibited their achievements in the arts and sciences—presented in an equally important illustrated catalogue. More than 1700 items pictured with accompanying text—ceramics, textiles, cast-iron work, carpets, pianos, sleds, razors, wall-papers, billiard tables, beehives, silverware and hundreds of other artifacts—represent the focal point of Victorian culture in the Western World. Probably the largest collection of Victorian decorative art ever assembled—indispensable for antiquarians and designers. Unabridged republication of the Art-Journal Catalogue of the Great Exhibition of 1851, with all terminal essays. New introduction by John Gloag, F.S.A. xxxiv + 426pp. 9 x 12.
22503-8 Paperbound $5.00

A HISTORY OF COSTUME, Carl Köhler. Definitive history, based on surviving pieces of clothing primarily, and paintings, statues, etc. secondarily. Highly readable text, supplemented by 594 illustrations of costumes of the ancient Mediterranean peoples, Greece and Rome, the Teutonic prehistoric period; costumes of the Middle Ages, Renaissance, Baroque, 18th and 19th centuries. Clear, measured patterns are provided for many clothing articles. Approach is practical throughout. Enlarged by Emma von Sichart. 464pp. 21030-8 Paperbound $3.50

ORIENTAL RUGS, ANTIQUE AND MODERN, Walter A. Hawley. A complete and authoritative treatise on the Oriental rug—where they are made, by whom and how, designs and symbols, characteristics in detail of the six major groups, how to distinguish them and how to buy them. Detailed technical data is provided on periods, weaves, warps, wefts, textures, sides, ends and knots, although no technical background is required for an understanding. 11 color plates, 80 halftones, 4 maps. vi + 320pp. 6⅛ x 9⅛. 22366-3 Paperbound $5.00

TEN BOOKS ON ARCHITECTURE, Vitruvius. By any standards the most important book on architecture ever written. Early Roman discussion of aesthetics of building, construction methods, orders, sites, and every other aspect of architecture has inspired, instructed architecture for about 2,000 years. Stands behind Palladio, Michelangelo, Bramante, Wren, countless others. Definitive Morris H. Morgan translation. 68 illustrations. xii + 331pp. 20645-9 Paperbound $3.00

THE FOUR BOOKS OF ARCHITECTURE, Andrea Palladio. Translated into every major Western European language in the two centuries following its publication in 1570, this has been one of the most influential books in the history of architecture. Complete reprint of the 1738 Isaac Ware edition. New introduction by Adolf Placzek, Columbia Univ. 216 plates. xxii + 110pp. of text. 9½ x 12¾. 21308-0 Clothbound $12.50

STICKS AND STONES: A STUDY OF AMERICAN ARCHITECTURE AND CIVILIZATION, Lewis Mumford.One of the great classics of American cultural history. American architecture from the medieval-inspired earliest forms to the early 20th century; evolution of structure and style, and reciprocal influences on environment. 21 photographic illustrations. 238pp. 20202-X Paperbound $2.00

THE AMERICAN BUILDER'S COMPANION, Asher Benjamin. The most widely used early 19th century architectural style and source book, for colonial up into Greek Revival periods. Extensive development of geometry of carpentering, construction of sashes, frames, doors, stairs; plans and elevations of domestic and other buildings. Hundreds of thousands of houses were built according to this book, now invaluable to historians, architects, restorers, etc. 1827 edition. 59 plates. 114pp. 7⅞ x 10¾. 22236-5 Paperbound $3.50

DUTCH HOUSES IN THE HUDSON VALLEY BEFORE 1776, Helen Wilkinson Reynolds. The standard survey of the Dutch colonial house and outbuildings, with constructional features, decoration, and local history associated with individual homesteads. Introduction by Franklin D. Roosevelt. Map. 150 illustrations. 469pp. 6⅝ x 9¼. 21469-9 Paperbound $5.00

THE ARCHITECTURE OF COUNTRY HOUSES, Andrew J. Downing. Together with Vaux's *Villas and Cottages* this is the basic book for Hudson River Gothic architecture of the middle Victorian period. Full, sound discussions of general aspects of housing, architecture, style, decoration, furnishing, together with scores of detailed house plans, illustrations of specific buildings, accompanied by full text. Perhaps the most influential single American architectural book. 1850 edition. Introduction by J. Stewart Johnson. 321 figures, 34 architectural designs. xvi + 560pp.

22003-6 Paperbound $4.00

LOST EXAMPLES OF COLONIAL ARCHITECTURE, John Mead Howells. Full-page photographs of buildings that have disappeared or been so altered as to be denatured, including many designed by major early American architects. 245 plates. xvii + 248pp. 7⅞ x 10¾.

21143-6 Paperbound $3.50

DOMESTIC ARCHITECTURE OF THE AMERICAN COLONIES AND OF THE EARLY REPUBLIC, Fiske Kimball. Foremost architect and restorer of Williamsburg and Monticello covers nearly 200 homes between 1620-1825. Architectural details, construction, style features, special fixtures, floor plans, etc. Generally considered finest work in its area. 219 illustrations of houses, doorways, windows, capital mantels. xx + 314pp. 7⅞ x 10¾.

21743-4 Paperbound $4.00

EARLY AMERICAN ROOMS: 1650-1858, edited by Russell Hawes Kettell. Tour of 12 rooms, each representative of a different era in American history and each furnished, decorated, designed and occupied in the style of the era. 72 plans and elevations, 8-page color section, etc., show fabrics, wall papers, arrangements, etc. Full descriptive text. xvii + 200pp. of text. 8⅜ x 11¼.

21633-0 Paperbound $5.00

THE FITZWILLIAM VIRGINAL BOOK, edited by J. Fuller Maitland and W. B. Squire. Full modern printing of famous early 17th-century ms. volume of 300 works by Morley, Byrd, Bull, Gibbons, etc. For piano or other modern keyboard instrument; easy to read format. xxxvi + 938pp. 8⅜ x 11.

21068-5, 21069-3 Two volumes, Paperbound $10.00

KEYBOARD MUSIC, Johann Sebastian Bach. Bach Gesellschaft edition. A rich selection of Bach's masterpieces for the harpsichord: the six English Suites, six French Suites, the six Partitas (Clavierübung part I), the Goldberg Variations (Clavierübung part IV), the fifteen Two-Part Inventions and the fifteen Three-Part Sinfonias. Clearly reproduced on large sheets with ample margins; eminently playable. vi + 312pp. 8⅛ x 11.

22360-4 Paperbound $5.00

THE MUSIC OF BACH: AN INTRODUCTION, Charles Sanford Terry. A fine, nontechnical introduction to Bach's music, both instrumental and vocal. Covers organ music, chamber music, passion music, other types. Analyzes themes, developments, innovations. x + 114pp.

21075-8 Paperbound $1.50

BEETHOVEN AND HIS NINE SYMPHONIES, Sir George Grove. Noted British musicologist provides best history, analysis, commentary on symphonies. Very thorough, rigorously accurate; necessary to both advanced student and amateur music lover. 436 musical passages. vii + 407 pp.

20334-4 Paperbound $2.75

CATALOGUE OF DOVER BOOKS

JOHANN SEBASTIAN BACH, Philipp Spitta. One of the great classics of musicology, this definitive analysis of Bach's music (and life) has never been surpassed. Lucid, nontechnical analyses of hundreds of pieces (30 pages devoted to St. Matthew Passion, 26 to B Minor Mass). Also includes major analysis of 18th-century music. 450 musical examples. 40-page musical supplement. Total of xx + 1799pp.
(EUK) 22278-0, 22279-9 Two volumes, Clothbound $17.50

MOZART AND HIS PIANO CONCERTOS, Cuthbert Girdlestone. The only full-length study of an important area of Mozart's creativity. Provides detailed analyses of all 23 concertos, traces inspirational sources. 417 musical examples. Second edition. 509pp.
21271-8 Paperbound $3.50

THE PERFECT WAGNERITE: A COMMENTARY ON THE NIBLUNG'S RING, George Bernard Shaw. Brilliant and still relevant criticism in remarkable essays on Wagner's Ring cycle, Shaw's ideas on political and social ideology behind the plots, role of Leitmotifs, vocal requisites, etc. Prefaces. xxi + 136pp.
(USO) 21707-8 Paperbound $1.75

DON GIOVANNI, W. A. Mozart. Complete libretto, modern English translation; biographies of composer and librettist; accounts of early performances and critical reaction. Lavishly illustrated. All the material you need to understand and appreciate this great work. Dover Opera Guide and Libretto Series; translated and introduced by Ellen Bleiler. 92 illustrations. 209pp.
21134-7 Paperbound $2.00

BASIC ELECTRICITY, U. S. Bureau of Naval Personel. Originally a training course, best non-technical coverage of basic theory of electricity and its applications. Fundamental concepts, batteries, circuits, conductors and wiring techniques, AC and DC, inductance and capacitance, generators, motors, transformers, magnetic amplifiers, synchros, servomechanisms, etc. Also covers blue-prints, electrical diagrams, etc. Many questions, with answers. 349 illustrations. x + 448pp. 6½ x 9¼.
20973-3 Paperbound $3.50

REPRODUCTION OF SOUND, Edgar Villchur. Thorough coverage for laymen of high fidelity systems, reproducing systems in general, needles, amplifiers, preamps, loudspeakers, feedback, explaining physical background. "A rare talent for making technicalities vividly comprehensible," R. Darrell, *High Fidelity*. 69 figures. iv + 92pp.
21515-6 Paperbound $1.35

HEAR ME TALKIN' TO YA: THE STORY OF JAZZ AS TOLD BY THE MEN WHO MADE IT, Nat Shapiro and Nat Hentoff. Louis Armstrong, Fats Waller, Jo Jones, Clarence Williams, Billy Holiday, Duke Ellington, Jelly Roll Morton and dozens of other jazz greats tell how it was in Chicago's South Side, New Orleans, depression Harlem and the modern West Coast as jazz was born and grew. xvi + 429pp.
21726-4 Paperbound $3.00

FABLES OF AESOP, translated by Sir Roger L'Estrange. A reproduction of the very rare 1931 Paris edition; a selection of the most interesting fables, together with 50 imaginative drawings by Alexander Calder. v + 128pp. 6½x9¼.
21780-9 Paperbound $1.50

AGAINST THE GRAIN (A REBOURS), Joris K. Huysmans. Filled with weird images, evidences of a bizarre imagination, exotic experiments with hallucinatory drugs, rich tastes and smells and the diversions of its sybarite hero Duc Jean des Esseintes, this classic novel pushed 19th-century literary decadence to its limits. Full unabridged edition. Do not confuse this with abridged editions generally sold. Introduction by Havelock Ellis. xlix + 206pp. 22190-3 Paperbound $2.50

VARIORUM SHAKESPEARE: HAMLET. Edited by Horace H. Furness; a landmark of American scholarship. Exhaustive footnotes and appendices treat all doubtful words and phrases, as well as suggested critical emendations throughout the play's history. First volume contains editor's own text, collated with all Quartos and Folios. Second volume contains full first Quarto, translations of Shakespeare's sources (Belleforest, and Saxo Grammaticus), Der Bestrafte Brudermord, and many essays on critical and historical points of interest by major authorities of past and present. Includes details of staging and costuming over the years. By far the best edition available for serious students of Shakespeare. Total of xx + 905pp. 21004-9, 21005-7, 2 volumes, Paperbound $7.00

A LIFE OF WILLIAM SHAKESPEARE, Sir Sidney Lee. This is the standard life of Shakespeare, summarizing everything known about Shakespeare and his plays. Incredibly rich in material, broad in coverage, clear and judicious, it has served thousands as the best introduction to Shakespeare. 1931 edition. 9 plates. xxix + 792pp. 21967-4 Paperbound $3.75

MASTERS OF THE DRAMA, John Gassner. Most comprehensive history of the drama in print, covering every tradition from Greeks to modern Europe and America, including India, Far East, etc. Covers more than 800 dramatists, 2000 plays, with biographical material, plot summaries, theatre history, criticism, etc. "Best of its kind in English," New Republic. 77 illustrations. xxii + 890pp. 20100-7 Clothbound $10.00

THE EVOLUTION OF THE ENGLISH LANGUAGE, George McKnight. The growth of English, from the 14th century to the present. Unusual, non-technical account presents basic information in very interesting form: sound shifts, change in grammar and syntax, vocabulary growth, similar topics. Abundantly illustrated with quotations. Formerly Modern English in the Making. xii + 590pp. 21932-1 Paperbound $3.50

AN ETYMOLOGICAL DICTIONARY OF MODERN ENGLISH, Ernest Weekley. Fullest, richest work of its sort, by foremost British lexicographer. Detailed word histories, including many colloquial and archaic words; extensive quotations. Do not confuse this with the Concise Etymological Dictionary, which is much abridged. Total of xxvii + 830pp. 6½ x 9¼. 21873-2, 21874-0 Two volumes, Paperbound $7.90

FLATLAND: A ROMANCE OF MANY DIMENSIONS, E. A. Abbott. Classic of science-fiction explores ramifications of life in a two-dimensional world, and what happens when a three-dimensional being intrudes. Amusing reading, but also useful as introduction to thought about hyperspace. Introduction by Banesh Hoffmann. 16 illustrations. xx + 103pp. 20001-9 Paperbound $1.00

POEMS OF ANNE BRADSTREET, edited with an introduction by Robert Hutchinson. A new selection of poems by America's first poet and perhaps the first significant woman poet in the English language. 48 poems display her development in works of considerable variety—love poems, domestic poems, religious meditations, formal elegies, "quaternions," etc. Notes, bibliography. viii + 222pp.

22160-1 Paperbound $2.50

THREE GOTHIC NOVELS: THE CASTLE OF OTRANTO BY HORACE WALPOLE; VATHEK BY WILLIAM BECKFORD; THE VAMPYRE BY JOHN POLIDORI, WITH FRAGMENT OF A NOVEL BY LORD BYRON, edited by E. F. Bleiler. The first Gothic novel, by Walpole; the finest Oriental tale in English, by Beckford; powerful Romantic supernatural story in versions by Polidori and Byron. All extremely important in history of literature; all still exciting, packed with supernatural thrills, ghosts, haunted castles, magic, etc. xl + 291pp.

21232-7 Paperbound $2.50

THE BEST TALES OF HOFFMANN, E. T. A. Hoffmann. 10 of Hoffmann's most important stories, in modern re-editings of standard translations: Nutcracker and the King of Mice, Signor Formica, Automata, The Sandman, Rath Krespel, The Golden Flowerpot, Master Martin the Cooper, The Mines of Falun, The King's Betrothed, A New Year's Eve Adventure. 7 illustrations by Hoffmann. Edited by E. F. Bleiler. xxxix + 419pp. 21793-0 Paperbound $3.00

GHOST AND HORROR STORIES OF AMBROSE BIERCE, Ambrose Bierce. 23 strikingly modern stories of the horrors latent in the human mind: The Eyes of the Panther, The Damned Thing, An Occurrence at Owl Creek Bridge, An Inhabitant of Carcosa, etc., plus the dream-essay, Visions of the Night. Edited by E. F. Bleiler. xxii + 199pp. 20767-6 Paperbound $1.50

BEST GHOST STORIES OF J. S. LEFANU, J. Sheridan LeFanu. Finest stories by Victorian master often considered greatest supernatural writer of all. Carmilla, Green Tea, The Haunted Baronet, The Familiar, and 12 others. Most never before available in the U. S. A. Edited by E. F. Bleiler. 8 illustrations from Victorian publications. xvii + 467pp. 20415-4 Paperbound $3.00

MATHEMATICAL FOUNDATIONS OF INFORMATION THEORY, A. I. Khinchin. Comprehensive introduction to work of Shannon, McMillan, Feinstein and Khinchin, placing these investigations on a rigorous mathematical basis. Covers entropy concept in probability theory, uniqueness theorem, Shannon's inequality, ergodic sources, the E property, martingale concept, noise, Feinstein's fundamental lemma, Shanon's first and second theorems. Translated by R. A. Silverman and M. D. Friedman. iii + 120pp. 60434-9 Paperbound $2.00

SEVEN SCIENCE FICTION NOVELS, H. G. Wells. The standard collection of the great novels. Complete, unabridged. *First Men in the Moon, Island of Dr. Moreau, War of the Worlds, Food of the Gods, Invisible Man, Time Machine, In the Days of the Comet.* Not only science fiction fans, but every educated person owes it to himself to read these novels. 1015pp. (USO) 20264-X Clothbound $6.00

LAST AND FIRST MEN AND STAR MAKER, TWO SCIENCE FICTION NOVELS, Olaf Stapledon. Greatest future histories in science fiction. In the first, human intelligence is the "hero," through strange paths of evolution, interplanetary invasions, incredible technologies, near extinctions and reemergences. Star Maker describes the quest of a band of star rovers for intelligence itself, through time and space: weird inhuman civilizations, crustacean minds, symbiotic worlds, etc. Complete, unabridged. v + 438pp.　　　　　　　　　(USO) 21962-3 Paperbound $2.50

THREE PROPHETIC NOVELS, H. G. WELLS. Stages of a consistently planned future for mankind. *When the Sleeper Wakes,* and *A Story of the Days to Come,* anticipate *Brave New World* and *1984,* in the 21st Century; *The Time Machine,* only complete version in print, shows farther future and the end of mankind. All show Wells's greatest gifts as storyteller and novelist. Edited by E. F. Bleiler. x + 335pp.　　　　　　　　　(USO) 20605-X Paperbound $2.50

THE DEVIL'S DICTIONARY, Ambrose Bierce. America's own Oscar Wilde—Ambrose Bierce—offers his barbed iconoclastic wisdom in over 1,000 definitions hailed by H. L. Mencken as "some of the most gorgeous witticisms in the English language." 145pp.　　　　　　　　　20487-1 Paperbound $1.25

MAX AND MORITZ, Wilhelm Busch. Great children's classic, father of comic strip, of two bad boys, Max and Moritz. Also Ker and Plunk (Plisch und Plumm), Cat and Mouse, Deceitful Henry, Ice-Peter, The Boy and the Pipe, and five other pieces. Original German, with English translation. Edited by H. Arthur Klein; translations by various hands and H. Arthur Klein. vi + 216pp.
　　　　　　　　　20181-3 Paperbound $2.00

PIGS IS PIGS AND OTHER FAVORITES, Ellis Parker Butler. The title story is one of the best humor short stories, as Mike Flannery obfuscates biology and English. Also included, That Pup of Murchison's, The Great American Pie Company, and Perkins of Portland. 14 illustrations. v + 109pp.　　21532-6 Paperbound $1.25

THE PETERKIN PAPERS, Lucretia P. Hale. It takes genius to be as stupidly mad as the Peterkins, as they decide to become wise, celebrate the "Fourth," keep a cow, and otherwise strain the resources of the Lady from Philadelphia. Basic book of American humor. 153 illustrations. 219pp.　　20794-3 Paperbound $2.00

PERRAULT'S FAIRY TALES, translated by A. E. Johnson and S. R. Littlewood, with 34 full-page illustrations by Gustave Doré. All the original Perrault stories—Cinderella, Sleeping Beauty, Bluebeard, Little Red Riding Hood, Puss in Boots, Tom Thumb, etc.—with their witty verse morals and the magnificent illustrations of Doré. One of the five or six great books of European fairy tales. viii + 117pp. 8⅛ x 11.　　　　　　　　　22311-6 Paperbound $2.00

OLD HUNGARIAN FAIRY TALES, Baroness Orczy. Favorites translated and adapted by author of the *Scarlet Pimpernel.* Eight fairy tales include "The Suitors of Princess Fire-Fly," "The Twin Hunchbacks," "Mr. Cuttlefish's Love Story," and "The Enchanted Cat." This little volume of magic and adventure will captivate children as it has for generations. 90 drawings by Montagu Barstow. 96pp.
　　　　　　　　　(USO) 22293-4 Paperbound $1.95

THE RED FAIRY BOOK, Andrew Lang. Lang's color fairy books have long been children's favorites. This volume includes Rapunzel, Jack and the Bean-stalk and 35 other stories, familiar and unfamiliar. 4 plates, 93 illustrations x + 367pp.
21673-X Paperbound $2.50

THE BLUE FAIRY BOOK, Andrew Lang. Lang's tales come from all countries and all times. Here are 37 tales from Grimm, the Arabian Nights, Greek Mythology, and other fascinating sources. 8 plates, 130 illustrations. xi + 390pp.
21437-0 Paperbound $2.50

HOUSEHOLD STORIES BY THE BROTHERS GRIMM. Classic English-language edition of the well-known tales — Rumpelstiltskin, Snow White, Hansel and Gretel, The Twelve Brothers, Faithful John, Rapunzel, Tom Thumb (52 stories in all). Translated into simple, straightforward English by Lucy Crane. Ornamented with head-pieces, vignettes, elaborate decorative initials and a dozen full-page illustrations by Walter Crane. x + 269pp.
21080-4 Paperbound **$2.00**

THE MERRY ADVENTURES OF ROBIN HOOD, Howard Pyle. The finest modern versions of the traditional ballads and tales about the great English outlaw. Howard Pyle's complete prose version, with every word, every illustration of the first edition. Do not confuse this facsimile of the original (1883) with modern editions that change text or illustrations. 23 plates plus many page decorations. xxii + 296pp.
22043-5 Paperbound $2.50

THE STORY OF KING ARTHUR AND HIS KNIGHTS, Howard Pyle. The finest children's version of the life of King Arthur; brilliantly retold by Pyle, with 48 of his most imaginative illustrations. xviii + 313pp. 6⅛ x 9¼.
21445-1 Paperbound $2.50

THE WONDERFUL WIZARD OF OZ, L. Frank Baum. America's finest children's book in facsimile of first edition with all Denslow illustrations in full color. The edition a child should have. Introduction by Martin Gardner. 23 color plates, scores of drawings. iv + 267pp.
20691-2 Paperbound $2.50

THE MARVELOUS LAND OF OZ, L. Frank Baum. The second Oz book, every bit as imaginative as the Wizard. The hero is a boy named Tip, but the Scarecrow and the Tin Woodman are back, as is the Oz magic. 16 color plates, 120 drawings by John R. Neill. 287pp.
20692-0 Paperbound $2.50

THE MAGICAL MONARCH OF MO, L. Frank Baum. Remarkable adventures in a land even stranger than Oz. The best of Baum's books not in the Oz series. 15 color plates and dozens of drawings by Frank Verbeck. xviii + 237pp.
21892-9 Paperbound $2.25

THE BAD CHILD'S BOOK OF BEASTS, MORE BEASTS FOR WORSE CHILDREN, A MORAL ALPHABET, Hilaire Belloc. Three complete humor classics in one volume. Be kind to the frog, and do not call him names . . . and 28 other whimsical animals. Familiar favorites and some not so well known. Illustrated by Basil Blackwell. 156pp.
(USO) 20749-8 Paperbound $1.50

EAST O' THE SUN AND WEST O' THE MOON, George W. Dasent. Considered the best of all translations of these Norwegian folk tales, this collection has been enjoyed by generations of children (and folklorists too). Includes True and Untrue, Why the Sea is Salt, East O' the Sun and West O' the Moon, Why the Bear is Stumpy-Tailed, Boots and the Troll, The Cock and the Hen, Rich Peter the Pedlar, and 52 more. The only edition with all 59 tales. 77 illustrations by Erik Werenskiold and Theodor Kittelsen. xv + 418pp. 22521-6 Paperbound $3.50

GOOPS AND HOW TO BE THEM, Gelett Burgess. Classic of tongue-in-cheek humor, masquerading as etiquette book. 87 verses, twice as many cartoons, show mischievous Goops as they demonstrate to children virtues of table manners, neatness, courtesy, etc. Favorite for generations. viii + 88pp. 6½ x 9¼.
22233-0 Paperbound $1.25

ALICE'S ADVENTURES UNDER GROUND, Lewis Carroll. The first version, quite different from the final *Alice in Wonderland,* printed out by Carroll himself with his own illustrations. Complete facsimile of the "million dollar" manuscript Carroll gave to Alice Liddell in 1864. Introduction by Martin Gardner. viii + 96pp. Title and dedication pages in color. 21482-6 Paperbound $1.25

THE BROWNIES, THEIR BOOK, Palmer Cox. Small as mice, cunning as foxes, exuberant and full of mischief, the Brownies go to the zoo, toy shop, seashore, circus, etc., in 24 verse adventures and 266 illustrations. Long a favorite, since their first appearance in St. Nicholas Magazine. xi + 144pp. 6⅝ x 9¼.
21265-3 Paperbound $1.75

SONGS OF CHILDHOOD, Walter De La Mare. Published (under the pseudonym Walter Ramal) when De La Mare was only 29, this charming collection has long been a favorite children's book. A facsimile of the first edition in paper, the 47 poems capture the simplicity of the nursery rhyme and the ballad, including such lyrics as I Met Eve, Tartary, The Silver Penny. vii + 106pp. (USO) 21972-0 Paperbound
$1.25

THE COMPLETE NONSENSE OF EDWARD LEAR, Edward Lear. The finest 19th-century humorist-cartoonist in full: all nonsense limericks, zany alphabets, Owl and Pussycat, songs, nonsense botany, and more than 500 illustrations by Lear himself. Edited by Holbrook Jackson. xxix + 287pp. (USO) 20167-8 Paperbound $2.00

BILLY WHISKERS: THE AUTOBIOGRAPHY OF A GOAT, Frances Trego Montgomery. A favorite of children since the early 20th century, here are the escapades of that rambunctious, irresistible and mischievous goat—Billy Whiskers. Much in the spirit of *Peck's Bad Boy,* this is a book that children never tire of reading or hearing. All the original familiar illustrations by W. H. Fry are included: 6 color plates, 18 black and white drawings. 159pp. 22345-0 Paperbound $2.00

MOTHER GOOSE MELODIES. Faithful republication of the fabulously rare Munroe and Francis "copyright 1833" Boston edition—the most important Mother Goose collection, usually referred to as the "original." Familiar rhymes plus many rare ones, with wonderful old woodcut illustrations. Edited by E. F. Bleiler. 128pp. 4½ x 6⅜. 22577-1 Paperbound $1.00

TWO LITTLE SAVAGES; BEING THE ADVENTURES OF TWO BOYS WHO LIVED AS INDIANS AND WHAT THEY LEARNED, Ernest Thompson Seton. Great classic of nature and boyhood provides a vast range of woodlore in most palatable form, a genuinely entertaining story. Two farm boys build a teepee in woods and live in it for a month, working out Indian solutions to living problems, star lore, birds and animals, plants, etc. 293 illustrations. vii + 286pp.
20985-7 Paperbound $2.50

PETER PIPER'S PRACTICAL PRINCIPLES OF PLAIN & PERFECT PRONUNCIATION. Alliterative jingles and tongue-twisters of surprising charm, that made their first appearance in America about 1830. Republished in full with the spirited woodcut illustrations from this earliest American edition. 32pp. 4½ x 6⅜.
22560-7 Paperbound $1.00

SCIENCE EXPERIMENTS AND AMUSEMENTS FOR CHILDREN, Charles Vivian. 73 easy experiments, requiring only materials found at home or easily available, such as candles, coins, steel wool, etc.; illustrate basic phenomena like vacuum, simple chemical reaction, etc. All safe. Modern, well-planned. Formerly *Science Games for Children*. 102 photos, numerous drawings. 96pp. 6⅛ x 9¼.
21856-2 Paperbound $1.25

AN INTRODUCTION TO CHESS MOVES AND TACTICS SIMPLY EXPLAINED, Leonard Barden. Informal intermediate introduction, quite strong in explaining reasons for moves. Covers basic material, tactics, important openings, traps, positional play in middle game, end game. Attempts to isolate patterns and recurrent configurations. Formerly *Chess*. 58 figures. 102pp.   (USO) 21210-6 Paperbound $1.25

LASKER'S MANUAL OF CHESS, Dr. Emanuel Lasker. Lasker was not only one of the five great World Champions, he was also one of the ablest expositors, theorists, and analysts. In many ways, his Manual, permeated with his philosophy of battle, filled with keen insights, is one of the greatest works ever written on chess. Filled with analyzed games by the great players. A single-volume library that will profit almost any chess player, beginner or master. 308 diagrams. xli x 349pp.
20640-8 Paperbound $2.75

THE MASTER BOOK OF MATHEMATICAL RECREATIONS, Fred Schuh. In opinion of many the finest work ever prepared on mathematical puzzles, stunts, recreations; exhaustively thorough explanations of mathematics involved, analysis of effects, citation of puzzles and games. Mathematics involved is elementary. Translated by F. Göbel. 194 figures. xxiv + 430pp.   22134-2 Paperbound $3.50

MATHEMATICS, MAGIC AND MYSTERY, Martin Gardner. Puzzle editor for Scientific American explains mathematics behind various mystifying tricks: card tricks, stage "mind reading," coin and match tricks, counting out games, geometric dissections, etc. Probability sets, theory of numbers clearly explained. Also provides more than 400 tricks, guaranteed to work, that you can do. 135 illustrations. xii + 176pp.
20335-2 Paperbound $1.75

MATHEMATICAL PUZZLES FOR BEGINNERS AND ENTHUSIASTS, Geoffrey Mott-Smith. 189 puzzles from easy to difficult—involving arithmetic, logic, algebra, properties of digits, probability, etc.—for enjoyment and mental stimulus. Explanation of mathematical principles behind the puzzles. 135 illustrations. viii + 248pp.
20198-8 Paperbound $1.75

PAPER FOLDING FOR BEGINNERS, William D. Murray and Francis J. Rigney. Easiest book on the market, clearest instructions on making interesting, beautiful origami. Sail boats, cups, roosters, frogs that move legs, bonbon boxes, standing birds, etc. 40 projects; more than 275 diagrams and photographs. 94pp.
20713-7 Paperbound $1.00

TRICKS AND GAMES ON THE POOL TABLE, Fred Herrmann. 79 tricks and games— some solitaires, some for two or more players, some competitive games—to entertain you between formal games. Mystifying shots and throws, unusual caroms, tricks involving such props as cork, coins, a hat, etc. Formerly *Fun on the Pool Table*. 77 figures. 95pp.
21814-7 Paperbound $1.25

HAND SHADOWS TO BE THROWN UPON THE WALL: A SERIES OF NOVEL AND AMUSING FIGURES FORMED BY THE HAND, Henry Bursill. Delightful picturebook from great-grandfather's day shows how to make 18 different hand shadows: a bird that flies, duck that quacks, dog that wags his tail, camel, goose, deer, boy, turtle, etc. Only book of its sort. vi + 33pp. 6½ x 9¼. 21779-5 Paperbound $1.00

WHITTLING AND WOODCARVING, E. J. Tangerman. 18th printing of best book on market. "If you can cut a potato you can carve" toys and puzzles, chains, chessmen, caricatures, masks, frames, woodcut blocks, surface patterns, much more. Information on tools, woods, techniques. Also goes into serious wood sculpture from Middle Ages to present, East and West. 464 photos, figures. x + 293pp.
20965-2 Paperbound $2.00

HISTORY OF PHILOSOPHY, Julián Marias. Possibly the clearest, most easily followed, best planned, most useful one-volume history of philosophy on the market; neither skimpy nor overfull. Full details on system of every major philosopher and dozens of less important thinkers from pre-Socratics up to Existentialism and later. Strong on many European figures usually omitted. Has gone through dozens of editions in Europe. 1966 edition, translated by Stanley Appelbaum and Clarence Strowbridge. xviii + 505pp. 21739-6 Paperbound $3.50

YOGA: A SCIENTIFIC EVALUATION, Kovoor T. Behanan. Scientific but non-technical study of physiological results of yoga exercises; done under auspices of Yale U. Relations to Indian thought, to psychoanalysis, etc. 16 photos. xxiii + 270pp.
20505-3 Paperbound $2.50

Prices subject to change without notice.
Available at your book dealer or write for free catalogue to Dept. GI, Dover Publications, Inc., 180 Varick St., N. Y., N. Y. 10014. Dover publishes more than 150 books each year on science, elementary and advanced mathematics, biology, music, art, literary history, social sciences and other areas.